Books by Joseph C. Goulden

The Best Years   1976

H. L. Mencken's Last Campaign   1976

The Benchwarmers   1974

Meany   1972

The Superlawyers   1972

The Money Givers   1971

Truth Is the First Casualty   1969

Monopoly   1968

The Curtis Caper   1965

THE BEST YEARS

YEARS

1945–1950

THE BEST YEARS

YEARS

1945–1950

Joseph C. Goulden

ATHENEUM 1976 New York

Library of Congress Cataloging in Publication Data

Goulden, Joseph C
   The best years

Includes bibliographical references and index
1. United States—Social conditions—1945–
2. United States—Politics and government—1945–1953.
I. Title.
HN58.G66   1976   309.1'73'0918   75–41852

ISBN 0–689–10708–0

Designed by Kathleen Carey

Ho, ho, the date draws nigh,
How the time doth drag by.
Noon-on-the-nineteenth, the vow was made,
Memories, expectation, they do not fade.
The best years approach, for you and I.

GI DOGGEREL, NINE DAYS
BEFORE V-J DAY

Contents

THE BEST YEARS
YEARS
1945–1950

How We Began

I N AUGUST 1944, Hollywood producer Samuel Goldwyn was leafing through *Time* magazine when his eye fell upon a photograph of eleven travel-soiled soldiers hanging from the window of a grimy Pullman car—some smiling, some seemingly bewildered, some almost grimly expectant. Below the window were chalked two words: "Home Again!"

A shrewd movie-moneyman, Goldwyn immediately saw a potential market in those faces; after all, some 15,000,000 men and women would be "home again" once the war ended. Later that day he telephoned writer MacKinlay Kantor in Palm Beach and said, "Write me a picture about America and Americans." Goldwyn wanted a story about the "living, loving people, working, playing, loafing, in the American way of peace." Kantor liked the idea, and over the next year he wrote a novel entitled *Glory for Me,* about three homecoming veterans. Pleased, Goldwyn turned the book over to playwright Robert Sherwood for a script, and signed top director William Wyler (who had just won an Academy Award for *Mrs. Miniver*) for the filming.

But Sherwood had problems with the script. One of Kantor's veterans had come out of the war with an injury that made him spastic, a condition difficult to portray on the screen. He and Wyler tried several approaches to a screen treatment but couldn't satisfy themselves or Goldwyn. They kept working.

Meanwhile, the same month the *Time* photograph stirred Goldwyn, a young paratrooper named Harold Russell was undertaking a movie experience of an entirely different sort. Russell was in Walter Reed Army Hospital in Washington, painfully learning to use the cold metallic hooks that were to substitute for the hands he had lost during a training accident, and worrying about whether he could hold down his prewar job as a meat cutter. Often, when the ward lights went out, Russell would lie in his bed and stare at the ceiling and play a game of "if." *If* he had gone into the air corps rather than the airborne infantry. *If* he had dropped the grenade a split second earlier. *If* he had lost his eyes instead. The answer always came down the same way: Harold Russell was going to go through life without any hands.

One day officials from the Veterans Administration came around Walter Reed scouting for a lead character for a film about rehabilitation of crippled soldiers.* "I was the only double-arm in the place, and a four-star general, the first one I ever seen, told me I would make the movie," Russell says. "I replied, 'Yes, sir.' " The twenty-five-minute film, *Diary of a Sergeant,* traced Russell from an opening scene on the operating table, where he anguished over his future, through his struggle with the artificial hands, to a tolerably upbeat homecoming and entry into college, with a girl friend. "It was a damned good job," Russell said of *Diary.*

The film was so good, in fact, that the government decided to use it at war bond rallies. Wyler, still working with Sherwood on the Kantor script, saw it in Hollywood one night, persuaded the bond officials to lend him a print, and took it home and called Goldwyn. "This was two in the morning," Russell said, "but right away the wheels started to turn. They ran the film a couple of times, and Wyler says to Goldwyn, 'Sam, we'll use this guy, this is great.' Sam bought the idea, and that was it." The next day Goldwyn's office called Russell, by now attending Boston University, and persuaded him ("No, this is *not* a joke") to come west to star in the movie.

"At first it was very demoralizing. Here I was, an amateur among professionals. One of the first things Goldwyn did was send me to drama school. I mentioned this to Bill Wyler at dinner one night, that I was going, and he said, 'Who the hell told you to do that?' I told him Goldwyn. Bill called Goldwyn on the spot and said, 'Look, forget it, this guy's not an actor, and I don't want to make an actor out of him.' That was the end of that. 'I want you to play yourself,' he told me.

"Wyler was very high on veterans, and he issued an order that veterans would have first preference on jobs on the set. So we had maybe ninety percent vets. The spirit was good. It was more than a motion picture, it was a kind of mission, a crusade."

The story was of three servicemen returning to the fictitious Midwestern town of Boone City, and the way they went about picking up the threads of their prewar existence: Dana Andrews, a bombardier captain with ambitions beyond his old job as a soda jerk, and tired of his addle-brained wife, Virginia Mayo; Fredric March, who found his bank job stuffy after serving as a middle-aged infantry sergeant; and Russell, cast as former sailor Homer Parrish. The movie did not pretend that homecoming was easy. Banker March, for instance, became so disillusioned

* The war left 14,648 soldiers minus one or more limbs: one hand, 3,322; one foot, 10,405; two hands, 64; two feet, 731; one hand and one foot, 114; one hand and both feet, 10; both hands and both feet, 2.

with loan discriminations against veterans that he went on a glorious drunken bender and delivered a heavily satirical lecture on the "virtues" of big business to a formal gathering of company officers. March's daughter, meanwhile, had a sputtering affair with the unhappily married Andrews. But, of course, all the snarls are resolved, and toward the end of the movie someone concludes that they are really enjoying "the best years of our lives."

Robert Sherwood thought those six words more aptly expressed the thrust of the movie than Kantor's original *Glory for Me*. Goldwyn wasn't so sure: What did the public think about the postwar years? Were the American people really all that enthused about what had happened since V-J Day? Goldwyn cautiously hired the Gallup polling organization to do a survey on what the public considered to be "the best years." The answers were most upbeat. A thirty-year-old housewife answered, "This year—right now. My husband's come home from the army, I'm having a baby, and this is the most challenging time I've yet seen. If I don't have any more years, this one [1946] is fine." A twenty-three-year-old veteran agreed: "Oh, boy, this last year will be hard to beat. Got discharged from the army, got married, got back into college . . ." As RKO General Pictures later exclaimed in releasing *The Best Years of Our Lives*, "These and scores of other answers had a special significance for Mr. Goldwyn. They told him that America was still living, loving, dreaming."

Nonetheless many persons in Hollywood told Sam Goldwyn he was a damned fool even to consider such a movie. "The 'professionals,' whoever the hell they are," Harold Russell said, "told Sam: 'This thing will never go. With all your good intentions, you just can't show an amputee in a motion picture. This movie is not good box office.' " If Goldwyn ever worried or listened, no hint of it came through to Russell or other persons in the cast.

The Best Years, released in October 1946, won nine Academy Awards, including an Oscar for amateur actor Harold Russell, and the New York film critics called it the best movie of the year. After the promotional tours Russell thought awhile about staying in Hollywood, either as an actor or as a public relations man for Goldwyn's organization. But his friend Wyler discouraged the notions. "How much future is there in the motion picture industry for a guy without any hands over a period of five or ten years?" he asked. Russell agreed, and went back to Massachusetts, where he is now—in 1976—a businessman in a Boston suburb.

"I can look back at that period now and say they truly *were* 'the best years,' " Russell says. "The guys who came out of World War Two were idealistic. They sincerely believed that this time they were coming home to build a new world. Many, many times you'd hear guys say, 'The one thing I want to do when I get out is to make sure that this thing will never happen again.' We felt the day had come when the wars were all over, we were going to break down the bonds that separated people."

Russell shook his head. "I could give you a long lecture on what went wrong. But the important thing is that the postwar years *were* a great period for our country, and you had a tremendous feeling just being alive. Periods of readjustment are always difficult, but they are also interesting. We had problems, sure, but they didn't dominate us; we face the same things now, and we despair."

The Best Years is a reasking of the question that the Gallup surveyors asked citizens some three decades ago on behalf of Sam Goldwyn. *The Best Years* is an attempt to re-create what was happening in and to America from the end of World War Two to the start of the Korean War. August 1945 to June 1950. What years! And, in the beginning at least, as Harold Russell has told us, what a national spirit! Two vivid flashes of light over Japan, two ugly, churning mushroom clouds, and suddenly the war was over, a full year ahead of expectation. Americans rejoiced in the ultimate euphoria of victory over people whom even our schoolchildren had been taught to hate, in a conflict where defeat meant national and personal subjugation. Four years of common sacrifice gave Americans a reason for shared joy, and a rare sense of national unity and superiority, reinforced with an overriding moral righteousness only slightly diminished by the fact that the penultimate events of the war were the first uses of nuclear weaponry. Once again we had bailed out the British and the French in the nick of time, and the Russians as well. Oh, the Allies helped, certainly, but *we* provided the decisive striking power, when all appeared lost for the rest of western civilization. So America basked in collective self-glory.

August 1945 found America victorious on places other than the battlefield. The Great Depression fell along with the Axis powers, and the word "want" took on a new and not entirely negative meaning: when citizens wished to buy something, the shortage was not of dollars, but of articles to carry home from the stores. When the war ended, Americans had jobs (53,000,000 of them, with unemployment less than two percent) and Americans had money ($140 billion in liquid savings, in war bonds and in banks and in their wallets, about three times the national income in 1932). Although most people expected some inevitable painful bumps as the economy shifted from war to peace, Americans nonetheless entered the postwar era confident the bread lines were gone forever.

Above all, Americans had the future. And here a clear departure from the post-World War One mood, which journalist/historian Mark Sullivan described in *Our Times:*

Of all the nostalgic longing for the past that man has experienced since theology first taught him to look back toward Eden, hardly any was greater than the homesickness with which much of the world in 1920 looked back toward the world of 1914, in vain. That homesickness was responsible for many of the votes that Warren G. Harding got when he ran for President of the U.S. in 1920; of all the speeches he made in his campaign, the three words that most appealed to the mood of the country, the one phrase for which he was most applauded, was "back to normalcy."

But why look backward in 1945, when prewar "normalcy" meant 8,000,000 men out of work, and a take-home pay, for the average industrial worker, of less than $25 weekly (versus $44.39 on V-J Day)? Americans read the Sunday supplement features about the future, and they believed it would work: futuristic automobiles and jet planes that would whisk them around the world (seven of ten Americans had never even flown in an airplane in 1941), even to the moon, as they luxuriated in the twenty-five-hour week made possible by the arcane technologies developed in secret war laboratories. The American's new house—and Americans needed them, about 15,000,000 in all, to make up for construction lost during the Depression and the war, and to catch up with the population jump—would be made of glass and plastic, with perhaps a supporting slab or two of steel or aluminum; a buyer would order one from Macy's in the morning; the men would bring it out in the afternoon, and assemble it on his lot in time for dinner. Radiant heat would keep the house warm in freezing weather, even with the windows open for fresh air, or comfortably cool in the summer. No outside noise, no dust, no termites, no germs (ultraviolet lamps would take care of them). New plastic clothing would be so cheap a man would wear a suit two or three times and toss it in the trash.

Or transportation. Within a decade after the war ended, aviation wizard Igor Sikorsky promised in 1943, "Hundreds of thousands of helicopter aircraft will fill the skies here, providing cheap, safe, intermediate transportation." The wonder drugs of the battlefield, those long clumsy words ending in "my-o-cin," would rid society of most illnesses. Another chemical proven in Burma and the swamps of the South Pacific, dichloro-diphenyl-trichloro-ethane (DDT, the scientists mercifully abbreviated it), would rid the outdoors of flies and mosquitoes and other flying bugs. There would be consumer goods in abundance: After all, had not American industry built 297,000 planes and 86,338 tanks and 71,060 ships and vessels during wartime? Did not this mammoth industrial capacity mean a surfeit of autos and refrigerators and cook stoves once a few gauges were changed on the machines? Television would mean Betty Grable and Bob Hope and Dorothy Lamour and

Clark Gable alive (well, practically alive, anyway) and performing in one's living room.

A restiveness to return to the peacetime economy and to begin enjoying the material fruits of victory was highly visible even before the formal peace. As hundreds of thousands of GIs streamed from the European to the Pacific theater, and naval bombardments of Japanese coastal cities reinforced the steady air bombings, defense officials had trouble keeping the public's mind on the fact that civilians still had a role in the war. The lassitude was reflected in sudden and unfillable job vacancies in war plants. In California, a shortage of shipyard workers became so critical that the United States Employment Service (USES) resorted to shock tactics. Rather than continuing to conceal the extent of shipping damages, they threw open Terminal Island and Los Angeles harbor to visitors so citizens could see the effects of kamikaze attacks on the destroyer USS *Zellars* and the hospital ship USS *Comfort*. The USES set up booths to recruit shipyard workers. On a single weekend, 250,000 persons visited the ships. Only 2,500 paused at the USES stands, and of these only a handful expressed an interest in defense jobs. In Michigan City, Indiana, an army plane dropped thousands of leaflets seeking 300 workers for the local Pullman plant, which was doing defense work. As a Labor Department official commented, "Workers in war plants have had their noses to the grindstone for three or four years now. Many have been foregoing vacations, working overtime, sacrificing home life. They are told that continued work is necessary to win the war against Japan, but they see war plants closing down. . . . They want to blow off steam." The July 30 *Newsweek* cover, two weeks before peace, revealed the deepening public dichotomy: The cover photo was of a scrawny Japanese soldier with a three-day stubble of beard, with the caption: "The Jap: How Long Can He Take It?" Page nine was a full-page color ad from General Motors on "What's ahead at Oldsmobile." The text noted that production lines released from war work were being swiftly converted to private cars: "Under this new 'combined operations program,' America's Oldest Car Manufacturer soon will be serving the home-front as well as the war-front—building vitally needed motor cars for essential transportation." Americans read the car ads (few could buy autos, however; even after a partial conversion following V-E Day, Ford produced only ten vehicles per day) and they had their first fleeting taste of consumer goods (when a Philadelphia department store advertised 100 electric irons at $9.20, the supply lasted fifteen minutes). And so the citizenry waited, with whetted appetites and overflowing wallets, for the economic cornucopia of peace.

Looking abroad, Americans also saw reasons for optimism. A series of Gallup polls found their confidence about winning the war matched only by their confidence in keeping the peace. A clear majority did not expect war again for at least twenty-five years. Americans believed in the United Nations, in the Yalta agreement, even in the Russians, to the extent that public sentiment favored a continuing military alliance. (The Gallup surveys also found strong sentiment for harsh treatment of the vanquished Germans: two out of three people wanted a death sentence for Hermann Goering, the ranking surviving Nazi, and many of these wanted him tortured before the execution.) In the words of Gallup editor John Fenton, "Our excitement in the onrush of events made us a little giddy perhaps, a little inclined to see anything and everything in a hopeful light." "The war for human decency is done," *Fortune* editorialized in September 1945, "and now the United States stands out as the inheritor of more power and more responsibility than any nation on earth. . . . Partly against its will—certainly without seeking the prize —it has become the guardian and standard-bearer of western civilization."

And, above the general euphoria, a broad national confidence, both in the future of individuals and in the country's ability to solve any postwar problems that arose. The mood was caught by a young Swedish exchange student named Olof Palme, later his nation's prime minister. "I wrote the first review for the Swedish press of Mailer's *The Naked and the Dead*. I remember the thrust of the last paragraph: 'The spirit of the world is ours for the taking.' This statement was typical of postwar American youth. America was a country with a lot of social and economic problems, and ideological differences. But it was not a divided country. I returned [to Sweden, in 1948] with a deep affection for America, for the vitality, for the openness." Hear, too, Les Cramer, a navy veteran of the South Pacific who went back to college in Ohio: "You had a mixture of feelings. I wanted to make up for the fun I had missed while overseas, and I also wanted to start moving professionally. I had not the slightest doubt that I would be able to do both, and that I would make a comfortable living when I graduated." Charles Lehman, a Missouri veteran, remembers, "I was a twenty-one-year-old lieutenant with a high-school education, and my only prewar experience was as a stock boy in a grocery store. But on V-J Day, I *knew* it was only a matter of time before I was rich—or well-off, anyway." (Lehman is now an insurance man in a Kansas City suburb—"comfortable, but by no means rich.") Stan Monto, who grew up in rural northern California, says, "The war taught me there was another world out there, beyond the vegetable patch." When he was discharged from the marines in 1946, "I never gave a thought to going back to the country; I headed straight for San Francisco, because I wanted something better out of life than a permanent assignment at the end of a hoe. If I hadn't been exposed to something else, I never would have had the confidence to leave home."

Peace. The return of more than 15,000,000 men and women from war. The strong probability of continuing economic plenty. National confidence. A high degree of unity, born of the shared adventure and triumph of war. An acceptably popular President, even if Harry S. Truman himself recognized that, for the moment at least, he wore the mantle of FDR by inheritance only, not by mandate of the electorate. (The first Gallup poll on Truman's popularity found 87 percent of the public approving of the way he was handling his job; only three Americans in a hundred expressed any disapproval. Neither Roosevelt nor Eisenhower ever achieved such a peak.) Americans truly had reasons to anticipate the best years of their lives.

By contrast, five years later the national mood had done a complete turnabout. Discord was widespread. The unions and the corporations fought one another with a savagery that had the verbiage, if not the overt violence, of class warfare, with management attempting to overthrow the New Deal legislation that made mass unionism possible. A stranger wandering into the strife would have heard that Communistic labor barons were bent upon creating a socialist workers' state in America; or that the corporate statism of Adolf Hitler was alive and thriving in the board rooms of the National Association of Manufacturers. Such were the things that boss and worker shouted at one another as America suffered the most crippling series of strikes in its history. In the South, racists forgot about the "brotherhood" of war, and chilling three-paragraph stories about lynchings of blacks sprinkled the nation's newspapers. Only a threatened black boycott of the Selective Service System, organized by A. Philip Randolph, the unionist, forced the military forces to abandon segregation.

The fear of a nuclear confrontation with the detested Russians—the same people who, five years before, were courageous, all-sacrificing allies—permeated national thinking, so much so that one's Americanism was gauged by the ferocity of his denunciation of any ideas even vaguely parallel to Communist ideology. In the United States Senate, the mere mention of a government functionary's name by a jowly, long-ignored backbencher named Joseph R. McCarthy sent newspaper makeup men scampering for their largest, blackest type. In one typical week (in March 1950) a Washington *News* headline read: NEW STATE DEPT. PERVERT HUNT ON, while the Washington *Post* promised MCCARTHY WILL ACCUSE STATE DEPT. BIG SHOT. Further, much of the press coverage gave heavy evidentiary weight to any snippets of gossip McCarthy uttered as "proof" of his accusations. Thus the public read in the Washington *News* on March 13, 1950, that "Senator Joseph McCarthy, backing up charges government payrolls are padded with Reds and sympathizers, named as a 'pro-Communist' a former adviser to President Roosevelt, ———." The person named, a former diplomat, eventually repudiated McCarthy's charge, but only after grave damage to his reputation, career, and pocketbook.*

The Truman Administration, McCarthy's ultimate target, at first did not take him seriously. At one point the Senator charged that the wife of Secretary of State Dean Acheson (a man too elegant of speech and dress for much of middle America) belonged to a suspect organization. Years earlier she had contributed two dollars to the Washington League of Women Shoppers, later merged into another women's group which McCarthy called a "Communist front." Acheson took time off from his premiership of the Cold War against the Soviet Union to compliment McCarthy for his "contribution to the gaiety of the situation," and told a little story to a press conference: Communist agitators tried to break up a mass meeting, prompting intervention by the police, who arrived with flailing clubs. When one struck the innocent chairman, he protested, "Hey, I'm an anti-Communist." The policeman retorted: "I don't give a damn what kind of Communist you are—you're under arrest."

Acheson's wry tale, however, is the last recorded instance where any official American considered Joe McCarthy a laughing matter. Although McCarthy was some months away from his demagogic apogee (as late as August 1951 the Gallup poll found that two out of three people did not know who he was), by 1950 he was a most visible menace to Americans in general and to the Truman Administration in particular. And more than any other public person he symbolized the anxieties, the fears, the outright hatreds that marred what Americans had hoped, had expected, would be an era of tranquillity and prosperity.

So the best years led to Joe McCarthy. They were also the birth of national television and the concurrent death of national radio. They were Kathy Fiscus, the three-year-old girl who in 1947 fell into a water pipe near her home in San Marino, California, and there remained for three days until rescue workers removed her lifeless body—one of the first tragedies caught live by television cameras. The best years were builder William Levitt converting a Long Island potato patch into a mass of production-line houses—"little boxes," social critics called them, but Levitt's production portended the suburbization of America and the deification of the automobile. The best years were the Tucker automobile, whose promoter produced more windy promises and worthless stock than vehicles; Jorge Pasqual and his Liga Mexicana de Beisbol challenge to established big-league baseball; California teenagers' discovery of a risky new sport called drag racing. The best years were the give-'em-hell-Harry campaign of 1948, the one Truman couldn't win, and Taft–Hartley and Alger Hiss and frozen foods and the

* Not wishing to revive this man's embarrassment, I am leaving him nameless in the text.

long-playing phonograph record. *Forever Amber,* the first lurid national best-seller a woman could read under the hair dryer. The discovery of flying saucers (in a rare jest, the fierce Soviet ambassador, Andrei Gromyko, suggested, "Some say it is a Russian discus thrower training for the Olympic games who does not realize his own strength"). The Boudreau shift. Lena the Hyena. Kaiser-Frazer. Computers. Billy Graham. Borden's Hemo. The Ingrid Bergman–Roberto Rossellini affair ("the most famous confinement in nineteen hundred and fifty years," quipped a Broadway columnist). *Death of a Salesman.* William ("Catch me before I kill more") Heirens. "Open the Door, Richard." Howard Unruh, the Camden killer. Glenn McCarthy and the hydrogen bomb and the "Friendship Club" pyramid chain letters. The first drive-in bank and the Berlin airlift. The Coke machine and Thomas E. Dewey. Gorgeous George and the Kinsey Report. The 0–0 tie between Army and Notre Dame in 1946. *Bongo bongo bongo, I don't want to leave the Congo.* . . .

Enough. Regardless of the chaotic end of the period, the years 1945–50 are in most probability the last time Americans will have the chance even to attempt to enjoy the aftermath of a world war. What I have sought to do in *The Best Years* is to tell what America was doing and thinking—how its citizens lived and changed, from the Japanese surrender on August 15, 1945, until the North Korean army swept across the thirty-eighth parallel on June 25, 1950. And here a word of personal perspective is in order. At the beginning of the period I was a totally apolitical eleven-year-old in small-town East Texas, more interested in Captain Marvel comic books and catfish-skinning techniques than in Dumbarton Oaks and the economic reconversion policies of the Truman Administration. Five years later I had "progressed" to the check-out counter of a Piggly Wiggly grocery, and to earnest (and usually futile) pursuits of nubile maidens at the Fox Drive-In Theater. What few intrusions I suffered from the contemporary world outside Harrison County (and what local boosters called the "Ark-La-Tex trade area") were through the notably narrow and parallel columns of the Dallas *News,* the *Reader's Digest* and the *Saturday Evening Post,* the core reading material in our household and publications not intended to excite one's imagination.

One remembrance is a sufficient benchmark of my political acumen circa 1948: In these pretelevision days the people in small towns such as Marshall received local election results by gathering on the courthouse square after sundown and watching a harried deputy county clerk enter them, ward by ward, on a blackboard borrowed from the agricultural agent's office. The Lions Club sold soda pop, the Wesley Guild had the hamburger concession, and I recollect too the presence of greasy, cold popcorn. This particular evening another kid grabbed my arm and pulled me close so he could whisper in my ear as he pointed to a young man standing nearby: "Do you know who *that* is?" No, I didn't. "Well, that's Buster White's brother, and my daddy says he's a CIO organizer down at Port Arthur."

I couldn't believe my ears! A *union* organizer right here in Marshall, walking around on the street, and the police not even bothering him. We all knew—either from reading the Dallas *News* or from listening to our parents—what a CIO organizer was: a deputized agent of Stalin, with the social standing of a child molester or someone who cheated at dominoes. I kept an eye on this White character the rest of the evening, wondering whether Sheriff Rosborough would finally notice him and get him off the street and away from us decent, law-abiding citizens. (I told this story to George Meany in 1971. He didn't think it amusing.)

All of this is a roundabout way of saying that the world sailed right past me during 1945–50 and that I took little notice of cultural developments any more significant than the St. Louis Cardinals (whose batting order and pitching rotation I still know by rote) and the styling changes Detroit made in its automobiles each season (it remains my conviction that the downfall of the Ford Motor Company began in 1948, the year it switched from the rounded body to the square-back rear end). Hence *The Best Years* is a product of what I've read about the period and what people have told me. An interesting lot of people, too, ranging from Mad Man Muntz, an odd but highly successful purveyor of automobiles and cheap TVs, to personages of the world such as Clark Clifford, who made decisions in the Truman White House that set the course of the Cold War, and the editor of the Kinsey Report. I conducted interviews for more than two years, and I read an incredibly huge pile of printed material, ranging from small-town newspapers and politicians' memoirs to the infuriated letters people sent Harry Truman about rent controls and the high price of pork chops. (A more formal recitation of sources and acknowledgments follows the text.)

My operating principle has been to avoid hindsight and revisionism: Americans behaved on the basis of information contemporaneously available to them, and my purpose is to explore the political and social environment as it appeared to them in the 1940's—not as it does through the long-distance prism of history.

I

The Veterans:
Home Again,
Sixteen Million
Strong

A Remembrance of Marshall: I

For the Goulden family, the homecoming GI was personified by my father's brother Carl, a rakish young man whose gift for electronics was surpassed, perhaps, only by his enthusiasm for beer and late hours. Carl worried people, especially the women in the family. In his mid-teens, before the war, he unilaterally declared his schooling at an end—without the formality of notifying either parents or the principal—and spent the daytime hours of most of an autumn sitting in a tree house, calling radio hams around the country with a transmitter he built from scratch. When the school finally called to ask Carl's whereabouts, Grandmother Goulden was philosophical. "Carl's that way," she said. Because of chronological happenstance, Carl was the only one of three brothers caught up by the military and sent overseas.

My direct memories of the wartime Carl are vague: a pleasant, red-faced young man in the woolly brown uniform of the air corps, sittting on our couch with a can of Falstaff in his hand and a dozen or so others close by in the ice box; once or twice a jolly, giggling girl named Dolly or Reba beside him, young ladies from Shreveport or Dallas who were not quite like my sister's high-school friends, but in ways I could only sense, not fully understand. My parents' discussions of Carl tended to break off in mid-sentence when a child appeared, but I learned several things about him during the war years. The military discipline would "make Carl settle down and make something out of himself," the fervent hope of my mother and Carl's sisters. The exposure to the outside world would "let Carl know there's more to life than Marshall and Shreveport, Louisiana," in the words of my father, who at times seemed somewhat envious that his kid brother was seeing Manila and Tokyo and Seoul at government expense, and enjoying cold beer as he did so.

Carl finally came home, some months after the peace, preceded by a huge trunk and a duffel bag, which arrived by rail, and postcards from the West Coast. He was in the living room one afternoon when I came in from school—the same red face, the woolly brown uniform, the can *of Falstaff. He grunted hello, and I said I wanted a war story. He gave me one. The bomber on which he was a radio operator put down at a strip in the Philippines. A few minutes later, as another American craft landed, its guns jammed, and Uncle Carl and the other men ducked into a ditch to escape the bullets. Carl kept drinking Falstaff, and during dinner he told another story. His crew took Philippine beer on runs over Japan and dropped empty bottles along with the bombs. "Might as well put empty bottles to good use," Carl said.*

A day or so later I heard my mother sigh in the kitchen and say to my father, "I don't think the army did much for Carl. He's the same old boy he was in 1941." "Why the dickens should the army have had any effect on Carl?" my father asked. "Nothing else ever bothered him." Carl drifted on to Shreveport and an engineer's job at a radio station and an apartment whose ice box always contained a can or two of Falstaff. Six years later, when we were moving, my mother asked if he wanted the old army trunk that had sat, unopened, in a back closet since the day he returned from Asia. "I'd forgotten all about that thing," he said. "Throw it away. There's nothing in the air corps that could interest me now anyway."

dents, time in the military, and age. These findings in hand, the War Department announced its first demobilization policy on September 6, 1944: that discharges would be on an individual, not a unit, basis; and that surplus soldiers would be mustered out as quickly as possible after Germany fell. The department warned that some men fighting in Europe might be shipped to the Pacific and said that details of the point system would be announced in due course. Endorsing the policy three weeks later, President Roosevelt noted it was one "based on the wishes of the soldiers themselves."

Press and public reaction, for the most part, was favorable. But loose high-level lips caused problems. Major General Lewis Hershey, head of the Selective Service System, had said several times during the year the army should hold men until jobs were available for them, even after peace. Hershey said, "We can keep people in the army about as cheaply as we could create an agency for them when they are out." Thomas E. Dewey, the Republican presidential candidate in 1944, picked up the Hershey statement and charged that the Roosevelt Administration intended to maintain a large army just to avoid a high unemployment rate. Actually, Pentagon thinking was just the opposite. When the idea of "coordinating" releases with "employment opportunities" was floated, a key demobilization planner, Brigadier General F. H. Osborn, sharply dissented. By doing so, Osborn wrote, the army would be "making itself into a sort of preventative WPA." Such a policy would prevent many men from entering into fair competition with civilians for available jobs, he said. The idea died, and a Pentagon directive ordered Hershey to stop talking publicly about policies of which he was ignorant.

To the American GI the September 1944 announcement, vague and hedged though it was, offered the first faint promise of home. The soldiers made the most of their hopes. The army magazine *Yank* bannered the story PLAN FOR DEMOBILIZATION and talked in a tone that made GIs begin looking around for the boat. "Demobilization is all set to go. X-Day, that is, the day the resistance ends, has been officially designated as the starting gun. So it is possible that by the time some GIs in outlying bases read this story, the process of discharging surplus soldiers and sending them home may actually have begun." Later on in the piece *Yank* did say some European ground troops, "even including those who have had combat, *may* have to be shipped to the Pacific" (italics added). But to weary GIs the very mention of "demobilization" stirred eager expectations.

That demobilization was going to make a lot of people unhappy, regardless of how the military carried it out, became painfully obvious beginning with the German capitulation in May 1945. The mechanics of the point system, revealed the day after V-E Day, relied heavily upon servicemen's preferences gathered in the Research Branch survey. The system gave one point for each month in the service; one for each month overseas; five for each campaign star or combat decoration; and, if the GI was a father, twelve for each child under age eighteen, to a maximum of three children. The army's first "magic number" for immediate discharge was eighty-five points, and GIs the world over scrambled for pencil and paper to compute their totals. Inequities were inevitable, and aggrieved soldiers quickly made them known via Congress. Typical was the letter of a staff sergeant serving with an army air forces group:*

> A man who does the engine changes on our planes is in the service group and gets no stars, but the man who drives the gas truck to fuel the planes is in the bombing group and gets four stars. A man who keeps a 2½-ton truck of the service group in top condition to haul bombs and other vital needs rates no stars; a man who keeps a 2½-ton truck of the bomb group in top condition to haul these very same needs rates four. A bomb group man in headquarters is handed twenty points; a service group man at the next desk, doing the same work, is handed, it would seem, a gold-braided TS ticket.

Black spokesmen also complained. Edgar G. Brown, director of the National Negro Council, noted that blacks, who seldom earned combat points because of their assignments to service units, "will be the last to return home."

But the most severe criticism hit at the size of the armada the military intended to hurl at Japan. Far, far too many men, opined the Chicago *Tribune,* noting that the Pentagon was sending 11,000,000 men to fight a single enemy in the Pacific, and that only a million or so more had been enough "to fight a two-front war on both sides of the globe against six nations and their auxiliaries." The *Tribune* saw a simple solution—confirm the officers in their temporary ranks and discharge the enlisted men: "The army and its officer hierarchy cannot expect the country to endure without complaint a roster that seems to have less reference to military necessity than to a padded political payroll in a whoopee era." But the Los Angeles *Times* felt "obviously the most important consideration had to be military necessity . . . the job of beating Japan."

Shipping battle veterans from Europe to the Pacific caused the military even louder problems. Men of the 28th Division, during their transit through the United States from one war theater to another, dispatched protesting telegrams to editors saying regular army officers wanted to keep surplus divisions intact "for the retention of their temporary wartime ranks." The 95th Infantry Division petitioned congressmen, "Why should we serve on two fronts when there are many who never served on

---

* It should be remembered that the air force was part of the army during the Second World War.

one?" Major General Harry L. Twaddle, the division's commander, said the situation approached "open sedition and mutiny," and he indirectly confirmed the soldiers' chief gripe. The "principal disturbing elements" in the 95th, Twaddle said, were "high-point men who had been transferred into the division prior to departure from Germany." The voice of every angry GI was amplified by relatives and friends. America had won half the war. Why should not half the army be permitted to come home? And why should not fresh conscripts, rather than combat veterans, go to the Pacific? Responding, the War Department insisted that most combat veterans had been screened from the divisions. Secretary of War Henry L. Stimson also pointed out that the Japanese army still had 2,250,000 trained soldiers in the home islands alone, and an equal number in Pacific and Asiatic territories. The United States must disarm these men, he said, and ships going to the mainland must be prepared for combat if necessary. He also felt it "risky" to use green troops for occupation duty. John L. Lewis' militant United Mine Workers of America demanded the early release of 30,000 coal miners. So, too, did the railroads, arguing they needed extra help to handle troop movements. Senator J. H. Bankhead of Alabama wanted farmers out immediately. Secretary of War Stimson refused to bend policy to accommodate the farmers, the railmen, or the miners. But he did issue strict orders for commanders to search out men holding nonessential jobs, and hasten their discharges. Personnel oversights were legendary. An inspector general wrote, "One corporal with a silver star was found driving a garbage truck, and a private with two purple hearts was discovered tending a hot water heater in a WAC barracks."

But for all the criticisms and the wide newspaper publicity given the horror stories that inevitably pop up in an undertaking involving a bureaucracy and millions of people, public sentiment overwhelmingly supported the demobilization policy. A Gallup poll in June 1945 reported 73 percent of the public felt the point system to be fair, and only 15 percent opposed it. As Gallup noted, seldom is three-quarters of the American people supportive of *any* governmental policy.

The flow of discharges, once it began, quickly became a gush. Between V-E Day (May 7) and mid-September the army alone mustered out 700,000 men, surging toward a goal of 25,000 daily. The navy, preparing to return some 4,000,000 men from abroad in the first year of peace, hurried landing and cargo craft into yards for conversion to troop carriers (three weeks and $280,000 were required to transform a stubby Liberty ship, workhorse of the navy's freight fleet, into an ersatz liner capable of holding 550 men). In July the *Queen Mary* sped westward across the Atlantic with its lights ablaze for the first time since 1939, carrying 15,278 troops happy to crowd into space designed for 2,000. The soldiers slept in bunks three and four tiers high, in cabanas and lounges; they got only two meals a day and the chief pastime was carving names into the once-luxury liner's teakwood deck railings. The army sent out *Welcome Boat Q-200*—featuring a twenty-eight-piece all-female band led by Warrant Officer Marybelle Nissly—which bobbed alongside troop ships steaming into New York harbor. Troops lined the rails to cheer as the band blared out "One Meatball" and "The Pennsylvania Polka." In Boston, also an important port of entry, an eager lieutenant jumped fifteen feet to the dock to collect a kiss offered by a pretty girl. He broke his ankle but got his kiss before a stretcher carried him away. Some months later, when the carrier USS *Saratoga* sailed home from the Pacific wars, the navy crammed more than 2,000 extra sailors aboard. They slept on the open flight decks, in the pilot ready rooms, even in the admiral's sacrosanct flag office. By autumn of 1945, the navy had 843 troop and combat ships ferrying men to the states, ranging from the *Queen Mary* (which Britain finally retrieved late in the year to take its own men home from India and Burma) to the converted freighters. "It took us three and a half years to get the men overseas, and it will take us only ten months to get them back," Admiral William M. Callaghan, the director of naval transportation, told an inquiring Senate committee.

But for the individual GI, the troop ship home could be the last great adventure—and frustration—of the war. Some of the civilian-soldiers managed to laugh about the round-the-clock chow lines, the crowding (bunks were stacked six and eight deep in the holds of some freighters), the lack of exercise space (on some ships enlisted men were allowed fifteen minutes daily above decks), the shipboard discipline enforced by officers and noncoms bent on demonstrating that, peace or no peace, the GI remained government property.

One person repelled by the diehard hold of the military caste system was the American Communist leader Elizabeth Gurley Flynn, who got passage aboard the troop transport USAT *Edward M. Alexander* en route home from a European meeting of the International Congress of Women. Mrs. Flynn said that even though the enlisted men ate franks and sauerkraut for breakfast while officers enjoyed eggs and fresh fruit, they were "initially philosophical." But morale took a nasty turn on Christmas Eve when enlisted men lined up for a USO show for which tickets had been distributed. "The announcement came over the loudspeaker that the performance was 'for officers only,' and military personnel [enlisted men] would return to quarters. They drowned out the voice in catcalls and boos." The men glumly returned to the hold; the next day, the ship commander ordered a rerun of the entertainment for them. Mrs. Flynn concluded, somewhat jubilantly, "Agitation pays even on an army transport, especially one headed towards home."

*   *   *

C. K. Hollomanberg worked as an executive for a New York hotel chain before going to Europe as a fighter pilot. A man who appreciated his comfort, Hollomanberg recoiled from the possibility of traveling home in the hold of a troop ship. "I spent much of my military career keeping out of uncomfortable mob situations," he said. "Uncle Sam had given me a fighter plane to ride in for more than fifty combat missions, and I really thought he could find one for me one more time." Uncle Sam couldn't, at first, because Hollomanberg was neither ranking brass, a VIP, wounded, nor facing a family crisis that warranted priority transport. But one asset Hollomanberg did possess was ingenuity.

"At the main demobilization terminal in Roussefls I scouted around until I found the guy, a lieutenant, who controlled the shipping rosters. I laid it down for him directly: 'You get me a plane ride home, my good young man, and when you get home, I expect you and your wife to spend a week in New York as a guest of my hotel.'

" 'Sit right there,' the lieutenant told me, and hurried away. I was scared shitless. I expected him to come back with an MP and have me hauled off to Lichfield* for attempted bribery. I almost got up and sneaked out. Then here came the lieutenant, with a file of papers. 'Here is the drill,' he said. 'You are a compassionate case, so you get priority, that's what these orders say. If anyone asks any questions, you turned all the papers over to the shipping center here, and "the sergeant" insisted that he had to keep them. See you in New York this fall, Captain.'

"I went off without a question. Fifty-three hours later I was in the states, and within a week I was back at my desk. The lieutenant? Well, I got a letter from him later that year. He was out, but he couldn't afford to come to New York just then, so I told him any time. I got a Christmas card from him each year, and he'd jot on it, 'Soon, I hope.' When he finally did come East, in 1953, I had left the hotel business and moved to Erie. But I kept my bargain: I had the chain send me the bill for his week, and I laid out something like $140 for him and his wife. Troop ships were pretty far from my mind by that time, but what the hell, you make a deal, you keep it. I sure the hell would have handed him $140 in the summer of forty-five."

For men in the Pacific, the vast expanses of water separating them from home caused seemingly ceaseless weeks of tedium. Under optimum conditions a transport required more than a month from Manila to San Francisco. But the ships didn't always sail the more direct route at top speed, for they had to pick up servicemen from the dozens of remote Pacific atolls where war had scattered them. One GI, home from the

---

* A military prison in France notorious for brutality toward inmates.

Philippines, wrote his senator: "I have just arrived here [San Francisco] on October 14, 1945 . . . with 1,200 other enlisted men. We spent 81 days from July 26 to October 14 in arriving at our destination. I carried my seabag and personal gear across the gangplank exactly 27 times." Another reported living aboard a ship at anchor for twenty-seven days in the Olithi islands group, awaiting sailing orders that were delayed for some reason never made clear to the troops. During his spare time—which was considerable, as the GI wrote—he counted no less than 200 ships of varying sizes in the anchorage, and asked why the navy could not put them to use ferrying men home. The navy, responding to scores of such complaints before the Senate Naval Affairs Committee, said many small ships didn't carry enough men to make such use worthwhile. The navy could not sail a 40,000-ton vessel, with a 40-man crew, 12,000 miles over 2½ months "just in order to return twenty or thirty passengers," said Admiral Callaghan.

Stateside transportation had problems as well. With most of America's autos and buses worn out during four years of war and air passenger service a novelty, the railroads handled the bulk of long-distance traffic. Restless civilians, eager for long-delayed vacation trips, competed with returning servicemen for the few available seats—so vigorously, in fact, that by late summer the railroads and government attempted to keep them at home. A Pullman Company advertisement pictured wounded vets en route to hospitals in Pullman cars, and civilians clustered around a ticket counter. The text warned that "the military load on trains will probably be greater—for the next few months at least—than at any time since we have been at war." The Association of American Railroads advertised: "If it comes to a choice between your taking a trip—and a returned soldier getting to see his home folks—we know you will understand who deserves the right of way." Lines to Cape Cod and the Berkshire Mountains canceled summer excursions to keep trains available for soldiers. Still the civilian travelers persisted—even after the Office of Defense Transportation prohibited reservations more than five days in advance, in hopes of discouraging trips to mountain and shore resorts. Five hundred vets almost rioted during an eight-day odyssey from Massachusetts to California when they heard rumors, which turned out to be untrue, that German POWs were riding in Pullmans at the front of the train. A troop train arriving in Denver had two clogged washrooms for fifteen cars; signs painted on the sides told the vets' gripes: "So this is America?" "Nothing's too good for the returning Yanks—oh, yeah?" An air corps lieutenant reported traveling thirty-six hours with sixty men in a dirty antiquated coach in a train that also carried a vaudeville troupe, which had an entire Pullman for its comfort.

As noted earlier, the War Department had anticipated an eighteen-month lag between V-E and V-J days. Hence the sudden collapse of

Japan after the nuclear bombing of Hiroshima and Nagasaki meant an unexpected acceleration in the pace of demobilization. The army had expected to muster out 1,100,000 men during the eighteen months, and another 4,500,000 the year after peace, bringing its postwar strength down to around 2,500,000 men. Instead, the demobilization rate was increased fivefold, with a target of 5,500,000 by the end of June 1946.

In terms of getting men home and out of uniform, the War Department performed well; indeed, it far exceeded its own goals (for instance, the army had planned on discharging 750,000 men in December; the actual figure was 1,168,000). But in terms of long-range policy goals, demobilization proved a disaster, one that effectively wrecked the United States military.

The reasons are several. Most important, perhaps, the Truman Administration talked of one policy only to execute another. As the war ground to a close, first President Roosevelt and after his death President Truman spoke repeatedly of the United States' intention to assume vast peacetime responsibilities for world security—language that could mean only that hundreds of thousands of American troops would remain on foreign soil indefinitely. General Marshall spoke of the need for "strong American forces abroad to protect the fruits of victory." Truman even gave specific numbers. In a letter to the House Military Affairs Committee in August 1945, he noted that since Generals Eisenhower and MacArthur needed 1,200,000 men for occupation duty, planning for the postwar army should start from that base figure. He estimated an army of 2,500,000 men by July 1946. Even so, Mr. Truman foresaw problems. At the then-rates of induction and demobilization, the army would have only 800,000 volunteers and draftees at that time. Thus he said the difference of 1,700,000 men "must be made up by holding additional numbers of veterans in the service."

After stating the policy, the Truman Administration proceeded to ignore it. Instead, it bowed to public and congressional pressures and set about dispersing the army as rapidly as possible. A scant month after Mr. Truman's pronouncement about the 2,500,000-man army, General Marshall was telling a congressional committee that the demobilization rate "has been determined by transportation facilities and the availability of trained personnel to carry its administrative requirements out. It has no relationship whatsoever to the size of the army of the future."

In fairness to the Truman Administration, its surrender to expediency could have been avoided only at great political cost. As early as March 1945 the chief Pentagon lobbyist had warned General Marshall that "the attitude of Congress is beginning to approach that which exists towards the military establishment in normal times of peace. . . . Until recently, Congress has responded to the army as the desperate householder whose home is in flames welcomes the fire department: Drive over the lawn, chop down the doors, throw the furniture out the window, but save the house. Now, with the flames under control, the Congress, like the householder, is noting for the first time the water damages and thinking that if the fire department had acted differently, the lawn would not be torn up, the doors smashed, and the furniture broken." The lobbyist counseled that the Pentagon treat Congress gingerly if it expected passage of such priority legislation as an extension of the draft.

Congress's major offensive against the military commenced August 4, 1945, only days before V-J Day, in a letter from Senator Edwin C. Johnson of Colorado to Secretary Stimson, demanding an immediate reduction in the size of the armed forces. Johnson, a self-elected point man for the congressional dissidents, asserted there was a "widespread feeling in Congress and the country now that the War Department is tenaciously holding millions of men it does not need and whom it cannot use."

Editorial criticism, although scattered, was from influential sources. The Chicago *Tribune* asked in an editorial, "Has the army heard of peace?" and demanded force reductions. Returning to the same "outrage" a few days later, the *Tribune* saw no explanation other than "incompetence and selfishness. . . . It often has been pointed out that the more rapidly the army is reduced from its wartime strength the more rapidly its higher officers will be reduced in number, rank and influence. It would be hard to imagine a worse reason than this one for keeping millions of men in the army, but what other reason is there?" The *Wall Street Journal*, noting that the army alone would still have 6,000,000 men by the end of 1945, declared, "On the basis of any information available to the public, that is a policy that is perfectly idiotic. If the United States saw any other country pursuing a similar policy we would be crying to high heaven about 'militarism' and what not." The *Journal* charged that the army "is deliberately pursuing a policy of 'gradual' demobilization. . . . We wonder if anyone in Washington has any adequate idea of the resentment that is being built up in this country."

Washington was not deaf. Under Secretary of War Robert P. Patterson, called before the Senate Military Affairs Committee to account for the "slow pace of demobilization" (at a time, ironically, when discharges ran 30 to 45 percent ahead of schedule), protested that the Pentagon was doing the "best job possible," mustering out 10,000 men daily. "We are getting 10,000 *letters* a day," shot back Senator Johnson, who complained that former combat troops were "mowing lawns with bayonets" to kill time while awaiting discharge. Representative Homer V. Ramey of Ohio complained that he and colleagues spent so much time handling citizen gripes about the military that they acted as "harried errand boys at a time when other vital questions" demanded attention. All that the Pentagon could do was avow that it was trying and plead for patience. But any ground it gained was promptly, if inadvertently, squandered by an offhand remark by General MacArthur. The Japanese had proved so docile and cooperative, the general said, that he needed only 200,000 occupation troops rather than the previously estimated 500,000. (A later army study called MacArthur's announcement "another of the public relations errors that characterized the demobilization period.")

As autumn wore on, critics attracted more and more attention. A group calling itself "The Service Fathers' Release Association" claimed branches in more than 300 cities and demanded that elected officials down to the local level join its drive to get the release of everyone from the service, regardless of his time in uniform. "Bring the Boys Home by Christmas," financed largely by liberals and leftists in organized labor, stirred up a blitz of postcards directed to President Truman. On December 17 alone, 60,000 cards swirled down on the White House, carrying this message:

Dear Mr. President:

I urge you as commander in chief to press into service every ship flying our flag to bring back our troops by Christmas.

Ships for private commerce, ships laid up in United States ports and United States meddling in China are keeping GIs from being reunited with their families.

I urge every ship be made a troopship.

Sincerely yours,

Other outcries were more spontaneous. A GI's wife wrote the Wyoming *State Tribune:* "He's fat, sway-backed—with a crick in the sway—chipped elbow, has several teeth missing and hobbles into age thirty-eight this month. . . . But he has a nice smile—with what teeth he has left—and I love him. So why don't you send him home?" An Oklahoma Republican congressman got a terse letter from a constituent in Manila: "You put us in the army, and you can get us out. Either demobilize us, or, when given the next shot at the ballot box, we will demobilize you."

The climax came in January 1946 when the War Department was forced into a grudging admission that it had promised faster discharges than it could deliver. In September General Marshall had told Congress that all men with two years or more service would be discharged by late winter.* By January, the rate of demobilization was so rapid that the Pentagon decided it must take immediate steps to stop it. It fell to the

---

* According to a later army study, General Marshall apparently misunderstood a briefing given him by demobilization planners, and accidentally promised something the army had never intended.

lot of Secretary of War Robert Patterson (who had succeeded Stimson in September) to tell the public that the military must renege on Marshall's promise. An army internal memo said Patterson "feels that it would be better to admit that we have made a mistake than to try to qualify any announcement." The announcement pushed the discharge of two-year men back to July 1, 1946.

And it also pushed GIs and the Congress into open revolt. The unfortunate Patterson was just beginning an inspection tour of Pacific bases when the statement was released. When he arrived in Guam, angry demonstrating soldiers burned him in effigy. At each stop thereafter worried local commanders arranged for him to meet soldier delegations to vent the GI ire. But on successive days in Manila he faced shouting mobs of up to 10,000 soldiers and sailors. The Pacific edition of *Stars & Stripes* bannered PATTERSON CALLED NUMBER ONE ENEMY BY JEERING MOB. Other GIs marched through Manila with banners protesting the cancellation of ship sailings that were to take them home. "We want ships, we want to go home," they chanted. A colonel ordered them back to their barracks, exclaiming, "You men forget you're not working for General Motors. You're still in the army." (The United Auto Workers was striking General Motors at the time.)

The protests spread rapidly around the world. The same January week that thirty-eight-year-old Major General James Gavin led 13,000 members of the 82d Airborne Division up Fifth Avenue from Washington Square, in the sort of joyous procession civilian America delighted in watching as well-cadenced evidence of peace, virtually every U.S. command witnessed demonstrations against the "slow-down" order. Soldiers booed their commanding officers at mass meetings and passed their service caps for money to buy ads in state-wide newspapers. Military police noted sharp increases in arrests for drunkenness, reckless driving, and slovenly dress. Hundreds of GIs marched down the Champs Elysées waving magnesium flares and shouting "scab" at men who wouldn't join them. In Frankfurt, 2,000 soldiers gathered outside the quarters of Lieutenant General Joseph T. McNarney, the occupation commander, and dared him to talk with them. "Service yes, serfdom no," they called. "Japs go home—how about us?" In London, a chanting but good-natured crowd of soldiers and airmen marched on Claridge's Hotel and asked that the visiting Eleanor Roosevelt help them. She received a delegation and later wrote a note to General Eisenhower, now the chief of staff: She said the "boys" were "very well behaved, and, I thought, very logical." The former First Lady recounted some of the specific complaints about inequities of the point system and idleness ("one boy said he would give anything to do one good day's work") and expressed the "hope that something can be done." She concluded, "They are good boys but if they don't have enough to do they will get into trouble. That is the nature of boys, I am afraid, in any situation."

Stars & Stripes reported frequently on enlisted men's complaints of idleness and boredom; if no meaningful work existed for them, why not permit them to go home?

And an anonymous GI poet directed a message to the President through the European *Stars & Stripes:*

> Please, Mr. Truman, won't you send us home?
> We have captured Napoli and liberated Rome;
> We have licked the master race,
> Now there's lots of shipping space,
> So, won't you send us home?
> Let the boys at home see Rome.

GIs griped about being treated as second-rate citizens while officers enjoyed liquor, the best housing and clubs, and the company of nurses and Red Cross girls. Soldiers and sailors came out of the war "hating and detesting military life," *Stars & Stripes* said. "A caste system inherited from Frederick the Great of Prussia and the 18th-Century British navy is hardly appropriate to the United States . . . the aristocracy-peasantry relationship characteristic of our armed forces has a counterpart nowhere else in American life."

An unmeasurable factor in the bring-our-boys-home sentiment was traditional feminine jealousy on the part of wives, girl friends, and blue-nosed busybodies; and maternal concern over the sort of company Sonny might be keeping abroad. The woman at home heard enough dire warnings to stimulate any imagination. One reason Senator Johnson of Colorado claimed he opposed the draft was a fear that "every boy drafted will be thrown in the path of diseased prostitutes and lewd women in the foulest human cesspools." In the *Christian Century,* the Reverend Renwick C. C. Kennedy, an army chaplain overseas for twenty months before returning to the moralistic community of Camden, Alabama, wrote that the "average" GI had "primitive" interests. "They are chiefly three: (1) to find a German woman and sleep with her; (2) to buy or steal a bottle of cognac and get stinking drunk; (3) to go home." Kennedy described the overseas GI as a pitiful creature: "There he stands in his bulging clothes, fat, overfed, lonely, a bit wistful, seeing little, understanding less—the Conqueror with a chocolate bar in one pocket and a package of cigarettes in the other." Kennedy claimed that the rate of venereal disease was up to 427 cases per 1,000 men in some areas of Germany, and that "army headquarters in Frankfurt had to prepare special armbands for U.S. wives to protect them from wolves." American females read of such peccadilloes with fury: when the Gallup poll asked in mid-1945 whether American soldiers should be permitted to date German girls, 70 percent of the American women under thirty voted no. The U.S. command for several months flatly banned fraternization of any kind, subject to a $65 fine. Accepting reality, the army in

July 1945 eased the ban to permit soldiers to walk with girls in "public places" but not to visit them at home or entertain them in their own quarters. Soldiers still could not "drink, play games nor dance" with Germans.

The spectacle of an army in near mutiny jarred the military. On the other side of the world, General MacArthur said the turmoil made it difficult to turn Japan toward true democracy because "real democratic leaders are afraid to speak, not knowing how long U.S. troops will be here to protect them." After General Eisenhower ordered an end to demonstrations upon pain of court martial, the Milwaukee *Journal* called some of the GI complaints "fantastic," especially those that soldiers were being kept overseas to enforce "imperialism" and to enable the "brass hats to maintain large commands to keep their own rank or to 'play at war.' " The *Journal* did not believe that President Truman, "who must answer to the American people and the 15 million American vets at the polls, would dare to resist the clamor of these soldiers overseas unless he was convinced that the welfare of the nation and the world required him to do so."

Army intelligence reports claimed that by demonstrating "large numbers of American soldiers gave support to the Communist Party line and were not even aware of it."* As supporting "evidence" the reports cited the similarity of questions that enlisted men put to officers during protests in Seoul, Shanghai, Manila, and New Delhi: "Are we out here to protect Wall Street? Is this Yankee imperialism? Did you bring the 86th Division to suppress the aspirations of the Philippine people? Are we protecting the 'British Lion'?" Intelligence agents also smelled suspiciously leftist sentiments in statements GIs made during hearings conducted at Pacific bases by a Senate investigating committee later in 1946. For instance, one noncommissioned officer testified the January protests were prompted in part by an announcement "by the chief of staff of the 86th Division to the effect that the . . . division would undergo training along battle lines to exert . . . American influence in prospective disturbances in the Philippines," which were preparing for elections in advance of promised independence on July 4, 1946. The noncom asked the senators whether they felt the army should "be used to maintain vested interests in property and jobs in the Commonwealth?" Another soldier said GIs felt they were kept in Luzon as a "potential strike-breaking force."

* Peculiarly, the reports still bore a "secret" classification in late 1974, more than a quarter of a century after they were written. The United States Army Center for Military History denied me access to a study entitled "Intelligence Activities of the Army Ground Forces During the Demobilization Period, 1 September 1945–10 March 1948," compiled in 1948, on the grounds of secrecy. The information cited above is taken from a broader army study of demobilization, which incorporated the intelligence reports.

If the protesting soldiers indeed were "dupes" of Communist propaganda, so, too, were many members of the Congress, for the slow-down order touched off the loudest yells of the postwar period. Seeking to force the Administration's hand on fast demobilization, Mississippi Representative John E. Rankin, chairman of the House Committee on World War Veterans Legislation,* and Representative D. A. Reed of New York, among others, introduced bills releasing any man with eighteen months' service. "The war is over," cried Rankin. "We do not have an enemy on earth that would dare bat an eye at us today. Why should we have an army of occupation in the Philippines?" Representative Emanuel Celler of New York wondered what U.S. troops were doing in "a place such as India." Republicans McCowen of Ohio and Gillie of Indiana accused the army of committing a "breach of faith with those who served us so well." Representative A. H. Andresen of Minnesota said the slow-down order "smacks of military dictatorship."

To keep matters in a semblance of perspective, much congressional whooping must be dismissed as airy bluster. Congress, then as now, is an easily excitable body when confronted with an emotional issue. For all its threats and thinly prepared "investigative" hearings into demobilization, not a single law or even resolution resulted. When the House Military Affairs Committee refused to report the eighteen-month release bills to the floor, sponsors could not get the required 218 signatures on a petition to bring it out of committee for a vote, and the reason was obvious. The Democratic leadership did not intend to embarrass its own administration by forcing changes in demobilization policy. A degree of political caution was also involved: as Massachusetts' Senator David I. Walsh argued on the floor, "If I . . . were to submit a resolution declaring that the war emergency was over, we would be accused of interfering with the orderly ending of the war, as well as with leaving the army and the navy up in the air and crippling the necessary work of preserving the property of the army and navy, and getting our ships back to America." But what does a politician do when constituents mail 200 pairs of babies' booties to Washington with notes reading, "I Miss My Daddy," a package that the nervous Senator Elbert Thomas of Oklahoma found in his office mail one morning? The reaction is as should be expected: the politician dances with rage and shouts nasty things at the people responsible for disturbing the voters. Experienced Washingtonians learn to pay no heed to such tantrums, especially when nothing concrete accompanies them.

The immensely popular General Eisenhower finally invoked his personal prestige and charm to hush Congress. On January 15 he appeared before members assembled in the Library of Congress (braving hissingly

* Now the House Committee on Veterans Affairs.

angry women pickets who demanded, "How do you think we feel when we see pictures of our men walking with the Germans and the Japanese?") and delivered a most polite challenge. In his quiet, slow-paced delivery, Ike went right to the point: The military was slowing demobilization because if the present rate continued "we would literally run out of soldiers." The military had been told by "higher authority" to perform certain functions. If Congress insists on cutting the military's strength, it should also specify the functions to be discontinued. Ike professed sympathy for the women pickets and other aggrieved relatives of servicemen, but added, "If we should take every father today, authorize his discharge, and start him home, the army simply cannot do his job."

Eisenhower convinced the congressmen. Critics thereafter complained of isolated instances of supposed injustice, but never again attacked the overall demobilization policy. But in the minds of the military leaders, grave damage, perhaps irreparable damage, had already been done: in their estimates, the "willy-nilly discharges" and the "national hysteria to demobilize" (the words of Major General St. Clair Streett, deputy commander of the continental air command) had disabled the armed forces.

And indeed by the end of 1945 the once-mighty American fighting forces were a hollow, echoing shell. Even President Truman conceded in his memoirs, "The program we were following was no longer demobilization—it was disintegration of our armed forces." Truman did his part to speed along the process: In January 1946 he told the Pentagon he wanted an overall military strength of 2,000,000 men, about a million fewer than planned. The army, Mr. Truman directed, should be cut to 1,000,000, or some 50,000 less than what the brass had called the minimum "bedrock requirements." Congress went even further. During debate over the draft extension in the spring of 1946 the military was cut even deeper, to 1,070,000 men effective July 1, 1947.

To career military men the cuts portended disaster. Major General Clovis E. Byers, chief of staff of the Japan occupation forces, warned, "None of our divisions is up to full strength. . . . If any group of Japanese decided the time was ripe for revolt, they would certainly pick a time when they believed there was dissatisfaction in the American Army. It appears that subversive forces are deliberately at work, for obscure reasons, attempting to undermine the morale of our army," Byers concluded darkly. The army desperately cut training cycles for recruits from seventeen to thirteen weeks, then to eight; once a soldier finished basic training, he was shipped directly to Germany or Japan. By mid-1946 the army was not a closely integrated military machine but large groups of individual replacements. General Carl Spaatz, the army air force commander, reported that only two of fifty-five air groups passed their 1946 proficiency tests: "Airplanes were stranded in all parts of the globe for lack of maintenance personnel to repair them . . . serviceable and even new aircraft, equipment and material were left to deteriorate for lack of personnel to prepare them for storage." In June 1946 the army's four "active" divisions in the United States included the 2d Armored Division, with only 20 percent of its authorized personnel; and the 3d Infantry, "which existed only on paper with a complement of sixteen officers and twelve enlisted men." So great was the rush to speed men abroad that the army suspended combat rifle firing tests save for units marked for strategic reserve: "Greater emphasis was placed on an information and education program than almost anything else," commented an army report.

Field commanders—and U.S. diplomats—felt the reduction in a variety of ways. In the Far East, the turnover of skilled staff officers was so brisk that it slowed the trial of accused Japanese war criminals; not until June 1947 was a full complement of ten courts operating. When a "send-us-home" rally in Seoul in 1946 coincided with U.S.–Soviet negotiations over the division of Korea, the American commander, Lieutenant General John R. Hodge, commented that the Russians "would take great pleasure in our embarrassment and unwillingness to continue as soldiers." The conferees didn't reach any agreements. And years later General Marshall recalled the tribulations of trying to talk tough with the Soviets at a time when U.S. forces had melted to nothing:

> I remember, when I was secretary of state, I was being pressured constantly, particularly when in Moscow, by radio message after radio message to give the Russians hell. When I got back, I was getting the same appeal in relation to the Far East and China. At that time, my facilities for giving them hell—and I am a soldier and know something about the ability to give hell—was one and one-third divisions over the entire United States.
>
> That is quite a proposition when you deal with somebody with over 260 [divisions] and you have one and one-third. We had nothing in Alaska. We did not have enough to defend the air strip up at Fairbanks.

In its postmortems on demobilization, years after the war, the army itself could not decide whether the operation was a success. From the human standpoint, a group of social scientists working with contemporary War Department polling data gave passing marks to the concept, if not the execution, of the program. Their report concluded, "Although in retrospect history may find that the greatest American army ever created was broken up too rapidly, history also will record the irresistible political pressures to 'bring the boys home' and the impatience of the soldiers themselves, some units of which behaved in a manner hardly describable in terms other than mutiny." The team felt that if the army had used unit discharges, freeing short-service men in Europe while combat veterans continued fighting in the Pacific, "the morale situation would have been explosive. . . . In taking its calculated risk, the army won its gamble. . . . [T]he War Department chose correctly when it broke all precedent and went to the enlisted men for their opinions before promulgating its redeployment and demobilization policy." The Research Branch polls never found a majority of the men surveyed giving negative answers about demobilization, even during the post–V-J Day period when "almost every expression about the army . . . was negative by a decisive proportion." But the army's official history of demobilization—written in 1952, after the agony of Korea had demonstrated the dangers of letting an army lapse into disrepair—had as its concluding sentence, "When future scholars evaluate the history of the United States during the first half of the 20th Century, they will list World War Two demobilization as one of the cardinal mistakes." Yet a later army study, published in 1968, took a middle view, saying judgment "depends on the vantage point from which it is viewed." The 1968 study stated:

In terms of what were actually the national objectives during the 1945–46 period—rapid return of soldiers to civilian life and rapid reconversion of a wartime to a peacetime economy—it was a success. From the vantage point of preserving necessary American forces to support American diplomacy, it was a failure.

But to America of 1945–46, the long-range implication of rapid demobilization was a question to be ignored. The public demanded the physical presence of its loved ones as proof that peace had truly returned to America. And the civilians, concurrently, were in the midst of their own preparations for the best years, earnestly studying how to cope with that mysterious creature known as The Veteran.

2

Preparing for Ulysses

A S T H E W A R drew to a close, the American public awaited the return of its combat servicemen with a curious ambivalence: On an individual basis, of course, every family wanted its own Johnny home as quickly as possible, although realizing he might not be quite the same young man who went off to war. But Americans looked at that vast all-inclusive generic class of "veteran" with more than a little anxiety, as if U.S. shores were to be assaulted by some sort of domestic Wehrmacht. Could the "veteran" abandon overnight his blood lust for killing? Was it really safe to put bayonet and judo experts into civilian society? In seeming seriousness, several congressmen proposed "demilitarization centers" where dangerous servicemen could be rehabilitated before release. A vestryman asked the War Department whether his returning pastor was fit for the pulpit after exposure to mayhem. Rumors seeped through the land. The Marine Corps had set aside remote Pacific islands where especially vicious veterans of "killer battalions" would be detained for life. When the European war ended, commanders would sort out their most depraved fighters, men incapable of rehabilitation, and group them into special units for supposed priority shipment home. A ruse: once the ships got out of sight of land, submarines would torpedo them, consigning the "hopeless cases" to death.

Both plans, of course, were nonexistent nonsense, but such talk was encouraged by pop experts on veterans in the press and the supposedly learned professions. The Boston *Post* found a psychologist at Boston University who warned that unless the government started a program "of reeducating the soldier, sailor and marine not to kill, we will endure a crime wave of proportions that will exceed by far that which followed World War One." Agreeing, the *Post* editorialized, "A great number of boys who have been educated to kill cannot, immediately upon discharge from the armed services, readjust themselves to the ways of normal life; therefore, they will lean toward a life of crime." An FBI agent warned publicly of the crafty veteran: "They have learned to utilize every sneaking and ferocious trick known to savages. They know how to make an enemy unaware and slit his throat or garrote him with a piano wire. Against Germans and Japs they have found that it is suicidal to be merciful." This agent, and other policemen, wondered how beat patrolmen could handle ranger-trained hoodlums. (One possible motivation for this particular genre of scare stories was that the police "fears" always seemed linked to pleas for more men and higher salaries.)

Any former serviceman who got into trouble was seized upon as empirical support of the War-Crazed Veteran theory. Daily newspaper headlines exploited the fears, and the following were not atypical:

VETERAN BEHEADS WIFE WITH JUNGLE MACHETE

EX-MARINE HELD IN RAPE MURDER

SAILOR SON SHOOTS FATHER

TWO VETS HELD AS ROBBERY SUSPECTS

A Bill Mauldin cartoon depicted a couple reading a newspaper headlined VETERAN KICKS AUNT. The man remarks, "There's a small item on page 17 about a triple ax murder." But what newspaper could ignore the twenty-three-year-old combat veteran, on guard duty at a POW camp in Salina, Utah, who one midnight sprayed tents with .30-caliber machine gun fire, killing eight Germans and wounding twenty? The youth said he had planned a "mass murder" for some time and "was not sorry." Then there was the Louisville soldier who became angry when denied a streetcar seat, sat on the floor brandishing a German Luger, and ordered everyone out. In St. Louis, a vet denied housing threatened to "get me a machine gun and find me some space on my own." But to the veterans' chagrin a returning GI who drank too much beer and threw a glass at the barroom mirror was apt to find himself under the headline CRAZED VET GOES BERSERK. When veterans' groups protested sensationalized treatment, editors replied that a policy against identifying ex-GIs as criminals would make veterans a specially privileged class. Nonetheless organized veterans did get pro forma assurances of fairness: in 1947, for instance, Alan J. Gould, an Associated Press executive, told the Conference of State Directors of the Veterans Administration that AP would "refrain from unnecessary or gratuitous use of the word 'veteran' in connection with crime stories."

The veteran problem. Luncheon-club speakers and feature writers fretted over the subject energetically and at great length, and literally hundreds of magazine articles titillated, alarmed, reassured, and informed the public on what to expect. "Don't Go Sympathizing," counseled *Time.* "Don't Let the Veteran Down," pleaded the *Saturday*

Evening Post. Parents' Magazine listed "Do's and Don't's for Veterans" (an example: don't ask about combat experiences unless he volunteers to talk). "Readjustment Hardest for Good Soldiers," cautioned the *Reader's Digest.* "Has Your Husband Come Home to the Right Woman?" asked the *Ladies' Home Journal.* "Prisoners May Be Gloomy," alerted the *Science Newsletter.* One subject on which the public preferred to be optimistic (if editorial treatment of it indeed is indicative) was the fate of GIs maimed in battle. So Americans read articles with such grisly-upbeat titles as "Advantage of Handicaps" (*Rotarian*); "They Make Blindness an Asset" (*Saturday Evening Post*); and "Convalescing Can Be Fun" (*Recreation*). And specialty publications pursued their own interests: "What Is Broadway Doing for the Veteran?" asked *Theatre Arts,* while *Recreation* told "What the Serviceman Expects from His Home Town in the Way of Recreation." (A veteran browsing through 1945 periodicals must have sighed happily when he finally came to a *Survey* magazine article: "Stop Calling Them 'Problems.'")

The image of the veteran that emerged from contemporary analyses is muddled. As Benjamin C. Bowker noted in a 1946 study, contradictions abounded:

Veterans had lost their moral sense in battle, yet they returned highly critical of the nation's peccadilloes.

Veterans had lost initiative in the routine of service life, yet they would organize so strongly they would dominate the nation.

Veterans were physical and mental wrecks, yet they threatened to set up a reign of terror through cunning and brawn.

Veterans hated the uniform, yet they intended to force universal military training on their sons and brothers.

Veterans had gorged themselves on creature comforts denied civilians, yet they intended to seize all remaining assets through communism.

Veterans were returning "vicious and godless," even though there had been "no atheists in foxholes."

The armed services, concurrently, ran their own orientation programs to prepare the veterans for their reintroduction to civilians. Typical was a slim, pocket-sized booklet, "Coming Home," prepared by a team of air force psychiatrists and published in 1945. The booklet's foreword obliquely suggested that becoming a civilian might be tougher than anticipated: regardless of whether the vet felt an immediate need for the booklet's counsel, he should retain it for later days when he feels "good or bad or just mixed up." One strong recommendation was that men feeling restless should vent their stresses by boxing, hunting, chopping wood, or "jitterbugging, too. . . . Of course, it would be fine if he [the veteran] could have all of his former values restored by just blowing a whistle. But it takes time, sometimes lots of it, to 'decondition' or 'detrain' after a session of combat." The booklet also emphasized that any man who felt stress while still on active duty should seek immediate psychiatric counseling. But a few weeks after the booklet was released (and publicized in *Newsweek*) an anonymous GI wrote the magazine that such advice was easier given than followed. Men feeling the onset of emotional instability "are shamed back to duty by gruff, disinterested doctors and accused of 'goldbricking.' Can you imagine a soldier—nervous, emotionally out of gear—trying to tell a doctor his troubles in front of about 30 other men who are also on sick call?" the soldier wrote *Newsweek*.

Once in civilian clothes again the veteran could be distinguished by his eagle-in-circle discharge button—the "ruptured duck" as it soon became known. To insure wide publicity for the emblem the War Department urged corporations to refer to it in their advertising. Ford and Texaco explained, "In the days to come, the ranks of those who wear this proud insignia will grow. Let all of us give them our grateful thanks and recognition." But J. C. Furnas, who studied returned veterans in Elmira, New York, for the *American Legion Magazine* shortly before the war ended, found few vets would wear the button. "The public doesn't know what it means," one vet told Furnas. "It's too small—you can't tell what it is two feet away." If a vet wore the button he was apt to be asked "how you got shipped home when the other guys are still out there somewhere fighting." Furnas commented, "One dischargee, veteran of Tarawa, you hear, leaves his button off because he takes special pleasure in socking busybodies who ask him the wrong question. More of him would help a lot." The button's unpopularity notwithstanding, energetic merchandisers sought to peddle similar commercial memorabilia to the multimillion-man ex-GI market. A choice medium was the *American Legion Magazine*. For $1, a Newark firm offered a car reflector with the honorable discharge insignia; for $5, a Chicago company would supply a vet with a "Liberator Genuine Leather Discharge Case," with his service insignia "engraved in gold," and with room for discharge documents, medals, and campaign bars and citations. A vet could buy a beer mug with his unit emblem, miniatures of his medals and ribbons, a ring with the words VETERAN WORLD WAR II emblazoned on the stone.

On a more elaborate scale, monument manufacturers urged cities and veterans' organizations to memorialize their dead. The Bronze Division of Gorham Company in Providence, Rhode Island, offered "free counsel on your Honor Roll or War Memorial. From earliest stages of your planning, the facilities of Gorham Bronze Designers are available without obligation to help you obtain good taste and good value in your war memorials." But the writer Louis Bromfield, after surveying some of the obelisks that sprouted after the Spanish-American War and the First World War, urged communities to plan carefully. Most existing monuments "are dead piles of stone and metal, most of them of an antiquated ugliness of which a certain quaintness is their only attraction. In many towns and cities they obstruct traffic. In others their actual removal would benefit the general appearance of the community." As an alternative Bromfield suggested "living monuments" such as camps, trails, playgrounds and stadiums.

America threw open its arms in other ways as well. The *Reader's Digest* offered half-price subscriptions to veterans. Taylorcraft, a manufacturer of private planes, announced 25 percent of its production would be reserved for veterans: "Just show your discharge papers and go to the head of the line," the company advertised. Posters depicting the ruptured duck promised America was determined to "Honor This Emblem"; others said a grateful nation would not forget "They Have Served." Virtually every neighborhood had its own poignant version of The Homecoming: the hand-painted banner welcoming Johnny or Horace or Carl or Darrell or Joe or Robert or Isaac, with a picnic table in the back yard, a nervous prewar girl friend peering around the corner, and Sunday-best-dressed relatives ready to buss the returning serviceman. As a Philadelphia clergyman sermonized in September 1945: "Gather close, our returning warriors, to the most sacred of shelters: the loving and warm bosom of thy own family."

But did a "family bosom" always await the returning vet? Thousands upon unhappy thousands of men returned "home" to discover that it had not survived their absence; that their marriages no longer existed, in emotion or in reality. The mobility of warfare shook the institution of marriage to its core. Hurried, lonely people made frightful mistakes in choosing mates, and in 1945 and 1946 discovered they really didn't care that much about their spouses. After hearing 2,000 divorce cases in the last four months of 1945 Judge Edwin A. Robson of Chicago mourned, "I point to my record not with pride but with shame—shame for the people of my county, state, and country." During 1945 the United States achieved the highest divorce rate in the world—thirty-one divorces for every 100 marriages, double the prewar rate, a grand total of 502,000. The record surpassed even that of the First World War, when the divorce rate jumped 40 percent for 1918–20, then settled back to prewar norms. Oklahoma City and Dallas, in the last ten months of 1945, recorded more divorces than marriages. As Benjamin C. Bowker wrote, "It was a symbolic though shocking event to the services when the babyfaced Bill Mauldin, an idol of the European Theater of Operations . . . filed suit for divorce on adultery grounds shortly after his release from the army." Between January and V-J Day 1945, some

2,500 servicemen obtained divorces for adultery in New York alone. Sociologists noted wide geographic disparities. Of 324 cases heard by a Chicago judge in one month, 82 percent involved pre-Pearl Harbor marriages. But 67 percent of the divorces in Los Angeles split war marriages.

In their instant analyses marriage specialists were reluctant to blame all the splits on faithless war wives and fraternizing GIs. They cited separation as the largest single factor. Another was the increased economic independence of women. For the first time in her history the American woman learned she could find and hold a job, drive and maintain the family car, keep the checkbook in balance—without the help of a man. "Keeping women in the home following this war may prove as difficult as keeping the boys down on the farm after they'd seen Paree," opined *Newsweek*. In terms of the entire postwar decade the prediction proved wrong; the American woman settled into an outwardly contented domesticity centered around her new postwar refrigerator and "togetherness." But nonetheless, because they had learned to fend for themselves, women did not view divorce with the stark terror of earlier generations: if a marriage didn't work, why ruin two lives by continuing it? The respectability of numbers stripped divorce of much of its old stigma. No longer would divorce be a word whispered in the shadows. As one woman told a New York *Post* interviewer in early 1946, "I used to think that I'd cut off my head before I went back to Ohio and admitted that I made a bust of marriage. But now, so what? Of the first five girl friends I made in New York, three are divorced, and I'm on my way. I'm not blasé about it, because it hurt. But I'm not wearing sackcloth and ashes either." Reported an advertising executive, formerly an army captain: "Maria and I married right before I went into service, and we had only a month or so together steadily. After that it was hurried weekends for six months, a day here or there, then overseas for three years. I can't tell you why it happened—I came home, and we looked at one another, and we knew right away we didn't want to stay married. Oh, we tried, and went through all the motions, but we just lost interest. When I finally moved out, it was no more significant than changing college roommates or finding a new apartment."

Which is not to suggest that all partings were painless. One of the more poignant cases involved a Chicago man who married his high-school sweetheart in 1939 and went into the army two years later. In Germany, a mine mangled his legs and one arm. Both legs had to be amputated. Back in the states in the hospital, he discovered his wife had deserted him for a forty-nine-year-old meat buyer she met at the firm where she worked as a typist. The maimed corporal sued for a divorce and for an accounting of $2,500 in savings and allotments he had sent the wife. (He also asked $50,000 from the meat buyer for alienation of affections.) In other well-publicized Chicago divorce cases, a sailor returned from the Pacific to find his wife and four-year-old son living with a man who was also wearing *his* civilian clothes. A machinist's mate found his wife had borne a child fourteen months after he left for the Pacific. The cases so angered Chicago citizens that State's Attorney William J. Tuohy announced he would prosecute for adultery wayward wives or husbands spotlighted in divorce cases. "These women deserve the limit," stormed Judge Victor A. Kula. "And I mean a term in jail or prison, and not just a small fine." In Newark, Judge P. James Pellecchia, Jr., was even sterner: "If I had my way, soldiers' wives who are unfaithful would be branded with scarlet letters and have their heads shaven." Pellecchia noted that some primitive tribes decreed death for faithless wives of men at war. But rather than resorting to the branding iron and shears, Pellecchia went after adulterous wives' pocketbooks: in a score of cases he forced the women to surrender their army allotments upon pain of going to prison.

When they had the choice, legislative bodies generally took the side of the homecoming veteran over the wife. For instance, the California legislature haggled over something called the indiscreet wives bill which would have permitted a woman to adopt a child fathered by someone other than her serviceman husband, or put it out for adoption, without notifying her husband. Existing law assumed any child born to a married woman was the product of her husband, who had to sign adoption papers. Proponents said that notifying a GI that his wife had borne another man's child while he was off fighting would be disruptive to morale and the war effort. But *Stars & Stripes* attacked the bill as a "deception" on servicemen, and it died. Judge C. P. McClelland of Columbus, Ohio, took the opposite view. "The court must look to the welfare of the child and not to the possible embarrassment of the parents in all such cases as these," he held. Since such children legally were fatherless, McClelland ruled it was not necessary to notify the women's husbands of adoption proceedings. He placed for adoption children born to women whose husbands had been absent as long as twenty-two months. Such a clamor arose from servicemen, however, that the Ohio legislature passed a law reversing McClelland.

Wives, in turn, were counseled to take a charitable view toward sexual adventures of their servicemen husbands. In a popular 1946 book entitled *Sex Problems of the Returned Veteran,* Dr. Howard Kitching advised, "It is impossible to tell men to go and kill an enemy and risk their lives in doing it, and expect them at the same time to be honest, chaste, kind and unselfish all the time." In the next breath, however, Dr. Kitching said men should mind their sexual manners. Suppressing sexual feelings, he said, "will inevitably cause mental discomfort and frustrations . . . but will not in itself be harmful . . ." Such frustrations "will just have to be borne. They are not going to go on forever. They are one of the major sacrifices that have had to be made in order to win the war." Actually, Kitching maintained, continence under "necessary" circumstances can result in "a strengthening of self-respect and a legitimate feeling of increasing power over oneself . . . which later on pays excellent dividends in the form of mental serenity and poise." Once a man has taken "such a reasonable view he will not be inclined to worry or to punish himself with guilty feelings over nocturnal emissions or occasional masturbation." Kitching found it hard to generalize whether wife and husband should tell one another of outside sexual experiences; nonetheless "the transient, physical rare occasions which happen in wartime to the best-intentioned of people, under the stress of frustration, boredom or bitterness, are best ignored. In relation to the marriage, they have little meaning. . . . This does not mean that they are to be condoned or permitted to become a habit." Kitching urged that vets and their wives treat themselves to a "second honeymoon" soon after homecoming: "They should have a period in which to satisfy each other, to discharge their sexual tension, to renew their knowledge of each other, and to see what changes have occurred."

Dr. Alfred C. Kinsey, whose definitive study *Sexual Behavior in the Human Male,* published in 1948, drew upon material collected during the war years, disputed the wide belief that military service encouraged sexual adventure. He found that only a "small portion" of men in service "materially modify their pattern of behavior after they leave home." Male sexual patterns are generally set by age sixteen, Kinsey said, and rarely change thereafter. "It is true that many a man has had his first experience with heterosexual coitus after he got into the armed forces; but most of these men would have begun coitus at about that age if they had stayed at home," Kinsey wrote. "The men who have the most coitus after getting into the armed forces are, for the most part, the men who would have had the most coitus if they stayed at home. . . . Similarly, the married men in the armed forces turn to extra-marital intercourse, or avoid extra-marital intercourse, largely in accord with the patterns that have guided their behavior previously in their lives." Kinsey's empirical data notwithstanding, many American men came home feeling that they had discovered something about themselves sexually, whether with a female war worker encountered casually in a San Francisco bar, an English servicewoman, or one of the prostitutes who embarnacled the invasion forces driving up the Italian peninsula. And it was these men who could feel empathy for Thomas Rath, the central character in Sloan Wilson's best-selling postwar novel *The Man in the Gray Flannel Suit,* who fathered a child while serving in Europe and had to explain the affair to his wife when he decided to give the mother financial support. The poignancy of a foreign love that cannot be sustained, the swiftly achieved intimacy of lonely strangers, the joy of a spontaneous physical encounter—such experiences did not convert themselves easily into Dr. Kinsey's charts and bar graphs; nonetheless they were in many a soldier's emotional baggage as he returned home.

E. V. (Ev) Faber, now a purchasing agent for a Cleveland manufacturer, was in a marriage that didn't survive his return from the military. "Janie and I had been together a couple of years, and we didn't have the money to start our family. As I remember it, we paid about $45 a month for an apartment in Chicago and I was making take-home of about $38 a week. Sure, I misbehaved, both in the states and overseas. I guess I was lucky in having access to women. I was a flier, and I didn't have the paunch then, and I decided, What the hell, the war might last forever, and I might not even come out of it alive. So why stop living for X years? Nothing serious, although I did see one girl quite a lot when we were in Surrey. Of course, once you got into bases in France, all that ended.

"Anyway, when I got home, the first few days were pretty good. But after that, it didn't seem that Janie and I had anything to talk about. I ran through my war stories, the combat stuff, and eventually, out of boredom if nothing else, I got around to the other stuff, the women and the parties and the drinking. She listened for a couple of days, and made no particular comment one way or another, just asking a question here and there. Then one morning, she said, 'I guess you realize that we can't stay married, not after what you've done.' Without thinking much of what I was saying, I answered, 'I suppose you're right.' Thinking back on it now, I realized I'd already decided I didn't want to stay married with Janie, and that we were going through some playacting—me giving her an excuse to call it off, and not objecting when she took it. So she saw the lawyer, and we cut it, snap, just like that.

"There's an ironic aftermath to this. A couple of years later, after I had done some pretty extensive roaming and bumming around, I got tight one night during Christmas and called her to say hello. First time we'd talked since we left court. Friendly conversation, sort of bringing ourselves up to date on what we'd been doing. And then she blurted out this thing that she felt awful about making me take all the guilt, because she deserved some too, and I asked her what she meant. She said she'd had a lover too, a naval lieutenant, out at Great Lakes [naval air station near Chicago] and they were serious enough to start planning marriage. Then he was sent overseas, and she got tied up with one of his friends, and so on.

"That really jolted me. At first I was mad, and I told her some pretty nasty things, and hung up. Later, though, I realized she had gone through the same thinking I had, and I couldn't blame her for screwing

around. Hell, I'd certainly done the same thing. I sent her a note apologizing, and saying I'd like to hear from her. But that was the last of it. I got it through friends later that she had remarried, but I don't have the slightest idea where she is."

By his own testimony, as revealed through sociological and other polls, the veteran saw the war as a direct loss, personally and professionally. The war cost him years away from school and/or a career; would he ever be able to regain the lost time and money? An uncomfortably sizable minority wondered whether the stated goals had been achieved—or even whether the United States had fought on the right side. A War Department survey in September 1945 of men still in Europe found 51 percent feeling that although Hitler was wrong in leading the Germans into war, he did Germany "a lot of good" before the war. Twenty-four percent thought the Germans had a "very good" or "fairly good" argument when they said that since Germany was the most efficient country in Europe, it had the right to be the controlling influence on the continent. Twenty-two percent felt Germans had "some good reasons" for "being down on the Jews." (Another 10 percent were undecided on this question.) And 19 percent felt Germany had a "good deal" or "some" justification for starting the war (11 percent were undecided). In fact, more GIs had "very favorable" or "fairly favorable" opinions about the Germans than they did about the French (61 percent versus 59 percent). The War Department also ran a periodic check on the question: "Do you ever get the feeling that this war is [was] not worth fighting?" The answer "sometimes" or "very often" increased from 18 percent in July 1943 to 48 percent in August 1945, while "never" dropped from 68 percent to 29 percent in the same time span.

The same general aura of negativism turned up when pollsters asked veterans about the personal impact of the war. When questioned about "undesirable" changes wrought by the war, 41 percent of one group listed such factors as "more nervous," "high-strung," "restless," "jumpy," "tense," "want to be 'on the go,' " "can't concentrate." The group felt itself "more irritable," "short-tempered," "quarrelsome," "belligerent" (17 percent); "sadder," "lacking 'pep,' " "no longer carefree" (10 percent); and " 'dumber,' " "intellectually narrower," "wilder," "less moral," "more given to drinking and gambling" (two percent). Asked directly "Do you feel that army life changed you?" 37 percent listed only undesirable changes; 22 percent only desirable changes. (Some of the latter included "intellectually broadened," "think deeper," "understand things or people better," 16 percent; "and quieter," "more settled," "less given to running around or drinking," 13 percent.)

Another poll, by the National Opinion Research Center in February

1947, asked a cross-section of the public whether the war changed "your own life" for better or for worse. The results showed significant differences between veterans and nonveterans:

	Vets	Nonvets
Life worse	48	35
Life changed, but don't know whether better or worse	6	3
Life better	24	9
No change	21	52
No answer	1	1

The differences came across even stronger in interviews that the War Department's Research Branch conducted with returned veterans. Many vets expressed anger at profit-minded civilians whose home-front lives had not been as arduous as servicemen were led to believe. One aim of propaganda directed toward men abroad was to stress the "sacrifices" of the people at home. A veteran told a Research Branch interviewer: "We were over there and we heard how tough it was and we thought people were starving. We thought they had it worse than they did. That's why I probably have this feeling, like when I hear someone complain about not getting tires or something. I think, 'you *civilian.'* " About a third felt estranged from civilian life, even after mustering out: their friends weren't around anymore, food was scarce, prices high, and gasoline nonavailable. Many felt homecoming was a letdown. "Every guy thinks it will be the greatest thing in the world, but somehow I didn't quite get the thrill I thought I would get." One in five felt completely hostile to the civilians: "When you come back they treat you just like scum. They act just like you was the unlucky guy that got the dirty end, and that's just too bad. We figured we had done something and we find out we won't be shown any partiality. If you ever get the boys all together, they probably will kill all the civilians. They [the civilians] aren't worth anything anyway." The polls revealed hostility on the part of the veterans toward labor unions, Jews, and blacks (half the group covered by one War Department survey predicted racial "trouble" before the decade ended). A few felt wartime contact with blacks improved their tolerance. One GI said, "I saw what these boys did on the Burma Road. I had closer contact with them in the hospital and all. It explodes a lot of things you hear. You realize they have the same abilities—they just haven't had any breaks." But an even larger group reported reinforced antiblack attitudes: they maintained blacks were "poor soldiers" who stayed behind the combat lines and led unacceptable social lives. (Ironically, military propaganda services devoted more effort to publicizing the fighting efforts of Japanese-American nisei units than they did predominantly black outfits.) The War Department quoted one soldier: "They [the blacks] went with English girls. We practically had a war over there. Our men were supposed to be given a twenty-four-hour pass and we were going to town and wipe every Negro out, but some of the officers said we had a war of our own to fight first."

Jerry ——— is a prosperous insurance agent in East Texas, a confident, poised man in his sixties who is high in his town's economic power structure. But deep inside him linger resentments against some of the people with whom he now must do business and whom he sees socially on the golf course at the local country club. He spent four of the war years in the army as a noncommissioned officer:

"The draft board here didn't do an equitable job deciding who went into the service. They listened to too many excuses, especially from the big business houses and the farmers. I was just a kid then. I was nothing in ———, nor was my family. So I was among the first to go, right after Pearl Harbor. I was kind of burned, because many of the kids I'd gone to high school with got deferments on the grounds they were essential to the farm work, or to their father's business.

"When I came home I was even madder. Here these people were, who had sat out the war, they had made money hand over fist while the rest of us were away; they had a big head start and they made the most of it. I had some cash I had saved, and the first day or so I went down to a car dealer—one of those who had managed to slip around the draft, even though he was my age and in good physical shape—anyway, I asked him about buying a car, and he wanted money under the table, a subterfuge to beat the price freeze.

"I told him to go to hell, that I had fought a war for the cause of decency and honesty, and that I wasn't going to be shaken down by some damned profiteer. Boy, was I mad. I decided I'd rather walk when I went around selling insurance than pay any damned kickback for a second-hand car.

"I guess I was pretty belligerent that first month. I wouldn't get a haircut, I shaved when I felt like it, which wasn't very often, I didn't even keep myself clean. I was saying to the slackers, 'To hell with you, I won't play your game.'

"Of course, I was only hurting myself, because I realized after a few weeks that going around mad wasn't helping me sell insurance. I cleaned myself up, and I started doing better. But I never did pay money under the table to get a car. I waited until the market straightened out before I bought.

"One thing, though, I still remember the bastards who thought the war was nothing more than another way of making money. I'm polite with them now, and socialize with them, and buy stuff from them. But I'll never respect them."

*   *   *

GI antipathy extended even to homecoming fetes. Four sociologists who studied veteran problems in an Illinois town of 6,000 persons (Midwest, they called the community to ensure its anonymity) found the servicemen edgy when given too much attention. "I wanted to see the relatives all right, but I wanted to see them one at a time," one veteran told the interviewers. "So what do they do? The first thing my mother does is haul us out there, clear out in the country in no-man's land, for a picnic with all the relatives, and I had to stand around with all of them and answer their darn fool questions." Another said: "The folks had everyone in for a big party. There was all the noise and excitement—people banging me on the shoulder and wanting to know how it seemed to be back. After a while I just froze up. I told my dad I was going to have to take off for a little while. I guess he thought it was sort of funny, but I couldn't help it. I went outdoors and smoked a cigarette, and then I went back in again, and after that it was all right. But it just seemed like there was too much going on—too much pressure for me to take."

In some instances—apparently isolated—servicemen suffered from deliberate cruelty. The journalist J. C. Furnas recounted some problems he found in the factory town of Elmira, New York: "In one shop a nerve-shattered boy's benchmates insisted it was fun to make sudden noises to make him jump and turn white. In another a veteran shrinking from the racket associated with his old job asked for outside work—only to be refused and eventually laid off as inefficient, even though he had offered to take a lower pay outside." Another man, a quiet dischargee, worked normally until a low-flying plane came over the plant. "He dived under the desk in a panic of collapse and it was days before he could face work again. In case after case a boy back on his old factory job can't take the racket of nearby presses crashing down, and he has to be shifted to outside work." (Elmira had no psychiatrist to help such persons readjust, Furnas said, nor were there VA facilities.)

Faced with these and other pressures, unable (or not ready) to find a job, flush with savings and mustering-out pay, many servicemen roamed —three or four friends pooling their resources to buy an old auto and the gas and oil for a leisurely drive to whatever spot on the map struck their attention.

Bob Moses, now a Baltimore accountant, was perhaps typical of the wanderers. "I came home in late August and if I had pushed it I could have entered college the next week. But what the hell—I had been away for thirty months, and I wasn't ready to settle into a routine. I loafed around the house awhile, and spent a week over at the shore, and made a half-assed attempt to get a job. Big deal. I could have become a stock clerk in an automotive supply house for $32.50 a week, as I recall it. No *thanks. I had more than $500 in savings, so I talked with a couple of buddies from high school, and we went in on an old '37 Chevvie sedan, for around $700, and we headed west. Nowhere in particular, just roaming. We'd see a kink in a river on the map, and head there. Low key all the way. We'd stop in some small town, and drink beer with the locals, and make a half-assed attempt to meet some girls. Sometimes we did, sometimes we didn't, but let's not get into that at this late date.*

"Two of us were members of the Legion, and that helped, too. In one town in Wisconsin we pulled a real bullshit deal. We went in for a beer late in the afternoon and ran into the post commander, and on the spur of the moment we told him our Baltimore post had chosen us 'young vets of the year' and sent us on this goodwill mission to get new recruiting ideas from other posts, and hadn't he received the letter about our tour? Nothing could be too good for 'our visiting brothers,' and we sat in their clubhouse far into the night, drinking their booze and eating steak dinners. They even brought in a photographer from the local newspaper.

"When we got to San Diego one of the guys looked up an old girl friend he had met in the navy and decided to stay. I thought about it myself, and even went so far as to apply for a civilian job at the navy base. But what the hell. The very act of moving around was beginning to be a bore. My restlessness was of a different sort—I wanted to find a place to stop. So we sold him our interest in the car and caught a bus home. Man, Baltimore looked good, better than it did when I came home from the army, even. I did odd jobs until the first of the year, then started college on the GI Bill. Relaxed, with the army and the war out of my blood. By the spring it was as if I had never been away."

Boredom. Ennui. An end to military regimentation, and the necessity for men to make their own decisions—men in many instances who had gone into the army straight from high school with no experience in the adult world. The loss of group identification—first, the status and security of being a member of a specific military unit; next, the rapidly diminished novelty of the "ex-serviceman," who by the end of 1945, in general public opinion, had been home long enough not to be considered anyone special. The chance to carry out those "the-first-thing-when-I-get-home" fantasies that occupied the imaginations of millions of men at war. "All the time I was overseas," said one of the veterans covered by the Midwest study, "I was promising myself that I'd spend two days on the front porch here at home, doing nothing but sit, for every day I had to spend on that damned island. And I'm telling you, that's exactly what I'm going to do." Wives and the community were initially tolerant of men who wanted nothing more than "join the 52-20 Club and take a long rest."

The 52-20 Club. One benefit for vets was a "readjustment allowance" of up to $20 weekly for fifty-two weeks for men who either were unemployed or earned less than $100 a month. During the four years of its existence, the 52-20 Club had 8,500,000 members who drew $3.7 billion. The vast majority accepted benefits only briefly, while finding jobs and getting back into the economy. But a conspicuous number deliberately loafed away the entire year. In New England, vets even made up "52-20 Club" emblems to sew on old Ike and fatigue jackets. A poignant *Life* magazine photograph depicted scores of young men sitting idly in a Long Island soda shop, faces empty of any interest even in the people around them. Veterans in the Midwest called the 52-20 benefits "rocking chair money" but many who did not apply for it felt it was "causing a lot of trouble." One veteran told an interviewer, "It's ruining a lot of these guys. They're sitting around on their dead asses forgetting what a day's work is like."

3

Veterans–or Citizens?

THE 52–20 CLUB FLOURISHED because Americans accept as a matter of faith that men who go to war should be rewarded when they return home. Land grants, cash bonuses, free medical and hospital care, pensions, gratis fishing and hunting licenses, preferential hiring for governmental jobs, streetcar passes, even lifetime movie passes—such is the largess a grateful country has bestowed upon its fighting men after battle. "There aren't going to be any apple sellers on the street corners after this war if we can prevent it," vowed Lieutenant General Brehon Somervell, chief of the army service forces. President Roosevelt, in a 1944 letter to Congress, said, "It is impossible to take millions of our young men out of their normal pursuits for the purpose of fighting to preserve the nation, and then expect them to resume their normal activities without having any special consideration shown them." FDR instructed federal agencies to give preference to veterans in their hiring. (The Washington *Post* disagreed: "Why not give veterans' preference benefits to former servicemen who might want to run for election in the national legislature? The status of these men can only be debased by treating them as inferiors incapable of securing jobs through free competition with their fellow citizens.") That a program would be created for World War Two servicemen was never doubted; the only questions were how much and in what type of package.

Fiscal conservatives expressed wariness of locking the country into an open-ended program of cash benefits, fearing that euphoric generosity at war's end would burden future generations. Veterans' programs do have a marked tendency toward longevity: not until March 1946 did the government finish paying off claims from the War of 1812, upon the death of an eighty-eight-year-old Oregon woman, daughter of a soldier who fought in the Battle of New Orleans. The operative criteria, based upon congressional decisions beginning in 1944, were to give the veterans enough to "catch up" with civilians who had not gone off to war, but to avoid turning the national treasury into a cornucopia that would make former servicemen an overprivileged class. Overhanging the debate was the political realization that if history could be considered a guide, veterans would come home howling for hard cash, payable immediately, and that the initial mass public reaction would be, "Give our boys anything they want." Even before the war ended, the Veterans of Foreign Wars lobbied for $5,000 in paid-up cash or in bonds maturing over five years. The Philadelphia *Bulletin,* in a poll in November 1945, found citizens favoring some form of bonus by a margin of 14–1— greater even than the 10–1 sentiment of veterans. Precedent existed for a cash bonus: after the First World War veterans received $1 for each day of service in the United States and $1.25 for each day overseas. But the House Committee on World War Veterans Legislation, in a report in May 1944, opposed a cash bonus, pointing out that, at the First World War rates, the cost would be $20 billion cash immediately. Nonetheless Congress found itself uneasy. As a body Congress' instinctive nature is to take the least hazardous available path: if the public cried for a free Cadillac and $50 a week for each returning GI, many politicians would oblige and worry about the consequences later. Many congressional elders had been around Washington during the traumatic Bonus March of 1932, when thousands of veterans descended on the capital to demand a bonus for their war service. Army troops dispersed the marchers, brutally but efficiently, an experience no one in government wished to relive.

In all the clamor for benefits, the loudest voice of the organized veteran belonged to the American Legion. Boasting 2,000,000 members when the war ended, and a chapter system that made it visible in every American hamlet, the Legion towered over rival groups like some elephantine colossus. When the Legion's Washington office growled, politicians paid attention. One index of the Legion's political eminence is that officeholders of all parties found it expedient to join. When Congress convened in 1946, 44 of 96 senators carried Legion cards, and 195 of 435 representatives. President Truman was a Legionnaire; so were five of his cabinet members, three Supreme Court justices, and twenty-six state governors. At the end of 1945 the Legion was signing 70,000 new members weekly, more than the combined membership of AMVETS and the American Veterans Committee, and comfortably ahead of the archrival Veterans of Foreign Wars. Although the Legion charter prohibited enrolling men still on active duty, Legion recruiters literally camped outside the gates to await dischargees. A field office in Honolulu, manned by four publicists, distributed pony editions of the *American Legion Monthly,* disbursing both news and appeals to stay away from VFW recruiters (who could sign active servicemen). Many vets came home to find that their Legionnaire fathers had already signed them into the local post. In small-town America the Legion built phenomenal strength: in Luray, Kansas, the Legion had 234 members of a total population of 380 persons; the entire town turned out for meetings. Although Luray was an extreme example of hyper-Legionism, other tank towns approached its enthusiasm. In Bagley, Minnesota, the Legion post had 448 members in a population of 1,248; in Loris, South Carolina, 604 of 1,298.

Incentives to join the Legion were many. Often the local Veterans Administration official was a Legionnaire and gave fellow members preferential treatment. The Legion had tight liaison with the VA at all levels, and its Washington office could expedite claims. In small towns such local powers as the banker, insurance agent, leading merchants, even the police chief and sheriff, were often Legionnaires. For a young veteran, membership was the chance to hobnob with people who could give him a job or approve his loan. In middle America the Legion exuded a respectability rivaling that of organized religion. As a Legion national commander once said, "The time should come soon, and I think it will be here soon, when any man eligible to become a member of the Legion who does not belong will be looked upon with suspicion, and justly so, by the community where he lives." And, finally, there was the social factor. In the bone-dry towns of the Bible and corn belts, the Legion hall was the only place in town where a man could buy a bottle of beer and idle away a Saturday afternoon shooting pool. In larger cities, the Legion bar was popular because as a private, nonprofit club it undersold competitors and followed loose closing hours. The Legion sponsored dances and picnics and showed movies; veterans (and their families) gravitated to the Legion hall often because the town offered no other social attractions.

Politically, the Legion's consistent demand was that the country "not forget" the veteran once the immediate postwar euphoria subsided. The Legion's stated goals—to help veterans get better education, housing, and medical care—had undeniable surface attraction. But the fine print in the specific programs the Legion was willing to accept on the veteran's behalf is yet another story, and one that can be explained only in the context of the group's origins, its internal politics, and the causes it espoused over the years.

A group of army officers who served in France in the First World War is credited with planning the Legion. Headquarters had asked the officers how to improve morale. Lieutenant Colonel Theodore Roosevelt, Jr., son of the former President, suggested a veterans organization, and the Legion resulted. According to an official history published by former Legion publicist Richard Sellye Jones in 1946, "There was a general concern about the postwar attitude of the average soldier toward extreme political radicalism." Officers worried about "rumors and reports from America on radical, Communistic movements," and the formation of "soldiers' and sailors' councils among men who had been discharged quickly after the armistice. . . . Even the restless lack of discipline in the [army] itself was vaguely attributed by some to Soviet ideas. A safe and sound organization of veterans might be the best insurance against their spread." Thus did "antiradicalism" become a leitmotiv of the American Legion. On the positive side the Legion helped the individual veteran in his dealings with the mare's-nest bureaucracy of the Veterans Administration, and the Legion's employment service in the 1920's surpassed anything offered by official agencies.

Concurrently, however, the Legion spent almost as much time helping authorities suppress the politically suspect. Labor organizers especially were harassed. In agricultural areas of California Legionnaires wearing overseas caps and Sam Browne belts and acting as "special deputies" helped bully migrant farm workers into staying on jobs that paid near-starvation wages. The Legion maintained close ties with such groups as the National Association of Manufacturers (which underwrote the Legion's annual national high-school oratorical contest), the American Medical Association, and the real estate industry. Coincidentally or not, the views of these friends were consistently reflected in the Legion's positions when it began working in Congress for post-World War Two veterans' benefits.

The Legion's first concern was the inability of the Veterans Administration to care for thousands of servicemen discharged because of disability. The law provided that they be hospitalized and given compensation. But the VA, a horror house of red tape and inefficiency, could not do its job, and thousands of veterans received neither money nor care for months on end. The VA, as did other wartime federal agencies, suffered manpower problems. More crippling, however, was its hypercautious director, Brigadier General Frank T. Hines, a fussy bureaucrat who had run the VA since the 1920's. (Hines' title was real: he had enlisted as a private in the Spanish-American War, and earned his brigadiership in 1918.) So far as anyone could deduce, Hines ran the VA on the theory that the less he did, the better his chances of avoiding trouble. A conservative, anti-New Deal Republican, and a favorite of economy-minded congressmen, Hines ran the VA as penuriously as possible. Not even the start of the war and the prospect of caring for millions of veterans in one manner or another stirred Hines into preparing the VA for its expanded responsibilities. Although hospital care for veterans was a major VA function, Hines' attitude toward medicine was not only ignorant but hostile. Brushing aside criticisms of his refusal to permit VA hospitals to associate themselves with medical schools, Hines once said, "I don't want any interns experimenting on my veterans." So when the wounded began returning home the VA sat immobile, unable to care for them or to pay their benefits promptly. Many cases dragged for months. One particularly pitiable and publicized incident involved a GI, blinded in combat, who was discharged June 20, 1943, and who still awaited his first VA pension check on November 29. The American Legion, which itself had close relations with General Hines (the Legion, after all, itself reflexively opposed most federal spending), finally cried "enough." If anything was to be done for veterans, initiative must come from other than the Veterans Administration. So the Legion began a vigorous lobbying campaign with separate but overlapping purposes: the immediate reform of the VA, so that it could process the increasing flow of disabled dischargees; and a package of long-range benefits.

Harry W. Colmery, an attorney from Topeka, Kansas, who had been both Republican national chairman and national commander of the Legion (both in the 1930's), took responsibility for writing specific legislation. Working in the Legion offices overlooking K Street Northwest in downtown Washington, often through the night, Colmery saw two broad purposes in the GI legislation. When veterans returned to civilian life "they should be given the opportunity to reach that place, position or status which they normally expected to achieve, and probably would have achieved, had their war service not interrupted their careers." Secondly, Colmery thought it "sound national policy" to adopt a benefits program "to see us through the troublous times which [are] ahead of us, by giving stability and hope and faith to the men and women who would return." Veterans should be assured of their benefits before leaving the military. "When the time comes to get out," Colmery said, "most men will sign almost anything, without any thought of the fact or the future." So the bill contained a section to the effect that no predischarge declaration should be held against a veteran if he asked for benefits later. In one public talk asking support for veterans legislation Colmery declared:

> There are those who worry about making the veteran shiftless, and unwilling to work, and desirous of loafing and leaning on the government for sustenance. Would you take that position toward the boy in need of a job, without whose fighting you wouldn't have any government on which to lean or depend to protect your freedom?

As a lobbying ally, the Legion relied upon the not inconsiderable publicity resources of the Hearst newspaper organization. David Camelon of Hearst's Washington bureau had helped the Legion in a 1943 campaign to boost the mustering-out bonus from the $300 sought by the Roosevelt Administration to $500. Although Camelon favored the benefits as "a matter of principle," a personal feud gave added fire to his enthusiasm. He and the Legion had thought the bonus was in hand until

Representative Andrew Jackson May, chairman of the House Military Affairs Committee, went home to Tennessee in late December before adjournment, permitting the legislation to die. Camelon wrote that May had "slipped out of Washington." A few days later, after returning to town, the angry congressman bearded him in a Capitol corridor. "If you say any more about me sneaking out of Washington, you make arrangements with the undertaker before you do—because, brother, you'll need him." According to Camelon, May's threat "made it my personal fight." Concurrently, the Hearst organization concluded that fighting for veterans would be good promotion for the newspapers as well as good citizenship, so an extraordinary thing happened in early 1944. On the orders of William Randolph Hearst, Ted Sloan, political editor of the Chicago *Herald-American,* sought out Legion national commander Warren Atherton, a fellow Illinoisan, and offered him "all the facilities of the [Hearst] organization to help the Legion insure passage" of the bills. Hearst said he wanted no credit, just the legislation. According to Camelon, "three Hearst men—Frank Reilly [of the Boston *American*], Roy Topper, crack promotion manager of the [Chicago] *Herald-American,* and I—were assigned to the Legion's Washington headquarters for the duration of the campaign. We functioned as aides in the Legion's public relations department. The Legionnaires accepted us completely; they made us a part of the team. We sat in on all conferences—we were in the fight every minute, and we shared all the heartaches and the joys of the long campaign. We did whatever we could to help under their leadership." The Hearst team wrote "news stories" about veterans legislation while acting as Legion lobbyists. During a brainstorming session at Legion headquarters one afternoon Jack Cejnar, a Legion publicist, came up with a catchall slogan describing the benefit package—a phrase that became an integral part of the veteran's vocabulary, one so much a part of the American language that it is a subject heading in encyclopedias: "The GI Bill of Rights." Camelon felt the slogan "was something close to genius. It was short, punchy, easily grasped. It told the whole story—and it became a fighting slogan from coast to coast."*

Yet did the American Legion strike the best deal possible for the veterans it purported to represent? Returning veterans read in the papers of the splendid benefits being readied for them—only to find that in reality not all that much had been changed. And the American Legion, in the legislative infighting on the GI Bill, consistently took conservative positions that worked to the disadvantage of the veteran.

* The bill's formal title was "The Serviceman's Readjustment Act of 1944." Another version of the source of the name "GI Bill" came from Chester Bowles, director of the Office of Price Administration, who proposed that President Roosevelt spell out a "Second Bill of Rights" in his 1944 State of the Union message. Roosevelt used the title, but extended coverage of the "rights" to all Americans, not just veterans.

A prime example was housing. One section of the GI Bill provided financing for veterans who wanted to buy or build homes. The real estate lobby (specifically, the National Association of Real Estate Boards and the National Association of Home Builders) liked the concept of the bill, for it was certain to touch off a postwar housing boom. But the real estate people wanted a bill of their own design. A key issue was whether the home-finance section of the bill should be administered by the existing Federal Housing Administration or the VA. The FHA was the logical agency, for it had the staff and experience. The VA would have to create a duplicate bureaucratic apparatus. The real estate interests, however, distrusted the FHA because of its involvement in public housing (an unpleasant association in their industry) and did not want to give it a toehold in the veterans' program. So the Legion fought alongside the real estate lobby for VA control. Another issue was a proposal in the original version of the GI Bill that the government make housing loans outright for three percent. Again, there was strong business opposition: the real estate industry and its allies (including the Legion) argued for conventional financing through banks and savings and loan associations. As a result, the GI paid higher interest than necessary when he went into the home market. One close critic of the Legion's role in the GI Bill, Justin Gray, commented that, contrary to popular expectation, the legislation did *not* provide new housing for veterans; it ended up "merely helping the vet finance a house if he could find one." Another critic, Charles G. Bolte, a founder of the progressive American Veterans Committee, found any number of flaws in the Legion's handiwork. Under its provisions, Bolte wrote,

. . . the veteran could resume his education, *if* he could live on $50 a month; could get the government to guarantee up to $2,000 of a loan at four percent interest to buy a house or a farm or to go into business, *if* the lending agency thought he was a good risk; could get up to $20 a week unemployment compensation for up to 52 weeks, *if* he was unemployed through no fault of his own within two years after his discharge or after the end of the war, whichever was later.

Bolte charged that the bill was sold "like a new breakfast food," to the grave disappointment of GIs, who discovered they simply couldn't walk into a bank and ask, "Where's my $2,000?"

The Legion groused about "outrages" of another sort—the realization that it would not be permitted to dominate the Veterans Administration after the war. Soon after peace, President Truman dismissed General Hines and installed General Omar N. Bradley as head of the VA. One of the most popular field commanders of the war, a brass hat who convinced the GI he was a true friend, Bradley agreed to try to straighten out two decades of administrative chaos. He made headway. For instance, he persuaded the nation's seventy-seven leading medical colleges to let doctors work as resident physicians for the VA while completing three years of specialist training. In a year's time Bradley reduced the average hospital stay from forty-two to twenty days. But in remaking the VA, Bradley also alienated old-line allies of the Legion, and brought all sorts of troubles on himself. For one thing, Bradley told his physicians to buck up and not admit patients just because a Legion "case officer" had promised them a hospital bed, needed or not. Bradley also had the audacity to refuse to build a hospital in Decatur, Illinois—a project dear to an Illinois politician named John Stelle, the Legion's postwar commander. When Bradley supported legislation limiting on-the-job training payments to $200 per month, Stelle jumped him for "breaking faith with the veterans" and all but dared the general to defend himself at the Legion's convention.

Bradley did. He took out after the "high-salaried professional veterans . . . who forget that the veteran has paid, and is paying, for all that he gets. . . . More dangerous than the German army is the demagoguery that deceives the veteran today by promising him something for nothing." As the Legion hierarchy listened in pained silence, Bradley said, "Anyone, whether he be the spokesman of veterans or any other group of American citizens, is morally guilty of betrayal when he puts special interests before the welfare of this nation. . . . The American veteran is first a citizen of these United States. He is thereafter a veteran." (Bill Mauldin, at the convention as an amused observer, said, "From the stony silence that greeted his speech . . . one would have thought the general had recommended the use of veterans for vivisection.") Stelle replied at the convention, "The main difference between General Bradley and myself, apparently, is that the general thinks that the citizen should be considered first and then the veteran." After a year Bradley fled back to the army, exhausted (according to Mauldin) from "wading through political slop and dodging floating pork barrels."

Despite its defects, the GI Bill did avoid the obvious pitfall of simply paying off servicemen with a lump-sum bonus and leaving them on their own. And, in the long run, the approach of the GI Bill was economical to the nation as well as beneficial to the veteran. The total cost of the World War Two GI Bill, for education and training, was $14.5 billion when it ended July 25, 1956.* During its twelve-year existence,

---

* By one estimate, the government made a net profit on the GI Bill. According to the Department of Labor, a male college graduate will earn (and pay income tax on) in excess of a quarter-of-a-million dollars more in his lifetime than the high-school graduate. The VA asserts, "The federal tax on this added income alone will be several times the total cost of his GI Bill education and training assistance from VA."

7,800,000 veterans (50 percent of the 15,600,000 eligible) received training: 2,200,000 in institutions of higher learning; nearly 3,500,000 below college level; 1,400,000 on-the-job; and almost 700,000 in institutional on-farm courses.

The GI Bill notwithstanding, enough veterans preferred immediate cash payments to make the "war bonus" a major political issue in state after state. And the bonus seekers wanted more than token payments. At a rally in Boston in March 1946, veterans hooted and howled at speakers opposed to increasing the Massachusetts state bonus from $100 to $1,000. The clamor over bonuses irritated *Time:* "The country had promised to cushion the shock of their return and the country, for the most part, had made good. No soldier could deny that. If anything, the cushion was too soft." *Time* said the GI Bill and other benefits made previous veterans' programs "look like nickel jitney rides." But such criticisms did not deter the bonus seekers, who had mixed luck at the state level. In West Virginia voters rejected a new state sales tax to raise the $90,000,000 needed for bonuses; similarly, New Jersey rejected a $105,000,000 state lottery. The Pennsylvania legislature, however, approved a $500,000,000 bond issue without a dissenting vote. By mid-1949, according to a survey by the American Legion, eleven states and two territories had approved bonus payments, ranging from South Dakota's 50 cents a day for U.S. service and 75 cents daily for overseas to $10 and $15 monthly in Pennsylvania.

But was material gain all that should concern the veterans? Should not veterans' organizations deal with matters more important than a pension check, cut-rate license tags, and cheap after-hours beer? One person who looked beyond the bonus and benefit checks was Gilbert A. Harrison, who had gone from UCLA to the air force. In 1943 Harrison wrote about twenty-five college friends in the service suggesting that they keep in touch through a regular channel so they could share their thoughts about postwar America. Most of the men had backgrounds in UCLA's University Religious Conference, an ecumenical umbrella under which campus liberals did good works rather than simply talk about them. Harrison's friends liked the idea, and the URC supplied the logistics for a periodic bulletin through which servicemen could vent their thoughts. Many were frightened at the prospects of postwar America. A serviceman from overseas wrote: "We'll have all the ingredients for a first-class fascistic government—all that's needed now is a catalytic agent, such as a breakdown of our internal structure. A military group returning to find their services no longer needed, a working class without jobs, a middle class a thing of the past, governmental irresolution, are fatal ingredients. We will have all of them if we don't begin now to decide what we are going to do with them."* Another man wrote: "See how everyone is preparing for the postwar grab. . . . People who organize seem to do so for the purpose of going out to grab, and the ones who pay are the poor devils who have not learned the ropes, or do not care to play in a game where life is valued in decimals."

So what should be done? Harrison and his friends realized the practical futility of "reforming" the far-flung American Legion from within. Better to create their own organization of like-minded persons rather than squander energy with internal fights. Eventually Harrison got to Charles G. Bolte, a Dartmouth graduate who had joined the British army before Pearl Harbor, lost a leg in the battle of El Alamein, and come home to write news copy as a civilian for the Office of War Information. Bolte heard of Harrison's loosely organized correspondence group, they talked and found their ideas markedly parallel, and so in January 1944 Bolte became chairman of the American Veterans Committee. Bolte tells what happened thereafter:

"At the end of the war the magazines were full of stuff about what the veteran would or wouldn't do, and how he was a new force that could dominate the country politically. That was a lot of crap. Most of us just wanted to get home and rescue our lives again. Most veterans expressed their individuality by not joining any organization at all—a majority of them, in fact. They said to hell with the Legion, the VFW, the AVC— 'Thanks very much, but I'll be my own spokesman.'

"Our guiding philosophy at the AVC was that we were 'citizens first, veterans second.' We didn't want special privileges—we wanted a better society. At our peak we didn't have more than 100,000 members, but we made about as much noise, and attracted as much attention, as the American Legion. The columnist Thomas Stokes once asked why the AVC got so much publicity, and answered his own question: 'Because every single son-of-a-bitching one of them owns a typewriter.' That was true; we had a heavy concentration of members in publishing and the media, and we took advantage of it.

"The lack of numbers didn't bother us. We were not deliberately elitist—in fact, we made a deliberate appeal to political moderates and conservatives—but we did not aim at signing up everyone we could. When we were still talking about the kind of organization we wanted,

---

* Demagogues certainly expected sunshiny times. The Reverend Gerald L. K. Smith said in 1944: "My time will come in the postwar period—the election of '48. The candidate will not be me—it will be a young veteran of this war, but I'll be behind him." Smith forecast inflation, widespread unemployment, and farm foreclosures because "professional politicians are too cautious" to face up to readjustment. "Then the flame will spread, and the extreme nationalist will come to power."

Gil Harrison and I visited Walter Lippmann. He listened with care and said, 'Go ahead, but keep it small. Try to get men who are going to govern the country in twenty-five years, and don't let the big numbers join.'

"Well, we beat Lippmann's goal by ten years. Five members of JFK's first cabinet were AVCers* and there were many, many more at the under secretary level.

"Thoughtful congressmen were grateful for AVC because it gave them a chance to say that 'not all veterans are for this particular grab.' Our emphasis was on benefits for all, without veterans' preference. For instance, we wanted a national medical care program for all Americans, not just the ex-GIs. We wanted the Wagner-Ellender-Taft housing bill to give good low-cost housing to everyone in the country, not just our people—as hard up as vets were for housing. Our attitude was that what is good for the nation is good for the veteran; that what vets needed was help in picking up the threads of civilian life, not continuing handouts.

"The Communists wouldn't join AVC at first because they thought we'd be a small elitist group. They went to the Legion and found they could get nowhere there; it was too tightly controlled. So they came back to the AVC.

"For most people the transition period was very short. The veteran lost his novelty in a hurry. After the first few hundred men came home the fact that you were a veteran didn't make that much difference. By late '45 they were nothing special—less than a dime a dozen. This was good. One of our chief objectives was to reassimilate veterans into the general community as fast as possible, so they would not stand apart and feel oppressed.

"My fears of fascism, which were very real near the end of the war, wound down very fast—that is, until the end of the decade, when McCarthyism was upon us. The day I stopped worrying was when the FBI came around checking on an AVC member who was accused of involvement in radical activities of one sort or another. The agent asked, 'Was he with you or with the Communists?' I realized the FBI was getting sophisticated, when it could look at an organization as complex as AVC, which did have a Communist problem, and realize that not everyone in it should be so tainted."

Measured against the bread-and-potatoes goals of the Legion and the VFW, the AVC's aims had a refreshing visionary appeal for veterans not content with the same old prewar world. The Legion's banana-republic zest for pomp, ceremony, and fancy uniforms amused even its own members. A letter writer to the *American Legion Magazine* sug-

---

* Dean Rusk, Orville Freeman, Stewart Udall, Arthur J. Goldberg, and Abraham Ribicoff.

gested that old-timers stop cluttering their uniforms and caps with medals showing past offices and honors. "The caps together with the hardware are worn pulled down over the ears in order to carry the weight of scrap," he said. If an *American Legion Magazine* editorial rumbled with suspicion about "entanglement" with the United Nations, a letter to the *AVC Bulletin* suggested that AVC members volunteer for a (nonexistent) UN military reserve. While the VFW fretted over obscure details of pension bills, the AVC discussed the idea of having GI Bill benefits made available to children of vets who did not wish to attend college. While Legion lobbyists sat jowl-to-jowl with the real estate people before congressional committees, the AVC was the sole veterans' group to testify for continued federal rent controls. The AVC staged public forums and demonstrations across the nation in favor of low-cost-housing programs; 2,500 members and families slept overnight in MacArthur Park in Los Angeles to dramatize the need for the Wagner-Ellender-Taft (W-E-T) Housing Bill, which the Legion denounced as "radical," despite the conservative pedigree of Senator Robert A. Taft, one of the authors. The AVC spoke the truths other veterans' groups ignored: in the words of Clinton E. Jencks, of Denver, vice-chairman of its mountain states region, all that veterans received from the housing programs were "a few army barracks reconverted down by the stockyards and railroad shops," while contractors busied themselves with "bars, garages, beauty parlors, ski shops, supermarkets."

The AVC did not hesitate to call names. Franklin D. Roosevelt, Jr., a national AVC officer, termed the Legion's opposition to W-E-T a surrender to the real estate interests. "One wonders what the privates in the Legion think of it." He called the Legion's then national commander, Paul Griffith, "the principal errand boy on Capitol Hill for the powerful real estate lobby." Editorially, the *AVC Bulletin* charged that the Legion "is well on the road to making suckers of the veterans of World War II. It has enrolled several millions of veterans of the last war with rosy promises. But the kingmakers of the Legion are paying no heed to the promises they made."*

Inevitably, of course, the AVC's nervy activism got it dangerously

* Whether Legion opposition to W-E-T and other housing measures represented rank-and-file sentiment is undeterminable. World War Two vets comprised 70 percent of the Legion's membership in 1947—but only 5 percent of the delegates to the national convention. Commander Griffith would not permit W-E-T advocates to speak; when a resolution supporting W-E-T came to a vote, he ruled that any delegate absent from the floor would be considered in opposition, and so recorded. The VFW hierarchy used another form of parliamentary legerdemain on housing issues. A few days after a national convention approved W-E-T, national commander Louis Starr said the resolution was not binding; acoustics in the auditorium were so poor, Starr said, that members didn't understand what they were voting on. Starr's ploy did not work: a young VFW housing enthusiast named John F. Kennedy, a first-term Democratic congressman from Massachusetts, made the commander back down.

crosswise with the Legion, the VFW, and other powerful adversaries. The AVC insisted on its chapters and meetings being integrated, even in the South, and it supported the fair employment practices commission and antilynching and antipoll tax legislation (the latter three the civil rights causes célèbres of the late 1940's). So Representative Rankin, the avowed white supremacist from Mississippi who chaired the House Veterans Affairs Committee, banned AVC from appearing before his committee to testify on legislation—some of which, ironically, AVC had written. Rankin did so by restricting testimony to organizations whose members were "exclusively active, participating veterans of American wars." AVC had on its rolls 400 merchant seamen and men, such as Bolte, who had served in foreign armies. (The VFW had demanded just such a legislative rule for months.) Rankin's order survived only briefly before the full committee overturned it, but it did set an irksome precedent. Later in 1947 the California and North Carolina legislatures, at Legion urging, used the same excuse to bar AVC from public facilities. In 1948, when AVC pressured Army Secretary Kenneth C. Royall to end segregation in the army, he retaliated by withdrawing its accreditation as a bona fide veterans' organization (meaning AVC could no longer use military bases for meetings and other activities).

Threatening though the external foes were, the issue that ultimately stifled AVC was an internal one: a traumatic fight against Communists who attempted to seize the organization and turn it into a propaganda arm of the far left. The AVC's leadership's first tactic was to admit Communists to membership, and then to work hard to outvote them when they ran for national office. The very presence of the Communists prompted the right-wing press to denounce AVC as a fellow traveler of Moscow or worse, and AVC civil libertarians spent considerable time in pained and often murky explanations of their containment of the infiltrators. For example, in early 1947 the Washington *Times-Herald* published a vitriolic series of articles citing Communists active in various AVC chapters, and depicting AVC as a sort of veterans' wing of the Communist Party, USA (CPUSA). The attack touched a sore spot, for one non-Communist AVC faction was arguing that taking a hard line against the internal Communists was nothing more than "red-baiting." Rebutting, Franklin D. Roosevelt, Jr., wrote in the *AVC Bulletin* that while communism was not an issue in many chapters, "there are no civil liberties or anti-Russian issues involved in the necessity of non-Communist members of AVC being organized to combat Communist influence and infiltration . . . to maintain AVC as a genuine independent organization." Merle Miller, the writer, who was a member of AVC's national planning committee, disagreed with "those wonderfully honest progressives who think that a liberal movement in America must accept the help of the Communist Party." He wanted continued election of

AVC leaders "whose understanding of independent liberalism as against Party-line thought is clear and unmistakable."

The climactic confrontation with the Communists came in 1948, when the AVC decided that the advantages of taking Communists as members were far outweighed by the dangers. In midsummer a federal grand jury indicted John Gates, editor of *The Daily Worker,* and a member both of the CPUSA and the AVC, under the Smith Act. The AVC national governing board promptly expelled him on grounds it was "inconsistent" for him to "sign the preamble to the [AVC] constitution in good faith while a member of the Communist Party." Because the CPUSA was a "tight conspiracy" demanding "rigid adherence . . . a member of the CPUSA is neither a free agent in his own party nor in AVC. As a party member he can join AVC only for the purpose of furthering the objectives of the CPUSA." Gates called the statement "too childish to answer," but his supporters took the issue to the floor of the AVC convention in November. They lost, and Gilbert Harrison, running for AVC president, easily beat down a Communist-supported candidate. The convention declared Communists ineligible for AVC membership, and instructed the national officers to purge them.

The Communists fought no longer. Communist-dominated AVC chapters in Los Angeles and elsewhere simply vanished, with members moving into leftist organizations such as the "Progressive Veterans of America." But for non-Communist members victory proved Pyrrhic. As Roosevelt admitted, "From a flowering, inspiring group of young Americans, interested in the nation's welfare, we have become a tattered and torn group."

The American Veterans Committee survives today, but only tenuously. Although its national advisory council boasts eight congressmen, two senators, and two United States district judges, AVC is virtually anonymous in Washington; the windy "position papers" that flow from its second-floor walk-up offices in a ramshackle old building south of Dupont Circle are apparently read (and heeded) by few save its 50,000-odd members. Nonetheless Bolte* thinks AVC did what needed to be done in the postwar years. "We were an alternative to the American Legion, and a loud one," he said. "For one hundred thousand of us, at least, the AVC was a way of saying that winning the war didn't mean a damned thing unless the end result was a better country, a better world. Am I satisfied? Oh, one looks at any situation, any outcome, and thinks about 'what could have been.' At least we provided a forum for the thinking veteran."

* Bolte ended his career as an official of the Carnegie Endowment for International Peace, from which he retired in 1973.

4

Books and Bonuses

CHESTERFIELD SMITH, *a curly-haired, booming-voiced kid from rural Florida, never seemed able to settle down before the war. When he entered the University of Florida for prelaw studies in 1935, "I'd go to school a semester and then drop out a semester to earn enough money to return. I chose the easy life in college: I'd rather drop out and work than skimp in school." He worked as a clerk in the Florida legislature, jerked sodas at a tourist fishing resort in Boca Raton, ranged over central Florida as a debt collector, and sold tobacco and candy from a route truck. Smith's childhood sweetheart, Vivian Parker, whom he married in 1944, said of him: "He was just a poker-playing, crap-shooting boy who wouldn't settle down." Between 1935 and 1940 Smith managed to complete only 3½ years of school. "I'd had the highest average in my high-school class, but I had few targets, and I never worked very hard." In 1940 he went on active duty with the National Guard, attended officer candidate school, and served with a field artillery battery in France, beginning "about D-Day plus 45," through the Battle of the Bulge to peace. Smith saved $5,000 from his army pay, won another $3,000 shooting craps on the homeward troop ship, and re-entered the University of Florida in 1946.*

"Something happened to Chesterfield's attitude in the war," Mrs. Smith said of her husband years later. "I don't know just what, but he was a serious man when he returned." Carefully budgeting his money ("What with the GI Bill, the money from the war, and a teaching job, beginning my second year in law school, we had more than most") and his hours (he found time to golf five times weekly), Smith led his class academically and politically, and took about every BMOC honor available. "I didn't go drink coffee or sit out on the bench and bull it all the time. I never missed a day of class. I kept a work schedule just like I had a job. If I had a paper due in three weeks, I started it right away and finished a week early. Hell, here I was, almost thirty years old—I wanted to get that law license and get into practice and make myself

some money. The idea of playing around a university for unnecessary months or years had no appeal to me whatsoever."

Twenty-five years later Smith was the lead partner in a prestigious Tampa-Orlando firm, with a six-figure annual income, and held the presidency of the American Bar Association. "The way I was going before the war," Smith said, "I don't think I would ever have made it through law school. But after the war I felt I had something invested in my country—five years of my life. I said to myself, 'Boy, you've got to settle down and make something of yourself, otherwise you ain't agonna 'mount to nothin'.' My classmates in the forties, after the war, we wanted to get on with our lives. We were men, not kids, and we had the maturity to recognize we had to go get what we wanted, and not just wait for things to happen to us."

In terms of sheer revolutionary impact upon American society, the most important feature of the GI Bill was higher education. Through its financial assistance, the GI Bill brought a college degree to within reach of millions of persons who otherwise would have gone directly into trades or blue-collar jobs. Between 1945 and 1950, according to VA figures, 2,300,000 veterans studied in colleges and universities under the GI Bill. The GI Bill provided a special incentive to older veterans and to those whose families were ill-educated and low-income. Educational Testing Service, in a study of postwar vets, found that 35 percent of the older GIs (twenty-two years or more) would not have attended college had not the GI Bill existed. For all the vets, 10 percent "definitely" would have forgone college; another 10 percent "probably" would not have gone. Even so, the GI Bill had a more profound implication: It marked the popularization of higher education in America. After the 1940's, a college degree came to be considered an essential passport for entrance into much of the business and professional world. And mass America, once the GI Bill afforded it a glimpse at higher education, demanded no less an opportunity for successive generations. Pushed beyond their prewar capacity by the glut of veteran students, colleges and universities vastly expanded their physical plants. Once the space existed, academia filled it, and the educational boom was on. Some decade-apart statistics show the intensity with which postwar Americans pursued higher education. In 1939–40, U.S. colleges and universities conferred 216,521 degrees. In 1949–50 the number more than doubled, to 496,661.

America's postwar affluence and emphasis on technology undoubtedly would have boosted college enrollment even if the GI Bill had not existed. But the GI Bill was important because it was tantamount to a forced feeding of the universities: the veterans demanded schooling, and in a hurry, and their very presence jolted academia into a double-time expansion inconceivable to an earlier educational generation. Further, the GI Bill marked the first federal contributions to higher education since establishment of the land-grant colleges in the late 1800's, a political precedent of no little significance. That the spending was "for our boys" enabled legislators to brush aside engrained prejudices against federal aid to education. The money went not only to the veterans, but to the colleges as well, $9.65 for every credit hour taken by a student enrolled under the GI Bill.

Colleges realized even before the war ended that they faced unprecedented enrollments once the servicemen returned home. A War Department survey taken in 1944, before the benefits of the GI Bill were firmly set, showed that at least 8 percent of the 16,000,000 people in uniform intended to enter college. So the universities began to think seriously about what veterans would expect of them. Beginning in 1943, Columbia University sent its former students in the military a periodic "Memorandum from Morningside" to tell them what was happening on their old campus. Near the war's end, 1,200 servicemen were asked what they wanted from Columbia, both as students and as humans. Virtually every man who responded urged that he and fellow veterans be treated exactly like other students. They asked only that recognition be given their age, their varied experience, and their desire to make up for lost time. An officer aboard the USS *Chief,* in the Pacific, reported, "Much as I'd like to, I don't expect to take very much more liberal arts work. By the time I get back to school, I'll be getting on in years, and with several more years of professional study contemplated, the problem of when I'll start earning a living will begin to be a serious one." The officer nonetheless had mixed feelings about suggestions that Columbia accelerate its courses. "Education is too important to me now to be raced through. I want to have the feeling of leisure to do an honest job with the most valuable time of my life." Going to a year-round three-semester plan "would turn college into a factory." But a P-51 pilot was not worried about twelve unbroken months of classes: "I remember how we used to think that a full year would be a tough grind, but it was probably laziness that prompted that feeling."

A condescending tone frequently crept into college bureaucrats' house organs as they discussed what to do with the veteran. As was much else of America, the educators were prepared to treat the veteran as somewhat of a special animal, and they didn't know quite what to expect of him, or vice versa. "Because the veteran fought our fight," President Paul Klapper of Queens College wrote in *School and Society,* "because the victory he brings is purchased all too frequently at the expense of his health and his integrated personality, ours is the obligation to make him at home in the society he has served." But Klapper warned that universities "must guard against mawkish generosity toward the veteran-student. If he receives a substandard education because of our mistaken kindness, he will become a substandard member of his vocational and cultural group." Klapper didn't like the notion of accelerating classes, regardless of what the eager veterans demanded: to permit a veteran to finish college in less than three years "is a delusion and a snare. One must live with ideas to understand them. Unless they are applied and reapplied in successive challenges, they degenerate into mere words, mere mouthings."

Klapper was not alone in his worries about the demands the vet would make upon universities. Frederic W. Ness, assistant to the vice-chancellor of New York University, said many veterans came to college with unrealistic expectations, foxhole and barracks dreams they had scant chance of realizing. A navy storekeeper, twenty-five years old, married with three children, his only formal education a single year at a commercial high school, wanted to be a doctor. Another veteran "whose campaign ribbons outnumbered Hermann Goering's medals" wanted three business courses but lacked the required preparatory schooling that would enable him to understand the material. Both men had to be rejected. Ness did not disguise his frustration with vets who acted as if earning a college degree involved nothing more than showing up for classes: "If we think that the primary objective of a college course in French is to give only a speaking acquaintance with the language, then we limit the function of a college," he wrote. "Why bother to pass a GI Bill of Rights to send the veteran to college? Let us buy him a set of Victrola records!"

The fretting of the academics, however, was beyond the earshot of the veteran student, who saw considerable visible evidence that the colleges were preparing for him. College after college created special programs tailored for the veteran. The University of Nebraska, for example, waived its entrance requirement of a high-school diploma for anyone who could prove his "capability" of doing college-level work; it created one-, two-, and three-year curricula for veterans wanting to rush through specialized courses. North Dakota Agricultural College added a "school of veteran education" to "provide for the returning veteran such training as will prepare him for a pleasant and profitable place in the postwar world." Chancellor Robert M. Hutchins of the University of Chicago worried about "educational hoboes" who would drift into school for lack of anything better to do. Western Reserve University in Cleveland set up a course in small business management for the veteran. At North Carolina State College, the navy closed its diesel engineering school, which had trained hundreds of technicians for sea duty, and the head of the ceramics department returned from service with the War Production Board. The universities were ready for peace.

"Being somewhat of a sentimentalist," former paratrooper Jack Fisler wrote in *The Technician* at North Carolina State College in 1946, "I just couldn't keep that lump in my throat from bobbing right up and knocking a few very dry tears out of my eyes as I gazed on our beautiful Memorial Tower last March after three long, long years of drilling, KPing, griping, jumping from airplanes, and in general, making a monkey out of myself and the Japs." A columnist in *The Texas Ranger,* student magazine at the University of Texas, wrote in the September 1946 issue: "This is a different campus now, even if the buildings look the same. You see fellows in prewar saddleshoes, but when you get close you hear them trading baby formulas." Goodfriends, a campus area women's shop, advertising in the same issue, advised coeds, "That guy, who was someone nice to send your letters to last year, is back in your college life. Vaulted corridors will resound once more to the tread of size twelve brogans. And what a welcome change the boys make in your college life, in your college wardrobe. . . . Even campus and class-room fashions are softer, prettier, packed with man-appeal. G. I. (Guy Interest) is the theme song of Goodfriends campus college. . . ." And North Carolina State's *Technician* directed an editorial at newcomers that was both a welcome and a warning:

> You new freshmen comprise a class unique in the history of State College because of the wide variance in age range, amount of experience, and maturity of the different individuals. . . . Only one of three new entrants graduate, even in peacetime. . . . So it appears that if you are starting in college just to have a good time, it would be best to stop now before you have wasted too much money and too much of your own and other people's time.

For veterans who had been in college before the war, homecoming had its disappointments. The demands of war had stripped campuses of many of their old traditions and activities, and now the Veterans Association elbowed aside prewar political blocs and established itself as the most powerful student group on many campuses. For example, at North Carolina State it ran the United War Fund Drive (campus form of the community chest), lobbied through reduced ticket rates for vets at the little theater, formed a cooperative store, and won four of six sophomore offices. The Interfraternity Council, nervous about the depletion of Greek letter societies, pledged to eliminate the "old collegiate snobbery" by broadening fraternity membership so that returning veterans "will find on the campuses a true manifestation of the democracy for which the war was waged." Unimpressed, vets on some campuses formed their own highly informal fraternity: Chi Gamma Iota, whose Greek letters are X-G-I. Old customs also withered at Duke University in nearby Durham. Campus editor Clay Felker* wrote that shouts of "Button, freshman," were replaced by "Square that hat,

* Now editor of *New York Magazine.*

sailor," during the war, when naval officers trained at Duke, and somehow never revived. First-semester freshmen sat on the broad steps of Duke Chapel, off limits to them before the war. Upperclassmen dutifully handed out "blue dinks"—beanies bearing class numbers which traditionally had been worn until the Duke-North Carolina football game (and to Christmas if Carolina won). The veterans threw them away. And when nonveteran upperclassmen attempted to revive "Rat Court" hazing of freshmen, student columnist Jack Fisler cautioned, "Being an enlisted veteran of the parachute infantry, we understand that no strong-arm tactics would be advisable to apply on indifferent freshmen of the veteran group."

An air of solemnity pervaded. There was a determined preoccupation with books and study, a frenetic hurrying to *finish*, to earn the degree and enter the job market, to "make up for lost time," the five words that summarized the overriding goal of the postwar campus veteran. A *Time* reporter, asking graduating vets about their "problems" in June 1947, got this answer from a student at Indiana University: "Pardon me, but you'll have to hurry, because I've got to get along. Problem? The main problem of everybody is to catch up. We're all trying to get where we would have been if there hadn't been a war."

Late in the war University of Texas sociologists Drs. Harry Moore and Bernice Moore speculated on what the returning veteran would think of the coed: "He will not be staggered if when he returns she has changed not at all; if she has refused to grow up; if she has not kept up with the times; if she has not learned what the war really meant. He expects and needs a *woman* [the sociologists' emphasis] when he returns." But did the coeds fit the veterans' definition of "woman"? And were coeds fresh from home prepared for men three, four, five years older, and experienced in subjects other than warfare? In retrospect, no other aspect of postwar campus life had such long-range insignificance as the debate over boy-girl relationships, an argument waged with windy fury in dormitory bull sessions, the letters columns of campus newspapers, college political campaigns, even in quasi-learned sociological tracts; so intense, in fact, that when the *New York Times* published an article by a veteran comparing American girls unfavorably with Europeans ("being nice is almost a lost art among American women"), the storm of protesting mail was so immense that the *Times* self-defensively devoted two full pages to the females' rebuttal.

For the veterans, a major irritant was a frequently outrageously one-sided male-female ratio. At the University of Texas, an archetypical large state university, the ratio was three males for each woman, a figure that provoked an ominous opinion from a professor of anthropology: "Not even warfare has ever put such a strain on any civilized or primitive society. There have been isolated cases of such a ratio, but it is definitely an artificial phenomenon." John Bryson, writing in a special issue of *The Texas Ranger* devoted to women, commented, "The contrast between ego-inflated young girls, blessed with such a ratio, and the women the veteran met in a realistic outside world has provided a comparison that only invites unpleasantness and hard feelings. The female excuse, 'Look how unhappy we were during the manpower shortage; we have to make up for lost time,' is hardly logical to men who spent their formative years enduring the loneliness of jungles, trenches, and barracks in similar lost time, intensified by the ultimate in suffering."

Another Texas veteran, Downs Matthews, wrote that ex-GIs knew what was "wrong" with the average coed but were at a loss on how to go about improving her. "The biggest factor involved is one of contrast," Matthews wrote. "Through a quick, sobering maturity and the sweeping education of war travels, they know what they want in a woman. They have been awakened to possibilities in the female by association with women all over America and the rest of the world. Not loose, wild women without morals. Just women, not girls." In the next lines, however, Matthews made some criticisms that tended to confirm the direst suspicions of coeds: that the phrase "lack of maturity" was a euphemism for girls who refused to be bedded in a motel or the back seat of a car. Matthews complained that the college girl "expects too much of her boyfriend, and gives too little in return. She makes no attempt at being a good date, or trying to show the boy, who is willing to spend his time, money and efforts in obtaining her company, that she is appreciative." Matthews frowned at coeds who "pretend . . . to be shocked at the mention of a drink or talk of going off to another city for a party and football game. . . . The college girl has absolutely no concept of what pleases a man." By contrast, Matthews wrote, "working girls . . . have learned the hard way that such attitudes do not pay. They are forced to face the unadorned facts that if they want to have a good time they will have to have something to offer the man. Being thrown into the terrific competition of the working world, where there are few opportunities to meet eligible men, girls get terribly lonely and bored with nobody asking for a date every day or so. When a date comes along, they really appreciate him and they do their utmost to show their appreciation of his attention." Veterans writing to *The Daily Texan* drummed home much the same theme. One student defiantly called upon all male students to make three dates for the night of February 8, then gather for a stag party, standing up the entire female population of the university. A few weeks of such treatment, the veteran suggested, would result in "the most cowed, trustworthy group of women to be found anywhere in the world outside Moslem India." Said another writer: "There's really nothing wrong with those Texas coeds that a change of diapers wouldn't cure." Responding, females generally equated criticisms as reflections upon their virtue. A letter signed by three coeds stated: "We regret that we cannot measure down to the standard you lived by in the streets of Paris, London, Frisco, and a few other hot spots of the universe. Perhaps [the veterans are] confusing immaturity with chastity. The average girl on the campus does not want to be a mature woman in the sense that she forfeit her gaiety, her laughter, and even her coquettishness. We are proud to be young and full of life. We are proud to be innocent." Some coeds found a self-assurance among the vets that set them apart from the younger undergraduates. Mary Matossian, as a freshman at Stanford in the 1940's,* dated many older vets and found them more pleasant, mature company than the run-of-the-mill sophomore. "They treated you like a lady, they knew you were young and inexperienced, they didn't spend all their time trying to lay you," Dr. Matossian related. One of Dr. Matossian's colleagues at Maryland (she begged anonymity) said, "I had offers and propositions made to me at UCLA and Michigan, by these horny vets, that were so direct I won't repeat them even today, and I consider myself a broad-minded person." And Ivamae Brandt, in a letter to the University of Iowa's *Daily Iowan* in 1946, warned, "Your [the veterans'] prewar manners need a little brushing up. You're no longer the fair-haired boys the war has made you. Girls like to have doors opened for them, to be called respectable names, and to be treated with what chivalry there is left in the world. You fellows are going to be hard up unless something is done about your repulsive selves in a hurry." Joan Walker, giving the women's viewpoint in *The Texas Ranger* symposium, scoffed at the vets as crybabies, and suggested some self-examination:

The women think you're the ones that have changed, and I agree with them. You've ruined the curve on quizzes. You're too self-sufficient. You talk about radar and the cap'n and the B.O.Q. You spend too much of your time living over your buzz-boy days. You're still in that period that's called "postwar readjustment." And I could go on. But you don't hear women griping much. We're glad to have you back—the pickin's were pretty slim for a long time. But we're beginning to get a little tired waiting for your "Here-I-am-welcome-me-with-open-arms" attitude to be over, and we're beginning to be a little tired of your complaints. We're not so bad.

So shut up, remember where you are, look around, and there she is. I know some guys that have already done this, and they're just that far ahead of you.

But where to live, and where to study? Increased enrollments staggered the capacity of colleges to absorb the gush of students. A *School and Society* survey of 450 institutions found increases of up to 580

* Now a professor of history at the University of Maryland.

percent in teachers' colleges; 125 percent in agricultural and engineering colleges; 280 percent in arts and sciences. The surge surprised even the educational bureaucrats: In early 1946 the U.S. Office of Education had estimated that college enrollments would reach 2,000,000 in 1949 and 3,000,000 some five years later. But by November 1946 enrollments were 2,062,000, of whom 1,073,000 were veterans (and 667,000 were women). Further, the demands came after more than a decade of financial starvation for the colleges, whose income dropped precipitously during the Depression and war years because of lower investment income and decreased enrollment and gifts.

So the colleges scrambled. "Education proceeds with a student, a teacher, a book and a laboratory," President Henry Wriston of Brown University said in 1946. "Students there are in plenty but everything else is scarce." Temple University in Philadelphia bought an old aircraft-parts plant and converted it into classrooms. The state of New York set up a college at a naval training station near Geneva, and enrolled 12,000 students. "Let's get them in this year even though you will have to sacrifice some of your standards," Governor Thomas E. Dewey told state college presidents. The University of Connecticut took part of a coast guard facility at Fort Sampson; the University of Oklahoma got a naval air station at Norman. Colleges and universities in New York City combined to convert barracks at Camp Shanks into housing for 2,400 families, and buses hauled the students to and from classes. The Federal Public Housing Authority dismantled more than 100,000 housing units built for war workers and transported them, complete with surplus furniture, to campuses. The University of Wisconsin established branches in thirty-four cities to give the first two years of college work; the University of Illinois managed to obtain an old amusement pier in Chicago, used for navy classes during the war, and squeeze in 4,000 students. Texas Christian University in Fort Worth put its geology labs in a gymnasium. Wisconsin bedded 1,866 vets in an old munitions plant thirty-five miles from campus, another 1,600 at an airbase.

Student ingenuities were no less active. At the University of Iowa, three students found living space in the basement of a funeral parlor. Les Cramer, a navy vet at Ohio Wesleyan University, rented a house trailer in a preacher's back yard and got water through a garden hose. At the University of Southern California, two men lived in an auto for seven months, studying at night under a street light. At Auburn University in Alabama, two students persuaded a sympathetic Episcopal minister to let them live in the belfry of his church. At North Carolina State, engineering student Charles C. Elder, Jr., who spent eighteen war months in remote weather stations in Canada and Greenland, balked at leaving his wife in his home town when he couldn't find conventional housing. So Elder made himself a trailer of wood and sheet metal and friends helped him haul it to Raleigh—twenty-four feet long, eight feet wide, seven feet tall, but a temporary home nonetheless. Princeton, breaking a 200-year tradition, let student wives live on campus. At Rhode Island State, housing officials crammed eleven students into each Quonset hut.

Gripe though they did, most student vets philosophically accepted the housing mess as an unpleasant extension of wartime hardship, a discomfort that could be endured because school, unlike war, had a definite completion date. The vets and their families lived in tight camaraderie: in "villages" of house trailers, Quonset huts, plywood houses, and old army barracks that had been hauled to campuses and converted into housing. Many of the dwellings were little more than sparsely furnished housekeeping rooms. At North Carolina State, for instance, the majority of couples lived in quarters without cooking facilities. But the vets built a markedly cohesive community.

Consider Monroe Park, an enclave of ninety-five house trailers for vet families at the University of Wisconsin, dubbed the "state's most fertile five acres" because of the high birth rate the year after former servicemen and their wives reunited and settled down to study. (In one week in the spring of 1947 babies were born to five Monroe Park families.) Monroe Park was as tightly organized as an army battalion, albeit on a more convivial basis. It elected a mayor (term: one semester) to serve as liaison with university and town officials. Six "constables" had arrest power but, aside from quieting roisterous Saturday night parties, spent most of their time handling such emergencies as defective oil heaters. The park's cooperative grocery store grossed $5,000 weekly and gave eight vets part-time work; its prices were about 10 percent lower than private stores'. The park sponsored a bowling league, a softball team, semimonthly dances at a community recreation center (with music by radio or jukebox), and classes on sewing, cooking, and child care. The Monroe Park vets skimped. Trailer rent ranged from $25 to $32.50 monthly, including electricity for light and cooking, and oil for heating (but no running water). Estimated expenses for a family with one child were $150 monthly, $60 more than the GI Bill stipend. But a park resident, Pauline Durkee, wife of an engineering student and mother of girls eight and nine, was philosophical when she talked with a writer for the *American Legion Magazine*. Although she clerked in a grocery store to help balance the family budget, Mrs. Durkee found time to be the Monroe Park social chairman, and she said it was "good discipline" for the families to haul their own water and live communally. "It keeps us from becoming softies, and makes us remember that our forefathers had to go without conveniences we consider indispensable, and thought nothing of it."

Michigan State College boasted its own fertile valley in a vet village of apartments, trailers, and prefabricated huts. A count in April 1947 turned up 800 children of less than five years among the 2,000 veteran couples; 288 wives were pregnant. Here, too, the families banded closely together. A young wife named Marian McGregor, shocked by general loneliness when she moved into the village in 1946, began bringing women together for picnics and discussions on homemaking. The response was so warm that Mrs. McGregor arranged a mass meeting in a college ballroom to organize a formal association, Spartan Wives. College officials detailed a woman professor and the director of the adult extension division to help develop a program. Soon the Spartan Wives had classes on subjects ranging from swimming to motherhood and how to make kids' clothes from cast-off GI garb. The wives sponsored a weekly program on the campus radio station on such subjects as "How to Live on $90 a Month." Their cooperative store undercut local grocers by 10 percent. But more important than the formal programs, Mrs. McGregor mused in 1947, was the cohesiveness the Spartan Wives brought to the village, and the excitement of a shared adventure. "Our men didn't sit around and gripe when they were overseas fighting; they went ahead and did the job. The least we wives can do is to make the home life as easy as possible while they finish the other job, that of getting their degrees."

Dick Mullan* was a freshman at Pennsylvania State College when drafted into the infantry for "three kind of grim years." At age twenty-one, he and his new wife, Peggy, returned to State College, Pa., in 1947 to pursue a degree in biochemistry. They lived briefly in a small upstairs apartment with no stove or refrigerator. "We kept things outside the window to keep them cool, milk and cream for breakfast. We tried to cook on a hot plate, cleaning the dishes in the bathroom sink." Mullan car-pooled with neighbors to the campus, three miles distant, often waiting hours in the library for a ride home at night. Peggy had problems getting to and from her job in the graduate school. Hence they felt themselves lucky when a vacancy suddenly developed for an apartment on Beaver Street, State College's main thoroughfare near the campus.

"Our new apartment was really a front porch, right on the main street, with venetian blinds separating us from the outside world. The 'living room' consisted of a desk and a chair. The stove had three gas burners. We had some sort of tin contraption, a Dutch oven, which we put on top of the stove for an oven. But we did all sorts of wild things with it. We'd bake cakes and roasts. One time my brother came for dinner and said, 'Peggy, sometimes I think you are going to open that thing and take out a suckling pig!'

"But the bathroom was the real riot. There was no shower, no bathtub. We were never really sure how the landlady expected us to keep clean; I guess she really didn't. Everything in the bathroom was minia-

* Now an executive with a national food chain, living in a Philadelphia suburb.

ture—little tiny john, little tiny sink. The problem was to figure out how to take a bath. I could always go up the street and take showers at the fraternity house. But this really wasn't going to do for Peggy.

"I was down at Sears one day and saw a collapsible bathtub—a camping type of thing, which you opened up like a cot and filled with water, using a pan or a bucket. You had to be careful about scraping or tearing the thing—which we did at the end, anyway—but it worked, sort of. Since we lived right on the main street, if you wanted to take a bath you had to pull the blinds and lock the front door. If anyone came to the door, you quickly said, 'Sorry, I'm taking a bath.' " ("*When I got pregnant, it was a real drag,*" recollected Peggy Mullan. "*It was hard enough getting in and out, but there was no way I could fill or empty it, no way.*")

"The landlady didn't even know we had the thing until we moved; I don't think she was particularly interested in how we kept clean, if we did. I really felt we were not too welcome by the town, that the people wanted to exploit us. When we finally left, though, after one and one-half years, we sold it to her at the price we had paid for it, leak and all.

"The bedroom was approximately seven by eight feet, with a double bed six and three-quarters by seven and three-quarters feet. It took up the whole room. You walked in and fell right into bed—the bedroom was really that, a bedroom." ("*You crawled in from the end,*" Peggy Mullan said. "*That got funny when I was pregnant—I needed Dick to pull me in from the foot of the bed.*")

"The front porch had no insulation. We'd start a bridge game, and it would get colder and colder and colder; there was no answer but for everyone to go home. Sometimes we'd come in from a weekend outing when the temperature was ten below zero, and there was a big rush to get hot chocolate and crawl into bed and attempt to get warm."

Peggy Mullan was 8½ months pregnant the snowy February day in 1950 when Dick received his degree. ("There was a real baby explosion the last year at State College, when everyone was finishing; most all of our friends were pregnant.") They returned to the apartment and crammed their belongings into a 1938 Plymouth. "The last thing we put in was the broom we used to sweep the snow off the top of the car. We had a drink with a fraternity brother and drove away in ten inches of snow, ready for the world.

"It was one of the best times of our life. We were young. What we had to contend with was more in the pioneer tradition of the country. We survived, and we learned, which was good for all of us."

As inflation pushed the cost of living steadily upward, Congress heard an increasing crescendo of cries by veteran students that they could not survive on GI Bill payments. A conference of veterans, labor, and education officials in January 1947 produced considerable data to support the complaints. Stipends at the time were $65 monthly for a single vet, and $90 for a man with dependents. The VA also paid up to $500 annually for tuition, books and supplies. But for most vets the GI Bill was a supplement, not a supporting income. A survey of 132 campuses by veterans' groups found single vets paying as much as $120 monthly for living expenses (the low was $32 monthly, the average $53.33). The range for married ex-GIs was from $47 to $165 monthly, with an average of $79. Regardless of the disparities in living costs, however, vets received the same amount, no matter where they lived and the amount they spent for subsistence. So in early 1947 the veterans lobby put forth a bill increasing stipends to $75 for single students and $100 for married vets, plus $15 for the first child and $10 per child thereafter. The vets had the statistics on their side, a fact everyone conceded; nonetheless surprisingly diverse protestants opposed any increase. Dr. Francis J. Brown, speaking for the 829 colleges and universities in the American Council on Education, endorsed higher pay for couples with children, but for no one else. Brown acknowledged the vets' financial plight. Yet the purpose of the GI Bill, he noted, was to "assist" and encourage vets to go to college, "not to give them a free education." A token $5 monthly increase would cost the Treasury $150 million a year, he noted. Charles A. Shields, a student at Haverford College outside Philadelphia, supported Brown: "It would be just expense money, spending money," Shields testified before the House Committee on Veterans Affairs. "We never had it so good." A committee member, Representative W. Howes Meade of Kentucky, chimed that the majority of committee members were Second World War veterans, and all had a college education. "So far as I know," he said, "all had difficult times. Yet, without any assistance from the government, they got their college education." Representative Olin Teague of Texas, a wounded combat hero, was also cool. He put into the record a letter from a college student saying single vets griped chiefly because they were too lazy to earn money to supplement the GI Bill. "Not only do the majority of them refuse to work, but they all drive nice automobiles, take weekend trips practically every weekend, and . . . spend considerable money on whiskey and beer." Other congressmen were hostile because two-thirds of the vets were not in programs of any sort; hence why give more money to those in college?

Student supporters of an increase talked about both immediate needs and the long-range benefits of the GI Bill. Gary Reynolds, student editor of *Mail Call,* the veterans magazine at George Washington University, Washington, D.C., said about 10 percent of the 6,000 vets at the school couldn't find part-time jobs; that his personal monthly expenses were

$100, including $69 for a boarding-house room. Without an increase, Reynolds said, veteran enrollment would drop by half. James T. Roberts, a student at the University of Baltimore, said he wouldn't wave the flag for more money, but that he would talk about practical reasons: "I am sick and tired of hearing this 'I faced death' stuff," Roberts said. "I don't want anything for that, but I do want an education, and I feel I can serve my country better as an educated man than I can as 'John Doe, ditch digger,' or a man who runs a machine."

The veterans' demands were irresistible: In 1948 Congress kicked up the benefits to $75 monthly for a single vet; $105 for a couple, $120 for a family with a child. Budgets nonetheless remained tight, but the veterans tugged their belts and kept at their studies.

Regardless of their desires to blend into the general student population, veterans did retain a separate identity. Because of their intensity of purpose, the conventional wisdom among college bureaucrats was that they accomplished far more academically than did nonveterans. But the difference was more imagined than real. The Educational Testing Service studied 10,000 veteran and nonveteran students at sixteen colleges during the late 1940's and arrived at the carefully hedged conclusion that among freshmen "there is a tendency for veterans to achieve higher grades in relation to ability than do nonveteran students." But ETS said the "actual magnitude of the difference is small, however. In the most extreme case, the advantage of the veterans would on the average amount to no more than the difference between a C and a C-plus." But for "interrupted veterans" (that is, those who had attended college before military service, and then returned) there was "marked superiority" at four of five large universities studied. ETS also turned up an apparent anomaly: despite their seriousness, the veterans "on the whole . . . attached less importance to college grades and to college graduation than the nonveterans." They attended college to obtain higher-paying jobs, not to prepare for a profession.

The veterans' emphasis on the practical offended many professorial sensitivities. Were the universities destined to be nothing more than academic factories, producing graduates in assembly-line fashion, with the emphasis upon speed rather than quality? Must the popularization of higher education mean also its vulgarization?

But according to S. N. Vinocour, a veteran who taught speech at the University of Nevada, "If pedagogic desks were reversed and the veteran now in college were given the opportunity to grade his professor, he would give him a big red 'F' and rate him as insipid, antiquated and ineffectual." Reporting on a 5,000-mile research tour of campuses in *School and Society* in 1947, Vinocour wrote that many vets feared an economic depression was imminent. Hence they wanted career training rather than theoretical courses. The veteran, Vinocour maintained, did not want to "fritter away his time cramming inconsequential facts, such as learning the names of all the signers of the Declaration of Independence, conjugation of the vulgar Latin verbs, memorizing the date that Shakespeare first said 'Hello' to Ann Hathaway, or how many hours Benjamin Franklin had to stand in the rain with his kite." The veteran felt he entered college as a full-fledged and mature citizen, "not as an adolescent high school graduate eager to participate in the old rah-rah days of Siwash." He considered the collegiate atmosphere "not only very stupid, but a definite hindrance to his acquiring an education." Vinocour argued that the veteran wanted more practical courses (such as radio technique) and "more realistic English courses," rather than the "minor poems of Milton" and "history of oratory." Concluding, Vinocour charged that veterans are "living and studying in a vacuum covered with the moss of the professor's yellow lecture notes."

Such a broadside, of course, could not go unchallenged. *School and Society* bristled with angry rebuttals from professors claiming that the indolent veteran was the major educational problem of the nation. Most of the vets, asserted the correspondents, would be better off in trade schools, not universities; they decried their lack of intellectual curiosity and abhorrence of serious scholarship. So frothful was the debate (or, more accurately, the attack upon Vinocour) that it eventually burst from the pages of *School and Society* into other academic trade journals. One must speculate at the magnitude of the classroom slight that prompted the retaliatory outburst of the venerable Professor Bayard Quincy Morgan, of Stanford University, in the *Pacific Spectator,* a West Coast intellectual quarterly. Morgan scoffed at the complaint about "professors mumbling from notes yellow with age" (a paraphrase of one of Vinocour's laments). He asked: "Does that mean to you that the ideas embodied there are *necessarily* flyblown and fit only for the ash can? Must I write a fresh set of lecture notes every year, ignoring everything I said the year before?" Morgan continued: "They want a degree, oh yes, but about as a man buys a railway ticket or secures a passport. . . . [A]nything that doesn't contribute directly and demonstrably to the quickest acquisition of a degree is not only not wanted, it is resented." Veterans wanted "training" rather than "education." Morgan summarized their attitude: " 'Never mind the theory; that takes too long, and we won't understand it anyway. What we want is the know-how.' So they demand just enough English to talk to a day laborer; just enough of a foreign language to order a meal or engage a hotel room; just enough mathematics to check the bills and the bank statement."

Beneath Morgan's wrath was a serious criticism of an ominous drift in American higher education. The new generation of students, he said, was resentful of courses that did not provide "results." Confronted with a course outside their narrow professional field, they asked, "What good will it do me?" The veterans, he maintained, were scornful of free discussion of political, economic, and social ideas. Morgan felt he knew why: "The armed forces were always intent on 'getting the job done,' and always in a hurry. They rushed the recruits through 'just enough' of everything, trusting . . . to the exigencies of actual fighting to augment the scanty education of the trainee. It is not surprising if the veteran thinks all education is like that, and expects the college to give him the same kind of training he got in the army or navy." (Critical as Morgan was of the veteran, he said academicians should listen to the complaints, and, "perhaps, with the veteran's help and counsel, improve on our present system.")

Guy Owen is a writer who has earned more satisfaction, and quiet reputation, than money. His The Flim Flam Man and The Apprentice Grifter, *published in 1972, the truly uproarious account of the adventures of a con man in rural North Carolina, is at once a handbook on how to fleece larcenous rednecks and a comic narrative of the genre of Mark Twain's* Huckleberry Finn. *The book sold 3,000 copies, the movie was not the box office success it had promised to be, and Pocket Books remaindered the paperback edition. But these matters are inconsequential to Owen himself. He has staked for his personal literary province the changing character of the coastal regions of North Carolina, the subject of three other novels; he writes poetry; he teaches English at North Carolina State University; and he has been active in the civil rights and peace movements. After graduation from high school in 1942, the seventeen-year-old Owen lied about his age to get a job as a welder in a shipyard, and made so much money that he was reluctant to leave to enter the University of North Carolina. He managed one year before being drafted, and eventually landed with the 13th Armored Division under Major General George S. Patton. Owen won't—or can't—talk about his specific war experiences, other than to say that he heard "considerable gunfire."*

"There is a reason my story is not 'typical.' I came out of the war mentally . . . [Owen paused many seconds] mentally wounded, I guess you would say. I spent a month in a hospital in California. I don't think I was batty or anything like that, but I had nervous tics in my face. The psychiatrists gave me a fifty percent disability. So a good part of the postwar years, so far as I was concerned, was spent trying to find myself, to prove to myself that I was not sick.

"Looking toward peace, for me the main thing was to get back to a sane world where the ground would not buckle under your feet, to a world that was not a slaughterhouse. I was young and sensitive, maybe hypersensitive; after all, I'm a youngster who published poetry in high school, mind you. But during the war me and other soldiers, we just turned ourselves into monomaniacs, in a way. The main thing was to stop the Germans, stop the Japs. There was no arguing about it, it damned simply had to be done. There was no romance about it.

"I guess what happened to me, when I returned to Chapel Hill [*site of the University of North Carolina*], was a gradual withdrawing into a safe world, a little island, a retreat into an aesthetic world, away from the brutality of the shipyards and the army. I had two goals: to prove that I could make it in the world even though I had been labeled fifty percent disabled; and to get a college education. I did this by going to my private inner island. I cut off relations with the church and became an agnostic; I had no interest in politics, no belief in economic salvation, no thoughts about science. I didn't even care enough about politics to argue them.

"Financially, I was better off than before the war; I didn't have to wait tables. I didn't have a lot of money to throw around, to buy records and books I wanted. But I didn't miss it, because I never had it. It was a pretty austere life, living in those little old boxed-up Quonset huts and 'victory villages.' I couldn't get any work done in a crowded dorm, so I'd take off to the library: after all, how do you study in a double-bunk bed?

"But I don't think I bitched very much. There were people who couldn't even get into the university because they didn't have a place to stay. I remember a few tents thrown up around the campus. Plus the fact that when you are in the army, and a private, you are used to sleeping on the ground. I felt grateful running my hands over the smoothness of a clean sheet.

"For the vets, college was a sort of no-nonsense thing. They worked hard, they concentrated on the main thing, the degree, married or not. Oh, there were blowups on the weekends, when people would sit around and drink beer. But the main thing was, 'Man, I've got three, four, five years down the drain; we've got to work.' Myself, I graduated in three years by going to summer school.

"Sure, we felt an apartness from nonveterans. I resented it very much when I went home on my furlough from overseas, and going up and shaking hands with a man on the street who said, 'Hello, there, where have you been?'

"It was like we were in a cancer ward looking out the window at people who were very healthy, and who couldn't communicate with us.

"I don't think it was a fun time for us. I worked too hard. Those days, I didn't even drink, so I kept out of the weekend parties. A part of it was that I came from a very small high school, and was not ready for Chapel Hill; I was always sort of running scared.

"Also, there was this 'fifty percent disabled' label put on me, and *having this psychiatrist tell me, 'You are going to make it okay, but don't try to do anything that will tax you too hard, don't get too involved, don't set your goals too high.' I still resent that. I got rid of the percentages in a few years, and I was no longer getting a $10 check each month to remind me that I shouldn't try too hard.*

"*The GI Bill, I can't emphasize enough, really saved me. I don't think I would have been able to go on for the doctorate. Sure, I would have gotten an AB, but that would have meant teaching in a high school, where I wouldn't have the spare time to write the novels. The GI Bill took me well into my doctorate, and enabled me to get outside the state, to places such as the University of Chicago, where I had different experiences from what I would have ever seen in Carolina.*

"*The war is something I've tried to dismiss, and I've done a pretty good job of blanking it out. Anybody who can't tell you the name of his first sergeant—and I can't—has it out of mind. Still, when I hear machine-gun fire, I begin to tremble. I wouldn't go see* Patton [*a film with George C. Scott in the title role*]. *I had the shaking experience just last week watching Charlie Chaplin's* Modern Times *again. It doesn't hurt me, but my body still takes over.*

"*I thought, when I was floundering around at Chapel Hill, that if I had any story to tell, it was about the war. A lot of GIs who wanted to be writers felt the same way, mostly as a means of working off grudges against officers and sergeants, and the waste of war—the horror, the boredom, the regimentation, the dehumanizing things. I remember once drawing up a list of things I'd like to write about, and one of them was the war. But I haven't written anything about it. For a long time I was so close to it, so haunted by it, that I couldn't be objective.*

"*Going back to my immediate postwar feelings: sure, I was apolitical. (I'm not now: I helped organize peace vigils in Raleigh, and marches against the [Vietnam] war, and I made trips to Washington, and I helped integrate Raleigh by demonstrating in the streets.) But I make no apologies for the postwar period. We* did *stop the Japs, we* did *stop the Germans. I'm a little bit impatient with youngsters who want to picture us as American Legionnaires and hard hats and whatnot. This is all that anyone has the right to demand of my generation: that we stopped the Japs, we stopped the Germans.*

"*Now if we want to turn on the TV, drink beer, even to vote for George Wallace, it may be that we should be forgiven in a sense. We cut away everything to make up for those lost years. Maybe that's why my generation was called the 'silent generation.' "*

Summing up the first full campus year of peacetime, *The Texas Ranger* at the University of Texas noted, "All in all, it was a year of everyone trying to return to normal. Khaki leftovers from the army gradually disappeared from the campus as clothes became available to the new civilians. There was less and less talk about old outfits and more and more discussion of what lies ahead. All in all, it looked like American college life was on the way back."

So, too, was the American economy, but with a mass of problems that far surpassed any troubles faced by the academicians. The question, in essence, was whether business and labor could survive peace.

II

The Economy: From Guns to Fords

A Remembrance of Marshall: II

My father roared through the war years—quite literally—in a muffler-less *1936* Pontiac whose blattering thunder of a morning, I realize in pained, honest retrospect, must have been a damnable nuisance to anyone living within a block of our home on North Fulton Street. The car suffered other problems as well. One of the rear doors, in perpetual confusion, could not decide whether to jam shut, resistant to the most strenuous of adult tugs and admonitions, or to swing open on curves, unexpectedly and frighteningly to those of us in the back seat. My sister and I once ate half a watermelon on the rear seat on a lazy, rainy Sunday afternoon, to the outrage of both my father and the upholstery. Why, I remember wondering, did our Pontiac's speedometer provide for registering a speed of *100* miles an hour, when neither we nor anyone else ever went above *35* (which I later came to realize was the wartime limit).

But so what? Everyone else in town coaxed along a similar clunker, wondering which would collapse first—the tires or the Japanese. Model A Fords toughened by the hard wear of the Depression. Ramshackle pickup trucks. Chevvies with rumble seats and rusty running boards and wooden-spoke wheels. The *1939* Fords with grilles snaggled-toothed from the loss of vertical chrome bars. Rusting fenders and turtle-shell lids that flapped on rough roads. (*Turtle shell.* A much better word than *trunk.* Whatever happened to it?) Blue-black clouds of oily smoke and dripping crankcases that black-pocked the streets. The collective over-riding postwar ambition of America—the practical wish, once you got beneath the folderol about "building a better world" and "preserving lasting peace," the high-flown sentiments voiced more by editorial writers than by the people who actually *are* America—was to ride around in a new automobile.*

---

* The car hunger gnawing at Americans is shown by raw statistics. In 1941 about 29,500,000 passenger cars were registered in the United States. By 1945 the total was down to 25,350,000, and many of these were so decrepit they qualified as

The Gouldens' wish materialized one spring day in 1946, in the bulbous form of a maroon four-door Nash sedan, an off brand but the only car available. The details of this auto are somewhat vague, other than first-sight memories of some trappings it carried from Detroit: excelsior padding around the arm rests; heavy packing paper sheathing the rear seats; cryptic grease pencil marks on the windshield; the pervasive smell of new rubber and paint and fabric and petrochemicals.

The first few days, when my father drove home for lunch, my sister and I played in the Nash, sitting behind the wheel and pretending we were speeding along the narrow Texas highways to Beaumont and San Angelo and perhaps even the beach at Galveston—the faraway places where cousins abounded, denied to us during the war. In the evenings, after a supper of chicken-fried steak or liver smothered in onions, my father would announce, "Let's drive around the Loop and cool off," meaning a spin around Pine Crest Drive, below Marshall to the south, touching the stately old southern houses with antebellum pines and wisteria and columned porches; and "Yankee Stadium," the cluster of two- and three-bedroom bungalows built to house the influx of workers, many of them nasal-twanged northerners, who had come for war jobs at the Longhorn Ordnance Works, fourteen miles northeast of town ("the only thing in East Texas the Germans would want to bomb," according to war strategists at Van Zandt Elementary School). Some evenings we would push farther into the countryside, the three oldest of us in the back, our little sister scrunched in the front, singing "The Old Gray Mare" and listening to my father boom out Rice Institute fight songs and trying to learn lyrics that really didn't mean much at the time ("Don't send my boy to Baylor, I'd rather see him dead . . ."). After dusk we would find a country store, at a crossroads or a lumber mill, and my oldest sister and I would climb the wooden steps and cross the rickety porch past the coal-oil pump. (These things were made of metal and painted red and smelled like a fire hazard, even to a subteen kid. The sight of one would give a modern fire marshal the shaking palsy; yet the chronicles of East Texas as recorded by oral historians do not reveal a single instance where one ever caused a fire. But coal-oil lamps had other even more deleterious effects: The sawmill and farm kids who studied by them reeked of oil smoke the next morning, and perhaps for a few days thereafter. Those of us who enjoyed electric lights were known

---

vehicles in name only. By one estimate, Detroit had an immediate postwar market for 10,000,000 to 15,000,000 cars. And the manufacturers were so eager they began advertising even before any cars were available. Buick, for instance, dipped into its archives for a picture of a yellow 1942 convertible and advertised it in July 1945 as a promise of "the high standards to be surpassed in new models now being made ready. . . . Victory in Europe is releasing many fighting men to come home—and permitting the country to turn, at least in part, to the making of things they will find nice to come home to. To many a fighting man, this will mean such pleasures as an open road, a glorious day—and a bright and lively Buick."

to complain of the stench, cruelly and occasionally at personal risk, as witness the savage schoolyard fight the winter day Bobby Price said something funny but nasty about R. C. Marshall's odor, and lost a tooth, the original contour of his left cheekbone, and his rating as the baddest-assed guy in the sixth grade.) But I digress from the 1946 Nash: Inside the country store my sister and I would grope in the cold-drink box for twelve-ounce Pepsi-Colas; probably Cokes or Seven-Ups for Mother and Dad; a big orange for Marinel, the little one; a Barq's root beer on the evenings I would sacrifice four ounces of quantity vis-à-vis a Pepsi for my favorite flavor. A nickel for each, and if we didn't have empties rattling around the back seat, a two-cent deposit on the bottles (or, more frequently, the storekeeper would holler to my father, "Bring them by the next time you're out around here, Mister Joe").

But something about the Nash irritated father. The first day or so he spoke vaguely about its being "air-conditioned," a luxury we had enjoyed on an occasional trip to a restaurant in Shreveport, the metropolis across the state line in Louisiana, or at the local Paramount Theater. But air-conditioning in a car? *Wow! Summer came, but not the air-conditioning, no matter how Dad adjusted the dials. The Nash had a powerful fan out of sight under the dashboard, but the air didn't match the frigid, popcorn-scented gales that swept across the Saturday afternoon cowboy-double-feature crowds at the Lynn Theater.*

A visiting Aunt Ruth brought the issue into the open. "Joe," she told my father as we rode along Pine Crest Drive one July evening, "I thought you wrote us your new Nash was air-conditioned." *Silence. "Well, why don't you show us how it works?" A longer silence, then, "If I wanted to, I could make it so cold in here you'd want to go home for your coat." "Then why don't you?" "I don't want to," in a tone that said the subject of Nash air-conditioning thereafter was nondiscussable.*

Two decades later, while researching this book, I ran across an advertisement in a June 1946 issue of Time *that supplied the missing ingredient to the story. The new Nashes, the ad said, feature "the Nash* Eye Conditioned Air System *that furnishes fresh, filtered air—warm as you dial it—without dust or drafts." Semantical flimflam, to be sure, and enough to beguile an East Texas appliance dealer who expected and wanted his postwar auto to have a modernistic feature, and was quietly mad when it did not.*

No matter, for the newness, the fun, the virginity of that Nash were ruined one autumn noon. A WHAMP! of a crash in the street as we ate lunch, a rush to the door, the face-tightening sight of another car, a prewar one, jowl to jowl with the new Nash, the jointure point a mess of smashed metal and leaking fluids and broken glass. My father said a nasty word, something he normally didn't do in front of us. The man who got out of the other car was sincerely apologetic.

"Mr. Goulden," he said, "I was headin' back downtown, and thinkin'

how pretty your new car was, and I guess I got to lookin' at it so hard that I just run right into it."

The insurance company fixed the car, after a fashion. But what is the satisfaction in owning a dented dream—be it a car or a vision of the future?*

* Before the decade ended, Detroit inflicted its own dents on the auto, with bloated, low-slung cars that sacrificed headroom for a totally subjective concept called "modern design," to the discomfort of any person who had the misfortune to grow beyond six feet tall. Outsized hoods and sweeping fenders, often topped with a worthless "fin," added empty girth. Nash bragged of a "completely aerodynamic car . . . nearly eighteen feet long, 6½ feet wide . . . *only shoulder high.*" For several makes, the entire engine had to be removed before the mechanic could get at the crankcase for repairs. Angled windshields gave more vision, but also admitted more glare, and drivers had trouble seeing over the puffed-up hoods. Bric-a-brac and dubious "optional equipment" encrusted postwar cars like so many flashy barnacles. John Keats, the social critic, listed the electrical apparatus crammed into "overblown, overpriced monstrosities built by oafs for thieves to sell to mental defectives":

Four headlights, two stop lights, two tail lights, parking and signal lights, dome lights, courtesy lights, rear license lights, beam indicator light, shift indicator light for automatic transmission, light switch "escutcheon" lamp, ash tray lamp, cigar lighter and lamp, heater control light, instrument cluster lights, glove compartment light, parking brake warning light, temperature indicator light, turn signal indicator light, electric clock—with light—underhood light, rear compartment light, two backup lights, radio dial light, spotlight, fuel gauge, oil pressure warning light, generator warning light, ignition switches, radio, heater, air conditioner, window motors, seat adjustment motor, defroster fan motor, radio antenna motor, automatic radar light dimmer, and windshield wipers.

5

Popping the Controls Cork

SPEAKING FROM THE WHITE HOUSE a few hours after the Japanese surrender, Chester Bowles, the price control chief, happily announced the economy's first small move toward prewar normality. Gasoline rationing was at an end, Bowles said over national radio. "Now you can take your gasoline and fuel oil coupons and paste them in your memory book. Rationing has been lifted, too, on canned fruits and vegetables. It's a pleasure for us at last to be able to bring you good news." That same evening, the Office of Price Administration canceled orders for 187,000,000 books of ration coupons—the green and white stamps that had been as necessary as money for wartime shoppers.

Other announcements were more foreboding. In Philadelphia, the navy declared a two-day holiday for most civilians at the shipyard, not so they could sleep off victory celebrations, but to await word from Washington on the future. The navy had ninety-five ships under construction at Philadelphia and yards elsewhere, including a battleship, two aircraft carriers, and twenty cruisers. Quite obviously these vessels would never sail into battle, but what should be done with their partially completed hulls? Curtiss-Wright, the big aircraft firm, told 150,000 workers in sixteen plants to go home and wait for further instructions. In Seattle and Renton, Washington, skilled metalworkers stood in the cavernous plants of Boeing Aircraft, the slam-wham-shriek of production lines suddenly and ominously silent, and listened to a company official's voice over the public address system: the air corps wanted 50 B-29s in September, instead of the 122 ordered; 10 rather than 20 in October. The official was sympathetic, but what could he really say? The war had ended, and with it the lush wages and premium overtime pay of defense work. In a single day Boeing laid off 21,200 of the 29,000 persons employed in the two plants. Within forty-eight hours of peace the army sent manufacturers 60,000 form telegrams canceling contracts worth $7.3 billion; the air corps, a few days later, kicked the totals to 70,848 contracts valued at $15 billion.

Thus the first impact of peace upon the American economy, a swift braking of an industrial machine that had pushed the gross national product, in dollar-dripping bounds, from $101.4 billion in 1940 to $215.2 billion in 1945. With Washington expecting the Pacific war to continue for another year or more, postwar economic planning was rudimentary. The sudden deceleration and the overnight stilling of the factories sent chill tremors through many persons, once the initial relief of peace passed. Was the prosperity of wartime illusionary? With the gushing pump of defense spending halted, would civilian demand keep the economy churning? The frenetic pace of war had pumped average weekly earnings to almost twice their 1940 level—$44.39 versus $24.20, with much of the bulge due to the extra overtime pay in the standard forty-eight-hour week. More than one worker guiltily suppressed the reflexive thought, "Peace is going to cost me an awful lot of money."

"There should be no mincing of words," said John W. Snyder, the Truman Administration's ranking reconversion planner. The end of war spending would cause "an immediate and large dislocation of our economy," with the "severity of this shock . . . increased by the sudden ending of the war." Nonetheless, Snyder made plain the Administration did not intend to "continue the manufacture of useless armaments for as much as one day to cushion the shock. We will not manufacture a single shell, nor a single piece of equipment above absolute minimum military needs, for the purpose of reducing the shock of terminating war work. We will not keep a single soldier or sailor in uniform longer than he is needed . . . in order to hold down the totals of temporary unemployment."

Some raw statistics show the challenge that peace brought to economic planners. Consider, first, the manpower problem. In August 1945 the civilian labor force was at a historic peak of 53,140,000, and some 12,120,000 persons remained in the armed forces, the bulk of them scheduled for swift mustering out. With the rapid paring of defense work forces, manpower experts somberly forecast that civilian industry could not possibly absorb homecoming soldiers. Before the sudden Japanese collapse, planners had hoped for a "frictional float" of perhaps 2,000,000 jobless persons during reconversion. But the uncertainty of August 1945 pushed the guesses even higher: 8,000,000 jobless, according to the government's stable of economists; anywhere from 10,000,-000 to 20,000,000, by organized labor's guess. Labor, it must be noted, wanted tight controls and heavy government spending to cushion reconversion; hence its figure was more scare than science. The National Association of Manufacturers, conversely, which wanted all controls lifted immediately so that "industry can get back to work," pooh-poohed the prospects of massive unemployment; although the jobless figure might reach 1,500,000, the level would not be sustained for more than thirty days, the NAM said.

And the persons who retained their jobs would be demanding more money. Because of rationing and tight price controls, the cost of living remained markedly stable in 1940–45, rising only about 30 percent (instead of the 100 percent of the three years before and during World War One). When overtime was excluded, however, base pays had been permitted to increase only 15 percent, hence labor was ready for catch-up bargaining once wage controls were lifted.

Another dangerous ingredient, paradoxically, was a cornucopia of spendable wealth that civilians and soldiers alike had piled up during the war.

Early on, the Roosevelt Administration had decided to finance the war through the sale of bonds, rather than confiscatory taxation—a policy that Marriner Eccles of the Federal Reserve Board called "mone-tization of the public debt," equivalent to the printing of money. This decision, combined with strictures on wartime spending and the dearth of consumer goods, enabled Americans to accumulate enormous sums of readily available cash. For the last two years of the war, citizens soaked away about 25 percent of their take-home pay, and by midsummer 1945 their liquid assets totaled an astounding $140 billion in savings accounts and war bonds—three times the entire national income in 1932. Add in the individual incomes of $120-plus billion for 1945, and Americans had a quarter of a trillion dollars to spend during the first year of peace—a mountain of wealth sufficient to make any economist blink. And by the estimate of the Federal Reserve Board, the savings were spread fairly evenly across the populace. About 60 percent of it was in the pass books of persons with less than $5,000 in savings. Of one sample cross-section of adult New Yorkers, surveyed by the Fed, only 7.9 percent reported no savings at all; 84 percent owned war bonds (many of them doubtlessly because of mandatory savings programs).

And after years of denial and listening to surly clerks snarl, "Don't you know there's a war on?" citizens literally itched to spend their money—for homes, for cars to replace the 1930's clunkers they nursed through the war, for refrigerators and juicy red steaks and nylons and anything else that caught their eye.

Thus the ingredients for a monumental economic tangle: a threatened shaking out of the work force, with high unemployment; an avaricious public hunger for consumer goods, more by far than industry could produce in the predictable future; worker restiveness for higher wages; a gnawing fear that the Depression had only been interrupted, not ended; and the complex task of turning factories back to civilian production. As a complicating factor, peace brought a quickening of the ideological debate over whether government should "quit meddling" with the fortunes of its citizens and businesses, and permit the economy to "return to a free market." Many Americans had accepted economic controls only grudgingly because of the back-to-work aberrations of Depression and war, and a sizable and outspoken minority still fondled hopes of reversing the New Deal. Conservatives made themselves jittery with a scholarly treatise entitled *The Road to Serfdom,* written just before the war ended by Friedrich A. von Hayek,* an obscure Austrian-born economist then living in Great Britain. Hayek argued—turgidly, but convincingly enough for nervous conservatives—that Nazism and the New Deal shared the same headwaters of national economic planning. Any form of collectivism, be it socialism, communism, liberalism, or Nazism, led inevitably to totalitarianism (i.e., "serfdom"). For the American right wing, Hayek's thesis carried the special warmth of reassurance, and a copy found its way to veritably every conservative nightstand and coffee table in the land. Corporations bought thousand-lot copies for mass distribution, and *Serfdom* stayed on the best-seller lists for months. And the Truman Administration itself grappled with the questions, What should Washington do to ease the pangs of economic reconversion, and How involved should the federal government become in labor-management disputes and the workings of the marketplace?

Government planners' overriding concern as the war ended was what to do about the quaky mountain of cash savings that threatened to crash down upon the economy with avalanche force. By one estimate, Americans had the money to buy three times as much consumer goods as could be produced the first year of peace even if reconversion went smoothly. If free spending is permitted in such circumstances, run-away inflation inevitably results. Chester Bowles, the director of the Office of Price Administration, feared a repetition of the post-World War One situation, when Bernard M. Baruch, in charge of price and production controls, resigned the day after the armistice, saying his job was done. The economy fell with a thud the next winter, and the jobless total reached 8,000,000 before recovery. There were 110,000 business bankruptcies and more than 400,000 farmers lost their land; nearly half the inflation took place after the guns stopped firing. In Bowles' estimate, "after World War One economic fumbling delayed orderly peacetime conversion for more than two years." He called the situation in August 1945 "one of the most dangerous periods in our country's economic

---

* The 1974 Nobel laureate in economics.

history." Bowles was pleased that "we had built a price, wage and rent control dam with surprisingly few leaks." Nonetheless the amount of savings behind that dam was "steadily growing. If the public should become convinced that the dam was about to be removed or to collapse, those savings would inundate the market to bid up prices, and the inflation would quickly get out of hand." The long-range solution was increased production, but it would take months until industry put out enough washing machines, autos, and radios to soak up the surplus purchasing power. The stopgaps of higher taxes and compulsory savings programs appealed to neither Congress nor the Treasury Department. So Bowles asked for continued controls, to help the economy over an expected two-year hump.

Mechanically, controls made much sense. Politically, they proved impossible. Americans endured wartime regimentation of the marketplace in the patriotic spirit of national emergency—and at the same time detested the OPA and the 73,000 people who served it. Now they wanted to shake off the restraining hands of Washington bureaucrats who tried to tell them that they couldn't have that new refrigerator or sirloin steak or auto tire; "economic reconversion" required that they suffer longer, as much as eighteen months longer, according to a "hold the line" order issued by President Truman on August 18, 1945. Not no, but *hell no,* shouted the American consumer. And the American manufacturer eagerly egged on the protests. Controls ran counter to the American tradition. Full production could be achieved only in a free market: What sane businessman would strain himself producing trousers and bathtubs to be sold at cheap, controlled prices? (The same businessman envisioned all the while hordes of consumers bearing down on his store, war-savings dollars held aloft, eager to pay twice the controlled price for virtually anything on the shelf.) Senator Joseph Ball of Minnesota called the OPA "the single most important collection of American fascists we've got," and *Time* suggested lifting controls and giving the populace its head: "The good sense of the American people, sometimes overlooked by paternal busybodies in Washington, could help." New York businessman Sidney W. May indignantly wrote the White House: "My Dear President: With so many automobiles around, how did they gather so many horses' asses and put them in the OPA? If you desire that I explain in detail I am ready to come to Washington at two minutes' notice." Senator Kenneth Wherry of Nebraska claimed in a floor speech that OPA bureaucrats were so stupid they could not distinguish "between male and female critters. That's the truth. They once issued an order forbidding the slaughter, for sixty days, of female steers."

Cheating the controllers became a boasted-about national pastime, with buyer and seller alike finding gimmicks to put a patina of legitimacy on bribes. A slaughterhouse owner in Kansas, before selling a beef carcass, would tell the eager buyer, "I'll bet you $100 you can't hit the barn door with your hat from a hundred yards." The buyer would take the bet, couldn't hit it, of course, and handed over the $100. Auto dealers would sell only to persons willing to buy odd accessories—a lap robe for $100, or an extra jack for $125, or another battery for $150. An Oklahoma dealer reputedly insisted on "throwing in" an old hound dog for an extra $100 each time he sold a car. The dog dutifully loped back to his lot within an hour or so. Another tactic was for a customer to buy a secondhand car from a dealer for $800, and immediately trade it back on a new car for $400. (At the most crass level, a buyer would simply drop $100 on the table and look away for a few seconds, confident it would vanish into the automan's pocket.) A New Yorker who wanted a fifth of Scotch might be required to buy, as well, bottles of rum, gin, and cheap wine. In San Francisco, a man who wanted a bathtub also had to purchase a medicine cabinet, an ironing board, a garage-door handle, and panel molding—and he still paid $8.25 above ceiling price for the bathtub.

The farmers were particularly restless. James Reston, touring the Midwest for the *New York Times,* found law-respecting farmers flouting OPA rules without fear of community censure. As in Prohibition days, citizens considered the regulations unfair, so they simply ignored ones they didn't like. One farmer told Reston he had been offered a Chrysler sedan as a bonus if he would sell his last carload at the ceiling price. The "bonus and barter" system was so prevalent that a farmer tried to place an ad in a Kansas City newspaper stating that he had been forced to raise his livestock on black market feed, and asking for contact with a "black market operator" who would dispose of his cattle. The farmers, Reston found, were not sympathetic to groups benefiting from various price control and export programs: "They do not think in terms of feeding starving human beings abroad, but in terms of 'feeding Europe' and 'feeding Asia,' and keeping prices down not for the 'people in the cities,' but 'for labor,' which, they assert caustically, goes on strike when it likes and forces up prices which the farmers have to pay." They also detested a "set aside order" requiring that the farmer must sell to the government one-half of the wheat he took to the grain elevators—an order acceptable in wartime, but anathema to rural independence after August 1945. On a more sophisticated level, manufacturers scouted for loopholes in the regulations. When the OPA permitted textile plants to return to full civilian production, for instance, the industry turned its energies to curtains and bedspreads, no longer price controlled, and ignored pajamas, shirts and other clothing still under controls. OPA took public blame for the shortages. And the public no longer felt queasy dealing with a type of businessman who during the war years had

been considered as much a national enemy as Hirohito: the black
marketeer.

In August 1945 Clifton (Clif) Bronk clung to solvency by the tips
of his wits. The sign on the highway in the Washington, D.C., suburb
said he ran a used-car lot.* "Fact of the matter, though, during the last
months of the war I'd have my own car parked there, and a few old
clunkers. The stuff that I was selling I kept at a house I rented out
around Laurel, Maryland. Some guy who'd come in, and smell like he
had money, I'd sound him out and make sure he wasn't an OPA man,
then suggest he take a ride out in the country with me. I wasn't about to
leave stuff on the lot that could bring a good price; that was an invitation for OPA trouble. 'Course, you didn't have to put on a big display,
'cause it was definitely a seller's market. Anything that started, rolled,
and stopped, you could sell.

"In those days I was a good cosmetics man on a car. I could take a
heaving wreck and with some paint, a rubber hammer, and some sawdust
I could make it smell like it just left Detroit. Sawdust? That's good for
tightening up a transmission. For a few miles, anyway. [Laughs.] I'd
also get some of the heaviest damned oil you can imagine, something the
navy developed for its ships. Put a few quarts of that stuff in a motor,
and it might be tight starting but, man, it would run smooth for enough
miles to sell.

"During forty-five I played it pretty cautious. I wasn't above barter-
ing. Say a guy wanted a thirty-nine Chevvie that OPA might let me sell
for $400. Well, that wasn't enough; hell, by the time I scouted up a car
in those days, and did any work at all, I was already out that much, or
more, and I'm a businessman. I had the car, somebody wanted it, and
was willing to spring for $700, even $800. I never would make the first
suggestion that they pay over ceiling. My lawyer told me I was on safer
ground just listening to other people's propositions, and just nodding
and smiling. You know, in case OPA sent out a man to check on me.

"What I'd do is say something like this: 'Well, I'd really like to let you
have this car, but some other fellow was in here first looking at it, and I
should give him first refusal. He's a man I know will be interested in
doing business with me after the war, when all the shortages are over,
and I'm trying to build up a string of customers who will stick with me.'
Most people got the drift of what I was saying, that they were going to
have to top another buyer. I'd like them to take the burden of figuring
out a way to get me that extra $300, $400. You'd get all sorts of deals.
A fellow in Baltimore came up with seven brand-new tires that he had
conned out of some soldier in a quartermaster depot, one way or an-*

---

* A pseudonym.

other. I got $35 each for them, so that was like handing me $245 cash.

"Cash was crude, but I didn't mind it. A guy would take a ride around the block and come in the office and talk price, then go for another ride. Then he'd say, 'Why don't you go check the front seat—I think a spring is busted.' Of course, he'd leave two or three bills there, and I'd put them in my pocket and tell him, 'I tightened it up, you've got a deal if you want it.'

"The accessory gimmick was popular with some dealers, but I thought it kind of risky, so I stayed away from it. Oh, the dealer would say the buyer needed a new rear-vision mirror, and sell him one for a hundred bucks. Or they'd trump up an 'engine overhaul' that went with the sale. The dealer would change the oil and maybe shine the top of a spark plug, and charge $200.

"I was cagey about putting stuff on paper, so I wanted something that could be done directly between me and the buyer, without any traces. I wasn't too proud to barter, either. I even let a carpenter build a shed for me as an 'incentive' for me to let him have an old truck.

"I confess that I was a pretty arrogant SOB in those days. Some character would see a car on the lot, and look up the OPA list price, and try to hand me the cash. One thing we were permitted to do, though, was to try to insist on a trade-in, and I could turn away a lot of them that way. Or I'd say, 'Sorry, that one's already sold, I just never got around to putting the sign on it.' If they persisted, I'd tell them to get their ass off my lot.

"It must have been 1949, 1950, when I had opened up this agency, when a guy came in and let me go through the whole spiel, trying to sell him a new car. We were in a recession then, and you couldn't sell cars for hell, and I was hurting. Anyway, he let me run on for half an hour, and he put me through all kinds of paper figuring—what it would be for twenty-four months, for thirty-six months, with and without all sorts of accessories and insurances; I was getting irritated as hell, but trying to be nice at the same time because I wanted that sale.

"So finally he looked at me and said, 'You red-faced son of a bitch, you don't remember telling me to get the hell out of your office when I tried to buy a car from you in the fall of forty-six, do you?' I had to admit I didn't. He went on, 'I just thought it would be fun to see what you looked like when you were off your high horse. Kiss my ass, you bastard.' And he walked off.

Controls—scrap them or keep them?—gave the fledgling Truman Administration its first major political test. Uncomfortable with the newness of its power, the pecking order around the President not yet established, the Administration was already heaving with quiet but

vicious jousting matches between FDR holdovers and Truman intimates. Many of the Roosevelt people treated the new President as
somewhat of a bumpkin unworthy of the Rooseveltian mantle; their
intrinsic loyalty was not to Truman, but to FDR's programs and ideals.
The Trumanites, for their part, bridled at the notion that any decision
must be prefaced with the question, "What would President Roosevelt
have done?" And the divisions were acutely visible in the controls fight,
one in which the Truman Administration (to public appearances, at
least) seemed to be in a contradictory set of positions.

As an "overriding goal" the Administration declared it wished to
return to civilian production as rapidly as possible, "vastly expanded
over anything this or any other nation has ever seen," with the American
people "as *individual customers* [determining] what businessman and
farmer are to produce [the government's emphasis]." Yet the Administration was not quite ready for a totally free economy, and its
policy guidelines on controls, announced the day the war ended, were
wondrously subjective:

Wherever immediate removal of controls will help to get expanded production under way faster, they will be removed.

Wherever the removal of controls at this time would bring a
chaotic condition or cause bottlenecks, or produce a disruptive
scramble for goods, controls will be kept and used.

But how to draw the line on which controls should be lifted? On this
question the President's men divided sharply, in style as well as in
substance. As his chief economic adviser Truman relied heavily upon
John Snyder, an old National Guard friend who had held minor bank
jobs in small-town Arkansas and Missouri before entering the Treasury
Department bureaucracy during the New Deal. Snyder spent most of the
prewar years in assignments outside Washington, and in many ways he
embodied the Midwesterner's abhorrence of government "meddling" in
other people's business. Nor was Snyder a great thinker. A dry man with
a pinched, worried face—one former associate said, "His mouth looked
like a tight capital *O*"—Snyder's favored path was containing least
resistance; in the words of a contemporary observer, his "primary im-
pulse was a psychologically frantic desire to put the difficulty behind
him." Snyder was unwilling to spend more than two or three minutes
reading memos staff people prepared to guide him on important decisions. "We've got to press on," he said, time and again. That his decisions might be wrong apparently did not disturb Snyder. If someone
complained loudly enough to be heard, Snyder's reflexive reaction was
to yield, thereby relieving the pressure. The subtleties of controls were a
concept that Snyder either did not understand or did not accept. "Snyder
lacked an overall picture of what planners were trying to do with the

economy," said a former associate, "and he was also averse to the idea of controls themselves."

Pitted against Snyder was Chester Bowles, whom President Roosevelt had summoned to Washington early in the war to oversee the price controls program. The energetic Bowles carried impeccable business credentials. A cofounder of the Benton & Bowles advertising agency, a Madison Avenue titan, he had earned his fortune, and he was personally friendly with the men who dominated American commerce. Nonetheless Bowles moved smoothly into the Democratic Administration. Cerebral, articulate, witty, skilled at bureaucratic and political infighting, Bowles felt not at all uncomfortable around government (even if he was a reluctant postwar carryover), and he did not shudder at the thought of Washington exercising power over business. Further, Bowles feared that the hard-won price stability achieved by wartime controls—an accomplishment of considerable personal pride to Bowles—could be washed away overnight. Although he publicly supported the White House's goal of a quick end to controls, Bowles thought they should continue through mid-1947. Bowles enthusiastically promoted the extension of OPA, due to expire New Year's Day 1946 unless Congress said otherwise. And here Bowles came into direct confrontation with yet another, even tougher, set of opponents: the business community and their titular spokesman in Congress, Republican Senator Robert A. Taft of Ohio.

Working through the National Association of Manufacturers and lobbying adjuncts, business laid siege to Washington beginning in the autumn of 1945 in a crusade with the victory-or-else fervor of an ideological war. Warning of a "regimented economy," industrialists and merchants marched by the dozens into the vast Senate Caucus Room, where a tolerably sympathetic Senate Banking Committee clucked over predictions of bankruptcy and ruin. Resolutions, telegrams, and letters swirled down upon the Capitol, and rare was the congressional office that did not reverberate with the raised voices of a visiting business delegation. The business position, as articulated by Robert P. Wason, president of the National Association of Manufacturers, was that the best means of stopping inflation was an end of government regulation and reinstatement of "price control by the American housewife." Few outside the business community took Wason's proposal seriously. The Chicago *Sun* jeered: "That hollow laughter you hear comes from the American housewife. . . . You cannot blame the lady for a certain mirthless skepticism. When Mr. Wason says that price control by the housewife is 'real price control . . . the kind that has made America great,' she remembers that the price of oranges and lemons shot up 50 to 100 percent within a few days after OPA removed the ceilings. When Mr. Wason shows Congress a set of slick charts to prove that 'prices are fixed by competition in free markets,' she recalls that when coconut was decontrolled, its price multiplied fourfold within thirty days. She knows about 'competitive' real estate prices, too."

The protesters went after OPA in general and targeted individual controls as well. For instance, Bowles was anxious that new cars go onto the market at prices roughly comparable to those of October 1941. By OPA edict, the 2.5 percent increase in manufacturers' cost was to be absorbed by the dealers, whose gross profit margin ran around 25 percent. Bowles's experts computed that the resulting margins would give the dealers profits far in excess of their actual prewar earnings. In a radio speech, he declared, "Automobile dealers today are doing a very profitable business, thanks to repairs on old cars, the sale of used cars, and the sprinkling of newly produced cars, which will soon grow to an increasing flood." The National Automobile Dealers Association reacted as if Bowles wanted to force America back to the horse and buggy. Some 400 embittered dealers appeared for hearings before the House Small Business Committee on a resolution demanding that OPA do nothing to affect auto prices "pending an investigation"—that is, to let the retailers charge what they wished. More than 300 members of Congress appeared as well to demonstrate support for these well-heeled constituents. OPA won this particular skirmish; Chairman Wright Patman, the Texas Democrat, heard the dealers out and adjourned without permitting any action.

Control advocates countered with their own lobbies—housewives, labor unions, consumer groups, ordinary citizens—which staged rallies in large cities and sent telegrams and delegations to pressure congressmen. Although they lacked the organization and direct financing of the business groups, the procontrols factions enjoyed the not-inconsiderable support of OPA's public relations apparatus. Bowles used, on behalf of OPA, the same sort of advertising techniques his old Madison Avenue agency had developed for business clients. Cards prepared by OPA went into envelopes with military allotment checks:

> Danger ahead, Americans. Watch the price line. Refuse to pay a penny over the price ceiling. Be sure you get full weight.

An OPA cartoon booklet depicted a restaurant with signs offering a blue-plate special for $300; golden brown waffles for $125; the "best coffee in town" for $33.50. The counterman says to a customer: "The blue plate's $295 for discharged sojers—that leaves ya $5 fer th' streetcar." An OPA radio spot opened, "Sorry. I'll have to give you your change in thousand-dollar bills. I'm all out of the large denominations. . . ." An announcer's voice continued: "That sounds ridiculous now, doesn't it? But the time could come when that speech would be an everyday occurrence."

These and other commercials engaged such controls foes as Senator

Taft, who thought it downright immoral for a government agency to spend $2,500,000 a year promoting its own existence. Taft charged that "such propaganda certainly implies a general crookedness on the part of retail merchants" and was part of an OPA strategy of "getting all the consumers it could to go after the businessman." Although Bowles protested that the messages were intended to curb black marketeering, Taft felt they were designed to "stir up public opinion in favor of continuing the OPA, and to bring down upon us [members of Congress] some of the letters we have already received."

With the price control "debate" reduced to shouted simplistic slogans, reasoned conviction soon ceased to be a factor in the shape of the postwar economy. As the columnist Marquis Childs lamented:

> The idea of government by pressure . . . assumes that officials should base their decisions not on the merits of an issue, but on the degree of pressure which can be focused on a given point. It's the principle of a steam boiler. If a lobby can generate enough heat to force the needle in the gauge up to the proper notch, then action must automatically follow.
>
> What is more, Congress seems to accept this technique.

To Harry Truman the business assault on price controls was part of a broad Republican drive against his presidency. Some in the White House felt the GOP would risk economic chaos and runaway inflation as an acceptable price for discrediting the Democrats and beginning a systematic rollback of the New Deal. Citizen mail to the President was broadly supportive of continued controls. "Millions of citizens already suffering from inflation are likely in extreme disgust to turn down Democratic leaders like yourself for some traitorous fascist group or individual," Robert H. Ellis, of Portland, Oregon, telegraphed Mr. Truman. "They are depending on you, Mr. President, to protect them from the racketeers." Emma Everson, writing for the Maryland Division of the American Association of University Women, pleaded, "Don't let special interest groups dictate. Hold the price line." Mrs. W. L. Keene, wife of a schoolteacher in Richmond, Kentucky, asked that Truman protect "the unorganized many," writing, "There are so many of us, Mr. President, but we cannot be heard above the clamor of organized interests." Samuel J. Kingdon, of Brooklyn, asked, "Please hold the line against inflation and those greedy money pigs who never have enough." "Appeasement of economic royalists with a little inflation can only bring disaster to your administration," counseled Charles W. Eliot, of Pasadena, California.

But in Congress a working "Republocrat" majority, composed of Republicans and sympathetic southern and other conservative Democrats, had the votes to emasculate OPA. Although the Republocrats gave lip service to Truman's goal of keeping OPA alive, they tacked on amendments that made a farce of enforcement. Perhaps the most cumbersome, sponsored by Senator Taft, required that OPA price schedules reflect a manufacturer's profit on each item, an administrative impossibility. Passage put Truman in a dilemma. Either he must sign an unworkable bill, or see all controls expire on June 30, 1946, with an unavoidable surge in inflation. Politically, Truman's choice was equally chancy. If he signed a bad bill, and inflation soared, he *might* be able to put blame on Republicans in that fall's mid-term congressional elections. Again, however, he might not. Despite the loud critics, opinion polls showed a majority of the public favoring continued controls. A Gallup poll in May, for instance, found 75 percent of the respondents favoring food price controls; 78 percent, rent; 70 percent, autos. A *Fortune* magazine survey a month later found even 58.3 percent of Republicans wanted controls. But were these supporters sophisticated enough to understand that the "controls" bill passed by the Republocrats was in fact a sham? Could not a veto be interpreted as an Administration license for price gouging? Robert R. Nathan, one of the architects of the controls program who was now back in private practice as a consulting economist, also wanted a veto, even at the cost of an end of controls. "There is no point in beating a fast retreat under a hopeless law," Nathan wrote the President. "It is quite possible that, if OPA is hamstrung or abolished, the cost of living will rise 30 or even 40 percent by next November." Nathan suggested a "fireside chat" in which Truman would lambaste the Republicans for playing politics with the economy. Responding with a personal note, Truman told Nathan: "I can't for the life of me understand the attitude of our friends down the street. They certainly don't appreciate what would happen if OPA suddenly stopped. There is no doubt but what the Republicans have played politics with this vital economic issue."

Most of the cabinet urged Truman to sign for "better than nothing" reasons; so, too, did Alben Barkley, the Senate majority leader, and Sam Rayburn, the speaker of the House. Barkley, one of Truman's closest friends in the Capitol, ended a half-hour conference by putting his hand on the President's shoulder and saying, "Harry, you've got to sign this bill. Whether you like it or not, it's the best bill we can get out of this Congress, and it's the only one you're going to get." Truman's lips tightened, and he replied, "We'll see, Alben, we'll see." Clark Clifford, the President's counsel, and Paul Porter, Bowles's successor as head of OPA, had been sitting on the other side of the room, desultorily drafting a veto message which they thought the President would never use, and monitoring the conversation. "You heard all of that?" Truman asked them. They had, Porter replied, and if Truman signed the bill, "I don't feel I could honestly stay on as OPA administrator." Truman smiled. "What the hell makes you think I'm going to sign it? You fellows are writing a veto message, aren't you? Well, get to it. And I want a thirty-minute speech to go on the radio with tomorrow night to tell the people *why* I vetoed it."

The next evening, in a broadcast heard by 32,000,000 persons (98.4 percent of all radios in use at that hour were tuned to him, according to ratings), the President called a veto the "only honest solution." Truman said he knew "how weary you all are of these restrictions and controls. I am also weary of them. I spend a good deal of my time listening to complaints. I know how eager every one of you is for the day when you can run your own affairs in your own way as you did before the war." And Truman came down hard on congressional Republicans:

> Are you a veteran planning to build a home for yourself and family? The Taft Amendment would have added immediately a minimum of twenty percent to the cost of your building materials. . . .
>
> Do you need a new low-priced automobile? If so, what effect would the Taft Amendment have had on the price of your new car? It would have increased immediately the price of the popular makes of automobiles by $225 to $250 per car.*
>
> Are you a housewife who has been waiting for years for that new washing machine or refrigerator? The Taft Amendment would have made it cost one-third more right away. . . .

Congress promptly overrode Truman's veto, leaving OPA a powerless hulk. Prices spurted. Sirloin steak went from fifty-five cents to one dollar a pound overnight; butter from eighty cents to a dollar; milk from sixteen cents a quart to twenty. A grocer advertised in the Tulsa *Tribune:* "Shrimp. We have it. But it's too high. I wouldn't buy. Regular 20¢ size now 89¢." PRICES SOAR, BUYERS SORE, STEERS JUMP OVER THE MOON headlined the New York *Daily News*. The Bureau of Labor Statistics' food index jumped 16.1 points the first week controls ended. The rent situation was even worse, with increases reported of from 15 to 1,000 percent. Landlords gleefully evened scores with tenants who had refused to pay a dollar more than the legal rent limit, a New Jersey apartment owner writing his occupants, "It is with the greatest of pleasure that I announce . . . I'm giving you one month's notice to vacate, get out, in other words to scram!" OPA reports to Truman said its field offices "have been bombarded with complaints from anxious tenants protesting against rent increases and eviction notices. Despite appeals by

* The Taft Amendment said manufacturers should receive the same per-unit profit as 1941 *plus* all costs incurred since that time. Truman noted 1941 profit margins "were fifty percent greater than in the banner year 1929." But Henry Ford II claimed the manufacturing cost of a 1946 Ford was $1,041.26, compared with the OPA wholesale ceiling price of $728, meaning a built-in loss of $313.26.

real estate organizations and civic bodies urging landlords to exercise moderation, unofficial reports from all sections of the country were uniform in citing large numbers of immoderate rent increases and a sharp rise in eviction proceedings by landlords." OPA ticked off some percentage increases: Eugene, Oregon, 33 to 55; Chicago, 20 to 150; Oshkosh, Wisconsin, 33 to 300; Birmingham, 15 to 75. Seemingly the only restraint on landlord greed was fear the public would stomach only so much gouging. Thus associations representing Miami and Miami Beach apartment owners voted in July to forgo immediate increases on their 25,000 units, following the advice of their former president, E. J. Minges: "Don't kill the goose that laid the golden egg—yet. We're all tired of collecting low rent, but for goodness' sake, let's wait until this corpse is buried. Don't do anything until they get the marble slab on tight. Stay down for a few months. The winter is coming and when that slab is down tight, you can work rents up and then there won't be any OPA for them to fall back on."

In late July 1946 Congress passed (and Truman approved) legislation reviving OPA, although in much-emasculated form. The act succeeded in temporarily stemming rising prices, and in some instances—notably meat—rolling them back to wartime levels. But in the end, however, OPA simply fell apart by bits and pieces, its bureaucracy weary from the constant fighting with the congressional majority and business, its top echelon demoralized by the constant sniping by Truman's economic hierarchy. The congressional tinkering with OPA, performed in the name of increased efficiency, had the net effect of inserting new administrative layers into a structure that was already a cumbersome organization. For instance, a Price Decontrol Board had the authority to overrule the OPA, the Department of Agriculture, or any other agency on what goods should be removed from restrictions. The OPA had to compute prices for binder twine and casein, for shellac and for wood pulp imported from Finland. It spelled out increases for auto dealers to the odd dollar: $2,191 for a Lincoln Model 73 with custom interior, for example, and $1,366 for a Nash Ambassador.

By autumn of 1946 the control system was in near collapse. Meat virtually vanished from America's dinner tables, with farmers and ranchers keeping cattle off the market because of low prices, and stores closing because of lack of supplies. In one week in September 1946 Armour's main Chicago plant slaughtered 68 cattle rather than the average 9,000; two of three butcher shops in New York City were closed. A *Time* survey of 139 cities found only 6 without acute meat shortages. In Olympia, Washington, butchers opened only two days weekly; in Indianapolis, the only meat available was frankfurters and bologna. ONLY 87 MEATLESS DAYS UNTIL CHRISTMAS headlined the anti-Administration Washington *Times-Herald*. In Kansas City, a woman entered a shop and was handed a wrapped package priced $4.65. "What is it?" she asked.

"A pot roast," the butcher replied. "How much does it weigh?" "Lady, we don't weigh it, we sell it by the piece. Do you want it?" In Detroit, a strange woman entered a butcher shop and asked for meat. A clerk asked the boss who she was. "I don't know—starve the old bitch," he replied. "All during the war I hewed to the line," lamented an Illinois farmer. "I did everything the government told me. I even gave up my three boys, and they are back now, and I'm grateful for that. But now that the war is over, I am going to take these cattle back to Illinois, feed them some good corn, and then I am going to be one black market son of a bitch."

For established packers, the black marketeers were unbeatable competition. James D. Cooney, a vice-president of Wilson & Co., the big Chicago packer, complained to the White House that almost 75 percent of the nation's beef was going to the black market, chiefly via fly-by-night firms that ignored price ceilings. "During the week ending June 16," Cooney wrote, "36,604 head of cattle were received at the Chicago stockyards. We had fifteen active cattle buyers on this market and they were unable to buy a single head at legal compliance prices." During another week, Swift buyers at eleven markets around the country were able to buy only 575 head—of more than 141,000 put on the market.

With the public howling for meat—and for the scalps of an Administration that had allowed the shortages to develop—frightened Democrats pleaded with Truman to relent and remove controls. Speaker of the House John McCormack of Boston, whose hospital patient constituents ate horse meat because no other meat was to be had, asked the President for a sixty-day moratorium on meat controls. Robert E. Hannegan, Truman's postmaster general as well as Democratic national chairman, also asked for decontrols. Truman at first resisted, and persuaded a reluctant Democratic National Committee to stand with him. Defending continued meat controls, Truman argued the shortage was due to extraordinarily heavy slaughters during two summer months when controls had been lifted and packers took advantage of temporarily higher prices. Abandoning controls would cause long-run difficulties, Truman insisted. This was on September 26. On October 3 Truman predicted there would be no "meat famine," and said he was watching the situation closely; he was "uncertain" whether the shortage would continue into the winter. On October 10, the first question asked Truman at a press conference was whether action was imminent on lifting controls. "No," he replied. But on the evening of October 14,* Truman went on national radio to abandon price controls. He retreated under a covering fire of oratory,

* Several hours earlier the White House announced that the President would make a major statement on price controls. New York butchers promptly took the sparse remaining supplies of dressed meat from their display counters. The next day, with controls dead, the meat went back on display—with price tags 50 percent or more higher.

charging that a "reckless group of selfish men" in Congress gambled for political advantage on destruction of the controls program. The people who killed controls, the President said, were the "same bunch which fought every attempt at social reform initiated by the New Deal" and "hated Franklin D. Roosevelt and fought everything he stood for." This group, Truman said, "is thinking in terms of millions of dollars instead of millions of people."

TRUMAN SURRENDERS—NOW WATCH ALL PRICES SPURT! sputtered New York's *PM*. Anti-Administration newspapers chortled over the policy switch. "Bravely, and somewhat unexpectedly, President Truman entered a plea of political bankruptcy," the New York *Herald-Tribune* said. "To cling to meat price controls would have been to nail his flag to a sinking ship. To abandon them is a confession that the ship was badly designed, imperfectly caulked and certain to sink in any event." The Washington *Times-Herald* saw the end of a political era: "[E]ven Democratic diehards admitted the New Deal concept of government was at an end . . . the planned economy of a past era is dead."

So, too, was OPA. On the last business day for the agency's Consumer Price Division—Friday, November 24, 1946—a group of "mourners" carried a flower-decked coffin into a fourth-floor office known as the Chapel, formerly the room where businessmen came to plead their cases for higher prices. A "corpse" was in the coffin, fashioned from sheafs of old price regulations. The wall bore signs such as "Taft, Wherry, Walcott, Inc., Architects of Destruction."* On one door was a sign "Guaranteed Profits Division. Closed." A five-gallon, white-enameled electric washing machine stood on a desk; from its spigot poured a gin punch. There were philosophical speeches by Leon Henderson, OPA's founder, and Paul Porter, its last chief. There were gibes at Senator Taft and other Republicans. But as a Washington *Post* reporter wrote, "Everybody did his best to be bright and cheery, and to look on the sunny side. But as the guests . . . left, they walked down long halls that bore little resemblance to the bustling wartime days. Desks stood empty in every office. Coat racks were as barren as an oak tree in January. OPA was dead and buried."

---

* Referring to three GOP foes of controls.

6

We Want More!

S T E V E   H U T C H I N S O N   W A S   *twenty-four years old the winter the big steel strike began, a semiskilled operator in the finishing mill of United States Steel Corporation's vast Pittsburgh plant, a many-acred mélange of noise and searing heat and grime. "I got a little more than a year in before I went to the marines, went to work at Steel right out of high school. I had been back only about that long when we went out. Buck thirty-seven an hour I earned. Geez, that sounded like all the money you could stack up then, especially after what I had made in the marines. But it was damned tight trying to get by on it. I guess you could say I had real mixed feelings about striking. You give up that immediate cash, the weekly paycheck, in hopes that you'll come out better in the long run. But I admit to being scared shitless.*

"Shirley and I, at the time, had this one-bedroom apartment over in Duquesne. Our big expense was the rent, $37 a month, and we also paid the coal, which ran another ten or so during the winter. We kept about even. Shirley worked during the war, and put some away, maybe $500, what with the allotment from me and her being able to live with her folks. But we knocked a big hole in that the first month I was home, taking a trip up to Canada and just goofing around, staying in a big hotel we really couldn't afford and eating in fancy restaurants. And, of course, we put a kid in the hopper right away too, born nine months and two days from the day I got back to Pittsburgh.

"Oh, we weren't flat out broke, but things were tight. I couldn't have bought a car even if there had been one to buy. I car-pooled with another guy on my shift, paid him $1.50 a week to ride back and forth. We took in a movie maybe once a month, I hung around the Legion hall and shot some pool on Saturday afternoon; buy a couple of beers and maybe spend a buck total during three hours. Groceries? No, she didn't spend much, but we ate OK. Thing was, what I got and what we spent pretty well evened out at the end of the month.

"When the union officers began talking strike I got nervous, I admit. Here we were, with Stevie only a few months old, and me with damned

little put away. But what the hell—we read in the papers about what the big corporations were making, and you could tell that U.S. Steel sure wasn't hurting. [Laugh.] A week or so before we took the strike vote, one of the Pittsburgh papers ran a story about a big party one of the steel executives gave for his daughter, at a country club. I don't remember the exact figure, but we figured out that it was more than the five of us in the car pool earned put together—way up over $20,000. That sort of stuff made us realize, hell, we had to bite the bullet, else we'd always be living a nickel-and-dime life; the bosses sure didn't give a damn for us. The way I had it, I'd rather risk losing pay for a few months then, when I was young, than take an ass-kicking the rest of my life. I pretty well knew I'd be in the mills until I died, so why not make what you can?

"*Anyway, the vote came, and we voted to go out. The union got up picket schedules, and we were on the bricks, roughly following our regular work shifts. There were some strike benefits but they didn't amount to much—maybe ten or fifteen bucks a week, at the start. But our spirit was good when we went out. A lot of the guys were just out of the service, and we had this feeling of togetherness, almost like we were on another combat mission.*

"*Oh, there was hollering. The public attitude was that we should get back to work, settle for anything U.S. Steel offered, just so people could start buying cars and refrigerators again. The hell with that. I think the more the newspapers yelled the tighter we dug in. I felt that way, anyway.*

"*How do you live on strike? [Laughs.] Tight, that's how. I told Shirley right off, 'We'd better cut to the bone, because this one will be a long one.' And we did. I still remember some of those damned meals. She'd buy a big old soup bone, something with just a small bit of meat on it, and boil it in a pot of white beans. That was lunch and dinner and maybe lunch again the next day. Day-old bread, no sugar in the coffee, hamburger when we had meat, which wasn't often. I even gave up cigarettes, and me a two-pack-a-day man.*

"*The picket line itself wasn't so bad. We'd fill a big steel drum with scrap lumber and pour some kerosene over it and stand around. Of course, no problem in anybody trying to get into the mill. Steel's like that: you shut down a mill, you turn off the furnaces and everything stops. This isn't something where management can run in a handful of scabs and foremen and keep the thing in operation.*

"*Christmas I guess was the rough time. Shirley and I talked about exchanging presents, and she finally said, 'I tell you what, let's just give each other real big smiles.' When we woke up Christmas morning she said, 'Wait in bed a minute and close your eyes.' She ran out and came back and handed me a card she had written out in her own big flowery handwriting, 'I love you. Merry Christmas! I hope Santa brings you twenty cents an hour.' I gave her a big hug and wanted to cry.*

"When the settlement came we were one happy bunch of guys. The first paycheck, me and Shirley went out to a nice Italian place and loaded up. You never really catch up financially after a strike, because you do have a big hole. I figured once that it took me more than two years to make back what I had lost if we hadn't gone out and had kept working the old rate. But what the hell—U.S. Steel, the bosses, they don't go around handing out dollar bills on the corners. You got to kick them in the ass, make it tough on them, else they keep you working 'round the clock for nothing. My uncles, when they came to U.S. Steel in the twenties, they sometimes got on a seven-day week, twelve hours a day.

"I'm not no economist. I wasn't in forty-six, and I'm not now. But it seems to me that when you have this pie of money, every feller that works to make it should get a fair share of it, that when they do, business is better for everybody. We steel millies buy more, the people downtown make more, the bosses make more. Hell, that's all we wanted in that strike—the right size slice of pie. And we got it, too."

A month after the war ended, the *CIO News,* organ of the Congress of Industrial Organizations, reported a beguiling "five year study of war profits." The study told a remarkable success story. Prepared by the United Steel Workers of America, it showed a 113 percent rise in after-tax profits in the steel industry between the five-year periods 1935–39 and 1940–44, from $576 million to $1.225 billion. Assets of the steel companies increased from $4.86 billion at the beginning of 1940 to almost $6 billion at the first of 1945; dividend payments those years amounted to $705 million. But the steel workers union cited these statistics not in praise of corporate efficiency, but as a war cry that set alarm bells to ringing in board rooms across the nation. Philip Murray, president both of the steel workers and the parent CIO, pointed to the billion dollars added to the companies' assets during wartime, and the near three-quarters of a billion paid out to stockholders. "Contrast this with the financial position of America's 475,000 steel workers," Murray said. "In five years of war work, they have accumulated only . . . $285 million in savings, or $600 a worker." Further, the steel companies expected an additional bonus in the form of $149 million in tax refunds during 1946.

Management understood Murray's implied threat: now free of its no-strike pledge, labor intended to fight for what it considered to be a fair share of the war profits hoarded by business. Further, the unions wanted to bring incomes into tolerable balance with the cost of living, essentially by gaining, for the standard forty-hour week, the same take-home pay workers made for forty-eight hours during the war.

Statistically, the unions had a strong case. A University of California study headed by Dr. Walter Heller* reported in late 1945 that a family of four persons in an average American city required $2,700 (around $50 weekly) to maintain a "decent standard of living." At the same time, the Labor Department's Bureau of Labor Statistics said the average factory worker earned only $40.98 weekly, with wide variations between industries: $44.81 for auto workers; $45.60 for steel workers; $41.25 for electrical workers; $27.42 for textile workers; $23.75 for garment workers. Even during the boom year of 1945, about one-fifth the city families had incomes below $1,500.

From management's viewpoint, the wage situation was considerably more complex. With price controls destined to sputter on indefinitely, the corporations argued they did not have the money for higher pay. The uncertainties of reconversion, the loss of defense contracts, an undefinable fear of the unknowns ahead in the postwar years—these and other factors made manufacturers wary of locking themselves into high-pay contracts. Management's willingness to fight the unions, and strikes be damned, was enhanced by some glitteringly attractive loopholes in the tax laws. During wartime, business had to pay destructive taxes on excess profits, a levy that was to expire at the end of 1945. By the last quarter of 1945, many corporations reasoned, they had earned the keepable limit; any further profits would go to the government, so why not let the unions shut down the plants? As one executive told *PM,* "A strike might cost us production, but it won't cost us money. Better to let the union go out when it won't hurt us—and it will hurt them." Further, any losses sustained in 1946 (because of strikes or otherwise) could be offset by refunds from years in which companies paid the excess-profits tax. Thus a cotton mill operator in Union Point, Georgia, when his workers walked out, confidently informed shareholders in a bulletin: "We think it will take four months before our strikers decide to come back to work. Any loss we sustain in 1946 will be made up to us by government out of our profits in 1944 and 1945," years when his company had a "nice profit."

Management also hoped to capitalize on public disenchantment with the seemingly open-ended expectations of unions and with demands the average citizen considered outright silly. For instance, a local of the painters union in Detroit maintained that a man who rented a room in his home to an insurance agency must hire union painters for touch-up work in his living room because it was an "office building." *Time* had continuing sport with James C. Petrillo, the head of the American Federation of Musicians—invariably "James Caesar Petrillo"—who would "loll back in his well-upholstered chair" and "dictate" letters to people "demanding" that they do his bidding. And what biddings. Petrillo once

* Chairman of the Council of Economic Advisers in the Kennedy–Johnson administrations.

asked the movie studios for a package that included a 100 percent pay raise (meaning $10,400 annually for a ten-hour week); the rerecording of musical scores, at full pay for the orchestras, when 35-millimeter film was transferred to 16-millimeter; 30 percent extra pay if a musician was required to bring more than one instrument or suit of clothes to work; and a limit for recording time of two minutes in any given hour. When the producers protested the grab bag would boost their costs 1,200 percent, he angrily replied they were a bunch of damned liars: the cost wouldn't be a cent more than 900 percent. (He eventually got a 33 percent pay increase.) A typical Petrillo maneuver is exemplified in a soliloquy with a reporter from the Chicago *Tribune,* explaining his "ruling" that radio stations must ban musical programs originating in any foreign country save Canada:

> We're just trying to keep foreign musicians from getting our jobs. Look at the tariff laws. The manufacturers are always lobbying in Congress to keep cheap materials out of the country. There's the immigration law. The government—everybody—protects themselves against cheap labor.
>
> Why the hell should musicians be suckers? You know what happened to Swiss watches. The watchmakers union muscled the State Department into stopping sending them into the country. We're trying to keep out foreign musicians in person or on the air.
>
> For a long time the orchestra conductors came from London, all the music stars of Europe. They'd stay in this country, several months, make a lot of dough, and then go home to Europe. I said, "Hey, you boys get into the union!" There was a hell of a holler from the long-haired boys about that. Well, what about it? . . .
>
> I'll tell you where a lot of those bangs I get come from. There are 900 radio stations, 300 owned by the press. Every time I make a move against radio, the press—not all of it, though—goes after me. You won't hear any musicians saying anything against me.

Petrillo asking $10,400 a year for men who "played horns and banged drums" for two minutes an hour. John L. Lewis calling out the coal miners twice during the war ("Speaking for the American soldier," the service paper *Stars & Stripes* had said on its front page, "damn your coal black soul!"). Walter Reuther and his brother Victor, the United Auto Workers powers, men who had actually lived and worked in *Communist Russia!* CIO farm and textile organizers, ruffling the status quo of the South. *The damned unions. Labor barons. Goons. Commies. Crooks. Featherbedders.* Such were the epithets heaped upon American labor as it entered the postwar period.

"Is anybody interested in getting the work done?" the New York *Daily News* demanded in an autumn 1945 editorial. Apparently not, for the wave of strikes was seemingly endless, with 3,500,000 persons in-

volved in walkouts during 1945, chiefly the last few months. Trans
World Airlines pilots wanted $20,000 annually and finally they settled
for $12,500. At the New York Stock Exchange, the tickers fell silent for
two hours when 400 clerical employees walked out. Barbers, butchers,
bakers struck. Stoppages interrupted the production of copper wire,
Campbell's Soup, castor oil, Christmas toys. The Pittsburgh Pirates,
near the cellar in the National League, took a strike vote in midsummer,
but decided to continue playing. On successive days in January 1946
unions set strike deadlines in three major industries: 800,000 steel
workers on the fourteenth; 200,000 electrical workers on the fifteenth;
125,000 packing house employees on the sixteenth. Even organizers for
the United Auto Workers threatened to strike when the union began
layoffs in an economy drive. And many of the stoppages touched off
ripples that lapped against persons and businesses far removed from the
dispute itself. When 3,500 electric company workers struck in Pittsburgh, plant closings idled 100,000 other persons as well. Trolleys
stopped running, street lights went out, office buildings closed for fear of
elevator failure, residential areas were blacked out in rotation. "This is a
disaster," Mayor David Lawrence said over radio in pleading with the
strikers to return to work. An elevator operators strike in New York
City meant that uncounted scores of thousands of office workers could
not get to their jobs. Manhattan suffered the simultaneous indignity of
strikes by truck drivers and maritime unions, meaning a complete stop-
page of shipments in and out of the city. General Motors kept a log of
supplier strikes affecting its production: 116 one week, 83 the next, 55,
63, 47, and so on through the fall and early winter of 1945. Greyhound
buses in Birmingham. Mail deliverymen in Albany. Casket makers in
Tennessee. Fishermen in Boston. "People are somewhat befuddled and
want to take time out to get a nerve rest," Truman wrote his mother in
Missouri. "Some want a life guarantee of rest at government expense
and some I'm sorry to say just want to raise hell and hamper the return
to peacetime production to obtain some political advantage."

As an added frustration, employers felt the sting of jurisdictional
fights between rival unions which sought to organize the same workers,
or to control certain jobs. So the sheet metal workers union picketed
(and halted) a housing project at Rutgers University because the iron
workers union handled metals of a controversial thickness. That both
unions were brotherly affiliates of the American Federation of Labor
made no difference. At Idlewild Airport in New York, AFL and independent unions quarreled for fourteen months over the right to lay 500
feet of telephone cable. In Hollywood, picket lines formed over the issue
of which union should install false bosoms in actresses' gowns. Why?
Well, some of the falsies were cloth, others foam rubber. The motion
picture costumers union claimed jurisdiction over one variety, the
makeup artists and hair stylists union over the other.

Although unions greeted peace with a firecracker string of minor strikes, the big confrontation was two months in the shaping, with the United Auto Workers and General Motors as protagonists. The UAW's choice of GM as a target was both tactical and political. The other industry giant, Ford, had fallen on hard times during the 1930's, because of the eccentric conduct of aging founder Henry Ford, and was losing money heavily until the war started. The UAW feared that too vigorous a shove just might push Ford out of existence. GM, conversely, evoked no such cautions, for it had piled up vast wartime profits, much of them possible because of wage curbs. (The freeze did not affect executive compensation. President Charles E. Wilson's salary went from $288,178 in 1941 to $459,014 in 1943; and those of vice-presidents O. E. Hunt and Albert Bradley from $235,000 and $250,000, respectively, to $350,000 each.) But GM was off balance. It lost $2 billion in defense contracts in a single swipe on V-J Day, and it was sweating and straining to convert its 102 plants to peacetime production, with the battle cry of "from tanks to Cadillacs in two months." To be shut by a strike during reconversion could throw GM behind competitors in the postwar market. Internally, the UAW feared its own very survival was at stake. Some 140,000 of its members went off GM payrolls when the war ended, and the surviving 180,000 found their pay envelopes shrunken by about 25 percent because of the loss of overtime. Hence the UAW had a militancy born of fright. And in Walter Reuther, the UAW's GM department had a leader to give firm voice to that militancy. Reuther was then only thirty-eight years old, a fastidious, slightly built redhead of German/socialist origins, a unionist whose head had been bloodied in organizing Ford workers a decade earlier. He was articulate, visionary, and highly ambitious. Reuther wanted the UAW presidency, and one route into the office was by establishing himself as a more forceful man than the incumbent, R. J. Thomas. So Reuther found his political aspirations in happy juxtaposition with a situation that veritably demanded that he, as a union leader, move vigorously to protect rank-and-file members.

The Truman Administration, nervous about being caught between two such powerful adversaries, squirmed to keep out of the argument. The record suggests that the White House felt it best to let labor and management settle their business without government meddling. At one point William H. Davis, the director of economic stabilization, estimated that industry could push wages up as much as 40 or 50 percent without price increases. Truman repudiated the statement. A few days later, at a press conference, Truman announced that Davis' agency was being moved under the jurisdiction of the Office of War Mobilization and Reconversion.

"Mr. President," a reporter asked, "what does that do to Will Davis?"

"I guess that leaves him out of a job," Truman replied.

Davis at the time was in another part of the White House for a routine meeting, unaware he was being dismissed until a functionary hurried up with news of what the President had just said. A bit later that day Davis' chauffeur returned to the office without him. Davis' secretary asked, "Herbert, what did you do with Mr. Davis?" The chauffeur replied, "He said he wanted to walk back to the office. Kind of looked like he had something on his mind."*

Another unsuccessful peacemaker was Chester Bowles, in his last weeks as head of OPA. Acting secretly (and beyond his jurisdiction), Bowles met with Reuther, Philip Murray, and William Green, president of the American Federation of Labor, and asked if it would be possible to work out a new wage-price formula that would avoid strikes. They gave "cautiously affirmative" approval to a Bowles idea that all hourly wage rates would be boosted 10 percent immediately by the Wage Stabilization Board, while the OPA "would do all it could to minimize the impact" of the increase on prices. In return, labor would "agree to forgo all strikes for one year." Green, Murray, and Reuther felt they could sell the deal to rank-and-file unionists. Still working behind the scenes, Bowles next persuaded a group of business leaders headed by Eric Johnston, president of the United States Chamber of Commerce, to accept the proposal. But Bowles's victory proved short-lived. Lewis B. Schwellenbach, an old senatorial friend of Truman's, had been just named secretary of labor, and he was determined to be a more active policy-maker than his predecessor, Frances Perkins. Schwellenbach laughed at Bowles, saying his fear of inflation was exaggerated, that the 10 percent pay raise was unneeded. Truman sided with Schwellenbach, and the deal fell apart.

And with disastrous results. When bargaining began, Reuther asked pay increases of 30 percent—three times the amount he had been willing to accept under the Bowles compromise. Further, Reuther argued that GM could pay that amount without increasing prices, and that the increased buying power made possible by higher wages would in turn lead to even more profits for the auto and other industries. He dismissed as "coming-in-on-a-wing-and-a-prayer economics" the notion that savings and the pent-up demand for consumer goods would prevent the nation from tailspinning into deflation. Specifically, Reuther asked a base pay of $1.45 hourly, versus the $1.12 then earned by the average GM worker. This would give UAW members $58 weekly, roughly equal to the take-home pay they earned with overtime during the war. After

---

* Dr. Walter S. Salant, a Davis aide who tells this story, said the dismissal was "generally regarded as a rather gauche way of handling things, and there were accusations he [the President] wanted a crony . . . in the position." Davis' much reduced job in fact did go to an old Truman friend, J. Caskie Collett, who had been a United States district court judge in Kansas City.

weeks of jockeying and public name-calling with the GM president, Charles Wilson, who decried "the monopolistic power of your [Reuther's] union," the UAW rejected a GM counteroffer of ten cents an hour and voted six-to-one to strike. In December 1945 some 195,000 men walked away from 95 GM plants, and the first big postwar strike was on.

To GM executives Reuther went far beyond the acceptable bounds of collective bargaining. Reuther's linkage of pay increases to GM's supposed "ability to pay" and his demand that GM's books be opened to an arbitration panel were ideas anathema to industry. "It is none of your damned business what the OPA does about prices," Harry Coen, the GM assistant personnel director, yelled at Reuther during one session. Reuther disagreed.

REUTHER: Unless we get a more realistic distribution of America's wealth, we don't get enough to keep this machinery going.

COEN: There it is again. You can't talk about this thing without exposing your socialistic desires.

REUTHER: If fighting for equal and equitable distribution of the wealth of this country is socialistic, I stand guilty of being a Socialist.

COEN: I think you are convicted.

REUTHER: I plead guilty.

Appealing beyond the bargaining table to public opinion, GM ran full-page advertisements in major U.S. newspapers declaring HERE IS THE ISSUE:

Is American business to be based on free competition, or is it to become socialized, with all activities controlled and regimented? . . .

America is at the crossroads! It must preserve the freedom of each unit of American business to determine its own destinies. Or it must transfer to some governmental bureaucracy or agency, or to a union, the responsibility of management that has been the very keystone of American business!

Conservative economic columnist Henry Hazlitt wondered how many persons would support Reuther's "ability-to-pay" notion were the proposition to be restated: "If such a principle were sound for wages, it would be equally sound for prices. When you asked the salesman of an automobile, 'How much is it?' he would reply, 'How much have you got?' and insist on prying into your bank account and rifling your safe deposit vault before stating what the price would be to *you*." On yet another level, GM arranged quiet luncheons for businessmen around the country to hear company spokesmen argue that "the principle involved [in the strike] definitely affects your business and hours." At these luncheons—held in such diverse places as Allentown, Pennsylvania, and Manhattan's Hotel Commodore—GM distributed booklets charging that the central issue of the walkout was whether wages would be set by a "political bureaucracy," meaning, of course, the Truman Administration. As labor writer Victor Riesel commented, "Obviously, those who control the giant GM Corp. have declared political war on Harry Truman. These executives are turning GM clubs into a countrywide network of political centers for indignant and embattled auto salesmen, bank presidents and store owners who fear that the CIO is tearing apart the profit system."

Reuther also played for public opinion. He urged strike commanders to make "special efforts . . . to have veterans in prominent positions on the picket line. . . . Ask the veterans to wear their service uniforms. Special picket banners should be prepared, 'I did not fight over there to protect GM's billions over here,' etc." He wrote letters to merchants in Detroit and other strike areas: "How many of the du Ponts do you have among your customers?" The Michigan state CIO asked every member to donate a can of food per week to help the strikers. But the strikers hurt. The Chicago *Tribune* visited Flint, Michigan, where 50,000 GM workers were out, and found an aura reminiscent of the Depression. "Strikers are cashing hundreds of thousands of dollars of war bonds. Savings accounts of many are being depleted rapidly and the number of personal loans made by them has risen sharply." More than a thousand strike families there were on welfare rolls.

In the end, happenings elsewhere cut the ground from beneath Reuther and UAW. In January 1946 panic rushed through the Truman Administration as industry after industry fell idle to strikes: the steel mills; the meat packing houses; the electrical equipment factories. Three key industries, with more than 1,600,000 workers, *plus* the 175,000 auto workers, plus dozens of smaller unions were idled. At the end of the war, President Truman had promised he would not "lay down the law" to business and labor, that he looked to "free and fair collective bargaining" to bring industrial peace. But with management and unions bargaining with holy-war ferocity, as if their very survival were at stake, Truman realized normal bargaining techniques were not enough. So he intervened with fact-finding panels in the auto and steel disputes. In recommendations issued in the same January week, the panels made parallel findings, as follows: The cost of living had jumped about 33 percent since before the war, while the wartime wage freeze had limited pay increases to around 15 percent for the average industrial worker. Allowing for regional variances in the cost of living, and "circumstances peculiar to particular industries," the panels called for wage increases to a level 33 percent above that of January 1941. For the auto industry, the recommended increase was 19½ cents an hour; for steel, 18½ cents.

But there was a major difference. The auto pay jump would not be coupled with an increase in car prices, whereas the steel panel recommended a $5 per ton increase in steel prices, which the Administration announced it would support. United States Steel, titular leader of the industry, at first refused to accept the panel's terms, with President Benjamin Fairless demanding a $6.25 per ton price increase. Whereupon labor heard support from some unexpected voices: *Life* magazine said editorially, "Mr. Fairless should pay 18½ cents; right or wrong, the President picked it, and we've got to get on with the job." The New York *Daily News* editorialized, "Fairless Made a Big Mistake." Fairless and steel settled, and workers' pay went up an average $32 monthly, the largest single raise in the history of the industry. GM, however, would not be pressured. It refused to follow the "unsound principle" that a rich company should pay higher wages than a less profitable one (i.e., Ford) and offered the UAW 18½ cents on a "take it or leave it" basis.

Reuther suddenly found himself an isolated labor leader. His own rank and file bickered over continuing a "penny an hour strike," especially when other unions accepted the 18½-cent increase. Internal CIO politics were also involved: Reuther simultaneously jousted with a Communist faction in the UAW and with Philip Murray, president of both the CIO and the United Steel Workers, and a man deeply suspicious of his younger rival. Rightly or wrongly, Reuther felt the Communists and Murray would toss the GM strikers overboard for their own ends. The White House put the final squeeze on Reuther, refusing to reenter the negotiations and urging that he settle for 18½ cents. In March, after 113 days of bargaining, the UAW broke and signed while insisting, for purposes of face, that improved seniority provisions and a dues checkoff system were worth an extra penny. Within the next four months the government permitted GM and the other auto makers no less than three rounds of price increases. "The plain fact," commented *Time,* "was that the people everywhere, not caring much who got what, sensing that both higher wages and higher prices were in the air, wanted labor and industry to get back into production on almost any terms."

During a 1946 floor debate on legislation restricting powers of labor unions, Nebraska's Republican Senator Kenneth Wherry denounced the "unionists who fatten themselves at the expense of the rest of us." Wherry wondered "how long America will tolerate big labor's use of the strike bludgeon to get . . . inflated, unrealistic pay scales that hamper productivity, slow reconversion, and deny goods to the average American." Wherry concluded: "Big labor, beware; the people are tiring of your arrogance, and your increasing privileged position."

Among the 195,000 workers who joined the General Motors strike was William Michael (Bill) Nation, thirty-seven years old in the winter of 1945–46. Born in Pennsylvania of Serbian parents, Nation in 1932 had gone to work in Plant 18 of the Fisher Body–Ternstedt Division of GM in Detroit. His job was to inspect window moldings for GM cars— Chevrolets, Buicks, Oldsmobiles, and Cadillacs. At first GM paid Nation twenty-four cents an hour for a ten- or twelve-hour day; his normal week was six days; often, however, he worked seven days. Nation's most lucrative year was 1944, when war overtime enabled him to earn $3,602, often as high as $90 weekly. This money almost, but not quite, offset the bleak year of 1941, when Nation was ill much of the time and earned only $846.

Nation lived ten miles south of Detroit in Lincoln Park, in a three-bedroom house he bought in 1941, just before the war started, obligating himself to pay $32 monthly for twenty years. Nation and his wife, Vangie, of Polish descent, had five children, so the house was cramped: Mrs. Nation and the girls occupied the two downstairs bedrooms; the one upstairs was for the boys and "usually the old man."

The Nations hadn't been to downtown Detroit in so long that in 1946 Bill couldn't even remember the last trip. The couple had never attended a stage production or a movie. Nation's social life consisted of occasional card games with his brothers-in-law, during which he would drink "a few bottles of beer," and an infrequent Sunday drive in the family's 1939 Plymouth. Nation owned two suits, both bought before the war; at work he wore suit pants, a blue work shirt, and a tie and vest (the latter because inspectors were a rung above production workers in the GM industrial caste system). The entire family bathed on Saturday night and set aside clean clothes to wear to Sunday Mass.

After the 1945–46 strike, Nation's pay was set at $1.47½ per hour, or $59 weekly, which the family spent as follows:

Mortgage payment	$ 8.00
Food	25.00
Coal	1.49
Electricity	.75
Telephone	.75
Gas	.41
Water	.32
Insurance premiums	1.96
Social security	.62
Group hospitalization	.39
Union dues	.37
Cigarettes, lunch	2.50
Gasoline and oil	3.00
Total	$45.56

These fixed expenses left the Nation family with $13.44 weekly for clothes, doctors and medicine, household expenses and repairs, movies, magazines and comic books. Because of the number of dependents,

Nation paid no income tax. He generally spent "$58 of the $59," and saved nothing. Nor could he make any payments on a $350 debt he had run up during the strike.

Nation computed that the strike cost him $1,000 in lost wages; nonetheless, he was not discouraged. He had always made out one way or another, and he expected to keep on doing so. His only ambitions, beyond surviving from day to day, were expanding a plastics workshop in his basement and putting his sons through college. Nation paid no attention to international affairs, and he had no interest in visiting relatives in Serbia.

In retirement Nation could look forward to a social security income of $65 to $70 monthly (GM had no pension plan at the time). And Nation was understandably sore when he read press accounts of the "unreasonable demands of labor." The 18½-cent raise won by the UAW made it possible to feed his kids, nothing more.

"If I had one of the top GM guys' salary for just three months," Nation told an interviewer in the summer of 1946, *"I'd be fixed for the rest of my life."*

A few months after Harry Truman became President, labor specialist Louis Stark wrote that "organized labor has taken [his measure] . . . and found it to be friendly and disposed to be reasonable." True, the White House had no labor confidant approaching Sidney Hillman, a man so close to Roosevelt that during brainstorming on Truman as a vice-presidential possibility, FDR ordered, "Clear it with Sidney." That Truman was approved by Hillman bespoke labor's confidence in him.

For his part, Truman in his early presidential months frequently felt labor to be unrealistically critical, and unsympathetic to the political problems he had with the Republocrat majority in Congress. As the wave of strikes began in late 1945, for instance, R. J. Thomas, the CIO vice-president, wrote Truman a snippish three-page letter on the veterans' housing crisis. Every conscious American realized the problem existed, but Thomas outlined it at carping length and noted that the Roosevelt Administration found solutions to national problems during war: "Are we willing to admit that we can only solve such problems in the presence of military urgency?" Truman didn't like Thomas' tone. He scrawled an angry note across the bottom for Judge Samuel Rosenman, the White House liaison man with labor:

> Tell him if he'll get his gang back to work the things refered [sic] to here can be worked out.

But Truman's differences with labor soon escalated beyond informal notes. The Administration picked its way through the auto and steel strikes without offending the unions; indeed, the general public attitude (and especially among businessmen) was that the White House was outrageously prolabor. The miners and the railroad workers soon thought otherwise.

In the rail case, the unions received a tart taste of the famed Truman temper. An arbitration panel had haggled with the carriers and twenty rail unions for weeks, finally getting the agreement acceptable to all parties save the two largest unions: the Brotherhood of Railroad Trainmen, headed by A. F. Whitney; and the Brotherhood of Locomotive Engineers, led by "Grand Chief Engineer" Alvanley Johnston, both old political friends of the President. Truman summoned the men to his Oval Office three days before a strike deadline and told them sternly, "If you think I'm going to sit here and let you tie up this whole country, you're crazy as hell." Whitney apologized, "We've got to go through with it, Mr. President. Our men are demanding it." Whereupon Truman rose with tight lips and gave the men a forty-eight-hour deadline for settlement. "If you don't, I'm going to take over the railroads in the name of the government."

Although the strike deadline was shoved back five days, the talks got nowhere. So on Friday morning, May 24, 1946, the workers having resumed their strike, Truman strode into a cabinet room bristling with anger. He announced he intended to ask Congress for the most Draconian labor law in U.S. history: the authority to draft strikers into the military without regard to age or number of dependents when their walkout threatened a national emergency. Truman even brought along a handwritten speech he would deliver over radio that evening. Never had such angry words been put onto paper by a President for public utterance. While America's young men faced "bullets, bombs, and disease" to win the war, "some people worked neither day nor night and some tried to sabotage the war effort entirely. John L. Lewis called two strikes in wartime to satisfy his ego, two strikes that were worse than bullets in the backs of our soldiers. He held a gun at the head of the government. The rail unions did exactly the same thing." When peace came, Truman continued, union leaders "all lied to him" when they promised to help reconversion. When he wanted cooling-off legislation to halt the auto strike, "a weak-kneed Congress didn't have the intestinal fortitude to pass the bill. Mr. [Philip] Murray and his Communist friends had a conniption fit and Congress had labor jitters. Nothing happened. . . ." The more Truman wrote, the madder he got, and his windup was a call for mob action:

> Every single one of the strikers and their demigog [sic] leaders have been living in luxury, working when they pleased and drawing from four to forty times the pay of a fighting soldier.
>
> I am tired of the government's being flouted, vilified and misrepresented.
>
> Now I want you men who are my comrades in arms, you men

who fought the battles to save the nation just as I did twenty-five years ago, to come with me and eliminate the Lewises, the Whitneys, and the Johnstons; the Communist Bridges* and the Russian Senators and Representatives and really make this a government of, by and for the people.

I think no more of the Wall Street crowd than I do of Lewis and Whitney. Let's give the country back to the people. Let's put transportation and production back to work, *hang a few traitors* [emphasis added], and make our country safe for democracy.

Come on, boys, let's do the job.

Truman's entourage read the message with open-mouthed horror; one man remembers thinking, "My Lord, had Mr. Truman given that speech, he would have been ridden out of Washington on a rail. A President just doesn't go around demanding that the country lynch labor leaders." Under urging by press secretary Charles Ross and White House counsel Clark Clifford, Truman softened the speech to an indignant diatribe ("This is no contest between labor and management. This is a contest between a small group of men and their government") and said "this emergency is so acute" he would appear personally before Congress the next afternoon to request the legislation.

Scorched by the full fury of presidential temper, the rail unions scrambled for cover. Truman's chief labor adviser, a burly, drawling Alabamian named John Steelman, hammered at Whitney and Johnston in a room at the Statler Hotel. In late afternoon Steelman advised Clifford that a settlement could be reached momentarily. But nothing was definite when Truman entered the House Chamber and began his talk. Minutes later Steelman frantically telephoned Clifford, standing by at the Capitol, to report, "It's over, they've signed." Clifford scrawled a note, "Mr. President, agreement signed, strike over," and a Senate functionary ran to the podium and dropped it atop Truman's text. Truman broke off in mid-sentence and his somber face creased in his familiar broad grin. "Gentlemen," he said, "the strike has been settled." There were cheers and wild applause, and Truman continued, saying the draft legislation was needed anyway. The House obliged that same evening, 306–13, but the Senate was not to be so easy. Robert A. Taft, arguing the bill smacked of fascism, dissuaded the Senate from acting. The bill eventually died.

Truman emerged from the fuss with a mixed balance sheet. Whitney and Johnston swore terrible retribution, the latter vowing to spend his union's "$47 million treasury" to defeat the President in 1948. (Johnston later backed down when a reporter looked at his union's books and

* Harry Bridges, president of the West Coast International Longshoremen's and Warehousemen's Union, spent more than a decade fighting attempts to deport him to his native Australia for alleged Communist ties.

discovered nowhere near that amount was available—unless he intended to put pension funds into a political campaign; the liquid assets totaled only $2.5 million.) Thousands of leftist New York unionists jammed Madison Square Park in a rally sponsored by the CIO's Political Action Committee; they carried placards assailing Truman as a "fascist" and a "labor hater." The newspaper *PM* devoted its full tabloid front page to a single exclamatory headline: AN APPEAL TO REASON: A PROGRAM TO SAVE AMERICA FROM TRUMAN'S PLAN FOR MILITARY FASCISM. An inside picture showed 1930's German workers, in uniforms with swastika armbands, marching to their jobs in military formation. *PM* suggested a new military recruiting slogan: "Join the Army! Your government needs you to defend the country and break strikes!" The New York *Daily Mirror,* at the opposite end of the political spectrum, was angered into an incomprehensible yelp: "What public opinion needs to do is kick this ward-heeling, petty, small town, two-by-four administration into when [sic] it came upon us." Lowell Mellett of the Washington *Star* felt Truman's rail strike legislation "cut short his own political career." The labor vote was "washed out." Victor Riesel agreed: "He has just thrown away virtually all labor support by asking Congress to empower him to put strikers in the Army. A quick check of every important labor headquarters here [Washington] and in New York and visiting union chiefs discloses that Mr. Truman no longer has a single important friend in labor circles." (Riesel's labor sources apparently were a mercurial lot: three weeks later, commenting on the "good" pay increases recommended by Truman's labor appointees to fact-finding boards, Riesel claimed that the President "now has the tough union chieftains more solidly behind him than did FDR." But even as labor meetings around the country denounced the draft bill as "repressive" and "un-American," the majority of the nation's press supported it editorially as a means of curbing labor strife.

Truman had no such public opinion problems during his showdown with the bristly-browed John L. Lewis, of whom even friendly biographer Saul Alinsky wrote in 1949, "no man in our history has been so hated for so long a period." To Americans of the 1930's and the 1940's Lewis' coal strikes were as much an annual ritual as the first sighting of the ground hog, or a President throwing out the first baseball of the season. A forbidding, hulking man who glowered at the world between strands of tousled gray hair, Lewis made a theatrical production of each sentence, and his seemingly impromptu insults left the tarnish of public ridicule on several generations of prominent persons. Former Vice President John Nance Garner carried to his grave Lewis' brand as a "poker-playing, whiskey-drinking, labor-baiting, evil old man." Lewis said of his archrival American Federation of Labor, "The AFL has no head; its neck just growed up and haired over."

In the 1940's Lewis was the renegade of organized labor, his mine workers out of the CIO (which he was instrumental in organizing) because of his refusal to join its support of Roosevelt's third term in 1940, his feud with the AFL leadership so virulent that some members of its hierarchy feared him physically. But Lewis' power was real: he was callous and brutal to the public, but his miners—and the possessive is deliberate—revered him as a flesh-and-blood saint; in the homes of many miners, two pictures were on display: one of the Virgin Mary, the other of John L. Lewis.* Further, America needed the coal these men produced. Coal heated more than half the houses in the country. Coal powered 95 percent of the nation's locomotives; coal fired steel furnaces and provided the thermal-electric power for most of American industry. Lewis knew, and appreciated, his power. "When we control the production of coal we hold the vitals of our society right in our hands," he once told an interviewer. "I can squeeze, twist, and pull until we get the inevitable victory. Whenever we strike, time is always on our side, for coal is basic to our economy. Stop coal, and you stop steel. Stop steel and you stop autos and then tires and every part of our economy." Although press, public, and government hostility built against the miners, the auto and steel industrialists would counterpressure the coal operators to accede to the union's demands so that "their own fabulous profits will not be interrupted."

Perhaps prophetically, the second major news story in the United States the day Harry Truman succeeded to the presidency involved John L. Lewis: his grudging acceptance of a coal contract that temporarily put his miners back to work. He took his men out twice again before the year ended and then in April 1946, just as the nation was recovering from the auto and steel strikes, Lewis called yet another strike. This time the issue was a demand that a miners' welfare fund be financed by royalties on each ton of coal produced. When Truman publicly questioned the legality of the plan, Lewis snorted: "Truman doubts the legality of our demands? What does Truman know about the legality of anything?" As coal stockpiles dwindled that dreary spring, the government ordered dimouts of twenty-two eastern states; railroads laid off 51,000 men, the struggling Ford Motor Company another 110,000; New Jersey declared itself in a "state of emergency." But just as a general economic collapse seemed imminent, Lewis sent his miners back to work in a two-week truce—a tactic typical of the cunning Lewis, dancing away just as an infuriated nation prepared for drastic retalia-

* The miners loved Lewis because his willingness to strike meant money to them. A Bureau of Labor Statistics survey of the fifteen basic manufacturing industries (auto, steel, printing, shipbuilding, etc.) for 1935–39 showed the coal miners ranking twelfth, with an average weekly wage of $22.16. By 1949 Lewis had brought the average miner's pay to $76.84—an increase of an astounding 246.8 percent, and the highest level of any manufacturing industry.

tion. Only Lewis didn't jump quite fast enough: when further negotiations stalled, Truman ordered Julius A. Krug, the secretary of the
interior, to seize the mines. "Let Truman dig coal with his bayonets,"
jeered Lewis, and the miners ignored Krug's order that they return to
work. The government capitulated in nine days, and Lewis got his welfare and retirement fund, financed by a five-cent levy on every ton of
coal mined.

Lewis wasn't satisfied. In the fall he demanded that Krug reopen the
negotiations and increase both vacation pay and contributions to the
welfare plan. Rebuffed, he ordered another strike. The mood inside the
White House was a mixture of fear and exasperation. Roosevelt had
been unable to take the wily Lewis to the mat even in wartime. Should
Truman risk yet another public bloodying? But, again, unless the line
was drawn, would not Lewis taunt Truman for the rest of his presidency, striking at will regardless of contractual obligations? While a
senator, Truman had come to detest Lewis; in a letter to his family he
had called him a "racketeer" and said the coal strikes hurt the war
effort. Truman's anger deepened at each flamboyant Lewis outburst.

The night of Saturday, November 16, Truman attended the annual
banquet of the White House Photographers Association ("The One
More Club," he always called it) and around midnight returned to his
second-floor study for talks with Krug, Attorney General Tom Clark,
and counsel Clark Clifford. The men talked until the early hours of
Sunday, and the decision was to carry the fight with Lewis through to a
showdown, regardless of the political and other risks. Truman saw the
case as something much greater than a quarrel over wages, hours, and
working conditions. He believed the sovereignty of the United States
government was at stake, since the Interior Department still controlled
the mines. The miners' walkout was not so much a strike as an insurrec-
tion, a blow at every man, woman, and child in the United States. The
time had come to find out which was the stronger, Lewis or the government; and whether one element of American society could penalize the
entire country and get away with it. Truman directed Clark to ask a
court order restraining Lewis and the UMWA from breaking the contract provision against strikes. The U.S. courts were an institution that
Lewis could defy at his own peril. "The instructions were to fight to the
finish," Truman said in a file memo written later. (He also noted that
Lewis was boasting he would "get Krug first . . . and then he would
wait until 1948 to get the President.")

Another decision that night was to refuse to be drawn into Lewis'
traditional "war of nerves," in which the mine leader trumped up an
atmosphere of national crisis to pressure adversaries. Truman moved
out of the picture entirely and left the mechanics of confrontation to
Clark, Krug, and Clifford. U.S. District Court Judge T. Alan Golds-

borough granted the injunction, and Truman boarded his plane, the *Sacred Cow,* and flew to his Key West retreat for sun and rest. He took a daily swim, he fished for barracuda, he submerged in a captured German U-boat, he went sightseeing in the Dry Tortugas. As Lewis blustered around Washington, denouncing "government by injunction" and a "yellow dog labor-hating administration," Truman fended off press questions about the miners. When he returned to the White House Lewis—by now adjudged in contempt of Judge Goldsborough—telephoned several times, presumably to talk peace; Truman wouldn't accept the calls, saying the matter was in the hands of the courts.

Truman's strategy tossed Lewis completely off balance: the legalities of his walkout were to be resolved, not by political dictates, but in a court of law. And Lewis didn't like the prospects. When he came to court for sentencing, on December 4, according to one observer, his eyes were sunken, his skin flappy, his mop of hair gray, dry, and scraggly. He denounced the "ugly recrudescence of government by injunction," then sat quietly as government lawyers asked a fine of $3,500,000 (based on the loss of $250,000 revenues daily during the fourteen-day strike).

Lewis' lawyers argued such a staggering fine was intended to "put the United Mine Workers out of business," one of them, Welly Hopkins, storming: "Shame upon a government representative that would undertake to perpetuate such an outrage. I denounce it with all my heart and soul. I denounce it as a day of infamy when you come into this court and ask that a crown of thorns be placed upon a man merely to satisfy the political program of an administration." Hopkins paused and stamped his foot. "Double shame!"

Lewis arose. "Mr. Hopkins, may I shake your hand? I associate myself with every word you have uttered."

"It was from my heart, sir," said Hopkins, wiping away the sweat.

Under questioning from Judge Goldsborough, Lewis said he earned $25,000 annually and owned two houses. "Aside from that, I have nothing left except enough money to pay my bills, but don't let that deter you from levying any amount that you wish to levy on me personally."

"Don't get into contempt of court, Mr. Lewis," Goldsborough warned.

"Sir, I have been adjudged in contempt of court."

"I know, but that is another contempt."

Lewis shut up and sat down, and listened to Goldsborough's summation in fidgeting silence. "This is not the act of a low law-breaker," Goldsborough said, "but it is an evil, demoniac, monstrous thing that means hunger and cold and unemployment and destitution and disorganization of the social fabric. . . . It is proper for me to say . . . that if actions of this kind can be successfully persisted in, the government will be overthrown." He fined the UMWA the requested $3,500,000 (of a treasury of $13,500,000).* Lewis ordered his miners back to work.

"Well, John L. had to fold up," Truman matter-of-factly wrote his mother. "He couldn't take the gaff. No bully can."

"Let's be fair about it and give the devil his due," Philip Porter wrote in the Cleveland *Plain Dealer* a few days after the strike ended. "It was the forgotten man, Harry S. Truman, who faced down John L. Lewis and made him call off the coal strike. It was Truman who had the guts to bring the porkiest of all the labor monopolists to heel. It was Truman who refused to compromise. It was Truman who forced Lewis to admit that the government was bigger than Lewis." Clark Clifford said years later that the showdown with Lewis marked the "moment when Truman finally and irrevocably stepped out from under the shadow of FDR to become President in his own right." Biographer Saul Alinsky felt that Lewis "was so accustomed to dealing with a subtle, brilliant, wary Roosevelt that he could not anticipate the directness of a politically insensitive Truman." Lewis was to bluster on for several more years but his days as a reigning national ogre were over.

Despite its surface erraticism Truman's labor policy was consistent at its core. He was "friendly" to the unions in the same sense that he was "friendly" to other sectors of the nation, and he realized that much of his political support came from the men and women of organized labor. As did most union leaders, he felt government should stay out of the collective bargaining process. Yet when a strike situation threatened the entire nation, as was the case in the rail and coal crises, Truman looked beyond the unions to his broader constituency, the American public. Several times during the turbulent winter of 1945–46 he said to White House aides, "I don't give a hang what the unions say about me, or do to me politically; that isn't my job. But when they run a balance sheet on Harry Truman, they'll realize they got a fine fair shake."

While the strife in big industrial centers commanded national head-lines and presidential attention, quiet, most intense struggles disrupted old patterns in the backwaters of American labor—among unskilled and farm workers in the South. War industries siphoned hundreds of thousands of these persons out of low-pay areas. Once exposed to city life and shipyard and aircraft-factory wages, they were never quite the same again. To the South, especially, a major shock of peacetime was that the dirty work of agriculture and commerce no longer would be performed for pennies. The situation flabbergasted the South; and its business establishment spent many postwar months trying to convince the populace (and itself, for that matter) that the high wages of war were a transient phenomenon best forgotten by all concerned, and as rapidly as

* The U.S. Supreme Court the next spring cut the fine to $700,000.

possible. The people who ran the South anguishedly cried out for a return of the remembered old days, when everyone knew his place—in the economy and elsewhere—and did not measure local wages against the benchmark of a shipyard in Pascagoula or an oil refinery in Houston. "Cotton Pickers, Where Are You?" pleaded the Memphis *Press Scimitar*. Mrs. Clara Kitts, director of the Memphis office of the United States Employment Service (USES), found it peculiar that farmers were "begging for pickers" even though they paid $2.10 per hundred pounds in Mississippi and $2.05 in Arkansas. "A good picker can average 300 to 400 pounds a day," Mrs. Kitts said. "A whole family picking can bring home lots of money. The weather has been warm and beautiful. There are lots of people idle. But still nobody comes out to pick. I don't understand why." In prewar days, she said, the office dispatched 16,000 pickers daily. Now only 3,000 could be found. Nor were men interested in working for sixty cents to $1 an hour in the citrus groves around Bradenton, Florida, a situation the local *Herald* could not understand: "They prefer to idle and spend their wartime savings. . . . [A] good many men now idle would be earning good wages right along if they could be persuaded that it is a more sensible thing to be in gainful occupation at reasonable pay than to indulge in a foolish hope that wartime wages and jobs are coming back and that one is warranted to wait for the return." In Jacksonville, Florida, where job seekers wanted "double the pay offered by industry," George Main, the local USES officer, commented, "The principal conversion problem in Jacksonville is the reconversion of our minds to current conditions."

Nor on the whole were black women eager to return to prewar conditions. The Associated Press, in a survey of southern cities in the fall of 1945, reported that "negro [sic] maids and cooks and yardmen aren't beating paths back to their old jobs." Persons who made ninety cents an hour or more in defense jobs preferred to "take the claim" (i.e., for unemployment compensation). Although one USES official expressed optimism about a "gradual return to their old jobs," the AP concluded that "very few people expect to see a return of the days when there was a cook in every kitchen in the south—when negro servants were paid as little as $3 a week for long hours." In Orlando, Florida, matrons found maids demanding fifty cents an hour, whereas prewar servants worked from 8 A.M. to 7 P.M., six days a week, for $4 to $7 (or 9 A.M. to 2 P.M. for $3). In West Palm Beach and Miami, a domestic wouldn't consider less than $25 weekly. In Manhattan, New York *Sun* reporter Patricia Brown wrote, "Sure, you can get help—providing you're willing to pay through your olfactory organ, but even then, dears, this is the age of specialists." Cooks demanded $250 monthly, butlers $150 to $225; chauffeurs were "plentiful" at $60 weekly, "but they won't do housework on the side." And domestics had learned something of fringe benefits, Ms. Brown reported: "Gone beyond recall is the era when she would be content in a room in the attic, or the little cubicle off the kitchen which frequently contained, in addition to her bed, the ironing board, laundry basket and, as often as not, little Willie's tricycle. Annie is holding out for a room of her own, with private bath—if she'll sleep on the premises at all."

Conservative southern editorialists fumed about the "free-loaders" and "parasites" who took unemployment pay rather than slipping back into their prewar jobs (at prewar pay, in many instances). The *Lakeland* (Florida) *Ledger* complained about southern blacks ("and some whites") who went north to "the defense plant employment and cosmopolitan living of centers like Detroit or Chicago, found contentment there, and have not come back." But the *Ledger* was confident that nature eventually would side with the citrus growers: "For one thing, colder weather will chase some of the hesitating blacks and whites southward to work. . . . Some [blacks] said in a kind of whisper that northern unions are discouraging southward migration of negro labor so as to tighten the shortage here." In Marion, South Carolina, the *Star* felt that cutting off unemployment pay would help speed the "loafers" back to work: "It will do the culls good to suffer for a short while and it will give them time to think it over and get off their high horse. Then when they realize who they are and why they are—that we are members of a society that lives by the sweat of its brow—then the period of transition will gradually begin to progress into a state of normality." The *State,* of Columbia, South Carolina, wished the jobless would go away. "Instead of scurrying home after losing their jobs in defense plants, thousands of the people are still hanging around the town for better jobs than they left behind and showing no disposition to return home until their unemployment pegs out. Perhaps six months hence when the free hand-outs have been spent, few jobs might be going begging." The Raleigh, North Carolina, *News & Observer* led into its denunciation of the "lazy" with a vintage southern anecdote: "The Negro new husband offered to buy his bride a wash tub. 'No,' she said, 'I prefer a mirror.' The husband replied, 'Well, you can have your choice. You can take in washing and have food in the house, or you can stand in front of the mirror and watch yourself slowly starve to death.' " The *News & Observer,* saying the unemployed should not be "coddled or petted," concluded, "If they can get jobs and refuse to take them, they ought to be forced to 'watch themselves starve.' "

Many southern states heatedly resisted paying unemployment compensation to persons unwilling to work for prewar wages. In Georgia, the State Department of Labor held that anyone refusing such a job was unemployed by choice, and hence ineligible for benefits. It cited a woman who refused a job paying $2.50 a day plus meals and tips. "This job would have paid her much more than she had made on any job before the war. Before going into war work as a riveter for 85¢ an hour she had worked for a laundry for $12 per week and as cashier in a filling station at from 30¢ to 35¢ an hour." In Tennessee, Commissioner W. O. Hake of the Tennessee Labor Department sent letters to unions and employers asking them to identify persons drawing benefits to whom they had offered jobs. Unions replied that Hake was attempting to "induce employees to establish a state-wide spy system." Some of the jobs deemed "suitable" by Hake, the unions said, paid the "miserably low wage" of $16 weekly, only $1 more than the unemployment benefit.

So adamant was employer resistance to higher wages, so intent the determination to bludgeon workers back to prewar conditions, that several industries even appealed to the War Department that German prisoners of war be kept in the United States for extra months past peace so that they continue in their assigned jobs. The pulp and paper manufacturers of Florida wanted a thousand POWs; so did citrus growers around the big POW camp at Winter Haven; so did the cotton barons of Virginia. The Pentagon refused, citing a policy of shipping the POWs home as rapidly as possible, and thereby denying the employers a pool of dirt-cheap labor.

For returning vets the pay disillusionment was especially jolting. For months these men had heard—and believed—the barracks gossip about the big money earned by war workers. Now they were home to share the new prosperity and could not seem to find it. So the restless vets skipped from job to job, unable to decide in advance whether they would really enjoy the work—many with no specific goal in mind other than the first paycheck, their gut-confidence shored by the knowledge that a 52-20 Club stipend was always there for the asking, resistant to menial jobs and often reluctant to return to their prewar employer. (Big New York companies, for instance, reported a scarcity of office boys—sixty to sixty-five cents an hour—in the immediate postwar months.) But the veterans found that the high war wages had melted away. A USES official in Florida, calling the GIs "disillusioned and disappointed," commented, "It's a terrible letdown for the veteran when he finds out what kinds of wages are actually being paid." One vet told the New York *Sun:* "One problem is that we got so used to bragging and lying to one another about the super jobs we were going to find after peace that we lost touch with reality. You heard more big yarns and dreams about the money you made than on almost any subject except women." What career could there be for a twenty-one-year-old fighter pilot who had earned $400 monthly during the war—but who had no college training and whose practical experience consisted of shooting down other people's airplanes? *National Aeronautics Magazine,* after study of the potential job market in late 1945, suggested that most of the 3,000,000 men and women in military aviation should forget about flying as a peacetime avocation, even though a survey indicated perhaps half of them wished to continue. "The peacetime aviation is governed, not by the law of national necessity, which justified the greatest expenditures in history, but by the law of economics, which decrees that an airplane or an air service must show some signs of paying for itself. . . . Aviation probably will be no more remunerative than the washing-machine business."

Moving On

*"I wish I was a bird—because people are build-
ing houses for them to live in."*
—One veteran to another in a cartoon caption in
the *American Legion Magazine*, November 1946

T HE END OF THE SECOND WORLD WAR found the United
States facing a "housing shortage of unparalleled magnitude,"
in the words of a government study. The Depression had staggered the
home-building industry. New starts dropped to 93,000 in 1933, from a
peak of 937,000 in 1926, and recovery was barely underway when the
war sent construction into yet another tailspin. With the nation concentrating on munitions during the forty-five war months, most housing
starts were hastily constructed quarters for defense workers—poor
quality stuff intended to last only a few years. The building materials
industry fell dormant. To cite two items among many, brick and bathtub
production in 1945 was only one-fifth the 1941 level. Existing housing
was in ill repair, with scant materials and workers available for maintenance.

The young veteran felt the shortage more keenly than any other
group, for he was the person whose prewar home had been with his
family or in an apartment. Now married and eager to form his own
household, he found "no vacancy" signs plastered everywhere he
looked. By October 1945, when only 3,000,000 persons had been demobilized, and another 11,000,000 awaited discharge, the government
estimated that 1,200,000 families already lived "doubled up." The California Department of Veterans Affairs found that about 27 percent of
that state's 500,000 former servicemen lived with friends or relatives;
Democratic Representative Helen Gahagan Douglas said the homeless

far outnumbered those left without shelter by the San Francisco earthquake.

Veterans tried to joke about their situation, but the humor bore the frantic hollowness of desperation. A couple wanted to rent the bedroom set on the stage of a Broadway theater for use during nonperformance hours. Another couple actually moved into the display window of a Manhattan department store for two days, until sympathetic publicity brought them an apartment. Bill Mauldin's Willie and Joe, the doughboy characters of wartime, now "reconverting" along with everyone else, moved into a barn, where they told the inquiring farmer who came out with a shotgun and lantern, "If ya want character references, Mister, write to Signor Pasticelli, Venafro, Italy. We occupied his barn for seven weeks." Walter B. Mansfield,* a marine captain who served with the Office of Strategic Services in Asia, reported spending most of his terminal leave searching for an apartment in Manhattan. "Peace is sure hell," Mansfield told a reporter. He said it was easier to find a sniper in China than an apartment in New York. In Chicago, GIs and families filled garages, coal sheds, and cellars; in San Francisco, vets "lived" in autos parked on city streets, using the restrooms in the public library and cooking over wood fires in the park. Chicago put 250 streetcars on sale for conversion into "homes."

The emotional volatility of the housing crisis was not lost on the White House. One poignant letter among thousands received was from a Los Angeles man who wrote President Truman:

> Tonight coming home I met a first class medical sergeant and his wife. She was crying. She had a little boy on her lap. I said, "Sergeant, what's the matter?" and he said, "I've no place to go tonight and my wife is having another baby." I have them with me tonight.

The man expressed confidence in Truman's ability, but urged, "Do *something.*"

The Truman Administration tried a multipronged solution. Truman sought to continue rent controls for as long as possible, to prevent landlords from gouging tenants in the scarce market. "You can't turn the chiselers loose," he wrote a friend, John B. Pew, a Kansas City lawyer. If rent controls ended he feared "it will make the Florida boom look like a Sunday school picnic. . . . Naturally the landlords and real estate owners want to see the boom because they all figure that they can get out without being hurt—that simply can't be done." Truman directed that materials be channeled into construction of medium-income houses, rather than nonessential buildings such as restaurants and shopping centers. This order, in April 1946, halted an estimated $14 billion of construction in the blueprint stage, bringing an angry editorial grump

* Now a U.S. district court judge in New York.

from the *Wall Street Journal:* "The drastic order, if tightly enforced, will halt what is potentially the largest nonresidential building spree in history." And Truman tried to devise a program that would push the construction industry into mass production of houses that low- and middle-income families could afford, rather than concentrating on luxury homes.

But Truman recognized the practical problems. When an old friend, Bernard F. Hickman, the postmaster in St. Louis, complained about slow progress, the President replied in a personal note, "You must remember that there isn't any possible way of waving a wand and getting houses to spring up. For four years we have concentrated on the war effort and it will take time to get the necessary houses constructed. . . . The construction industry is disorganized—there are more strikes in the building trades than in all the other industries combined. . . . [M]aking speeches and blaming somebody for something which can't be helped is not going to help the shortage."

Truman did not suffer from a lack of citizen advice. Oscar Cooley, a radio commentator in Indianapolis, suggested that Truman set an example by taking one or more veteran families into the White House. Another writer would use the "much wasted service spaces" in churches for veterans. Ex-GIs at the Missouri Valley College, in Marshall, Missouri, asked Truman to give them fuselages from surplus B-29, B-24, and B-12 bombers for conversion into living quarters. A man in Florida claimed to have perfected a building material made of the "inexhaustible scrub palmetto of Florida, cement and old newspapers"; he offered to send Truman a sample. The shortage was so tight in Washington that J. Edgar Hoover, the FBI director, pleaded with the White House to give housing preference to agents "who are engaged in security activities essential to the national defense." (The agents received the preference.)

But each initiative the Truman Administration attempted encountered vehement opposition. Builders claimed that inflation, both of wages and material costs, made it impossible for them to construct the low-cost housing demanded by veterans. By one 1946 survey, three-fourths of the persons searching for houses could pay no more than $50 a month, limiting them to houses costing $6,000 or less; only 6.8 percent could afford to pay $75 or more a month. Yet builders claimed they could not build a $6,000 house that anyone would want. Contractor Clarke Daniel in 1945 duplicated three two-bedroom houses he had put up before the war in suburban Prince Georges County, Maryland. The 1941 versions cost $6,230; the 1945 ones, $9,919, an increase of 59 percent. Daniel complained that although he paid laborers ninety cents an hour, rather than the prewar sixty cents, "they do only about two-thirds the work; they are very inefficient." Builders elsewhere reported similar escalations.

But even as they complained that economics prevented them from satisfying the low- and middle-cost markets, the builders vigorously opposed any federal programs to encourage cheap housing. The industry, through its powerful Washington lobby, the National Association of Home Builders and the National Association of Real Estate Boards (NAHB and NAREB), fought any direct government role in housing, other than guaranteeing loans for housing units costing $10,000 and more. The NAHB argued that any government move to undercut interest rates of conventional lenders (banks and savings and loan associations) to spur low-cost homes would "lead to socialized housing." Even in the emergency months just after the war ended, when veterans slept on relatives' couches and begged for cold-water tenements, the NAHB scorned moves to give them temporary lodging in unused military barracks. Indeed, the thrust of the industry argument was that the problem was not so much a *shortage* of housing as it was an *oversupply* of people with the money to pay for decent places to live, an exercise in logic that many persons in official Washington and elsewhere found difficult to understand.* For instance, the National Association of Apartment Owners, at its 1947 convention in Cleveland, complained that "stenographers and clerks" were earning so much money they lived alone in apartments that previously housed four or more persons, a situation possible because of rent controls. The association's president, John E. Owens, said that in Los Angeles alone the removal of controls would enable apartments to absorb 80,000 more tenants. "There are simply too many people occupying space they don't need," Owens said. "A rent increase would take care of a lot of that." (But a more objective observer could find evidence the problem went deeper than controls. In early 1946 the Des Moines *Register & Tribune,* cross-checking local realtors' claims that the housing crisis had passed there and controls could be removed, published an advertisement offering a nonexistent apartment for rent. During the next three days 351 callers asked for it. Of these, 56 told a reporter they lived in hotels or sleeping rooms, 68 with parents; 14 planned to be married, 137 "wanted something better.")

The salvation proved to be the GI Bill, with its guarantee of low-cost loans for veterans. From the program's inception in late 1944 through the end of 1947, some 1,056,771 veterans received home loans, 540,000

* The conservatism of the real estate lobby is best illustrated by a letter from Herbert U. Nelson, the Washington lobbyist for the National Association of Real Estate Boards, written to an NAREB superior in 1949, and later procured by a Senate investigating committee. "I do not believe in democracy," Nelson wrote. "I think it stinks. I believe in a republic operated by elected representatives who are permitted to do the job, as the board of directors should. I don't think that anybody but direct taxpayers should be allowed to vote. I don't believe women should be allowed to vote at all. Ever since they started, our public affairs have been in a worse mess than ever."

in 1947 alone. The average GI house cost $7,300, although four of ten sold for more than $8,000, and one in twenty for more than $12,000. The organized veteran groups such as the American Legion lobbied strenuously for GI housing but opposed any govenment programs for the general public. When Senators Taft, Ellender, and Wherry (an odd trio of a conservative Midwestern Republican, a moderate southern Democrat, and a big-city liberal Democrat) proposed a slum-clearance program involving construction of 1,625,000 units annually for four years, the Legion's first worry was that Congress might try to finance the program by "depriving veterans of some of their other hard-won benefits." Besides, the Legion argued, "public housing is not *veterans* housing." (The next issue of the *American Legion Magazine* offered one solution to the housing crisis, an article entitled "How I Built My Own Home.")

The mass market opened by the low-cost GI loans ultimately was satisfied by a revolution in housing construction: a revolution with dubious long-range effects, to be sure, but nonetheless a genuine one, in which builders turned out homes literally on an assembly-line basis. The revolution had several interrelated ingredients: standardization, the automobile, and the willingness of harassed buyers to pay for homes that an earlier generation would have scorned as junk.

Standardization resulted from an eagerness of builders to follow designs that could be erected swiftly by someone other than skilled carpenters, who, although they did good work, also demanded union wages. The most visible result was the proliferation of the so-called Cape Cod house in the immediate postwar years, not so much by buyer preference as by builder dictate. "Postwar homes," the *American Builder,* the journal of the NAHB, said in 1945, "have to be designed for the greatest possible economy. This demands straight lines without many breaks in the foundation and roof. It means the elimination of dormers, almost to extinction." It meant "the almost unbroken foundation lines of the true Cape Cod, and the simplicity of framing . . . with which most carpenters are familiar." It meant, in other words, a decision by builders to demonstrate their expertise by housing a generation of Americans in an architectural style reminiscent of a string of boxcars. At the end of 1945 the *American Builder,* which purported to speak for the entire industry (and there is no evidence to the contrary), pridefully pointed to a Chicago builder who had planned an entire subdivision with only four basic house designs, each intended to "give the feeling of being individually planned and oriented to suit each family. . . . All [the builder] needs to do to gain this ideal is to adapt a varied color styling scheme and alternate the setback lines of the houses. He will then have a subdivision with individuality."

Appliance manufacturers urged on the trend to standardization. In

July 1945 the American Gas Association, a trade group, persuaded the entire appliance industry to agree upon standard sizes for both kitchen cabinets and appliances, maintaining that a streamlined kitchen should not belong exclusively to the housewife who could afford custom workmanship. Working space would be thirty-six inches above the floor. To prevent toe stubbing, cabinets, stoves, and other fixtures would have a "toe cove" three inches deep and four inches high. Counter tops could extend 25¼ inches from the wall, allowing half an inch overhang from the cabinet base. The standardization agreement, which attracted absolutely no public attention, nonetheless was perhaps the most significant thing to happen to the American woman's kitchen* since the invention of the gas stove, in terms of aesthetics, convenience, and economy. Unsightly gaps and bumps between cabinet units and appliances would plague her no longer; she could buy new items without throwing her entire kitchen out of kilter. For the builder, standardization meant easier construction: manufacturers soon supplied packaged kitchen units that could be melded together, cabinet with sink with stove, with the ease of a child stacking toy blocks. The standard package concept spread to other parts of the house as well. For instance, in 1947 the Borg-Warner Corporation displayed what it called a "core unit" for heating, plumbing, and electrical facilities—essentially a console affair containing the central heating plant and the main terminals for the household plumbing and electrical outlets, compact enough to be rolled into the house by a single workman, at a considerable saving in both space and installation costs.

Fritz Burns, a seasoned Los Angeles builder, had ideas of his own on how to make postwar housing more attractive to potential buyers. "Builders made two mistakes. They either went way out in designs—I remember a round house that revolved with the sun—or dusted off their prewar plans, only on a scale so small they were inadequate. My idea was to be innovative, but not so abruptly you would scare away people.

"A good example: I built the first house in Los Angeles that contained a garbage disposal unit. You heard all kinds of objections about those units. They were supposed to 'clog the sewers,' among other things. That isn't true, of course; the residue acts the same as any other sewage roughage, it clears the pipes. I rigged the unit with a plastic pipe running from the garbage disposal to the outlet, and in demonstrations we used a beet. People could stand there and watch the bright red juice go through the plastic. It convinced them.

"The same house† contained the first thermal pane windows used in

---

* To feminists who might object to my assignment of ownership of the kitchen, may I say only that the American woman held clear title in 1945–50.
† At 4950 Wilshire Boulevard, now used as an office for Fritz Burns & Associates.

Los Angeles—two glass plates with an air space. I experimented with the U-shaped counter for the kitchen; we called it the 'no-stoop counter' in our ads, and women loved it. At the rear and sides we used conventional windows, but in the front we used jalousies that admitted air for ventilation but screened off the living room. Why have a front window when you looked out onto Wilshire Boulevard traffic? People couldn't believe this: you'd hear them exclaim, 'My goodness, there are no front windows.' At that time you had to have a picture window with a lamp sitting in it.

"People were so hungry to see new housing they tried to get in even during construction. When we finished we left up the construction fence and charged a dollar admission to see the model house. Since we didn't want to be called profiteers, we gave the money to a different charity each day. We had to do something to keep away the idle curious. What times!"

During the war years many builders gained experience in hurry-up production techniques when called upon to erect housing for defense workers. One such contractor, and a man whose name became synonymous with "postwar development builder," was William J. Levitt, who built nearly 2,500 units during the eighteen months after Pearl Harbor in the Norfolk, Virginia, area. Levitt then joined the navy and served the remainder of the war in the Pacific. Returning home at age thirty-nine, he sensed several things that were about to happen to America. The economic realities of postwar building meant that developers could not build any appreciable number of new homes inside existing cities. The automobile gave the American family the mobility to live ten, twenty, even thirty miles away from the place of work. The country-to-city population flow would inevitably lead to a proliferation of service industries and satellite communities around the big cities.

So Levitt and his father, Abraham, and brother, Alfred, bought hundreds of acres of potato fields on Long Island, scoured the country for scarce building materials, and set out to construct a 1,000-home new town. The supplies came into a railhead near his building site, and a "factory" rapidly assembled such standard components as interior partitions, roof trusses, and door and window units. Levitt split his work force into crews: one group built foundation forms down one side of the street, crossed over, and came back down the other side, followed by another crew pouring concrete that had been mixed in a central plant; next would come carpenters to erect the framework—crew after crew, each performing a specialized job, and then hurrying to the next house in line. In the 1920's and 1930's a master carpenter was required to know everything about building a house from foundation forms to roof gables; for Levitt's assembly-line purposes, all that was necessary was that the man be able to perform a single job, which he repeated hour after hour. Levitt used nonunion workers; thus his painters could work with sprayguns, rather than the archaic handbrush, for an estimated time saving of 60 percent. The unions, although unhappy, never succeeded in organizing Levitt. By the end of 1946, his first homes nearing completion, Levitt advertised in New York newspapers:

It's Mister Kilroy now . . . for $70 a month.

By the hundreds the home-hungry veterans drove out to Long Island and listened to salesmen recite Levitt's offer: $1,000 down, $70 monthly, for a three-bedroom house with a log-burning fireplace, a gas range, venetian blinds, a gas heater, and a landscaped lot of 75 by 100 feet, all for a total price of $9,990.

Levitt's idea stood the test of the marketplace. He continued cutting costs (by cutting "frills" from the house, and refining his building procedure). In 1947 he gave the name Levittown to another thousand farm acres near Hempstead, Long Island, built 150 homes weekly, and sold them for $6,900—a 25-by-30-foot two-bedroom bungalow, to be sure, and austere, but the veterans bought them. Levitt had an eye for savings. He provided a "full basement," but an unfinished one; if the buyer wanted a recreation room, or a work room, he built it himself. The "third" bedroom in the fancier models did not have a closet; instead, Levitt stuck a metal cabinet behind the door, and told buyers this gave them "more usable space." There were differences in the exterior trim, in the colors, in the spacing of shutters and windows, in the setbacks from the street; yet anyone who looked closely could detect that there wasn't really all that much difference in the four basic Levitt houses. Levitt used asphalt tile for the floors, even in the living room and dining area (*area,* not room), and explained that the traditional hardwood floor was not available because of shortages. Since most of his buyers had never owned a home, why should they know enough to object? Buyers didn't. By 1949 more than 4,000 persons annually were buying Levitt homes, and he enjoyed a reputation as the "Henry Ford of the postwar builders."*

Builders elsewhere used variations of the Levitt technique. In Dallas, for instance, Angus W. Wynne, Jr., produced a finished house in twenty days in his 2,200-home Wynnewood development. Roofs and walls went up first so that inside work could be done even in the rain, and Wynne expected brick masons to finish one house daily. Wynnewood homes had air-conditioning, which Wynne's ads called "an innovation for South-

---

* Two decades later Levitt's houses remained livable, even if not totally satisfying. We lived in one briefly, in New Jersey in the 1960's, and survived, although my wife avowed that she would have been batty in another month because of the isolation and sterility of the neighborhood.

western homes in the $10,000 price range." Wynne helped popularize
the so-called ranch style house, which meant rooms were joined hori-
zontally rather than vertically. Developers of Oak Meadows, a low-
priced development near Oak Lawn, Illinois, a Chicago suburb, used an
overhead conveyor belt to haul fabricated sections from a central work-
shop to home sites, and they built 1,200 units in slightly more than a
year. Traditional carpentry vanished: workmen used glue and automatic
nailing guns to bind precut panels to precut frames, and the "accepted
expectation" of a six-man crew was to erect the frame and roof trusses
of two houses daily.*

Although most of the builders gave lip service to "individuality" and
promised that variations of their basic designs would make houses distinctive, even if mass-produced, the cost cutting and the dedication to
the "elimination of frills" (which is only another way of saying cost
cutting) took a toll on the American home that was both aesthetic and
practical. In 1948–49, for instance, a Houston company put up a 4,700-
unit development that included not a single porch or garage; a slight
overhang on a roof eave—little solace from the South Texas sun—was
considered such an "innovation" that the builder mentioned it in advertisements. To call these homes—and others—boxes was to insult the
container industry. The goal of many builders seemed to be how little
house they could sell for how much money. What they offered, all too
often, was two bedrooms atop a concrete slab, containing little more
space than one would find in a two-bedroom apartment. The buyer's
choice was between a house that he didn't particularly like and the
exorbitant rents that greeted the end of controls in late 1946. Complaints poured into Washington by the tens of thousands, and in 1948
the Office of the Housing Expediter concluded, "The chisel was the tool
most often used to construct the postwar development house."

A House investigating committee headed by Representative Olin
Teague, a Texas Democrat, and a much decorated veteran himself,
catalogued the horrors found in a 26-city survey. Builders substituted
linoleum for tile in bathrooms, pine for oak, plywood for pine; they
used one coat of paint, rather than three. Floors were splintery, knotty

---

* The on-site innovations notwithstanding, conventional builders continued to
sniff at prefabricated housing, on which the work was done at a remote location.
In 1945, Jacques Willis, a Chicago builder who pioneered the use of plywood in
home construction, demonstrated the construction of his "Home-Ola" house between 9 A.M. and 5 P.M. Willis said he chose a trademark deliberately suggestive
of a soft-drink name because he thought small houses should be available through
lumber dealers "just as easily as you buy a bottle of Coca-Cola." Willis sold
thousands of the homes for $3,220, yet the National Association of Home Builders
cautioned, "Erroneous talk by government planners, plus the fertile imaginations
of Sunday supplement writers, convinced many prospective home owners that in
a matter of months, houses would be coming off production lines like autos did
before the war—and that they would be about as easy to buy and move on a lot
in some subdivision." The NAHB seemed pleased that the public was "becoming
realistic."

horrors; tops and bottoms of doors were left unsealed and unpainted. Not only did some developers neglect to build promised driveways and paved streets, in some instances a three-bedroom house turned out to have only two. Lawns washed away with the first rain. In Corpus Christi, Texas, a builder did not connect the bathtubs to the sewer pipes, so the waste water drained under the house into the crawl space beneath the bedroom. Tighe E. Woods, the housing expediter, said his "prize horror case concerns a new house built in Sacramento of such inferior construction that a nine-year-old boy threw a baseball through the solid wall." Yet builders would not take responsibility for shoddy work. Some sales contracts were so indefinitely worded, the Teague committee found, that they "actually fail to indicate the veterans will receive a house."

The psychic toll and social costs of the jerry-built developments were another matter. Dr. Charles Winslow, professor emeritus of public health at Yale University, angrily told an American Institute of Architects forum in 1948 that many of the "inferior type of small house being provided by speculative builders to meet the veteran demand . . . [were] doll houses which out-slum the slummiest of our prewar slums." He predicted that "families living in these houses might suffer serious mental and physical ills." But the architects professed helplessness, one of them responding that the policy of government lenders was to "adopt the view of the builders and ignore the views of the architects."

The developments lacked a focus for community interest. Many did not have a single store, park, even a neighborhood school. Thus residents fell back upon one another to break the tedium of the day, with devastating effect. Howard Mendelson, of the American University Bureau of Social Research, who spent considerable time probing life in the new suburbs, concluded, "In these communities there is no real privacy. The women become involved in one another's emotional problems. And, unless they take part in community activities, they are apt to be shunned and lead incredibly lonely lives, surrounded by the endless monotony of the development itself and trying to cope with the monotony of their children and housework. Their husbands may drive off to the city each day, but for the women, there is no escape. It's often a tough life for them." For surcease the women turned to television ("the twentieth century's built-in babysitter," Mendelson called it) and the mass-market magazines—which, in turn, led to further emotional and intellectual inbreeding, because everyone else in the development watched and read the same things. Dr. Leonard J. Duhl, a staff psychiatrist for the National Institute of Mental Health, foresaw a long-range effect on children raised in a matriarchal society, knowing fathers only as "nighttime residents and weekend guests." Duhl wrote that the suburbs, with their one-class conformity, denied the child the chance to "try out new ideas, feelings and himself . . . to see what fits."

There was another drawback as well. Many veterans went into the quickie developments with the intention of moving on to more traditional housing as soon as it became available or affordable. Prewar Americans (or many of them, anyway) bought houses with the intention of living in them for a lifetime; in the 1940's, however, and thereafter, people thought of a house as they did an automobile: use it until the new wears off, or you see something better. John Keats, the social critic, wrote bitingly of what happened to the mass suburban developments once the first generation of veterans began moving elsewhere. "Secondhand development houses were sold to the kind of people who buy secondhand automobiles solely out of need. People, in other words, less financially responsible; less able to give the same degree of care to the house than the original veteran-purchaser gave to it."

In sum, the cheap developments gave the veterans—and other Americans—*houses;* all too frequently, however, they did not provide *homes.* And a vague unease was noted by sociologists and other students of the public: The American was discovering that all too often his "home" turned out to be the same overadvertised, overpriced, under-quality junk as did his car. Thus did his dream of a better postwar world slip a bit further toward disappointment.

III

Culture: Serials and Other Sagas

A Remembrance of Marshall: III

The console radio stood head high in the corner of the living room, a massive affair more furniture than appliance, a dark-stained wooden lyre and heavy brocade cloth covering the speaker; dusty in the ornate crannies; the veneer faded to yellow and splitting at floor level. One listened to the radio flat on the floor, nose nuzzling the outside of the speaker, a friend or a sister (and a stack of salt crackers) hard by. Above, the soft orange of the panel light illuminated a dial set, more or less permanently, just to the left of the numeral 12, the frequency for station KWKH in Shreveport, thirty-eight miles distant across the Louisiana border, the foremost cultural influence in what local boosters called the Ark-La-Tex area.

The radio. Four o'clock on a winter afternoon in 1946.

"Hen-reeeeee! Hen-reeeee Al-drich!"

"Coming, Mother."

We liked Henry Aldrich because he carried the special quality of credibility. Henry was awkward, and he made mistakes, and the teachers and his parents fussed at him, just as they did at us in real life. Henry Aldrich lost his cap. Henry Aldrich forgot to do his homework. He played football enthusiastically, but not very well.

The dashing Jack Armstrong, the other boy star of the afternoon serials, was a different sort of character altogether. We admired Jack's airplane, the Silver Albatross, *and his dirigible, the* Golden Secret. *We even learned the words to the Hudson High fight song that opened Jack's program:*

> *Wave the flag for Hudson High, boys,*
> *Show them how we stand!*
> *Ever shall our team be champions*
> *Known throughout the land!*

But could any of us consider Jack Armstrong a real boy? If he really attended Hudson High, how did he find time for adventures in the Sulu

Sea and the Amazon Basin? We could not picture Jack joining our pick-up football games in the dust bowl, the pasture-cum-athletic-field behind East Texas Baptist College. Better to make a friend of Hen-ree Al-drich, who would sneak off to the woods during recess and throw chinaberries at other kids during the Saturday afternoon cowboy double features at the Lynn Theater. And get caught, as well. We usually were.

8

Afternoons of Soap and Hope

CULTURAL HISTORIANS ARE of a single mind about American diversions once peace returned. Americans opted for frivolity in literature and in film; they sang nonsense lyrics ("Bongo bongo bongo I don't wanna' leave the Congo, I refuse to go. . . ."); they enjoyed bizarre national fads, either as active fools or as gawking audience (to boost the fortunes of a popular radio show called "Truth or Consequences," a man journeyed to the fringe of a jungle in the Philippines and wailed a song as nonsensical as the program itself: "Chloe, where are you? I can't find you. . . ."). Their support made gossip columnist Walter Winchell the nation's highest-paid newscaster ($520,000 in 1948 from American Broadcasting Company, plus perhaps that much more directly from the sponsoring Jergens Lotion Company), even though he was so unreliable as to be a journalistic joke, and so hypervocal he was almost unintelligible to a casual listener.

Crazes sputtered unpredictably across the land. In the winter of 1948–49, serious adults began forming "pyramid friendship clubs." To avoid postal strictures against chain-letter schemes, members met personally to exchange money. With local variations, the schemes worked as follows: At his first party, a new member handed over $4 and became one of many "number 12's" at the base of the pyramid. To the next meeting he brought two new members, each with $4. Subsequently, as new members multiplied and formed pyramids behind him, he was pushed toward the peak. On the twelfth night, if things went well, he received $4,096 for his original $4 investment. According to the newspapers, people won anywhere from $800 to $1,500, the jackpot depending upon the size of the opening ante. In a Los Angeles suburb a crowd cheered a judge who ruled the clubs violated no laws. By March 1949, when the craze reached New York, the first payment in some clubs soared to $5, with a possible payoff of $10,240; reporters chased rumors of a Wall Street club with a $100 ante and a payoff of $204,800. The clubs defied reason and mathematical tables. By one computation, 16,777,216 players would be required to keep a club going for 25 days. But no one listened to the warnings. Suddenly, in the spring of 1949, the clubs vanished overnight. Their replacements, at the teen-age level, included "slam books," in which New Orleans schoolgirls exchanged brutally frank comments on friends; and "scratching," an automotive sport in which Atlanta youngsters put their fathers' cars in reverse, roared backward in a tight circle, then slammed into low gear and sped forward, at unestimated cost to gears and nerves of adult bystanders.

Christopher Morley complained in 1946: "The American muse, of strong and diverse heart . . . was in 1946 drinking gin and eating horsemeat; uttering hyperthyroids of pain, or else climbing backward to anesthetic in Henry James and Sherlock Holmes and *Alice in Wonderland.* For the first time in a number of years, the current product in books was so obviously second-rate that older classics were rediscovered and reprinted in good supply." John Mason Brown felt much the same about the first postwar drama season: "The war's nearness cast its inescapable shadow over the entire season. It explained the continued absence of new young talents, and the confusion with which older playwrights approached the world, once again supposedly at peace. It also explained why revivals contributed to the season more than their usual quota of interest." Americans had had the forced draft of seriousness during the war: now, for God's sake, let us relax; no more challenging thoughts or uplift, if you please, we wish to enjoy the peace.

And radio proved the medium that struck a happy common denominator with the entire country—from teen-aged kid in Texas to housebound mother to big national advertiser. Radio, of course, had cemented itself in national popularity for years—as a curiosity during the 1920's; as the poor man's theater during the Depression; as a messenger with the voice of immediacy during the war. By 1947, 34.8 million of the 38.5 million households in the country had at least one radio receiver; there were 8.5 million in use in automobiles; and another 21.6 million in stores, hotels and institutions; in short, an American had to go out of his way to avoid the cacophonous din of music and commercials. Radio reigned as America's sole "national" means of communication. With listening patterns enhanced by the war, people got into the habit of switching on news broadcasts and forgetting to turn off the radio when they ended.

What Americans heard fell into three broad daily cycles: Beginning in midmorning, housewives could follow a most unique aural-literary form known as the soap opera—Balzacian tales of domestic tragedy, unrequited love, and medical curiosa. At three o'clock or thereabouts the programming switched abruptly to the juvenile serials—improbable high adventure and derring-do in which justice prevailed and girl-boy relationships were most platonic. Finally, during the dinner hour, radio reached out for every ear in the family with situation comedies, quiz shows, and music. According to polling data, the average American child listened to radio about fourteen hours weekly, and adults (especially the women) didn't trail far behind.

The soap operas stood as an industry unto themselves, a merchandising dynamo that generated about 60 percent of advertising revenues for the four major networks, and sold more boxes of washing powder, more bathtubs of suds, more varieties of feminine gimmickry, than anyone ever bothered to count. Procter & Gamble alone spent $14.9 million in 1946 for the soap dramas "Road of Life," "Right to Happiness," "Life Can Be Beautiful," and "Ma Perkins." The "soaps," as they were known, contained built-in advantages. They were cheap: two fifteen-minute segments could be produced for about a third the cost of a half-hour music show featuring a name band such as Fred Waring. And they certainly were addictive. Although one survey by the Federal Communications Commission claimed that about three-fourths of the radios in America fell silent during soap hours, the advertisers' figures held that 50 to 60 percent of American women swore fanatic loyalty to at least one show, and most often three or four, the sort of listenership convertible into a buying audience of millions of persons. Speaking through one of his characters in the best-selling 1946 novel *The Hucksters,* former ad executive Frederic Wakeman wrote that the soap operas worked "like magic. . . . The more you irritated them with repetitious commercials the more soap they bought. . . . The announcer reminded him of the hucksters who used to shout their vegetables in the streets. . . . Huckster—that was a good name for an advertising man. A high-class huckster who had a station wagon instead of a pushcart." And, finally, the soaps—or, more accurately, the people responsible for them —showed not the slightest concern for critics who denounced them as a callous vulgarization of the nation's taste. The soaps had the redeeming candor of lack of cant and pretense: They existed for the sole purpose of making money, and money they indeed made. In the words of Mary Jane Higby, for eighteen years the star of "When a Girl Marries," soap opera "may well have been the lowest point ever reached by dramatic art . . . but make no mistake about it, as *advertising* it was just great. Dollar for dollar, it may well have been the greatest value the advertiser ever got for his money."

The brain trust of the soaps was the husband-and-wife team of Frank and Ann Hummert, veterans of Chicago advertising, who first experimented in the genre in the early 1930's, with a serial entitled "Just Plain Bill," about a Midwest barber who "married out of his station." A folksy, decent chap, Bill endured condescending relatives and spent more time trying to solve other people's problems than he did cutting hair. Bill wasn't always successful, either, and seldom did his episodes have the heart-warming happy endings of conventional pulp fiction. Housewives worried about the Depression could empathize with poor old Bill, and his vast audience convinced the Hummerts that emotional voyeurism was a marketable commodity. They formed a production agency in New York that was a veritable factory for daytime radio "drama," producing fodder that by the end of the war filled about one-eighth of network air time.

The Hummerts and the other soap kings marketed distress. Their central characters spent their lives either in a swamp of trouble or offering a helping hand to others bogged there. As was the case with "Just Plain Bill," seldom did anyone find real happiness. The Hummerts packaged these woes in fifteen-minute lumps, broadcast live five days weekly. Little programming other than the serials could be heard on midday radio: in September 1945, to cite a not untypical month, the National Broadcasting Company had four and three-quarter hours of soaps daily, CBS, four and one-half.

The serials opened with distinctive theme music, Pavlovian in intention, to alert the housewife to put her radio alongside the ironing or sewing she could do as she listened to the daily installment. Usually a Hammond organ provided the overture, for its cathedral solemnity implied the program was serious business, not sheer frivolity. But there were other instruments as well. "Helen Trent" opened to the strains of a ukulele, "Just Plain Bill" to a plaintive mouth organ, "Mary Marlin" to a tinkly piano rendition of Debussy's *Clair de Lune*. The overture was invariably followed by a brief recap of the continuing story line—words that faithful listeners could recite along with the announcer:

> And now—"Our Gal Sunday"—the story of an orphan girl, named Sunday, from the little mining town of Silver Creek, Colorado, who in young womanhood married England's richest, most handsome lord, Lord Henry Brinthrope. The story that asks the question, Can this girl from a mining town in the West find happiness as the wife of a wealthy and titled Englishman?

> "The Romance of Helen Trent"—the story of a woman who sets out to prove what so many other women long to prove in their own lives, that romance can live on at thirty-five and even beyond.

> We give you now—"Stella Dallas"—a continuation on the air of a true-to-life story of mother love and sacrifice, in which Stella Dallas saw her beloved daughter, Laurel, marry into wealth and society and, realizing the difference in their taste and worlds, went out of Laurel's life.

Then the story bowed to the first commercial: laundry flakes ("Rinso White, Rinso White, happy little wash day song . . ."), or toothpaste, or bleach. This interruption, plus another commercial break at midpoint of the program and the close-out echo, left only eight minutes for the writer to remind the audience of what had happened yesterday (the soaps never made the mistake of overestimating listeners' intelligence; moreover, even the most dedicated fan missed an average of two shows weekly, according to radio polls); to make perceptible progress in the plot; and to contrive an ending suspenseful enough to entice people to "tune in again tomorrow, same time, same place on your dial, for another thrilling episode in the . . ." Hence writers fell upon a variety of techniques that had a single redeeming literary quality: they worked. Hear, for instance, a typical recap that led into the daily action on "Mary Marlin":

> In Cedar Falls, Mary Marlin is pondering the strange fate which has revealed to her the fact that Joe may still be alive, while Joe, in Freedom Outpost, is reminded by Simone of the love he once had for Mary; of how he could love her still if he had not put her out of his life; or of how he could love someone like her—like Simone; while up on the hill, Mr. Crayley looks upon the whole thing as an invasion of his privacy.

An especially innovative writer relied upon a character to work the recap into the script—murmured over low organ music which peaked into occasional "stings" (a sudden, treble boing-nnng-nng that alerted the listener that something awful might happen momentarily.) Thus a soliloquy from a character on "Lora Lawton":

> Here I am, Adam Collingwood, a discredited diplomat, walking up and down outside the country club—while inside Lora is having lunch with Lester Coleman. What is Lora saying to Lester? What is Lester saying to Lora? . . . This is a contingency I had not foreseen!

Often a character would pop out a line such as, "Good afternoon, Mr. Baker, this is my college roommate, Charles Peter, whose wife died in an air crash last year, and who is studying to become a brain surgeon."

Writers added dramatic girth to the soaps by lacing the basic story lines with subplots. Confusion reigned, but audiences loved complex situations. Moreover, the padding delayed the inevitable hour when the heroine must face a crisis and resolve it. Gilbert Seldes, the critic, although astounded that a sane adult could "listen so long to so little," nonetheless recognized the utility of the soaps' amble-along pace: "The woman at the center of the serial is a strong character, but if she were permitted to function in strength, the plot would blow up in a few days;

she has to be harried and chivvied and above all prevented from taking action." Keeping these subplots in motion along with the main story required liberal use of scene shifts. A character might enter an elevator on Monday and not reach the seventh floor until Thursday of the following week. "Meanwhile, at the office of Dr. Nolan," or "meanwhile, as the country club dance reaches a peak of gaiety," other characters went about their business. Ma Perkins once stood at her kitchen table for two weeks and a day, wondering whether to open a suspiciously long and thin package. (It proved to contain a poisonous snake, sent by a villain.)

One quality the soaps never achieved—nor intended—was reality. The soap world was a mélange of tense courtroom scenes as characters fought over wills and the custody of children; of lost mates who roamed the world like so many descendants of the Flying Dutchman; of treacherous lovers, invariably male, whose backgrounds were blurred by mysterious dark happenings; of an incidence of amnesia that would defy medical probability tables. The epidemic of amnesia came about by sheer accident, according to Mary Jane Higby. A character on "Mary Marlin" developed amnesia and awoke in a hospital, asking: "Where am I? What's my name? What town is this?" The show's rating increased by half overnight. Miss Higby explained: "Havoc broke loose in the networks and agencies. Plot lines were abandoned, characters were dropped, writers were changed, and in a trice, half the leading men on the air were saying, 'Where am I? What's my name?' " The next time the ratings were issued, "Mary Marlin" was back in its old position. Someone checked the figures and found the earlier high rating was an error. The soaps spent weeks restoring the senses of various characters.

Yet women loved the soaps, and each time a critic raised his carping head network executives hurled public opinion at him, saying, in effect: "Don't gripe at us—blame public taste if you don't like what we are offering; the only persons who agree with us are the American people." H. L. Mencken, although by no means a fan of radio, accepted the broadcasters' theory, although not in a complimentary sense. "The real villain, only too obviously, is the public taste," Mencken wrote to *Fortune* magazine in 1947 in challenging an article that blamed the networks for the abysmal quality of programming. Mencken blamed the situation on a "serious deterioration in the American stock, perhaps mainly due to long-continued dysgenic breeding."* Niles Trammell, the NBC vice-president, apologized neither for the soaps' popularity nor for their content; indeed, his explanation was pragmatic in a 1946 talk to the National Association of Broadcasters:

* Mencken further traced the decline of public sense to the public school, which he charged "is an implacable enemy of every intellectual decency, and is steadily growing worse. The same may be said for the newspaper. . . . The old-time leadership of journalism has pretty well vanished and is now simply a panderer to imbecility."

I am reminded of an old European proverb that "the culture of a nation is determined by the use of its soap"—that the United States with six percent of the world's population uses one-third of the world's soap supply. Broadcasters are mindful of the fact that the sponsors of serial drama pioneered in the daytime use of radio. They helped broadcasters build a new daytime service; and in doing so they brought pleasure and relief from drudgery to millions of American housewives. . . .

It seems appropriate to state one very simple proposition. It is this: the broadcasting of any radio program which a substantial portion of the available audience wants to listen to at the time it goes on the air is an example of broadcasting in the public interest.

The soaps ended in mid-afternoon, clearing the air waves for the kid serials—sagas that were, in a sense, a continuation of the grand story-telling tradition that traced its origins to the campfires of antiquity, but also were a literary form devised to make the breakfast food industry profitable. Children love good stories, and always have. What difference if they are told by a village elder on the steppes of Asia Minor, by the books of Bret Harte or Mark Twain, or by a radio character who interrupts a wheezy organ rendition of Saint-Saens' symphonic poem *Le Rouet d'Omphale* with the mocking question-and-answer: "Who knows what evil lurrrrrrks in the hearts of men? *The Shadow knows!* Hmmmmmmmmm-hmmmm-hmmmmmmm." And what imagination the creator of the Shadow used on behalf of uncountable thousands of kids huddled around radio sets:

> The Shadow, who aids the forces of law and order, is, in reality, Lamont Cranston, wealthy young man about town. Years ago, in the Orient, Cranston learned a strange and mysterious secret, the hypnotic power to cloud men's minds so they cannot see him. Cranston's friend and companion, the lovely Margo Lane, is the only person who knows to whom the voice of the invisible Shadow belongs. Today's story begins . . .

On the surface the cereal-serials that so fascinated youngsters had the same content, and intent, as the soap operas that mothers listened to four hours earlier in the day. Both worlds were make-believe; both existed to peddle a product. And anyone who chuckled about the con-trived plot of "The Romance of Helen Trent" should wonder about the origins of "The Lone Ranger." A band of outlaws ambushed six Texas Rangers and left all for dead. An Indian passerby, one Tonto, came upon the scene and found John Reid gravely wounded but alive. The crafty Tonto dug six graves to delude the bandits into thinking all the Rangers were dead, and spirited Reid away and healed him. Then off they rode, Reid on his wild stallion Silver, Tonto on his trusty paint Scout, with gunfire crackling in the background, and the announcer intoning excitedly, "A cloud of dust, a galloping horse with the speed of light, a hearty *Hi-Yo, Silver! The Loooo-oooone Ranger!"*

Youngsters liked it, and believed it; why should not the Lone Ranger be capable of standing down every badman in the West, in two-dozen lots when necessary, and eluding death and torture and capture by villains? Was not the Lone Ranger essentially good, because he never killed his adversaries, only shot the pistols from their hands? Nor did it really matter that the elders guffawed about Tonto's famed goof: when the Long Ranger called, "Let's go, Tonto," the Indian scout reflexively replied, "Gettum-up, Scout"—even though the setting was a second-floor room.

The cereal-serials were good for youngsters—and for the country, for that matter—because they buttressed the continuing national consensus that good *could* triumph over bad in those best years. The serials were miniature morality plays: they taught us to brush off the dust of temporary defeats, and to persevere. Villains lied; heroes told the truth. The "decent townspeople" spontaneously banded together in adversity. Doctors were kindly old men who never lost a patient (nor dunned them about the bill). The serials even avoided the imminent sexual crises of adolescence: The Shadow and constant companion Margo Lane traveled together, had late-night chats in apartments and hotel rooms, and generally behaved as if they were friend-boy/friend-girl—yet the sleuth never even bussed the fair lady. What really happened between Buck Rogers and his pretty copilot Wilma Deering during those weeks-long flights into space in a comfortable cabin? It never occurred to us to ask.

Nor did our mothers. For one thing, few adults could endure the gamma-ray battles and cattle stampedes for enough consecutive afternoons to become aware of what we were hearing. They reserved the same scorn for "The Green Hornet" that children did for "One Man's Family." Further, and perhaps most important, using a persuasion far more plausible than that available to any real adult, the serials convinced us to take spoons to otherwise unacceptable breakfast stuff. Buck Rogers' Cocomalt would have sold on its own, for it made milk palatable, even appealing; so, too, could Ovaltine, assiduously huckstered by Little Orphan Annie ("Leapin' lizards! For a swell summer drink there's nothing like a cold Ovaltine shake-up mug, eh, Sandy?" "Arf! Arf!") But Ralston shredded cereal was another matter entirely, a food without any redeeming culinary values whatsoever. Yet not only did Tom Mix persuade us to eat Ralston, we eagerly sang his theme song—a commercial—and convinced ourselves that the cereal *was* good.

> When it's Ralston time for breakfast
> Then it surely is a treat

To have some rich, full-flavored Ralston
Made of golden western wheat.

(*Chorus*)
Wrangler says it is deee-licious
And you'll find before you're through
With a lot of cream—boy, it sure tastes keen
It's the tops for breakfast too.

Ask your mother in the morning
To serve you up a steaming plate.
It's a grand, hot whole wheat cereal
And the cowboys think it's great.

(*Chorus*)
Once you try it, you'll stay by it.
Tom Mix says it's swell to eat.
Jane and Jimmy, too, say it's best for you—
Ralston cereal can't be beat.

Further, the formal oath of obligation to Tom Mix's "Square Shooter Club" required the consumption of a minimum of three bowls of Ralston weekly. The honor system was explicit. It was hokum, but it worked.

But choking down ungodly grain concoctions carried material compensations beyond good health and parental approval. The cereal-serials offered a treasure chest of premiums, available only via the magic passbooks, box tops. And who could be without them? If a magic compass enabled Tom Mix to find his way from an arid desert, a Square Shooter deserved the same protection. Magnifying glasses, mock pistols, Ranger badges, sun dials one could wear on the wrist, pocket magnifying glasses, code kits, makeup masks—did we buy the cereal, or the box top? (The manufacturers, of course, didn't care.) And, to be sure, the premiums were valuable items. During one period, "Captain Midnight" ended each day's episode with an encrypted message that could be translated only with a "code dial" the faithful listener wore on his wrist. Bearers entrusted with such codes were expected to take the rituals seriously and guard their confidentiality; Little Orphan Annie's admonition was on the cover: "Anyone who finds this book should return it at once, *without reading,* to the owner whose name is on the back cover."

"My sister married an Irishman."
"Oh, really?"
"No. O'Reilly."

"We have potatoes."
"Oh, really?"
"No, *au gratin.*"

"My sister came from the southwest."
"Oh, really?"
"No, Oklahoma."

—Lines that America found outrageously funny on the Danny Kaye radio show, circa spring 1946.

The approach of dusk mercifully ended the daily soap/cereal drama; whatever kid-momma drama existed during the evening hours tended to be weeklies, longer shows that resolved a single plot situation within a tight half-hour. Evening radio made special demands upon the broadcaster. By custom, a large percentage of families listened to the radio together, often from dinner through to bedtime. People fell into this habit during the Depression, when there wasn't enough money to seek outside entertainment, and continued it during the forced austerity of war. Hence a show that sought to capture the vast family audience had to be intelligible to everyone in the household, from subteens through grandparents. This core fact about the broadcasting industry must not be forgotten: the people who controlled radio saw themselves, first, as businessmen; any discussion of the intellectual or other merits of a program began with the core question: "How will it do in the ratings?" While the broadcasters might have been Philistines, they were certainly not fools. Specifically, the need to sell an all-ages market resulted in some programming that was substandard, in some other that was at worst escapist, and at the best entertainment of classic quality.

Through fortuitous circumstance, both the popular ratings and the dictates of good taste agreed upon the man who was the best, both as a salesman and as a master of his art. His name was Jack Benny, and he stood atop the ferociously competitive world of radio comedy for more than a decade. Benny mastered radio's special demand for a blend of intimacy and elusiveness. He conjured up a living, visual world in the listener's imagination through word and sound—and, frequently, silence, for the affronted pause was a Benny trademark. The disembodied voices of Benny's entourage became personal friends to Benny's audience—as did Benny himself, the aural personification of Everyman, moseying and stumbling through a bewildering world. "Straight man for the whole world," fellow comedian Steve Allen once called him, and it was not a bad line.

Benny's continuing gags, and he drew them out for years, never grew stale. His old Maxwell touring car sputtered and coughed, and he refused to buy a new one. Benny's violin rendition of "Love in Bloom" invariably began with a screechingly wrong first note. And his tightness. When Benny made his "annual" visit to his vault (although memory says he went there far more often), guarded by an ancient retainer, he fumbled with an endless series of locks, and the seldom-opened doors swung wide with creaks and groans. No guest borrowed a cigarette from Jack Benny, nor used his phone for free; the pay phone and cigarette machine in his living room noisily gobbled up coins. Benny grieved that the knees were getting baggy in his suit—after only seventeen years' wear—and that postal rates were increasing by a penny. In one bit a bandit confronted Benny with a pistol and demanded, "Your money or your life." Silence. More silence, with the laughter from the audience gradually swelling into a roar. The robber repeated his demand. Benny, in earnest desperation, stammered, "I'm thinking, I'm thinking."

Laughter. Warmth. Immediacy. Radio personalities brought their friendly banter into the living room weekly; not for them the Olympian remoteness of movie stars. When Bob Hope bantered with Bing Crosby in their incessant mock-feud, America listened as if to neighbors:

"As I live," Crosby greeted his rival. "Ski snoot!"

"Mattress hip," Hope retorted.

"Shovel head."

"Blubber."

"Scoop nose."

"Lard."

A pause by Hope, then, "Yes, Dad."

And so on, into the evening. The radio comedians were quick to seize upon routines that turned on audiences and to convert them into running jokes. Kenny Delmar, a so-so bit player on the Fred Allen show, used a quip that brought a laugh from the audience but no response from the character opposite him. He leaned forward and exclaimed in an exaggerated southern accent, "That's a joke, son." Thus was born one of radio's most quoted catch lines, and a character that brought Delmar fame and fast money: Senator Beauregard Claghorn, a heavy but good-natured caricature of a cornpone southern legislator. Claghorn was an unreconstructed rebel. "When in New York ah only dance at the Cotton Club. The only dance ah do is the Virginia reeel. The only train ah ride is the Chattanooga Choo-Choo. When ah pass Grant's Tomb ah shut both eyes. Ah never go to the Yankee Stadium! Ah won't even go to the Polo Grounds unless a southpaw's pitching. In college ah was voted the member of the senior class most likely to secede, and ah was graduated magnolia cum laude."

Another newcomer to radio comedy, Danny Kaye, thirty-three years old in 1946, soared to sixth place in the ratings with an act based on occasionally intelligible gibberish which resembled a sputtering lawn mower. Kaye's opening and closing signature went something like this:

Git-gat-gittle-giddle-di-ap-giddle-de-rap gipple-de-tommy, riddle-de-biddle-de-roop, de-reep, fa-san, skeedle-de-woo-da, fiddle-de-wade, reep.

When Broadway asked Kaye to lend his unique talent to the show *Lady in the Dark,* he scatted through the names of fifty Russian composers in an Ira Gershwin lyric in forty seconds, with tight diction and control:

> There's Malichevsky, Rubinstein,
> Arensky and Tchaikovsky,
> Sapelnikof, Dimitrieff, Tscherepnin,
> Kryjanovsky . . .

That Kaye could learn such linguistic gymnastics in a single afternoon enabled him to earn half a million dollars a year from radio, movies, and the stage.

Unfortunately for radio—and the people who relied upon it as their major medium of entertainment—the Bennys, the Fred Allens, the Danny Kayes were scarce. Bing Crosby could charm the nation with his Wednesday night radio show ("Bingsday," the promoters called it) and his use of a song could mean 50,000 sales in record stores the following day. But Crosby pursued a parallel career in movies—and why should a true fan settle for El Croono's voice alone when he could be seen full face (and heard) at the neighborhood theater? Despite its strengths, radio suffered from a surfeit of the same old voices. As the radio critic John Crosby noted at the end of 1946, "the fifteen programs with the top radio ratings contained seven names—Fred Allen, 'Lux Radio Theater,' Jack Benny, Bing Crosby, 'Amos 'n' Andy,' Eddie Cantor, and Walter Winchell—who had been in the first fifteen ten years earlier. Others on the list, such as Charlie McCarthy, Red Skelton, Fibber McGee and Molly, and Bob Hope, were hardly new faces. There were no new ideas."

But this appraisal is not precisely accurate, for radio *did* try some new programs in the 1940's—although whether they qualify as "ideas" is questionable. There were give-away shows and disc jockeys—one long dead, victim of an edict of the Federal Communications Commission, and the other quite literally having kept radio in business into the mid-seventies.

The progenitor of the give-aways was Ralph Edwards, whose popular "Truth or Consequences" inspired a succession of imitators. Under the "Truth or Consequences" format, a contestant who flubbed a question was dispatched on a treasure hunt bounded only by the vast imagination of the show's staff. Typical was the assignment meted to Mr. and Mrs. Albert J. Anderson, of Los Angeles, in 1947: a cigar butt from Winston Churchill, a hair from Jack Benny's toupee, another from union leader John L. Lewis's eyebrow; a salt cellar from Senator Claude Pepper of Florida, a copy of the "Missouri Waltz" autographed by President Truman and Senator Robert A. Taft, his archrival. If the couple succeeded, the prizes awaiting them included a washing machine, a man's wardrobe, a diamond ring, a vacuum cleaner, a radio-phonograph, two watches, a refrigerator, an electric range, a seventy-two-piece silver service and a home freezer.

In another gambit, the show put the nation in a tizzy over the identity of "Miss Hush," who mouthed such clues as,

> "Second for Santa Claus, first for me, thirteen for wreath, seven for tree. Bring me an auto, a book and a ball, and I'll say Merry Christmas in the spring, not in fall. What does the wreath have to do with the tree? It's second for Santa Claus, first for me. Santa Claus comes by sleigh, but I prefer an auto."

Miss Hush kept the nation guessing for almost six months, with 10,000 letters daily fluttering down on the NBC offices, and an audience estimated at 20,000,000 persons. Tip sheets intended to decipher the weekly clues sold for $1. When NBC suggested that prospective entrants enclose $1 with their letters, with proceeds to charity, the March of Dimes amassed $325,000 very quickly. Finally, for prizes including a 1947 convertible and a trip to Hawaii, Ruth Subbie, a Fort Worth, Texas, housewife, named Miss Hush: Martha Graham. Edwards, who introduced the gimmick as a burlesque of other give-away programs, found himself trapped by the contest's popularity, so next came Mr. Hush, a "Walking Man" who strolled past the microphone each week, not saying a word, his hollow, echoing footsteps audible above the jingle:

> Bing bong bell
> It's ten and only one can tell.
> The master of the metropolis
> Fits his name quite well.

The "Walking Man" got 114,000 entries in a single week, and the American Heart Association, the designated charity, netted more than a million dollars. His identity was Jack Benny, an answer that brought a $22,500 prize for a sixty-eight-year-old Chicago widow who earned $30 weekly as a department store checker.

Hysteria, once set into motion in the second half of that decade, was inexplicable and unfathomable, and the give-away craze swept on in seemingly incessant waves. Mrs. William H. McCormick, of Lock Haven, Pennsylvania, who won $17,590 in a Mrs. Hush contest, found that strangers would stand on her lawn, just to look at her. Shrewdly, she put this public attention to practical use by running for the school

board, and winning. Two women proposed marriage to Richard Bar-
tholomew, twenty-five, who identified Jack Dempsey as a later Mr.
Hush. When Edwards offered to do his tenth anniversary show in any
United States town that would change its name to Truth or Consequences, the citizens of Hot Springs, New Mexico, promptly obliged, by
a vote of 1,294 to 295. On the Mutual network, "Queen for a Day"
offered "new future" prizes of a home in the San Fernando Valley north
of Los Angeles, a Kaiser automobile, and a choice of jobs. In one
jackpot drawing that attracted 3,000,000 mail contestants, actress Billie
Burke drew the name of Mrs. Edgar Parrett, fifty-six, who lived on a
Navajo Indian reservation near Shiprock, New Mexico. Mrs. Parrett
answered no questions, wrote no essay, in fact she didn't even hear the
winning broadcast. No matter. Here is what she won:

> A house, a home freezer, an auto and trailer, a Persian lamb
> coat, a trip to Manhattan, Vermont and the Bahamas, a ten-piece
> wardrobe, an electric refrigerator, more canned goods than space
> allows one to mention here, a set of china and silverware, a
> coffee brewer, new carpeting, a washing machine, a ten-piece ma-
> hogany bedroom set, a stove, a calf handbag, an ironer, four end
> tables, a scarf, a pressure cooker, an electric mixer, and a year's
> supply of bed linen.

Then, the National Association of Broadcasters began to look
askance at such blatant Philistines and advised members, "Any
broadcasting designed to 'buy' the radio audience, by requiring it to
listen in hope of reward, rather than for quality of entertainment, should
be avoided." But the networks paid about as much attention to the NAB
as would small boys commanded to stop picking up stray dimes found in
the street. Learned clergymen lamented that the people running radio
would instill "something for nothing" hopes in the populace, and called
upon them to stop, under pain of ecclesiastical censure, or worse. The
Reverend Martin Stearnes, a Presbyterian dignitary in New York, in-
toned: "What a spectacle! The time our good American women and
men squander on these contests could best be used in the service of Our
Lord, who certainly would not smile at the spectacle of His children
indulging in such wishful pursuit of riches. Does being 'Queen for a Day'
mean so much to a woman that she would risk losing her soul and
becoming 'Damned for Eternity'?" Although the Reverend Stearnes provided no biblical documentation for his condemnation of radio, even
nonbelievers could sympathize with his contention that the country was
wasting too much time on the give-aways.

The FCC finally cracked down on the shows in the fall of 1948, by
barring the awarding of prizes "dependent in any manner upon lot or
chance" and keyed to listening to the program, or knowing past broad-

cast clues, or writing a letter or answering the phone when the contents of either the letter or the conversation were to be broadcast. It should be noted that ironically the FCC acted for economic reasons on behalf of the networks, not for altruism: The radio networks were investing heavily in television research and the scramble for prizes was draining them of more than $100,000 weekly. Because of the give-aways' popularity, the networks dared not halt the shows on their own, hence they quietly asked the FCC to pronounce the death sentence.*

No such restrictions hobbled the other "idea" radio unleashed upon the public in the 1940's: the disc jockey. Prior to 1940, a radio station that played records had to announce the fact frequently. For some reason that has escaped both sociologists and radio historians, these announcements supposedly stigmatized the station as being too cheap to hire live musicians. Another inhibiting legal consideration was that such well-known performers as Paul Whiteman, Bing Crosby, and Guy Lombardo put warning notices on their records, "Not Licensed for Radio Broadcasting," with the intent of protecting the exclusivity of their live network programs. But federal courts struck down the ban in 1940, holding that once someone purchased a phonograph record he could do with it as he wished, regardless of the desires of the artist or the manufacturer. The American Federation of Musicians, under president James C. Petrillo, and the American Society of Composers and Performers (ASCAP) threw up temporary roadblocks over musician job security and royalties, but by 1945 the radio revolution was complete: live programs were the exception, rather than the rule. A stack of records, an Associated Press or United Press wire with items tailored for a three- or five-minute "newscast," an announcer who could read and speak English, an engineer, and an advertising salesman (especially the latter)—such was the staff of many a postwar radio station. The format of canned music interspersed with many, many commercials was a businessman's delight. The National Association of Broadcasters, the lodge of the moguls making the money from radio, was blunt about its place in the scheme of things. J. Harold Ryan, the NAB president, deposed in a speech:

> American radio is the product of American business! It is just as much that kind of product as is the vacuum cleaner, the washing machine, the automobile and the airplane. . . . If the legend still persists that a radio station is some kind of art center, a technical museum, or a little piece of Hollywood transplanted strangely to your home town, then the first official act of the second quarter century [of commercial radio] should be to list it along with the local dairies, laundries, restaurants, and filling stations.

---

* As should be obvious to any listener to contemporary rock stations, the ban on give-away calls has long since been lifted.

With such an attitude at its upper echelons, and with merchants literally begging for advertising time, radio sogged itself with commercials. The ad men somberly attempted to pass some of them off as new and significant forms of artistic expression—humbuggery, of course, but enough to entice *Time* to give the firm of Batten Barton Durstine & Osborn a rating of "number one on the jingle-jangle hit parade" for a bouncy little ditty with a calypso beat extolling the care of bananas:

> I'm Chiquita Banana and I've come to say
> Bananas have to ripen in a certain way. . . .
> Bananas like the climate of the very, very tropical equator
> So you should never put bananas in the refrigerator.*

A catchy tune, to be sure, but did not radio exist for reasons other than huckstering? The "Unseen Audience" cartoon on the radio page of the New York *Herald Tribune* depicted a couple in easy chairs before their console: "Rodman," the wife said, "I'm getting sick and tired of headache remedies and laundry soaps. Let's listen tonight to hair tonics and cosmetics and toothpaste." "Radio makes me sick to my stomach," said Victor Norman, the fictional advertising executive in Frederic Wakeman's *The Hucksters*. "I never listen to radio on my own time. I take the position that if a thing is not worth doing at all, it's not worth doing well." Reacting to wide citizen complaints, Clifford J. Durr of the Federal Communications Commission ordered a survey that confirmed the worst suspicions about radio. KIEV, of Glendale, California, typical of the disc-jockey stations, devoted 88 percent of its air time in a specimen week to transcribed music, broken by 1,034 commercials (and eight "public service" announcements). The champion, if the word be appropriate, was KMAC, of San Antonio, Texas, which squeezed 2,215 commercials into a single week—16.7 per hour of air time. WTOL, of Toledo, Ohio, originally licensed to broadcast during daylight hours only, received permission to go full-time in 1938 on the representation it would air the local civic opera and give programming time to the Boy Scouts, the American Legion, churches, and the YMCA. The management promised to devote more than 80 percent of its evening hours to

* The men who wrote the singing commercials wanted a tune that would stick in the inner recesses of a listener's consciousness, and bob to the surface periodically to remind him of the product even without the prompting of a radio. I must concede these craftsmen could be infuriatingly successful, for the writing of this chapter jarred loose a jingle that had been stored in my own mind for a quarter century:

> Pepsi-Cola hits the spot
> Twelve full ounces, that's a lot,
> Twice as much for a nickel too,
> Pepsi-Cola is the drink for you!!
>   Nickel, nickel, nickel,
> Trickle, trickle, trickle, trickle,
>   Nickel, nickel, nickel, nickel . . .

live local public interest programs. As things worked out, however, WTOL was more than 90 percent commercial, its sole local programs being twenty minutes of sustaining features—ten minutes of local sports news and ten minutes of bowling scores. Durr's report quoted a typical WTOL broadcast log during the dinner hour:

6:39:30   Transcribed spot announcement
6:40:00   Live spot announcement
6:41:00   Transcribed spot announcement
6:42:00   Transcribed spot announcement
6:43:00   Transcribed spot announcement
6:44:00   Transcribed spot announcement

During some periods, Durr found, WTOL went as long as twenty minutes without airing anything other than commercials. And WTOL, while perhaps an extreme example of shoddy programming, was by no means unique; much of American radio was a mess, daytime or nighttime.

Commissioner Durr's findings were issued in an FCC report that became known as the Blue Book. The broadcast industry, instead of challenging his facts, attacked his supposed motivation. *Broadcasting* magazine, the industry organ, couldn't decide whether Durr was fascist or Communist, or perhaps even both. It viewed his criticisms as a forerunner of governmental controls of programming, and editorialized:

> Have we forgotten so soon the fanatical Pied Pipers of destruction who led the German and Italian people down a dismal road by the sweet sound of their treacherous voices on a radio which they programmed? . . . There is at stake the pattern of American life, and you can find that truth in the charred ruins of a chancellery in Berlin.

Two months later *Broadcasting* was at Durr again, calling him a knight errant riding down from the "commission's castle on the Potomac" to protect the public:

> He enters the jousts in righteous splendor, garbed in an academic grey suit and gripping tightly in one hand—the Blue Book. And the banner he bears high—is it the white of purity, or is there a tint of pink?

Having commissioned the study, the full FCC proceeded to ignore it. Durr singled out for criticism as a "horrible example" Baltimore's WBAL, which had the impolite habit of cramming sixteen commercials into a 45-minute period—one every 2.8 minutes. A group headed by Washington columnists Drew Pearson and Robert S. Allen tried to win the WBAL license away from the holders, only to be declined by the FCC, chairman Charles R. Denny saying programming "is principally in the hands of the licensees of the thousands of stations throughout the country."

Durr, of course, did not intend for the FCC to dictate ideological content; what he wanted was more entertainment and fewer commercials. But even had he won, would the listening public have been any better off? The lifting of the ban on recorded music, and the resultant rush of broadcasters to deejay programs, fell into unfortunate juxtaposition with another development that had profound effect upon postwar American "culture"—the nonsense song.

The most revelatory thing that can be said about the nonsense songs is that teen-agers loved them, and they learned them by listening to the radio. They learned them, and sang them over and over again, to themselves, with friends, to weary parents. Just why the songs struck America's fancy is as inexplicable as a taste for bubble gum, or cocktails made of gin and Dr. Pepper; they existed, they were sung, and they occupied an inordinate amount of radio time. For months the people of the world's most powerful nation bestowed their collective approval on such "music" as:

> Open the door, Richard,
> Open the door and let me in,
> Open the door, Richard,
> Rich-ard, why *don't* you open the door?

A black jazz-band leader, Jack McVea, based the song on a vaudeville skit written in 1919 by John Mason, who got half the royalties after his lawyers coughed politely. Five versions of "Richard" went on sale the first month, with a dozen more performers rushing their renditions to the public (including The Yokels, who sang it in Yiddish). A mention of the word "Richard" by Bob Hope, Fred Allen, or Bing Crosby set radio audiences to guffawing. And the song's success commenced a scramble for yet more nonsense:

—Musicians George Tibbles and Ramey Idriss, working with piano, a guitar, and their memories of a movie cartoon character, dashed off both words and lyrics in half an hour to:

> Ha ha ha ha-ha,
> Ha ha ha ha-ha,
> Tho' it doesn't make sense,
> To the dull and the dense
> Ha ha ha ha-ha
> That's the Woody Woodpecker song.

After four weeks the song topped *Variety*'s list of the most-played juke-box tunes.

—James Anderson, of Port Arthur, Texas, spent much of his army career pushing a mop, and he got to humming as he worked:

"M, I say *M-O, M-O-P, M-O-P-P* . . .
R, I say *R-A, R-A-G, R-A-G-G* . . ."

Anderson didn't know how to write music on paper, so he just sang it, and sent the recording to a friend of Johnnie Lee Willis, a western singer. It soon topped the "Hit Parade" of popular tunes.

—Bob Merrill, the son of a Philadelphia candy manufacturer, wrote down every cliché he could think of on the astute assumption that "clichés make the best songs." He went to songwriter Al Hoffman, who had just produced a song entitled "Mairzy Doats." Hoffman scratched his head over Merrill's list, and his eye fell on an old rural saying, "If I knew you were comin' I'd have baked a cake." Hoffman then jotted down a song using those words, and little else, as the lyrics. No matter. The "song" had record sales of more than a million, and it led the "Hit Parade" for a solid month.

—Four songwriters driving back to Los Angeles from a jaunt to Las Vegas passed an old prospector plodding through the desert:

> Mule train (looooo, loooo, loooooo)
> Mule train (loooooo, loooo, loooo)
> Clippity-clopping over hill and plain,
> Seems as if they never stop,
> Clippity-clop, clippity-clop.

"Mule Train" sold two million records in two months.

—Late in the nineteenth century students at Amherst College put together tonsil-tangling doggerel to sing over their ale mugs late at night, proving at once their sobriety and intelligence. One version went:

> In China there lived a little man
> His name was Chingery-ri-chan-chan.
> His feet were large and his head was small,
> And this little man had no brains at all.
> Chingery-rico-rico-day ekel tekel happy man.
> Kuan-a-desco canty-o gallopy-wallopy-china-go.

In 1945 songwriter Jo Proffitt pulled the Amherst lyrics out of the archives and changed the Chinaman to a chicken who got bored with saying "chick chick chick" all day.

> Chickery-chick cha-la cha-la
> Check-a-la-romey in a ba-nan-i-ka . . .

Despite the flash popularity of the nonsense songs, Americans were distinctly dichotomous in their taste for popular music. In October 1947, a not untypical month, four of the top ten tunes on *Billboard's* list were at least sixteen years old ("That's My Desire," "I Wonder Who's Kissing Her Now," "Peg O' My Heart," and "When You Were Sweet

Sixteen"). The year's best-selling record was Francis Craig's "Near You," followed closely by "Peg O' My Heart," which had been written in 1913. Frank Sinatra, the screen idol of the wartime teen-agers, did not produce a hit record that year; he was completely outdistanced by a handsome onetime barber named Perry Como.

Dance bands were an immediate casualty of the deejays and the jukebox. For one thing, night-club operators and dance promoters found that the public would no longer pay $3 per couple for music they heard for free on the radio. The teen-agers' penchant for undanceable music also hurt: kids might learn the lyrics to "Bongo bongo bongo (I don't wanna' leave the Congo)" but no one ever devised dance steps for it. In the winter of 1946, Harry James, whose reputation as a trumpet player and band leader was well established (almost as impressive, in fact, as his envied position as the husband of the movie star Betty Grable), was forced to cut his asking price from $4,000 to $2,000 a night, and yet he still couldn't find enough bookings to survive. He folded his band before the year ended. Two years before, in 1945, *Metronome* had named Woody Herman's Herd the band of the year; it, too, fell silent, in an eight-week period in 1947 that also saw the demise of the bands of Benny Goodman, Tommy Dorsey, Les Brown, and Jack Teagarden. The teen-agers who still danced preferred the hot beat of jitterbug music, to the worry of oldtime bandleader Art Mooney, who feared for the physiques of America's women: "piano legs, wide bottoms, thick waists, and hefty bosoms."

So radio was king. And though it entered the postwar era with great potential, it never rose above its lowest-common-denominator philosophy of programming. At its best, radio offered fleeting mass entertainment; at its worst, it justified the outburst of Robert Ruark, then a columnist for the Scripps-Howard newspapers: "Nearly everything [in radio] is either corny, strident, boresome, florid, insane, repetitive, irritating, offensive, moronic, adolescent, or nauseating." "The American radio currently represents one of history's most amusing, yet disturbing instances of mankind's technology getting ahead of its culture," *Life* editorialized in 1946. "In twenty-five years radio has advanced technically from the cat whisker and crystal to almost full color video. But in the same time it has progressed from Graham McNamee to Gabriel Heatter . . . from Jack Pearl to Milton Berle. We have the new theater, plush seats, gold curtain, but where is the show?"

The broadcasters conceded nothing. Shortly after the FCC's Blue Book report on advertising, the National Association of Broadcasters commissioned the National Opinion Research Center of the University of Denver to probe public attitudes about radio. The center reported 82 percent of Americans felt radio did a job "between good and excellent"; 62 percent felt the number of ads was fine; 81 percent could get programs they liked when they liked. An NAB contest for the 200 best letters on the subject "What I Think about Radio" produced these comments:

> The radio has become a constant companion and friend. Of course, there are times when I become annoyed with "my buddy" and then I am likely to turn a haughty back to it, only to return, repentant and lonely, after a few days . . .
>
> I can do without radio—the way I can do without food and drink.

When the NAB held its annual meeting in Chicago in 1946, Lee De Forest, the inventor of radio, was not invited to attend. Asked by the Chicago *Tribune* what he might have had to say had he addressed the broadcasters, De Forest did not mince words:

> What have you gentlemen done with my child? He was conceived as a potent instrumentality for culture, fine music, the uplifting of America's mass intelligence. You have debased this child, you have sent him out on the street in rags of ragtime, tatters of jive and boogie-woogie, to collect money from all and sundry for hubba hubba and audio jitterbug.
>
> You have made of him a laughing stock to intelligence, surely a stench in the nostrils of the gods of the ionosphere. . . . Soap opera without end or sense floods each household daily. . . . This child of mine, now thirty years in age, has been resolutely kept to the average intelligence of thirteen years. Its national intelligence is maintained moronic, as though you and your sponsors believe the majority of listeners have only moron minds.

To close observers of the broadcast industry, however, the most significant event of the era was not the merits of the soap opera, nor the taste of commercials, but a prizefight. On June 19, 1946, some 45,000 persons watched heavyweight champion Joe Louis pound Billy Conn into unconsciousness in Yankee Stadium, while an estimated 100,000 others saw the same knockout on television receivers in New York, Philadelphia, and Washington. In the opinion of radio critic John Crosby, "RCA's miraculous new image orthicon camera brought the television audience a crystal-clear and far more intimate view of the fight than that of the stadium audience." Radio's days as the prime national medium of expression were rapidly dwindling away even as it enjoyed its golden hour of primacy.

9

Birth of the Tube

In the mid-1940's national magazines promised America it soon would be watching Broadway shows, college classes, and baseball games on the equivalent of a living-room movie screen. My father, as an appliance dealer, awaited the advent of this miracle of the media with understandably deep curiosity. As long ago as 1931, he had witnessed a crude demonstration of the principle of video at a trade show in Chicago, and now we watched with him as something called "coaxial cable," which carried the TV signals, inched westward from New York.

The cable reached Shreveport, Louisiana, late in the winter of 1949, and by early spring our region's first TV station was on the air, even if out of range of any conventional home receiver. But my father had plans. During the past two decades he had sold Philco and Motorola radios, both battery powered and electrical, to perhaps half the households in Harrison County, and he did not intend to let his archrivals Joe Woods and Ed Dahmer get ahead of him in the new market. He put a seventeen-inch set in our living room and a fifty-foot antenna on the roof. He turned on the set, and we witnessed only the same dancing whiteness we had seen on the set during the dry runs before the arrival of coaxial.

A higher antenna definitely was needed. My father and I went outside, and studied the tall pines in the side yard. But how could an antenna be anchored amidst the sparrow warrens of the upper branches? So my father's attention turned to the chapel under construction at East Texas Baptist College, several hundred yards up the hill from our house. He stood in the street and regarded the steel girders towering far above the neighborhood. As an agnostic, my father retained formal diplomatic relations with the fundamentalist ecclesiastics who controlled the college, but little more. He had taught electronics there during the war, and though he had friends on the faculty, he made no secret of his opinion that ETBC was a citadel of ignorance, and that the majority of its fledgling ministers pursued service-to-Jesus as a comfortable alternative *to sharecropping. Thus how would a self-avowed heathen approach the Baptists on Sunday afternoon for permission to use their premises to bring a Mammon of unknown qualities into a Christian home?*

My father wisely resolved the question by ignoring it. "The Baptists," he said, "are all in prayer meeting. Besides, this is a legitimate scientific experiment." Soon one of his cautious young servicemen, driven by curiosity as much as loyalty, had climbed to the uppermost peak of the soaring girders, fastened an antenna with metal clamps, and dropped a roll of lead-in cable to the ground.

The further course of the cable posed another problem, but one also easily ignored. With only 17,000 citizens and a community attitude rooted in populism and independence, Marshall city government was conducted on the principle that it is best not to bother people. You could keep cows and even pigs inside the city limits as long as they didn't run loose, and whatever you did on your own property was generally considered to be your own business, unless your activities caused undue annoyance to a neighbor. (A decade or so earlier the city government had had trouble inaugurating traffic lights: drivers either ignored them or shot them out with .22 rifles.) So in stretching a cable between the Baptist college campus and our house my father did the traditional thing. Not bothering to ask city officials or anyone else for permission to bridge three city streets, he simply went ahead. In an afternoon we strung the cable down the hill through the college's magnificent oak trees (scene of grisly Afro-American lynchings earlier in the century), across North Grove Street using the poles of Southwestern Bell Telephone Company, and paused long enough to ask Mr. J. D. Denny for permission to go atop his house "just for a minute" to keep the cable off the ground. By this time residents from a ten-block area had gathered to watch "Mr. Joe bring us TV to Marshall," and my father was able to draft volunteer workers and select the most agile pole climbers. By 5:00 P.M. we had spanned North Gregg Street and cut across yet another neighbor's lot to our house and the noise was a rising curve of shouting, "Mr. Goulden gonna' bring tee-veee to their house."

As many of the crowd as were able came inside to the living room to see my father connect the set to his hundreds of yards of lead-in cable, and adjust the fine-tuning dials. The dancing white dots separated and formed into battalion ranks, some in dark uniforms, others not so dark. The sound evolved from buzz to heavy static, with occasional lower-pitched growls that could have been voices.

After study of the screen and consultation with the program guide in the Shreveport Times, my father decided we were witnessing either a Texas League baseball game (the Shreveport Oilers v. the Dallas Eagles) or a performance of the Shreveport Symphony Orchestra.

The crowd stayed an hour or more, the children pressing their noses to the picture screen, the adults warily keeping their distance. Perhaps significantly, no one complained about either the quality of the picture or the nature of the program they assumed they were viewing. "The future" had come to Marshall, and whatever it was, people watched it.

S OON AFTER TELEVISION came to Manhattan, a housewife marveled to a journalist, "The hours between play and bed used to be the most hectic part of the day. Now I know where the children are. The television set is the best nurse in the world." Adrian Murphy, a vice-president of Columbia Broadcasting System, felt television would "re-cement" the American family. "I talked with a man who had seen his teen-age daughter for the first time in two months. He bought a set, and now she brings her boyfriends home." David Sarnoff, the president of Radio Corporation of America, felt television would force a revolution in election campaigns. "Political candidates may have to adopt new techniques. . . . Their dress, their smiles, and gestures . . . may determine to an appreciable extent their popularity." But a Sarnoff subordinate, John F. Royal, a vice-president of National Broadcasting Company, felt the change would benefit American politics: "Television will strip the phony, the mountebank, the demigod, as bare as the day he was born."

Not all these plaudits and predictions held water through the end of the decade, as things turned out, but their underlying message did prove true: television was destined to make great changes in America. Television began as a diversion, a toy, an entertainment that few persons felt could challenge the preeminence of radio. The fetus quickly grew into the *enfant terrible* of the best years, one radically revising not only America's entertainment patterns, but the conduct of politics, dissemination of news, the huckstering of consumer goods. For better or for worse, television stood as the most important "new" product of the postwar period, and one marked to this day by the operating principles it acquired in its youth. Its evolution is not without irony. Television came into being during years when America was painfully realizing that radio was a medium that shamelessly peddled its birthright for a handful of hucksters' dollars. Yet the promising new medium, viewed at first with unabashed idealism, was handed unquestioningly to the same men who had debased radio. It is not surprising, then, what came in the decades to follow. But the 1940's were significant years for TV not so much as for what happened on the screen as for the political-economic decisions on who was to control the new medium. In both areas, however, the end result was determined by traditional laissez-faire capitalism.

The broadcast companies had nibbled at TV several years before the war, with RCA producing the first commercial telecast on February 26, 1939, from the New York World's Fair. "Amos 'n' Andy" went before cameras in blackface, and a few weeks later Franklin D. Roosevelt became the first President to speak on TV. RCA began marketing sets with five- and nine-inch screens, at prices ranging from $200 to $600. Programming was rudimentary—variety shows from Radio City Music Hall, puppets and jugglers, an occasional cooking demonstration, snippets of drama. A mobile unit picked up everything from Columbia University baseball games to wrestling in Brooklyn, ice skating in Rockefeller Center, even pictures of planes landing at La Guardia Airport. CBS and DuMont joined in, and by the end of 1941 about two score stations were on the air, on the East Coast and in Los Angeles. But with only 10,000 or so sets in the country, and the FCC and the industry unable to agree on the technology of the new medium, television was definitely a novelty. And, with the approach of war, civilian development stopped altogether as the government commandeered technicians to work on the ultrasecret radar.

RCA quickly resumed its lead in 1945, promising in August to have sets on the market by the next summer. RCA's ads reflected the uncertainty of TV technology. They lauded both "direct view" receivers, with persons looking directly at a six-by-eight-inch screen, for normal living-room use; and a "projection" screen of eighteen-by-twenty-four inches for larger groups. RCA, employing the considerable lobbying prowess of President David Sarnoff, pressured the Federal Communications Commission to begin licensing immediately, and to let the industry work out the technical problems on the basis of operational experience. But a major difficulty was color television. The early work emphasized black-and-white transmissions, but experts prophesied that color could not be far behind. In the interim, such industry leaders as Zenith's Eugene McDonald complained it was unfair for the FCC to permit the sale of any black-and-white sets "without putting the public on notice that they will be obsolete." CBS was first with a color system in 1947, an incredibly complex one involving rotating color wheels, positioned in front of both camera and receiver, that sorted out the spectrum and produced strikingly vivid images. But the CBS system had practical drawbacks. A CBS home receiver required a cabinet three times as large as the picture tube because of what one TV expert called "this damned Ferris wheel that ran in front of the tube." A similar wheel spun in front of the camera. More grievously, the CBS system was not compatible with existing black-and-white sets, which meant that if the FCC accepted the CBS system, every set in the country would be obsolete. RCA's David Sarnoff told the FCC to bide its time, that his engineers would have a comparable color system ready in six months with the added advantage of being compatible with existing black-and-white sets. How did he know the engineers would succeed? Erik Barnouw, the radio historian, quotes him as replying: "I told them to."

CBS, meanwhile, was content to let television develop at a leisurely pace, for several reasons: the high costs of putting TV stations on the air; the uncertainty of advertiser willingness to pay the higher prices when sight was added to sound; the postwar boom in radio profits. In a study given the Federal Communications Commission in 1946, CBS argued that whatever its ultimate values, television faced "seven lean years" of huge outlays and meager returns, with radio income dwindling as advertisers shifted to the new medium. In effect, CBS asked, why starve for seven years when you can continue to feast on radio profits? CBS's lack of faith was demonstrated when the network rejected four of the five station licenses allotted to it by the FCC (several years later, CBS paid tens of millions of dollars to buy these discarded licenses).

NBC, conversely, strove to maintain its early technological lead, acquiring licenses for a total of ten stations. In February 1946 NBC made the first Washington–New York transmission via 225 miles of coaxial cable, depicting General Dwight Eisenhower placing a wreath at the Lincoln Memorial. The image came into Radio City as blurred and jumpy as an old Charlie Chaplin movie, but no matter—RCA had proved intercity transmissions were technically feasible. A year later NBC televised the opening session of Congress, a camera roaming the outer halls, then focusing on children sitting in their fathers' laps in the two chambers. By the summer of 1947 a "network" linked New York City with Philadelphia and Schenectady.

By the spring of 1947 NBC was on the air almost thirty hours weekly, and the predominant voice was that of an oldtime sportscaster named Robert S. Stanton. NBC covered all Giant baseball games at the Polo Grounds, it went to the United Nations for debate on the Palestine issue, it put together crude studio dramas, it doted on boxing, one of the few sports confined to a tight, easily photographed arena. Baseball caused problems. Stanton, who announced the Giant games, had only two cameras at his command, and he relied upon a variety of hand and voice cues to tell them where to focus, delivering his commentary with studied deliberation so that the description didn't get too far ahead of the picture. Radio techniques were so ingrained that they proved hard to break, and NBC used Stanton essentially as an off-stage voice who seldom was pictured. An old radio professional, Stanton, with some disdain, called himself "merely a stooge for mechanical contraptions." However crude these programs were, the public liked them, especially bar habitués. In late 1947 an estimated 12,000 sets glared at drinkers in Manhattan alone—the most serious affront to saloon civilization since the abolition of the free lunch, in the view of an ignored minority—and bartenders reserved screenside seats for regular patrons; drop-ins were shunted to the back of the bar, away from the tube. "There are millions of people in New York who don't even know what television is," quipped comedian Fred Allen. "They aren't old enough to go into saloons yet." The Roosevelt Hotel installed sets in forty rooms and added $3 per day to the bill.

What did the enraptured citizenry witness during this early period? Not very much. A typical day might have been one in January 1948 that began with live coverage of President Truman's State of the Union Address on three major networks (NBC, CBS, and DuMont). NBC chose for its background music in the House chambers the *Scheherazade Suite.* During the speech, the cameras stared unrelentingly at Truman's face, with only occasional side glances at his audience. When the President finished, NBC and DuMont signed off for the rest of the afternoon, while enterprising CBS traveled to a supermarket in Jackson Heights, Queens, for a customer-participation show called "Missus Goes A-Shopping," highlighted by children imitating animals.

At 5 P.M. programming resumed. NBC presented a kid show entitled "Playtime," with a woman "Popit Hostess" dressed as a clown and introducing short films: a picture tour of Italy, a lesson in how to make a beanie out of felt, and a marionette show. DuMont, meanwhile, offered "Big Brother's Small Fry," featuring an animated film, "Cubby the Bear," and shorts on how to brush teeth and hang up clothes. At 6:45 P.M. DuMont had a newscaster, followed by films on hunting dogs and wild birds, and then a dance band. Oddly, from contemporary perspective, ads were few: there was one for Lucky Strike cigarettes and another for a device whose purpose was to make the TV image clearer. From 7:30 to 8 P.M. NBC presented a program of classical music, but no picture except for the station's name and cards advertising coming attractions. At 8 P.M. NBC featured "Americana," a version of the popular radio quiz show "Information Please." DuMont, meanwhile, had a live musical program featuring Sylvie St. Claire, a singer, shown sitting on a couch, holding a telephone and singing "Melancholy Baby." Then DuMont switched to a grade-B movie. NBC rebounded with "Kelvinator Kitchen," devoted to a demonstration of how to prepare oysters Rockefeller.(The show was tantamount to a quarter-hour commercial, as Kelvinator products stood in conspicuous view the entire time.) At 9 P.M. CBS went to a pro basketball game, DuMont to a fashion show, NBC to a live production of A. A. Milne's play *The Truth about Blayds.* NBC signed off (at 10:20 P.M.) with a large eye on the screen slowly closing to the Brahms lullaby.

For economy reasons, television learned early to leech off other entertainments and events, to train its cameras on spectacles produced by others, and transport them into the living room. Obviously, TV in its infancy could not begin to compete with Hollywood dramatic presentations. In the late 1940's a single minute of finished movie film cost from $15,000 to $25,000, equal to what TV would spend on an entire hour of drama. The movie studios, as might have been predicted, at first refused to take television seriously as a competitor. But then, quick to sense the threat television posed, the studios refused to license films for TV display. Consequently, television looked to the ball parks, the boxing arenas, the college football spectacles, even to the roller derbies. By logical progression, TV found itself at the national political conventions in 1948.

The relationship was immediately symbiotic. The Republicans convened first at massive old Convention Hall, in the heat of a Philadelphia summer, and commanded a television audience of 10,000,000 persons, the largest ever for television—indeed, equal to almost half the vote Thomas E. Dewey had received in the preceding election. (The record stood a week, until the Joe Louis–Joe Walcott heavyweight fight.) In terms of live coverage, television devoted forty hours to the convention and its outrider activities—twenty minutes more than the radio networks, by the computations of one journalistic watchdog. Working in tandem with *Life*'s convention staff, NBC received wide praise for its "Room 22" show, to which reporters took every major candidate, as well as a duke's mixture of delegates, for live interviews. The chief interviewer, Frank McNaughton, spent so much time before cameras he complained of "video sunburn" because of the pancake makeup. Tom Dewey's major press conference went out live from "Room 22." In idle moments, films of past conventions were shown. But the scorching glare of television lights drove many convention veterans to cool shelter. "I began to wilt and go blind," wrote H. L. Mencken, "so the rest of my observations had to be made from a distance and through a brown beer bottle"—via a monitor the networks put in the press lounge. Still, television's debut was impressive. "An unpolished but very promising reporter," *Time* said.

The Democrats, convening a week later, had noted enough GOP gaffes to come prepared for a professional performance. The Democratic National Committee sent mimeographed warnings to speakers and state chairmen: "Millions throughout the country can see as well as hear all convention activities. . . . We must not forget that millions of curious eyes are on us at all times, as well as many more millions of ears turned to the broadcasts. Our attention to these points means votes." Stay alert while in Convention Hall, the DNC counseled; anyone who wanted to refresh himself from a bottle in a brown paper bag should find a discreet corner in the corridor. The Democrats had the foresight to bring along Hal King, of the Max Factor Company, to decorate speakers —9 N pancake for the men, 6 N for the women, applied with sponge and water. Even with such elaborate preparations, there were mishaps. A camera crew focused on two couples on the platform as an announcer identified them as two governors and their wives. A few moments later they stepped forward and sang "The Star-Spangled Banner," and the embarrassed network confirmed they in fact were a musical quartet. Even so, television gave mass America its first live glimpse of two national conventions and of political personalities. It was kinder to some than to others. *Broadcasting* magazine gave high marks to Harry Truman, to Arthur Vandenberg, the Michigan senator and would-be GOP nominee, and to Henry Wallace, the Progressive Party candidate. But Thomas E. Dewey suffered because of his moustache; Harold Stassen, because of his youth; General Douglas MacArthur, because of his baldness. (MacArthur didn't appear live; he was still in Japan, commanding occupation forces, so his "appearances" were via still photographs.) Robert A. Taft had the shakiest rating of all because of his stern physical appearance and stilted speech.

The vast audiences the conventions attracted to television meant the infant had come into its own. And each surge of the new medium drove aged and infirm radio closer to the grave. At the National Association of Broadcasters convention the next spring, Merlin Aylesworth, a former broadcast executive and NAB president, now an advertising man, predicted radio as the country then knew it would be wiped out in three years. Wayne Coy of the FCC agreed. "Make no mistake about it," he said, "television is here to stay. It is a new force unloosed in the land. I believe it is an irresistible force."

That television grew in four short postwar years into an "irresistible force" is attributable to a number of factors, not all of them an encouraging confirmation of American manners and taste. In its early days television commanded public attention as a novelty. The existence of a picture, not the content of a program, drew people to television sets, and they watched whatever appeared. Quite naturally, national advertisers took note of this audience's presence and moved to exploit the popular new medium. In doing so they followed a natural progression that had its roots early in the century, with the rise of such mass circulation magazines as the *Saturday Evening Post* and *McClure's,* which enabled a manufacturer to advertise his product nationwide. Radio, of course, followed. At the beginning of the Second World War only about one-third of network radio had commercial sponsorship; by 1945, it was up to two-thirds. But there was a significant difference between advertisers' relations with the popular magazines and the radio networks. Although advertisers certainly affected magazine editorial policy—philosophically if not directly—such *Post* editors as George Horace Lorimer and Ben Hibbs, to name two of many, chose their own editorial content and took no nonsense from the business office, which tried to push them toward or away from specific articles. Radio, on the other hand, was a different matter entirely. Advertising and production agencies packaged major programs, such as the Bob Hope comedies and the Bing Crosby musicals, and sold them directly to the networks, whose control over program content was minimal. No detail was too trivial to be beneath the attention of the ad men. Mary Jane Higby, the soap opera veteran, recollects an episode with immediate repercussions. She loaned a fur coat to her maid during an episode of "When a Girl Marries." Whereupon "corporate memos drifted down like snow" from the sponsor, Prudential Life Insurance Company. Prudential did not sell personal property insurance. Nonetheless its executives feared that if the soap opera inspired listeners to lend fur coats to their maids, and they lost them, other insurance companies would suffer, to the detriment of the entire industry. "I and my silvery tones, the company feared, would skyrocket insurance rates all over the country," mused Ms. Higby.

Unsurprisingly, the hucksters gained the same stranglehold on television. The tremendous investments required for a program left little margin for failure. Consequently, the advertisers and networks demanded programs that would attract the widest possible audiences— salable mass-cult entertainment. In a widely discussed 1946 book on the broadcast industry, Charles A. Siepmann astutely forecast that television would probably "conform rapidly to a few . . . stereotyped conventions. It will be technically ingenious and inventive but artistically poor. Except on rare occasions, and for some time to come, its true scope as a medium of expression will not be fully realized." Siepmann's prediction was of psychic accuracy. NBC signed Chesterfield cigarettes to sponsor New York Giant games; CBS countered with Old Gold for the Dodgers. NBC drew mass audiences with comic Milton Berle; CBS answered with Sid Caesar.

But advertisers were never a breed to be intimidated. Statistics bear this out. During television's pioneer days of 1946, advertising revenues were minuscule; seldom did a station gross more than $1,000 of the $3,000 cost of an hour's operating time. By 1950, however, TV ad revenues were approximately $100,000,000—four times the 1949 level, and almost one-fourth those of radio. For Madison Avenue, the trend toward television was obvious. According to a survey by Young & Rubicam, a superagency, 94 percent of advertisers opted for television when they had a choice with radio. "When these two stand up and slug it out," said Peter Langhoff, Y&R's research chief, "there is little doubt who is the coming champ." Duane Jones Company, a Manhattan survey firm, found marked changes in the habits of persons once they bought television sets. Of the sample group, 92.4 percent listened to less radio than before; 80.9 percent cut their moviegoing; 58.9 percent spent less time with books, 48.5 percent less with magazines; 23.9 percent even cut back on newspaper reading. (But more than 70 percent reported an increase in visitors.)

A major problem of television was to find interesting ways to spend the flow of ad dollars. The early commercials were largely ineffective. As late as 1948 an unblinking camera would be focused on a soap bar while an announcer discussed its fragrant virtues. Disembodied hands fondled cigarette lighters or whipped up a foamy lather of Ivory Snow. Fairfax M. Cone, of prestigious Foote, Cone & Belding, blamed these early crudities on both bad habits inherited from radio and the generally shabby quality of the rest of television. The lack of substance in "so much television advertising is in accord with the lack of substance in so much television programming," Cone observed. "Television is directed at the lowest common denominator of public tastes and the excesses in advertising on the little screen are in keeping." During its first years, according to Cone, "television was little more than vaudeville brought into the country's living rooms." Originality was such a scarce quality that Lucky Strikes received wide praise for an animated ad featuring squads of marching cigarettes. Connoisseurs of disasters had their moments of joy. A refrigerator company proudly unveiled a model with a door that opened from either side. The first time the magic door was exhibited on live TV it fell off and hit the announcer's foot. He jumped up and down and yelled in pain. A Gillette razor disintegrated midway during a demonstration. A pretty woman chattered about Lipton's tea as she busily brewed a pot of Tender Leaf—the latter the sponsor, and an unhappy one.

That television would surpass radio was foreordained because the same broadcast companies controlled both media, and without exception they decided television had much more long-range potential. For radio, the "race" was particularly ironic because its profits paid for TV development costs. In the view of broadcast historian Erik Barnouw, "This meant that radio, provider of funds, had to be kept going at maximum profit and minimum expense." So high-brow shows such as NBC's "University of the Air," with no commercial sponsors, fell silent, diminishing radio's appeal to whatever intellectual supporters remained at the time it needed them most. Other similar shows were edged into fringe time periods, then dropped.

By the late 1940's, as the coaxial cable carried television across the nation, only one serious obstacle remained in its path: the price of a set. For less than $20 a family could buy a radio capable of picking up any network program with acceptable fidelity. Television prices, however, began around $300 and went about as high as a buyer's ambitions, with elaborate mahogany consoles retailing for $4,000. With median family income just over the $3,000 mark, not every family could afford to spend a tenth of its annual earnings on an unproven, nonessential appliance. The manufacturers tried hard to cut costs to bring television within range of the mass market. Ross Siragusa, president of the Admiral Corporation in Chicago, decided to get out of what he called "the furniture business," and began stamping out plastic cabinets for about one-third the cost of wooden ones. He undercut competitors by $50 (to $249.50) on a ten-inch set. Still, by mid-1948 not more than one American in ten had witnessed a television program. There were only twenty-eight stations (radio had more than 1,600), and of the 325,000 sets in the nation, half were clustered around the New York metropolitan area. It was obvious that television needed a mass merchandiser.

During the first part of the 1940's, a Los Angeles auto dealer named Earl "Mad Man" Muntz acquired a national reputation for offbeat advertising gimmicks. Freeway billboards depicted a slightly cockeyed Muntz in Napoleonic dress, with such captions as "My wife says I'm crazy because I give such good deals on cars." When the auto boom began to die down, Muntz decided to explore the profitability of television.

"I had been hanging around with Jerry Colonna [*the radio comedian*] and Gene Autry [*the cowboy movie star*], and the TV thing caught my eye. I had a pretty good background in radio when I was a kid, so anything to do with electronics excited me. In these days right after the war, because of the space shortages, if you stayed in a hotel you had to move every seventy-two hours, that was a law. If you had a permanent place you were sitting pretty. The manager at the Hotel Warwick, a nice guy named Bradbury, was happy to line one up for me because that meant he had a car to use every weekend. This began when I still ran the Kaiser-Frazer sales in the New York area.*

"Anyway, I got a permanent small suite in the Warwick, and I started playing around with television. I bought an RCA set, they delivered it, I plugged the damned thing in, and it caught on fire. I come to find out that the Warwick Hotel didn't have AC current, they had DC current, and I told Bradbury, the manager, I was going to move. I wanted to do something with this television thing, and I needed the juice.*

" 'Oh, you don't have to do that,' Bradbury said. He had a guy upstairs in what he called the old Marian Davies suite. [*Publisher William Randolph*] Hearst had bought the entire top floor for her when he was going with her, and made two apartments out of it. Later a guy had it who was a pinball-machine freak, who had spent $1,500 to have AC current brought up to the floor. Quite a place. He had a living room the size of one of my auto showrooms, and a couple of bedrooms, and more damned outlets than you could count, and a pinball machine plugged into every damned one of them. It rented for $1,000 a month, which was good money to pay for rent in those days in New York. You never seen so many pinballs, that's all this guy did, he was a nut.*

"So what I did was to buy a line model of every kind of set I could find, and get inside them to see how they worked. RCA and all the rest were carrying thirty, maybe thirty-two tubes. I started taking out tubes and changing the wiring, and seeing how I could make them work with less—what the set really needed and what was padding. I finally got the set down to eleven tubes. Everybody called it 'the gutless wonder' but it worked like a son of a bitch. We built it with eleven tubes to save* *money. Funny thing, it worked better that way. The fewer tubes you had in the set, the longer it would run without trouble because heat was the thing that was raising hell with the cathode rays.*

"I don't believe it gave as good a picture as a brand-new Admiral or a brand-new RCA, but when it was two years old it was still just as good as the day you got it.* The tube manufacturers, the people like National Video Company, the largest producer of cathode ray tubes at the time, said tubes would go maybe six times as long in a Muntz as in an RCA because we were only drawing 75 watts, instead of 200 to 250 watts.

"But what we were doing was trying to build a set as simple as possible, and as low priced as possible. We got the eleven-tube thing going, and we did our first sales in Los Angeles, where people knew me by reputation as a guy who would do them right. There was an old western-type entertainer, named Stu Hamlin, who was very popular in Los Angeles in those days. He'd get on the radio and sing songs and tell people to go buy something and they'd do it. Our big point, other than the price, was a one-knob picture control. We had vertical and horizontal controls on the back, but only one knob up front; RCA and the other fellows had knobs all over the place. We advertised, 'So simple a child can operate. Have a television in your home within an hour. Stop staring at your radio.'

"Stu Hamlin went on the air and actually burnt up our telephone, so many calls came in. They'd call and ask for a set, and we'd say, 'You want a demonstration?' 'Nah,' they'd say, 'Brother Stu says it's OK, that's good enough for me. Just bring it out.'

"When we went into New York we had this skywriting plane write 'MUNTZ TV' around town for as much as fifty times a day. We'd give a phone number, and set up a warehouse, and put our trucks on the street, with our name big and flashy on them. No door-to-door stuff, nobody does that except the Fuller Brush people. We'd set it so that people would call us and ask for a demonstration, and we'd try to give it within an hour. This was the beautiful part. We'd put the set in their house and get it adjusted with that single knob. They usually didn't need an antenna, because we sold the metropolitan areas that were close in to the transmitter. Our salesmen would say, 'You like the set, it stays right there, it's yours.' Most times, it did.

"We knocked the price down all the while. We got under the $200 barrier, then we put out a metal cabinet job we called the Pumpkin. A helluva good little set. We made a buck out of it, and we gave TV to people who wouldn't have it yet had they waited to screw around with RCA and the other companies.

* My father disagreed. When Muntz sets drifted into East Texas a few years later, he refused to accept them for repair. "Damned junk," he said of the Mad Man's gutless wonder. Not too long ago I met a lady whose father repaired TVs in the Los Angeles area in the same era. What did he think of Muntz's sets? "Damned junk," she replied.

"Were these the best years for me? Jeez, I don't know, they've all been pretty good. When you are young like that, you don't give it a thought. I had everything I wanted. If I wanted to buy something, I bought it. I'd like to go through the whole thing again knowing what I know now." (Laughs.) *

Inaugurating its new television section in its issue of May 24, 1948, *Time* predicted that "chances are that it [television] will change the American way of life more than anything since the Model T." Jack R. Poppele, president of the Television Broadcasters Association, said that television "is as expansive as the human mind can comprehend. Television holds the key to enlightenment which may unlock the door to world understanding." Children would attend classes in their own living rooms, presidential candidates would win elections from the studio, housewives would see on the screen the dresses and groceries they wanted, and shop by telephone. Television—the educational, entertainment, and commercial nirvana of the future.

In 1949, 75 percent of the Americans who owned television sets watched the weekly program of a comedian named Milton Berle, "Texaco Star Theater." Berle, aged forty, had been in the "theater" and its environs for thirty-five years. He acted as master of ceremonies of the show: a helter-skelter clown who could sing—after a fashion—dance, juggle, do card tricks, imitations, and acrobatics, ride a unicycle, and mug underwater. He changed costumes at least five times each show— Superman, Li'l Abner, Santa Claus, the Easter bunny, Father Time, Rosie O'Grady, an organ grinder, and a snaggled-tooth rube. He loved to burlesque Carmen Miranda, the explosive Latin singer. He took a horse on stage, and he persuaded the Metropolitan Opera's Lauritz Melchior to appear in blackface and Gracie Fields to sing in a bathing suit. Brash, obnoxious, Berle would do just about anything to provide a laugh, and not everyone in his profession liked him; fellow comics called Berle "The Thief of Badgags."

Berle didn't worry at scoffers, at critics who called his show warmed-over vaudeville. He cared only for the television audience in the twenty-four cities that carried "Texaco Star Theater." And close observers began to note some patterns beginning shortly before eight o'clock on Tuesday evenings, when Berle went on the air. Restaurant business dropped sharply. Some stores closed altogether. Tuesday became "dead night" at movie theaters. The other networks simply got out of the way. Three of every four Americans watching television were tuned to comedian Milton Berle—the most popular personality that television could offer to the public.

---

* I interviewed Muntz on June 23, 1973, at his used car lot in Van Nuys, a Los Angeles suburb. He also operates a chain of car-stereo stores, and says, "I'm making my third fortune."

10

Some Books, and a Man Named Kinsey

In the spring of 1948 the trade magazine Retail Bookseller *foresaw a great future for* Parris Mitchell of Kings Row, *a sequel to the best-selling novel* Kings Row: *"It has everything in it that made its predecessor sell: horror, sex, madness and depravity—all handled with dignity and restraint."*

ASKED ONCE WHY Book-of-the-Month Club membership increased by more than 300,000 during the war years (from 508,000 in 1941 to 848,000 in 1946), founder and president Harry Scherman matter-of-factly replied, "It was hard to get other things." Gasoline rationing forced people to stay at home. Shortages of consumer goods reduced the ways they could spend money. Most competent professional athletes went away to war, and their replacements, despite a certain novelty, didn't warrant many trips to the ball park. During the war the New York Giants had boasted an outfielder, named Danny Gardella, who did handstands while waiting his turn at bat, and in center field between innings; the St. Louis Browns had employed a brave but mediocre one-armed outfielder, Pete Gray. Neither survived the years after 1945. Radio indeed had its mass audience, but there were many Americans who didn't choose to squander their leisure hours on soap operas and "Amos 'n' Andy." So they bought books, a trend that continued after the war ended.

There are several barometers of public taste in books during a given period. One is the best seller charts; another the annual year-end reviews of the serious critics; and another the dusty, well-thumbed volumes a bibliophile finds two decades later at second-hand sales chartered by college alumni groups. All three indices reveal marked inconsistencies in what Americans liked to read after the war. Initially, they continued the trend of escapist fare begun during the war to get their minds off events around them: Daphne du Maurier's *The King's General,* about a centuries-ago militarist, seemed more palatable than a novel on the realities of North Africa and Normandy. During the first three months of 1946 six new novels ran up sales of more than half a million copies: du Maurier's novel sold a million copies; *David the King,* by Gladys Schmitt, 825,000; *Arch of Triumph,* by Erich Maria Remarque, 750,000; and *The Foxes of Harrow,* by Frank Yerby, and *Before the Sun Goes Down,* by Elizabeth Metzger Howard, each 600,000. And despite the many earth-shaking events of 1945–46—the first use of atomic energy, the multifold problems of peace and reconversion—the best-selling nonfiction work was *The Egg and I,* by Betty MacDonald, a light-hearted account of life on a primitive Oregon chicken farm. The MacDonalds shared the countryside with such neighbors as the Kettle clan, dominated by Ma Kettle, a mountainously fat woman in a very dirty housedress. Bob MacDonald once went down to complain about the Kettles' cattle eating his garden. "The dignity and force of his entrance were somewhat impaired by the fact that as he came abreast of the back porch he found himself face to face with Mrs. Kettle, who was comfortably seated in the doorless outhouse reading the Sears, Roebuck catalogue, and instead of hurriedly retiring in confusion, she remained where she was and took an active part in the ensuing conversation." *The Egg and I* sold 1,038,500 copies; Hollywood bought it for a movie, and television later carved out Ma Kettle for a separate comic series.

The first distinctive shift in taste was to introspection on national problems. *The Snake Pit,* by Mary Jane Ward, gave a sickening portrait of conditions in mental hospitals. The Book-of-the-Month Club offered the novel with some trepidation, but Dorothy Canfield Fisher, of the selection committee, said the feared adverse reaction never materialized. "Changes in subject and in taste move pretty rapidly—by that time, studies of abnormal mentality were well received, without too much surprise," she said. *The Lost Weekend,* by Charles Jackson, recounted the binge of a middle-class Manhattan executive, the sort of person with whom many bookbuyers could relate. Frederic Wakeman's *The Hucksters* ripped the paving stones off Madison Avenue and hurled them at the admen who worked there. (Wakeman spent a month writing the book. It sold 750,000 copies, and he computed his profit at $100,000 a week, including the movie sale. He never returned to advertising.) "The public cavorted in this Hall of Mirrors," wrote Joseph Henry Jackson, book critic of the San Francisco *Chronicle,* "and the novels that did the reflecting, especially when they showed the reader to himself in poses of a downright unpleasant nature, found enormous audiences. Americans were in a mood to be told off, and they embraced most warmly the writers who scolded hardest."

Yet another phase, as the Cold War approached, was a keener interest in serious nonfiction about current world affairs, especially the Soviet Union. According to Scherman, the Book-of-the-Month Club detected a sharp shift to nonfiction in its periodic "satisfaction" poll, which probed whether people actually read the books they purchased and what they thought of them when finished. Nine of the top ten books were nonfiction. "People were more interested in what was going on than in their private world," Scherman concluded. "I think there was a definite change as a result of the war."*

The war was one subject on which tastes changed slowly. Predictably, the first years brought a plethora of memoirs and I-was-there stories, in substance little removed from the everything's-rosy wartime potboilers intended to pump up civilian and soldier morale. Two best sellers mark the parameters of what Americans were willing to read (or write) about the war, and when. *Mr. Roberts,* by Thomas Heggen, published by Houghton Mifflin in 1946, was a jolly story about the experiences of a junior officer on the USS *Reluctant,* a cargo ship whose regular run was "from tedium to apathy and back." Boredom and cranky senior officers, not Japanese bullets, were the main danger. Two years later came Norman Mailer's *The Naked and the Dead,* a war novel of another genre entirely.

Mailer in a 1948 photograph, taken for the dust jacket. Tweed suit, dark tie, white shirt, several rows of tight black curls parallel to his forehead, canted slightly upward right; cigarette in right hand. Stiff. "The greatest writer to come out of his generation," Sinclair Lewis says in a cover blurb. Mailer, twenty-five, looks slightly scared. But not surprised. "I may as well confess," he confessed many years later, "that by December eighth or ninth of 1941, in the forty-eight hours after Pearl Harbor, while worthy young men were wondering where they could be of aid to the war effort, and practical young men were deciding which branch of service was the surest of landing a safe commission, I was worrying darkly whether it would be more likely that a great war novel would be written about Europe or the Pacific, and the longer I thought, the less doubt there was in my mind. Europe was the place."

Army personnel minions did not give due consideration to Mr. Mailer's literary planning once he had finished Harvard. They sent him to the Pacific, where his experiences paralleled, more or less, what he

---

* The copyright date says John Gunther's best-selling *Inside U.S.A.* was published in 1947, which is a surprise, for it means I first comprehended a land outside of Texas at age thirteen, when I read my father's copy in new condition. How America has grown. A contemporary in Washington journalism, Neal R. Peirce, is now walking Gunther's footsteps, trying to put America between hard covers. He is on his fourth volume, and half a continent remains. Gunther capsulized a nation in 920 pages plus 59 pages of notes and indices. In his informal fashion he stands as a twentieth-century de Tocqueville.

was to describe in his book. Discharged in 1946, he moved to Paris with his wife and their war savings, and "lived like a mole writing and rewriting seven hundred pages in . . . fifteen months," at the rate of twenty-five draft pages a week.

The Naked and the Dead was built on an army platoon on an arduous and dangerous combat patrol across a Pacific island, a novel that told of gut wounds and diarrhea, of grime and sweat and of savagery, by American and Japanese alike. Mailer was not the man to tell land versions of funny wardroom stories about college-boy-turned-bumbling-officer. He described the climax of the exhausted soldiers' mission:

> Every minute or two someone would stop and lie huddled on the rocks, weeping with the rapt taut sobs of fatigue that sound so much like grief. In empathy a swirl of vertigo would pass from one to the other and they would listen with a morbid absorption to the racking sounds of dry nausea. One or another of them was always retching. When they moved they were always falling. The climb up the rocks slippery with mud and vegetation, the vicious thorns of bamboo thicket, the blundering of their feet against the jungle vines, all blended into one vast torment. The men groaned and cursed, stumbled on their faces, reeled and skidded from rock to rock.

There was more. The U.S. soldiers killed Japanese prisoners. ("The platoon leader looked at his watch . . . and sighed, 'We're going to have to dump them. . . .' The sullen Jap seemed to know what he meant, for he stepped off the trail and waited with his back turned. The shot caught him behind the ear. Another soldier came up behind the prisoner with the swollen genitals and gave him a shove which sprawled him on the ground. He gave a single scream of pain before he was killed.") The U.S. soldiers didn't trust their women at home, and they used naughty words such as "fugging" (a Mailer concession to contemporary literary mores) in talking about them. ("Listen, they're no different from you and me, especially the ones that've had their screwing. They like it just as much as men do, and it's a helluva sight easier for them to get it. . . . What do you think your girl friend is doing now? I'll tell you what. It's just about six A.M. now in America. She's wakin' up in bed with a guy who can give her just as much as you can, and she's giving him the same goddam line she handed you.") The U.S. soldiers detested fellow citizens who had escaped the military. ("All I know is there's a fuggin' score to be paid off, a score to be paid off. There's somebody gonna pay, knock the fuggin' civilians' heads in.")

Critics and readers couldn't decide exactly what to make of this young man and his graphic realism, the cynicism with which his soldiers went about their killing, the libido-quickening sexuality of flashback remembrances. John Chamberlain called it "disillusion with a vengeance." He continued: "The really disillusioning element in the novel is the author's implied conclusion that even our military successes in World War II were the result of certain horrifying traits of character"— a gunman's delight in murder, sexual maladjustment, hatred of a father, coldness toward humanity in general. Did men remain in battle solely for fear of officers? Did a pathological quest for domination, rather than a crusade to win a better world, motivate military leaders? Mailer asked these questions, and strongly implied both answers were Yes, and in so doing he made previous books about the war appear to be so much sentimental tosh. Many people howled, and the professional veterans reviled Mailer as a son of a bitch, or worse, for revealing the unspoken secrets of the barracks and the battlefield to the mothers of America. What Mailer wrote about the people who fight wars was certainly no secret to anyone with exposure to the military: armies are composed of bystanders and the brave, of cowards and sadists. Further, men kill in battle, and not always nicely, and with diverse motivation. Yet does a victorious nation care to be reminded of the dark shadows of its own triumph? The major complaint with Mailer was not that he told untruth, but that he told at all. Nonetheless people bought the book. Its first year on the market *The Naked and the Dead* sold 137,185 copies in the bookstores and another 60,000 through book clubs.*

Mailer had left Harvard in 1943 with a degree in aeronautical engineering. He never used it. America had its first major postwar literary figure. "The only war novel of any distinction to appear hitherto," George Orwell said a few months after publication of *The Naked and the Dead*.

Although the subject is one on which the serious critics are silent, the best-read snatch of literature circulating among East Texas teen-agers circa 1947 was two pages ripped from Erskine Caldwell's 1930's novel of the white-trash South, God's Little Acre. *The book was a savagely low-key commentary on the hypocrisy of fundamentalist Protestantism. The central figure, a quasi-literate farmer, pledged the annual proceeds from one acre of his farm "to the service of God." But the fellow craftily hedged his promise. He had a vision of finding gold on the property, and he insured that whatever acre he happened to be digging was not designated for the Divinity. The portion that produced the poorest yield each year was set aside,* ex post facto, *as "God's little acre." Caldwell's theme alone was enough to cause a furor, for one does*

---

* As an indication of Americans' bifurcated literary tastes, and of the dangers of trying to "prove" trends through best-seller lists and critics' choices, the year's top seller was Lloyd C. Douglas' biblical novel *The Big Fisherman*, with 366,693 copies. Many Mailer-haters invoked the name of Douglas' central character in denouncing *The Naked and the Dead*.

not safely jest about Jesus in the Bible belt. Even worse was the "sala-cious" paragraph beginning at the bottom of a page and continuing over to the top of the next. A farm hand reached the penultimate stage of se-duction with a precocious girl, and paused to reconnoiter his next objec-tive. Low on her belly, between her legs, "it looked like somebody had stuck their finger in a balloon, and the place had stayed there."

Caldwell's snippet of anatomical description carried the special cachet of credibility, at least as perceived in our circles. The first time I saw the two pages they came from a hidden pocket in the wallet of David "Fat" Ford, my closest friend and himself the son of a lay minister in the Church of Christ (and a respected butane dealer in the secular world). Within a week I had procured my own two pages—purloined from Uncle Carl's copy—and put them into circulation on a samizdat *circuit rivaling in efficiency (and secrecy) that now maintained by the Soviet literary underground. Confiscations were rare. I confess to no lasting psychic damage from Caldwell's lines, and so far as I know none of the readers is now confined in either the Texas state penitentiary at Hunts-ville or a lunatic asylum. Curious minds found interesting fare, and read it, and went on to other matters.**

Which is a round-about means of moving to yet another feature of postwar publishing. Mass America tolerated frank discussions of alco-holism and mental hospitals, but demanded a retreat to euphemisms, both of language and of scenes, when a writer turned to sex. A pseudo-historical novel such as *Forever Amber* (1,750,000 copies) required a randy frame of mind for maximum enjoyment; under strict rules of evidence, no reader was certain what really happened to the heroine, although innuendo and suspicious circumstance abounded.

In 1946 Edmund Wilson, who was then the book critic of *The New Yorker,* stood in the front ranks of English-speaking criticism, an intel-lect whose interest in literature was notable for its gusto, open-minded-ness, and curiosity. Although Wilson had spent a vigorous quarter cen-tury commenting upon the works of other men he had himself produced only one mediocre novel, *I Thought of Daisy,* published in 1929. Thus the publication of his new work, *Memoirs of Hecate County,* a synthesis of six longish "short stories," was hailed as a major literary event. Even Wilson's friends put him on notice that *Memoirs* would receive close scrutiny. The *Saturday Review of Literature* stated:

> When the man who was the sharpest and most readable literary
> critic of our time produces a long work of fiction he is laying

* In fact, in rereading the book I find that another even more torrid sequence, involving cunnilingus, sailed right over my twelve-year-old head. Elder censors were more discerning. Although *Acre* won its first court battle in New York in the 1930's ("The court may not require the author to put refined language in the mouths of primitive people," a trial judge said), it was being banned elsewhere as late as 1947.

himself open to attack. He who has assaulted so many fly-blown reputations and flattened so many writers who were hailed as budding geniuses may expect to find himself in a direful position of the armed knight of old who was pushed off his horse and lay helpless on his back where the common soldier might have a go at him.

Alas for Wilson, the bulk of the public debate over *Memoirs* concerned not its literary merits but whether it was pornographic. The longest of the six stories, "The Princess with the Golden Hair," contained a number of sexual episodes, some lyrical, some explicit, some both. The central character, a genteel Communist (he spread his *Daily Worker* on a damp park bench so a girl friend could sit in comfort), had simultaneous affairs going with an Irish working girl and an aristocratic neighbor. The passage that most aroused the bluenoses concerned the latter's visit to his apartment one sultry summer afternoon, obviously ready for their first act of intercourse. In an enraptured description of the woman's body Wilson deposed as follows:

. . . [W]hat struck and astonished me most was that not only were her thighs perfect columns but all that lay between them was impressively beautiful, too, with an ideal aesthetic value that I had never found there before. The mount was of a classical femininity; round and smooth and plump; the fleece, if not quite golden, was blond and curly and soft; and the portals were a deep tender rose, like the petals of some fleshly flower. And they were doing their feminine work of making things easy for the entrant with a honey-sweet sleek profusion that showed I had quite misjudged her in suspecting as I had sometimes done that she was really unresponsive to caresses. She became, in fact, so smooth and open that after a moment I could hardly feel her. Her little bud was so deeply embedded that it was hardly involved in the play.

Reviewers either loved *Memoirs* or hated it. Ralph Bates, in the *New York Times,* called it "a good, a distinguished book." *Time* thought it "pretty certainly the best contemporary chronicle, so far, of its place and period." But the Catholic publication *Commonweal* wrote off *Memoirs* as a "pathological joke—a string of satiric stories, which, in their aimless offensive vulgarity . . . defied description." *Memoirs* sold 50,000 copies within a month and hit the *New York Times Book Review* best-seller list in mid-July 1946. The success brought out the censors in full bay, led by the Hearst newspapers, which denounced *Memoirs* as "printed filth," and by the New York *Daily News,* which professed to see nothing of literary merit in the volume. *"Memoirs* is [Wilson's] first score on the best-seller list," the *News* said, "and the only reason it was there for several weeks is because word got around that oh, boy, you ought to get a load of this. The book is tough reading.

Everybody keeps talking all the time* and not about anything that seems to matter much except in certain circles of well-to-do suburbia."

Memoirs broke even in obscenity tests in California—a Los Angeles jury banned it as obscene, a San Francisco panel could not agree—but the censors saved their major effort for New York, hoping to cut off the book in the nation's most lucrative literary market. The New York Society for the Suppression of Vice, Anthony Comstock's old vigilante group, obtained an obscenity indictment against Doubleday & Company, the publisher. A three-judge panel ruled two-to-one the book indeed was obscene, fined Doubleday $1,000, and forbade further publication or sales. The U.S. Supreme Court, which ultimately reviewed the case, hung four-four, thus allowing the New York decision to remain in effect.

The furor over *Memoirs* is subject to several interpretations—each of them, in fact, voiced at the time. America's core Puritanism remained unshaken by the war, and any writings about sexual conduct would remain couched in euphemisms or wrapped in plain covers. Even the editors at *Time* felt constrained to complain that although Truman Capote's *Other Voices, Other Rooms,* published in 1948, revealed "gifted invention and imagery . . . the distasteful trappings of its homosexual theme overhang it like Spanish moss." The ban on Wilson's *Memoirs* was a dying-breath gasp of the Society for the Suppression of Vice, successful only because of the power of the Hearst newspapers. Mailer's *The Naked and the Dead,* published two years later, attracted ten times the readership of *Memoirs* (and boasted ten times the sexual directness as well); yet *Naked* encountered minimal censorship problems. Wilson got into trouble because he was a serious writer of established reputation who wrote serious books; America could tolerate a Kathleen Windsor, because housewives could read *Forever Amber* under the hair dryer with a feeling of naughtiness but not guilt, but permitting established authors free rein would turn the nation into Gomorrah. Or so it was said.

That the public worried about sex being discussed explicitly, even in books, was indicative of a peculiar ambiguity that permeated American life. Seldom has such a gulf separated public myth and private reality—a nation professing obedience to ageless moral and biblical credos, yet all the while pursuing *verboten* sexual pleasures, furtively and guiltily. For centuries the accepted societal dogma was that sexuality remained dormant until a person fell in love and married. Any sexual activity prior to (or outside of) marriage was sinful, and perhaps illegal as well. Theologians insisted on these strictures, society approved them, the courts enforced them—and people ignored them.

The conflict was shoved out of the shadows in 1948 by a book that

* Not exactly accurate; in truth, *Memoirs* is notable for a lack of dialogue.

was a publishing and cultural phenomenon, *Sexual Behavior in the Human Male,* by Dr. Alfred C. Kinsey.* A zoologist at Indiana University, Kinsey spent the first years of his professional life achieving a reputation as the world's ranking authority on the wasp, collecting scores of thousands of specimens. An inquisitive observer, Kinsey became fascinated with disparate sexual mores he witnessed on field trips to Latin America (of the Guatemalans, for instance, who insisted that visitors to their villages wear long-sleeved shirts on the grounds of decency, but who happily splashed around naked, men and women together, when bathing in a river). In 1938 Indiana University asked Kinsey to coordinate a marriage course, and he found there was so little data about human sexual activity that he could offer only guesses to his students. So Kinsey set about gathering his own case histories, eventually compiling them on 5,300 white males. He asked about the incidence and frequency of orgasms through six sexual outlets: masturbation; nocturnal emissions; heterosexual petting; intercourse (premarital, marital, extramarital, postmarital, and with prostitutes); homosexual encounters; and animal contacts. The analysis was in terms of race, marital status, age, educational level, occupational class, familial and religious background, and place of residence. Kinsey's conclusions, after almost a decade of work, dashed about every prevailing conception of the seldom-mentioned subject of sex:

—Sexual activity begins at an early age. Kinsey found 22 percent of preadolescents attempted intercourse between age ten and the onset of puberty. Among males who went to college, 67 percent had coital experience before marriage; for those who went to high school but not beyond, 84 percent experienced premarital intercourse. In the "lower social levels," Kinsey wrote, it "appears to be impossible to find a single male who has not had experience by the time he had reached his middle teens." The greatest sex drive seemed to come between ages sixteen and twenty. But the statistical difference between classes was not great. "The general impression . . . that the middle class is the one which most rigorously upholds the social traditions is obviously based on the expressed opinions of this group, rather than upon the record of its actual behavior," Kinsey observed wryly, noting that "there is no sort of sexual behavior which has been more often condemned than premarital intercourse."

—About half of all men have extramarital intercourse at some time in their lives. Kinsey found men with the least education the most active in their earlier years, but they tended to decrease extramarital activities as they grew older. College men, while late starters, increased their frequency steadily; even at age fifty, 27 percent of college males were

* Although Kinsey shared credit for authorship with two research associates, Wardell B. Pomeroy and Clyde E. Martin, he bore responsibility for it.

having extramarital affairs. (Oddly, American wives told the Gallup poll in 1946 that philandering was not their chief worry. "Drinking with the boys" was the chief complaint women expressed; "other women" ranked a distant fifth, after "failure to bring home candy," "tendency to domineer," and "problems over money.")

—Sixty-nine percent of all college graduates continued masturbation after marriage, although the frequency decreased from 2.7 times weekly to "about once in two weeks in early marriage, dropping a bit in the later years." Kinsey found no evidence "that the boy who begins masturbation at an early age suffers any more harm than the boy who delays the beginning of his experience until some time in adolescence or later." The only adverse effects, psychological ones, came from parents who "upset the child's peace of mind" by reprimand, humiliation, or unwarranted warnings. Indeed, Kinsey included among his case histories that of a track star who said he broke a national record within an hour after masturbating.

—Thirty-seven percent of the total male population "has at least some overt homosexual experience to the point of orgasm between adolescence and old age. This accounts for nearly two males of every five that one may meet." Thirty percent had "at least one incidental homosexual experience" between the ages of sixteen and fifty-five.

—Men who began sexual activity at an early age tended to maintain a higher incidence for thirty-five to forty years, and exercising one's sexual capacities did not seem to impair them. These early-adolescent males were often more "alert, energetic, vivacious, spontaneous, physically active, socially extroverted, and/or aggressive individuals." Late starters tended to be "slow, quiet, mild in manner, without force, reserved, timid, taciturn, introvert, and/or socially inept."

—"Petting"* to one degree or another was almost universal among males, with only slight variations between the college group (92 percent) and those who did not go beyond grade school (84 percent). Kinsey found that more people were petting than in the preceding generation, at earlier ages, and frequently to climax. Many, he discovered, substituted petting for intercourse, satisfying their consciences with what he called "curious rationalizations":

> The fact that petting involves erotic contacts which are as effective as genital union, and that it may even involve contacts which have been more taboo than genital union, including some that have been considered perversions, does not disturb the youth so much as actual intercourse would. By petting, they preserve their virginities, even though they may achieve orgasm while doing so. They still

* Kinsey's definition of "petting" went through gradations from body contact and kissing to oral-genital stimulation.

value virginity, much as the previous generations valued it. Only the list of most other activities has had new values placed on it.

—No definite "American pattern" of sexual behavior could be isolated, for in some instances practices and frequencies varied widely between socioeconomic groups. The largest difference concerned the origins of moral taboos: upper-level people rationalized their behavior on the basis of right and wrong, the lower social levels on what was "natural and unnatural."

—Although intercourse was the most prevalent sexual activity, a surprisingly large number of males found outlets elsewhere. At age fifty-five, for instance, college males "derive only 62 percent of their total outlet from marital intercourse, and . . . 19 percent of the outlet at that age is derived from the dream world which accompanies masturbation or nocturnal emissions."

Aware in advance the book would create a furor, Kinsey attempted to make its release as dignified as possible. On the advice of the Indiana University president (who also pleaded that the report not be published while the Indiana legislature was in annual session), Kinsey arranged to have the book published under the dignified imprimatur of W. B. Saunders Company, an old and respected Philadelphia medical publisher.

Helen Dietz had edited books at Saunders for five years, and the Kinsey volume was her first major assignment, although initially she did not consider it anything out of the ordinary.

"It must be naïve at this point, but we had books here every day that talked about sex and showed explicit pictures, and it never occurred to us that this would be any different. In fact, I found it very dull reading, and even when I was editing it I had no idea it would be a popular best seller. Nor did Mr. [Lawrence] Saunders, our president. It simply never occurred to us that this could be a popular best seller. We did not have the alliances with the popular book stores. We sold to and through the medical profession, and we only gave dealers a twenty percent discount, rather than the forty percent that is normal for commercial trade publishers.

"As an editor, I found Dr. Kinsey to be a good author, but a very stubborn one. Every word and every comma was important to him, and he read his manuscript aloud to himself to insure that it 'sounded' right. He was meticulous; when he realized you had to draw lines down the page to indicate tables should be indicated, he insisted on using a ruler; a free-hand line would not suffice.

"The response hit everybody here by surprise. Why did it take off? One reason is that Dr. Kinsey wanted it to be generally disseminated, because the more people who knew about the work, the easier it would

be for him to receive more case histories. Dr. Kinsey was well known in the scientific community, so he began with a good amount of professional respect.

"When we realized it wasn't going to be 'just another book' we brought in our lawyers for a talk with Dr. Kinsey, so as to be prepared if any legal actions occurred. That proved not to be a problem. But many people here at Saunders were somewhat concerned that we would spoil our image. We had always been rather terribly scientific, and some of our more conservative medical authors objected to the publicity. We knew this wasn't going to be our bread and butter the rest of our lives; we had to think of our whole reputation.

*"To me, the revolution was to have sex discussed in this dispassionate way. Medical men are very conservative in this field. They always have been. But, again, when the manuscript first came into the office we considered it another medical text."**

The office qualms notwithstanding, Saunders was astute enough to direct a first press run of 10,000 copies, rather than the 2,000 to 3,000 standard for medical texts. Saunders' advertising was minimal, but no matter. Working from advance copies, newspapers and magazines seized upon Kinsey's raw data—especially the high incidence of extramarital sex—and billed the book as a sensational exposé of sexual mores. The general tone, despite Kinsey's efforts to ensure that any publicity was accurate, depicted America as a vast sexual playpen; that people should feel free to try any activity they wished, because their neighbors were already doing it. As the prerelease publicity swelled, Saunders crossed its fingers and increased the first-print order to 25,000 copies. "The general feeling around the office," said a Saunders executive, "was that we were getting involved in a very sensational matter. We had ambivalent feelings. We wanted the sales, but we also had our reputation to consider." A Saunders book carried a certain prestige, and some people there felt "it was most undignified to be associated with a 'popular' best seller."

Which is what the Kinsey Report promptly became. The formal publication date was January 5, 1948. By the first week of March, 200,000 copies had been sold, and Saunders had two printing companies working around the clock to meet the demand. The book itself weighed three pounds and contained 804 pages of pedantic text and tables; the reviewer who called it a "dreary morass of technical jargon and statistical charts" knew whereof he wrote. But for anyone who poked through the

---

* Nonetheless the book carried a rare "Publisher's Foreword" that concluded: "This book is intended primarily for workers in the fields of medicine, biology, psychology, sociology, anthropology, and allied sciences, and for teachers, social workers, personnel officers, law enforcement groups, and others concerned with the direction of human behavior." The last cited group presumably accounted for the bulk of the sales.

material, the content matched the sensational billing: what Kinsey had accomplished, quite simply, was to tell American men about their collective sexuality: that each man's fantasies, even his activities, were shared by a plurality of his neighbors.

The immediate response was what can be expected when a forbidden subject is mentioned in public: snickers. A radio comedian knew he could mention the Kinsey Report with the assurance of hearty guffaws ("He's at the awkward age—you know, too old for the *Bobbsey Twins,* and too young for the Kinsey Report."). According to the omnipresent observers of *Time,* copies were supplied in cabanas at resort hotels in Miami Beach; a Kansas City grain dealer gave his mistress a copy coyly inscribed, "I hope this will help you to understand me better"; a playboy supposedly sent copies to fifty girl friends. A cartoon in the *New York Times Book Review* depicted a suburban matron sedately reading a copy tucked inside a magazine called *The Home Gardener.* Librarians reported the volume was popular with thieves. At Harvard, students sang:

> I've looked you up in the Kinsey Report
> And you're just the man for me.

Although five of six Americans told the Gallup poll they thought it was a "good thing" (rather than a bad one) to have the Kinsey data available, theologians, scientists, and sociologists roundly denounced the report, and on several grounds. Geoffrey Gorer, a noted British anthropologist, declared that Kinsey's sample group was so small and ill-chosen that it did not portray the entire U.S. male populace, that in fact it was representative only of white male college graduates in six northeastern and Midwestern states* where the bulk of the interviews were conducted. Kinsey admitted to having only skimpy data from men over fifty, very young children, rural residents, factory workers, blacks, and members of certain religious groups. Sociologists questioned whether boasting and memory lags tarnished the reliability of subjects, to which Kinsey replied he felt he received straight stories by "looking an individual squarely in the eye and firing questions at him at maximum speed." The Kinsey interviews, furthermore, began with the assumption "that everyone has engaged in every type of activity." Thus interviewers asked subjects *when,* not *whether,* they first did certain things. "This places a heavier burden on the individual who is inclined to deny his experience," Kinsey wrote. To critics of the statistical reliability of his data base, Kinsey expressed hopes of compiling 100,000 case histories, thereby sampling a broader cross-section of Americans. (To his disappointment, Kinsey failed; when he died in 1956, at age sixty-two, he had only 18,000 histories.)

* Indiana, Illinois, Ohio, Pennsylvania, New York, and New Jersey.

The list of dissenters was impressive. Dorothy Thompson, in her heyday as an outspoken liberal columnist, conceded that the Kinsey Report "may be corrective of attitudes having no relationship to reality." But she felt it also "holds the danger of being used to justify unbridled license. If this interpretation is drawn from a report so dubiously representative, its results may do more evil than good." Margaret Mead, the cultural anthropologist, argued that societies needed social strictures as a stabilizing influence, even if their chief purpose was "apparently to reward men for staying home at night, which doesn't seem to be biologically necessary." Dr. Mead feared that Kinsey's findings "may increase the number of young men who may indulge in 'outlets' with a sense of hygienic self-righteousness." The Reverend Harold Gardiner, the editor of *America,* a Jesuit periodical, took a similar view. He did not think that the high incidence of sexual activity warranted any changes in laws or community attitudes. If a study showed that 99 percent of American boys stole, the country would not demand revision of the laws against larceny; changing sex laws as a result of Kinsey's findings would be equally senseless. "Indiscriminate knowledge improperly acquired and applied is an incentive to a lack of virtue," Father Gardiner wrote. He wanted the book sold only to the clergy, doctors, police, penal authorities, judges, and social workers, and not to the lay public. Two University of Pennsylvania sociologists, Dr. A. H. Hobbs and Dr. R. D. Lambert, felt the fact that the "actualities of sexual behavior . . . fall somewhat short of the ideals . . . does not necessarily lead to the conclusion that the ideals are wrong, nor that they should be abandoned."

But it was exactly on the issue of whether ignored ideals should be discarded that the serious post-Kinsey debate centered. What are the bounds of the law's effectiveness in curbing the more stubborn impulses of human nature? Dr. G. M. Gilbert, a professor of psychology at Princeton University, in a widely discussed essay, maintained that people should no longer delude themselves about male sexual morality: that Kinsey simply confirmed what he and other professionals had long known (or suspected) about sexual laxity. Without proper sex education, the problem would only be perpetuated; parents having failed, Gilbert urged that schools take up the task of teaching youngsters about the facts of life. Gilbert was particularly concerned about sexual needs of college students. For persons who complete their education at age seventeen or eighteen, sexual needs could be met through marriage.* But the college group must cope with the unnatural lag between adolescence and married adulthood that is apt "to be prolonged until strong emotional

---

* According to Kinsey, at age twenty-one only 49 percent of men with some college education have indulged in premarital intercourse, while 84 percent of the grammar-school group and 77 percent of the high-school group have done so.

conflicts or tawdry promiscuity are almost inevitable." The situation carried serious implications for the entire nation, Gilbert argued:

> Because of the socio-economic standards set for family life at the upper social and educational levels, the delay is apt to be prolonged far beyond the additional four years of college. The bulk of the nation's leadership in all fields today comes from the rank of the college population, but society seems to demand prolonged sexual frustrations as the price of training for such leadership.

Professor Gilbert urged that college students be "permitted, even encouraged, to marry without discontinuing their studies." He found no reason to believe that "petting to climax" and other substitutes for intercourse were preferable to early marriage. And another professor, Dr. Robert M. MacIver, a sociologist at Columbia University, argued against continuation of laws and moral strictures based upon ignorance or distortion of the evidence about the effects of sexual activity. He wrote, "Those who would 'clean up' society, sexually, in effect are suggesting that 95 percent of us be put in penal institutions to be watched over, neutralized, or reformed by a hypothetically pure 5 percent."

Stung by the criticisms, acutely sensitive to persons who attacked him as a charlatan or sensationalist, Kinsey remained generally aloof from the debate, content to confine his role to a continuing compilation of data. As the 1940's ended, he was well along on work on his second volume, *Sexual Behavior in the Human Female,* published in 1953. But his findings brought to Americans the first stirrings of what was to become the sexual revolution, a concept the public could talk about after his book, even if not accept.

The lively discussion about the Kinsey Report aside, did the American public really care about serious writing in the postwar period? In 1949 the nation brooded over the Berlin airlift, the Soviet acquisition of the atomic bomb, the fear of a "shadow government" of Communists and sympathizers in Washington. In this year of fear and trembling, the nonfiction best-seller list, based upon trade sales in stores, went as follows:

> *White Collar Zoo,* by Clare Barnes, Jr., a series of animal photos humorously captioned to relate them to familiar office characters and situations.
> *How to Win at Canasta,* by Oswald Jacoby, capitalizing on the current card craze.
> *The Seven Storey Mountain,* by Thomas Merton, an autobiography of the Trappist monk.
> *Home Sweet Zoo,* by Barnes, the photo book idea transported to the household.

Cheaper by the Dozen, by Frank B. Gilbreth, Jr., and Ernestine Gilbreth Carey, on how an efficiency expert raised a family of twelve children, and made the experience sound more fun than common sense would suggest.

The Greatest Story Ever Told, by Fulton Oursler.

Canasta, the Argentine Rummy Game, by Ottilie H. Reilly and Alexander Rosa. Yet another card book.

Canasta, by Josefina Aratayeta de Viel. And another.

Peace of Soul, by Fulton J. Sheen.

A Guide to Confident Living, by Norman Vincent Peale.

In sum, America's interest in these, the best years, was distinctly escapist: four religious books, three books on a card-game fad, three books of humor. Events beyond the individual American's control were gradually tugging him toward a share of a collective responsibility for the rest of the world. But he did not care to read about what this new obligation would require of him.

The Movies Flicker Out

During the filming of The Outlaw, *a not-so-true-to-history story about Billy the Kid, the script called for the leading lady, Jane Russell, to submit to Indian torture. She was tied by her wrists between two trees, bound by leather thongs soaked in water. As the thongs dried and threatened to tear the hapless lady apart, her chest was thrust into even greater prominence than an abundant nature had provided.*

Still, the contours did not satisfy producer Howard Hughes. His concern was understandable, for the industry consensus was that Miss Russell's body overshadowed her acting ability. So time and again he, Miss Russell, and the wardrobe mistress vanished into the dressing room where he applied his engineer's skill to the lady's brassiere. The production crew watched the up-and-down progress of the Russell breasts with professional fascination. "They're a little higher this time," a cameraman said. "No, it's not that," replied someone else. "I think they're a little lower, actually; it's just you see more of them." Hours passed before Hughes grunted approval: regardless of how Miss Russell twisted between the trees, the brassiere rather pointedly fixed everyone's attention on what Hughes had in mind.

Months later the marquee on Radio City Music Hall broadcast enticing slogans that attracted turn-away crowds:

THE MUSIC HALL GETS THE BIG ONES!
WHAT ARE THE TWO GREAT REASONS FOR JANE
RUSSELL'S RISE TO STARDOM?

When the movie industry's censorship board accused Hughes of "violating standards of decency," he blandly replied, "How? Do you fellows have dirty minds?" He escalated. Another ballyhoo line in advertisements asked, "How would you like to tussle with Russell?" In St. Louis Outlaw *drew the largest crowds in history. In South Texas, the bishop of the Catholic Archdiocese of Galveston called for a year-long boycott of theaters that displayed Miss Russell's charms. Church protests caused cancellations of* Outlaw *showings in St. Paul and Minneapolis. Still the crowds came. "The censors may not like it," Hughes chortled in a two-page ad in* Time, *"but the public does." What the public "liked" especially was a scene where Ms. Russell decided the only way "to keep Billy warm," as he lay wounded and unconscious, was to peel off her clothes and snuggle under the covers with him. According to the teen-ager underground, the "uncut" version actually "showed them doing it." Although women's liberation remained a generation distant, many females took exception to a scene in which Billy and Doc Holliday gamble and cannot decide whether the winner should take Ms. Russell or a horse. The higher value ultimately was placed on the horse—a necessity in the West, whereas a woman was simply an expendable luxury.*

Goaded by ministers, authorities in San Francisco went to court to try to have Outlaw *banned as obscene. During the days preceding the trial, attendance shattered all records. Twelve jurors saw the movie and voted that it was not obscene. Judge Twain Michelsen agreed. He saw no signs that the movie left the jury "in a state of moral suspense, or of mental lewdness . . . bewitched or seduced." He continued:*

> *We have seen Jane Russell. She is an attractive specimen of American womanhood. God made her what she is. There are some fanatical persons who object to Miss Russell in a low-necked blouse. The scene is in the desert—hardly a place for woolens or furs. Life is sordid and obscene to those who find it so.*

THE OUTLAW is not afforded a place in history as a great film, and aside from anecdotal interest is mentioned at length only because so very little of substance happened in the movie industry during its declining years. The peace years almost killed Hollywood. The movies began the period in seemingly robust health, with a ready-built market of patrons apparently ready to pay a dollar to view almost anything projected on a screen. Crowded housing conditions encouraged people to get outside their homes for diversion, and millions of veterans had acquired the movie habit via constant exposure at USO shows and canteens. Movie box offices clicked out an average 95 million tickets a week during 1946, 10 million more than the best prewar year; industry profits doubled the first year after peace.

The boom didn't last. After those first golden months, the movies fell into a cost-quality squeeze which made the stock lavish musical too expensive to support. Restrictive taxes by foreign governments, notably the British, effectively sealed off a market that had given Hollywood about one-third its total profits. A Red scare over alleged Communist influence in film making threw the entire industry into the shaking jitters; in response Hollywood virtually destroyed itself while trying to "save" itself.* Then, of course, the new bugaboo, television, caught the eye of the mob known as the American entertainment public and suddenly the movie houses stood empty on Saturday nights. In the words of veteran Hollywood agent H. M. Swanson, "You can't dictate to a man what his recreation is going to be. You can entice him, but you can't force him to relax." And of the two media, television definitely was the more enticing. By 1950, a scant four years after its record profit-attendance records, Hollywood carried the mark of *facies Hippocratica,* the term a doctor uses to describe the facial appearance of someone who is about to die.

As a popular art form, movies inevitably attempt to reflect contemporary events and public moods. The record suggests that Hollywood consistently guessed wrong in the late 1940's. Initially, Hollywood "knew" —as did everyone else in the nation—what Americans would be wanting after the war. The veteran needed advice on how to readjust to civilian life. The civilian wanted reassurance that the veteran was the same human as everyone, his battle traumas notwithstanding. So Hollywood offered *Pride of the Marines,* starring John Garfield, dealing with a blinded veteran's problems; *Tomorrow Is Forever,* in which Orson Welles played a man so deformed by war wounds that he let his wife believe him dead (inexplicably, Welles's character was from the First World War, not the Second World War); *Lonely Journey,* about an amnesiac veteran, exploiting a theme dear to radio soap operas; and *That Man Malone,* featuring John Wayne as an itinerant blacksmith who returned home to find his wife had become a political power. And, of course, there was *The Best Years of Our Lives,* about double-amputee Homer Parris and two other troubled veterans.

But with the exception of *The Best Years of Our Lives,* these films were destined to fail at the box office. Movies about the war fared little better. Early in 1945 John Ford began work on a film version of W. L. White's *They Were Expendable,* the fictionalized story of a flotilla of PT boats that harassed Japanese battleships in the Philippines, delaying the invasions and permitting General Douglas MacArthur to escape with a small army. Ford intended to release the film on December 7, 1945, anniversary of the Pearl Harbor attack. By that time, of course, the war was long over, and despite gripping battle scenes with documentary realism and a stirring story (the opinions of critics), the public greeted the film coolly. Bosley Crowther of the *New York Times,* most impressed with *They Were Expendable*'s artistic merits, concluded, "If this film had been released last year—or the year before—it would have

* See Chapter 18, "The Mood Turns Sour."

been a ringing smash. . . . Now with the war concluded and the burning thirst for vengeance somewhat cooled, it comes as a cinematic postscript to the martial heat and passion of the last four years." Hollywood abandoned the war as a story source: in the words of a leading director of the era, King Vidor, "I certainly didn't want to make war movies. You got fed up with it, having read about it every day in the papers for years. You guess the public has had it, too. I've never had a formula as to what the public wants, but let me say this: if a thing is entertaining to me, I have a chance to make it entertaining to the public. In fact, the public, they don't want anything, they don't *know* what they want. They want what you can give them, in an interesting way. But the war, no. The public had had enough of it, and so had Hollywood." (Perhaps appropriately, John Wayne's next film marked the only pacifist role in his long career—*Angel and the Badman,* about a beautiful Quaker girl who converts an ornery gunslinger from shooting to loving his neighbors. It flopped and Wayne returned to what he did best.)

To Hollywood's advantage, the industry boasted dazzling technical expertise. Lavish musicals, fluffy comedies, tough melodramas with maximum action and minimum message—studios ground them out "with skill and chromium-plated production finish," in the words of critic Howard Barnes of the New York *Herald Tribune.* When it so decided, Hollywood was capable of painstaking excellence in whatever genre it chose to work. Metro-Goldwyn-Mayer spent eight years adapting *The Yearling,* the Pulitzer Prize novel by Marjorie Kinnan Rawlings, about a small boy growing up in the Florida bayou country immediately after the Civil War. *The Jolson Story,* a glamorized biography of the mammy singer; *Blue Skies,* a happy musical with Bing Crosby and Fred Astaire; and *Night and Day,* with a profusion of Cole Porter tunes, showed the industry at its commercial best. *Gentleman's Agreement,* based on the novel by Laura Z. Hobson, exposed the social and economic sores of anti-Semitism. *Pinky,* about a black woman who "passed" for white, explored a new area of racial prejudice.

Yet Hollywood was also capable of productions that blasphemed the word "entertainment": Deanna Durbin in musicals that never quite came alive. Judy Canova making her pigtails stand on end in spook movies. Donald O'Connor mugging and grimacing in hayseed comedies. Jon Hall, Sabu, and Turhan Bey in exotic desert adventures inconceivable even by the undemanding standards of a bored teen-ager. The overworked *Road* series of Messrs. Hope and Crosby. A talking mule named Francis. In the words of Kyle Crichton, movie critic of *Collier's* magazine, "a great scurrying about for 'escape' brought [movies] . . . from which the only escape was provided by the audiences." Hollywood found itself copying even bad films when it scented the possibility of commercial success. A good example was *Duel in the Sun,* which despite some admirers was generally dismissed as a "knowing blend of oats and aphrodisiac" (the comment of the *Time* reviewer, who also said the movie proved that even if illicit love doesn't pay, "it appears to be loads of fun"). King Vidor, who directed the film for David O. Selznick, found he had problems other than anticipated bluenose bans. "Mrs. Selznick was very upset at the entire idea. David was a heavy breather when aroused, and she didn't want him to make a pornographic film and fall over dead with a heart attack." Selznick survived, and *Duel* made money—boosted along, Vidor felt, by comedians who called it "Lust in the Dust" and "Drool in the Sun," among other things.*

Hollywood's vision of American taste, its idea of what adults would pay to see at their local cinema, is best summarized in the industry's own words, in the form of a Paramount Pictures advertisement circa February 1946:

She's the Woo-Woo of the Year

The cameraman on the picture hadn't been around to collect his check for three weeks running. "Don't you want your money?" someone asked him. "What?" he said. "You mean Paramount lets me photograph Dorothy Lamour and pays me, too?"

So with that double incentive he cranked out 8,000 wonderful feet of Lamour at her luscious loveliest in the danciest, romanciest treat of the year—*Masquerade in Mexico.*

It's a lavish Pan-American paradise through which Dottie wanders in the most gorgeous gowns you've ever "ooohed" and "aaaahed" at. . . .

Masquerade in Mexico is Woo-Wow entertainment with the Woo-Woo girl of the year.

Or, again, Columbia Pictures touting *Down to Earth,* a 1947 quasi-drama:

Who is she? Where is she from? They say she kissed 2,000 men . . . She's out of this world, and down to earth in Technicolor with music. . . . She sings! She dances! She's terrific! But who is she? The answer, of course, is that she is Aphrodite.

Also known as Rita Hayworth, born Margarita Carmen Cansino on the upper West Side of New York twenty-nine years previously, a woman *Life* put on its cover as a "Love Goddess," and an actress whose talents studio publicists listed in press releases: "Height 5 ft. 6 in.; weight 116 lbs.; bust 36, waist 26; hips 35; thigh 19; calf 14; ankle 9."

---

* *Duel in the Sun* also stands as a good example of how Hollywood felt that promotion would bring success even to a so-so movie. *Duel* cost $6,000,000 to produce. Selznick invested another $2,000,000 in advertising, including such stunts as dropping 5,000 parachutes containing promotional material at the Kentucky Derby, and distributing beach stickers that spelled out the movie's name.

*   *   *

*On another level entirely, Hollywood possessed the magic formula for making southwestern kids happy, an alchemy known as the Saturday afternoon cowboy movie/serial. For nine cents I could buy an afternoon at the Lynn Theater, and a long afternoon at that—a double feature with Roy Rogers, Gene Autry or Lash LaRue in one movie, perhaps Johnny Weissmuller as Tarzan in the other, and a segment of a fifteen-episode serial with Hopalong Cassidy and his sidekick Smiley Burnett. In addition, of course, there were at least two cartoons and advertisements of the next eight or ten movies on the schedule. The lines began forming at the box office at 12:30, little boys clutching dimes in tight fists, the doors opened at 1 P.M., and we didn't stagger back into daylight, eyes bleary, until 5:30 or 6 P.M. The serials relied upon much-tested devices for keeping suspense alive from one Saturday to another, and they always seemed to work: How many times did the stagecoach plunge over the cliff, our beloved Hoppy aboard, just as the episode ended? How many times did the wagon laden with burning hay crash into the ranch house containing the besieged hero, his girl companion (she was not his girl friend, for we didn't tolerate such things), and his faithful saddlemate? We knew Hoppy had leaped from the back of the stage at the penultimate moment, out of camera range; we knew the hero and entourage had slipped from the ranch house—nonetheless the nagging thought that this time they might not have escaped tugged us back to the Lynn Theater the next Saturday. And the next. And the next. A research note informs me that Gene Autry made nineteen westerns during the years 1945–50; those that I saw (probably all of them) I liked, although try as I may, I can remember no details save vague images of Gene riding a horse, alone and in a pack, sometimes singing, sometimes firing a pistol. I am not saddened that Autry had no more lasting impact, for such was not his function: he entertained me on a Saturday afternoon, and the nine cents was well spent.**

Hollywood's artistic stagnation was compounded by other problems. Years of acrimonious labor-management relations erupted into strikes in 1946–47, throwing production schedules into disarray and splitting the community asunder. When a truce came, the wounds remained, and the average picture cost twice what it had six years previously. As revenues dwindled, bankers and outside managers supplanted the flamboyant individuals who had long dominated Hollywood. To such directors as King Vidor, the turnabout was a disaster for the industry. "These men

---

* Movie houses were a bargain during the 1940's regardless of one's age. In our town the admission escalated to thirty cents at age twelve, and to sixty-five cents at eighteen. As a kid I could always find a dime for the movie at least once and often twice weekly; my boys are not nearly so successful at coming up with an extra dollar.

were individuals, showmen; they had a feeling that they knew what the public wanted. You could tell a story, simply and directly, and they could decide whether they wanted to go ahead.* But then the agents, the businessmen, the bankers, the conglomerates took over. They wiped out the individual producers."

Another crucial blow to the industry was the loss of foreign markets. In 1946–47 four of every five movies shown in Great Britain were American-made, and the profits earned there were pure gravy. In an attempt to stem the flow of foreign exchange dollars, the British government clamped a 75 percent tax on the earnings of foreign-made films in the British Isles, whereupon Hollywood decided to boycott British films in retaliation.

As earnings plummeted, the studios were forced not only to cut back on personnel, but to change the kinds of pictures they made. The glorious Technicolor musicals of the past years were replaced by stark black-and-white dramas intended to shock rather than amuse. A Saturday night at the movies meant no such froth as *Weekend at the Waldorf,* but *Johnny Belinda,* about the rape and impregnation of a deaf-mute girl, or *Body and Soul,* a prizefight drama marked by the graphic photography of James Wong Howe. Pictures such as *Arch of Triumph* were destined to lose $2,000,000, despite the talented presences of Ingrid Bergman and Charles Boyer. No longer would the bankers risk financing such gambles.

Further, in a small but significant number of pictures Hollywood dropped its traditional the-good-guy-wins attitude toward America, a shift that Robert Thom, a film historian, feels was a natural concomitant of a deeper feeling of the years. Thom developed this thesis: "In foreign affairs we helped the loser as never before; we did not pause very long to feel triumphant. We had had five years of the worst movie-making propaganda possible, being told every day how horrible Japan and Germany were. General Marshall organized the defense of the country and destroyed Japan and Germany, and then came up with the notion, in the form of the Marshall Plan, that to avoid future war, we could not enjoy triumph. A most anomalous situation: to build up the very industries that we had just bombed out, to insure that Krupp was on top again. This was very confusing to the ordinary American, and to the educated American as well. The same attitude of 'loser-wins' was reflected back at them in the movie theaters." To Thom, the most telling moment in

---

* Individuals, indeed. Harry Cohn, the omnipotent, if rough-hewn, head of Columbia Pictures, made his own decisions on details down to script dialogue. Reading an advance script of *The Bandit of Sherwood Forest,* he was disturbed by the frequent use of such early Anglo-Saxon expressions as "Yea, sire," and "No, sire." He flicked on his interoffice microphone and bellowed for the author's presence. "This story is colossal," he told the man, "but this is a medieval drama, see? Who wants modern slang in a medieval drama? What's all this 'yes sir-eee,' 'no sir-eee' stuff?"

American movies during the period came in *Red River,* when a younger, smaller Montgomery Clift beat up John Wayne in the climactic scene. "The 'loser' won, an unusual occurrence in movies. But it was a time of 'losing winners,' when people fantasized with the loser. There was a revulsion with success—perhaps because the artistic people who conceived of movies, and dominated the industry briefly, saw that the 'success' of winning the war was being compromised and tarnished with what happened after peace. So you have *Duel in the Sun* ending with everyone losing, with the two leading lovers, Jennifer Jones and Gregory Peck, mortally wounding one another and crawling into one another's arms to die. The movie makers featured the tortured, suffering, the young American who didn't know where he was going, whose whole value system had been destroyed." To Thom, the epitome of the anti-hero was Montgomery Clift: "I didn't have a single girl friend in this entire period who wasn't wildly in love with Monty."

That this trend coincided with a precipitous dip in movie revenues convinced many in the industry that Hollywood was committing artistic suicide. In the words of W. R. Wilkerson of the *Hollywood Reporter,* the leading industry voice:

> During the past five or six years our production efforts have been just too damned arty. We've been shooting over the heads of our ticket buyers . . . and audiences have not been happy . . . because, seemingly, our producers all forget about their tastes. . . .
>
> What's happened to Hollywood? . . . What inspired the effort to go intelligentsia instead of making the type pictures that made this great business what it is, or was? . . . This Academy Award thing has done a lot to twist the type of shows from entertainment to artistic successes. . . . Audiences are yearning for some good belly-laugh comedies and pleading for those great love stories of yesterday and the homespun yarns that sent them home happy.

By 1950 the movies had degenerated to the point where drive-in theaters drew serious consideration as a salvation. A thousand or more were strewn around the country, an idea so new to most Americans that the Shell Oil Company felt compelled to describe drive-ins in a 1948 tour guide of Los Angeles: "This type [of theater] consists of an open-air amphitheater and an outdoor screen. The patron drives into the darkened area with lights dimmed and runs his car into a specified parking space. The front of the car slopes upward at a 5° angle, permitting a view of the screen from inside the car, and the sound is amplified so that dialogue is easily followed. Thousands of patrons have voted it a novel and a comfortable way of viewing a movie." Movie trade papers facetiously called them "ozoners" and "airers" but the industry gladly accepted any dollar available. In Denver, 1,500 cars sat in a driving rainstorm as occupants watched the first world premiere ever for a drive-in, *Colorado Territory*. The drive-ins offered all sorts of subsidiary attractions: barbecue pits so that families could come early and cook supper before the movie began; bottle-warming service for the baby; shuffleboard. Concession business ran around four times as high per ticket as at a sit-down movie. When business got really bad an operator would offer a weeknight game of "speedometer bingo," in which the prize went to the motorist whose odometer displayed the right sequence of digits.

All things considered, however, the drive-ins really weren't the movies.

IV

Truman: Trying to Take Charge

A Remembrance of Marshall: IV

Somehow we just couldn't accept the haberdasher in the king's chair. A Midwestern machine politician—and a corrupt machine at that, one of the very worst, according to the esteemed Reader's Digest*—posturing as leader of the western world, sitting alongside such titans as Churchill and Stalin, while his big-bellied cronies, men whose horizons did not soar beyond a gravel contract or a patronage job for a ne'er-do-well brother-in-law, elbowed aside the elite of Mr. Roosevelt's New Deal. Most of us in Marshall missed Mr. Roosevelt, the only President we had ever known. The day he died people stood around the courthouse square and cried, and the preachers had special church services that evening so that we could pray for him.*

But Truman? Common people, I fear, distrust their very own. One looked at Truman and saw not a President of Rooseveltian stature, but a man as ordinary as Mr. Bradbury, who ran the men's wear store in Marshall, or Sam Hall, the Harrison County judge. Imaginations would stretch, but not so far as to put either of these men in the White House. So why Truman?

One index of a politician's standing is whether people laugh at him. Here Mr. Roosevelt was blessedly equipped with a marital lightning rod, Ell-aye-nore of the protruding teeth and the strange ideas about nigras. In East Texas circa 1945 an Eleanor joke could be told with impunity at a Methodist covered-dish supper, or even by a third-grade teacher, yet no one dared jest at the Great God Roosevelt himself. Truman was another matter entirely. Indeed, the man seemed designed for ridicule, with his thick, sissyish glasses; his ordinary suit-with-vest; his flat, uninspiring speech. Savage jests abounded:

"To err is Truman."

"Don't shoot the piano player. He's doing the best he can."

"I wonder what Truman would do if he were alive?"

Had Roosevelt lived, of course, the demobilization of the soldiers would have gone faster and smoother; there would have been no post-

war shortages of automobiles and lard; everyone would have had a new house and icebox within a year, at prewar prices; the "labor goons" would not have shut down factories; the farmers would have enjoyed three inches of rain in July and August; and the Marshall Mavericks and their ace quarterback, Y. A. Tittle, would have beaten the Lufkin Panthers in the bi-district football playoffs. None of these things happened, of course, and in Marshall we wanted someone to blame, just as did people elsewhere.

So why not Harry?

12

Exit the New Dealers

AMERICANS FOUGHT A WAR for a better world; they came home to find their country run by an accidental President, a man of such obscurity and seeming mediocrity that he was little known outside official Washington and the provincial bounds of his native Missouri. What blurred image the general public had of Harry Truman, an image derived chiefly from his subdued vice-presidential campaign, was that of a not especially bright fellow who could be anyone's next-door neighbor; nice enough, in his own way, but did one really trust him with the country?

The things one read about Truman did little to help his cause. A few days after he succeeded to the presidency he let an old Missouri friend, Roy Roberts, managing editor of the Kansas City *Star,* into the White House for a discursive chat. In a widely syndicated article, obviously intended to be sympathetic, Roberts tried to explain his fellow Midwesterner to the general public. "The new President is the average man," Roberts opined. He felt it significant, even commendatory, back-handed as it may have sounded, that when the late-blooming Truman was "approaching forty" he was "still looking at the rear of the horse as he plowed the corn rows." Roberts thought this could be "his greatest asset as he undertakes these new overpowering responsibilities." That Margaret Truman found Roberts' analysis "almost laughable" is irrelevant; Roberts' average-man characterization is what Americans were told of their new President, and the one they accepted. The sophisticates at *Time* dismissed the new leader with a regal sniff: "Harry Truman is a man of distinct limitations, especially in experience in high level politics. He knows his limitations. . . . In his administration there are likely to be few innovations and little experimentation." The skepticism reached even into the Truman household. At one of his first White House meals the housekeeper served Truman brussels sprouts. The President shoved them aside, and daughter Margaret told the woman not to offer them again. She did anyway, on successive nights. Bearded by Mrs. Truman, who laid out specific menus for the family, the woman huffily replied, "Mrs. Roosevelt never did things that way." A couple of weeks later the White House had a new housekeeper.

The hostility was deepest among certain Roosevelt intimates, for several reasons. Liberals resented Truman as the displacer of Henry Wallace on the 1944 ticket, an antagonism Wallace did nothing to quiet. "How I wish you were at the helm," Minneapolis Mayor Hubert H. Humphrey wrote to Wallace a few days after FDR's death. Eleanor Roosevelt, in a private letter to Wallace, expressed her own indirect misgivings about Truman. "I feel that you are peculiarly fitted to carry on the ideals which were close to my husband's heart," she wrote. Wallace, shoved far down the prestige ladder by Roosevelt to Secretary of Commerce, was left with nothing other than the titular leadership of American liberals. Although willing to credit Truman as an honest and devoted senator, the liberals dismissed him as representative of a narrow, small-town mentality, lacking any guiding ideology to handle the fundamental issues facing America and the world. David E. Lilienthal, chairman of the Tennessee Valley Authority, and a powerful intellectual force in the New Deal, wrote in his journal that he felt "consternation at the thought of that Throttlebottom, Truman. . . . The country and the world doesn't deserve to be left this way." (Lilienthal changed his mind within a few weeks, when Truman nominated him for a new term as TVA chairman despite venomous Senate opposition.) Further, the Roosevelt Administration was so entrenched in Washington, after thirteen years, that the people serving it acted as if they owned the government. Truman was a newcomer, a usurper, a man close to "The Boss" neither before nor during his vice-presidency. The fact is that Truman saw Roosevelt only three times between his nomination and the inauguration, and they never shared a campaign appearance. During the days of Truman's vice-presidency Roosevelt found time for only three cursory meetings; he didn't bring Truman into the inner circle of his Administration, tell him anything of substance about that Administration, or give him any responsibilities. The exclusion troubled Truman, but he dutifully kept quiet and spent much of his time presiding over the Senate, his only constitutional role, and enjoying Washington's reviving social world. On some nights he and Bess Truman graced as many as three cocktail parties before adjourning to a formal dinner party. "Currently, the new Vice-President is the most fed gentleman in Washington," a columnist reported. "He has guzzled at more feed troughs than Whirlaway" (a recent Kentucky Derby winner). To an out-of-town newspaper reader Truman's only publicity of note was a picture of him playing the piano for a group of grinning reporters at the National Press Club, while film star Lauren Bacall sat on the piano and stretched out her long, lovely legs for the photographers. This was the man suddenly thrust into the White House, and the Roosevelt people there didn't like it a bit.

For that matter, however, Truman thought little of them. In a long chat with Clark Clifford, a St. Louis lawyer and naval officer who was to become his key adviser, Truman huffed about the staff he inherited. "Most of the people Roosevelt had close around him were crackpots and the lunatic fringe," Clifford quoted the President as saying. Truman had no use for most of them. "I want to keep my feet on the ground; I don't want any experiments; the American people have been through a lot of experiments and they want a rest from experiments."* In the same conversation Truman told Clifford he didn't like the words "progressive" or "liberal," preferring instead "forward-looking." It was not surprising then that Truman cleaned house. Within four months he accepted the resignations of all cabinet officers except Wallace, retained as a gesture toward the left wing, and Secretary of the Interior Harold Ickes. "I don't know how I ever got out of that mudhole," Truman later told speech writer Jonathan Daniels, referring to the FDR cabinet. Truman's misgivings aside, the turnover was natural because history has proven that any President works best with a team of his own choosing. Indeed, as was candidly admitted by Harry Hopkins, FDR's most intimate aide, "Truman has got to have his own people around him, not Roosevelt's. If we were around, we'd always be looking at him and he'd know we were thinking, 'The President wouldn't do it that way.' "

But the quality of HST's appointees caused stirs. Tom C. Clark, named as attorney general, carried such a reputation as a reactionary lightweight and a politician that his predecessor, the patrician Francis Biddle, pleaded with the President not to appoint him. Biddle supposedly told Truman, "They have quite a record on Mr. Clark both in the Justice Department and in the office of the Collector of Internal Revenue." Truman ignored him.† Fred Vinson, who replaced Henry Morgenthau as secretary of the treasury, was another conservative of limited vision, frank in stating he didn't believe in "social experimentation." (Clark later followed Vinson onto the Supreme Court bench.)

At the working level, Truman followed tradition and found room for countless old political friends from Missouri and his Senate days. "The Missouri Gang," the newspapers called these men, an oblique suggestion that the caliber of the Truman Administration—moral and otherwise— was of a class with the notoriously corrupt "Ohio Gang" of Warren G. Harding. Ed McKim, a sergeant in Truman's First World War artillery

---

* The Gallup poll bore out Truman's statement: in October 1945, 55 percent of the public wanted HST to pursue policies "in the middle of the road."

† Henry Wallace recounted the Biddle quotation in his diary. Truman, in his memoirs, however, asserted that "I asked Biddle whom he would recommend to take his place, and he suggested Tom Clark. . . ." The Truman memoirs, unfortunately, are somewhat less than perfect history.

battery, and an erstwhile insurance salesman, took over the White House administrative staff. When he found stenographers answering the flood of condolence letters that had been sent to Mrs. Roosevelt, he halted the work with the pronouncement, "Mrs. Roosevelt is no longer riding the gravy train." The story got into print, and it didn't please people who admired the Roosevelts. Harry Vaughan, an old Missouri National Guard friend and Senate factotum, came in as military aide and self-styled court jester (a reserve colonel, Vaughan was swiftly upped to brigadier general, and then to major general). A bulky fellow with a droopy Saint Bernard face, Vaughan whooped around the White House like a conventioneering Legionnaire, telling unprintable jokes and bolstering the President with such assurances as: "I'm still with ya, Chief." Vaughan once offered this assessment of the Truman presidency vis-à-vis FDR: "After a diet of caviar, you like to get back to ham and eggs."*

Such was the image exuded by the Truman White House in its formative early months. In the contemporary words of journalist I. F. Stone:

> . . . [T]he little name plates outside the little doors began to change. In Justice, Treasury, Commerce and elsewhere, the New Dealers began to be replaced by the kind of men one was accustomed to meet in county courthouses. The composite impression was of big-bellied, good-natured guys who knew a lot of dirty jokes, spent as little time in their offices as possible, saw Washington as a chance to make useful "contacts," and were anxious to get what they could for themselves out of the experience. They were not unusually corrupt or especially wicked—that would have made the capital a dramatic instead of a depressing experience for a reporter. They were just trying to get along. The Truman era was the era of the moocher. The place was full of Wimpys who could be had for a hamburger.

Another journalist, Willard Shelton, wrote in November 1945 that a "visit to official Washington is a depressing experience these days. Pessimism runs through the capital like an epidemic; in a two-week period I found few observers who had firm confidence in President Truman's over-all leadership or much confidence at all in Congress. . . . [T]he aftermath of war in Washington has a very unpleasant taste." Labor columnist Victor Riesel, after listening to an HST cabinet member

---

* Some of Vaughan's later activities were to cause Truman grave embarrassment. For example, during the height of the housing shortage he intervened to produce scarce building materials for a race-track operator. He permitted a shady character named Johnny Maragon, later convicted of influence peddling, to use his White House office and telephone while pursuing smelly deals. But Truman would hear no criticisms of Vaughan; when the President wanted to relax over the poker table, Vaughan was always handy with a bottle and a joke. During one of HST's cruises to Key West, Florida, Vaughan was green with seasickness. He took the ordeal philosophically. "What the hell," he told someone, "it tastes just as good coming up as it did going down."

attempt to inspire a labor-management conference, wondered, "Who is the power behind that drone?"

Truman had begun his presidency with an "approval" rating of 87 percent, higher even than FDR's peak of 84 percent—a rating John Fenton of the Gallup organization felt reflected more what the public *hoped* he would do than the record of what they actually thought he had *done* during his first two months. The positive ratings came from both liberal Democrats who desired HST to continue New Deal policies and from conservatives and Republicans who saw him as "safer" than Roosevelt. Both businessmen and labor thought he would be friendly to their causes.

But as labor-management problems swept the nation, idling scores of thousands of workers, and economic reconversion developed painful kinks, public opinion turned against the President—slowly, at first, slipping to 82 percent in early November 1945, to 75 percent later in the month; then with a rush down to 63 percent in February 1946 and to 50 percent in April. Thereafter Truman was more often a minority than a majority President in the Gallup polls; well over half the time a majority of the public disapproved of his performance in office.

A Roosevelt he wasn't. An FDR fireside chat seldom failed to draw at least a thousand letters. In January 1946 Truman went on radio to denounce Congress for failing to approve key parts of his economic program. Fewer than a hundred letters from citizens across the country resulted. Respected men raised doubts about Truman's ability to master the presidency. "There is an American myth and legend," wrote Walter Lippmann, "that the 'plain people' like mediocre men in their government. . . . This is a politicians' fable. . . . The cult of mediocrity, which is a form of inverted snobbery, is not democracy. It is one of the diseases of democracy." The Hearst newspapers, in a series entitled "The Tragedy of Truman" (written by Samuel Crowther, a onetime ghostwriter for auto mogul Henry Ford), had absolutely nothing nice to say about his first nine months in office. "Now it stands revealed that Harry S. Truman . . . is president . . . in name only. We have been robbed of our birthright and stripped of our honor because President Truman and his picked associates . . . have had neither the wit nor the courage to face their duties." Then, picking up a theme that was the first tremor of a campaign that was to cause anguish for the Truman Administration thereafter, Crowther wrote, "This group is at its core communistic and takes its orders from Moscow.* . . . Nero fiddled while Rome burned. Truman plays the piano."

What tenuous ties Truman retained with the Democratic left wing

* More intelligent observers were denouncing the Truman inner circle—John W. Snyder, Vinson, Tom Clark, and James K. Vardaman, the naval aide—for a variety of supposed shortcomings, chiefly stupidity, but that this conservative crowd would embrace Marxism was a possibility that never occurred to most persons.

snapped with a twang in 1946. Labor fell upon him because of the railroad strike legislation that would have given the government the power to draft strikers into the armed forces, and union leaders seemed engaged in a contest to see who could contrive the nastiest comment about a "labor-hating" President. Two holdovers from the FDR cabinet noisily exited in 1946, accentuating the strains within Truman's official family both on domestic and foreign policy issues. First to go was Harold Ickes, the self-proclaimed "Old Curmudgeon," Roosevelt's interior secretary from the very beginning, the personification of militant progressivism. As secretary he had headed the vast Public Works Administration from 1933 to 1939, notable for honest and careful spending; he also involved his department heavily in public power and housing projects. A short, heavy-jawed man with a profound distrust of big business and monopolies, Ickes stood as the archetypical New Dealer. Yet Ickes had his personality difficulties: Petty, vicious, a tart-tongued gossip who eagerly took on hatchet assignments for Roosevelt, Ickes was graspingly possessive of his bureaucratic territories. Convinced that an independent Missouri Valley Authority would undercut powers of his Interior Department, he helped New Deal opponents sabotage an MVA bill, even though FDR wanted it; he constantly harassed David Lilienthal and the Tennessee Valley Authority. Nonetheless Ickes was fiercely and unquestioningly a Roosevelt man, and his presence in the Truman cabinet symbolized continuity.

In January 1946 Truman nominated Edwin Pauley, a California oil man and Democratic treasurer during the 1944 campaign, as undersecretary of the navy. Truman regarded Pauley highly for his firmness in negotiating with the Russians on war repatriations. Pauley gave Truman several helpful cushions during the frantic hours when his vice-presidential nomination was in doubt. Eventually Truman wished to put Pauley in charge of a unified defense department (even though unification was several years distant) in the belief he could make order of the chaotic national defense establishment. Ickes did not share Truman's enthusiasm for the Californian. After a cabinet meeting on January 30, he cornered the President and said the Senate Naval Affairs Committee had asked him to testify on the Pauley appointment. Ickes did not volunteer the reason, nor did Truman ask; all the President said, by his account, was, "Tell 'em the truth, and be gentle to Ed." Several days later Ickes told the Senate committee that Pauley had offered the "rawest proposition ever made to me." On the funeral train returning from Roosevelt's burial in Hyde Park, Pauley, then the Democratic national treasurer, had told Ickes the party could raise several hundred thousand dollars if the federal government dropped a suit asking for title to tidelands oil fields, an issue under Ickes' domain. Ickes said that Pauley should not be put into a post that gave him purview over naval oil reserves, the wellspring of the Teapot Dome scandal of the Harding era.

Truman stood behind Pauley. Asked about the charges at a press conference, he replied firmly, "Mr. Ickes can very well be mistaken the same as the rest of us." Whereupon Ickes sent Truman a lengthy letter of resignation that implicitly asked that the President back down and admit he was wrong. Truman, already suspicious of Ickes as a "trouble-maker," wasn't to be cowed by threats. He accepted the resignation, and curtly rejected Ickes' suggestion that he remain in the Interior Department for six weeks because "there were so many things that only he would know how to attend to." Truman gave him three days to get out of his office, and said the resignation ended "all" Ickes' activities within the Administration. The furious Ickes replied that "I assure you that I have no secret desire . . . to hold onto any other office under your jurisdiction." At a press conference he said, "I could no longer retain my self-respect and stay in the cabinet of Harry Truman." He warned "of a cloud, now no bigger than a man's hand, that my experience sees in the sky." Ickes signed on as a columnist for the New York *Post,* and added his masterfully honed insults to the cacophony of insults resounding around Truman. "President Truman has not 'elevated' Tom C. Clark to the Supreme Court," he snarled a few months later, "he has degraded the court."

The Henry Wallace firing was a good deal more complex, for it involved one of the more mystifying figures ever to hold high public office in America. Not even the people closest to Wallace purported to understand him. A skilled campaigner, capable of arousing intense devotion among followers, he nonetheless was "shy, ill at ease in public places, sloppy in his dress, tousled of hair, and completely incapable of small talk," in the words of his biographer and contemporary, Frank Kingdon, who knew him well. Wallace lived on several planes simultaneously. A plant geneticist by training—and a good one, who developed several hybrid strains of corn—Wallace followed his grandfather and father into the editorship of *Wallace's Farmer,* one of the most widely read and respected farm papers in the country, although its blend of agriculture and religion mystified many subscribers; why, for instance, should a story on infant damnation run alongside a discussion of hog cholera? Wallace went into the Roosevelt cabinet in 1933 as secretary of agriculture and presided over the radical farm legislation of the early New Deal: chiefly, attempts to boost prices by controlling crop acreage and slaughtering calves and piglets. Wallace gradually expanded his interests beyond agriculture to become a leading spokesman for New Deal ideas; FDR, after making him Vice-President, also used him extensively to articulate American war aims.

But Wallace had problems. Were it not for his high office, his staggering inconsistencies of word and action and his predilection for foggy speech that masked even foggier ideas would have brought him swift dismissal as a classic Washington misfit. A health enthusiast to the point of fanaticism, he could—and would—talk at length on the marvelous medical properties of garlic, eaten raw. While in the cabinet Wallace became smitten with the idea of a soybean diet. According to Louis H. Bean, an associate and one of the few people trusted by Wallace, "he had the head of the Bureau of Home Economics [in the Department of Agriculture] prepare meals out of soybeans. For a week or two we were served various products made out of soybeans, because he wanted to experiment." Foremost among Wallace's many preoccupations was religion, and exactly what he believed might defy the comprehension even of a trained theologian. While professing adherence to High Episcopalianism, he concurrently dabbled in mysticism and astrology. He would draw horoscopes for visitors, and he maintained that the future could be predicted from certain markings on the Great Pyramid. "It's conceivable that he had some psychic gifts, but I wouldn't know," said Louis Bean. "Sometimes you'd see him looking at you, as if he was really probing deeply into you." The inspiration he drew from the Old Testament prophets was so intense he frequently seemed to identify with them: "to believe that he talked for God as well as *to* him," in the words of one observer. He once wrote of the need for a "modern Isaiah" who "would go to the people of the different nations and call for a New Deal among nations." When a business delegation protested that a Wallace agriculture program couldn't possibly work, he stood upright and his flashing eyes looked toward Heaven: "I have faith that Divine Providence will provide a means to fit the times," he said. Further, as appeared in due course, Wallace was moved to put some of his more idiosyncratic religious musings into writing. However, he showed no signs of recognizing his limitations, nor his dependence upon the tight clique of advisers who influenced his thinking. When pressed, he employed the gambit of closing his eyes and lapsing into, or feigning, sleep, frequently during important conferences.

Mindful that Wallace was anathema to vast segments of the Democratic Party, especially the big city leaders and fund raisers (including Pauley of California), irritated at Wallace's public feuding with cabinet members in direct violation of a presidential order, Roosevelt decided in early 1944 to nudge him off the ticket. The strategy contained devilish tricks that bear the mark of vintage Rooseveltism. In mid-May FDR dispatched Wallace on an essentially senseless "fact-finding mission" to Siberia, China, and Outer Mongolia that kept him out of the country until July 6. Wallace's foes undercut him deeply during the absence. For whatever reason, he didn't realize the significance of his exile and ignored a series of signals FDR gave him during a White House talk on July 10 that would have been painfully obvious to most men. Roosevelt spoke in oblique terms, but his meaning finally became clear even to Wallace, as was confirmed later in Wallace's own account. Roosevelt said "visitors" had been telling him Wallace would cost the ticket from one to three million votes; that "many people looked on me [Wallace] as a communist or worse"; that he could not bear the thought of Wallace's name being put before the convention and rejected ("You have your family to think of. Think of the catcalls and jeers and the definiteness of rejection," FDR said. "I am not worried about my family," Wallace replied). Eventually, of course, FDR tilted the convention to Truman.

Although he continued as secretary of commerce in the Truman cabinet, Wallace was far from comfortable. By late spring 1946 he was convinced that such key presidential advisers as Admiral William D. Leahy were "vigorously getting ready to fight Russia," by establishing bases from Greenland all the way across northern Canada and the Pacific to Okinawa. The attitude of Charles E. Bohlen, leading Russian expert in the State Department, "was frankly one of pulling chestnuts out of the fire for England," in Greece and elsewhere. In July 1946 Wallace sent Truman a long memorandum contending that U.S. actions were unnecessarily provoking hostile responses by the Soviets. He listed the atomic bomb tests at Bikini; continued production of B-29 bombers and plans to go ahead with the larger B-32; the proliferation of air bases around the world; a $28-billion defense budget; and indiscreet high-level talk about the possibility of preventive war. In this memo and in speeches Wallace pleaded for better understanding of the Soviets, and their better understanding of the United States. When columnist Joseph Alsop, in a private talk, warned Wallace that he was "in a completely indefensible position in the cabinet," Wallace deduced that "Joe in effect was a secret agent sent by the get-tough-with-Russia boys in the State Department to come over and sound me out. . . . Joe was on the verge of hysterics." Another journalist visitor took the opposite view. Walter Lippmann told Wallace that postwar negotiations "are being conducted by a bunch of amateurs and the final result is bound to be very bad." According to Wallace, Lippmann thought both Senators Arthur Vandenberg and Tom Connally, ranking members of the foreign relations committee, "unbelievably ignorant." Nor did Lippmann think that Dean Acheson, the undersecretary of state, "had so very much on the ball."

From Truman's vantage point, Wallace's constant buzzing made him a nuisance, and he regretted Wallace's self-appointment as a foreign policy adviser. He felt that Wallace "lacked . . . common sense" and that his claims the United States was pursuing anti-Soviet policies were "sabotage." Truman was upset when Wallace intervened in a special Manhattan congressional election on behalf of Johannes Steel, an American Labor Party candidate running with Communist support, over a Democratic opponent with a solid progressive record who was backed by both the Liberal Party and the New York *Post*. But how would he get rid of Wallace without unnecessary fuss?

Wallace forced Truman's hand in the fall of 1946. On September 12 he was to address a Madison Square Garden rally sponsored by two leftist political groups, the National Citizens Political Action Committee (NCPAC) and the Independent Citizens Committee of the Arts, Sciences, and Professions, the latter chaired by the eminent sculptor Jo Davidson. Both groups contained heavy infestations of Stalinists, but Davidson, a political greenhorn, didn't mind. "We know no more who are communists than who are Republicans and Democrats," he said. "We ask no one what their political affiliations are." The slant of the groups is important because it was to this forum that Wallace chose to make a major speech criticizing the Truman Administration's conduct of U.S.-Soviet relations.

Wallace knew he was venturing onto quaky ground. Rather than submitting the speech to the State Department for review, the usual procedure, he went directly to Truman. And, by Truman's account, Wallace hoodwinked him. After some talk about Commerce Department matters Wallace mentioned vaguely that he intended to make the speech, and read Truman some sample lines. For instance, he said, "I am neither anti-British nor pro-British—neither anti-Russian nor pro-Russian." Truman said Wallace suggested that was the way America should conduct its relations with the USSR, and the President nodded agreement. Wallace also read enough anti-Soviet lines to persuade Truman he was moving closer to the Administration policy. But Wallace's account is somewhat different. He claimed that he and Truman spent an hour together, and that Truman went over the speech with him "page by page," occasionally chiming, "That's right," and "Yes, that is what I believe." Truman didn't suggest a single change, and Wallace asked if he could say the White House endorsed the speech. Truman agreed.

The morning of September 12 Truman had a press conference, and William Mylander of the Cowles newspapers, holding high a text of what Wallace was to say that night, began asking about it. Truman interrupted; he could not answer questions about a speech that had not been delivered.

"Well, it's about you," Mylander said. "That's why I asked."

"What's the question?" Truman answered, smiling.

Mylander quoted from the speech, including a line following the sentence about Wallace being neither pro-British nor anti-British. Wallace had inserted, "When President Truman read these words, he said they represented the policy of this administration."

"That is correct," Truman said.

Mylander continued. "My question is, Does that apply just to that paragraph or the whole speech?"

"I approved the whole speech," Truman said.

Well, was the speech a departure from policies that Secretary of State

James Byrnes had been enunciating at the Paris Peace Conference that very week?

No, Truman said, Wallace's remarks were "right in line" with Byrnes's views.

The Madison Square Garden rally that evening was a hornets nest of anti-Administration sentiment. One resolution charged that the "aims of President Roosevelt have been placed in jeopardy by the 'get tough with Russia' policy, the refusal to withdraw American forces from China and support for British imperialism." Senator Claude Pepper of Florida urged a return to friendship with the Soviets, and accused Truman of appeasing "imperialists in the Republican Party." Pepper continued: "With conservative Democrats and reactionary Republicans making our foreign policy, it is all we can do to keep foolish people from having us . . . drop our atomic bombs on the Russian people." (Byrnes, it must be noted, at that very moment was trying to assure the Soviets at the Paris conference that the United States had no militaristic designs.)

By comparison Wallace sounded moderate; nonetheless, as a ranking figure in the Administration his direct criticisms of policies of the President he served were tantamount to political treason.

> We are reckoning with a force which cannot be handled successfully by a "get tough with Russia" policy. . . . Throughout the world there are numerous reactionary elements which had hoped for Axis victory . . . and continually try to provoke war. . . .
>
> We have no more business in the political affairs of Eastern Europe than Russia has in the political affairs of . . . the United States. . . . We are striving to democraticize Japan and our area of control in Germany while Russia strives to socialize Eastern Germany. . . .
>
> [T]he danger of war is much less from communism than it is from imperialism, whether it be of the United States or England— or from fascism, the remnants of fascism, which may be in Spain or Argentina.
>
> Let's get this straight, regardless of what Mr. Taft or Mr. Dewey may say, if we can overcome the imperialistic urge in the Western World, I'm convinced there'll be no war.

When Wallace ventured a mild criticism of the Soviet Union, many in the audience booed. He flinched but finished the sentence. Thereafter, however, he carefully dropped lines that the crowd might consider hostile—a sentence, for instance, about "native communists faithfully following every twist and turn in the Moscow party line." Another theme was that America should accept geopolitical reality and recognize that the Soviets would dominate a third of the world, the United States much of the rest, assisted by Great Britain. Three years previously Wallace had advocated "One World." Now he had retreated to "two spheres of influence," a change that sickened many long-time admirers.

For several stunned hours neither friend nor foe knew what to make of Wallace's speech. Conservative columnist John O'Donnell of the New York *Daily News* cheered Wallace (and seriously) as a late arrival among isolationists. The *New York Times* wondered how good an internationalist Wallace really was. Even the first editions of the *Daily Worker* denounced the speech.

But Truman felt he had been euchred. He called in the press and somewhat lamely explained that his answer as to whether he approved Wallace's entire speech "did not convey the thought that I intended it to convey. It was my intention to express the thought that I approved the right of the secretary of commerce to deliver that speech. I did not intend to indicate that I approved that speech."

Time called the statement a "clumsy lie." George Dixon, the Hearst columnist in Washington, explained why Truman was late for a conference: "He got up this morning a little stiff in the joints and he is having difficulty putting his foot in his mouth." Billy Rose suggested W. C. Fields for President: "If we're going to have a comedian in the White House, let's have a good one."

"Grievous official stupidity," the Miami *Herald* said of Truman. "Surely this has been one of the sorriest performances in the history of the presidential office," said *PM* of New York. "Inept," said the Richmond *Times-Dispatch*. "Mr. Truman either did not understand the Wallace speech when he read it or he does not know what the nation's foreign policy is," said the Milwaukee *Journal*.

Wallace's troubles escalated. Two days after Truman's tacit rebuke, columnist Drew Pearson surfaced with the July letter in which Wallace had warned of a "school of military thinking" which advocated "a 'preventive war' . . . *now* before Russia has atomic bombs." Truman thought Wallace responsible for the leak (Wallace said it came from the State Department) and called him over to the White House to try to persuade him to be silent on foreign policy, at least until Byrnes had finished the Paris peace conference. Truman was ready to take leave of Wallace, yet he hoped by keeping him in the cabinet a few more weeks he might be able to prevent further public statements until Byrnes's work was done. Previously he had never doubted Wallace's "sincerity or honesty of purpose"; now, however, "I was afraid that, knowingly or not, he would lend himself to the more sinister ends of the Reds and those who served them." Wallace was unrepentant. At one point he said that since the Democratic Party had adopted no formal platform on U.S.–Soviet relations he "did not feel bound" by loyalty to either party or Administration; further, that the party contained "the greatest diversity of opinion." He wanted policy alternatives and consequences discussed publicly before decisions were made. In the end, however, Wallace seemed to agree he should remain silent on foreign policy, and he and Truman so told the press in a joint statement. Yet within hours Truman learned that Wallace was giving the press details of the White House meeting.

In preceding days Byrnes and his Paris delegation had been filing an estimated 90,000 words daily of cabled reports (chiefly texts of speeches by the participants). But for three long days the teletype machines fell silent, save for perfunctory traffic. On the fourth day, Byrnes sent a direct message to the President which said, in effect, Wallace or me. "If it is not possible," he said, "for you, for any reason, to keep Mr. Wallace, as a member of your cabinet, from speaking on foreign affairs, it would be a grave mistake from every point of view for me to continue in office, even temporarily." Truman quickly pacified Byrnes directly via a teletype "conversation." Then he called in Wallace and fired him.*

The episode upset Truman, for it made a public fool of him at a time dangerously close to the congressional elections, and it encouraged the Soviets to behave obstinately toward Byrnes on the assumption that American policy was confused. But Truman had no regrets as to the outcome. Writing about Wallace a few days later in his diary, Truman opined:

> I am not sure he is as fundamentally sound intellectually as I had thought. . . .
>
> He is a pacifist 100 percent. He wants us to disband our armed forces, give Russia our atomic secrets and trust a bunch of adventurers in the Kremlin Politbureau [sic]. I do not understand a "dreamer" like that. The German-American Bund under Fritz Kuhn was not half so dangerous.† The Reds, phonies and the "parlor pinks" seem to be banded together and are becoming a national danger.
>
> I am afraid they are a sabotage front for Uncle Joe Stalin. They can see no wrong in Russia's four and one-half million armed force, in Russia's loot [sic] of Poland, Austria, Hungary, Rumania, Manchuria. They can see no wrong in Russia's living off the occupied countries to support the military occupation.

But the firing brought further scorn to Truman. The Chicago *Tribune* mocked an interview between Edgar Bergen and dummy Mortimer Snerd:

* The White House publicly denied at the time that Byrnes threatened to quit. Truman quoted the exchange of teletype messages in his *Memoirs*. Truman's current (1976) reputation as a candid President is frequently belied by comparisons of contemporary accounts with later "insider" accounts, both in his *Memoirs* and elsewhere.
† Kuhn and his Bund actively espoused the Nazi cause in the United States in the years immediately preceding the Second World War.

BERGEN: Mortimer, how can you be so stupid?

SNERD: Umph. What was the question?

BERGEN: Why did you fire the man who made the speech after you said you liked it?

SNERD: Did I fire him? I thought someone fired me.

BERGEN: Mortimer, you're hopeless.

SNERD: What was the question?

BERGEN: It wasn't a question. It was a statement. You're hopeless.

13

Had Enough? Yes!

F OR THE DEMOCRATIC PARTY, the exit of Henry Wallace loomed as the penultimate act of disaster in the November congressional elections. As early as June the Democratic National Committee, surveying the massive defection of labor and public anger over problems ranging from meat shortages and housing to the botched price control program, privately admitted the possibility of losing control of the House of Representatives. (The Republicans needed to win twenty-six new seats to control the House, and nine of sixteen seats up for election to gain the Senate.)

Republicans gleefully exploited every blunder and accused the Democrats of offering nothing more than "confusion, corruption and Communism." The GOP national chairman, Brazilla Carroll Reece, a Tennessee congressman, claimed the Democrats had fallen under the sway of "Red-fascists." To which Democratic publicity man Sam O'Neal retorted, "Chairman Reece and other stooges for the multimillionaires who control the Republican old guard once more are screaming communism and accusing 25 million Americans of having betrayed their country to Moscow." The *Republican News,* the GOP campaign organ, carried a front-page cartoon of an indubitably Russian bear wearing the false ears of the Democratic donkey, and an accompanying editorial signed by Reece:

> The party which bears the name of Democrat has ceased to exist as such. It consists today of three important elements—the Solid South, held in bondage by the chains of racial discrimination; the big machines—Kelly, Hague, Flynn, Pendergast;* and the radical group devoted to Sovietizing the United States. Of these three the last-named is the most important and the most powerful.

The predominantly Republican daily press, sensing a chance to purge the nation of detested New Deal reforms, stated as unchallenged fact the

* The reference was to Democratic leaders Ed Flynn of New York, Frank Hague of Jersey City, Ed Kelly of Chicago, and Thomas Pendergast, Kansas City.

charge that key Democratic units did the bidding of the Soviets. The Chicago *Tribune,* prominent among newspapers which abandoned any pretense of objectivity in its news columns, "reported" in a straight news story by Arthur Sears Henning of its Washington bureau:

> The CIO and other left wing groups have openly espoused Russian foreign policies, even at times taking the side of the Russians against American policy, and have become virtually a Russian fifth column in this country. The climax was capped recently in the blessing pronounced upon the CIO by the Moscow government.
>
> All of these developments have boomeranged in a violent swing of the political pendulum to the right in this country. The Republicans may be indebted to Russian Dictator Stalin for winning control of congress.

Did America truly face a threat of internal Communist subversion? And, if so, did the Communists exert inordinate influence in liberal and progressive circles? That GOP chairman Reece and the Chicago *Tribune* could make such charges, without evidence more substantial than the obvious fact that many Americans disagreed with Truman's foreign policy, can be credited in good part to J. Edgar Hoover, director of the FBI. Hoover's ability to scent changes of public opinion contributed in great part to his long tenure, and in 1946 he foresaw a virulent swing against domestic communism. In a speech to the American Legion convention in San Francisco on September 30, coincident with the Republican charges about the Red menace, and their "control" of the progressive movement, Hoover allowed that at least 100,000 Communists were running loose in America—in "some newspapers, magazines, books, radio and the screen . . . some churches, schools, colleges and even fraternal orders." The number of out-and-out Communists didn't scare Hoover; his fear was that ten sympathizers stood behind every card holder, "ready to do the party's work. These include their satellites, their fellow travelers and their so-called progressive and liberal allies. They have maneuvered themselves into positions where a few Communists control the destinies of hundreds who are either willing to be led or have been duped into obeying the dictates of others." The Hoover speech, with its obvious political implications, evoked a sense of helplessness and dismay at the Democratic National Committee. But no one in the Administration stepped forth to bell the redoubtable Hoover. When national chairman Robert Hannegan protested to Attorney General Tom Clark, Hoover's superior, Clark promised to "look into the matter." Nothing ever happened. Republican orators hurled Hoover's quotes at the Democrats for the remaining seven weeks of the campaign.*

* Columnist Marquis Childs, in a postmortem, concluded the communism charge "was one of the most potent forces in the shift from the party in power to the opposition."

Valid or not, the charges struck home in voting blocs that tradition-ally went Democratic. The Washington *Post's* Edward T. Folliard found "hatred of communism rampant" in all the states he visited. In Detroit, a Republican politician of Polish ancestry told Folliard: "You political reporters are overlooking something in this campaign. That's the foreign-born. They are off the reservation, and I mean off. Why, I can take you to clubhouses here where they have torn Roosevelt's picture from the wall." The politician cited clubhouses of Poles, Lithuanians, Estonians, and others who felt Roosevelt had betrayed their country to Russia at the Yalta Conference. In Pennsylvania, Governor Edward Martin, run-ning a successful campaign to dislodge Senator Joseph Guffey, con-stantly hammered at the "Communist" Political Action Committee (PAC) of the CIO. In Detroit rank-and-file members of the CIO refused to contribute to PAC, charging it was Communist. The Gallup poll, gauging campaign issues in late September, found "foreign policy and relations with Russia" ranked the most important. (The other issues, in order, were lowering the cost of living; curbing strikes and regulating labor troubles; working out world peace and making the UN succeed; housing; shortages of food, clothing, and other necessities; and veterans' welfare.)

A major imponderable in the election was "the veteran vote," a sup-posed bloc estimated at upward of eight million persons. "The hustings ring with cries of concern for the . . . demobilized GIs," Sam Stavisky wrote in the Washington *Post.* "Every platform and virtually every speech promises the former serviceman a panacea for his readjustment problems." The Democrats took credit for every piece of veterans' legis-lation passed since the Revolutionary War—a somewhat dubious claim, since the benefits would have passed anyway, given the veterans' special postwar standing; indeed, a Mississippi congressman named William M. Whittington was the lone man in either house to vote against terminal leave pay for enlisted men. The Republicans promised to do the same things, only better.

Several incidents in the summer of 1946 displayed veterans' potential political clout, and raised fleeting fears that they would use guns rather than ballots to achieve their goals. The most dramatic episode came in Athens, Tennessee, when supporters of the "G. I. Nonpartisan Ticket" felt the entrenched Democratic machine cheated them during a primary ballot count. Rival mobs gathered, the machine politicians took refuge in the courthouse, under protection of eighty-three deputy sheriffs, and hundreds of angry, armed GIs milled around outside. By *Time's* account:

A black-haired veteran walked up to the jail front and shouted, "We want the ballot boxes back where they belong or we'll open up on you." From the jail came a single shot. From the ridge rang a deafening volley. From everywhere all hell broke loose. . . .

Flames burst from an auto parked in no-man's land. . . . An ambulance seeking to rescue the wounded hastily retreated before sniper bullets. . . . Once the barricaded deputies called out a threat to kill three G. I. hostages, jailed during the day, unless the assault ceased.

After six hours the veterans blasted away the front of the courthouse with dynamite, and the deputies surrendered, with the plea, "Stop it. You're killing us. Let us give up." The veterans set up an interim government and called for new elections. Encouraged by their example, GIs in three adjacent Tennessee counties started organizing against their own local machines, and dissidents from throughout the South met in a "convention" at Alamo, Tennessee, to discuss a national political party. But Brigadier General Evans F. Carlson, famed Marine raider and much respected by organized veterans, dissuaded them: work within the framework of the national parties, he said, lest you create a fatal cleavage between ex-GIs and other citizens.

Nonetheless, any candidate who carried a war record into the 1946 campaigns began with a distinct advantage. In Pennsylvania, the Democrats persuaded a blinded former Marine sergeant, Al Schmid, to run for secretary of internal affairs, although he had no political experience whatsoever. (Schmid was to go down with the Democratic ticket.) Pennsylvania Republicans tried—but failed—to get native-son General Carl A. "Tooey" Spaatz, the air corps hero, to run for governor. DeLesseps Story Morrison, who won the Legion of Merit as a thirty-three-year-old colonel in the transportation corps, was in a separation center when New Orleans politicians asked him to run for mayor. He won and the victory pictures had him still in uniform. In Massachusetts, John F. Kennedy, running for Congress, frequently recalled a "promise" he had made while a PT-boat skipper in the Solomons: "When ships were sinking and young Americans were dying . . . I firmly resolved to serve my country in peace as honestly as I tried to serve it in war." In California, navy veteran Richard M. Nixon reasoned that a majority of veterans had been enlisted men for whom a politician campaigning in officer's uniform held little appeal. So Nixon threw out the military pictures, and the words "Dick Nixon" replaced "Lieutenant Commander Richard M. Nixon" on his literature. But Nixon did let voters know where he had been the last four years. Campaign literature described him as the "clean, forthright young American who fought in defense of his country in the stinking mud and jungles of the Solomons," while incumbent Congressman Jerry Voorhis "stayed safely behind the front in Washington."

Even a proveteran voting record was not enough to save many incumbents who had not gone away to war. In Oklahoma, three ex-GIs mounted an offensive against Congressman Lyle Boren, and beat him in the Democratic primary. In Wisconsin Joseph R. McCarthy demonstrated how to make the most of the "issue." He distributed 750,000 copies of a twelve-page brochure depicting him in the rear seat of a bomber and emblazoned with the slogan: *"Washington Needs a Tail-Gunner."* Newspaper advertisements read:

> JOE McCARTHY was a TAIL-GUNNER in World War II. When the war began Joe had a soft job as a Judge at EIGHT GRAND a year. He was EXEMPT from military duty. He resigned to enlist as a PRIVATE in the MARINES. He fought on LAND and in the AIR all through the Pacific. He and millions of other guys kept YOU from talking Japanese. TODAY JOE McCARTHY IS HOME. He wants to SERVE America in the SENATE. Yes, folks. CONGRESS NEEDS A TAIL-GUNNER. . . . AMERICA NEEDS FIGHTING MEN. . . .

The McCarthy literature contemptuously dismissed the record of incumbent Robert M. La Follette, Jr., who had been in the Senate since 1925: "sat out the war in Washington, lived on his Virginia plantation," enjoying his Senate salary and "fat rations" while "15,000,000 Americans were fighting the war and 130,000,000 more were building the sinews of war." McCarthy won by 5,396 votes.

By autumn *Army Times,* a service publication, counted 183 Second World War veterans who had hurdled the primaries to represent the major parties in congressional elections: 110 Democrats and 73 Republicans. Of these, 69 were elected, or about one out of seven members of the new Congress.

By late October the Democratic campaign was in such disarray that chairman Bob Hannegan fell back upon the memory of the sainted Franklin D. Roosevelt to try to stir voters into going to the polls. A series of nine-minute recordings, using professional actors, sought to dramatize campaign issues. In one of them the actors discussed the meat shortage, with one finally saying, "Here's what President Roosevelt had to say about it." Roosevelt's voice, taken from an earlier recording, then came in, explaining the necessity for fighting inflation. Next Truman was heard, explaining his actions in the meat controversy. Another platter dealt with veterans. Yet another featured a "man who remembers" looking backward to the Harding, Coolidge, and Hoover administrations. GOP chairman Reece called the recordings "one of the cheapest and most grisly stratagems in the history of American politics." Democratic chairman Hannegan replied, "Our Republican opposition does not like the sound of the name of Roosevelt." Reece, he said, no doubt "wishes most fervently that the American people might forget that voice and the profound words it uttered." The Alsop brothers, Joseph and Stewart, found the recordings odd both aesthetically and politically—a "touch of vaudeville" interspersed with the mournful dramas of the soap operas, in which an incumbent President was deliberately subordinated to a dead man. But they did see the recordings as evidence "Truman himself has faced up to the appalling loss of prestige and appeal which he has suffered in the past six months." Truman did no other direct campaigning. Richard L. Strout of the *Christian Science Monitor* thought it incomprehensible that the President would abstain from "participation in a campaign whose outcome may well spell his own victory or defeat in 1948." Truman was dubious about the strategy as well, but went along with the advice of chairman Hannegan—against his better wishes, according to Margaret Truman—on Hannegan's assurances that "the less the voters saw of the President, the better it would be for the party." One of the first things Truman did after the election was to fire Hannegan.

In early autumn 1946 Karl M. Frost, a forty-nine-year-old advertising man from Swampscott, Massachusetts, a Boston suburb, sat down with pencil and paper to devise a campaign slogan for state Republicans. Among those he submitted to the state GOP committee was the line:

HAVE YOU HAD ENOUGH OF THE ALPHABET?

Frost intended an indictment of the "alphabet soup" of government agencies and programs that had poured out of Washington since the New Deal, and especially the OPA. The line was gradually pared. "Of the alphabet" was dropped first; then "have you." Two natural words were added. After the committee editing, Frost's slogan read:

HAD ENOUGH?
VOTE REPUBLICAN!

Frost hired a prominent billboard on Dock Street in Boston and congratulatory phone calls inundated him. A press photograph of the sign was printed around the country. The Republican National Committee ordered fifty posters for display elsewhere, then a couple of hundred, then many thousands. A political slogan had been born—a negative question that promised nothing in return for the existing "enough," but that nonetheless summed up Americans' brooding, if unspecified, discontent.

Harry Truman went to bed early election night, on a special train bringing him from Missouri, where he had gone to vote, back to the capital. He woke up the next morning with a bad cold and a Republican Congress—the House split 246 Republicans and 188 Democrats; the Senate 51 to 45.

* * *

The Chicago *Tribune* puffed with joy the morning after the election. "Those who passed Tribune Tower yesterday," the paper editorialized, "saw the building wearing its holiday dress of flags, with an especially large one flying at the top of the mast. This was done to express our view that the outcome of the election was not so much a partisan success as an American victory. . . . The people were aroused by the manifest dangers to their country's future and to their own welfare. They won the greatest victory for the Republic since Appomattox. . . . They have broken the evil combination that so long has held the government of this country captive—the combination of corrupt metropolitan machines with disloyal Communists and no less loyal Anglomaniacs."

Other anti-New Deal newspapers fell over themselves with glee; for the first time since 1928 Republicans had cause to be happy in the wake of a national election. "The New Deal is kaput," gloated the New York *Daily News.* "It is finished. It is over. Historians to come will lift it out to study as a species, as they study the Thirty Years' War or the Black Plague and other disasters. . . . [I]t is like coming out of the darkness into sunlight. Like feeling clean again after a long time in the muck." The Washington *Times-Herald* said the Democrats lost by "hanging onto and intensifying the arrogant, papa-knows-best attitude which had come over them during the war. The Great Brain idea took possession of most of them—a notion that only a select few are capable of governing a nation." The Washington *Daily News,* in similar vein, attributed the Republican success in part to the "deep American conviction that it is unhealthy in a free government to keep one crowd in power too long." But there was another, more important reason for Americans' repudiating a government at a time of full employment and general prosperity:

The people were tired of being pushed around and being told what to do, tired of Washington's remote control over their daily lives and activities. They had wearied of endless directives, regulating what they should charge for the goods they sold, what they should pay for the goods they bought, what they could get for the hours they worked.

They had lost patience with the arrogance and stupidities of the Washington regulators. In wartime, they had accepted most of these harassments as necessary or inevitable. But when peace came and the regulators showed themselves loath to surrender their powers—when the ineptitude of these regulators was proved by such absurdities as the disappearance of meat from the dinnertables although cattle crowded the ranges—the people rebelled.

They had grown sick of unnecessary strikes, of government policies that seemed to promote industrial warfare, of government

officials who were all too ready to seek political advantage by
building up the power of ambitious labor leaders.*

Regardless of the reasons, Harry Truman faced two years as an
"accidental" and most unpopular President, opposed by a Congress
eager to assert its own voter mandate. And Truman definitely was now a
minority President. The New York *Herald Tribune*'s Bert Andrews, by
converting the congressional votes to state figures, computed that if the
election had been presidential, the Republicans would have won 357
electoral votes, Truman but 174 (compared with the 432–99 outcome in
the Roosevelt–Dewey race of 1944). The Republicans' popular vote
totaled 17.9 million, the Democrats', 14.7 million; twenty-nine states
voted Republican, nineteen Democratic.

With such a vote of nonconfidence, why shouldn't Truman speed up
the inevitable and permit a Republican to take the presidency? Marshall
Field, publisher of the Chicago *Sun-Times,* a Truman supporter, suggested he step aside. So, too, did Democratic Senator J. W. Fulbright of
Arkansas, who said Truman should appoint a Republican as secretary
of state, and then resign. Since there was no vice-president, the Republican would accede to the presidency. "If the change in sentiment is
strong enough to elect a Republican Congress," Fulbright said, "it indicates the people want a change. This ought to be done. What can be the
advantage of going along for two years in a stalemate?" Fulbright suggested that Senator Arthur Vandenberg was the logical successor.†

Carroll Reece, the Republican national chairman, quickly endorsed
Fulbright's proposal, saying the election results imposed a "moral obligation" upon Truman and the Democrats "to acquiesce in the verdict
and carry out the expressed will of the people." Reece generously suggested that "the method of acquiescence" was "something for Mr.
Truman to decide"—that he could either "accept the proffered cooperation of the Republican Party" or follow Fulbright's advice and make his

* The Chicago *Sun-Times* was one of the few national newspapers to disagree that
the election was a repudiation of the New Deal, on the ground that the GOP
offered no alternative programs. "Instead, they capitalized on discontent over postwar reconversion, some of it, no doubt, inevitable, but most of it resulting from
failure to hold the controls, and adopt new measures, which would have eased the
transition."

† Although this suggestion exploded as a postelection bombshell, Fulbright had
talked about the idea publicly for months. In March 1945 he testified on behalf
of legislation permitting the President to dissolve the government in case of a
deadlock between the executive and the legislative branches, and to call new elections to avoid "the anomalous and dangerous condition which arises when the
opposite party from that of the executive controls the Congress." A week before
the election Fulbright discussed the idea again at an informal luncheon of senators
and reporters; asked if he could be quoted, Fulbright first said no, then agreed if
by chance the Democrats did lose both houses, which he didn't expect to happen.
To his dismay, the Associated Press reporter used the story the morning after
election. "I was in terrible shape," he said later. "I had to defend it because it was
already printed."

own appointment. Although conceding Truman's legal right to office, Reece stated, "It is a matter between the President and his conscience." Truman never responded directly to the suggestions that he quit. But his "friends"—a press euphemism for White House aides who would talk—said he considered the proposal "fantastic and outrageous." A few weeks later Truman talked about Fulbright at an off-the-record dinner, and he was widely quoted as calling the senator "an overeducated Oxford SOB."

Harry Truman, minority President, intended to cling to office, even if under the most adverse political circumstances ever to confront an American chief executive. The Eightieth Congress whetted its knives, and Truman was a lame duck ready for the carving.

14

Enter the
Eightieth Congress

The week after the election Time *ran brisk profiles of twelve "new faces" who would "add much to the life, color, success or failure" of the Eightieth Congress. Among them were:*

> *Richard Milhous Nixon, dark, lank Quaker attorney who turned a California grass-roots campaign (dubbed "hopeless" by wheelhouse Republicans) into a triumph over high-powered, high-minded Democratic incumbent Jerry Voorhis. To beat Voorhis, ex-Navy Lieut. Commander Nixon, 33, passed around 25,000 white plastic thimbles labeled: 'Elect Nixon and needle the P. A. C.' He plugged hard for veterans' housing, end of controls, a bipartisan foreign policy; politely avoided personal attacks on his opponent.*
>
> *John F. Kennedy, 29, boyish, raw-boned, Harvard-bred son of ex-U.S. ambassador Joseph P. Kennedy. To win the Democratic primary in Massachusetts' 11th District, which has rarely sent a Republican to Congress, ex-PT boat commander Kennedy made 450 speeches, plumped first for international issues, then switched to such local matters as the restoration of Boston's port and the encouragement of New England industries. One of his biggest jobs: to convince 37 nationalities in some of Boston's grimmest slums that he was no Fauntleroy.*

SEVERAL DAYS AFTER the Republican-controlled Eightieth Congress convened, Representative Clarence Brown of Ohio looked over at the Democratic minority and announced his plans with a gloat: the Republicans, he said, intended to "open each session with a prayer and close it with a probe." The Republicans had campaigned on the thesis that the Democratic government was riddled by "communism, confusion and corruption"; soon the GOP had no fewer than thirty-nine investigative committees and subcommittees looking for confirmatory evidence. Republican distrust extended even to ecclesiastic matters. On opening day Senator Kenneth Wherry, the Republican whip, nominated the Reverend Peter Marshall, of the New York Avenue Presbyterian Church, as chaplain, replacing the Reverend Frederick Brown Harris, a Methodist who had served for four years. Alabama Senator Lister Hill said the firing of Harris was a "sorry business," that the chaplain position traditionally was not considered subject to political patronage. Wherry straight-facedly replied the Republicans wanted Marshall because he represented the church where Abraham Lincoln had worshiped as President. Hill shouted in reply, "What you are speaks so loudly I cannot hear what you say you are." Marshall was confirmed on a party-line vote. In the House, Representative George H. Bender of Ohio handed each new GOP member a new broom tagged, "Here's yours— let's do the job."

Yet exactly what was the "job" to be done? Reflecting the negative tone of the 1946 campaign, the GOP policy committees in the Congress laid out three main tasks: "Clear away the rubble of the New Deal and the war," which in translation meant returning the government to pay-as-you-go financing; curbing labor; and reducing spending and taxes by as much as twenty percent. For congressional Republicans the taste of power had broader meanings as well. The next two years they were to show the nation how *Republicans* ran things, the first such opportunity afforded their party since 1932. An uncountable number of these persons caressed thoughts of the presidency, either outspokenly or in their private moments. Power was there for the seizing. As a party of losers the Republicans swore fealty to no leader. Those from the party's Midwestern heartland suspiciously crossed their arms across vests at the approach of New York Governor Thomas E. Dewey, who had lost in 1944, and who looked toward 1948 with the infuriating expectation that the party "owed" him the presidency. The Easterners, conversely, thought the outlanders stupid and dated, typifying Republicanism that had died along with Warren G. Harding.*

It was through Congress, however, that the Republican Party had the opportunity to show its face to the nation. And the 1946 landslide

* The eastern "moderate" Republicans boasted their own quotient of gabbleheads. One of their "bright promising faces" in the Eightieth Congress was Hugh Scott of Pennsylvania, returning after an abrupt set-down in 1944. Scott had declaimed at a public meeting that Republicans "are the best stock. We are the people who represent the real grit, brains, and backbone of America." After penance—and wartime navy service—Scott won back his seat in 1946, and went on to become GOP national chairman.

propelled a peculiar mélange of characters into power—some of them considered downright peculiar even by persons and periodicals that spent considerable energy propagandizing the Republican cause. Representative Harold Knutson, the new chairman of the powerful Ways and Means Committee, responsible for tax legislation, was a diehard isolationist who had opposed defense appropriations to the very eve of the Second World War. Knutson had professed to see no reason to worry about what Hitler was doing in Europe. After the Wehrmacht moved into Scandinavia, Knutson said in a speech, "Hitler is displaying a forbearance that might be emulated by statesmen of other countries. Personally I cannot see much difference between Hitler's actions in Norway and the New Deal program in this country." Representative John Taber of New York, the new chairman of the Appropriations Committee, had the voice (and some said the brain) of a bull moose; when confused or in doubt, he shouted. During a debate on a labor bill he once bellowed so loudly he restored the hearing in the deaf ear of Representative Leonard W. Schuetz of Illinois, afflicted since birth. Schuetz thanked Taber. "I had spent thousands of dollars on that ear," he said. In the Senate, the Republicans were served by the likes of Wherry, a onetime mortician and tractor salesman who opposed any social legislation that reached the floor as "thinly disguised handouts," and who felt that most anyone who worked for the State Department was Communist, homosexual, or Anglophile (quite probably simultaneously). Wherry once got into a loud floor wrangle with Senator Tom Connally over a demand that the Administration make available "bimonthly reports" on the China situation from the Pacific military command.

> CONNALLY: We will try to accommodate the Senator. I have not seen any of the reports which the Senator says have been made every two weeks.
> WHERRY: No; bimonthly.
> CONNALLY: That is every two months.
> WHERRY: No, that is twice a month.
> CONNALLY: I said every two weeks.
> WHERRY: No; the Senator said twice a week.
> CONNALLY: No; I said every two weeks.
> WHERRY: Mr. President, will the Senator further yield?
> CONNALLY: I yield.
> WHERRY: The bimonthly reports I am talking about are two reports a month, which have been made since 1946.

At this point, according to a journalistic observer, "even the Republicans were laughing at Wherry," and Connally sat down in frustration. And it was Wherry whom the Republicans trotted forth as their floor leader—ideally, a post for a man who thinks quickly on his feet and has expertise in parliamentary gamesmanship.

To the general public the Eightieth Congress was personified by Senator Robert A. Taft of Ohio—son of a President, "Mr. Republican" to
many in his party, who as GOP policy chairman was the intellectual and
ideological voice of the majority. Specifically, Taft was responsible for
devising alternative programs to the New Deal and the successor Fair
Deal, and in packaging acceptable both to the eastern moderates and the
Midwesterners. Taft's chief attributes were smartness and a belief in
principle: as one observer put it, he absorbed complex legislative issues
as swiftly as most congressmen could understand the dialogue in comic
strips. He had led his law class at Yale, and before his move to Washington he had earned a comfortable living in Cincinnati doing the
dullest, driest, most technical corporate and civil cases imaginable.
Taft's chief drawback was his dour personality. Somber-faced, most
comfortable in a dark, double-breasted suit with vest and a tight necktie,
Taft came across to the public more as a conservative banker than a
politician. When his father, William Howard Taft, was President, the
other Taft children pilfered large silver trays from the state dining room
in the White House and held bumpity-bump races down the stairs.
Robert Taft preferred studying to such play. An ardent religionist, a
man born to wealth and social position, Taft clung to the traditional
notion that the rich have a special obligation to show the poor how to
take care of themselves. He professed little sympathy for the down-
trodden; his motivation, in the words of one contemporary observer,
was the "historically deep-seated, experienced sense of responsibility for
the whole community characteristic of the genuine aristocrat." Executing such a role without appearing condescending is a ticklish feat, and
one that Taft could not accomplish. Though many senators respected
Taft, few liked him. Soon after becoming majority leader he matter-of-
factly informed colleagues he intended to push the smartest senators
forward, the dumbest to the rear, in making committee assignments.
When someone bearded him for his callous treatment of other senators
he replied, "It isn't honest to be tactful." "I think the senator is talking
tommyrot," he snapped to another Republican during a floor debate.
Taft's lordly demeanor infuriated Republicans who felt they, too, were
entitled to come out into daylight after so many years in political darkness. One of them told a journalist (from anonymity, because Taft
wasn't a man with whom even a senator trifled): "I don't mind one man
calling the signals, taking the ball, throwing the forward pass, running
around and catching it, making the touchdown and then marking up the
score. But I'm goddamned if I like it when he rushes over like that and
leads the cheer." When provoked, Taft's temper flared like a kitchen
match. Dean Acheson, frequently thrown into conflict with Taft as
undersecretary and secretary of state, found him an adversary of limited
abilities. Speaking of Taft and Wherry, the majority whip, Acheson said
since they "both totally lacked humor and possessed unlimited energy,

their opposition was undiscriminating and ubiquitous. This helped to make it dull, scattered, and less effective than it could have been." Acheson agreed with the wide consensus that Taft "had a wonderful mind until he made it up." And he could not resist teasing the somber senator, even with Taft in a position to do dreadful things to the Truman Administration.

Acheson and Taft served on the Yale Corporation, governing body of the university, and the Senator once arrived late and asked the subject of discussion. Improving science courses at Yale, Acheson whispered. Taft promptly interrupted the speaker: "Mr. President, *I* went through Yale without taking a single course in science."

The other trustees stared at Taft in blank surprise, and Acheson, who wanted better science instruction for his alma mater, spoke up. "Your Honor, the prosecution rests." Taft was not amused.

The persons who tried to know Taft well—they were few, for his stiffness discouraged them—sensed a different private man beneath his forbidding public exterior. Edwin A. Lahey, the iconoclastic labor and political writer for the Chicago *Daily News,* succeeded perhaps as well as anyone. Lahey's first article on Taft, based on careful research, concluded he was "civilized" on enough key issues (specifically, support of public housing and federal aid to education) to offset his general reputation as archconservative. Because of Lahey's reputation, the article was widely reprinted in labor publications. The Senator was appreciative, and thereafter trusted Lahey enough to confide in him occasionally. Lahey found Taft "afflicted with a sense of uncertainty and pain at not being liked." During one talk he "was almost forlorn in discussing the bitterness with which he was hated by Dewey," his chief rival for the 1948 presidential nomination. A fear that "he could be wrong" nagged Taft. Lahey heard him talk at length one evening about high taxes and deficit spending, and finally interrupted. "What the hell are we going to do if you become President and we run into a recession? Will you have any other alternative except deficit spending, which you treat like a mortal sin?" Taft replied, "I don't suppose there would be any other alternative." Lahey commented, "It didn't occur to him that he wasn't sounding the way he sounded on the platform." Taft seemed most pathetic the few times he tried to "act like one of the boys," as his political advisers insisted. On a campaign trip Senator George Malone of Nevada brought him into a Reno casino, a "real sawdust joint," in the words of Lahey, who was there shooting dice with other journalists. "All I could think of was that this was a preacher in a whore house. He just stood there kind of wishing somebody would take him out."

Taft stirred about as little passion in his colleagues as he did in the public (Senate Republicans, in a poll by the Washington *Post,* preferred Senator Arthur Vandenberg for President by a two-to-one margin).

Lacking charismatic leadership, the GOP congressional bloc was forced back upon the issues. And although they boasted of a "mandate," the Republicans went slowly in making any use of it. During the first three months they did little other than change the name of Boulder Dam back to Hoover Dam, reversing what the Democrats had done in 1933. Another diversion, and essentially a senseless one, was prolonged baiting of David Lilienthal, the New Deal veteran whom Truman nominated to run the new Atomic Energy Commission. An outspoken public power enthusiast as TVA chairman, Lilienthal spent almost four months convincing reactionary senators he was neither socialist nor Communist. Democratic Senator Kenneth D. McKellar of Tennessee, who had despised Lilienthal for years because the TVA didn't always do his exact bidding, happily signed on with the opposition for the hearings. Although McKellar carried a reputation as the quickest temper in the Senate, he wasn't much help to the Republicans. A single example demonstrates the intellectual depth of his participation. McKellar asked the birthplaces of Lilienthal's parents, then aged seventy-two and seventy-eight.

"It is in the vicinity of Pressburg, which is now a part of Czechoslovakia," replied Lilienthal.

"Czechoslovakia is now under the domination of *Russia,*" whooped McKellar.

The Republicans mounted a filibuster against Lilienthal on the floor, Taft calling him a "power-hungry bureaucrat" who was "temperamentally unfit to head any important government agency" and "soft on the subject of communism." Senator Vandenberg broke the filibuster's back in a floor speech citing his own place on "all Communist black lists around the world," and stating he found no evidence that Lilienthal was sympathetic to communism. Lilienthal won confirmation 52–38.

In terms of concrete legislation, the Republicans and conservative Democratic outriders did push through ponderously complicated legislation intended to "curb the powers of big labor"—the Taft–Hartley Act, named after Senator Taft and Representative Fred Hartley of New Jersey. An amalgam of more than one hundred antilabor bills that had kicked around Congress for a decade or more, Taft–Hartley was designed to outlaw a plethora of "unfair labor practices" by unions, just as the Wagner Act had barred "unfair management practices" at the start of the New Deal. Taft–Hartley proscribed the closed shop, jurisdictional strikes (in which rival unions contended for organizational rights in a plant or industry), and the secondary boycott (in which a union that is striking the Acme Company persuades other unions to strike the Bacme Company, with which Acme does business). Taft–Hartley revived the injunction to end strikes, although only on motion of the government. It provided wide governmental intervention in internal union affairs, on the assumption (anathema to union leaders) that rank-and-file members needed as much protection from their officers as they did from employers. Extensive financial reports had to be filed with the Labor Department. Officers of national unions were required to swear affidavits they were neither members nor sympathizers of Communist groups. Labor unions could not spend money directly or indirectly in national elections or primaries. On and on rolled Taft–Hartley, an act so complex that few union leaders understood it, much less the lay citizen; a generation later, it still provided work for a troop of labor-law specialists and federal bureaucrats.

Labor treated Taft–Hartley as a modern Armageddon and spent millions of dollars trying to beat it down. Labor failed, Congress overriding a Truman veto to approve the bill, but Taft–Hartley was to have a galvanizing effect upon the unions that had refused to support the Democrats in the 1946 congressional election. George Meany, a rising power in the American Federation of Labor and the chief spokesman against Taft–Hartley, said most American workers had refused to accept that "the class struggle could . . . be a national political issue." The AFL, resultantly, had declined overt identification with any political party, even when the insurgent Congress of Industrial Organizations became a tacit arm of the Democratic Party. But Taft–Hartley, according to Meany, changed the rules: "big business" and its "swollen treasuries" worked hand-in-glove with congressional Republicans to pass Taft–Hartley, leading the AFL to "wonder if the class struggle is about to shift from the economic to the political field." Taft–Hartley proved a Pyrrhic victory for the Republicans: it didn't significantly diminish union strength, and it brought labor back into Democratic politics with a vengeance—and, as shall be seen, helped tilt the balance in the 1948 presidential election.

In its pursuit of "corruption," the GOP experienced the heady thrill of ruffling the reputation of the late President Roosevelt, even if posthumously and indirectly, through FDR's son Elliott. As the wartime commander of an air corps photo-reconnaissance squadron, Elliott was detailed to find new types of planes, an assignment that brought him into the orbit of the industrially peripatetic Howard Hughes. Despite his reputation as an aviation genius, Hughes's record for actually building planes was something else. During the war he received about $60 million of plane contracts, but never delivered anything the air corps could put into the air. Just why was this so? In 1947 the Senate War Investigating Committee put its eager hands on the markedly detailed expense accounts of John W. Meyer, a pasty-faced, balding old Hollywood hand who served as a Hughes press agent and general nocturnal handyman. A regular Meyer duty was partying military brass with whom Hughes sought to do business, an item of concern to Congress because the expenses could be charged to the government as part of a contract cost or deducted from tax payments as a "necessary business expense." In either event, the vision of generals and bureaucrats living high at taxpayer expense during wartime—and the convivial Meyer grabbed $160,000 of checks on Hughes's behalf in less than four years—was a galling specter for Americans to contemplate. Further, an assortment of pretty girls wafted through the pages of Meyer's diary, and the committee promptly leaked enough information in advance of the hearings to hint at "squads of scantily clad models, actresses and whatnots running in and out of New York and Hollywood bars, house parties, nightclubs, swimming pools, hotels—hotly pursued by grinning generals and government administrators." And right in the midst of all these activities was Colonel Elliott Roosevelt. Committee Republicans Homer Ferguson of Michigan and Owen Brewster of Maine spun out each cent of the $5,083.79 which Meyer spent on Roosevelt in delighted detail.

A thousand dollars of race track tickets and hotel accommodations for the colonel and his date (and later wife), the lovely actress Faye Emerson. Another thousand dollars for a loan so Roosevelt could pay wedding expenses. A $106 dinner at Club 21 in New York. A $576.83 hotel bill at the Beverly Hills Hotel as a "wedding gift." A festive $850 wedding party, including $220 for champagne. After a nightclub party ($106.50), according to the Meyer diary, Meyer took $115 worth of liquor back to his apartment in the Ritz Tower so he could continue entertaining Roosevelt *et al.* "That is not too much," Meyer protested, "because liquor was quite expensive." Senator Ferguson had Meyer read his expenses item by item.

MEYER: It says, "Presents for girls, $75."

FERGUSON: How many girls?

MEYER: Two.

FERGUSON: Could you tell us more about that? Who were the girls? Do you know?

MEYER: I haven't any idea. . . .

FERGUSON: You have another item for $200 above there for presents for four girls; and then there is this item for presents for two girls, $75. Would they be girls eating at the same dinner?

MEYER: Certainly, certainly. Positively . . .

FERGUSON: Now, will you read the next item?

MEYER: The next item is the next day. . . . That is Miss Emerson, lunch at the Madison Restaurant, . . . seven and a half [dollars].

FERGUSON: The next item?

MEYER: That afternoon, some nylon hose that I bought for Miss Emerson as a present, $132.

FERGUSON: Now can you tell me why you were charging up to
[Hughes] Aircraft $132 for nylon hose for Miss Emerson?

MEYER: Because she had been very charming.

FERGUSON: Very charming.

MEYER: Girls are very pleasant.

FERGUSON: What has that to do with aircraft production?

MEYER: They just went along. Every company in business did it.

At another point Ferguson called upon Meyer to explain a diary entry
reading, "Some girls at hotels !ate." Meyer commented, "They obviously
didn't have dinner."

FERGUSON: How much did you pay?

MEYER: Fifty dollars.

FERGUSON: What do you mean "they didn't have dinner" when you
paid $50?

MEYER: No, they joined us at the Statler at the Embassy Room.

FERGUSON: How do you account for the $50? What is the $50?

MEYER: Probably some presents.

FERGUSON: Well, what does it have to do with the production of
aircraft?

MEYER: I charged it to the Hughes Aircraft Company. . . . Those
were my orders.

FERGUSON: Well, now, just look at the first sheet [of the expense
diary]. Colonel Roosevelt and the weekend totaled about $1,500,
did it not?

MEYER: If that is what it totals up to.

Roosevelt, demanding rebuttal time, charged Ferguson and Brewster
with attempting to smear his father "in the hope of building themselves
politically." Thumping his chest with his fist, he cried out, "I deny with
all my heart and soul that Johnny Meyer ever got me a girl." He dismissed Meyer's expense diary as fanciful nonsense; on some of the dates
the press agent claimed to have entertained him, he wasn't even in the
United States. Pointing to his unchallenged war record, Roosevelt demanded the committee produce proof of any wrongdoing. None was
forthcoming.*

Yet apart from the sideshow entertainment value, such extravaganzas
as the Meyer/Roosevelt hearings did little to help the Republicans.
After months of work the committee could display only one scalp of

* A bit later, Hughes spoiled some of the Republicans' fun with a dramatic appearance in which he charged Brewster with offering to call off the hearing if Hughes
would withdraw opposition to an airline merger the Senator was pushing. Brewster
and Hughes called one another liars under oath, but the committee ignored
Hughes's challenge to indict him for perjury. The citizens of Maine rendered a
verdict of sorts the following year when they turned Brewster out of office.

even passing importance: Major General Bennett E. Meyers, the second-ranking air corps procurement officer during the war. The Senate became interested in General Meyers when his name appeared in Johnny Meyer's diary. Investigators found that General Meyers was the invisible owner of an Ohio electronics firm that obtained hundreds of thousands of dollars of air corps contracts. By one computation, the general siphoned $140,000 out of the company in four years, and spent lavishly: $10,000 for decorating his Washington apartment; $3,000 for a Cadillac; $700 for a radio. Much cash also went to his attractive secretary and her husband. When questioned Meyers offered an intriguing explanation: the secretary was actually his mistress (with her husband's "knowledge, approval, and acquiescence"), and he created the private company so the couple could "live in the manner they wanted." Both the woman and her husband called Meyers a liar; a federal jury pronounced him a perjurer, and he went to prison in disgrace.

Locking up a career general, however, was not enough to convince America that a generation of Democratic officeholders was guilty of the pervasive corruption that had been charged during the campaign. The closest the GOP reached to Truman's official family was the disclosure that Brigadier General Wallace Graham, the White House physician, speculated in the commodities market at the very time Truman was denouncing speculators for unjustifiably puffing up consumer prices. "Five-percenter" and "deep freeze," words that came to be synonymous with Truman Administration corruption, had not been heard by 1948. And even as a minority President Truman constantly danced ahead of the Republicans on such traditional issues as taxes and spending. Twice in thirty-two days in 1947 Truman vetoed GOP tax-cut bills as disproportionately favorable to the rich. Try as they might, the GOP couldn't override him. In early 1948, with due regard for the approaching elections, Truman sent forth his own proposal: a $40 per head cut for every taxpayer and dependent, the something-for-everyone approach that warms the heart of every voter. Ways and Means Chairman Knutson was aghast. "My God," he exclaimed, "I didn't know inflation had gone that far. Tom Pendergast paid only $2 a vote and now Truman proposes to pay $40." "What, no mule?" asked Charles Halleck, the House majority leader.

So, in the end, the GOP turned to the last refuge of ambitious politicians: national security and communism.

V

Communism:
Fears Foreign
and Domestic

A Remembrance of Marshall: V

The band of Russian guerrillas clung to the red-clay embankment, homemade rifles at the ready, as the wheels of the freight train crunched over the grenade bombs tied to the tracks with heavy cord. An explosion rocketed the troop cars off the rails, and as the Nazis screamed and ran for cover the partisans slid down the slopes to mount a loud attack on the command car in the caboose. RATATATA-TAT-TAT-BOOM!

The brakeman on the Texas & Pacific Railroad train looked up from his paperwork and waved down as he passed us—me, Fat Ford, Billy Dan Cline, Bush Morgan, and Ray Key—as his train rumbled north toward Jefferson and Texarkana. We assembled new sabotage devices with fingers stiffened by the subzero temperatures of Mother Russia— old soup cans hand-packed with dirt and cinders—and climbed back up the embankment, impervious to the swirling red dust and the August Texas heat intensified by the asphalt roadway of the Water Street Overpass. Another successful sabotage by Russian guerrillas.

Under cross-examination none of the band could have distinguished a Communist from a logarithm. But we did know from movies that the Russians were brave and skilled partisans; in our minds their heroic stand at Stalingrad was equal to the defense of the Alamo.

A couple of years later I was to read about another side of the Russians, in the Reader's Digest. *As near as I can recollect the story went like this: An American naval officer was assigned to oversee the transfer of lend-lease vessels to the Soviets. His Russian counterpart arrived with a hefty inventory of the equipment that was supposed to be aboard. Some kitchen crockery could not be found, and the Russian began raising a commotion. The American's eye fell upon a chest laden with work tools—items not on the inventory. With a mock sigh he picked up a heavy machine wrench and tossed it into the sea. "What are you doing?" demanded the Soviet, outraged at seeing scarce equipment vanish into the deep. "Well," said the American, "since you intend to 'follow the book' on a ship that is being given to your country by the people of the United States, I must do likewise. According to those papers you are not entitled to these tools." He picked up another wrench and gave it a swing preparatory to throwing it overboard. "No, no, wait," cried the Russian. "Let us talk about this problem." In short order they reached agreement: The Russian wouldn't quibble about a few cups and saucers, and the American would release the tools, normal ship's stores on any U.S. vessel. Hands were shaken and smiles exchanged, and the Russians sailed away.*

My personal breach with the Soviets commenced with the reading of that anecdote. I was oblivious to the trouble over the oil fields in northern Iran and the seizure of such insignificant map dots as Lithuania and Estonia. But in this instance, they responded to our generosity with stupidity and bad manners. Why should the most powerful nation in the western world tolerate insults from a quasi-Asian nation of peasants ruled by a dictator?

15

Reconsidering the Russians

THE IMPACT OF A single anecdote upon a subadolescent East Texas mind is significant because it reflects, in a narrow microcosm, the great sea change of public attitudes toward the Soviet Union. In February 1945, as Russian troops sped westward across Germany toward a linkup with other Allied forces, seven of ten Americans were so enthused about the Soviets that they endorsed the idea of sending German men to the USSR to help rebuild cities devastated by war. By the middle of 1946, disillusionment had begun: Almost six of ten Americans felt Russia's actions in Eastern Europe and elsewhere portended an ambition to rule the entire world; about one in four was ready to go to war immediately to stop her. According to a systematic study by public opinion specialist Alvin Richman, the negative trend was "unusually steep" from September 1945 to March 1948, averaging four-fifths of a percentage point per month in "favorableness" toward the USSR, and one-half point per month in "expectations." Richman concluded: "By early 1948 approximately 70 percent of the American public viewed the Soviet Union unfavorably. It is reasonable to argue that the opinions of the large proportion of the remainder could not be affected under any circumstances." In this category Richman included "those whose views were particularly intense and rigidly pro-Soviet, those who were generally unaware of international events," and the hard-core "no opinions" who won't commit themselves on any subject whatsoever when polled.

The collapse of good feelings, although directly attributable to public conceptions of Soviet actions, is not nearly so drastic when viewed against a broader background of American attitudes toward the USSR following the Communist revolution. "Friendship" rested on a flimsy foundation. Although specific polling data for the 1920's and early

1930's is missing, the existing evidence is that Americans viewed the Soviet Union with a suspicion born of ignorance rather than of fear. In the words of John M. Fenton, long-time executive of the Gallup organization, "One hardly needs a public opinion poll . . . to surmise that the marriage of Douglas Fairbanks and Mary Pickford had far greater public interest than did the news of the Harding Administration's decision to withhold diplomatic recognition of the new Bolshevik government." Although what Americans knew of communism they did not like (in 1937 a majority favored banning firms that printed Communist literature), they preferred it as an alternative to fascism in Europe. If the Germans and Russians were to fight, 85 percent of Americans with opinions favored a Soviet victory, according to a 1938 poll; three in ten didn't care one way or the other. But Russia's image sank drastically with the Hitler–Stalin pact of 1939 and the invasions of small Poland and Finland. Then when the Wehrmacht turned on the Russians and surged deep into the USSR, American admiration of the "hard-working" and "brave" Soviets soared. Official and newspaper praise abounded. General Douglas MacArthur, Allied commander in the Pacific, in a 1942 statement lauded the "indomitable stand" of the Red Army against stronger German forces. "Today the free peoples of the world unite in salute to that great army and great nation which so nobly strives with us for victory, liberty, and freedom," MacArthur said. Secretary of State Cordell Hull declared the Red Army had won "the admiration of the liberty-loving peoples of the world" and deserved a place in history beside the Russian forces that beat back Napoleon a century earlier. Reporting on two major battles three months apart, the *New York Times* wrote somberly of Russian courage:

> Sevastopol is being subjected to ceaseless bombardment by German planes, guns and mortars, but the Russian reports do not indicate any flagging on the part of the defenders. . . .
>
> Only stone houses remain in Stalingrad. The German pattern of bombing has reduced many of these to ruins. Although only a few buildings are fit to live in, they still provide cover in the violent fighting. . . . Stalingrad is being converted into a honeycomb of defense for battles for every house and every street. Each house must become a fortress and each group of Red Army men a garrison.

Yet the sympathy contained anomalous ingredients, and more than a little condescension. Americans felt distinctly superior to the Soviets personally and intellectually. Even after Pearl Harbor one of four persons would tolerate a strong postwar Germany as a counterbalance to Soviet power. If Russia tried to bring communism to the rest of Europe, two of three Americans stood ready to "do everything we could" to contain her. A *Fortune* poll in mid-1943 found four of ten Americans fearing Russia would try to export the Bolshevik revolution to other European countries once the Germans were defeated.

The facade of official harmony masked deep misgivings about Soviet conduct, little of which seeped through to the general public during wartime. American policy toward the Soviets was ambiguous, perhaps necessarily so. President Roosevelt went into negotiations at Teheran and Yalta, in 1943 and 1945, with the notion that the Soviets could be cajoled and soothed into good behavior. Several factors guided him. The Joint Chiefs of Staff, their concerns concentrated on the battlefield, feared diplomatic haggling could diminish the Soviets' zest for pushing the European war to conclusion and give them an excuse not to enter the fighting against Japan. Recognizing Moscow's historic fear of invaders, FDR leaned over backward to heed demands that she have friendly powers on her borders when postwar Europe took shape. Fourteen times since 1800 invading armies had swept across the naked plains to Russia's west; Minsk had suffered 101 foreign occupations. Quite obviously the Soviets wished to fight any future wars in buffer states, not on their homeland. Winston Churchill, conversely, took a much darker view of the Soviets, arguing that the U.S. and Britain should begin preparing for how to cope with probable Russian designs on Europe. Churchill was doing just that on his own; in exchanges in 1943 he and Stalin reached tacit agreements that British influence should remain dominant in Greece; that Britain and the USSR would share Yugoslavia; and that the Soviets, through dint of occupation, could do pretty much what they wished in Rumania, Bulgaria, and Hungary. Neither kept his word, choosing to use these "agreements" as the starting point for further bargaining. Both also ignored the Atlantic Charter declaration of 1942 on the "freedom of choice" that would be afforded European nations once the war ended. Although not above compromise, Roosevelt proceeded on the assumption that the grand coalition could continue working during peace, as an alternative to the old power-bloc stratagems of world diplomacy. The result from these countering pressures was language wondrously broad and vague even by the standards of diplomatic-communiqué writing.

One has only to consider Eastern Europe and the Balkans. The Yalta language called for "processes which will enable the liberated peoples to destroy the last vestiges of nazism and fascism and to create democratic institutions of their own choices." Britain, the USSR, and the United States would "jointly assist" the nations in holding free elections. Churchill was privately aghast that the United States would so "cavalierly" discard other nations. He wrote, "It is true that American thought is at least disinterested in matters which seem to relate to territorial acquisitions, but when wolves are about, the shepherd must guard his flock, even if he does not himself care for mutton."

The section on Poland more accurately reflected the existing reality of

Soviet power, even if in oblique terms. Noting the "new situation . . . created in Poland as a result of her complete occupation by the Red Army," the agreement tacitly de-recognized the Polish government-in-exile that had been operating in London, in favor of a new regime created by the occupying Soviets. The Soviets did promise to include "democratic leaders from Poland itself and from Poles abroad," a point that quickly became a bone of contention between Truman and Stalin.

Another decision of great significance was not even alluded to in the formal communiqué—that the Anglo-American armies would halt their advance eastward into Germany at the Elbe River, permitting the Soviets to occupy Berlin. The agreement was not announced until May 1, 1945, after the converging armies linked up, and no reasons were given. Churchill violently disagreed, arguing that the Allies should drive as deeply into prearranged Soviet zones of occupation as possible and hold the territory for bargaining purposes. Truman, however, declined to break the agreement.

The Elbe episode—the root of repeated crises over Berlin for the next two decades—was received as a curious but not especially relevant happening. War correspondents with the Ninth U.S. Army wrote that they could not determine whether the decision was military or political. They pointed out the obvious tactical value in catching the reeling Germans in a "hammer and anvil" situation, with the Russians acting as the striking force, and in avoiding accidental encounters in which onrushing American and Soviet units could fire at one another before establishing identity. Reporters found no wide opposition. As the *New York Times* reported:

> While staff officers were disappointed, the American doughboys and tankmen who had to do the fighting and dying to get to Berlin expressed no regret. Almost to a man, they felt they could do without the final "glory" of getting to Berlin and the resulting expense in casualties.

The day of the linkup American GIs and Soviet infantrymen shook hands and spontaneously embraced. "They seemed instinctively to like one another," an Associated Press reporter wrote. Bureaucracy intervened swiftly: a frontier rigidly fixed the bounds of the two armies, and soldiers could not pass across the front without invitation. "The Russians simply do not want anyone, friend or foe, wandering around in their lines," the AP man observed.

Truman, too, was swiftly backing away from the openhanded policy of Roosevelt and following his instinctive feelings the Soviets should not be trusted. Averell Harriman, the U.S. ambassador to Moscow, warned soon after Truman's succession to the presidency that the United States faced a "barbarian invasion of Europe." Harriman said the Soviets would seek to impose their foreign policy and police-state system upon any nation they occupied and would likely ignore any "agreement" not to their advantage. He suggested give-and-take negotiations in which Truman would make plain he would not be shoved.

The first test came over Poland. Contrary to his Yalta promise, Stalin flatly refused to permit any members of the government-in-exile to join the provisional regime created by the occupying Soviet army. The United States and Britain, in turn, refused to permit seating of the "puppet" Polish delegation at the United Nations founding conference, which opened with great fanfare and expectations in April 1945 in San Francisco. Stalin gave every sign of pulling out of the embryonic UN if he did not get his way, an action that would have shattered hopes for a world organization to prevent future wars.

Harriman arranged for Vyacheslav M. Molotov, the foreign minister who was to head the Russian delegation to the UN conference, to stop in Washington enroute to San Francisco to meet the new President. Truman was furious. Before meeting Molotov, he told aides he felt he had walked a "one-way street" with the Soviets on agreements; if they didn't wish to cooperate "they could go to hell." He told Molotov much the same thing, and in only slightly more diplomatic language. Molotov talked in circles. He said his government stood behind the Yalta decisions but edged away to another subject when Truman asked him specifically about the breached Polish agreement. Finally Truman told him future friendship could only be on the basis of "mutual observation of agreements."

"I have never been talked to like that in my life," Molotov replied testily.

"Carry out your agreements and you won't get talked to like that," Truman replied.

Yet having talked tough, Truman didn't carry through. Stalin recalled twenty of the leading London exiles to Moscow, ostensibly to talk about their roles in a new government. No sooner had they arrived than he put sixteen of them on trial for inciting underground resistance to the Soviet occupation troops. As a sop to Truman, Stalin put the other four into the government, one as vice-premier. Unwilling to see the UN die over the Polish issue, and under pressure from other governments, Truman reluctantly agreed to recognize the puppet Warsaw delegation.

The Polish question also haunted the opening of the Potsdam Conference, in July 1945, at which Truman hoped the Big Three could start the hard business of writing formal peace treaties for Germany and its defeated satellite states of Bulgaria, Hungary, and Rumania. At Yalta Poland had been promised "substantial accessions of territory in the north and west," which Roosevelt and Churchill had interpreted as meaning a new eastern border near the Oder River. The Russian armies however, pressed much farther, to the Neisse, incorporating about a quarter of Germany's most productive agricultural land into Poland.

Stalin asked Churchill and Truman, in effect, What are you going to do about my *fait accompli?* Nothing was done. The Big Three kicked the "Polish question" into the future, to be resolved during drafting of an overall German peace treaty. (Three decades later, no such treaty has been written.)* Stalin took a similar attitude elsewhere in Eastern Europe: what the Soviets held, the Soviets intended to dominate, through docile "governments" that systematically excluded all save Communists. In the instances of Rumania, Hungary, and Bulgaria, the Big Three had earlier agreed to Allied "control commissions," which were to govern pending "free" elections. The Soviets hampered American and British members at every hand, ignoring their presence and so restricting their movements that they were effectively isolated from the countries they ostensibly were supposed to be running. Churchill, irked, snapped to Stalin that an "iron fence" had come down around the British mission in Bucharest, figuratively and literally. "All fairy tales," Stalin replied, equally snippily. For months the Soviets refused even to admit American and British control commission members to Vienna, despite clear agreement at Yalta for joint control of the Austrian capital. By the time they got in, the Soviets had installed a predominantly Communist government—whose leader, Karl Renner, a seventy-seven-year-old former chancellor, later succeeded in forming a tolerably representative administration.

On Germany, the most important issue, the Big Three made no progress whatsoever. At Yalta Stalin had demanded $10 billion in reparations; at Potsdam, this figure was put forth as a rock bottom minimum, with $20 billion as the top bargaining goal. All the while the Soviets busily dismantled entire factories in their zones of occupation—not only in Germany but in the Nazi satellite states, including oil refineries in Rumania that had been owned by British and American companies before the war. When Truman protested, Stalin replied it was a "trifling matter"; after all, the Russians needed refineries to replace those that the Germans had destroyed. "It was funny to watch him," Truman wrote later—albeit not in real amusement. "Every time there was something like this, where the Russians had stolen the coffin and disposed of the body, he was always very careful to insist that it be settled through diplomatic channels. But where it was a matter of France, Spain, or Yugoslavia [where Stalin wished to reduce the British influence], he was very anxious that the matter be put on the table and settled. I saw what was going on." Potsdam was a failure, although one cloaked from

---

* The Potsdam deliberations received yet another jolt in mid-course when the British electorate turned Winston Churchill and his Conservative Party out of office in what journalist Herbert L. Matthews aptly called "one of the most stunning surprises in the history of democracy." Clement R. Attlee, who had been sitting in on the talks as a member of the coalition War Cabinet, replaced Churchill as prime minister.

all but the handful of lay citizens with the insight to sense failure beneath the language of the final communiqué.

During an interlude at Potsdam Ambassador Averell Harriman fell into conversation with Stalin, congratulated him on the defeat of Germany, and remarked that he must be very satisfied to have the Red Army in Berlin. With a so-what shrug of his shoulders Stalin replied, "Tsar Alexander got to Paris." Harriman walked away stunned. The flip remark convinced him that Stalin was ready to spread Soviet communism to the banks of the English Channel.

With peace, and the end of censorship and boosteristic propaganda, the U.S.–Soviet differences no longer could be pushed out of sight. Almost daily the newspaper headlines told the public of yet another example of Soviet intransigence: the tightening of Communist regimes in Eastern European nations that passed swiftly from Nazi vassalage to the Soviet bloc; Russian support of guerrillas in Greece; Russian refusal to withdraw troops from the northern part of Iran; the incessant Russian demands for control of the Straits of the Bosporus, which if permitted would have meant the end of Turkey as a nation. From Moscow's viewpoint the preceding sentence could be restated as follows: the purging of Eastern European nations of the vestiges of the fascist governments that brought them into the war on the side of Nazi Germany; friendship toward insurgents attempting to overthrow an archaic monarchical rule in Greece that remained upright only because of the supporting prop of British imperialism; an attempt to end the Anglo-American monopoly of Middle Eastern oil; and a continuation of Russia's historic quest for warm-water access to the oceans of the world, for commerce and self-defense.

But American patience quickly stretched past the snapping point. Americans had spent four years fighting and working for a brave new world of peace; such had been promised them by their government, and in the swirl of postwar euphoria people tended to believe what they were told. Americans did not wish to burden themselves with the intricacies of unintelligible issues in far-away places; they wanted strife and war purged from the front pages. Our former allies "seemed to be going back to the old methods of seizing territory, dominating smaller nations, preparing strategic positions, restoring colonial nations," wrote John C. Campbell of the Council on Foreign Relations. "The greatest offender, in American eyes, was the Soviet Union." The shortcomings of Soviet society, the deep differences of the United States and Soviet economic and political systems, had been glossed over in the interest of the common war effort. The propaganda offensive against Nazi totalitarianism, as Campbell has noted, "was in many respects applicable also to the doctrines and practices of Soviet Russia." Hence, when the Soviets pressed ahead with their own political and strategic offensives, unilaterally and in violation of the principles of its wartime allies, "American opinion was conditioned to react strongly against them." The Russians stood as the most visible obstruction to world tranquillity.

For months Truman refused to share his own mounting anxieties with the American people. When Molotov harassed the hapless Secretary of State James Byrnes at a foreign ministers meeting in October 1945, Truman pooh-poohed the significance—merely a single step on the path toward an overall peace settlement, he told a press conference; the international scene would soon quieten, much as the domestic labor-management strife would run its course.

Stalin felt no such restraints. He publicly disavowed the wartime alliance in a speech to a party congress on February 9, 1946, that officially labeled the western nations, and especially the United States, as a graver threat than even Nazi Germany. Drawing upon the Marxist axiom that capitalism is fated to repeat boom-bust cycles, each worse than the last, he said the "capitalist ruling class" eventually would resort to aggressive war in quest of a solution for its economic problems. Stalin blamed the two world wars on such crises, and said a third must be expected because peaceful resolution of economic strife "is impossible . . . under present capitalist conditions of the development of world economy." Stalin announced a new Five Year Plan of economic development to bring the USSR to a war footing. "Only under such conditions," he said, "can we consider that our homeland will be guaranteed against all possible accidents." He predicted the confrontation would come during the decade of the 1950's, when America would have sunk into a disastrous depression.

Washington received Stalin's speech somberly. Supreme Court Justice William O. Douglas, a pillar of American liberalism, called it "the Declaration of World War III." A month later Truman publicly reverted to a get-tough policy himself, in a manner that was indirect—and, by the account of his daughter, Margaret, unintended. In March 1946, Winston Churchill, now a / private citizen—although certainly no ordinary one—accepted an invitation (endorsed by the President) to make a speech at Westminster College, in Fulton, Missouri. Truman rode with Churchill on the train from Washington, and introduced him with these words:

> I had never met Mr. Churchill personally until a conference we had with Mr. Stalin. I became very fond of both of them. They are men and they are leaders in this world today when we need leadership. . . . I understand that Mr. Churchill is going to talk about the sinews of peace. . . . *I know he will have something very constructive to say to the world.*

Churchill's speech, a harsh and eloquently phrased denunciation of Soviet aggression, contained a terse and evocative description of what lay ahead for the world:

> From Stettin in the Baltic to Trieste in the Adriatic, an iron curtain has descended across the continent. From what I have seen of our Russian friends and allies during the war, I am convinced that there is nothing they admire so much as strength, and there is nothing for which they have less respect than for weakness, especially military weakness.

Churchill pleaded for a resumption of the British-American "fraternal association" to discourage Soviet expansionism.

Truman, sitting on the speaker's stand behind Churchill, applauded at several points, and his staff told reporters he had read the speech enroute to Missouri. The special circumstances of the speech—Truman's role in the invitation, and his introduction—led to wide conclusion that he endorsed what Churchill said, and that the event signaled a hardening of the U.S. stance toward Moscow. Bert Andrews of the New York *Herald Tribune,* one of the better-informed Washington correspondents, wrote, "Mr. Truman went along largely with what Mr. Churchill had to say, if not entirely." Margaret Truman, in her memoir of her father's presidency, insists this was not the case; that Truman in no sense considered the speech a break with Russia. And, indeed, Truman did write his mother and sister a day or so later that while he thought the affair "did some good . . . I am not yet ready to endorse Mr. Churchill's speech."

Stalin thought otherwise. He denounced the Fulton speech as a "call to war against the USSR," and the whole Soviet propaganda machine busied itself with a barrage of vituperation against Churchill and his "fascist friends in Britain and America." (Three years later, in a newspaper interview, Truman revealed that Stalin sent him a private note protesting the Churchill speech. Whereupon Truman handwrote the Soviet leader a letter offering to send the battleship USS *Missouri* to bring him to the United States, and to escort him personally to Fulton for "exactly the same kind of reception, the same opportunity to speak his mind." Truman said Stalin refused.) Internally, the Soviet press did not report what Churchill said, only what Stalin replied. John Fischer, traveling in Russia at the time, wrote later, "Dozens of war-weary little people—farmers, train porters, bookkeepers, who normally took no interest in politics—asked me anxiously why these evil men were trying to set the world aflame again. And why didn't President Truman denounce these warmongers as Stalin had?" Thereafter the Soviet press carried items almost daily about America's "imperialist" motives in establishing bases in the Pacific and Iceland, and the soft treatment of "quisling war criminals" in refugee camps the United States ran in Germany. These statements were widely publicized in the United States, along with an article by P. F. Yudin, an authoritative spokesman for Marxist doctrine, who demanded a strengthening of the Red Army "because the Soviet Union is surrounded . . . by capitalist states which are constantly sending in a stream of diversionists and spies."

The same week Churchill spoke in Missouri, U.S. correspondents succeeded in entering Soviet-occupied Manchuria for the first time since the war ended. They did not report pleasant things. Factories were being dismantled and carted away to the Soviet Union by the veritable trainload. The populace was cowed. A factory manager who gave the correspondents an interview was shot within hours. The Russians kept the reporters cooped in their hotel and refused them transport; if they ventured outside, snipers fired at them. "The tommy gun is king and you see it everywhere," wrote A. T. Steele of the New York *Herald Tribune.* Robert Martin of the New York *Post* sensed a "studied and cynical freeze" directed against newsmen. "This correspondent walked through city streets after dark with chill fear gripping his stomach when challenges sounded,"

The journalist-editor John Fischer, who began studying the Soviets while at Oxford in 1933 and who spent several months in the USSR in early 1946 on a mission of the United Nations Relief and Rehabilitation Administration (UNRRA), tried to remain objective. In articles in *Harper's, Life* and *The New Yorker* in 1946, he explained the Soviets' pathological fear of outside invaders, wrote about the Russians as human beings, and counseled patience in dealing with them during the uncomfortable postwar years. Yet Fischer's exasperation leapt from his articles. He recounted talking with a Soviet official who argued that it would be an unfriendly act for the United States to direct shortwave broadcasts into the USSR, although the Soviets should feel perfectly free to broadcast its propaganda to America. Why? asked the befuddled Fischer. "A perfect example of reciprocity," he quoted the Soviet as replying. "Your laws provide for free speech, and we observe them. Our laws do *not,* and it would be improper for you to disregard them." Again, he told of a Russian official's explanation about why planes were not equipped with de-icers: "Sure we have a few more crack-ups. Maybe ten percent more than if we had all those safety devices. But by leaving them off, we can build fifteen or twenty percent more planes a year. So we are still five or ten percent ahead." Fischer thought it "characteristic that human life didn't enter into this calculation."

Because of the special audience of intellectuals and college-trained professionals and academicians who read *Harper's,* Fischer's articles had profound impact upon American opinion makers. Fischer was no belligerent yahoo, bellowing animosity at "Rooshian commies," a notable talent of the Hearst newspapers and the Chicago *Tribune:* he was one of the thinking class's very own, he had examined the Soviets with the objective eye of the scholar-journalist, and he found their system sorely wanting in human decency. More than any single writer Fischer had seminal effect upon America's postwar thinking about the Soviet Union, and especially upon liberals who had wanted to believe the best about Russia and were rapidly changing their minds. Raymond Gram Swing, the respected broadcaster who carried much credibility among liberals, said Fischer's account "breathes sincerity and fairness." The *Reader's Digest* condensed two of the articles, bringing them to an even wider audience. Published in book form (as *Why They Behave like Russians*), Fischer reached hundreds of thousands of other Americans via the Book-of-the-Month Club.

Concurrent with Fischer's gloomy reportage, Brooks Atkinson of the *New York Times* also wrote off the Soviets. Returning from a ten-month tour in Moscow in mid-1946, he called for drastic changes in the U.S.–Soviet relationship. "The familiar concepts of friendship" should be abandoned in attempts to establish workable relations with Moscow. "Friendship in the sense of intimate association and political compromise is not wanted, is not possible, and is not involved. . . . The Russian people are admirable people . . . but between us and the Russian people stands the Soviet government. Despite its sanctimonious use of the word 'democracy' it is a totalitarian government. . . . There are no freedoms within the Soviet Union. . . . [T]he government is a machine for generating power within the Soviet Union and as far outside as the power can be made to extend; and all attempts to deal with it in terms of friendship are doomed to failure.

"Although we are not enemies, we are not friends, and the most we can hope for is an armed peace for the next few years. . . ."

For younger veterans who came out of the war with idealistic hopes about world harmony, the Soviet break was an acutely painful wrench. Once sympathetic, Bill Mauldin now drew a cartoon of two Soviet bullies approaching an emaciated man in a dungeon. One carried a noose and said, "There's nothing to it, excellency. Comrade Popoff and I have committed hundreds of successful suicides." The same week Mauldin wrote a *mea culpa* letter to *Time:*

> I guess I'm a disillusioned fellow traveler. I'm angry with our former great Allies. It's an accumulation of many things, but principally it's because of Russia's behavior in the United Nations. The Russians are determined to break up the UN. We could take a lot of slaps at our own foreign policy, we've lost a lot of our moral right to criticize. We're all wrong, but Russia is wronger.

Soviet–U.S. détente a failure, the Truman Administration fell back upon a double-pronged strategy of nuclear superiority and military and economic aid to any nation willing to oppose the Russians.

16

The World Policeman

Soon after the Japanese armistice Dr. Philip Morrison, a scientist at the Los Alamos laboratory that constructed the first atomic bombs, visited Hiroshima to talk with officials about the impact of the blast. Morrison was awed by what he learned:

"When it [the atomic bomb] is detonated in the middle of a city, it is as though a small piece of the sun has been instantly created. There is formed what we have called the ball of fire, which is a hot glowing something about one-third of a mile across, with a temperature of about 4,000,000 degrees Fahrenheit in the center of it.

"There is a sudden creation and expansion which pushes away, with terrible violence, the air that once occupied this region. This air, shocked into motion, moves just like a blast wave from a great explosion of TNT. This pushing air creates an enormous pressure, even a great distance away. Behind the waves of pressure, there come great winds, 500 to 1,000 miles per hour, winds which damage and destroy all structures. . . .

"If you are near the sun, you must expect to get burned. The people near it are burned on the body; the people and the structures underwent terrific radiant heat. Instantly all organic material was burned up. Over some distance it burned the flesh. . . .

"At the instant of the explosion there are emitted from this small sun not only the great push through the air, the violent blast, the concentrated heat, there was also a great amount of radiation, like the . . . X-ray radiation used for the treatment of cancer. This radiation was very penetrating. There is no protection behind a foot of concrete, for example. Of those persons within a thousand yards of a blast, one in every house, or two—about five or ten percent—escaped death from blast or from burn. Many crawled out of their homes relatively uninjured. But they died anyway. They died from the effects of radiumlike rays emitted in great numbers from the bomb at the instant of explosion. This radiation affects the blood-forming tissues in the bone marrow, and the whole

function of the blood is impaired. The blood does not coagulate, but oozes in many spots through the unbroken skin, and internally seeps into the cavities of the body.

"It goes without saying that, like most of the scientists of the project, I am completely convinced that another war cannot be allowed."

IN LOS ANGELES the Burbank Burlesque Theater advertised "Atombomb Dancers." A farmer in Newport, Arkansas, sent a letter to the "Atomic Bomb Co., Oak Ridge, Tennessee," stating, "I have some stumps in my field that I should like to blow out. Have you got any atomic bombs the right size for the job? If you have let me know by return mail, and let me know how much they cost. I think I should like them better than dynamite." A cereal company advertised an "atomic viewer" as a premium—"peek through the hole and watch brightly colored atoms swirl past your eyes."

Lay America's ignorance of the superweapon that ended the Second World War with two blistering, mysterious flashes of light was profound; all that was known of it, with certainty, was that it worked, and that it substituted for a large standing army. Soon after Hiroshima an American corporal in Germany said what everyone seemed to be thinking: "It is downright stupid to keep a whole lot of divisions here now when a few bombers and some atomic bombs would keep the Germans in line." The Russians did not have The Bomb and although the scientists said they could build one within five years, using their own resources, no one really cared to worry about the future. The atomic bomb shielded the United States from the Soviet Union. Stalin might probe Eastern Europe and encroach on U.S. friends on the periphery of the iron curtain, but he would never risk the Armageddon of total warfare.

The irony of America's nuclear deterrence was that it was built entirely on bluff. Moscow raged about "nuclear diplomacy," and apparently assumed, as did most American citizens, that the United States had more atomic bombs in its arsenal; no one in a position of authority did anything to discourage the notion. In fact, however, after the Nagasaki and Hiroshima explosions, the United States assembled only two other bombs, both detonated in tests at Bikini in July 1946. Not until 1948 did the United States possess another nuclear weapon. Its stockpile during two of the most frigid years of the Cold War was exactly zero.

The nuclear issues America faced in 1945 were complex: whether the United States, through the United Nations, should share the nuclear secret with allies and potential foes; under what auspices, military or civilian, atomic energy should be developed for peaceful purposes; and whether scientists should be allowed to contrive more horrifying versions of the bomb.

The first issue, civilian control of nuclear energy, was resolved in rather short order. President Truman wanted it. So, too, did atomic scientists chafing under generals more interested in making bombs than power plants. The scientific community had high hopes for peaceful exploitation of nuclear energy. Robert M. Hutchins, chancellor of the University of Chicago, site of much of the wartime atomic research, had fulsome predictions about the future. "Heat will be so plentiful," he said in 1945, "that it will even be used to melt snow as it falls. . . . A very few individuals working a few hours a day at very easy tasks in the central atomic power plant will provide all the heat, light, and power required by the community, and these utilities will be so cheap that their cost can hardly be reckoned." The Atomic Energy Commission, created in 1946, took control of the nuclear establishment as what one scientist, Ralph Lapp, has called "the most total monopoly in the history of the United States." The act creating the AEC declared that development and utilization of atomic energy, "so far as practicable," should be for civilian purposes, "subject at all times to the paramount objective of assuring the common defense and security." The AEC swiftly became a major industrial force in America. By 1948 the AEC owned a larger investment in real estate, plants, and equipment than did General Motors; it ran more buses than the City of Philadelphia; its land holdings covered an area greater than Rhode Island. Its plant on the Savannah River near Aiken, South Carolina, was the world's most expensive industrial facility, costing more than $1.4 billion and representing a capital outlay larger than the total for the entire Bethlehem Steel Corporation. And despite the AEC's statutory emphasis on peaceful uses of atomic power, the military placed such demands on the AEC that at least 90 percent of its program was military.

Hopes of putting the atomic bomb under international control succumbed rapidly to U.S.–Soviet distrust, internal congressional politics, and Truman's unwillingness to run patently grave risks with the century's most important military development. The script was complicated. Initially the Truman Administration offered to share atomic data with the Soviets in return for an agreement on controls of its military use. But the two most powerful senators on the Foreign Relations Committee, Tom Connally of Texas and Arthur Vandenberg of Michigan, felt the draft agreement was so loose it amounted to "giving away . . . atomic secrets"; Vandenberg, especially distressed, felt "the 'exchange' of scientists and scientific information [to be] . . . sheer appeasement because Russia has nothing to exchange." Senator Allen Ellender of Louisiana feared that "if we should divulge the secret, it . . . may fall into the hands of unscrupulous leaders who might use it against us." The North American Newspaper Alliance polled congressmen on what should be done with the atomic secret. Thirty-nine of thirty-nine Republicans answering and thirty-seven of forty-seven Democrats would keep it. In one public opinion poll, 73 percent of the people would keep control of the bomb in U.S. hands, only 14 percent would turn it over to the United Nations. Representative George Bender of Ohio introduced a bill making it a felony punishable by death for anyone "in the know" to reveal the secret of the atomic bomb.

The Soviets, meanwhile, were receiving a steady flow of information on the U.S. program from espionage rings in the United States and England, and Stalin apparently was willing to risk developing his own bomb without American help rather than enter into a controls agreement that would violate the Russians' xenophobic fear of foreign inspection. The official Soviet press initially downplayed the importance of the Hiroshima–Nagasaki bombs. Foreign correspondents in Moscow found that censors struck any implication that the atomic bomb, rather than the Russian entry into the Pacific war, caused the Japanese surrender. Three weeks later, however, the Soviets warned against any "plans for world hegemony . . . based on intended utilization of temporary superiority in technical developments." And even later in 1945 the Soviet press accused the United States of "atomic diplomacy." *Krokodil,* a Soviet humor magazine, carried a cartoon showing two parents—John Bull the mother, Uncle Sam the father—pushing a baby carriage draped with an American flag embroidered "atomic energy." "How do you intend to bring up your youngster?" a bystander inquired. "In a strictly private boarding school," replied the parents. Soviet and U.S. officials talked at length about controls and information exchanges through 1945 and 1946, and Bernard Baruch, the financier and amateur statesman, operating under presidential injunction, developed a draft plan for international controls through the United Nations. Nothing came of any of these efforts; by late 1946 the deepening chill of the Cold War reduced them to formalistic rituals.

The Truman Administration, meanwhile, kept its nuclear monopoly on conspicuous display. In July 1946 the military staged two public tests of the bomb on a tiny atoll called Bikini, in the Marshall Islands, 2,000 miles southwest of Hawaii. Doomsayers—and many scientists—were aghast. Some predicted the explosions would send an enormous tidal wave rushing across the Pacific to inundate San Francisco. Others warned darkly about what might happen to the ocean when stung by the atom. The first bomb, decorated with a picture of the love goddess Rita Hayworth, was dropped from a B-29 into a flotilla of seventy-three ships—U.S., Japanese and German battleships, transports, landing ships, destroyers, even an aircraft carrier—from 30,000 feet. An audience of congressmen, reporters, and scientific observers from all nations gawked as the water boiled into a cloud of fire and foam. The vessels heaved and pitched; many burst into flames. But only five sank, to the surprise, even disappointment, of observers; one journalist dismissed the bomb as a "giant firecracker." Ralph Lapp, present as a government scientist, permitted himself an indulgent smile at the "prophets of doom [who had been] muttering in their beards and uttering their strange and dire incantations. . . . The wave which rolled toward the shore of Bikini . . . was no more than six feet high and it did not inundate the flyspeck island. Nor did the sea water ignite and consume the world in an all-embracing flame of destruction." A second blast three weeks later, however, this one underwater, showered the target fleet with a heavy contamination of radioactivity. The skeptics raised new specters: of a bomb exploding in a lake, a reservoir, a river, to snuff out an entire city beneath a deadly mist of radioactive haze during the night. The net result of the tests, however, was to soothe the fears of the American people almost as much as the bombs dropped on Japan had aroused them. William Laurence wrote in the *New York Times* that before Bikini the public "stood in awe of this new cosmic force." Now, he felt, "this feeling of awe has largely evaporated and has been supplanted by a sense of relief unrelated to the grim reality of the situation. Having lived with a nightmare for nearly a year, the average citizen is now only too glad to grasp at the flimsiest means that would enable him to regain his peace of mind." Major George de Seversky, in a *Reader's Digest* article, argued that the Hiroshima bombing was not nearly so awful as first reports indicated. Researchers from Cornell University, trying to assess public sentiment toward the bomb, found citizens unmoved by the prospects of nuclear annihilation. "I . . . take life as it comes," a man in North Carolina told the team. "If I have to live in a country where there are earthquakes, surely there would be no point in my going to bed every night in fear of an earthquake." Said another: "I'm not worrying about it. The government is sure to be taking precautions. Why should my heart be heavy over something I can't possibly control?"

But who *could* control the bomb? Labor declined. A group of pacifist workmen tried to demonstrate outside the Oak Ridge laboratory in 1946 against the use of atomic energy for war purposes; but CIO unionists in the factory halted the protest. Stopping production would endanger the jobs of workers, they said. Scientists declined. The Federation of American Scientists at one point was in the forefront of a drive to have the United States declare it would never use atomic weapons in warfare. But in the spring of 1947 sentiment had shifted sharply. A federation questionnaire asked, "Do you think the United States should proceed with the production of atomic bombs?" The answers: 242 yes, 174 no. At Los Alamos, where scientists presumably knew the extreme consequences of the bomb, the vote was 137 yes, 31 no. General Leslie R. Groves, director of the Manhattan Project, gloated, "What happened is what I expected, that after they had this extreme freedom for about six months, their feet began to itch. . . . Almost every one of them has come back into government research, because it was just too exciting."

And just too unavoidable, as well. In the last peacetime year of 1941, the total research budget for *all* universities was estimated at $30 million. The military in 1946 let it be known it intended to spend $135 to $175 million annually, a high percentage on secret work. *Time* reported that "thoughtful scientists are thoroughly alarmed" at the change. "Is the military about to take over U.S. science lock, stock and barrel, calling the tune for U.S. universities and signing up the best scientists for work fundamentally aimed at military results . . . ?" Yes. In October 1946 Philip Morrison, a nuclear scientist, complained that at an annual meeting of the American Physical Society, half the delivered papers were supported in whole or in part by one of the military services. Some schools, Morrison said, received 90 percent of their research support from Navy funds. Universities had greatly expanded their scientific departments and laboratories with wartime funds: the researchers wanted to keep them open, even if the price was purely military work. Science had gone beyond the capacity of the individual researcher, Morrison lamented. "He [the scientist] needs support beyond the capabilities of the university. If the [Office of Naval Research] or the new army equivalent . . . comes with a nice contract, he would be more than human to refuse." Many of the contracts were for general research rather than specific arms. But Morrison said fellow scientists feared that the results, "in the shape of new and fearful weapons, will not justify the expenses and their own funds will begin to dwindle. The now amicable contracts will tighten up and the fine print will start to contain talk about results and specific weapon problems. And science itself will have been bought by war on the installment plan."

During a Russian scare in 1947, Mortuary Science, *an undertakers' journal published in Chicago, approached the problem of how to handle the "remains" of victims of atomic blasts. Safety was paramount. Cremations would be unsafe because "radioactive particles . . . certainly would be borne away by the volatile gases." No undertaker should remain long near a body that was even slightly radioactive unless he was protected by lead-lined clothing.*

After consulting unnamed experts, Mortuary Science *reached its own conclusions. When radioactive bodies arrive at the mortuary "dispose of them summarily by sealing them in caskets . . . lowering the caskets into excavations floored by a copious layer of concrete and then*

completely surrounding them with more concrete poured to fill the exca-
vations. The graves, of course, would be located in a secluded spot
from which the public would forever be barred. . . .

"[S]*uch a body might be exhibited to public view provided the visi-*
tors file quickly past the bier."

With new designs of bomb in hand in 1948, the military and the AEC
set up a new series of tests on Eniwetok Atoll, some 200 miles west of
Bikini. Three bombs in all were detonated, this time under circumstances of utmost secrecy; no longer did the United States deign to invite
Soviet observers. The only public statement emitted by the AEC was a
single terse sentence: "Operation Sandstone [the code name for the
tests] confirms the fact that the position of the United States in the field
of atomic weapons has been substantially improved." A few weeks later
Senator Edwin C. Johnson of Colorado inadvertently gave the true
dimensions when he boasted in an interview that U.S. scientists "already
have created a bomb that has six times the effectiveness of the bomb
that was dropped at Nagasaki"—that is to say, a bomb with an explosive power of 120,000 tons of TNT.*

The inevitable happened one afternoon in late September 1949.
Charles Ross, Truman's press secretary, called in reporters for a brief
announcement in the name of the President: "I believe the American
people are entitled to be informed of all developments in the field of
atomic energy. That is my reason for making public the following information. We have evidence that within recent weeks [i.e., the third week
of September] an atomic explosion occurred within the U.S.S.R." Truman sought to downplay the importance, saying that "ever since atomic
energy was first realized by man the eventual development of this new
source by other nations was to be expected. This probability has always
been taken into account by us." Louis Johnson, the secretary of defense,
followed suit. "I warn you," he told reporters. "Don't overplay this."
"The calmer the American people take this, the better," said General
Omar Bradley, chairman of the Joint Chiefs of Staff. "It's the kind of
thing you can't think about on a straight line until you've put it aside for
forty-eight hours," said Senator Vandenberg.

The Chicago *Tribune* reminded readers that publisher Robert McCormick had already built himself a bomb shelter. The New York *Journal-
American,* the Hearst newspaper, ran a half-column picture showing

* Johnson had an irresistible urge to talk about atomic matters. On November 1,
1949, during a debate with scientists on the question "Is there too much secrecy in
our atomic program?" he blurted out, "Here's the thing that is top secret. Our
scientists from the time that the bombs were detonated at Hiroshima and Nagasaki
have been trying to make what is known as a superbomb." Referring to the
Entiwetok bomb, he continued, "They want one that has a thousand times the
effect of that terrible bomb—and that's the secret, the big secret, that scientists in
America are so anxious to divulge to the whole scientific world."

Manhattan engulfed in atomic "waves of death and havoc." America's nuclear monopoly was at an end. A few weeks later Senator Johnson made his statement about scientists working on the "superbomb," soon identified in the press as the hydrogen bomb. In February 1950 Truman said America indeed was building such a bomb. The nuclear race was on.

The immediate precipitant for military and economic aid to countries threatened by the Soviets was a sudden crisis in Greece in the spring of 1947. The war left Greece in economic and political chaos. German occupiers effectively destroyed much of the country trying to put down the resistance, burning 1,500 villages and destroying railroads, bridges, and highways. By one estimate, 85 percent of the Greek children were tubercular. The government was so decimated that "you had . . . a country without even a street sweeper in it," in the words of General George Lincoln of the War Department. During the war American and British intelligence had built the resistance movement around a core of Communist saboteurs and terrorists. Lincoln MacVeagh, long-time U.S. ambassador in Athens, said the war enabled underground Communists to become "the leaders of the national resistance movement, with our help. . . . [T]he best organizers in Greece, and the best men, are the heads of the Communist movement, the most vital fellows in the country." When the war ended, however, the British, dominant commercially in the country, reinstalled King George (whose unpopularity was enhanced by the fact that he was not even Greek) and brought in troops to suppress the resistance movement, which was insistent on sharing power. The ensuing fight, according to MacVeagh, was "not one of the nice old revolutions we used to have in the old days." World opinion widely condemned the British for being more interested in protecting investments than in the Greek people. A truce was finally called, and non-Communists won parliamentary elections of dubious authenticity. The United States helped celebrate King George's return by having planes from the carrier USS *Franklin D. Roosevelt* skywrite the letters "FDR" over Athens. Jonathan Daniels, Roosevelt's former press secretary, called the plan "the first forgery by air power."

The Communists took to the hills as guerrilla fighters, and the British army spent millions upon millions of pounds futilely trying to contain them. Concurrently, British money helped prop up Turkey, under pressure from the Soviets for territorial concessions and military bases around the Dardanelles Straits, the latter in keeping with the Russians' historic quest for warm-water ports. The Soviets attempted no internal subversion in Turkey, hoping instead to wear down Ankara through the economic attrition of supporting a large peacetime army.

Britain could not stand the pace. Its economy near ruin because of a congeries of postwar domestic problems, on February 24, 1947, the British government told the United States it could provide no further economic or military aid to either country. Diplomatically, the news came at a bad time. Secretary of State Marshall was only days away from a conference on the shape of postwar Europe, and the Soviets were probing Western Europe. With little internal debate, the Truman Administration decided to take up the burden the British were casting away. On March 12 the President asked a joint session of Congress for $400 million in aid for Greece and Turkey, as well as authority to detail military advisers. The speech was tantamount to a declaration of global policy that committed the United States to undertake, on its own, a job of world policing and unlimited economic aid to any nation opposing communism and the Soviet Union. Truman said:

> I believe that it must be the policy of the United States to support free peoples who are resisting attempted subjugation by armed minorities or by outside pressures. The world is not static, and the status quo is not sacred. But we cannot allow changes in the status quo in violation of the Charter of the United Nations by such methods as coercion, or by such subterfuges as political infiltration.

The Senate Foreign Relations Committee began hearings the next day, with Dean Acheson, acting as secretary of state in Marshall's absence, testifying in executive session as chief Administration spokesman. Acheson faced a tough job—to convince an opposition Congress to approve an expensive and somewhat open-ended change in foreign policy that conceivably could lead to war. Further, the panel's two ranking Democrats, Tom Connally of Texas and Walter George of Georgia, were openly suspicious of Truman's program, and both were respected figures in the Senate establishment. So essentially Acheson had to sell the program to both parties.*

Skeptics raised a host of questions and objections. Vandenberg said the detailing of military advisers "just scares me to death"; that the language "is quite provocative"; that it seemed "close to a blank check that comes pretty close to a potential act of war." Acheson disagreed. Press comments apart, the Soviets never protested formally British military activities in Greece. "The difference is," Vandenberg interjected, "that this is a century-old practice of the British, and here we are staking out a substantially new American policy." Acheson, scrawling

---

* The transcripts of the executive session remained secret until January 1973, when the Senate Foreign Relations Committee published them as part of a historical study of the formation of postwar U.S. policy. These hearings more accurately reflect Senate concerns than did the pro forma open hearings: in public opposing Democrats such as Connally and George remained tolerably quiet; in private they gave Acheson his rougher moments. In public Acheson even refrained from mentioning the Soviet Union by name. In private he said flatly the aid program was intended to stop Soviet expansion.

busily on a legal pad as Vandenberg spoke, offered substitute language, but in words beyond the comprehension of any citizen without access to a diplomatic library:

> The provisions of the Act of May 19, 1926, as amended, are hereby extended and made applicable to Turkey and Greece.

The cited act, Acheson informed the committee, permitted the military to send advisers to the banana republics of Central and South America. The new language stretched the obscure, two-decade-old law to cover Turkey and Greece. The masking satisfied Vandenberg.

Senator Alexander Wiley of Wisconsin asked whether the United States intended to replace Britain as a colonial power. "The people of America are mightily concerned about whether this is the opening wedge to our taking over the job that Britain has done so well in the last 150 years around the globe. They are concerned . . . as to our ability . . . and as to what it will do to our own economy if we charge our own economy with that strategic load." Senator Walter George was skeptical about whether the British economic problem was as bad as depicted, and whether the United States was being euchred. "In fact, if she [Britain] can unload a few more problems of this kind on us or someone else, she is going to be stronger than she has been since before World War I." George noted Britain was retaining investments in Greece.

But the toughest questions put to the Administration concerned its decision to bypass the United Nations, and whether Truman's broad language in fact meant the United States intended to become a world policeman. The UN bitterly disappointed persons, in Congress and elsewhere, who had taken the grandiose charter language at face value, and felt the Greek situation should be handled by the international community, and not by the United States acting alone. Vandenberg, however, felt that giving the UN the problem "would have all but ruined the United Nations" because nothing could have been done. Nonetheless he felt Truman made a "great error" not to notify the UN of his intentions before going to Congress. But he felt hamstrung: "Here we sit, not as free agents, because we have no power to initiate foreign policy. It is . . . almost like a presidential request for a declaration of war. When that reaches us there is precious little we can do except say 'yes.'" That aside, he saw no choice for the Truman Administration: "I think they [the Soviets] have never gotten it out of their heads that if they press us hard enough we will finally yield." He could "not escape the feeling that we have got to take a calculated risk and that there is less risk in standing up than there is in lying down." But Vandenberg insisted, "I do not think we can fool the American people about it. I do not think there is any use in trying to fool them. . . . There is no use in pretending . . . that for $400 million we have bought peace. We have done nothing of the sort. It is merely a down payment on the only hopeful program for peace."

Senator Pepper, testifying before the committee at one of the closed sessions,* saw a dangerous precedent in the authorization for the United States "to send a military mission to armed forces outside the Western Hemisphere" for the first time. Putting armed forces in Turkey would "invite military action" by Russia, he said. He noted that UN pressures had forced Russian troops out of Iran in 1946 "without a soldier being advanced and without a dollar being put out," either by the United States or Iran. Pepper also told of an interview with a British officer who had served with Greek guerrillas fighting the Germans. He quoted the officer as saying that although Communists undoubtedly were involved, "the great part of those people are sincere, patriotic people. . . . They are striving toward what they believe to be democracy in their country." Pepper was not disturbed that neighboring Communist nations armed the insurgents. "Is this border disturbance so serious as to justify the U.S. government taking . . . the primary responsibility for raising and equipping and maintaining a Greek army in Greece?" If soldiers had to go to Greece to stop the border arms traffic, "let them have 'US' on one shoulder and 'UN' on the other," Pepper said. Wiley, too was bitterly disappointed that America did not have representatives at the UN "who can seize this dynamic moment and make the United Nations what I think it should be and what the hope of the world is that it will be. . . . My America is stepping out into a new field, reaching out and, yes, without mincing words, assuming the function of the British Empire, which she so gallantly handled in the century that is past."

But did the Greek-Turkish aid in fact portend a new American policy of containment of the Soviets? Acheson, in somewhat equivocal language, would not put any advance limitation on similar American responses elsewhere in the world, should a friendly nation be threatened with Communist takeover. Senator H. Alexander Smith of New Jersey, pointing to "Communistic infiltration in South America," asked, "Are we going to be called on to finance resistance to communism in other countries like that? . . . I want to see what the implications are throughout the world." Acheson responded, "If there are situations where we can do something effective, then I think we must certainly do it." Senator Henry Cabot Lodge, Jr., of Massachusetts wanted more candor from Congress. "I can see where the State Department cannot go out and say this is a quasi-military measure, because it would hit the Russians right on the nose and make them sore. But I do not see why we

* Pepper had little credibility or respect in the Senate. Senator Carl Hatch of New Mexico, noting opposition to Greco-Turkish aid by Pepper and Henry Wallace, said, "They represent a certain group in this country that always takes sides when the Russian situation arises, and the side is against us."

in Congress cannot be very candid about it. . . . I think it will help a great deal in getting public support . . . to say this is a policy based on American national interest."

In making its case the Administration presented testimony from ambassadors to the two recipient nations. Both stressed the pragmatism of Truman's decision. Edwin Wilson, the ambassador to Turkey, said the U.S. intention was to "convince the Russians that we mean business in that area, and are not going to permit the expansion of the Soviets beyond where they have gone now." Wilson did not like many things about the Turkish and Greek governments; nonetheless "what we are doing here is not because we like the color of the eyes of the Turks or the Greeks or anything of that sort. We are doing it because it is in our own interest, and we would do it regardless of what regime was in Turkey or in Greece." Senator Connally was sanguine about where the U.S. help was going: "If you do not help either the totalitarians of the Communist breed or the totalitarians of the other, you are not going to help anybody in Greece."[*]

What especially galled Senator George was the feeling that Truman was trying to rush Congress in what he called "the most important step we have ever taken in our international relationships." Greece had received lush aid since the war ended ("Seven million people have had $700 million") and the guerrilla situation was not critical. "I know very, very well that this is simply the beginning of a program the end of which no man can foresee at the moment. . . . We are entitled to use common sense and not go any further than we ought to go. But once you take these steps, it is awfully hard to check. It is awfully hard to turn back . . . and that is the situation we are in." George conceded he was a "voice crying in the wilderness, but you are going to hear more voices, you do not need to doubt that, because the American people do not understand this thing, and when they do understand it they are going to ask a lot of questions about it."

To the Administration's relief, the general public accepted the Truman Doctrine, even if unenthusiastically and without signs they understood its full implications. A Gallup poll showed 56 percent favoring aid to Greece, 49 percent to Turkey. A majority regretted that the Greek problem was not put to the UN, and was "anxious to avoid military involvement of any kind in Greece." The vast majority of newspaper editorials favored the Truman Doctrine, albeit with reservations and misgivings. Many doubted whether communism could be fought with dollars, and suspected Truman had not told the whole truth. The San Francisco *Chronicle* was typical of the reluctant supporters:

[*] In its final report the committee stepped around the charge that the Greek government was fascist with the statement, "In Greece today we do not have a choice between a perfect democracy and an imperfect democracy. The question is whether there shall be any democracy at all."

". . . [T]he question inevitably arises, and neither the President nor Congress can dodge it, of where all this gets us. Are we to shoulder the mantle of nineteenth-century British imperialism? . . . Are we to set up a 1947 model WPA on the world scale? . . . And, finally, are we asking for a third world war? . . . America will demand answers to these questions."

The sharpest criticisms came from the left. TRUMAN SCRAPS FDR POLICY ON RUSSIA headlined *PM*'s story on Truman's speech; editorially, *PM* accused Truman of a demagogic appeal to the anti-Communist right. Fiorello La Guardia, the former New York mayor, said it was not worth the life of a single American soldier to keep the Greek king on his throne. The Chicago *Sun-Times* charged "naked imperialism." The *Progressive* refused to support the Truman Doctrine unless it was conducted through the UN and made contingent upon reforms of the recipient governments: "It was only five years ago that we were being implored to help Communism stop Fascism. Now, in effect, we are being urged to help Fascism stop Communism." In another vein, columnist Walter Lippmann called the conception of the Truman Doctrine "fundamentally unsound . . . a policy of holding the line and hoping for the best. . . . It would mean that for ten or fifteen years Moscow, not Washington, would define the issues. . . . The policy can be implemented only by recruiting, subsidizing and supporting a heterogeneous array of satellites, clients, dependents, and puppets, . . . a coalition of disorganized, disunited, feeble and disorderly nations, tribes and factions around the perimeter of the Soviet Union." But such liberals as Arthur Schlesinger, Jr., called the doctrine a welcome and overdue indication that Truman was capable of decisive action, and Hubert Humphrey asked the national board of Americans for Democratic Action to endorse his move.*

In the House the chief opposition came from a combination of far-left Democrats and far-right Republicans. Republican Representative J. Edgar Chenoweth of Colorado, referring to grave reclamation work then underway, stormed, "I should think that you who are trying to get us into World War Three would have the decency to wait until we get back the bodies of the 300,000 boys killed in World War Two." Rebutting, House Speaker Sam Rayburn said, "God help us, God help this world, if we do not accept our responsibility to help countries who do not want to be smothered by communism." In the end, Congress had little choice but to approve the Truman Doctrine—which it did in mid-May, by a

* Prominent Democratic liberals, many veterans of the New Deal, formed Americans for Democratic Action in early 1947 as what one founder, James Loeb, Jr., called "a declaration of liberal independence from the stifling and paralyzing influence of the Communists and their apologists in America." ADA stood thereafter as a non-Communist alternative to such groups as Henry Wallace's burgeoning, if as yet amorphous, Progressive Party.

67–23 vote in the Senate and 284–107 in the House. As John C. Campbell of the Council on Foreign Relations commented, "Truman had
issued a challege to the Soviet Union in one of the bluntest statements
ever made in peacetime by a head of state. Congress could not repudiate
him, or even amend his proposal substantially, without giving encour-
agement to Communists everywhere and dealing a blow to those whom
we wished to help."

Two parallel developments followed closely upon the Truman Doctrine to extend even further the policy of Soviet containment—the
Marshall Plan, indirectly, through economic aid to Europe; and the
North Atlantic Treaty Organization (NATO), a military alliance intended as a defensive shield against the Russians. Enacted against a
backdrop of brutal Soviet crackdowns on democratic dissidents in
Eastern Europe (notably Hungary and Czechoslovakia) the U.S. initia-
tives in 1947–48 ended any lingering public optimism about the postwar
world.

Secretary Marshall announced the plan bearing his name in a commencement address at Harvard on June 5, 1947, in characteristically
undramatic fashion. Speaking so softly as to be almost inaudible, gazing
steadily at the notes before him, and never for a moment looking at his
audience, Marshall laid out an unprecedented offer of international social responsibility: he offered all of Europe—including the Soviet Union
and its satellite states—aid for economic recovery. And Marshall tried
to make plain the plan was not antagonistic toward the Russians:

> Our policy is directed not against any country or doctrine, but
> against hunger, poverty, desperation and chaos. . . . At this criti-
> cal point in history, we of the United States are deeply conscious of
> our responsibilities to the world. We know that in this trying
> period, between a war that is over and a peace that is not yet
> secure, the destitute and oppressed of the earth look chiefly to us
> for sustenance and support until they can again face life with self-
> confidence and self-reliance.

Europe indeed needed help. The Soviet advance to the Oder River
had cleaved the continent in half, disrupting normal trade patterns. A
quarter of Europe's industry lay in ruins. Hundreds of thousands of
persons were displaced and either roamed aimlessly or huddled in refugee camps. Regardless of whether the "Russian menace" was real or
imagined, Europe needed help.

There were domestic considerations as well. In January 1948, during
debate on the scope of the Marshall Plan, Secretary of Agriculture
Clinton B. Anderson noted that American farmers were producing one-
third more food and fiber products than before the war and would
continue to need European markets. "We are going to have abundance

of agricultural production, and for many years to come we will need sizable export markets. . . . [T]he prospects of a collapsing European economy, providing little outlet for U.S. farm products, would not be pleasant to contemplate." The grandiosity of U.S. aid during the first four postwar years is documentable: $5.9 billion for the new World Bank; $3.4 billion for the United Nations Relief and Rehabilitation Administration; $3.6 billion for direct relief; $9.2 billion for loans and property credits; $17 billion for the first four years of the Marshall Plan—a total of $38.1 billion, which represents $20 for every man, woman and child on the planet.

The Soviets would have no part of the Marshall Plan (formally, the European Recovery Program, or ERP). Two weeks after Marshall's speech, at a ministerial conference in Paris, Soviet Foreign Minister Vyacheslav Molotov accused the United States of attempting to seize foreign markets with Marshall Plan funds to stave off an impending economic crisis. Molotov wanted each nation to draw its own recovery program. Attempts at a general European program, he said, would inevitably entail intervention in the affairs of individual states and "could not serve as a basis for collaboration among European countries." Molotov would deal out Germany entirely. The conference collapsed; the Soviets forced the satellite states to reject participation, and thus the Marshall Plan began as a Western European venture. The decision was especially painful for Czechoslovakia. Although President Eduard Benes and Foreign Minister Jan Masaryk expressed loyalty to their country's alliance with the Soviet Union and recognized their dependence upon Soviet goodwill, they also hoped to maintain economic and political ties with the United States. The Czech cabinet (including Communist ministers) voted to join in Marshall Plan talks, whereupon Masaryk was summoned to Moscow and ordered otherwise. In the words of John Campbell, "This decisive and humiliating intervention on the part of Moscow was convincing proof that no state in Moscow's orbit would be allowed to be a bridge over which American dollars and western influence might make their way eastward." Six months later Masaryk died in a mysterious plunge from his office window, and the Soviet control was complete. The death of Masaryk, son of a former Czech president and a friend of the West, dramatized, as few other things could have, the significance of what was happening in the Soviet satellite countries.

By the time the Marshall Plan went to Congress public opinion was solidly, if reluctantly, behind it. The chief criticism, from Republicans, was the cost—an opposition the Truman Administration deftly neutralized by convincing Senator Vandenberg to support the plan as if it were his very own. Many mornings Dean Acheson, the undersecretary of state, stopped by Vandenberg's apartment and read him top-secret diplomatic cables and briefing papers over breakfast, making him the Administration's foreign policy partner in fact as well as in appearance. The persuasion carried Vandenberg several light-years in his thinking, for he had ranked among the most committed of isolationists. He told an American Legion convention in 1939: "This so-called war is nothing but about twenty-five people and propaganda. They [the Europeans] want our money and our men." One of his two books on Alexander Hamilton carried the title-page motto: "Nationalism—not internationalism—is the indispensable bulwark of American independence." But as a matter of relaxation Vandenberg for seventeen years went to a different country annually and stayed there for as long as two months. Hence Truman and Acheson found him open-minded when they set out to convince him that European survival depended upon American help. At Vandenberg's suggestion, Acheson brought John Foster Dulles, the Wall Street lawyer and internationalist, into the State Department as an $11,000-a-year consultant. Dulles helped, even if his support was voiced in a rather backhanded way ("It is time to rally from a frustrating confusion that has its roots in mistakes of the past rather than in the circumstances of the present"). But Senator Robert A. Taft felt the Dulles appointment as a meaningless sop: "Bipartisanship is not accomplished by the appointment of a single Republican. . . . Bipartisanship is being used by Mr. Truman as a slogan to condemn any Republican who disagrees with Mr. Truman's unilateral foreign policy, secretly initiated and put into effect without any real consultation with Congress."

Vandenberg faced a severe challenge in persuading Republicans to go along with him. The House Republican whip, Leslie Arends of Illinois, proposed a national referendum before Congress voted on the Marshall Plan. "Are you willing to pay your share . . . if it means a minimum of ten percent increase in your cost of living, a withholding of at least thirty percent in your pay instead of the present twenty percent?" he asked. Representative Leo E. Allen of Illinois, chairman of the House Rules Committee, did not want to send any aid whatsoever to Europe's "armies of mendicants and loafers." Clare Hoffman of Michigan called the danger of world communism "a false doctrine." Dewey Short of Missouri opined, "There are times when one must be cruel to be kind. The more you give people, the more they will curse you for not giving them more." Taft called the bill a "wrong and fallacious approach" to solving Europe's problems.

On the Democratic left, Representative Vito Marcantonio of New York charged that the Marshall Plan benefited Wall Street, not the European people. In one lengthy speech on ERP's impact on Italy, he ticked off a series of charges: the Italian government, as a condition of receiving aid, had been forced to sell a $136,400,000 bond issue through Wall Street investment houses (J. P. Morgan and Company, Dillon, Read and Company, and the Chase National Bank, among others) to replace old Kingdom of Italy bonds valued at less than $10 million. The first loans made to Italy went to such industrialists as the Pierelli rubber family and the Montecatini chemical interests, who had supported the dictator Mussolini from 1922 until "Americans shed their blood and rid the world of him." ERP prohibited recipient countries from trading with nations not in the Marshall Plan—meaning Italy had to buy coal from the United States at $20 per ton when it was available in Poland for a quarter that price. The State Department warned that aid would cease if Italy elected a Communist government and that any Italian who voted for the Popular Democratic Front ticket would be denied immigration rights. Each of Marcantonio's charges contained a kernel of truth. But as a fringe figure unheeded even in the "respectable left" of his own party, his speeches made no impact whatsoever in Congress. Congress voted exactly what Truman asked for ERP's first year—$4.25 billion—and even threw in $1.5 billion as aid for the beleaguered Chinese government of Chiang Kai-shek. America had opened its purse to the world.

And its hearts as well. The Friendship Train, organized by columnist Drew Pearson, collected 266 boxcars of food (12,120 tons) during a California-to-New York tour. The American Silent Guest Committee of Plymouth, Massachusetts, had families donate the cost of one Thanksgiving meal to European relief. Hamilton College students in Clinton, New York, spent their Thanksgiving and Christmas vacations collecting food for distribution to the European needy through overseas alumni. The audacity of the Marshall Plan was that it equaled a U.S. promissory note for billions of dollars at the very time the Republican Congress had avowed to cut taxes, end government controls, and curb spending. The British economist Barbara Ward marveled at the concept. "I believe that the American people—the only people in the world who thought of an ideal first and then built a state around it—will prove in the long run happier, freer, and more creative when they carry that ideal of a free society out into the world, than if they sat at home to hug it to themselves. . . . I suspect that Americans will find initiative and action so much more to their taste than any panic-stricken waiting on what destiny may bring."

The Marshall Plan did as intended: American-supported factions remained dominant in both Greece and Turkey, and the Soviets swiftly lost interest in both countries. Yet another confrontation, this one in divided Berlin, brought even graver risks. Unable to reach agreement with the three western powers over the permanent status of the prewar capital, the Soviets in the spring of 1948 gradually began squeezing off access. The Soviets stopped trains and delayed traffic, and tore up streets leading to border crossings. In April a Soviet fighter plane buzzed a British transport; the craft collided and crashed. A month later, objecting to western issuance of a new currency for the allied zones of the city, the Soviets blocked all land routes whatsoever, with the unannounced intention of forcing abandonment.

The Americans and the British responded with a massive round-the-clock airlift of food, coal, and other essential supplies, with hundreds of planes daily lumbering into Templehof air base. Only four minutes flying time separated planes shuttling into the city—a southern corridor for inbound planes, a northern corridor for those returning west. Ground crews cut turn-around time to half an hour. The challenge was awesome: to supply a city of 2,500,000 persons, more than the population of Philadelphia. But the airlift worked. Berliners shivered through the winter months of 1948–49, and they tightened their belts, but the allies refused to back down. In late spring 1949, with the Soviets tiring of the tactic, flights increased to an incredible peak of 1,017 daily. In May the Soviets suddenly pulled back, and permitted ground traffic to resume.

Americans took quiet pride in the accomplishment: for the first time they had achieved a clear victory over the Soviets. The cost was high, in terms of money and men (the air force alone spent $400,000 daily on the flights, and seventy American and British airmen perished in crashes). Yet in the words of General Lucius Clay, the U.S. commander in West Germany, "Measured in terms of prestige, measured in the courage which it has brought to millions of people who desire freedom, measured indeed in comparison to our expenditures for European assistance . . . and national defense, its cost is insignificant." And in the words of historian Eric Morris, "Never again would there be any possibility of dislodging the Western powers from their position in Germany by putting pressure on Berlin."

Thus began the era of Pax Americana, a policy devised not so much by free choice of the public as by the lack of a palatable alternative; and one that led inexorably to U.S. involvement in such unforeseen places as Guatemala, the Dominican Republic, the Middle East, Chile—and Indochina. Stripped of diplomatic verbiage, the Truman Doctrine meant that the United States would use dollars and armed might to contain communism, with right-wing governments as partners if necessary.

17

The Spy Searches

In the spring of 1946 the Research Institute of America, specializing in business and political analyses, prepared a booklet on the Communist Party, USA, for its corporate clients. A major theme was "how to spot a Communist in your own business." The suggestions: Read the Daily Worker *for a guide on the often-changing party line. Watch workers for their attitudes toward such anti-Communist union leaders as Walter Reuther of the auto workers and David Dubinsky of the garment workers. The institute listed "characteristics" of Communist literature: violence of expression; "unreasonable criticisms"; charges that the opposition is fascist; and use of such Communist jargon as deviationist, Lovestoneite, and revisionist. When an executive suspected a Communist was at work in his plant the institute suggested he contact a labor relations specialist immediately.*

The Daily Worker *countered with advice on "How to Detect Capitalists in Your Industry." The paper wrote, "Don't expect to find the capitalist in your shop. Look for him on the golf course. It is there that he will tell you that without him, the industry could not function. . . .*

"He never comes before you and says, 'I am a capitalist.' He works through various front organizations: large sections of the Republican and Democratic parties; the 'free press,' the National Association of Manufacturers, the State Department and others.

"Watch out for the fellow who tells you that you, individually, are free to give U.S. Steel a run for their money. This is a trap. Do not try to manufacture steel. Examine the suspect's hands for calluses. But this is not conclusive. If his heart is callused, he's your man."

IN EARLY 1945 an analyst for the Office of Strategic Services, the espionage and intelligence organization that was to grow, during several mutations, into the Central Intelligence Agency, read with rapidly rising eyebrows an article in *Amerasia,* a scholarly journal on Asian affairs. The article, on British-American relations in the Orient, closely paralleled a top-secret report the analyst had written on the subject for OSS superiors. Entire paragraphs had been abstracted from his report; others were loosely paraphrased. Quite obviously the writer had had access to a document that should not be in public circulation.

Frank Bielaski, the OSS director of investigations, immediately started a probe of *Amerasia* and its editor, Philip Jaffe. Founded in 1937 as an offshoot of the Institute of Pacific Relations (IPR), an international grouping of Asian specialists, *Amerasia* was small (with only about 2,000 circulation at its peak) but vastly influential among the tight band of diplomats and scholars working in the field. Many of its contributors, such as Anna Louise Strong and Owen Lattimore, wrote critically of the Chinese Nationalist Government of Chiang Kai-shek, and reported the swelling popular support of the Chinese Communists. A cofounder of the magazine, Frederick V. Field, executive of the IPR's American Council, who owned 50 percent of the stock through February 1944, had a lengthy involvement with Communist causes.* So, too, did editor Philip Jaffe. Through surveillance the OSS established that he talked regularly with known Communists, contributed generously to pro-Communist causes, and wrote for *China Today,* a Communist publication, under a pen name. Jaffe's main income seemed to be from a printing plant that produced greeting cards.

On March 11, a Sunday night, Bielaski led a raiding party into the vacant *Amerasia* offices. In one room they found sophisticated photocopying equipment. In Jaffe's office were a suitcase and briefcases crammed with classified OSS reports—including the one used as source material for the article that had prompted the search. One document was stamped "top secret," the others "secret." Bielaski was flabbergasted.

> I took this stuff and spread it around. It covered almost every department in the government except the FBI. . . . There were documents from British intelligence, naval intelligence, G-2 [army intelligence], Office of Censorship, Office of Strategic Services. . . . There were so many we could not list them. These documents were from 3 or 4 to 150 pages. There were 300 documents. Every one of them bore the stamp that possession of these documents is a violation of the espionage act. . . .

* The *Amerasia* affair, in which Field was not involved as a defendant, did not deter his enthusiasm for the Chinese Communist cause. In 1949 he concluded an article in *Political Affairs,* a Communist journal, with the sentence, "It is our task as American Communists to help mobilize the forces of labor and all anti-imperialists in our country, and deal further blows at Wall Street, so that the [Communist] Chinese new democracy may consolidate its victories and move firmly and powerfully on the road toward socialism." Field went to jail in the late 1940's for contempt of Congress for refusing to answer questions about his political beliefs.

About that time one of my men who had gone into the library came in and said he had found something. He had an envelope which was not sealed. It was a large manila envelope. In that envelope were, I should say, fifteen or twenty documents. . . . In between these documents, . . . we found six top secret documents of the Navy Department. . . . One of them was entitled "The Bombing Program for Japan." . . . It showed how Japan was to be bombed progressively in the industrial cities, and it named cities.

The second one that I read gave the location of all the ships of the Japanese fleet, subsequent to the Battle of Leyte. I guess it was October 1944. It gave the ships by name, and where they were located.

Flipping through the papers Bielaski found an envelope with the cryptic label " 'A' Bomb." The notation meant nothing to him. He also came across a detailed breakdown on the strength and locations of units of the Nationalist Chinese Army. Still another hinted at one of the most closely guarded secrets of the war: that U.S. cryptographers had cracked Japanese military and diplomatic codes.

After carefully restoring the office Bielaski took away enough documents to show superiors the sort of information he had found strewn around the *Amerasia* premises. The OSS security chief, Archibald Van Beuren, was shocked into near speechlessness as Bielaski dealt out his sample. One of the papers, he was to recount later, was of "such secrecy" that its presence in the *Amerasia* offices struck him as "almost calamitous." In addition to the routine strictures on its face about disclosure to outsiders, the document was marked "for the eyes of chief of naval intelligence only." Internal time-stamps indicated the documents had come through the State Department, so the details eventually went to Secretary of State Edward Stettinius, Jr., who exclaimed, "Good God, if we can get to the bottom of this we will stop a lot of things that have been plaguing us."

The FBI put the *Amerasia* principals under tight surveillance for several months, with agents making several surreptitious entries into the offices to find even more documents. A bug on Jaffe's Washington hotel room turned up an interesting conversation with John Stewart Service, a career diplomat just back from China, where he had been posted to the headquarters of both Mao Tse-tung, the Chinese Communist leader, and Chiang Kai-shek. On May 8, during a discussion of Roosevelt's difficulties in dealing with China, Service reminded Jaffe, "Well, what I said about the military plans is, of course, very secret." He went on to state that if U.S. troops landed in Nationalist territory, "we would have to go on cooperating with them." But if the landings were in Communist territory, "they'd be the dominant force." When Jaffe asked whether it appeared likely Americans would actually be landed, Service answered, "I don't think it has been decided. I can tell you in a couple of weeks when [General Joseph] Stilwell gets back [from his former command in China]." In yet another conversation Jaffe asked Service for a document from the State Department's Division of Far Eastern Affairs. Service said he did not think he could obtain a file copy, but that he thought he could "run off" a copy and mail it to New York. Jaffe, concurrently, was found by the FBI to be meeting with Earl Browder, the head of the CPUSA, and Tung Pi-wun, who visited New York in the spring prior to attending the founding conference of the United Nations in San Francisco as a representative of the Chinese Communists.*

When the OSS case was ready for a grand jury, the Justice Department was told, apparently through Secretary of the Navy James Forrestal, that any prosecutions must be withheld until the end of the UN conference. The reason was that action might unduly antagonize the Soviets. Julius C. Holmes, the assistant secretary of state for security, was aghast. With acting secretary of state Joseph Grew, he went directly to the White House, and they told President Truman what was happening. The order to stop the case had gone to Myron Gurnea of the FBI.

Truman's reaction was direct. By Holmes's account, he said, "Well, get Mr. Gurnea on the phone for me." Holmes did, and he heard Truman tell Gurnea:

> This is the President speaking. I don't care who has told you to stop this. You are not to do it. Go straight ahead with this and it doesn't matter who gets hurt. This has got to be run down. If anybody suggests that you postpone, or anything else, you are not to do it without first personal approval from me.

Truman hung up and looked at Holmes and grinned. "Does that suit you?" he asked. "Yes, sir," Holmes replied.

Within a week six persons were arrested on charges of conspiring to violate the espionage act: editor Jaffe; diplomat John Stewart Service; Kate Louise Mitchell, the *Amerasia* coeditor; Andrew Roth, a lieutenant in naval intelligence until the day preceding his arrest; Mark Gayn, born in Manchuria of White Russian parents, and a long-time resident of China, now a free-lance newspaper and magazine writer specializing in Asian affairs; and Emmanuel S. Larsen, a China expert for naval intelligence and the State Department. Investigators found an additional 1,500 classified documents on Asian affairs when they made the arrests.

But the case ran into rough waters before the grand jury. Defense attorneys, in conferences at the Justice Department, argued that their clients were guilty of nothing more than the accepted journalistic prac-

---

* At Soviet insistence the Chinese Communists were permitted to attend the San Francisco conference, but they were denied formal membership.

tice of obtaining background material from government sources. For three of the defendants the argument was seemingly persuasive: indictments were returned against only Larsen, Roth, and Jaffe. The other three arrestees were cleared, and Service returned to full duty at the State Department, with James Byrnes, now the secretary of state, sending him a public welcoming message: "I am happy to approve the recommendation that you will be returned to active duty. . . . I predict for you a continuance of a splendid record."*

Even more grievous to the prosecution was a chance revelation to the defense. When the FBI was arresting Emmanuel Larsen in his apartment in suburban Arlington, Virginia, he overheard an agent say documents could be found in the middle drawer of a file cabinet. "That is the place," another agent replied. Once freed on bail, Larsen bearded his landlord, who admitted he permitted FBI agents to enter the apartment "two or three times" before the arrest. Larsen's lawyer, Arthur J. Hilland, told the Justice Department he would file motions asking dismissal of the case because of the "illegal entries." Justice Department lawyers realized Jaffe could make the same argument if he knew of the surreptitious raids on the *Amerasia* office, which were carried out without benefit of a search warrant. In the opinion of James M. McInerney, of the criminal division, should "the fountainhead of the evidence, Jaffe's office in New York . . . become inaccessible to us . . . the whole case would have been destroyed." Yet, inexplicably, Hilland did not relay his information to Jaffe's Washington lawyer, Albert Arent, so Jaffe remained officially ignorant of any allegations of illegal search and seizure.

McInerney decided his only hope was to squeeze a guilty plea from Jaffe before his lawyers realized what was happening. The afternoon Hilland was to file the motions, McInerney asked Arent to come to his office to discuss a possible plea. McInerney wanted an ironbound agreement on a plea, for "I knew that when [Arent] went out on the street, when I got finished with him, he would see Larsen's notice of motion in the newspaper, he would make a similar motion, and our entire case would be destroyed." So he kept Arent cooped in his office for four hours, and a deal was struck: the government would drop the conspiracy charge, and Jaffe would plead guilty to a lesser count of illegal

---

* Such was not to be the case. From 1945, loyalty and security hearings became an annual rite for the harried diplomat. He was cleared in 1946, 1947, 1949, 1950, and by a State Department board in 1951. But the Civil Service Loyalty Review Board ruled against him on December 13, 1951, when McCarthyism fervor about "the loss of China" was at white heat: "We are not required to find Service guilty of disloyalty and we do not do so, but for an experienced and trusted representative of our State Department to so far forget his duty to his trust as his conduct with Jaffe so clearly indicates, forces us with great regret to conclude that there is reasonable doubt as to his loyalty." Secretary of State Dean Acheson dismissed Service the same day. In 1957 the Supreme Court reversed the dismissal on grounds it violated departmental procedural rules.

possession of government documents. A court session was arranged for the next morning, a Saturday, and both sides played out the script: a $2,500 fine for Jaffe, $500 for Larsen; a dismissal of the indictment against Roth.

The reasons for the sudden denouement were shielded from public view. Prosecutor McInerney certainly could not boast of how he hoodwinked Albert Arent;* the defendants, similarly, had the common sense not to gloat about their narrow escape. Hence the outcome caused mystification. As the public saw it, a case warranting screaming newspaper headlines about "espionage" and "spy ring" suddenly vanished. The pleas were entered on a Saturday, when the federal courthouse was virtually deserted. The customary advance notice to the press about action in major cases was somehow overlooked. The entire presentation took about five minutes, and prosecutors agreed with Arent's plea that Jaffe was guilty of nothing more than "an excess of journalistic zeal."

The abrupt ending, and the wrist-slap sentences, caused consternation in much—but by no means all—of the American press. The New York *Herald Tribune,* hostile to the Truman Administration, called the arrests "Red-baiting," and said they were "a serious omen if they mean that everyone in the government [must] maintain a mouselike quiet if he is to the political left of the State Department." Better to have quietly fired the government employees involved, the *Herald Tribune* said, rather than fuss up public anger with arrests. But the Detroit *Free Press* simply ran a cartoon showing a trail of footprints labeled *"Amerasia* Fix" leading to the White House door.

Through intense public pressure the Republican minority in Congress forced the House Judiciary Committee to hold closed hearings on the charge that the case was a "cover-up." The Republicans hinted darkly that the Truman Adminsitration had backed away in a hurry when it realized the *Amerasia* principals were involved with a Communist espionage ring in the State Department. The most charitable explanation the Republicans would offer was that further revelations would upset the delicate Moscow-Washington friendship. A more damning explanation was that the Administration was so honeycombed with spies that it was unable to investigate itself.

Skeptics saw peculiar pieces of information. Consider Andrew Roth, who had doubled as a researcher for *Amerasia* while working as a lieutenant in naval intelligence. When Roth first entered the navy, security questions were raised because he was reported to be a Communist. But the navy held that "the fact that a man was a Communist was not a

---

* Years later McInerney conceded he might have erred in not pressing the case further. "I think now that Jaffe may have been an espionage agent, which information we did not have at that time." McInerney indicated lawyer Arent felt the Department of Justice had more evidence on Jaffe than had been revealed publicly, and hence was eager to resolve the case as painlessly as possible.

bar since we were at peace with Russia"—as indeed, we were, and hundreds of Communists served in the armed services, many of them bravely, and without a ripple of public protest. The House Judiciary Committee, when it finally got into the case, reported it found no evidence of a whitewash, although the Republican minority denounced the prosecution for bungling errors. The Democrats, in turn, pooh-poohed the importance of the papers found in the *Amerasia* office: "Few, if any, of the identifiable classified documents involved in this case had any real importance in our national defense or our war efforts."

For American conservatives, the *Amerasia* case was mightily suspicious because it dovetailed with a thesis that Chiang Kai-shek's problems were due more to sabotage by "crypto-Communists" and fellow travelers in the State Department than the defects of his regime. American journalists and diplomats alike depicted Chiang's rule as a corrupt dictatorship rivaling, in outright meanness, German Nazism. Was there any future for a government that "recruited" an army by marching twelve-year-old boys to the front in chains, handing them rifles only when they came within range of the enemy? But a powerful clique of businessmen with interests in Asia, China-buff publishers such as Henry Luce of Time, Inc., and zealot anti-Communist missionaries—a loose band that became infamous as "the China Lobby"—scorned this view; anyone who doubted the sagacity of Chiang was *ipso facto* ignorant or treacherous. Luce was particularly obstinate: after bitter wrangles with Theodore H. White, his correspondent in wartime China (who saw Chiang "as China's greatest enemy"), he ordered White to stop writing about the political situation and concentrate on military developments. Luce and White soon went their separate ways; the tone of *Time's* coverage thereafter was set by Whittaker Chambers, a onetime Communist now virulently rightist (and a man of whom we shall hear much more ere the period ends). Had Luce been a mere private citizen, his self-imposed ignorance would have been of little import; as America's most influential publisher, however, he could—and did—deliver his wholly subjective opinions to the general citizenry with Olympian authority. In fact, Luce unilaterally declared victory for Chiang in a *Time* cover story September 3, 1945:

> Now, at long last, Chiang's steadfastness and statesmanship had been vindicated. As the war ended, the great fact was clear: the Generalissimo had justified those [i.e., Luce] who had long held that his government was firmly embedded in popular support, and that given peace it could establish an effective administration in China. . . . Many of the bumptious propaganda claims of the Chinese Communists had melted in the face of facts. . . . Whatever military teeth the Communists once had, they seemed to have been drawn when Moscow withdrew its support. . . .

As the Communist problem fell into its proper perspective, the great problem before China was to organize the peace.

Less than a year later—and without a backward glance at its misplaced confidence in the Generalissimo—*Time* admitted that things were not going quite so well in China as forecast:

> [T]he news from China was bad—appallingly bad. China was hurtling into economic disaster and political anarchy. Its causes: (1) Communist rebellion; (2) failure of the U.S. to send enough prompt aid; (3) the corrupt inefficiency of the National Government. . . .
>
> The most important truth about China is that hardly anybody in China seems to have any faith in the ability of the present Government to run the nation wisely, well or honestly. Economically, China is decadent, living by an incestuous economy in which public officials sanction, if they are not leaders in, all depraving business practices of the day. . . .
>
> The question finally [sic] starting to bother Americans in China is "sovereignty for what?" The sovereignty so far is one of greed, ineptitude and Government preserved by force. . . .
>
> The present Government has been dissipating, selfishly and with utter callousness, American supplies and money.

Filling such a gap required much explanation. The American credo, by mid-1946, was emphatic that no freedom-loving nation voluntarily embraced communism. Chiang Kai-shek's inflated public image, pumped into gross disproportion by the necessities of wartime propaganda, remained real to Americans who had believed what they read in *Time* and elsewhere. So blame for his collapse was subtly reassigned. The *China Monthly,* emerging mouthpiece for the China lobby, ticked off a list of publications whose "first loyalty is to their ideology and adopted fatherland," Communist Russia—*PM, The Nation,* the Shanghai *Evening Post and Mercury,* and the New York *Herald Tribune.* The *Amerasia* arrests, in the view of *China Monthly,* proved its core conclusion:

> During the past months when waves upon waves of systematic and merciless criticism were striking China and her war effort, our constant conviction was that these attacks could not possibly be coming from sound and genuinely American minds. . . .
>
> The arrests of three newspapermen, two State Department officials and a naval officer prove that our observations have not been wrong.

So where were the spies? How could the suspicions be converted into gut-locking evidence? What was required to jar the public from its bliss, and make it see that America's problems in China and elsewhere were due in large part to domestic Communists serving the will of Moscow?

The same month the *Amerasia* case went to court, another "espionage" episode, this one unquestionably involving Soviet spies and subversion, began unfolding in Canada. The central figure was Igor Gouzenko, ostensibly a twenty-six-year-old civilian clerk in the Soviet embassy in Toronto, in actuality a Red Army officer assigned to transmit encrypted espionage reports of his superior, Colonel Zabotin. Originally a dedicated Communist, Gouzenko become disillusioned with the Soviet system the more he compared it with Canada's open democracy. Soviet hypocrisy distressed Gouzenko. Although Canada was directing hundreds of millions of dollars of military aid to Russia, he knew from Zabotin's cables that the embassy concurrently spied on its hosts through a wide network of agents. "Instead of gratitude for the help rendered, the Soviet government is . . . preparing to deliver a stab in the back of Canada—all this without the knowledge of the Soviet people," in Gouzenko's words. The night of September 5, his two-year assignment to Canada nearing an end, Gouzenko purloined scores of documents from Colonel Zabotin's files, went to a newspaper office, announced he was defecting, and asked that his story be published. As corroborating evidence he offered the pilfered documents—ones listing names of Canadian officials who had spied for the Soviets. Would the paper be interested in such a story?

Incredibly, no. Gouzenko packed up his papers and went home to his apartment in frustration. The next day he tried again, at various government offices and to a new face at the newspaper. He was unable to find anyone who would take him seriously. Knowing his absence from the embassy would be noted, and fearing for his wife and young son, Gouzenko sought refuge with a neighbor, a sergeant in the Canadian air force. In due course two Soviets beat down the door of Gouzenko's apartment, the police were called, angry threats were exchanged, and the Canadian government finally realized a defector of some importance had fallen into its lap. Investigators clamped a lid of secrecy on the affair and busied themselves learning the full identities of various Canadians referred to by code names in the Zabotin documents.

Gouzenko's story was staggering. The Soviet embassy was a mare's nest of spy rings, with military intelligence and the NKVD directing separate but parallel operations. The targets ran the gamut of Canadian military and political secrets—everything from the proximity fuse to antisubmarine devices, radar, and foreign policy objectives not only of the Canadians but of the United States and Great Britain. One person pinpointed fairly early was Alan Nunn May, a British scientist given temporary wartime assignment to atomic energy research in Canada. Unbeknownst to the British, May was an ardent, if secret, Communist, and through prearrangement Colonel Zabotin took him into tow under the code name "Alek." Arrested in Britain in February 1946, the trigger for the first public exposure of Gouzenko's information, May readily admitted spying for the Soviets. "I . . . had given very careful consideration to correctness of making sure that development of atomic energy was not confined to U.S.A. I took the very painful decision that it was necessary to convey general information on atomic energy and make sure it was taken seriously. For this reason I decided to entertain proposition made to me by the individual who called on me."* May admitted giving his Soviet contact wide information on Canadian nuclear research and tidbits on the U.S. program he gleaned from his work. He had also handed over several samples of uranium 233 and 235. Zabotin had considered the samples so important that he assigned an officer to carry them personally to Moscow. The coup had delighted Zabotin. Gouzenko quoted him as exclaiming, "Now that the Americans have invented it, we must steal it!" When May returned to Britain in early autumn 1945, the Soviets detailed how he should make contact with his new control agent:

1. Place:

    In front of the British Museum of London, on Great Russell Street, at the opposite side of the street, about Museum Street, from the side of Tottenham Court Road. . . . Alek [May] walks from Tottenham Court Road, the contact man from the opposite side—Southampton Row.

2. Time:

    . . . [I]t would be more expedient to carry out the meeting at 20 o'clock, if it should be convenient to Alek, as at 23 o'clock it is too dark. In case the meeting should not take place in October, the time and day will be repeated in the following months.

3. Identification signs:

    Alek will have under his left arm the newspaper *Times,* the contact man will have in his left hand the magazine *Picture Post.*

4. The password:

    The contact man: "What is the shortest way to the Strand?"
    Alek: "Well, come along. I am going that way."
    In the beginning of the business conversation Alek says, "Best regards from Mikel."

May pleaded guilty, and the sentencing justice denounced him severely: "How any man in your position could have had the crass conceit, let alone the wickedness, to arrogate to himself the decision of a matter of this sort, when you yourself had given your written undertaking not to do it, and knew it was one of the country's most precious

* May's awkward syntax is likely due to the fact that he handwrote it during the strain of interrogation by British counterintelligence agents.

secrets . . . that you could have done this is a dreadful thing." He sentenced May to ten years imprisonment. May's material gain, in addition to ideological satisfaction, was $700 and two bottles of whiskey.*

The court proceedings against May brought the Gouzenko disclosures into the open, and more arrests came quickly in Canada—an army captain who edited the official military journal *Canadian Affairs;* three scientists with the National Research Council who had helped develop such secret wartime equipment as radar and proximity fuses (one of them, Professor Raymond Boyer, of McGill University, was considered by the Canadians and Russians to be *the* leading expert on explosives in the Western Hemisphere); a Royal Canadian Air Force intelligence officer working directly with the joint chiefs of staff; a government economist; a high-level documents clerk in the Office of the High Commissioner for the United Kingdom in Ottawa; various munitions and procurement officials—fifteen persons in all, each in a position to provide the Soviets with military, political, or economic intelligence, and enough to justify Gouzenko's contention the Soviets had established a "fifth column" in Canada.

A Canadian investigating commission probed the Soviet ring from February through June of 1946 and concluded that domestic Communists no longer could be dismissed as harmless "parlor radicals." Secret Communist Party members "played an important part in placing other secret Communists in various positions in the public service which could be strategic not only for espionage but for propaganda or other purposes." Many of the Canadian bureaucrats implicated in the espionage network were persons with an unusually high degree of education, and many were well regarded [by colleagues] . . . as persons of marked ability and intelligence." All acted initially from ideological motivation, although some eventually took money or other gifts. The ring's two Canadian principals, both long-time Communists, cultivated recruits through "study groups" which gradually brought sympathizers to the point of uncritically accepting Soviet propaganda, and transferred their loyalty from Canada. Messages handled by Gouzenko told of parallel spy operations in the United States, Britain, and other countries.

In sum, the Soviet Union stood exposed as a nation willing to spy upon its friends, through its own agents and subverted converts—a violation of the then-norms of diplomacy.

---

* May proved to be a more valuable catch than it was first realized, even if indirectly. By cross-checking the information he admittedly passed to the Soviets, British intelligence surmised yet another agent was also active. Through a process of elimination the second man was identified as Klaus Fuchs, a German-born physicist who fled the Nazis and settled in England. Sent to the atomic installation at Los Alamos, New Mexico, in 1943, he maintained contact with Soviet espionage through Harry Gold, a meek little Philadelphia chemist. Fuchs named Gold when arrested in 1949; Gold, in turn, named his next-in-line contact as David Greenglass, a former army technician at Los Alamos. Greenglass pointed to Julius and Ethel Rosenberg.

18

The Mood Turns Sour

I F S O V I E T S P Y R I N G S indeed existed in the United States, as the Gouzenko evidence suggested, did they rely upon supporting networks of covert American agents and fellow travelers, as had the Canadian networks? In Congress, the responsibility for ferreting out and exposing foreign agents rested with the House Un-American Activities Committee (HUAC), a peculiar body on which few citizens were neutral. For liberals HUAC carried an especially odious reputation. In its early years, during the 1930's, under chairman Martin Dies of a backwoods Texas district, HUAC tended to equate liberals with subversives. Dies didn't like the New Dealers: "idealists, dreamers, politicians, professional 'do-gooders,' and just plain job hunters," he called them. (Interior Secretary Harold Ickes, in turn, called Dies an "ass," "moron," and "fascist.") By 1945 Dies had passed from the scene but his scent lingered, in the person of Representative John Rankin, a subject, his enemies would say, more for pathologists than political scientists. He disliked, in no particular order, Jews, Negroes, liberals, the foreign-born, unionists, most people who lived in cities, intellectuals, college professors, and anyone with even a tenuous connection with the Roosevelts and the New Deal. Rankin carried his anti-Semitism even into the halls of Congress. In a floor debate one day he referred to Representative Emanuel Celler as "the Jewish gentleman from New York." When Celler objected, Rankin replied, "Does the member from New York object to being called a Jew or does he object to being called a gentleman? What is he kicking about?" Again, in a floor speech he called Walter Winchell "a little slime-mongering kike." In more reflective moments Rankin blamed communism for the crucifixion of Christ.

Understandably, many congressmen held their noses when Rankin was about. But in early 1945 he succeeded in forcing a vote that made HUAC a standing committee of the House (rather than a special committee whose existence must be renewed at the start of each session), with great latitude as to whom it could investigate, and how. Rankin declined the chairmanship (preferring to remain as head of the House

Veterans' Affairs Committee) but wielded *ex officio* power under Representative John S. Wood of Georgia. In his random strikes around America, Rankin found grounds for excitement most anywhere he looked. From some source or another, he reported that 191 "loathsome paintings" executed by contributing artists for the *New Masses,* a far-left magazine, were owned by film stars. "I am sure," Rankin pronounced, "that some of them got into the home of Charles Chaplin, the perverted subject of Great Britain who has become notorious for his forcible seduction of white girls." He tried to get legislation requiring radio stations to publicize their commentators' names, places of birth, nationalities, and political affiliation. During a day of token testimony from Gerald L. K. Smith, a noisy old bigot associated with most nut causes of the 1930's and 1940's, Rankin chose not to explore the threat of neofascism in America. Instead, he threw Smith such questions as, "Would you say that [the New Deal] was more fascist or more Communist?"

Intermingled with all this was a single case of substance—and one that dropped on the Wood-Rankin committee by accident, rather than through investigative expertise. For ten years Louis F. Budenz ranked in the hierarchy of the American Communist Party, editing the *Daily Worker* and dutifully executing Moscow's policy. But Budenz, who came to communism after long involvement in the labor movement, saw things he didn't like. At his very first editorial board meeting, in 1935, a mysterious outsider with a heavy foreign accent berated the *Daily Worker's* editor-in-chief over a trivial issue. The editor sat silent, "as though he were a puppy deserving a kick." Budenz deduced (correctly, it developed) that the stranger represented the Soviet government, and that he carried enough clout to give orders to the American Communist Party. Budenz did not hesitate to obey Joseph Stalin as "leader of the revolutionary movement." But when he witnessed the immediate personal control of American activities by a Russian state agent, he was ill at ease. As he put it, "My American conscience revolted at the idea." Nonetheless Budenz remained in the party a full decade, surviving even the Stalin-Hitler pact. His latent misgivings swelled again in mid-1945, when the American party, at Moscow's direction, abruptly junked its advocacy of "peaceful cooperation" between the United States and the Soviet Union, and embarked upon a new policy line placing the entire responsibility for "future aggressions and wars" upon "American capitalism." In one meeting Budenz heard the *Daily Worker's* foreign editor (a man who doubled as a Soviet secret agent) declare that since the American "bourgeoisie" would never embrace socialism voluntarily, "international intervention" was required to establish a proletarian dictatorship. Budenz could stomach no more. A devout Catholic in his youth, he now grasped "the realities of the Soviet Union's concerted and unrelenting determination to crush both religion and our nation and to pursue . . . these objectives to the bitter end." In October 1946 he left the party and returned to the church, and began speaking and writing of Soviet control of American Communists. In Detroit he charged directly that "the equivalent of a representative of the Communist International"* still functioned in America. Budenz gave the spymaster an aura of mystery: "This man never shows his face. Communist leaders never see him, but they follow his orders or suggestions implicitly."

Within a week the man was identified as Gerhart Eisler, an Austrian-born Communist who had lived in the United States since 1941 under the name of Hans Berger. The FBI already had Eisler under watch, and snatched him up just as he was about to leave the country on a Russian ship for Leipzig, in the Soviet zone of Germany. The Immigration Service charged him with making false declarations on entering the country, and HUAC put in a bid for his testimony. In the interim, however, it listened at length to Budenz, who gave the committee its first recitation of personal testimony about Soviet control of the American party, and the key role of Comintern agents. Budenz carried great credibility because of his past stature in the party and his reassociation with the Catholic Church under auspices of the widely respected Francis Cardinal Spellman.† Budenz proved to have little direct evidence of Eisler's activity as a Comintern agent, although he did point to numerous articles in the *Daily Worker* and *The Communist* during 1941–44 which interpreted a rapidly changing party line to the faithful. Eisler, sitting in the audience, loudly demanded to reporters that he be given a chance to testify. Rankin, however, preferred to use Budenz as a sounding board for his own style of questioning: "Regarding these overrun countries, are you familiar with the rape of innocent women, the murder of innocent men, the plunder of the peasants, and the robbery of the helpless people in those areas by the Communist regime?" Budenz allowed he had heard as much.

HUAC didn't bring in Eisler until early 1947, by which time the FBI had put together a considerable dossier on his career. Eisler had no job; he did receive, under a false name, a $150 monthly stipend from the Joint Anti-Fascist Refugee Committee, a conduit for Soviet funds. Eisler's sister, Ruth Fischer, drummed out of the German Communist Party in 1926 for anti-Stalinist activities, a free-lance writer in the 1940's, denounced him as a "most dangerous terrorist." By her account,

---

* The Communist International—Comintern for short—was Moscow's agency for coordinating activities of domestic Communist parties through Soviet agents. With great fanfare the USSR announced disbanding of the Comintern during the Second World War as a friendly gesture towards allies. In actuality the Comintern remained most active, even if underground.
† After a year of religious retreat at Notre Dame University Budenz published a deeply personal account of his decade with the Communist Party, his disillusionment, and his return to the Catholic Church (*This Is My Story,* McGraw-Hill Book Company).

Eisler had acted as the Kremlin's agent in purging the German and Chinese parties of persons opposed to Stalin. She named as one of his victims Nikolai Bukharin, the renowned Russian economic theorist and Eisler's onetime protector. Another former party member testified he had met Eisler at a party training school in Moscow in 1931. Eisler's actual appearance was inconsequential, though dramatic. The committee counsel, Robert E. Stripling, directed, "Mr. Gerhart Eisler, take the stand." "I am not going to take the stand," shot back Eisler. A brisk but intense wrangle followed, with Eisler demanding that he be permitted to read a three-minute statement before being sworn, and calling himself a "political prisoner." J. Parnell Thomas of New Jersey, chairman of HUAC following the Republican sweep of the 1946 congressional elections, offered to let him make any statement he wished, "but first you have to be sworn."

"That is where you are mistaken," Eisler replied. "I have to do nothing. A political prisoner has to do nothing."

The committee cited Eisler for contempt and had him shipped back to Ellis Island, where he was being held on the illegal-entry charges. Eventually he went free on bail, and on May 7, 1949, slipped aboard the Polish liner *Batory* in New York and made his way to East Germany. (Eisler worked as an official of the German government until his death in 1968.) In the interim, Eisler's appeal of the contempt citation went to the U.S. Supreme Court, in company with cases of Eugene Dennis, general secretary of the CPUSA, and Leon Josephson, onetime lawyer for the International Labor Defense, who allegedly helped Eisler forge a passport application. In a six-three split, the high court refused to review the convictions, thus upholding the committee's asserted broad powers of inquiry. Justice Robert Jackson, although disturbed at some of HUAC's tactics, said the courts should "leave the responsibility for the behavior of its committees squarely on the shoulders of Congress." With House support assured—even congressmen with qualms about HUAC didn't risk "voting against anti-Communists"—and with U.S.–Soviet relations deteriorating, HUAC set to work with a reaffirmed mandate. If a ring like Gouzenko's existed in the United States, HUAC resolved to put it on public display.

Oddly, HUAC began its odyssey in Hollywood, capitalizing on the glamour of the movie industry to bring itself kleig-light publicity. Communists undeniably had made strong inroads in the movies during the 1930's and 1940's, for several reasons: The glamour of celebrity endorsements sells cigarettes, beer, and soap; it can also sell political ideas. The Communists wanted a base in Hollywood labor unions. Followers could neutralize or eliminate anti-Soviet and anti-Communist tones in American films. Further, in the words of the veteran anti-

Communist writer Eugene Lyons, the "cinema rebels . . . were genuinely angry at Nazis, and genuinely concerned for Spanish democracy, Spain's orphans, Chinese freedom and sharecroppers." They cared little about economic or political theory. "For nearly all of them, [communism] was an intoxicated state of mind, a glow of inner virtue, and a sort of comradeship in supercharity"—radical chic that gave a sense of worth even to writers of grade B movies. But these loose affiliates ended once the Cold War began, and the Communists lost their snap identification with popular causes. John Cogley, in a study of Hollywood communism, concluded that "in the brash, ego-centered, exhibitionistic film capital . . . the party had simply not succeeded in converting patriotism into Bolshevism."

The party activity, however, did provide the foundation for use of "the Communist issue" in violent labor disputes that erupted in Hollywood in 1945, and led directly to the HUAC probe. Movie unions long carried smelly encrustations of both corruption and communism. The largest was the International Alliance of Theatrical Stage Employees and Motion-Picture Operators of the United States (the IA), an AFL affiliate which during the 1930's was run by Willie Bioff, a onetime Chicago pimp, and George Browne.* Anti-IA unionists gravitated to the Conference of Studio Unions (CSU), chiefly due to the vigor of a rather abrasive and cocksure painters' union leader named Herb Sorrell, who concentrated on bread-and-butter issues. Sorrell readily formed alliances of convenience with the Communists, and his IA opponents charged (and he denied) that he was a party member. As the CSU grew, it inevitably quarreled with the IA over jurisdiction, and in March 1945 Sorrell ordered a strike. For two months the Communists opposed Sorrell, adhering to the party's no-wartime-strikes policy and denouncing him as "A Good Guy Gone Wrong" (an editorial caption in *People's World,* the party West Coast newspaper). But when the Communists abandoned the no-strike policy in the summer of 1945, the party swung behind Sorrell.

Now enters a new figure in the "anti-Communist" crusade: Roy M. Brewer, an AFL troubleshooter who had worked with the War Labor Board. The IA imported him to direct strategy in the fight with Sorrell and the CSU, and he chose to campaign against communism. Fliers described Sorrell as being "sympathetic and definitely interested in the communistic idea," and cited his past association with party causes: his opposition to the draft; his criticisms of President Roosevelt as a "warmonger" in 1940; his support of longshoremen's leader Harry Bridges in a deportation fight.

* Both Bioff and Browne went to prison as the result of an investigation stirred up by Los Angeles labor lawyer Carey McWilliams (editor of *The Nation* from 1952 to 1975).

The strike climaxed October 5, 1945, when pickets used stones, chains, bricks, and broken bottles against nonstrikers trying to enter the Warner Brothers lot. Some strikers concealed lead pipes in rolled newspapers; others battered open car doors and beat persons trying to drive through the lines. A fearful Jack Warner, watching from a studio roof, said, "The revolution has come to Hollywood." Even after mediation brought uneasy peace, animosities continued, with the Screen Writers Guild and the Actors Guild splitting over whether to support the CSU or Roy Brewer's IA. Actors such as Ronald Reagan, active in liberal causes that the Communists also supported, asked themselves, "Am I being used?"

Surprising alliances formed. Union leader Brewer associated himself and the IA with an ad hoc group called the Motion Picture Alliance for the Preservation of American Ideals, which had been formed in 1944 to combat "the growing impression that this industry is made up of, and dominated by, Communists, radicals, and crackpots." Despite its broad industry base, the Motion Picture Alliance was largely financed and controlled by studio heads, who saw it as a vehicle for "pro-free enterprise" messages. A guiding spirit, the novelist and film writer Ayn Rand, provided dos and don'ts for movie producers:

Don't smear the free enterprise system.
Don't deify the common man.
Don't glorify the collective.
Don't smear success.
Don't smear industrialists.

Miss Rand held that it was the *"moral* (no, not just political, but *moral*) duty of every decent man in the motion picture industry to throw into the ashcan, where it belongs, every story that smears industrialists as such." In early 1947 the Motion Picture Alliance sent emissaries to Washington to persuade Chairman Thomas of HUAC to hold hearings to expose "Communists" in the industry. And, finally, there emerged William Randolph Hearst—aging, his once-powerful press empire slipping both in influence and affluence, reclusive and eccentric to the point of looniness, but nonetheless a newspaper baron and one whose opinions could break a politician or an industry.

During the 1940's writer Adela Rogers St. John worked in the epicenter of the movie industry—as a story scout for Metro-Goldwyn-Mayer, responsible for locating suitable material for Clark Gable; as a personal troubleshooter for MGM head Louis B. Mayer, nursemaiding the drug-troubled young star Judy Garland; as a writer for the Hearst organization, frequently on movie subjects; and as a close confidante of William Randolph Hearst. Hence she observed at first hand Hearst's role in spurring the Hollywood investigation.

"Hearst had spent millions of dollars of his own money before Congress moved in with that committee. Everybody in Congress, in those early days, got all their material from us [the Hearst organization]. We had two floors of the Hearst magazine building on Eighth Avenue in New York devoted entirely to the testimony and investigative answers we had gotten. The Hearst crew put all the material together—chiefly through a man named Jack Clements, who knew more about communism than anybody else, and J. B. Matthews—and then the committee got into it. Mr. Hearst forced that.

"Mr. Hearst had always had a keen interest in movies, but I don't think that just because he liked the picture business he was willing to let Communists run it.

"Out of this, of course, came the Hiss case and the breakup of the group in the State Department. We made one fatal mistake—and how could anybody have known it? We were looking for a senator to carry the ball. I went down and tried to get Millard Tydings, the great senator from Maryland [Mrs. St. John's enunciation of the word "great" was not complimentary]. He said, 'Nooooo, noooooo, they'd beat you to death before you are through. I am willing to die for my country, but not that way.' Other senators wouldn't come anywhere near it. They saw the material, they knew we had it, no question.

"The only guy who would go was [Joseph] McCarthy.* We didn't know he was a drunk. If McCarthy hadn't been an alcoholic, the whole story would have been different, because we had the material, but he kept blowing it. He'd get drunk and say things he shouldn't.

"We had stuff on a man in China, a man we had just about pinned down, and McCarthy got drunk in a hotel in New York one night and told the whole tale, and messed it up. He made so much commotion we couldn't get it back together. Someone said, 'Why don't you take McCarthy out to New Jersey and lock him up and get him sober?' But it was no use—take your eye off him, he'd go get drunk again."

At the same time Mrs. St. John and other Hearstlings worked to move HUAC into Hollywood, lawyer Robert Kenny worked to keep it out. A former attorney general of California, defeated by Earl Warren when he sought the governorship in 1944, and an activist in the budding presidential campaign of Henry A. Wallace, Kenny for more than a decade was the ranking figure in California's non-Communist left. Kenny detected Hearst's influence in HUAC's hearings, and ascribed it to somewhat less lofty motives than those cited by Mrs. St. John.

"I was attorney for the Screen Writers Guild, an organization riddled with many professional jealousies, but nonetheless blessed with a num-

---

* McCarthy enthusiastically took up HUAC's work in the spring of 1950 and created more anti-Communist turmoil in two years than HUAC did in three decades.

ber of very progressive citizens, most of whom lived very well. Someone once called them the 'swimming pool pinks,' which says a lot about their ability to be good liberals and make a decent living at the same time.

"When HUAC began prowling here, Metro-Goldwyn-Mayer and some of the other studios threw out several of our members who had long-range contracts. We filed a lawsuit, and we began taking depositions early enough [before the hearings, when the industry went into a shell] that everyone was still speaking freely. When we asked Louis B. Mayer why he fired these people, he said it was 'his friend Mr. Hearst' who did it.

"Hearst would not support any movie studio that did not blacklist people he considered to be 'Reds.' Hearst thought he had been mishandled in the 1944 campaign, when he worked hard against Roosevelt, and that 'leftists' in the movie industry had reelected FDR through their favorable publicity for him.

"There was a personal pique as well. Some studio people continually made snide remarks about Hearst's relationship with Marion Davies, and about what an awful actress she was, and that if she wasn't screwing Hearst she wouldn't be able to work.

"Hearst became quite reactionary in his old age, and he had enough papers left to make life hell for people he disliked. He put out the word the Hearst newspapers would boycott any pictures from studios that did not 'check out Reds'—no reviews, no publicity, no advertising. And, to make it short, the studios turned tail and ran."

Despite the union turmoil, and the lobbying of the anti-Communist Motion Picture Alliance for the Preservation of American Ideals, Hollywood was not of a single mind on the hearings. One executive likened the hearings to calling four battalions of firemen to extinguish a blaze in a kitchen toaster: "In getting rid of harmless smoke they'll chop up the floor, knock out the ceiling, and leave six feet of water in your basement." Given its demonstrated penchant for irresponsible handling of witnesses and its suspicion of social ideas, HUAC could well torment the movies for months, destroying public confidence in the industry and forcing censorship.

When HUAC announced its intention of "exposing" communism in Hollywood, the movie industry's reflexive reaction was hostile. The Association of Motion Picture Producers threw down a challenge to Chairman Thomas: "Hollywood is weary of being the national whipping boy for congressional committees. We are tired of having irresponsible charges made again and again and not sustained. If we have committed a crime we want to know it. If not, we should not be badgered by congressional committees." Louis B. Mayer of Metro-Goldwyn-Mayer offered to show the committee any picture it desired, in Washington or elsewhere; he had personally viewed movies made by persons accused of Communist sympathies, and "they will speak for themselves." Star after star spoke out against HUAC's hearings. "Before every free conscience in America is subpoenaed, please speak up!" said Judy Garland, the singer. "Say your piece. Write your Congressman a letter! Airmail special." Frank Sinatra asked, "Once they get the movies throttled, how long will it be before we're told what we can say and cannot say into a radio microphone? If you make a pitch on a nationwide radio network for a square deal for the underdog, will they call you a Commie? . . . Are they going to scare us into silence?" Fredric March wondered who "they're really after? Who's next? Is it your minister who will be told what he can say in his pulpit? Is it your children's school teacher who will be told what he can say in his classrooms? Is it your children themselves? Is it you, who will have to look around nervously before you can say what is on your mind? Who are they after? They're after more than Hollywood. This reaches into every American city and town!"

The first round of public hearings, in Washington, confirmed the skeptics' worst suspicions. Using witnesses supplied by the Motion Picture Alliance for the Preservation of American Ideals, HUAC let prominent Hollywood personages lay the groundwork for charges of systematic and massive "communization" of the film industry. Producer-director Sam Wood (*For Whom the Bell Tolls*) named a long list of writers and other creative people as Communists. "If I have any doubt that they are [Communists]," Wood said, "then I haven't any mind. These Communists thump their chests and call themselves liberals. But if you drop their rompers you'll find a hammer and sickle on their rear ends." Wood was particularly upset about a rally of the Progressive Citizens of America (which was to become Henry Wallace's presidential springboard a year later). "Katharine Hepburn appeared and they collected $87,000. You don't think that money is going to the Boy Scouts, do you?" Wood charged a conspiracy to keep "good Americans" unemployed:

> For instance, a man gets a key position in the studio and has charge of the writers. When you, as a director or a producer, are ready for a writer you ask for a list and this man shows you a list. Well, if he is following the party line his pets are on top or the other people aren't on it at all.
>
> If there is a particular man in there that has been opposing them they will leave his name off the list. Then if that man isn't employed for about two months they go to the head of the studio and say, "Nobody wants this man."
>
> The head is perfectly honest about it and says, "Nobody wants to use him, let him go." So a good American is let out. But it

doesn't stop there. They point that out as an example and say, "You better fall in line, play ball or else." And they go down the line on it.

The veteran character actor Adolphe Menjou, resplendent in a brown double-breasted pin-striped suit and heavy shell-rimmed glasses, cheerily identified himself as a "Red-baiter" and added, "I make no bones about it. I'd like to see them all in Russia. I think a taste of Russia would cure them." Menjou said he had an infallible method of detecting Reds: "attending any meetings at which Mr. Paul Robeson appeared, and applauding or listening to his Communist songs." (Novelist-screenwriter Rupert Hughes told yet another technique: "You can't help smelling them.") Thanking Menjou for his testimony, committee member John McDowell, Republican from Pennsylvania, reported that he had recently examined the United States frontiers, and that "within weeks, not months but weeks, busloads of Communists have crossed the American border." The testimony continued for a week, with witnesses hurling accusations of communism at specific film people, HUAC members going through lists of supposed Communists and asking witnesses, "What do you know about his Communist activities?" They were gratified by much pseudoexpert testimony on party techniques. Lola Rogers, mother of actress Ginger Rogers, said the Communists were wickedly subtle. She noted *None but the Lonely Heart,* with its "despair and hopelessness." Its background music, by Hanns Eisler, a German Communist before immigrating to the U.S., was "moody and somber throughout, in the Russian manner." Roy Brewer, the IA leader, was permitted to denounce his rival Conference of Studio Unions as Communist, and to depict Hollywood's complex interunion struggle as a black-and-white contest between subversives and patriots. "We hope . . . that with the help of the committee the Communist menace in the motion-picture industry may be successfully destroyed, to the end that Hollywood labor may be spared in the future the strife and turmoil of the immediate past."

During this first phase of the hearings HUAC accumulated names of nineteen persons—writers, directors, and producers—who supposedly served the Communist cause. Parnell Thomas laid out a course of action. The nineteen would be put on the stand and be asked directly whether they were Communists. Then the industry would be asked whether it would support legislation barring Communists from employment in the movies.

At this point HUAC had nothing other than hearsay evidence about Communist influence in Hollywood, and not a scintilla of proof that they affected the content of a single picture. Besieged, the anti-HUAC forces mobilized. Dozens of stars organized "The Committee for the

First Amendment" under producers John Huston and William Wyler and writer Philip Dunne, declaring in a manifesto that "any investigation into the political beliefs of the individual is contrary to the basic principles of our democracy." The adherents included such names as Henry Fonda, Ava Gardner, Paulette Goddard, Benny Goodman, Van Heflin, Katharine Hepburn, Myrna Loy, Burgess Meredith, Gregory Peck, Barry Sullivan, Cornel Wilde, and Billy Wilder. The committee laid down a careful strategy. A select delegation would appear at the hearings to take the publicity away from Chairman Thomas and his sympathetic witnesses. Yet they would make plain they were not defending any Communists—only attacking HUAC's abuses of due process.

But the committee outsmarted the actors. On the day they appeared HUAC was to have heard Eric Johnston, the president of the Motion Picture Producers Association. Instead, Thomas craftily produced writer John Howard Lawson, a writer whom several witnesses had already named as the grand old man of Hollywood Communists. One writer, for instance, avowed Lawson was determined that five minutes of party doctrine go into every one of his films, and at such strategic junctures that they could not be deleted. An old Lawson article from a left-wing magazine was put into the record: "As for myself," he wrote, "I do not hesitate to say that it is my aim to present the Communist position and to do so in the most specific manner." (Lawson's films, upon sober analysis, proved him to be an inept propagandist; his 1936 film on the Spanish Civil War, *Blockade,* was so murky that an unsophisticated viewer wouldn't know whether to side with the Falangists or the Republicans.) Communist or not, Lawson succeeded in being almost as unmannerly as the committee—albeit with some justification. Preceding friendly witnesses had been permitted to begin their testimony with a statement. Thomas, however, denied any such right to Lawson. When the statement was handed up to Thomas, he didn't bother to go past the first line, which read: "For a week, this committee has conducted an illegal and indecent trial of American citizens, whom the committee has selected to be publicly pilloried and smeared."

"I don't care to read any more of the statement," Thomas said. "The statement will not be read. I read the first line."

"You have spent one week vilifying me before the American public—" Lawson began, and the row was on.

THE CHAIRMAN: Just a minute.
LAWSON: —and you refuse to allow me to make a statement on my
    rights as an American citizen.
THE CHAIRMAN: I refuse to let you make the statement because of
    the first sentence. That statement is not pertinent to the inquiry.
    Now, this is a congressional committee set up by law. We must

have orderly procedure, and we are going to have orderly procedure. Mr. [Robert] Stripling [committee chief investigator],
identify the witness.

Protesting all the while, Lawson answered questions on his date and
place of birth, and said he was a screen writer and belonged to the
Screen Writers Guild. But each time he was asked about past
associations, Lawson declared HUAC had no right to make such in-
quiries, Thomas punctuating his objections with smart raps of the gavel.

THE CHAIRMAN: The Chair will determine what is in the purview
of this committee.

LAWSON: My rights as an American citizen are no less than the
responsibilities of this committee of Congress.

THE CHAIRMAN: Now, you are just making a big scene for yourself
and getting all "het up." [Laughter] Be responsive to the
questioning, just the same as all the witnesses have. You are no
different from the rest. . . .

LAWSON: I am being treated differently from the rest.

THE CHAIRMAN: You are not being treated differently.

LAWSON: Other witnesses have made statements, which included
quotations from books, references to material which had no connection whatsoever with the interest of this committee.

THE CHAIRMAN: We will determine whether it has connection.
Now, you go ahead—

LAWSON: It is absolutely beyond the power of this committee to
inquire into my association in any organization.

THE CHAIRMAN: Mr. Lawson, you will have to stop or you will
leave the witness stand. And you will leave the witness stand because you are in contempt. That is why you will leave the witness stand. And if you are just trying to force me to put you in
contempt, you won't have to try much harder. You know what
has happened to a lot of people that have been in contempt of
this committee this year, don't you?

LAWSON: I am glad you have made it perfectly clear that you are
going to threaten and intimidate the witness, Mr. Chairman.

(*The Chairman pounding gavel.*)

LAWSON: I am an American and I am not at all easy to intimidate,
and don't think I am.

(*The Chairman pounding gavel.*)

Counsel Stripling finally got around to the important question: Was
Lawson now, or had he ever been, a member of the Communist Party,
USA? Robert Kenny, attorney for the writers, had advised them against
giving a direct answer to the question. Even if they had not been party

members, Kenny feared (and so stated) that committee zealots would forge cards and indict them for perjury. Hence he told them to attack the committee's right to ask the question, rather than answering it. Which is exactly what Lawson did, to climax his testimony:

STRIPLING: Mr. Lawson, are you now or have you ever been a member of the Communist Party of the United States?

LAWSON: In framing my answer to that question I must emphasize the points that I have raised before. The question of Communism is in no way related to this inquiry, which is an attempt to get control of the screen and to invade the basic rights of American citizens in all fields.

McDOWELL: Now, I must object—

(*The Chairman pounding gavel.*)

LAWSON: The question here related not only to the question of my membership in any political organization, but this committee is attempting to establish the right—

(*The Chairman pounding gavel.*)

LAWSON: —which has been historically denied to any committee of this sort, to invade the rights and privileges and immunity of American citizens, be they Protestant, Methodist, Jewish, or Catholic, whether they be Republicans or Democrats or anything else.

THE CHAIRMAN (*pounding gavel*): Mr. Lawson, just quiet down again. Mr. Lawson, the most pertinent question that we can ask is whether or not you have ever been a member of the Communist Party. Now, do you care to answer that question?

LAWSON: You are using the old technique, which was used in Hitler Germany in order to create a scare here—

THE CHAIRMAN (*pounding gavel*): Oh—

LAWSON: —in order to create an entirely false atmosphere in which this hearing is conducted—

(*The Chairman pounding gavel.*)

LAWSON: —in order that you can then smear the motion-picture industry, and you can proceed to the press, to any form of communication in this country.

THE CHAIRMAN: You have learned—

LAWSON: The Bill of Rights was established precisely to prevent the operation of any committee which could invade the basic rights of Americans. Now, if you want to know—

STRIPLING: Mr. Chairman, the witness is not answering the question.

LAWSON: If you want to know—

(*The Chairman pounding gavel.*)

LAWSON: —about the perjury that has been committed here and the perjury that is planned—

THE CHAIRMAN: Mr. Lawson—

LAWSON: —permit me and my attorneys to bring in here the witnesses that testified last week and permit us to cross-examine these witnesses, and we will show up the whole tissue of lies—

THE CHAIRMAN (*pounding gavel*): We are going to get the answer to that question if we have to stay here for a week. Are you a member of the Communist Party, or have you ever been a member of the Communist Party?

LAWSON: It is unfortunate and tragic that I have to teach this committee the basic principles of America—

THE CHAIRMAN (*pounding gavel*): That is not the question. The question is: Have you ever been a member of the Communist Party?

LAWSON: I am framing my answer in the only way in which any American citizen can frame his answer to a question which absolutely invades his rights.

THE CHAIRMAN: Then you refuse to answer that question: is that correct?

LAWSON: I have told you that I will offer my beliefs, affiliations, and everything else to the American public, and they will know where I stand.

THE CHAIRMAN (*pounding gavel*): Excuse the witness—

LAWSON: As they do from what I have written.

THE CHAIRMAN (*pounding gavel*): Stand away from the stand.

LAWSON: I have written Americanism for many years, and I shall continue to fight for the Bill of Rights, which you are trying to destroy.

THE CHAIRMAN: Officers, take this man away from the stand—

(*Applause and boos.*)

THE CHAIRMAN (*pounding gavel*): There will be no demonstrations. No demonstrations, for or against. Everyone will please be seated. All right, go ahead, Mr. Stripling. Proceed.

STRIPLING: Mr. Chairman, the committee has made exhaustive investigation and research into the Communist affiliations of Mr. John Howard Lawson. Numerous witnesses under oath have identified Mr. Lawson as a member of the Communist Party. I have here a nine-page memorandum which details at length his affiliations with the Communist Party and its various front organizations. I now ask . . .

Lawson's stormy behavior and his extensively documented record of Communist associations shocked many of the stars who had come to

Washington to protect their industry. None expected Lawson to cozy up to the committee, assuredly, but his shouting and doctrinaire denunciations (*"Pravda*-like prose," *Life* called it) made many in the group wonder whether HUAC just might be on to something. At a press conference after Lawson's testimony, the questions made plain to the delegation their presence was being interpreted as support for him. The same day the Washington *Times-Herald,* an unflinching HUAC supporter, stated that Sterling Hayden, one of the organizers of the trip, had a Communist background. William Wyler called a meeting to raise funds for a libel suit on Hayden's behalf. Hayden embarrassedly told them not to bother: the newspaper was correct; he in fact had been a party member for six months. After a couple of other witnesses emulated Lawson's performance, the actors' committee quietly withdrew to Hollywood, their attitude one of "We've been had," according to John Cogley. In all, HUAC summoned ten of the nineteen industry figures, none of whom would testify. Each was cited for contempt, and the "Hollywood Ten"* went away to federal prison.

Despite its plethora of old party membership cards and lists of people who sponsored front-group affairs, HUAC never produced anything to justify an affirmative answer to a somewhat central question: Did Hollywood Communists get anything into films that spread the party line? "The contents of the pictures constitute the only proof," said industry spokesman Eric Johnston. "It is the obligation of the committee to absolve the industry from the charges against it." This, of course, HUAC did not attempt to do. And the "evidence" of propaganda was laughably thin. For instance:

—A comedian who carried a party card whistled a few bars of "The Internationale" in a scene where he awaited an elevator. He credited himself with quite a coup. "Even in Brazil they'll know where I stand," he told a colleague. But even the party thought he was stupid to expose himself. In any event, the scene was cut, for nonpolitical reasons.

—In a script about a boys' school Lester Cole used a paraphrase of the old line "better to die on one's feet than live on one's knees." A handful of moviegoers perhaps would have recognized the source: the Spanish Communist La Pasionaria.

—In rewriting *Sinners in Paradise,* about a group of airline passengers forced to land on a deserted South Seas island, Cole transformed an amusing but harmless U.S. senator into a pompous ass interested in using his government influence in making "private deals" on war supplies ("it's very easy for the government to wink an eye"). A beautiful rich girl became a socially callous heiress "going abroad to absent her-

* The Hollywood Ten were Alvah Bessie, Herbert Biberman, Lester Cole, Edward Dmytryk, Ring Lardner, Jr., John Howard Lawson, Albert Maltz, Samuel Ornitz, Adrian Scott, and Dalton Trumbo.

self from the growing labor troubles at one of her great auto plants, which closed on strike." Some oil men were on the trip to explore munitions markets ("when these gentlemen dump their munitions in the Orient, they'll be responsible for . . . approximately 100,000 lives"). Whatever Cole's motives, the politicalization did little for the Communist cause, for the picture flopped.

When pressed by committee critics for chapter and verse on Communist taints in movies, Parnell Thomas fell back upon three wartime films that were undeniably pro-Russian. *Mission to Moscow,* about Joseph E. Davies' service as ambassador to Moscow, was depicted by critic James Agee in *The Nation* as "almost describable as the first Soviet production to come from a major American studio . . . a great, glad two-million-dollar bowl of canned borscht." Thomas also listed *North Star* and *Song of Russia.* The Russian-born novelist Ayn Rand told HUAC the latter was "terrible propaganda," and described it as a Potemkin-village USSR with children in operetta costumes and "manicured starlets driving tractors." (In the same testimony Miss Rand indicated she thought the United States had made a mistake taking on Russia as an ally, and that lend-lease equipment could have been put to better use by the American military.) In the end, however, even *Time,* whose coverage was generally friendly to HUAC, concluded the committee "had failed to establish that any crime had been committed—that any subversive propaganda had ever reached the screen."*

The uncertain ending notwithstanding, Hollywood capitulated to HUAC. All during the hearings Eric Johnston and other industry leaders denounced attempts at censorship and swore blood oaths they would not turn their backs on HUAC's targets. Within a month, however, fifty members of the three leading industry groups (the Association of Motion Picture Producers, the Motion Picture Association of America, and the Society of Independent Motion Picture Producers) met for two days at the Waldorf Astoria Hotel and adopted a policy statement intended to appease HUAC. It deplored the conduct of the Hollywood Ten. Although the moguls did "not desire to prejudge their legal rights, . . . their actions have been a disservice to their employers and have impaired their usefulness to the industry." Those under contract would be suspended without pay; none would be rehired until he was acquitted "or has purged himself of contempt and declared under oath that he is

* A study for the Fund for the Republic, Inc., published in 1956, concluded that "none of the 159 films credited over a period of years to the Hollywood Ten contained Communist propaganda," although the Communist Party did, on occasion, utilize films credited to the ten for propaganda purposes. The study also suggested that HUAC's attack resulted from a fear that "motion pictures—the most popular medium of our time—were beginning to devote themselves seriously to an exploration of some of the social, economic, and political problems of our time. There have long been some people—both in Washington and Hollywood—who regard these new trends in film subject matter as both unfortunate and dangerous."

not a Communist." The movies would not employ Communists or anyone else belonging to a group advocating forceful or illegal overthrow of
the government. "In pursuing this policy," the producers reassured
themselves, "we are not going to be swayed by hysteria or intimidation
from any source."

To attorney Robert Kenny, who defended the Hollywood Ten, Hollywood's turnabout was sheer cowardice. "Movies always behave as if
they have a guilty conscience," he said. "This dates to the Fatty
Arbuckle case,* when they feared the bluenoses would put them out of
business because of the antics of one drunken bum. In the early hearings, Hollywood stood down Congress because Hollywood had guts.
Will Hays, who ran the industry, wouldn't flinch. The difference in 1947
was Wall Street, which had many, many millions of dollars invested in
films. They said, 'Get rid of the Reds, quick,' and Eric Johnston, who
was no more than a glorified PR man for the industry, his high-faluting
title notwithstanding, went along.

"My big disappointment was the liberals. God protect me from hand-
wringing liberals. They fled at the first crackle of musket fire, and left
the ten all by themselves.

"A peculiar thing came up during their defense. Someone in the industry must have been a 'Red'—and I use the word facetiously—because I began getting carbons of correspondence between the industry
and an intermediary who was trying to make a deal with Parnell
Thomas. This fellow had been to New Jersey, where Thomas lived, and
interviewed him about being 'rewarded' if he would drop the hearings.
The industry was in one hell of a spot. The producers didn't want to
execute their best writers, people such as Dalton Trumbo and Ring
Lardner, Jr. I'll say this for Thomas: Although he went to jail later for
different reasons, he wouldn't make a deal with the industry. He kept on
with the hearings."

The Waldorf Declaration satisfied Congress. HUAC did not bother to
call the other nine persons on its "Red List," and the hearings trailed off,
although they did revive again in the early 1950's, when yet another
group of movie people took the stand to admit involvement with the
Communists, and to plead for absolution. Included was director Edward
Dmytryk, one of the Hollywood Ten. In an article he wrote for the
Saturday Evening Post in 1961, Ring Lardner, another of the ten, admitted membership in the party, but said he declined to admit it to
HUAC because he would have been compelled to name other persons,
which he could not do as a matter of conscience. The Waldorf Declara-

---

* Arbuckle, a famed comedian of the 1920's, fell from grace when a young girl
died after a wild drinking party aboard a train. Testimony indicated he had subjected her to unconventional sexual acts but he was acquitted when tried for
murder.

tion marked the beginning of a potent new weapon for "anti-Communists" to use in the entertainment industry: the blacklist.

Some time after his joust with the Hollywood Ten, Congressman Parnell Thomas was caught putting nonworkers on his office payroll and keeping their salaries for himself. Thomas offered no defense, and a Federal judge gave him a prison term of eighteen months—at the correctional institution in Danbury, Connecticut, where, as irony would have it, also resided the Hollywood Ten.

Once shorn of his office, Thomas no longer saw the movie people as threats to the republic. One day he said quite seriously to Ring Lardner, Jr.: "You've got a lot of influence; would you help me get a parole?" Lardner replied, "If I had any influence, I assure you I wouldn't be here myself."

Another time Thomas and Lardner found themselves on the opposite sides of an internal fence—the ex-writer cutting grass along a sidewalk with a sickle, the ex-congressman cleaning a chicken yard.

"Hey, Lardner," Thomas called, "I see you've got part of your old Communist emblem. Where's the hammer to go with the sickle?"

"I see you're up to your old tricks, Congressman—shoveling chicken shit," Lardner replied.

By 1948 anti-Communist militancy was sweeping the country, spearheaded by the American Legion, such newspaper chains as Hearst and Scripps-Howard, and any number of ad hoc business and "patriotic" organizations. Information on the Communist conspiracy, and the people composing it, was found to be a valuable commodity. One group with marked commercial success was "American Business Consultants, Inc.," formed by three former FBI agents in an old Madison Avenue office reachable only by freight elevator. The agents put together files (from HUAC and other investigative bodies, the *Daily Worker,* and the multitude of fliers issued by the Communists and their front groups) and offered their services to the business community. Did an employer have a question about a man's loyalty? For a fee, ABC would screen its material and "clear" the person. A periodic publication, *Counterattack: The Newsletter of Facts on Communism,* laid out a strategy for dealing with "dupes, stooges, fifth columnists, appeasers, and other innocents who help Communism."

Most important thing of all is to base your whole policy on a firmly moral foundation. Space should not be rented to the Communist Party or to any Communist front. Supplies should not be sold to them. They should not be allowed to participate in meetings. Communist actors, announcers, directors, writers, producers, etc., whether in radio, theater, or movies, should be barred to the extent permissible in law and labor contracts. . . .

The way to treat Communists is to ostracize them. How would you act towards men who had been convicted of treason? Would you befriend them, listen to them? Or would you treat them as outcasts?

Corporations ignored the "consulting firms" at their own peril, and in fact many of them smacked of blackmail operations. Merle Miller, the writer, in an exhaustive study of blacklisting, found an ad agency that was "advised" that a program sponsored by the Philco Corporation employed a "Commie actress," and offered to submit a dossier on her for $1,000. The agency declined. Less than a month later, the group's newsletter attacked Philco for hiring a "fellow traveler." The American Legion used even rougher techniques. In a periodic newsletter entitled "Summary of Trends and Developments Exposing the Communist Conspiracy," the Legion's Americanism Commission counseled:

Organize a letter-writing group of six to ten relatives and friends to make the sentiments of Americans heard on the important issues of the day. Phone, telegraph or write to radio and television sponsors employing entertainers with known front records . . . DON'T LET THE SPONSORS PASS THE BUCK BACK TO YOU BY DEMANDING "PROOF" OF COMMUNIST FRONTING BY SOME CHARACTER ABOUT WHOM YOU HAVE COMPLAINED. YOU DON'T HAVE TO PROVE ANYTHING . . . YOU SIMPLY HAVE TO SAY YOU DO NOT LIKE SO-AND-SO ON THEIR PROGRAMS.

James F. O'Neil, then the Legion national commander, cautioned members that the United States was infiltrated by "a secret battalion of some 75,000 or 80,000 trained Communists and an estimated auxiliary corps of 750,000 to one million dupes, camp followers, secret sympathizers, and casual supporters." To combat this internal menace, O'Neil urged local posts to organize "an unofficial advisory committee" of former FBI agents and navy or army intelligence officers, plus any "former C. P. members who have come over to our side."

When a known pro-Soviet apologist is slated to lecture in your city, to address a meeting, speak over a local station, or make any kind of public appearance, form a small delegation, assemble all your facts . . . then call upon those responsible for importing the out-of-town peddler of Soviet propaganda and in a friendly, helpful manner, call their attention to the fact that they have been misinformed as to the background and record of the individual in question or to the true intent and purpose of the allegedly bonafide organization.

Unsuspecting local citizens should be alerted when they endorse a Communist Party front. "Remember that you are trying to protect a local citizen from being made the fool, so belligerence and blustering are entirely out of order. If your local organization or citizen rejects your friendly, documented advice, then obviously you are dealing with a willful tool or with people who know exactly what they are doing and don't care.

"In other words, you will have uncovered another C. P. fronter."

Some other stratagems of the American Legion:

—Put "pro-American" literature into doctors' and dentists' offices.

—Watch the press closely. "Many newspapers and other publicity media have secret Communists on their staffs who regularly slip in a neat hypodermic needle full of Moscow virus."

—Announce boycotts of corporations and businesses that aid the Communists, either through employees or services. "Movie producers and producers of nationally advertised products have extremely sensitive pocketbook nerves."

The Legion's advice reached an appreciative audience. Adolph Covino, a Legionnaire in Pine Bush, New York, wrote the magazine his thanks for articles on "Commies" which he said "have been of inestimable value to us in the backwoods." Covino passed along a personal suspicion: "We parents and the teachers and the principals do not like the *horrors* created by the comics. Are the Commies behind these books, which appear in print by the thousands?" J. H. Killman, of Oklahoma City, wanted to carry surveillance into every hamlet. "We ought to work out a system whereby in each block in the city and in each neighborhood in the country someone can be made responsible for making sure that Commies are known for what they are." William LaVarre, who had spent time in Latin America, was much impressed by an internal passport system in Chile under which every person had to carry identification and to show it to authorities upon demand. "Thanks to a national passport system, it is no longer possible for disguised subversives and crooks to float around Chile and stir up trouble."

Harry Truman watched HUAC's work, and the spreading anti-Communist drives, with much apprehension. "When we have these fits of hysteria, we are like the person who has a fit of nerves in public—when he recovers, he is very much ashamed—and so are we as a nation when sanity returns." In internal security matters Truman preferred secrecy to publicity; he felt that "the security agencies of the government are well able to deal quietly and effectively with any Communists who sneak into the government, without invoking 'Gestapo methods.' " But the Gouzenko spy revelations, and the incessant din of HUAC, prompted Truman to do something publicly about "subversives in government." In 1946 he created a committee of subcabinet officers to review loyalty programs, both for prospective and existing employees, and recommend tightening where necessary.

After a year's work the committee called for an intricate system of loyalty review boards, which Truman promptly instituted, even though with misgivings. In his order Truman said he was trying to satisfy two requirements: to protect the government, since the presence of "any disloyal or subversive person constituted a threat to our democratic processes"; and to guard innocent employees against unfounded accusations. Under the system, a person accused of belonging to a subversive organization, or engaging in subversive activities, was given a first hearing before a board in his own department, with the decision reviewed by the department head. If the findings were adverse, the person could appeal to a national Loyalty Review Board, under the Civil Service Commission.

The system, with a misleading superficial fairness, contained grave civil liberties flaws. Although the accused was provided a résumé of the charges, anything considered secret was omitted. Confidential informants of the FBI and other investigative agencies were not required to testify, or even to be identified. Often the "evidence" consisted solely of a dossier seen only by the board members. Although the accused had right to counsel, the secrecy effectively made loyalty hearings star chamber proceedings. In his memoirs Truman wrote rather lamely that "by and large, it [the review system] did give anyone accused as fair an opportunity to have his case adjudicated as was possible *under the climate of opinion that then existed.*" [Emphasis added.]

Liberals shared many of Truman's doubts but generally accepted the review program as a necessity. The New York *Post* called it a logical response to attempts at subversion by "antidemocratic forces." The *New Leader* saw it as a "broom which would sweep the totalitarians out of Washington." But *The Nation* feared the program offered vast "opportunities for malicious gossip, character assassination, and the settlement of private grudges." So did the St. Louis *Post-Dispatch,* which felt Truman overreacted to a bogus "Red scare." The liberal columnist Thomas Stokes awaited the next step: "book burnings in front of the Capitol."

Truman's mournful commentary offered little solace to citizens caught up in the doomsday-machine operations of the boards and their Kafkaesque procedures. The most striking case to come to public view involved Dorothy Bailey, a fortyish bureaucrat in the United States Employment Service. Miss Bailey was of unquestioned professional competence. After receiving a degree from the University of Minnesota, she did graduate work in labor relations at Bryn Mawr and joined the government in 1933 as a junior clerk-typist for $1,440. In fourteen years she worked her way to a supervisor's job, at $7,911. Her chief outside activity was the presidency of Local 10, United Public Workers of America, a CIO affiliate frequently accused of Communist orientation, but never to the point of proof.

In 1948 Miss Bailey was handed a formal charge that the Civil Service Commission "has received information to the effect that you are or have been a member of the Communist Party or the Communist Political Association; that you have attended meetings of the Communist Party; and have associated on numerous occasions with known Communist Party members." It also claimed the commission had information that she had belonged to the Washington Committee for Democratic Action and the American League for Peace Democracy. Of the four groups, Miss Bailey admitted belonging to the latter briefly, and attending two meetings in 1938 or 1939. Her only contact with the Communist Party was in 1932, when she attended a meeting as part of a seminar in social economy while a graduate student at Bryn Mawr.

Miss Bailey and her attorney, Paul Porter, suspected the charge came from disgruntled union opponents. When her case came before the Loyalty Review Board they offered considerable evidence, through witnesses and documents, that she frequently took positions contrary to the Communists. But Porter was stymied when he tried to force the board to identify the source of what he termed "malicious, irresponsible, reckless gossip which has no foundation whatsoever in fact and stems from an internecine union controversy that we shall develop." Seth Richardson, a crusty Republican banker from New England whom Truman had made board chairman, cut Porter off.

RICHARDSON: I can only say to you that five or six of the reports come from informants certified to us by the Federal Bureau of Investigation as experienced and entirely reliable.

PORTER: We would like to have their names, and I would challenge any one of them to state it publicly in a nonprivileged forum. . . . [W]ould we be privileged to obtain at least this much information? Those informants which are judged reliable by the FBI, have they been active in the Federal Workers Union . . .?

RICHARDSON: I haven't the slightest knowledge as to who they were or how active they have been in anything.

PORTER: I think that is very relevant.

But Richardson wouldn't yield, even after Porter pleaded again that the obvious source of the accusations was union foes. The board was more interested in marching through the informants' charges. The difficulty Miss Bailey faced in knocking aside brickbats hurled from the dark was evident when she sought to answer questions from board member Murray Seasongood.

SEASONGOOD: Let me ask you now. Here is a statement that it was ascertained you were a member of the Communist Party in the District of Columbia as early as 1935, and that in the early days of her party membership she attended Communist Party meetings. What do you say to that?

MISS BAILEY: I have never been a member of the Communist Party. I have never attended a Communist Party meeting except the one I mentioned . . . when I was in college. I cannot understand how this allegation could be made. It seems to be completely unsupported. . . . Is there any evidence given by the person who made the charge that I was a member . . . ? We weren't able to obtain any evidence or any examples or instances and I find it extremely hard to defend myself in a case like this.

SEASONGOOD: You can say it is not true.

MISS BAILEY: Other than to say under oath that it is not true, that I have never been a sympathizer, and anyone who knows me could not help but corroborate this statement.

SEASONGOOD: Then another one says that it first came to the informant's attention about 1936, at which time she was a known member of the so-called "closed group" of the Communist Party operating in the District of Columbia.

MISS BAILEY: First of all, I didn't know, or don't know, that there is a "closed group." This terminology is unfamiliar to me. I can say under oath and with the strongest conviction that I was not then and have never been a member of the Communist Party.

SEASONGOOD: Here is another that says you were a member of the Communist Party, and he bases his statement on his knowledge of your association with known Communists for the past seven or eight years. That is part of the evidence that was submitted to us.

PORTER: It is part of the allegations. I don't think that can be considered evidence.

RICHARDSON: It is evidence.

PORTER: We renew our request, even though we recognize the futility of it, that some identification of this malicious gossip be given this respondent or her counsel.

RICHARDSON: Of course, that doesn't help us a bit. If this testimony is true, it is neither gossip nor malicious. We are under the difficulty of not being able to disclose this.

PORTER: Is it under oath?

SEASONGOOD: It is a person of known responsibility who has proffered information concerning Communist activity in the District of Columbia.

MISS BAILEY: You see that point in it worries me, because if I am convicted here that will make the persons who have made these charges considered reliable witnesses; and they are not, because the charges are not true, and whatever is said here should not add to their reliability.

Miss Bailey lost, and her case eventually went before the Supreme Court. She contended she had been deprived of her good name and livelihood without due process of law. The court upheld the verdict against her in a decision which Justice Robert Jackson bitingly described as "justice turned upside down." She left government service.

The Bailey case, although an extreme example of vicious secrecy, was not unique. Another hearing in 1949 involved a scientist who worked on nuclear projects for the Atomic Energy Commission. He held a "Q" clearance, necessary for atomic work, but encountered problems when he attempted to transfer to another agency. The challenges concerned associations and attitudes during the years 1934–38, when he was doing graduate work.*

EXAMINER: The commission's information is also to the effect that you admitted to a close associate that you were attending Communist meetings at the time [1934–38]. Do you have any explanation for that?

SCIENTIST: No, none. This just can't be true. May I ask, can it be found out who this person is?

EXAMINER: I do not know at this time.

SCIENTIST: Because this is just impossible. Whoever it was must have confused some other attendance at some open public meeting with this, but it just can't be true. I would like to know who this person is and confront this person.

EXAMINER: You understand that under this program we cannot always do that. We can only give you this information at this time, giving you every opportunity to explain it and bring out any matters that may explain it.

COUNSEL FOR THE SCIENTIST: I would like to ask what knowledge you have as to the individuals involved who reported. I realize the importance of keeping the names confidential, but I was wondering if there had been any check on the individual who gave this information to ascertain the character of the person who gave it.

* The case received scant publicity at the time, hence I see no reason to cause the man unnecessary embarrassment by using his name in this account.

EXAMINER: There has been considerable checking.

COUNSEL: Has that been checked by this board or is that only the—

EXAMINER: You understand that all our investigative work is done by the FBI.

COUNSEL: I have understood that the FBI would when questions were raised about confidential informants, that the FBI would give information they had to the Loyalty Board involved, telling them about the reliability of the person and giving them some background information, so that they might better appraise the informant even if the name of the informant remained anonymous.

EXAMINER: I do that when I can.

In its first year the loyalty program resulted in firings of 793 government employees; eighteen others quietly resigned under investigation. Arthur Flemming, head of the Civil Service Commission, under whose umbrella the boards operated, forecast that 3,200 workers (of two million) would be ousted during the first phase of screening. Reasons for the disloyalty findings varied, but the War Department said 158 of the 190 civilians it fired were "ineligible for employment for disloyalty involving Communism."

The loyalty panels' dragnets reached deep into American life. One guideline they used for judging loyalty was something that came to be called "the Attorney General's List." When serving as attorney general, Francis Biddle compiled a list of subversive organizations for agencies to use when evaluating prospective workers. Biddle wanted some uniformity among agencies, and the list was intended as a guide, not a blacklist. It was strictly confidential. However, Representative Martin Dies, while chairman of HUAC, obtained a copy and put it into the *Congressional Record*. In his executive order establishing the loyalty boards, President Truman said membership in any of the organizations was nothing more than a "factor to be taken into consideration" in determining loyalty. As a practical matter, however, membership in a group on the Attorney General's List could—and did—cost a person his government job, his teaching position, his pulpit, his position in private industry.

Nor was the list necessarily an exact index of subversive groups. Tom Clark, Biddle's successor, added the Socialist Workers Party, a virulently anti-Stalin faction of the Communist Party which operated as a legal political party (polling 13,000 votes in the 1948 presidential election) and which advocated socialization of all industry. But it disavowed violence. Nonetheless it went on the Attorney General's List.

In 1943 Private First Class James Kutcher, United States Army, lost his legs in the battle for San Pietro, Italy. When he returned to civilian life he resumed membership in the Socialist Workers Party and made no secret of the fact that he favored a socialistic society. He got employment as a $43-a-week clerk in the Newark office of the Veterans Administration. In 1948, to Kutcher's astonishment, he received a dismissal notice: because of the membership, he was automatically disqualified for federal service. "The Case of the Legless Veteran," columnist I. F. Stone called Kutcher's plight; he wrote, "The circumstances provide a *reductio ad absurdum* for the syllogism of suspicion which has hitherto served as rationale for the purge. . . . The case . . . demonstrates that the loyalty purge goes beyond any supposed necessity for protecting secrets so vital they justify the abandonment of traditional liberties. The political views and the job involved show that the effect is to punish a man for his ideas, irrespective of his conduct or his record. . . . No one could suspect a Trotskyist of trying to steal the atom bomb and ship it to the Kremlin, except perhaps with a mechanism attached to make it go off when Stalin turned the spigot on the office samovar."

Stone was one of few liberals to protest. America had found anticommunism, and it worked. In California in 1947, Superior Court Judge Newcomb Condee would not approve an estate settlement under which a Russian girl would be a beneficiary. "This court will take judicial notice that Russia is kicking the U.S. in the teeth," the jurist declared. In Carmel the same year, the Russian Inn changed its name to the Ocean Inn for what the owner said were "business reasons." He did not need to explain further. Hiram W. Johnson 3d, grandson of the California senator and onetime governor, resigned as a candidate for Congress: "In view of the international situation . . . a reserve officer in my status will not have time to be elected, much less serve." In April 1948, for the first time in history, the State Department refused a passport to a congressman. Leo Isacson, a Wallaceite elected on the American Labor Party ticket from the Bronx, wanted to attend a conference in Paris on aid for the Greek guerrillas. But the State Department said a sponsoring group, the American Council for a Democratic Greece, was a Communist-front group; that since it opposed the U.S. policy of aiding the established Greek government, issuing a passport would not be in "the interest of the United States."

The *New York Times* commented, "No citizen is entitled to go abroad to oppose the policies and interests of his country. . . . The State Department acted wisely."

19

HUAC Finds a Spy Queen

I N T H E A U T U M N O F 1945, according to the FBI, a frumpy, fortyish spinster named Elizabeth Bentley walked into its office and volunteered information on an American version of the Gouzenko spy case. Bentley claimed to have worked for a Soviet ring with access to the very inner sanctum of the White House, via Lauchlin Currie, a Harvard-trained economist who served as one of President Roosevelt's top domestic aides from 1939 to 1945. Bentley said her role was courier. She had traveled from New York to Washington on alternate weekends to pick up government documents stolen by separate espionage nets directed by Nathan Gregory Silvermaster, an economist for the Farm Security Administration and the Bureau of Economic Warfare; and Victor Perlo, an analyst in the Treasury Department. She reeled off name after name, more than a score of them. Harry Dexter White, an assistant secretary of the treasury, and a major architect of postwar monetary policy, was a Communist agent, her "most valuable source of information," a man able to place Communists and fellow travelers in key government positions.

By Bentley's account, she channeled her information to a Soviet agent named Jacob N. Golos, who was at once her lover and her superior.* Miss Bentley lived with Golos from 1939 to 1944, when he died in her

---

* Soviet recruiters readily bedded lovelorn women to lure them into espionage work. Before the decade ended a pretty Justice Department clerk named Judith Coplon claimed that romance brought her into the clutches of Valentin A. Gubichev, a Soviet employee at the United Nations. The FBI caught Miss Coplon handing documents to Gubichev. "She got an affection for him," her lawyer claimed at trial. "When you are in love with a person you don't care whether they are red or green. Love knows no bounds." Replied prosecutor John Kelley, Jr.: "Fornication has nothing to do with espionage." A jury convicted Coplon, but an appeals court set her free because the FBI admitted it had illegally tapped her phone, even during her trial. Judge Learned Hand wrote that Coplon's "guilt is plain" but that the FBI had ruined its own case.

arms, she whispering to him with a kiss, "Goodbye, *golobchik,* you have left me a legacy, and I will not fail you." Golos' successor spymasters, however, were an unromantic group who coveted the documents Bentley carried, not her body. As she would lament in her autobiography, "The international Communist movement, I realized, was in the hands of the wrong people." So she broke with the party and went to the FBI. (A counterintelligence expert mused some years later, "Had the Soviets detailed someone to give Elizabeth Bentley a good screw once a month or so, and show her some affection, she'd have stuck with them until the bureau caught her; she would never have walked in." But walk in she did, and with the special fury of a wallflower scorned.)

Such was the version of Miss Bentley's defection that the FBI released as her case gradually came out of the shadows. For one to accept this story unquestioningly requires considerable faith in the FBI. The main inconsistency, of many, was the assertion that the FBI knew nothing of Bentley's spying until she suddenly appeared and started talking.* Bentley's paramour, Golos, was no stranger to the FBI—nor, for that matter, to the newspapers. A native of Russia, Golos was an open Communist during the 1930's and edited a New York Communist newspaper. He ran World Tourists, a travel agency the Communists used to promote American travel to the USSR and to send recruits to the loyalist army in Spain. In 1939, the same year Bentley moved into Golos' apartment as his common-law wife, federal agents seized two truckloads of records from World Tourists and brought Golos before a grand jury twenty times. On January 2, 1940, Attorney General Frank Murphy accused Golos and World Tourists of "military espionage" for the Soviets; the *New York Times* ran the story. Three months later Golos pleaded guilty to failure to register as a foreign agent and received a suspended jail term and a $500 fine.

If J. Edgar Hoover's boasts of FBI efficiency are to be believed, the bureau thereafter knew of the existence of Golos and World Tourists. But by Bentley's account, Golos continued work as a master spy, without official interference. Nor should Bentley have been a stranger to an alert counterintelligence agency: she lived with Golos at the time of his arrest; she worked for a subsidiary of World Tourists and spent half her time at its office; she met regularly with Earl Browder, the head of the Communist Party, and Louis Budenz, a *Daily Worker* editor, often at appointments made over World Tourists' phone. Yet if the FBI is to be believed, Bentley came to the bureau as a total stranger.

According to what Hoover told a Senate committee later, he sent the

---

* Indeed, at one point the bureau said Bentley's first visit, to its office in New Haven, Connecticut, was to inquire about an erstwhile boyfriend who claimed to be a secret U.S. agent. She mentioned her own spying for the Soviets almost as an afterthought, and the agent took no formal statement from her. Because of a bureaucratic contretemps the FBI did not talk to Bentley again for nearly three months.

White House a "preliminary flash" on Bentley's charges on November 8, 1945, a day after her first thorough debriefing. The flash cited a "confidential source" as saying a "number" of government workers had furnished information for transmission "to espionage agents of the Soviet government." Later FBI reports identified one of the persons as Harry Dexter White, then in the process of being nominated as a director of the International Monetary Fund. But the FBI lacked hard proof. Bentley admitted she had never taken documents directly from White or Currie; so far as she could remember, she had never *seen* either man: her "knowledge" they were Soviet agents rested solely upon what other people told her. After much agonizing, Truman let the appointment go forward. To fire White without definite proof would permanently blacken his career, even if he should be found innocent later. Leaving him in place would enable the FBI to keep close surveillance on his activities; if White indeed were a spy, he should be caught in short order. White was confirmed by the Senate and served at the IMF until April 1947, when he quit to enter private business—taking with him a glowing letter of recommendation from President Truman.

The Justice Department, meanwhile, convened an ultrasecret grand jury in New York to hear Miss Bentley and any other witnesses the FBI could find to testify about Soviet espionage. The very existence of the jury was kept secret, as well as the identity of Miss Bentley and other witnesses. To the dismay of many of the agents working on her case, nothing happened. Witnesses trooped in day after day, and no espionage indictments resulted. Observers could mull several possible reasons. The espionage act carries a three-year statute of limitations, and conceivably no actual spying could be proved within this period. Conceivably Miss Bentley's story could not be corroborated enough to take to court in a criminal proceeding. Conceivably the Soviet sympathizers she charged had wormed their way into the government were now so powerful they blocked indictments. Conceivably the Truman Administration feared political embarrassment. Whatever the reason, more than a year passed with the grand jury silent on the subject of espionage.

The House Un-American Activities Committee, meanwhile, had gotten itself into difficulty. For some months Chairman Parnell Thomas had been charging that Dr. Edward U. Condon, director of the National Bureau of Standards, was "one of the weakest links in our atomic security." An esteemed physicist, Condon worked on development of the atomic bomb beginning in 1939, and he commanded broad respect in the scientific community as well as in government and industry. Condon was an unabashed liberal and had championed civilian control of nuclear energy, to the chagrin of the military and its congressional supporters. To many, the "case" presented by Thomas was laughably hollow. Among items cited in a formal HUAC report was such intelligence as that his wife was Czechoslovakian; he had been recommended for the

Bureau of Standards post, in 1945, by Henry Wallace, then secretary of commerce; and he had ties to such groups as the Southern Conference for Human Welfare. The report quoted a portion of a letter FBI director Hoover had written the Department of Commerce during an earlier security probe. It cited the contacts of both Condons with officials of the Polish embassy in Washington, and with Nathan Gregory Silvermaster, the government economist whom Elizabeth Bentley had named as an espionage agent. However, the report deleted the next, and most significant, line in the letter: "There is no evidence to show that contacts between this individual [Silvermaster] and Dr. Condon were related to this individual's espionage activities."

Truman considered the Condon case a challenge to his authority. Reassured the man was loyal, he stood down HUAC, refusing to let its investigators rummage through raw security files even when the House demanded access by a 219–142 vote. Truman felt his loyalty review program adequately protected the nation's security. In July 1948 the Atomic Energy Commission administered the coup de grace to HUAC insofar as Condon was concerned. After reviewing his entire file, including FBI reports, the AEC concluded that "his continued clearance is in the best interests of the atomic energy program." HUAC offered indirect apologies after the 1948 election, with Representative Richard Nixon conceding the committee's handling of the case might have been "unfair."*

HUAC's stumbling performance in the Condon case brought more embarrassment than benefit, to the dismay of Republican campaigners who depended on the committee to help elect Thomas E. Dewey. Parnell Thomas was to say years later the Republican national chairman, Representative Hugh Scott of Pennsylvania, "was urging me in the Dewey campaign to set up the spy hearings. At the time he was urging me to stay in Washington to keep the heat on Harry Truman." In the summer of 1948 the FBI offered HUAC what amounted to a lifeline out of its predicament. It handed over Elizabeth Bentley for public testimony. "The closest relationship exists between this committee and the FBI," Parnell Thomas was to boast that summer. "I think there is a very good understanding between us. It is something, however, that we cannot talk too much about."

Elizabeth Bentley took stage center on July 31, 1948, billed in advance as the "Beautiful Blonde Spy Queen" by the Scripps-Howard newspapers, with more expertise in creating drama than in appraising pulchritude. People scuffled and pushed for a chance to sit in the sweltering hearing room for her testimony, and her name made big black headlines on every front page in the country. Bentley loved it. Once

---

* The loyalty hounds bayed after Condon for years thereafter, even after he left government. In 1966 the air force apparently resolved the question once and for all by putting him in charge of its inquiry into the flying saucer phenomena.

again she recited the touching story of her love affair with Jacob Golos, and she littered the record with even more names of government officials in her spy ring. Even the skeptics had to admit a hard kernel of truth in Bentley's story: the woman had hustled industriously on behalf of the Soviets, and at least some of the people she contacted had highly suspect records. Nathan Silvermaster, for instance, had accumulated a thick dossier since entering government service in 1935. A Civil Service Commission report in 1942 concluded, "Nathan Gregory Silvermaster is now and has for years been a member and a leader of the Communist Party and very probably a secret agent of the OGPU" (predecessor of the KGB, the Soviet secret service). At the time, of course, nothing barred Communists from government service, and although Silvermaster knew the FBI had more than a casual interest in him, he not only kept his government positions but, according to Miss Bentley, utilized his house as a photographic lab to copy the scores of documents gathered by underlings, and to pass them to Miss Bentley. Conditioned by the press to receive Miss Bentley as a witness who carried the FBI's seal of approval, much of the public accepted her story without question. Even so, the gentlest of questions from the committee staff sent Bentley reeling into uncertainty. Much of what she "knew" had come from Golos, in the grave and beyond the reach of the committee; some other things she "surmised" on her own. An exchange with HUAC counsel Robert E. Stripling is illustrative of the Bentley style.

STRIPLING: May I ask you, Miss Bentley, was one _____ a member of this group?*

BENTLEY: Yes, he was.

STRIPLING: Was he a rather active participant?

BENTLEY: Rather remotely, Mr. Stripling, because at the time I had charge of the group he was in China. . . .

STRIPLING: Miss Bentley, did you collect the Communist Party dues from Mr. _____ and turn them over to Mr. Silvermaster? Do you recall doing that?

BENTLEY: Mr. Silvermaster gave me the dues for his complete group and I take it for granted those included Mr. _____. Since he was in China, I am not too sure about it.

STRIPLING: Did you ever meet Mr. _____ yourself?

BENTLEY: No, I never did.

Miss Bentley was even fuzzier as to the exact information she carted back to Golos, explaining that the bulk of it was undeveloped microfilm. But one piece of intelligence did stick in her mind, the exact timing of the D-Day invasion of Normandy. She brought up this point three times in her testimony. One of her sources, she said, was "in the Pentagon in the Air Corps, and through his connections with General Hildring's

* For obvious reasons, I am deleting this man's name.

office he had learned the date, and I remember it distinctly because with that knowledge he was betting with a friend of his when D-Day would be and, of course, he won the bet, since he knew it ahead of time."

If so, Miss Bentley's source knew more than General Dwight D. Eisenhower, the commander of the invasion force. Because of weather and logistical factors, the Allies set the operation for a time bracket, rather than a specific date, and indeed the decision to proceed on June 6 was not made until 4:15 on the morning of June 5, leaving scant time for the information to be transmitted to a Soviet spy in the Pentagon and relayed, via the peripatetic Miss Bentley, to Joseph Stalin. Even so, herein lies an absurdity. By the accounts of both Winston Churchill and Major General John R. Deane, head of the United States military mission in Moscow, the Allies kept the Soviets posted on invasion planning all along, including as approximate a date as possible.

Several of the persons accused by Miss Bentley acknowledged knowing her in wartime Washington, but under vastly different circumstances from those she described. One such man was a onetime law partner of General William J. Donovan, head of the Office of Strategic Services. The man came to Washington with General Donovan and acquired high rank in OSS himself. He testified he and his wife met Bentley socially (she used the name "Helen Grant") through the secretary to a Washington columnist and saw her regularly for some months. But Bentley soon became tiresome. The man testified:

> We came to the conclusion that she was a very lonely and neurotic woman, that she was a frustrated woman, that her . . . apparent liking for us was unnaturally intense. We began to feel she was an emotional weight around our necks and that really there was nothing in the acquaintance that justified the intense way she did follow us up.

Why did Miss Bentley make such accusations? The man felt she "used her social relationship with me merely to help her misrepresent to her employers for her own personal build-up that she had access through me to someone of the importance of General Donovan." The man flatly denied Bentley's accusation that he was a Communist agent or sympathizer, and implicitly challenged HUAC to attempt to prosecute him for perjury. HUAC did not accept the dare.

The Bentley hearings finished inconclusively, her charges accepted more or less uncritically by the part of the press that had vouched for her authenticity in advance, but worthless for court purposes, because of both the inconsistencies and the statute of limitations. One result of Bentley's appearances was that the provable falseness of much of her testimony, her erratic mannerisms and behavior, the inconsistencies in the FBI's accounts of how she came to be a witness, made many Americans—and especially liberal Democrats—reflexively suspicious of repentant Communists who decided to bare their souls to HUAC. The week that Bentley testified, reporters asked Harry Truman for an evaluation of the hearings. "A red herring," snapped the President. Any "spy ring" in Washington existed solely in the imagination of HUAC, he added. But Bentley served a more important purpose for HUAC. As Chairman Thomas said with obvious relish at one point, "We have been unearthing your New Dealers for two years, and for eight years before this."

The Monday evening of Christmas week 1948, Laurence Duggan, forty-three, "fell or jumped" (in the terminology of the police) from his sixteenth-floor office of the Institute of International Education in Manhattan. Passersby found Duggan's mangled body in a snowbank near the entrance to 2 West 45th Street; he was dead on arrival at Roosevelt Hospital. Duggan, a graduate of Exeter and Harvard, had spent fourteen years with the State Department, chiefly in Latin American affairs, before joining Carnegie as president.

Two weeks earlier, Representative Karl Mundt of North Dakota, a member of the House Un-American Activities Committee, had told newsmen Duggan had been named a member of a six-man ring in the State Department, including Alger Hiss, that passed documents to Soviet agents. Mundt cited as his souce Isaac Don Levine, an editor of an anti-Communist newsletter, who in turn was said to have acquired the information from a man named Whittaker Chambers.

After Duggan's death someone asked Mundt when the other "Communist agents" would be identified. "We'll name them as they jump out of windows," Mundt replied.

Several days afterward, Chambers said he had never met Duggan and had no personal knowledge that he had ever given secret government documents to anyone. Chambers said he had "found it necessary" to bring forth Duggan's name because of "second-hand information" he had received. Levine denied having called Duggan a Communist before the committee. He described him as a "high-minded person who may have committed some ideological errors."

Attorney General Tom C. Clark, after reviewing the FBI file on Duggan, called him a "loyal employee of the United States government." Mundt and another HUAC member, Representative Richard Nixon, conceded that their disclosure of the Levine "information" warranted "some honest criticism," and they sincerely regretted the "misunderstanding" and "misinterpretations" the public had of Duggan's death. So far as they were concerned, the Duggan "case" was a "closed book."

Duggan was buried on Christmas Eve from the Frank E. Campbell Funeral Church, 81st Street and Madison Avenue. In addition to his wife, Helen Boyd Duggan, he was survived by four small children, Stephanie, Laurence, Robert, and Christopher.

20

The Hiss Case:
An Ideal Tarnished

DURING HUAC HEARINGS on physicist Edward U. Condon in the spring of 1948, a New York journalist quietly passed a tip to Robert E. Stripling, the gaunt-faced, methodical Texan guiding HUAC's work as chief counsel. The New York grand jury, the reporter said, had been talking with a *Time* editor named Whittaker Chambers. According to corridor gossip, Chambers was spewing big names. Stripling dispatched two investigators to talk with Chambers, and on Tuesday, August 3, HUAC put him on the stand for a public hearing.

Despite his journalistic importance and his influence upon the content and tone of *Time,* Chambers was a little-known figure even at his own magazine, a man who avoided office confidences, worked with his door closed, and spent his off time at a farm in remote rural Maryland. A brilliant writer, equally at ease writing lush, baroque prose about medieval theology and chatty Timese about current events, the fact is that Chambers had spent the bulk of his adult life in the domestic Communist underground, and he had carried the secretiveness with him when he left the party—first, by his account, to avoid feared party retribution; later, as a matter of personal choice. Chambers' biography, *Witness,* reveals a tortured neurotic, a man incessantly pondering suicide, choosing to remain alive only because of what to him was a God-given mission to save western civilization. Even Chambers' advocates—and to believe in Whittaker Chambers meant unblinking faith in his word and his memory—recognized his abnormality.

Physically, Chambers was not an imposing figure. Reporters who watched him before HUAC, and in later court appearances, described him variously as "rumpled, moon-faced"; "perpetually rumpled and disheveled"; "a fat, sad-looking man in a baggy blue suit"; and "drab, middle-aged, hesitant of speech and manner." But Chambers' testimony, not his physique, was what counted. His story, in this initial public appearance, was as follows:

Chambers joined the Communist Party in 1924 because he felt western civilization "had reached a crisis . . . that it was doomed to collapse or revert to barbarism"; and "as an intelligent man I must do something," and thought he had found the answer in the economics of Marx and the politics of Lenin. Much of this time Chambers spent "in the underground, chiefly in Washington, D.C." He worked mainly with an underground organization developed "to the best of my knowledge, by Harold Ware, one of the sons of the Communist leader known as 'Mother Bloor.' " Chambers said he knew seven men at its top level:

> The head of the underground group at the time I knew it was Nathan Witt, an attorney for the National Labor Relations Board. Later, John Abt became the leader. Lee Pressman* was also a member of this group, as was Alger Hiss, who, as a member of the State Department, later organized the conferences at Dumbarton Oaks, San Francisco, and the United States side of the Yalta Conference.
>
> The purpose of this group at that time was not primarily espionage. Its original purpose was the Communist infiltration of the American government. But espionage was certainly one of its eventual objectives.

Chambers said that "in 1937" (a date to be noted) he repudiated communism because "experience and the record had convinced me that [it] is a form of totalitarianism, that its triumph means slavery to men wherever they fall under its sway, and spiritual night to the human mind and soul." For the next year he lived in hiding, "sleeping by day and watching through the night with gun or revolver within easy reach. That is what underground communism could do to one man in the peaceful United States in the year 1938."

In 1939, two days after the Hitler-Stalin pact, Chambers went to Adolph A. Berle, then the assistant secretary of state with security responsibilities, and told "what I knew about the infiltration of the United States government by Communists." Berle acted shocked. Chambers quoted him as saying that "we absolutely have to have a clean government service because we are faced with the prospect of war." But nothing happened. Chambers said he was especially galled to see Alger Hiss continue to rise through the State Department bureaucracy, from a minor post in the Trade Agreements Division to the director of the office in charge of United Nations affairs. In subsequent

---

* By 1948 Pressman had left government and served as general counsel of the CIO. He was also prominent in Henry Wallace's campaign for the presidency.

years FBI agents often called on Chambers (fourteen or fifteen times, in all, he later computed) but nothing happened to Hiss, who resigned from government in 1947 to become president of the prestigious Carnegie Endowment for Peace.

In going after Hiss, Chambers struck at the sort of man generally regarded as the best America has to offer. Hiss was archetypical of the urbane intellectuals who flocked into 1930's Washington to provide the operative brains of the New Deal. Hiss carried impeccable credentials. Born of Baltimore gentility, he attended Johns Hopkins University and Harvard Law School, and won the most cherished position available to a fledgling lawyer, a clerkship to the esteemed Justice Oliver Wendell Holmes. He came to Washington as counsel to the Nye committee investigating the munitions industry, worked awhile at the Agriculture Department, and then moved to State. His government service, culminating in administrative groundwork of the United Nations, put him on a career track that carried into the heart of the American establishment. He was selected for the Carnegie foundation post by none other than the redoubtable Wall Street lawyer/diplomat John Foster Dulles. In Chambers' eloquent words, Hiss had "put down roots that made him one with the matted forest floor of American upper class, enlightened middle class, liberal and official life. His roots could not be disturbed without disturbing all the roots on all sides of him." Only forty-four years old in 1948, Hiss had reason to anticipate even greater prestige and position—conceivably the post of secretary of state.

Certainly Hiss was not a man who could ignore Chambers' stain on his name. Self-preservation demanded that the testimony be rebutted. So Hiss telegraphed HUAC a strong denial of the charges, and asked the opportunity to appear publicly to refute them. And this he did, on August 5, in a skillful blend of subdued outrage and pained bemusement. Physically, Hiss was the antithesis of Whittaker Chambers. The journalist Murray Kempton, a Harvard classmate, once said, "I remember Alger Hiss best of all for a kind of distinction that had to be seen to be believed. If he were standing at a bar with the British ambassador and you were told to give a package to the ambassador's valet, you would give it to the ambassador before you gave it to Alger. He gave you a sense of absolute command and absolute grace." Slim, with handsome, defined features, Hiss "had one of those bodies that without being at all imposing or foppish seem to illustrate the finesse of the human mechanism," wrote the friendly British journalist Alistair Cooke. Graceful. Composed. Articulate, with the lawyer's insistence on precise phrasing. Charm, in a facile sort of way. And under risk of a perjury indictment he declared:

I am not and never have been a member of the Communist Party. I do not and never have adhered to the tenets of the Communist Party. I am not and never have been a member of any Communist-front organization. I have never followed the Communist Party line, directly or indirectly. To the best of my knowledge, none of my friends is a Communist. . . .

To the best of my knowledge, I never heard of Whittaker Chambers until in 1947, when two representatives of the Federal Bureau of Investigation asked me if I knew him and various other people, some of whom I knew and some of whom I did not know. I said I did not know Chambers. So far as I know, I have never laid eyes upon him, and I should like to have the opportunity to do so.

Hiss acknowledged knowing many of the people Chambers named, but as government and university colleagues, not as fellow conspirators. Lee Pressman, Nathan Witt, and John Abt had been on the legal staff of the Agricultural Adjustment Administration, but he had seen little of them since leaving that agency in the 1930's. "Except as I have indicated," he said, "the statements made about me by Mr. Chambers are complete fabrications. I think my record in the government service speaks for itself." When counsel Robert Stripling showed Hiss a press photograph of Chambers, he replied he would rather see the man than his picture, and that he would not care to testify that he had never seen him. When Stripling asked directly, "You say you have never seen Mr. Chambers," Hiss said, "The name means absolutely nothing to me, Mr. Stripling."

To the Hiss partisans, predominant in the hearing room, his statements came across as unequivocal denials. Hiss left the room in a cluster of admirers and friendly reporters, and one committee member muttered, "We're ruined." An irrefutable citizen had put the lie to a HUAC-endorsed witness in direct terms, and sentiment was strong for getting away from the Hiss–Chambers case as rapidly and gracefully as possible. But Representative Richard M. Nixon, the freshman Republican from California, demurred. He argued he detected distinct hedges throughout Hiss's testimony; the "denials" were not that he knew Whittaker Chambers, but that he did not know *a man named Whittaker Chambers*. Hiss's opening statement denying Communist Party membership or allegiance was also subject to negative interpretation: if Hiss truly was a deeply implanted agent, as Chambers charged, he likely was not a formal party member, and certainly would keep his public distance from identification with any Communist causes. "It is a little too mouthy," Nixon said of Hiss's looping sentences. At Nixon's insistence the committee decided to seek proof of whether Chambers had actually known Hiss, as he claimed. It created a subcommittee, with Nixon as chairman,* to question Chambers in closed session to discover what hard facts he knew about Hiss, his family, his personal life, the Georgetown

---

* The other members were Democrat F. Edward Hebert of Louisiana and Representative McDowell.

houses he had lived in. Then it would separately quiz Hiss on the same points and compare the answers.

Chambers gave Nixon, whom he described as "man of decision," total credit for keeping the Hiss case alive. He wrote in his memoirs, "If that small group of harassed congressmen had then acted out of their fears and dropped the Case [Chambers' capitalization] it is probable that the forces which for years had kept the Communist conspiracy in government from public knowledge would have continued to be successful in concealing it. Alger Hiss would have remained at the head of the Carnegie Endowment, exerting great influence in public affairs through his position and ramified connections. With him, the whole secret Communist front would have stood more unassailable than ever because the shattered sally against it had ended in ridicule and rout. Elizabeth Bentley's charges would almost certainly have been buried in the debris."

The decision then was to put Hiss and Chambers on a fateful collision course. It also put Richard Nixon on the road that eventually led him to the presidency.

The separate interrogations swiftly brought the committee back to total belief in Chambers. Answering brisk questions from Nixon, he ticked off detail after detail about the Hiss household. Much of the information was trivial and a matter of record in *Who's Who* and other standard reference works. But Chambers had a knack for flavorful details that went beyond public knowledge. Not only did he know that the Hisses were amateur bird watchers (a fact noted in several biographical reference books), he also recalled "once they saw, to their great excitement, a prothonotary warbler," rare in the Washington area. Others of Chambers' firm assertions were outright wrong. Chambers estimated Hiss's height at "five feet eight or nine"; actually Hiss is an even six feet. Shown a hearing-room picture of Hiss with a hand cupped over his ear, Chambers responded, "Mr. Hiss is deaf in one ear." He is not. Chambers called the Hisses teetotalers. Hiss is not. But the bulk of his answers indicated great familiarity with the Hiss household.

The methodical drumbeat of Nixon's questions, their tightly meshed sequence, suggest he was guided by something other than intuition. Given the tight coordination between HUAC and the FBI, it is probable, though it has never been proven, that Nixon primed himself with bureau reports of Chambers' many interrogations and of earlier background investigations of Hiss. In any event, his sixth question cut to the core of Hiss's carefully hedged denials that he knew anyone by the name of Whittaker Chambers. Asked if Hiss knew him in that guise, Chambers responded, no, "he knew me by the party name of Carl." Further, according to Chambers, neither Hiss nor any other member of the cell ever asked a surname, which would have been contrary to "Communist discipline."

How did Chambers know Hiss was a Communist? "I was told by J. Peters." Who was Peters, and what facts did he have? Mr. Peters was "the head of the entire underground" in the United States. Could Chambers provide "any other evidence, any factual evidence" to support his claim? No, "nothing beyond the fact" that Chambers knew him as a "dedicated and disciplined Communist" who faithfully paid his dues monthly for two years. As an underground agent, Hiss didn't carry a party card. Chambers made no mention of any espionage.

When Hiss went before the subcommittee on August 16 for private testimony, much of his previous self-assurance had vanished. Newspaper leaks of Chambers' supposedly secret testimony irked him. Accused of "hedging" by Congressman Hebert, he expressed indignation that Chambers, "a confessed former Communist and traitor to his country," should be given weight equal to his own. But under Nixon's lead, members took the unwitting Hiss over the household and personal material previously given by Chambers. Much of it jibed. What members considered a "clinching point" came when Hiss talked about bird watching.

McDOWELL: Did you ever see a prothonotary warbler?
HISS: I have right here on the Potomac. Do you know that place?
. . . They come back and nest in those swamps. Beautiful yellow head, a gorgeous bird . . .

A sudden hush fell over the subcommittee. How could Chambers possibly know such a fugitive detail from the past—unless he in fact had enjoyed a close relationship with Hiss? Nixon hastily asked another question to fill the void of silence.

The sparring continued for more than an hour; then, after a recess, Hiss abruptly stated he thought he could resolve at least part of the conflict. After sifting through his memory, and the leaked testimony that Chambers claimed to have lived in his house during the 1930's, he felt the man in question could have been a ne'er-do-well free-lance writer named "George Crosley," whom he had met in 1935 while working for the Nye committee. "Crosley" sought out Hiss for information on the munitions industry for use in an article. Hiss took a mild liking to the man, and let him and his wife and small child stay in his apartment a few nights during their move to Washington. Because Hiss and his wife were changing their own Georgetown residence at the time, they even let the Crosleys have their old apartment for a period when the leases overlapped, lent them some furniture, and gave them the use of a dilapidated 1929 Ford. Crosley, Hiss said, turned out to be a deadbeat who never paid rent on the apartment nor returned several small loans, and Hiss maintained he eventually drifted away. Hiss repeated his demand that he be brought face to face with Chambers. And even if Chambers and "Crosley" were the same man, he denied knowing him as a Communist agent.

The subcommittee thought Hiss's sudden surge of memory was play acting. Its interpretation (as expressed later by Nixon and Stripling) was that the nature of the questions alerted Hiss that Chambers had told so much about their personal relationship that a blanket denial would no longer suffice. Hence the change of strategy in mid-course.

Hiss's second testimony was on August 16, and the committee promised the long-sought personal confrontation would be arranged nine days later. Again, however, HUAC was caught up in a public relations crisis. On August 13, Harry Dexter White, the former Treasury Department official, appeared at public hearings to deny the Bentley-Chambers charges he was a Communist agent. White noted he was "recovering from a severe heart attack"—a claim Chairman Thomas received with open sarcasm—but bore up well under questions and was frequently interrupted by applause. He clearly carried the day. This was on a Friday. Over the weekend White suffered another heart attack, and on Monday, August 16, he died, his death presumably hastened by the strain of his HUAC appearance.

HUAC moved swiftly to ward off charges it "murdered" White. Staff members hustled Chambers to New York, and a cryptic telephone call to Hiss's office told him to report to Room 1400 of the Commodore Hotel in Manhattan late in the afternoon for unspecified reasons. Hiss arranged for a lawyer friend to accompany him. Enroute crosstown he saw newspapers headlining White's death. So he entered the Commodore "indignant at what I considered the committee's ruthless baiting of White and its callous attempt to divert public attention from his death."* But Nixon, presiding, brushed away his protests and directed that Chambers be brought into the room.

The two men stared at one another across the hotel suite—Hiss thinking that "I saw Crosley in the added pounds and rumpled suit," but uncertain until he heard his voice; Chambers considering it "great theater," Hiss's "performance . . . made . . . shocking, even in its moments of unintended comedy, [by] the fact that the terrible spur of Hiss's acting was fear." At Nixon's direction Chambers stated his name, and Hiss walked quizzically toward him, staring at his face, and asking, "Would you mind opening your mouth wider?" By Hiss's account he wanted a clearer view of Chambers' teeth, since one of "George Crosley's" distinguishing characteristics had been blackened, jagged front teeth. Chambers, amused, "felt somewhat like a broken-mouthed sheep whose jaws have been pried open and are being inspected by wary

---

* Nixon, in his *Six Crises*, denied any connection between White's death and the expedited August 17 session. He said he decided to move up the date to deprive Hiss of "nine more days to make his story fit the facts." Nixon's account, however, is belied by Chambers' description of frantic HUAC staff members hurrying him to the New York train. When he asked why the commotion, one of them "wrestled a newspaper out of his pocket and pointed to a headline" about White's death.

buyers at an auction." Congressmen and the HUAC staff watched with fascination. When Hiss said he wished to hear more of Chambers' voice Nixon handed him *Newsweek,* and he began reading a story about President Truman's search for a new labor secretary. After further straining and hesitations, Hiss said he could "positively" identify Chambers as the man he had known as Crosley. And he dared Chambers to repeat his charges outside the libel-proof forum of HUAC: "I challenge you to do it, and I hope you will do it damned quickly."*

The hearing ended with a decision to bring Hiss and Chambers together publicly in Washington on August 25. "Thank you," Congressman McDowell told Hiss as he left the Commodore.

"I don't reciprocate," Hiss replied.

"Italicize that in the record," McDowell said.

August 25 was a day of infernal heat, a discomfort that did not deter the curious from cramming the caucus room of the old House Office Building far beyond capacity an hour before the opening gavel. The strange new medium of television, adding its blistering lights to the torment, beamed most of the ten hours of proceedings to viewers along the eastern seaboard. The conventional pencil-and-paper press looked at the intruder with cocked eyebrow. The British journalist Alistair Cooke wrote:

> The cameras buzzed and roamed like speculative flies over the dripping audience; catching open-mouthed citizens in moments of unsuspected prurience or vanity; demonstrating to countless households . . . television's peculiar and terrifying gift for casting an intensely private eye on scenes of the greatest publicity; elbowing along the committee table and taking long, revealing glances at the darkly handsome Mr. Nixon; the unmoving bald head of Mr. Parnell Thomas, and the skeptical shruggings, ash-flickings, and nose-rubbings of Mr. Karl Mundt, who came to the point of saying out loud that at first he had been charmed by Hiss but was now inclined to share his wife's view that he had been taken in by the man's "suavity."

So, too, had concluded the other members, and their shaky neutrality didn't survive the opening moments, and a senseless semantical quibble by Hiss over whether he appeared in "response" to a subpoena, or voluntarily: "To the extent that my coming here quite voluntarily after having received the subpoena is in response to it—I would accept that statement." Another point subjected to tedious haggling was exactly

---

* The U.S. Court of Appeals two years later said a jury "well might have believed that [Hiss] had been less than frank in his belated recognition of Mr. Chambers. . . ."

how Hiss disposed of a ramshackle 1929 Ford. Chambers' story was that he used the car briefly while living with Hiss, and that later Hiss insisted on giving it to the Communists for use by "some poor organizer in the west." Chambers said Hiss made the gift through a Washington used-car company that the Communist underground regularly used as an unobtrusive channel for auto transfers. Hiss's story was somewhat different. The car had sentimental value only and was deteriorating in the street. So he "threw it in" when he let Crosley take his old apartment, as he by then had a new Plymouth. (Earlier Hiss had said he "sold" the Ford to the man he recalled as Crosley.)

The committee, however, had registration records showing that Hiss didn't buy the Plymouth for some months after he said he gave the old Ford to Chambers, and that he in fact had transferred the Ford via the "Communist underground" car firm in July 1936, a full year after the car supposedly was made available to Chambers. Pressed by Nixon to explain the discrepancy, Hiss replied he had testified from memory, not from records. Impatient, Nixon tried to elicit a direct answer.

NIXON: Now . . . did you give Crosley a car?

HISS: I gave Crosley, according to my best recollection—

NIXON: Well, now, just a moment on that point, I don't want to interrupt you on that "to the best of my recollection" but you certainly can testify "yes" or "no" as to whether you gave Crosley a car. How many cars have you given away in your life, Mr. Hiss?

Hiss, for the first time in the sessions, heard the ridiculing sound of unfriendly laughter. All he could (or would) say was, "I have no present recollection of the disposition of the Ford."

The committee, of course, was trying to lead Hiss into a flat answer on the car that could be proved a lie by its documentary material. But Hiss carefully avoided the bait. By committee count, on 198 occasions Hiss qualified his answers with a phrase such as "according to my best recollection." "You are a remarkable and agile young man," Congressman Hebert broke in at one point. And Chambers' testimony had shaken persons unwilling to believe the respected Hiss was a Communist agent. As the hearing drew to a close, near eight o'clock in the evening, Nixon asked whether a "grudge" motivated Chambers to testify against the man he had called "the closest friend I ever had in the Communist Party."

"I do not hate Mr. Hiss," Chambers replied. "We were close friends, but we are caught in a tragedy of history. Mr. Hiss represents the concealed enemy against which we are all fighting, and I am fighting. I have testified against him with remorse and pity, but in a moment of history in which this nation now stands, so help me God, I could not do otherwise."

* * *

The Hiss affair now took on a momentum of its own. His virtuoso HUAC performance notwithstanding, Chambers clearly was expected to accept Hiss's challenge: to make his charges publicly and risk a libel suit; or to be considered an untested witness. *Time* magazine, Chambers' employer, shared his discomfort. "Gee Whittaker!" wrote columnist Walter Winchell. *"Time* Marxes on." Winchell marveled that "Timemag was edited* all these years by [a] self-confessed Communist, accused perjurer and Russian spy! *Time* botches on!" When Soviet spy Valentin Gubichev was deported Winchell lamented, "Too bood. He would've made a wonderful senior editor at *Time*. . . . How can we get the Communists out of the State Dep't when we can't get them out of *Time* magazine's editorial dept?" Chambers threw down the gauntlet to Hiss on a *Meet the Press* broadcast on August 27, declaring flatly Hiss was a Communist, but declining to say whether he "now is or is not a member of the party." Chambers said he did not think Hiss would sue. And he chose his words carefully during a long series of questions aimed at eliciting whether Hiss acted as an espionage agent. Tom Reynolds, of the Chicago *Sun-Times,* asked whether Hiss ever did anything "that was treasonable or beyond the law of the United States." Chambers replied, "I am not familiar with the laws of treason."

REYNOLDS: Are you prepared at this time to say that Alger Hiss was anything more than, in your opinion, a Communist? Did he do anything wrong? Did he commit any overt act? Has he been disloyal to his country?

CHAMBERS: *I am only prepared at this time* to say he was a Communist.

REYNOLDS: It seems to me, then, sir, if I may say so, that in some respects this may be a tempest in a teapot. You say that he was a Communist, but you will not accuse him of any act that is disloyal to the United States.

CHAMBERS: *I am not prepared legally to make that charge.* My whole interest in this business has been to show that Mr. Hiss was a Communist.

A bit later, Chambers offered "clarification" of the group he said included Hiss. "That was a group, not, as I think is in the back of your mind, for the purpose of espionage, but for the purpose of infiltrating the government and getting Communists in key places." Influencing policy, he said, is "very much more important than spying."

The ball now was in Hiss's court, and when he did not sue immediately the Washington *Post* reminded him he had created "a situation in which he is obliged to put up or shut up." The New York *Daily News*

* Actually, Chambers was one of six senior editors answerable to a managing editor responsible directly to Henry Luce.

asked, in a one-sentence editorial, "Well, Alger, where's that suit?" In late September he filed, asking $50,000 damages; when Chambers, in a press statement, alluded to the "ferocity or the ingenuity of the forces that are working through him," he upped it by $25,000. Chambers now had to substantiate his charges in a courtroom, to the satisfaction of a jury.

The preliminary proceedings went poorly for Chambers, by his own admission. His lawyers did not put the same credence in his story as had HUAC, and for the first time Hiss, through his attorneys, had the opportunity to examine him under oath during depositions. By November, Chambers recited, "I saw that I might well lose . . . though it was not my nature to lose it without a fight." The sum demanded was "fantastic as compared with any ability . . . to pay it." Chambers' lawyers warned him that "if I did have anything of Hiss's" that would help prove the case "I had better get it."

By his story, Chambers made a weekend trip to Brooklyn, to the home of his wife's nephew, and found a cache of documents and microfilm he had hidden away as a "life preserver" when he broke with the Communist Party. Whe he found the packet in an old dumbwaiter shaft he felt as if an "act of God" had intervened. The material included sixty-five typed pages, copies of texts or summaries of confidential State Department papers, memos handwritten by Hiss and Harry Dexter White, and microfilms of papers from the State Department's Trade Agreements Division, in which Hiss had worked. But what should he do with the material? Chambers agonized for three days; at one point, according to his memoirs, he was on the brink of suicide. Chambers spoke of himself as the victim of "that great socialist revolution, which, in the name of liberalism, spasmodically, incompletely, somewhat form-lessly, but always in the same direction, has been inching its ice cap over the nation for two decades." The "forces of this revolution . . . had smothered the Hiss Case (and much else) for a decade, and fought to smother it in 1948." Simply, Chambers did not wish to entrust these unnamed "forces" with possession of all his documents. So he split them. The typed copies he gave to his libel lawyers, which were put into evidence at the depositions and (at Hiss's insistence) then surrendered to the Justice Department for safekeeping, because of their confidential nature. The microfilms he hid away on his Westminster farm, eventually in a hollowed-out pumpkin. HUAC got wind of their existence, and after some legalistic jockeying Chambers led committee investigator Don Appell into the field late the night of December 2, guided by flashlight, and pulled out what came to be known as "the pumpkin papers."*

The appearance of the papers cast the Hiss case in an entirely new

---

* A journalistic alliteration that was not exactly accurate; there were no "papers" in the pumpkin, only microfilm. But what headline writer could expect mileage from "pumpkin microfilms"? The entire packet eventually came to be known as the "pumpkin papers."

light. Now Chambers was offering *documentary proof* that showed Hiss to be not a mere intellectual follower of communism, but an active Soviet agent as well. Such was the thrust of the newspaper shouts the first weeks of December 1948. Public sentiment crystallized against Hiss overnight; as one of President Truman's political intimates remarked years later, "Had Chambers stuck his hand in that pumpkin before the November election, we'd've had Tom Dewey for president." The New York grand jury intensified its work, with HUAC members charging, darkly, that the Justice Department seemed eager to prosecute Chambers for perjury, but not Hiss.

For indeed Chambers' eleventh-hour revelations made him a self-confessed liar. Chambers carefully skirted charging Hiss with espionage both in his HUAC appearances and on the *Meet the Press* interview. But before the grand jury his denials that Hiss had done any spying were unequivocal. He had been asked on October 14:

> JUROR: Could you give one name of anybody who, in your opinion, was positively guilty of espionage against the United States? Yes or no.
>
> CHAMBERS: Let me think a moment and I will try to answer that. I don't think so, but I would like to have the opportunity to answer you tomorrow more definitely. Let me think it over overnight.

The next day the juror repeated the question.

> CHAMBERS: . . . I assume that espionage means in this case the turning over the secret or confidential documents.
>
> JUROR: Or information—oral information.
>
> CHAMBERS: Or oral information. I do not believe I do know such a name.

Chambers' explanation for withholding the espionage accusation was that he wanted to end Hiss's influence on American policy, but not destroy him as a human being.

The dates on the documents posed another problem for Chambers. In his first HUAC testimony Chambers said several times, both in prepared testimony and in answers to questions, that he left the Communist Party in 1937. He gave the same date in interviews with the FBI and State Department security agents. Later, during the public confrontation with Hiss, he edged the date forward to "early 1938." But the "pumpkin papers" bore dates as late as April 1, 1938; most were dated after January 1, 1938. Further, internal markings on many of the papers showed that they had never been handled in the offices where Hiss worked. All Chambers could do was revise his early testimony, claiming his "break" in 1937 was ideological, not actual, and that he did not succeed in leaving the party until 1938.

When HUAC began leaking the papers in early December, Hiss partisans had much sport with the committee's description of them as "vital to the nation's security." The papers contained such harmless chatter as the fact that the Italian and German armies had exchanged staff officers; that the Japanese were trying to buy a manganese mine off Costa Rica where the mineral was known not to exist; that the U.S. consul general in Vienna had warned Washington that "it seems possible Hitler is seeking a foreign political triumph at the expense of Austria." But the Democratic chortles faded when Hiss revealed that some of the documents "were of such importance" that he had asked the Justice Department to take possession of them. And Sumner Welles, the undersecretary of state at the time the papers were stolen, said certain of the papers had been transmitted in the "most secret code" and their possession by a foreign power could have caused the United States great harm.

Hiss spent eight days, off and on, before the grand jury. On the last day of its eighteen-month existence, it indicted him on two counts of perjury: for denying that he had given any government documents to Chambers; and for denying that he had seen Chambers after January 1, 1937. Congressman Nixon called the indictments a "vindication" of HUAC—a statement that Hiss termed "a frank admission of the committee's investment in the result." Liberal sympathy remained strongly, but not uniformly, on the side of Hiss. "I am going to believe in Alger Hiss's integrity until he is proved guilty," Eleanor Roosevelt said. The columnist Marquis Childs found it puzzling that Chambers waited a decade before producing his evidence. But the *New Leader,* which had first accused Hiss of Communist sympathies in 1945, was convinced of his culpability even before he went before a jury. And James Wechsler, a onetime Communist himself, recollected that the gloom of the Spanish Civil War and the Munich sellout convinced other sensitive and patriotic men that only the Soviet Union could halt the tide of Fascist terror. But most progressives and liberals saw the deeper significance of the trial. In the public mind, the New Deal stood in the dock with Alger Hiss.

During the six months between indictment and trial, the defense succeeded in locating what it accepted as an old Woodstock typewriter that had been in the Hiss household at the time he knew Chambers and that had been passed on to two young black brothers who helped the family move. Scientific tests showed that many of the "pumpkin papers" had been typed on the Woodstock; Hiss could offer no logical explanation, but this damaging evidence was made known to the prosecution. A drumbeat of hostile publicity intensified in the weeks preceding the trial. In a massive report entitled "Soviet Espionage Within the United States Government," HUAC pointed to Hiss as one of the "conspirators . . . [who] seek and indeed have influenced major decisions of government policy"—during the hours they were not maintaining "a steady flow of secret and confidential government documents to special couriers, which are quickly microfilmed for transmission to Soviet intelligence officers." Some 116 pages of the report were given over to reproduction of the pumpkin papers. On January 30, 1949, the New York *Journal-American* began serialization of the memoirs of HUAC counsel Robert Stripling; they continued until February 26, and virtually every episode vouched for Chambers' veracity. Two concurrent trials kept public attention on the Communist issue on the eve of Hiss' trial—that of leaders of the Communist Party, USA, for violation of the Smith Act, which began on January 16 in the same building where Hiss was to be tried; and the trial of Judith Coplon, accused of acting as a spy courier, in Washington on April 25. New York newspapers frequently paired stories on the Smith Act and Hiss trials.

The Hiss trial itself produced little new evidence. Although Hiss's counsel Lloyd Paul Stryker found yawning inconsistencies in Chambers' story—especially Hiss's access to the pumpkin papers, which Stryker sought to prove were actually stolen by Julian Wadleigh, another State Department official who had just confessed to Soviet espionage—the defense felt it was addressing closed minds, on the jury as elsewhere. Journalist James Reston visited the trial during its second week, before the defense began, and reported:

> It seldom happens that in the presence of such conflicting testimony men and women take a positive position for or against the accused. Yet this has happened in the case of Alger Hiss.
>
> Repeatedly in the last few days, counsel on both sides have asked for a recess, and the audience at the trial has retired to the outer hall. . . .
>
> There, the conversation has disclosed that, despite the gap between the two sides, few men are saying that they do not know whether Mr. Hiss is guilty or innocent. Though Mr. Hiss has not gone on the stand, men and women do not hesitate to pronounce their personal verdicts. . . .
>
> . . . [T]he quality of patent objectivity among the spectators seems remarkably small. . . . [M]ost popular impressions of the case were gained from Congressional hearings that did not disclose the discrepancies in the accuser's case.

Daily press coverage in New York was confused and contradictory. One might consider, for instance, headlines in the four morning newspapers on June 28, the day after Hiss's cross-examination began:

HISS ON STAND FOUR HOURS
HOLDS TO HIS STORY
CLEARS UP DISCREPANCIES ON AUTO
FOR CHAMBERS AND ABOUT TYPEWRITER
New York *Herald Tribune*

TESTIMONY OF HISS CONFLICTS NINE TIMES,
PROSECUTOR FINDS; CROSS-EXAMINATION BRINGS
OUT 15 MEETINGS WITH CHAMBERS—10 OR 11
WERE ADMITTED. CLASH ON MEMORANDUMS. DIFFERENCES ON
TYPEWRITER AND CAR TRANSFER DATES ALSO NOTED BY
GOVERNMENT.

The New York Times

GAVE CHAMBERS A JALOPY
AND A BRUSH-OFF, HISS CLAIMS

New York *Daily News*

HISS SAYS LEFTIST FRIENDSHIP
LED TO RED CHARGES

New York *Daily Mirror*

On the afternoon of the twenty-eighth, the New York *Journal-American,* the Hearst outlet in the city and an unblushing supporter of Chambers, came up with the following lead paragraph:

> The government ended its cross-examination of Alger Hiss at 3:01 P.M. today after forcing him to admit he was an associate of Mrs. Carol King, prominent legal defender of Communists, and a friend of Nathan Witt, ex-New Deal lawyer who was fired because of his Communist activities.

The lead was based upon the following testimony:

MURPHY:* Did you know Mrs. Carol King at the time?
HISS: I think I met her once or twice during that period.
MURPHY: So I think your answer is that you knew her?
HISS: *I said I think I met her once or twice; that is my answer.*
MURPHY: Was Nathan Witt one of the people in the association?†
HISS: I'm not sure whether he was or not. If so, that's how I met him. If not, I met him later while I was with the Department of Agriculture.

In his opening statement prosecutor Murphy said the government was content to stand or fall with Whittaker Chambers. "If you don't believe Chambers," he said, "then we have no case under the federal perjury rule, as Judge [Samuel H.] Kaufman will tell you, where you need one witness plus corroboration, and if one of the props goes, out goes the case." And Chambers was not enough. After two days' deliberation the

---

* Thomas Murphy, the government prosecutor.
† By "association" Murphy meant persons who worked together in the Agriculture Department.

jurors reported themselves hopelessly deadlocked, the foreman and three other persons for acquittal, the remaining eight for conviction. Judge Kaufman reluctantly discharged the panel, and the Justice Department announced it would bring Hiss to trial again as rapidly as possible.

In the interim, however, an angry storm of vituperation broke over Judge Kaufman's head—one touched off by Congressman Richard Nixon the day after the jury locked, with a demand for an investigation of the jurist's conduct of the trial. Kaufman's "prejudice . . . against the prosecution" had been "obvious and apparent," said Nixon, who never set foot in the courtroom during the trial. The anti-Hiss New York press eagerly grabbed cudgels and began flailing at Kaufman. HISS JUDGE PROBE DEMANDED, thundered the *World-Telegram*. DEMAND CONGRESS PROBE HISS JUDGE "PREJUDICE," said the *Journal-American*. Nixon moved to soggier ground the next day. He said Kaufman should have permitted testimony of two eleventh-hour witnesses put forth by the prosecution—Hede Massing, the divorced wife of Soviet agent Gerhart Eisler and an officer of the Washington car firm involved in the disputed Ford transfer. Nixon divined that "the average American wanted all technicalities waived in this case" (an accommodation that surely could not have pleased Hiss, who faced prison) and that the "entire Truman Administration was extremely anxious that nothing bad happen to Mr. Hiss."* To the *Journal-American*, Nixon hinted that jurors might be subpoenaed before HUAC. The *Daily Mirror* told why: "Those who voted for acquittal could not be convinced otherwise. . . . There might have been a Communist sympathizer in the group." Nixon declared, "When the full facts of the conduct of this trial are laid before the nation, the people will be shocked."

Nixon's exercise in judicial review inspired expertise elsewhere. The *Herald Tribune* found five jurors who felt Kaufman "biased for the defense." Representative Harold Velde of Indiana, HUAC member and former FBI agent, listed six "flagrant examples" of Kaufman's mishandling of the trial. (Most of them Nixon had cited earlier, a fact that did not deter their banner-headline treatment as "news.") The *Journal-American*, going an ominous step further, found that all jurors reported receiving calls and letters commenting on their stand. "Those who voted for conviction received expressions of approval while those who stood for acquittal reported 'threats.' " (After which the *Journal-American* obligingly provided the names and addresses for proacquittal jurors, presumably for the convenience of readers who wished to send along

* One of my instructors at the Army Intelligence School at Fort Holabird in 1956 was a former FBI agent who professed intimate knowledge of the Hiss case. According to this man, when the "evidence against Hiss" was laid out to the President, Truman replied, "Hang the son of a bitch." Truman doesn't even mention the Hiss episode in his memoirs. My instructor's scenario bears a close resemblance to Truman's reaction to the *Amerasia* case. See page 281 above.

their own threats.) One juror was told, "Go to Russia." A note told another, "We will trap you soon and that will be your end." A wife heard a phone caller say, "Tell your husband that he is a Communist, that he is on the top of our list, and that we will get him." The only warning note was sounded by Mary Hornaday of the *Christian Science Monitor,* who saw the attacks as a challenge to a free judiciary. If Hiss had been acquitted, she wrote, the attacks "probably would have been even more violent."

Citing the chilling impact of these attacks on prospective jurors, and the very real danger a fair trial was no longer possible in New York, the Hiss defense tried futilely to move the trial to Vermont, away from the pervasive influences of Hearst, Scripps-Howard, and the *Herald Tribune.* The motion was denied, a judge noting he had seen New York papers at his hotel while vacationing in Vermont, and Hiss went on trial again on November 17, 1949, this time before Judge Henry W. Goddard.

Goddard, an elderly judge with the profile of an American eagle, made it plain from the start he would rather err by letting extraneous testimony into the record than by keeping it out. He permitted Eisler's ex-wife, Hede Massing, to testify about meeting Hiss at the home of a party member in 1935, and bantering with him about the services of a prize agent. But in the main little new substantial evidence was developed, although Hiss's new lawyer, Claude B. Cross, drew a surprising revelation from Chambers. Confronted with an old passport photograph (in the name of David Breen, one of his many aliases), Chambers suddenly recollected he wore a moustache at the time he knew Hiss—something he had never mentioned earlier, even during the critical debate over identification.

Cross also craftily led Chambers through a chronology of the days he said he picked up stolen documents from Hiss, then repeated it to him in narrative form: Chambers would leave his government office in Washington, arrive at Hiss's house at five o'clock, wait for him (Hiss seldom got home before six), obtain the documents, go to Union Station, ride the train the forty-minute trip to Baltimore, go to the party photographer, wait for the lab work to be done, catch a late night train back to Washington, returning the documents to Hiss between midnight and two o'clock, return to his own home in Baltimore via train, and then be up and back on the train so he could be at his desk by nine the next morning. Was the description accurate? Probably, Chambers said.

Once again the jury debated two days. This time the verdict was guilty, on both counts, and Judge Goddard sentenced Hiss to the maximum five years. The Second Circuit Court of Appeals rejected his appeal, and the Supreme Court refused to review the case. On March 22,

1951, fourteen months after his conviction, Hiss went to prison at Lewisburg, Pennsylvania.*

In terms of its impact upon American political life, the Hiss case stands as the most important trial in United States history. The shoddy tactics of HUAC in the initial phase of the case (in permitting Chambers to make a public accusation without giving Hiss proper opportunity for rebuttal); the right-wingers' gusto in twisting the affair into a blanket assault upon all the New Deal stood for; Chambers' transparent instability, and the absurd twists and turns of his on-going confession; Richard Nixon's assault on the integrity of the judicial system after the first trial—all these factors encouraged liberals reflexively to throw a protective circle around Hiss and claim him as one of their very own. The guilty verdict left these people and their tradition in an awful position of exposure: the principles of fair play notwithstanding, the liberals had identified themselves with a convicted agent of what the right wing now called "the Communist conspiracy."

Many prominent liberals cut their losses after the second trial and disavowed Hiss. James Wechsler of the New York *Post* faulted Hiss for failing to explain the documents produced by Chambers; too many of Hiss's supporters, he charged, displayed residual nostalgia for the Popular Front. Chambers' testimony convinced the skeptical Bruce Bliven, editor of the *New Republic,* and Arthur Schlesinger, Jr., recent founding member of the anti-Communist Americans for Democratic Action. Eleanor Roosevelt stood with Hiss to the end—or past it, more accurately. So did Max Lerner of *PM,* who would "feel clearer in my own mind if the machinery for getting at the legal guilt or innocence of Hiss had functioned under circumstances of greater fairness."

Writing before the denial of Hiss's appeal, the British journalist Alistair Cooke said that if he indeed was guilty "what he owed to the United States and the people who had stood by him was a dreadful debt of honor." A congeries of horrors is directly attributable to Hiss's fate. A native American, a man groomed for national leadership, was shown

---

* A major handicap to the Hiss defense was that the typeface on his wife's old Woodstock typewriter matched that of many of the "pumpkin papers." At trial the best his lawyers could offer was a suggestion that Chambers or accomplices somehow sneaked into the Hiss household or that of the family that later owned the Woodstock, and typed the papers. Not even Hiss partisans put much credence in this unlikely happening. But in posttrial investigations, lawyers succeeded in having a Woodstock constructed with a typeface once again identical to that on the key papers. What supposedly was the Hisses' Woodstock proved, upon technical examination, to have markings indicating it was not the original machine, and in fact was itself a reconstruction. Despite a stone wall of unfriendly prospective witnesses, many of them silent assertedly by FBI demand, Hiss's lawyers presented a well-documented case of "forgery by typewriter" in a motion for new trial. They were denied. A quarter of a century later Hiss finally gained access to FBI files in an attempt to prove his innocence.

to be susceptible to subversion for a foreign power. HUAC's shabby cadre of Red hunters could now boast the special virtue of verification by jury. J. Edgar Hoover's FBI, under the umbrella of loyalty programs, acquired staggering powers of inquiry into the personal lives and political beliefs of hundreds of thousands of citizens; where else in the world, save Soviet Russia and its satellites, could a person be called upon to answer questions about a meeting he had attended two decades previously?

But the implications are profounder still. Most grievously, the Hiss case caused an entire generation of young Americans—the silent generation of the Eisenhower fifties—to draw a stultifying blanket of conformity over their heads. Why would one wish to experiment with a deviant political philosophy that half a lifetime later could be branded subversive? The Hiss case, in the judgment of Cooke, tended to "limit by intimidation what no Western society worth the name can safely limit: the curiosity and idealism of its young. It helped therefore to usher in a period when a high premium would be put on the chameleon and the politically neutral slob."

The jury voted Hiss's conviction on January 21, 1950. On February 9, Senator Joseph McCarthy of Wisconsin, who had been actively scouting Washington for "an issue that can get me reelected in 1952," spoke to the Republican Women's Club of Ohio County, West Virginia, in Wheeling. According to the account in the Wheeling *Intelligencer* the next morning, McCarthy brandished a document selected from a pile before him on the podium and said:

> While I cannot take the time to name all of the men in the State Department who have been named as members of the Communist Party and members of a spy ring, I have here in my hand a list of two hundred and five that were known to the Secretary of State as being members of the Communist Party, and who, nevertheless, are still working and shaping the policy in the State Department.

Thus was a squalid legacy passed from the 1940's into the 1950's, one that could be exploited for four tormented years, years that would bear the name "McCarthyism." Whether Hiss was guilty or innocent is irrelevant in the broadest of contexts: much of America's faith in itself died along with his conviction, and thereafter the nation looked not to its idealists for guidance, but to its McCarthys.

VI

The 1948 Election:
A Credo Affirmed

A Remembrance of Marshall: VI

Marshall lies on the fringes of the Old South, geographically and philo-sophically. As a remote backwater of the Confederacy, it was spared fighting in the Civil War; nonetheless persons were still around in the 1940's with direct memories: of the powder mill on Macedonia Road, north of town, that made cartridges for southern troops; of the army hospital near the present high school, extending across Whetstone Street to the land where my family later lived for two decades; of the clap-board house that housed the government-in-exile of the State of Mis-souri.

Other memories (and realities) were felt even more keenly: of the black officeholders installed during Reconstruction by the "damned Re-publicans in Washington," in the bitter words of our resident elder statesman and oral historian, Mr. Ike Hochwald; of East Texas' eco-nomic vassalage to eastern Republican bankers, a subject that our local congressman, Wright Patman, had been denouncing for three terms by the time I was born; of the way the fortunes of the Texas & Pacific Railroad, whose car shop was our major local employer, seemed to rise and fall upon the unpredictable whim of its Yankee owners. And, most especially, of the way "outsiders" complained of the attitude white Marshall took toward the 50 percent of its population that was black.

Here are some of the things a black man dared not do in Marshall circa 1946, as the best years began:*

—Buy a cup of coffee or a meal in a "white restaurant," or even get a glass of water in an emergency.

—Expect service from a white woman clerk in the dime stores or most department stores; he was expected to stand quietly in the store until a man noticed him and asked what he wanted. He could not try on garments for size; he likely was not even given a bag for his purchase.

---

* In anticipation of chauvinistic anger from fellow Southerners, I note in advance that many of these activities were also impossible for a black in Philadelphia, Chicago, and Seattle; I list what I saw firsthand at the time in my home town.

—Sit on the ground floor of the Paramount or Lynn theater. He bought his ticket at a separate entrance and climbed up to the balcony, or "nigger heaven." Discerning blacks learned to find entertainment elsewhere on days the Paramount featured such voluptuous white stars as Betty Grable or Rita Hayworth, lest their interest in the cinema be interpreted as lust for a white woman.

—Ride in a taxi driven by a white man; blacks were serviced by a separate fleet of ramshackle cars ("nigger taxis") run by a local undertaker. The back benches of city buses were "reserved" for blacks, with the white driver periodically adjusting the boundary marker (a card with arrows marked "white" and "colored"), depending on the composition of the traffic. Regardless of the number of blacks aboard, however, the marker was never placed forward of the midpoint of the bus, and "surplus" blacks stood, regardless of the number of empty seats in the white section.

—Drink from a public fountain that was not marked "colored." Department stores that sold to blacks had separate water coolers; they offered no restroom facilities for blacks whatsoever.

—Vote in the primary election for city and county officials. The dominant party, identical to the county Democratic organization in fact if not in name, considered itself "private" and did not admit blacks. A black who insisted on paying his poll tax and registering to vote in a state or national election risked losing his job, or worse.

—See his name or picture in the Marshall News-Messenger, *unless in a police story.*

—Swim in the "public" pool; take books from the library (private, but supported in large part by public funds); walk on the sidewalk if a white indicated he wanted the right of way; be sure of service at a gasoline station; have a paved road in front of his house, even though he paid city taxes; or be certain of gas, water, electric, or telephone service.

Most of these customs survived not so much from racial hatred (although hatred indeed existed) as through cultural inertia. Before the war began, for instance, blacks were not permitted to shop in stores on the east side of the courthouse square. For reasons that were never clear, this ban vanished sometime between 1941 and 1945. Whites who read learned that we could use the Carnegie Library at Wiley College, a school for Methodist blacks, with facilities far superior to our high-school and quasi-public libraries. Marshall did not worry about a "black problem," for it did not acknowledge that one in fact existed.

In 1948, however, Marshall and the rest of the South came into abrupt confrontation with a reality that it had hoped to avoid: the fear that the federal government (and one controlled by a Democratic Administration) intended to tell the white majority how to treat "our Negroes." We forgot Russia and domestic subversion and foreign aid and

*Taft–Hartley and the other issues: so far as Marshall (and the South)
was concerned, the sole question to be resolved in the 1948 presidential
election was whether a modern-day Democratic carpetbagger—and a
turncoat at that—would subject us to the same indignities that had been
inflicted by the Republicans sixty years earlier.*

21

Of Gideon,
Dixie, and Ike

I N L A T E 1947 a temporary surge of popularity attributable to the Marshall Plan pushed President Truman's standings in the polls to a "favorable" rating of 55 percent, highest in months and a welcome turnaround, but nonetheless a thin cushion to carry into an election year. The Gallup poll ran him in a trial heat with the two top Republican contenders, Governor Thomas E. Dewey of New York and Senator Robert A. Taft of Ohio, and he beat them decisively. The wise men of the Democratic Party took Truman's renomination for granted (although he was not to announce his candidacy formally until March 8 of the following year, in unconventional fashion. Senator J. Howard McGrath, the Democratic national chairman, left a meeting in Truman's office and told reporters, "The President has authorized me to say that if nominated by the Democratic National Convention, he will accept and run").

By the time of McGrath's announcement, things had fallen apart for Harry Truman—in Congress, in the left wing of the Democratic Party, in the southern conservative wing of the Democratic Party, in the Jewish community, in the ranks of big-city leaders wary of entanglement with a "loser," in the polls, which in a short three months showed him dropping from 52 to 36 percent favorable. If Harry Truman was to be elected President of the United States, he must do it on his very own.

ON THE LEFT: GIDEON'S ARMY

Journalist Dwight Macdonald, dissecting Henry Wallace with a vituperative typewriter in the fall of 1947, was tempted to declare the man a political corpse and be done with him. But he hesitated. Three times previously the pundits had buried Wallace—after he failed to get the vice-presidency in 1944; after his firing from the cabinet in 1946; after a European trip in 1947 devoted chiefly to praising Russia and denouncing U.S. foreign policy. That Wallace still possessed political vitality was a symptom of the anxiety gripping America, Macdonald concluded. "Wallace can make political blunders; he can make speeches, and write articles which are masterpieces of confusion, equivocation, and contradiction; he can identify himself with the Communists—but so long as he remains a symbol of hope and of dissidence, so long will he retain a mass following."

Wallace's promised "loyal opposition" to Truman's foreign policies evolved, by gradually heightening bounds, to a third-party candidacy. He took up the editorship of the *New Republic,* and enticed readers with such Wallacese sentences as "New frontiers beckon with meaningful adventure." In his famed Madison Square Garden speech he had spoken harshly of "British imperialism." But six months later, when facing a friendly British audience, it was the Truman Doctrine and the Marshall Plan that were imperialism, and the United States the chief obstacle to peace: "At the end of the war, America's main objective was a quick victory, followed by a quick return to normalcy. It was the normalcy of selfishness, nationalism, and power politics." He did not believe what the newspapers said about the status of civil liberties in Russia. "I have a hunch," he said in Great Britain, "that if I could speak Russian, Mr. Stalin would let me speak to the common people there just as I am speaking to you." (Perhaps, someone said, though not for the reasons implied.) To an audience in Norway, Wallace was not concerned about Stalin's dictatorship. "It would be unfortunate for world peace if anything happens inside Russia to upset its system of government at the present time." President Truman's new loyalty program, he said, would not keep Communists from government but would "tend to drive from public service the man who has ever read a book, had an idea, supported the ideals of Roosevelt, or fought fascism." In Paris, Wallace shared a Sorbonne platform with three prominent Communist politicians—Thorez, Duclos, and Cachin—and virtually every member of the audience was a Communist. Back home, conservatives called Wallace a traitor, accused him of violating the Logan Act, which bars citizens from negotiating with foreign governments, and demanded that his passport be revoked. Attorney General Tom C. Clark, presumably speaking for the President, declared that anyone "who tells the people of Europe that the United States is committed to a ruthless imperialism and war with the Soviet Union tells a lie."

Wallace returned home to find many of his most prominent followers running in the opposite direction. Senator Claude Pepper, for instance, shuffled away from Wallace in wall-eyed panic, to the extent that he even voted for the Greek-Turkish aid bill, which Wallace had denounced as "de facto U.S. aggression." Wallace muttered about "press misquotations" and set out on a speaking tour under the sponsorship of the Progressive Citizens of America, an umbrella group of leftists ranging from popular fronters to non-Marxist progressives. The reception shoved out of Wallace's mind the hostile reaction he had evoked during the European trip; the crowds turned out en masse, and they loved him: 3,000 persons in Cleveland; 6,000 in Minneapolis; 8,000 in Detroit; 20,000 in Chicago, at sixty cents to $2.40 per ticket (audience contributions added $10,000); 25,000 at Gilmore Stadium in Los Angeles; finally, 10,000 in Berkeley, students standing in the streets to hear him speak from the curbstone after University of California officials refused him a hall. "We want Wallace!" they chanted. "Wallace in '48."

Wallace's stated purpose metamorphosed in response to the cheering youngsters. At the outset he insisted all he intended to do was to "scare the Democratic Party leftward." But as the tour neared its end he had progressed to a near declaration of his candidacy: "If we can't make the Democratic Party liberal, we'll have to take what action is appropriate." He proposed, variously, a 10 percent reduction in taxes; increased wages to be financed from the "swollen profit structure"; a no-strings-attached handover of U.S. atomic weapons to the United Nations; a ten-year reconstruction program for the USSR, to be financed by the United States. Robert Kenny, the former California attorney general, defense lawyer for the Hollywood Ten, and the state's most prominent liberal, saw in the Wallace crowds "a mounting tide of popular opposition to the politics and leadership of both political parties." Kenny felt a new party would give voters "a clear choice between progressive and reactionary candidates for president." He and Wallace spoke of nationalizing coal mines, railroads, electric power facilities. By midsummer Wallace's vigorous campaigning, and his obvious charm for younger people, forced Democratic strategists to take a serious look at him. His supporters controlled the party machinery in Oregon and were close to doing so in Washington. Californian Kenny was organizing Wallace delegates to the 1948 Democratic National Convention, a task made easier because a feud between fund raiser Edwin O. Pauley and James Roosevelt, FDR's son, divided the state party. Colorado and Minnesota and Wisconsin Democrats looked favorably at Wallace; so did the American Labor Party in New York. In July the Alsop brothers forecast that Wallace would bring a "sizable minority bloc" to the convention, lose, and run on a third-party ticket, "wrecking the Democratic Party, at least temporarily . . . and electing the most stodgily conservative Congress in a great many years."

But Wallace found it increasingly difficult to command the support of big-name liberals. The failure of the Democratic Party in the 1946 elections, due in part to skillful use of the "Communist issue" by the

Republicans, handed anti-Communist liberals a new and convincing argument. The Philadelphia *Record* said flatly, "The Communist Party gave the kiss of death to Democratic candidates in many parts of the country"; it demanded that the party repudiate Communists who tugged at its coattails. Denouncing the "plague of communism" in many progressive organizations, columnist Thomas L. Stokes said the only solution was to "unmask the Communists and vote them out and root them out of the key spots as a matter of internal government and policing."

In January 1947 a strong cadre of veteran New Dealers—Chester Bowles, Paul A. Porter, John Kenneth Galbraith, to name a sampling—gathered in Washington to form an organization that would have a sizable impact on American politics: Americans for Democratic Action. The purposes were broad: to extend New Deal programs, protect civil liberties, stabilize the economy, work for world peace through the United Nations. A key sentence in the statement of principles threw down the gauntlet to the Progressive Citizens of America: "We reject any association with Communists or sympathizers with communism in the United States as completely as we reject any association with Fascists or their sympathizers." Many of the ADA founders had learned the futility of trying to work with Communists. The American party's open, if unadmitted, obedience to Moscow made 1940's communism repugnant to many of its early, idealistic followers. Thus was the line drawn between ADA and the Progressive Citizens of America. In a very telling gesture, Eleanor Roosevelt, long a Wallace admirer and friend, opted for ADA; so, too, did such labor leaders as James Carey, Walter Reuther, David Dubinsky, and Emil Rieve, each in a struggle with Communists in his own union* and desperate for support.

The liberal unions' alliance with ADA was a turning point for Wallace because it forced him to the farthest-left fringes of labor for manpower and dollars—almost invariably, Communist-dominated factions in CIO unions. At a convention of the United Electrical Workers in October, for instance, he appeared in support of party-liners Julius Emspak and James J. Matles, who expelled the anti-Communist James Carey and followers by a six-to-one majority for "disruption," i.e., demands that Communists in the union be expelled. Wallace beamed as the triumphant majority passed a resolution declaring that the government "has fallen under the control of Big Business. . . . By international Red-baiting and war scares they try to frighten us into panic under their extortionate greed. . . . [It] is the policy of the trusts to reestablish a reactionary Germany as economic dictator over Europe. . . ."

In December the CIO executive board met to debate endorsement of

---

* Respectively, the International Union of Electrical Workers, the United Auto Workers, the International Ladies Garment Workers Union, and the American Federation of Hosiery Workers.

the Marshall Plan for rebuilding Europe, which, of course, was imperialistic, in Wallace's view. Communists sought to undercut union support,
but they failed at the CIO. As a direct result, according to two unionists
in a position to know (Philip Murray, president of the CIO, and Michael J. Quill, president of the Transport Workers Union), the Communists received—and obeyed—a direct order to convert the Progressive
Citizens of America into a vehicle for fomenting opposition to the
Marshall Plan, with Wallace at its head as a presidential candidate.*

Thus was the die cast for Wallace. Prominent liberals tried to dis-
suade him from this course. Frank Kingdon, perhaps his closest supporter, quit PCA, charging Communist control. Alex Rose of the
Liberal Party charged that Wallace had "accepted the viewpoints of
Vishinsky and Molotov." Walter Reuther of the UAW called Wallace a
"lost soul. . . . Communists perform the most complete valet service in
the world. They write your speeches, they do your thinking for you, they
provide you with applause, and they inflate your ego." Wallace did not
listen. On a national radio broadcast the night of December 29 he
announced his candidacy, declaring:

> There is no real fight between a Truman and a Republican. The
> bigger the peace vote in 1948, the more definitely the world will
> know that the United States is not behind the bipartisan reaction-
> ary war policy which is dividing the world into two armed camps
> and making inevitable the day when American soldiers will be lying
> in their arctic suits in the Russian snow. . . .
>
> We have assembled a Gideon's army, small in number, powerful
> in conviction, ready for action. . . . We face the future unfettered
> by any principle but the general welfare. . . . By God's grace, the
> people's peace will usher in the century of the common man.

"Good riddance," commented Frank McHale, the Democratic
national committeeman from Indiana. "He is a much confused man and
always had his thingamajigs mixed up with his whatchamacallits." Senator Scott Lucas of Illinois said, "He won't get enough votes to wad a
shotgun." The sympathetic Ralph McGill of the Atlanta *Constitution*
lamented Wallace's "real genius for self-delusion [which] will make of
him an ignominious spectacle long before November . . . and I'm
sorry because I like him." The entire Roosevelt family disavowed the
third party, and Eleanor Roosevelt, Wallace's champion when he
worked for her husband, characterized him as a "naïve politician" being
manipulated by the Communists.

But Wallace plunged on with good initial omens. He spent several

---

* The Washington *Post*'s able national reporter, later to become managing editor,
Alfred Friendly, told of these machinations in a story published May 2, 1948. The
order was relayed by the CPUSA's general secretary, Eugene Dennis, and its
labor secretary, John Williamson.

days campaigning in the Bronx for Leo Isacson, American Labor Party candidate in a four-man special congressional election. Isacson won an astounding 56 percent of the vote, running 10,000 votes ahead of the Democratic candidate. Wallace said publicly he would "do the same thing nationally" in November, but whether he really felt so is doubtful. A few days after the election Louis H. Bean, a skilled statistician and old colleague from the Agriculture Department, visited Wallace and warned him not to attach too much importance to the Bronx election. "The man won because scarcely anyone turned out to vote," Bean said. "The vote was extraordinarily apathetic, and the Democrats had put up an unknown against a candidate [Isacson] who was a very popular state assemblyman. Also, the American Labor Party used virtually every worker in New York City in the single district." Bean said Wallace indicated he was not misled, citing a poll taken by Harold Stassen, then a GOP presidential contender, showing that his [Wallace's] support had slipped from 27 percent earlier to 10 percent. "I don't think he was fooled by or misinterpreted his position or his prospects," Bean said.

A week later Wallace acquired a runningmate, the flamboyant Glen H. Taylor, a freshman Democratic senator from Idaho. Son of a Presbyterian preacher, Taylor dropped out of school early to become a sheepherder and, later, a tent-show cowboy in a western stock show. An avid reader, he once boasted that his self-education "made me smarter than most folks in the Senate." He campaigned by singing western songs off the back of a soundtruck, accompanying himself on a guitar. An isolationist, he opposed the Marshall Plan and voted to cut foreign aid funds by more than half. When Wallace publicly invited Taylor to join the ticket, he saddled up his horse and rode off on a "peace tour" to get public sentiment. A pronounced liberal on most economic and domestic issues, especially civil rights, Taylor proclaimed, "I am not leaving the Democratic Party. It left me. Wall Street and the military have taken over." His decision was announced from horseback on the Capitol steps; Taylor waved his Stetson and said running would make him "feel real good inside."

Wallace and Taylor sputtered their separate ways in quest of votes. James Wechsler of the New York *Post,* traveling with Wallace, reported that "at virtually every stop the local left-wing stalwarts run the arrangements. . . . But the political complexion of the audiences is definitely broader. It is a cross-section of American discontent and insecurity." Violence, too, trailed along Wallace's path. In Evansville, Indiana, auto workers picketed him with signs, "Germany Had Hitler. Russia Has Stalin. We Don't Want Wallace for the U.S." Campaign manager Beany Baldwin and two aides were slugged. In Illinois eggs and vegetables splattered Wallace when he tried to talk to a coal-country audience. In Moline, people laughed when he said they had been afraid to park near the meeting hall lest someone identify their cars. "You laugh," Wallace shouted angrily. "But I've seen it happen in other places." And Wallace brushed aside warnings of Communist manipulation of his campaign, from Louis H. Bean and others. "I find nothing criminal in the advocacy of different economic and social ideas, however much I may differ with them." He suggested he was using the Communists as *his* tool, rather than the other way around. "If the Communists want to support me, they must do it on my terms," Wallace said. "If the Communists are working for peace with Russia, God bless 'em. If they are working for the overthrow of the government by force, they know I'm against them."

Taylor, working the southern states, gutsily challenged racial strictures. When he tried to speak to the Southern Negro Youth Congress in Birmingham, police commissioner Eugene B. (Bull) Connor* confronted him at the door: "There's not enough room in town for Bull and the Commies." When Taylor tried to press into the hall, through the "colored entrance," insisting he had a right to be heard, Connor ordered him arrested. The booking officer at the jail wasn't impressed with Taylor's importance. "Keep your mouth shut, buddy," he told Taylor. "God help the ordinary man," Taylor said when released. He returned to Washington displaying a four-inch scratch on his shin, suffered when a cop shoved him into a wire fence. He later paid a $50 fine by mail (a 180-day jail sentence was suspended).

The hostile press, the abandonment by prominent liberals who had urged on his criticisms of Truman, the ugly element in almost every crowd he faced, discouraged Wallace. In the days after the Bronx election political analysts such as James Hagerty of the *New York Times* had felt his candidacy could siphon away enough votes to throw New York, California, Michigan, Illinois, and Pennsylvania to the Republicans. Other pundits worried about Connecticut and even Harry Truman's home state of Missouri. No one of substance expected Wallace to win, but many Democratic leaders did fear him as a spoiler. Truman's nervousness was reflected in two jabs at Wallace that he ad-libbed into prepared speech texts. On May 17 he declared, "I do not want and I will not accept the political support of Henry Wallace and his Communists." Two weeks later he suggested that Wallace "ought to go to the country he loves so well and help them against his own country if that's the way he feels." But political adviser Clark M. Clifford counseled that such attacks could only hurt Truman's image and attract more attention for Wallace (who received free radio time to answer the first blast). Thereafter Truman was silent on Wallace. And by May Democratic fears were lessening, for the Wallace campaign seemed to be losing its initial steam and support. As *Time* reported in mid-month:

* Connor achieved national notoriety in the 1950's and 1960's for his handling of civil rights demonstrators in Birmingham and environs.

Wallace has become a bitter, dour man with a developing persecution complex. He would like to succeed to the mantle of Roosevelt but he does not know how to meet the common man whom he champions. His manner repulses people, and he in turn gets more and more resentful. He is a bore. . . . His speeches sometimes put people to sleep. He is completely humorless.

Nonetheless the polls showed Wallace with a tentative grip on the allegiance, and presumably votes, of almost 10 percent of the American people, votes Harry Truman needed for election.

ON THE RIGHT: THE DIXIECRATS

"That the United States is very nearly ten percent a black nation is known to everybody and ignored by almost everybody—except maybe the ten percent," John Gunther wrote in 1947. The civil rights "issue" simply did not exist in the early 1940's because the vast majority of Americans ignored blacks, and the cruel, petty, and efficient apartheid guiding his life. But the war brought race relations out of the shadows. About one million blacks served in the armed forces, and although the bulk of them were in segregated units (construction and labor battalions and the like), they moved around and saw new things and heard much talk from the government about the "rights of men" and freedom and democracy. Southern blacks for the first time were thrown into intimate contact with whites who treated them decently, even called them "Mister" and shook their hands. Those who got into the big eastern and northern cities saw blacks living in a more or less separate society, one suffering from manifold discriminations, to be sure, but nonetheless relatively free of the studied daily viciousness of the South. Many a black silently echoed the sentiment, if not the words, of the Alabama corporal who told the Pittsburgh *Courier* as the war neared its end, "I spent four years in the army to free a bunch of Frenchmen and Dutchmen, and I'm hanged if I'm going to let the Alabama version of the Germans kick me around when I get back home. No sirreee-bob! I went into the army a nigger; I'm comin' out a *man*." The black columnist George W. Crockett felt the black's chance of getting a decent industrial job increased during the war because of the government's fair employment practices and the acceptance of blacks into CIO unions. They learned other lessons as well. Crockett wrote:

> . . . Negro men literally saw the world. And they began to associate English imperialism in India, Chiang Kai-shek's autocracy in China, and Dutch despotism in Java, as part and parcel of the same brand of fascism they thought existed only here at home.

I do not believe that Negroes will stand idly by and see these newly opened doors of economic opportunity closed in their faces. Negro women will not be content to toil in other people's kitchens again for $3, $4, or $5 per week and a bag of left-over food scraps to take home to their poorly fed young ones.

Nor will Negro GIs permit our propaganda machine to forget that it did the world's best job when it sought to convince these same Negro GIs that this was really a war for democracy and against fascism.

Southern whites, concurrently, also became acutely conscious of the black, through the influx of black soldiers and defense workers to facilities located in warm climes. But these were new kinds of blacks: men who didn't shuffle docilely out of the way or doff their hat when a white man approached. And many whites never did accept the idea of a "nigger" wearing a soldier's uniform.

The confrontations were inevitable, swift, and brutal. During the war years the grisly southern institution known as the lynching had virtually vanished. During its "prime" the South lynched scores of blacks annually, the recorded peak being 235 cases in 1892, declining to four in 1941 and one in 1945. In the resurgence, beginning in 1946, in many instances the victim was a veteran who did nothing more than behave like a free citizen. In 1946, in Lexington, Mississippi, a thirty-five-year-old black tenant farmer, accused of stealing a saddle, was flogged to death and left to rot in a bayou. Five men admitted they hit the victim "a few licks." A jury acquitted them in ten minutes. In 1946, in Minden, Louisiana, a twenty-year-old black named John C. Jones and a seventeen-year-old boy were arrested on suspicion of trying to break into a white woman's house. Immediately after "release" a mob took them into the woods, chopped off both Jones's hands, and killed him by applying a blow torch to his head, throat, and body. The younger man, although severely beaten, survived. Local authorities claimed they could find no suspects. In February 1946, a black named Isaac Woodard received an honorable discharge and boarded a bus in Atlanta, still in uniform, for the trip to his home in South Carolina. The driver refused to let him use the restroom at a stop, and he argued back. At the next town, the driver called a policeman, one Lynwood E. Shull, who dragged Woodard from the bus, beat him, took him to jail, and ground out his eyes with his nightstick. Local authorities did nothing; after an FBI investigation, the Justice Department filed a criminal information (bypassing the all-white grand jury) charging Shull with violating Woodard's civil rights. Shull claimed self-defense, and a jury acquitted him in half an hour. Woodard was permanently blinded.

But federal interventions were rare, for prosecutions of such crimes as murder, even if by a quasi-official mob, were matters for individual states. The Department of Justice could enter a case under federal civil rights statutes only if an official or agent of the state was involved. Notoriously touchy on the subject of "states' rights," southern officials did not readily admit such involvement. Even if a case could be brought to trial, juror sympathies were solidly with the local citizen. "There has never been a successful federal prosecution for lynching, *per se,*" the *New York Times* noted in 1946.

The South vigorously excluded blacks from the polls. The nation's most notorious racist, Senator Theodore G. Bilbo of Mississippi, openly advocated terror against prospective black voters in his 1946 campaign: "I call upon every red-blooded white man to use any means to keep the nigger away from the polls. The best way to keep a nigger from voting is to have a little talk with him the night before."* Governor Fielding Wright of Mississippi said frequently that if the blacks of his state expected equality they should "move to some state other than Mississippi." The South used the poll tax and stringent property requirements to disenfranchise blacks (and poor whites as well, unless their votes were needed by the dominant machine). Some statistics illustrate how well the system worked. In 1946 Mississippi had about 1,250,000 citizens of voting age, of whom only around 180,000 went to the polls. In 1944 South Carolina had 989,841 citizens over twenty-one; only 99,830 of them voted. But South Carolina had six members in the House of Representatives—identical with the state of Washington, where 793,833 persons voted of a total voting population of 1,123,725. Liberals fumed about "political immorality" but could do nothing to change things. Three times the House passed a bill abolishing the poll taxes; three times the Senate killed it with filibusters.

Born of Confederate stock and raised in Jim Crow country, Harry Truman nonetheless considered official discrimination and racial hatred to be repugnant to the Bill of Rights. As he wrote of the postwar period, "my very stomach turned over when I learned that Negro soldiers, just back from overseas, were being dumped out of army trucks in Mississippi and beaten. Whatever my inclinations as a native of Missouri might have been, as President I know this is bad. I shall fight to end evils like this." In December 1946 he appointed a committee to investigate and report on the status of civil rights in America, hoping to prevent a repetition of the revival of the Ku Klux Klan following World

---

* A Senate committee held that these speeches did not constitute grounds for refusing Bilbo his seat. But a concurrent probe by the Senate war investigating committee found that Bilbo took bribes from at least half a dozen war contractors —his booty included more than $100,000 cash, a Cadillac, and a lake for his estate—and Senator Glen Taylor objected to his being seated when the Senate convened in 1947. By then Bilbo was mortally ill of mouth cancer, and the Senate simply ignored the question of his seating until he resolved it by dying.

War One. The committee recommended sweeping advances: an anti-lynching law; abolition of the poll tax; laws ending discrimination in voter registration; an end to segregation in the armed forces and in transportation and school facilities; establishment of a Fair Employment Practices Commission; and creation a permanent Commission on Civil Rights, a Civil Rights Division in the Justice Department, and a joint Congressional Committee on Civil Rights.

As a political realist Truman certainly realized the recommendations had little chance of enactment. But he had them drafted into specific bills, which were introduced in February 1948. By Truman's account, basic morality left him no choice: every Democratic convention since 1932 had "stressed the devotion of our party to the constitutional ideal of civil rights. . . . The platform of a political party is a promise to the public. Unless a man can run on his party's platform—and try to carry it out, if elected—he is not an honest man."

Even as he presented his program, Truman felt reasonably sure that at least part of the South would bolt the Democratic Party because of heightening antagonism toward blacks. Southerners barely tolerated the wartime intrusion of black soldiers and defense workers; they felt the Fair Employment Practices Committee (FEPC) to be the work of Satan, or thereabouts; the military establishment, with its deep roots in the South, strongly opposed integration. And immediate hot reaction to his civil rights package bore out the fears. Representative Ed Goss of Texas accused Truman of "kissing the feet of the minorities." Senator James O. Eastland of Mississippi said Truman was trying to "mongrel-ize the South." "Harlem is wielding more influence with the Administration than the entire white South," cried Representative Eugene Cox of Georgia. A week after the civil rights message the annual meeting of the Southern Governors Conference bristled with threats of rebellion against Truman and the Democratic Party. After four days of blustery oratory about the "carpetbagger" Truman and his many shortcomings, the conference sent a six-governor delegation to Washington to find out how serious the Administration was about civil rights. Governor Strom Thurmond of South Carolina, formal in his indignation, put the question direct to J. Howard McGrath, the Democratic national chairman:

> Will you now, at a time when national unity is so vital to the solution of the problems of peace in the world, use your influence . . . to have the highly controversial civil rights legislation, which tends to divide our people, withdrawn from consideration by the Congress?

McGrath stared back at Thurmond and replied, "No."

The southern revolt was on. Bills were introduced in Dixie legislatures taking the names of presidential candidates off the ballot, leaving only electors for each party. A postelection convention would instruct them how to vote in the electoral college. The threat was clear: Truman must withdraw the civil rights bills, or the South would deny him the presidency. In February 5,000 persons waved Confederate flags at a rally in Jackson, Mississippi, and shouted approval of a resolution calling on "all true, white Jeffersonian Democrats" to join the revolt. In March Senator Olin B. Johnston of South Carolina insulted the President publicly by buying a front table for the annual Jefferson-Jackson Day dinner at the Mayflower Hotel and leaving it vacant; news photos showed Truman speaking past the empty seats, while Johnston and party dined elsewhere. At the celebration dinner in Little Rock, tied in by radio, more than half the 750 diners noisily got up and left when Truman's voice came over the loudspeaker. Little of the Jefferson-Jackson money raised at southern dinners that night was sent to Washington. Senator John Sparkman of Alabama wished "very much that Truman would sense the situation and withdraw," otherwise Democrats would be "cut to ribbons." "We don't want to run a race with a dead Missouri mule," said Governor Ben T. Laney of Arkansas.

Truman didn't flinch. He visited the Virgin Islands and dined with William Hastie, the first black governor; a banner across St. Thomas' main street read, "Welcome, President Truman, champion of human rights." At the dedication of Colonial Williamsburg he cheerily shared the platform with Governor William Tuck of Virginia, an archfoe of the civil rights bill; when they shook hands for the photographers, Truman quipped, "They think we're going to fight." "Well, we certainly wouldn't fight with these clothes on," Tuck replied, pointing to the academic gowns they wore.

The Dixiecrats roared on. In May a conference of "States' Rights Democrats" brought together about a thousand key Democratic politicians. They walked to the brink of secession from the Democratic Party, then paused: party congressional leaders feared the loss of their seniority if they abandoned the Democrats. A third-party candidate held little realistic hope of winning, but voting Republican was anathema to a region nourished on hate of Yankee carpetbaggers (a sizable number of Southerners still feared that if a man voted Republican his hand would turn black, his hair would fall out, and his family would suffer genetic problems for three generations). Many Southerners lived with personal memories of the abuses of Reconstruction, and the pall it cast across Dixie until well into the twentieth century; the South feared "control by Washington" because of bitter experience, not paranoia. Economic vassalage rankled the South as well: northern corporations owned much of its industry; northern banks supplied much of its capital, often at exorbitant interest rates; northern-owned railroads charged the farmer and small merchant discriminatory shipping rates. The South's sole lev-

erage had been its power in the Democratic Party—and now that loyalty
was to be betrayed by what many Dixie leaders considered nothing more
than a "Democratic version of Reconstruction," in which federal bureaucrats, not local officials, would control communities. So the Dixiecrats put together a two-part strategy. First, they would attempt to block
Truman's nomination and substitute a prominent Southerner such as
Senator Harry F. Byrd of Virginia. Failing, they would convene immediately after the Democratic National Convention to choose a third-party
candidate who would siphon off enough votes to deny a majority to
either Truman or the Republicans, thus throwing the election into the
House of Representatives, where each state would have one vote. There,
the Dixiecrats felt, the South would dictate a president of its liking.

Whatever the outcome, Truman faced grave trouble below the Mason-
Dixon Line.

IN THE CENTER: WHO LIKES IKE?

Ideology fired the Dixiecrats and the Wallaceites, who disagreed with
the Truman Administration on specific issues (civil rights and foreign
policy) and offered alternatives. Not so for what must have been to
Harry Truman the most galling, and potentially the most threatening
opposition move: the Ike phenomenon.

Dwight D. Eisenhower came out of the war a truly popular hero, the
field commander of the largest expeditionary force ever mounted in the
history of man, a soldier-diplomat who meshed the Allied forces into a
victorious machine. Before 1941 few persons outside the military establishment had ever heard the name Eisenhower (indeed, his younger
brother, Milton, an academician, carried the greater reputation). But for
the next four years the military communiqués lauded Eisenhower as he
led Allied forces to victory—in North Africa, on the Normandy
beaches, through to the heart of Germany. His broad smile endeared Ike
to Americans: not for him the autocratic demeanor of General Douglas
MacArthur, the Pacific commander. MacArthur ruled; Eisenhower led.
The American GI, perhaps the most critical mass public ever assembled,
gave Eisenhower the ultimate accolade by naming his dress blouse "the
Ike jacket." When Ike came home victorious in June 1945, New York
City gave him a "reception of such overpowering bulk and enthusiasm
as to stun the beholder," in the words of reporter Frank Adams of the
New York Times. Some 4 million men, women, and children cheered
Ike along a 37-mile parade route, the largest and most enthusiastic
throng in the history of the city. "Every window, every fire escape, every
balcony, every rooftop along the way was crowded, and so were those
on side streets for blocks away from the thoroughfares on which the

motorcade was speeding if they promised to grant even a fleeting glimpse of the hero of the day." When he got back to his home town of Abilene, Kansas, and yet another surging crowd, Ike hugged his eighty-three-year-old mother and said, "Boy, I'm glad to be back here." When the crowd shouted "Our next President," he replied, "There's no use denying that I'll fly to the moon because I couldn't if I wanted to. The same goes for politics."

The popularity, and the presidential talk, followed Eisenhower into his postwar positions as army chief of staff and president of Columbia University. Ike reacted testily each time someone suggested he seek the White House. As early as January 1947, with "Ike for President" buttons sprouting over the country, the Washington *Times-Herald* broke out eight-column banner headlines to go with a supposed Eisenhower quotation: "I will run for President if the people of this country want me to run." "You know it's a lie," Eisenhower replied angrily. "I never said anything of the kind." Later that month, when a reporter innocently began a question about Ike's later political aspirations, the general cut him off. "Don't bring up that damnable subject of politics in which I have no damned interest."

The public hunger for Eisenhower was remarkable for several reasons. The people talking about him for President were not even sure whether he was Republican, Democrat, or neither (although the initial support was from the GOP). Eisenhower's views on national issues were totally unknown; as chief of staff, he had testified for universal military training, but beyond that the public record was barren. Nor, for that matter, did Eisenhower display any obvious qualifications for the presidency; indeed, the New York *Herald Tribune* was offended in mid-1947 when he was selected to become president of Columbia University, effective January 1948. "There will inevitably be regrets," the newspaper editorialized, "that the trustees were unable to find a scholar of the first rank qualified for the post. Plainly, in turning to General Eisenhower, they elected to subordinate the question of learning, of the skills in education, to the more practical issues of administration. . . ."* But the Ike devotees swept past these blank marks in his record. Public and professional politician alike scented a winner in the hero-general; regardless of his "qualifications," he would be a better national leader than the slumping Harry S. Truman.

* Professional academicians also looked askance at the appointment. Monroe Deutsch, vice-president and provost emeritus of the University of California, thought Ike's appointment a bad precedent, even though his fame would bring fringe benefits. Trustees should realize "that what a famous general says will always gain publicity, and he will be in constant demand," a boon for fund raising. But Deutsch asked: "Would a successful college president be able to step into command of an army? I doubt it." Eisenhower disagreed; if any of the Columbia trustees had suddenly taken command of his army, "the Battle of the Bulge would not have changed a bit."

So the Ike-for-President talk continued and gained momentum, regardless of how hard the general tried to stomp it down. At his final press conference as chief of staff, reporters wanted to talk only about the presidency, not the military, with specific reference to an assertion by Roy Roberts of the Kansas City *Star* that he would accept a genuine draft. The *Star* article noted that a draft without "conniving" was a political impossibility. "Now I assure you I am not going to give any authority for conniving," Eisenhower said. Would he run if nominated? "That is an impossible question. If I asked you what you would do if you were flying to the moon, and halfway up you met a friend who was flying to the moon, and he asked you what you were doing there—why, you'd say that was all impossible. It would be useless to answer the question." No one listened. Walter Winchell asked that listeners send Eisenhower a card or letter urging him to seek nomination. Some 20,000 pieces of mail fluttered down on Eisenhower's Columbia office the first week; eventually the crammed mail bags overflowed storage capabilities. In Milwaukee, Republican insurance executive Milton Polland, who had started the Willkie-for-President boom in Wisconsin in 1940, formed a national Draft Ike Committee and said Eisenhower would go on the primary ballot whether he wanted to or not. State polls of registered voters showed Ike leading Truman 48–39 percent. In January 1948 Republican Senator Charles W. Tobey of New Hampshire gave his blessing to a New Hampshire branch of the Draft Ike Committee, which entered a full slate of eight candidates in the primary. The committee announced it would enter Eisenhower in the Pennsylvania primary on April 27.

Things were clearly out of hand, so Eisenhower moved again to squelch the political career that people kept trying to push upon him. In early February he wrote a public letter to a New Hampshire newspaper stating he was convinced that "the necessary and wise subordination of the military to civil power will be best sustained . . . when lifelong professional soldiers, in the absence of some obvious and overriding reasons, abstain from seeking high political office. . . . [M]y decision to remove myself completely from the political scene is definite and positive. . . . I would not accept nomination even under the remote circumstance that it were tendered me." And so the Republicans reluctantly gave up on Eisenhower.

Not so for many Democrats, however, who found Eisenhower increasingly attractive as Truman's popularity plummeted during the late winter and spring of 1948. By one disputed account, in the fall of 1947 Truman himself offered to step aside as the Democratic nominee in favor of Eisenhower, via a message given the general by Kenneth C. Royall, the secretary of war. If Eisenhower was receptive, Truman "would not only help him get it but would offer to be his running mate for vice-president."* Samuel I. Rosenman, who continued as an informal adviser to Truman after leaving the White House in 1946, recollected also that "President Truman had told me that if Eisenhower wanted to run on the Democratic ticket, he would yield to him; but Eisenhower replied that he did not want to run." Truman, however, later denied making any such offer. In his own memoirs he agreed with the curt appraisal of Eisenhower offered by Speaker of the House Sam Rayburn when liberal Democrats began pushing Ike for the presidency: "No, won't do. Good man, but wrong business." Still, many years later, Truman told writer Merle Miller a more personal reason for opposing Eisenhower. By this account, soon after the war ended Eisenhower wrote General George C. Marshall, then chief of staff, that he intended to divorce his wife so he could marry Kay Summersby, an Englishwoman who was his secretary and personal aide from 1943 to 1945. In a blistering reply, Marshall told Eisenhower that "if he ever again even mentioned a thing like that, he'd see to it that the rest of his life was a living hell." Eisenhower dropped the idea; he never saw Miss Summersby again. Truman told Miller that "I wouldn't have *ever* supported Eisenhower under any circumstances for President even if I . . . hadn't known about his personal life." Publicly, of course, Truman said nothing about Eisenhower's availability or desirability.

To many liberals, however, Eisenhower was a practical favorite. Their hearts might belong to William Douglas, the Supreme Court justice, but their political acumen told them Douglas could not win. The Republican boom for Eisenhower had been dead but a month when anti-Truman Democrats took up his cause, signaled by a statement by the national board of Americans for Democratic Action that the party needed an open convention, and that "this nation has the right to call upon men like . . . Eisenhower and . . . Douglas if the people so choose." At a Jefferson-Jackson Day dinner in Los Angeles diners broke into prolonged applause when toastmaster Jimmy Roosevelt mentioned Eisenhower's name. Labor leaders James B. Carey, number-two man in the CIO, and Emil Rieve endorsed Ike. The revolt against Truman spread to state conventions. In Minnesota, Hubert H. Humphrey, the glib young mayor of Minneapolis, announced for Eisenhower, with Douglas a second choice; the state convention gave faint praise to Truman and sent an uninstructed delegation to the national convention. In California, ADA chipped away at Truman delegates, trying to stir interest in a draft-Ike movement. The intellectual Reinhold Niebuhr solemnly mourned, "We are sunk now and Eisenhower is the only pos-

---

* Arthur Krock, long-time Washington correspondent for the *New York Times,* heard of this supposed offer at the time, and wrote a long memorandum to himself about it; oddly, he never told the story in his own newspaper. A *Times* colleague, Cabell Phillips, revealed it publicly in his *The Truman Presidency,* published in 1966; the quotation is from the Phillips book.

sible candidate who could defeat the Republicans. I would support almost any decent man to avoid four years of Republican rule."

Dissenters remained, however, and important ones. When someone broached the idea of an Eisenhower-Douglas ticket, Douglas replied he was not interested in entering what might prove to be a "political whorehouse." The liberal commentator Elmer Davis scoffed at the Eisenhower movement. "If he runs, eventually he's going to have to say something, and then a lot of people might be surprised." David Lilienthal felt fellow liberals were succumbing to a "lynch-law atmosphere" and confided to his journal: "Did FDR ever stand up for public development of power, or human rights, or labor, essentially any more firmly than Truman? And who knows what Eisenhower would do on any of these issues? Bah!"

Wallace on the left. The Dixiecrats on the right. Eisenhower in the center. Could Harry Truman survive the Democrats' intraparty contests, much less the November elections?

22

HST:
The Underdog Plans

Y ES, HE COULD, because as President he still controlled the
machinery of the Democratic National Committee, and
through it the convention. Truman knew his contemporary political
history: that never in this century had a party rejected a sitting President's choice of either a candidate or a platform; that even the vastly
popular Theodore Roosevelt could not take the 1912 nomination away
from President William Howard Taft, despite the incumbent's many
problems in the Republican Party. "In 1948 I was in a position to control the nomination," Truman wrote in his memoirs. "When I had made
up my mind to run, those in the party who turned against me could do
nothing to prevent it." By early May, Truman had 423 of 620 delegates
named by state conventions, only 195 short of a majority; many of the
unpledged could be expected to vote for him. Thus weeks before the
convention Truman had clinched the nomination. The splinter candidates could provide a noisy convention, but they would have to seek the
presidency under a different banner.

Truman, therefore, looked beyond the convention to the campaign,
planning for which had begun in earnest after the 1946 congressional
debacle. Truman strategists worked from a thirty-three-page single-
spaced memorandum entitled "The Politics of 1948," written in September 1947 by James Rowe, a presidential assistant, after weeks of
interviewing politicians and others about the main problems facing
Truman and how he could overcome them.* Rowe's document was

* The strategy memorandum has been widely credited to Clark Clifford, a White
House counsel at the time, and the version that ultimately reached Truman's desk
bore his signature. In fact, however, Rowe was the primary author. Clifford asked
Rowe's help in writing the memo, and both men did extensive research in the
summer of 1947, assisted by other White House aides and Democratic politicians.
Rowe wrote a draft and gave it to Clifford, who added a new first paragraph and
some additional sentences in the civil rights section. The bulk, however, retained
Rowe's language.

coldly pragmatic. Policy suggestions, he wrote, "are based solely on an appraisal of the 'politically advantageous thing to do.' In a democracy, what is politically advisable may often accord with the merits of a particular policy; often it does not." Rowe did not attempt to "evaluate the merits; that is a matter of conscience for the Administration. For working purposes it is assumed here that the politically wise thing to do is also the best policy for the United States."

Many of Rowe's assumptions proved grossly wrong, the inevitable fate of any political prognosticator. The most striking example is that he took the South for granted. "It is inconceivable that any policies initiated by the Truman Administration, no matter how 'liberal,' can so alienate the South in the next year that it would revolt. As always, the South can be considered safely Democratic. And in formulating national policy it can be safely ignored." Five months later, of course, the Dixiecrat rebellion shook the party to its roots. Although stating flatly that Truman could not win "without the active support of organized labor," Rowe worried that the American Federation of Labor would strike a pragmatic bargain with the Republicans, and that the rival Congress of Industrial Organizations would be so divided over the Communist issue it would be impotent. Rowe especially distrusted George Meany, the AFL secretary-treasurer and a rising power in the federation; Meany, he noted, "has always been eager to make a trade when he thinks he has a winner," and had carefully confined his attacks to *"congressional* Republicans" rather than the party as a whole or potential candidates such as New York Governor Thomas Dewey, "with whom he is friendly." The fears proved baseless. Meany took the initiative in starting Labor's League for Political Education, the AFL's first direct intervention in a presidential election.

But the bulk of the document was incisive analysis and point-by-point scenarios for exploiting Republican weaknesses and capitalizing upon the many powers of the presidency. A Democratic victory, Rowe wrote, depended upon maintaining the "unhappy alliance" of the "three misfit groups" comprising the traditional Democratic majority—southern conservatives, western Progressives, and big city labor. With the South in hand, he urged concentrating on the West, with reclamation and public power projects, and on labor, with flattery and cajolery. Rowe forecast that the sole important domestic issue would be the high cost of living, with neither party likely to do anything to curb inflation because of fear of alienating the farmers. (". . . [F]arm price supports and large food exports abroad are the main reasons for high food prices. In an election year the farmer is everybody's friend.") Thus the "big political question is who will be blamed? The Republicans because they removed the OPA controls and refused to subsidize housing? Or the Democrats because of farm prices, labor 'coddling,' and 'restrictive' tax policies? . . . How the Administration dramatizes the high cost of living . . . can determine the next incumbent of the White House."

Rowe urged cultivating labor while rank-and-file members (political neuters in prosperous times) were still receptive because of anger over the Taft-Hartley Act. Labor leaders "must be given the impression that they are once more welcome" at the White House, with the stroking done by Truman personally. "The mere extension of an invitation to William Green, Dan Tobin, Philip Murray, [David] Dubinsky or any of the prominent leaders to 'come in and talk with me' has a stupendous effect on them and their followers. One by one they should be asked to 'come by' and the President should ask them for their advice on matters *in general*. (This is a question of delicate 'timing'—it is dangerous to ask a labor leader for advice on a *specific* matter and then ignore that advice.) No human being—as every President, from Washington on, has ruefully learned—can resist the glamour, the self-important feeling of 'advising' a President on anything, even if it is only his golfing backswing."

Rowe recommended that Truman deliberately antagonize the Republican-controlled Congress on the assumption no White House programs would be approved under any circumstances in an election year. "Its [the White House's] recommendations—in the State of the Union message and elsewhere—must be tailored for the voter, not the Congressman; they must display a label which reads 'no compromises.' The strategy on the Taft–Hartley Bill—refusal to bargain with the Republicans and to accept any compromises—paid big political dividends. That strategy must be expanded in the next session to include all the *domestic* issues." The White House should propagandize its economic programs through the press so that "by the time Congress convenes the people will know thoroughly what the President has been asking of them. He won't get it, his program will not get very far, but whatever *is* done will be regarded as a Democratic gain; and the Republican Party will be a sitting target for having been obstructionist." Even if the Republicans proposed good legislation it should be opposed: ". . . [I]n terms of 1948 the Administration simply cannot afford to allow a bill with Taft's name to pass." Rowe would also go after the special interest groups working with the Republicans. For instance, he advocated promoting a grass-roots movement against realtors because of their opposition to housing bills: "It is the essence of politics to wage an attack against a personal devil; the Real Estate Lobby should be built into the dramatic equivalent of the Public Utility Lobby of 1935. Purely on the merits, the performance of the real estate interests in their postwar gouging fully deserves everything they get in the way of retaliation. There can be no possible compunction about using such a tactic against them." Rowe doubted that a current Justice Department antitrust probe would be useful because of a "widespread suspicion that the department's motivation was purely political. . . . However, the useful material already gathered by the department's investigators should be made available to those who can make propaganda use of that material."

On black voters, Rowe cited the conventional political theorem that blacks held the electoral balance of power in New York, Illinois, Pennsylvania, Ohio, and Michigan. Roosevelt tore the black vote from the Republicans in 1932; now it showed signs of slippage, especially in New York, because of assiduous cultivation by Governor Dewey, who insisted that "his controllable legislature pass a state anti-discrimination act." Rowe warned that the black voter, "a cynical, hard-boiled trader," would return to the Republicans because southern Democrats had a hammerlock on Congress. "The Negro press, often venal, is already strongly Republican." The standard Democratic protestation about the blacks' improved economic lot "has worn a bit thin with the passage of the years. . . . Unless there are new and real efforts (as distinguished from mere political gestures which are today thoroughly understood and strongly resented by sophisticated Negro leaders) the Negro bloc, which, certainly in Illinois and probably in New York and Ohio, *does* hold the balance of power, will go Republican." Rowe made no civil rights recommendations. Clifford, in forwarding his version of the campaign memo, suggested that "it would appear to be sound strategy to have the President go as far as he feels he possibly could go in recommending measures to protect the rights of minority groups. This course of action would obviously cause difficulty with our southern friends but that is the lesser of two evils."*

So what should the Democrats do? One key suggestion was "to create in the public mind a vote-getting picture of President Truman." The "honeymoon" period had ended; so, too, had the months of "violently critical . . . public opinion. . . . Emerging instead is the picture of a man the American people like. They know now that he is a sincere and humble man and, in the cliché so often heard, that he is a man 'trying to do his best.'" Nonetheless Truman still came across as a politician, a person who "does not hold first place in the ranks of American heroes. Today's public picture of President Truman is not sufficiently varied. The people want something more." Rowe went on to say that the public pays little attention to what the President does as chief of state: "They really form their lasting impressions from watching his incidental ges-

* The eleven hard-core southern states had 147 electoral votes (Alabama, Arkansas, Florida, Georgia, Louisiana, Mississippi, North Carolina, South Carolina, Tennessee, Texas, and Virginia) versus 154 for the five states in which the black bloc vote was considered pivotal (New York, Illinois, Pennsylvania, Ohio, and Michigan). Ultimately the Democrats got 89 votes in the South, 53 in the North; the Republicans 101 in the North; the Dixiecrats 38 in the South. Thus the "race" vote proved a virtual standoff: 142 votes for the Democrats, 139 votes for the Republicans and Dixiecrats.

tures—when he appears as the representative of all the American people." Illustrating, Rowe noted that on a state visit to Brazil Truman received more warm publicity from a comic equator-crossing ceremony in which he was "changed from a pollywog into a shellback" than from formal conferences.

Yet the public wanted more than "stereotyped gestures" of visits with "a round-the-world flyer, or the little girl with the first poppy, or the Disabled Veterans, or the Eagle Scout from Idaho." Needed, Rowe said, were "gestures of substance" which through repetition "form a carefully drawn picture of the President as a broad-gauged citizen with tremendously varied interests." Specific suggestions followed:

—The President could lunch with Albert Einstein; it will be remembered he was the man who prevailed upon Roosevelt to start the atomic bomb project. At his next press conference he can explain that they talked, in general, about the *peacetime* uses of atomic energy and its potentialities for our civilization. He can then casually mention that he has been spending some of his leisure time getting caught up on atomic energy; he has been having "briefing sessions" from the AEC; and has also been doing some reading purely from the layman's point of view. He suggests to the newsmen it would do them no harm at all to read such and such a book (as long as he picks the right one) which he has just read. . . .

—Henry Ford II . . . is often in Washington these days. The President should casually invite him to lunch to just talk over matters "generally." This picture of the American President and the Young Business Man together has appeal for the average reader. Many other business leaders should be called in occasionally. . . .

—The President should concentrate on other fields. The literary field, for example, has its uses. A novelist with the latest best seller is just as good as an international banker for these purposes. Outstanding *women* in various activities should be invited.

Because custom dictated that Truman not do anything political until after the convention he "must resort to subterfuges—for he cannot sit silent. He must be in the limelight." Rowe concluded, "In national politics the American people normally make up their minds irrevocably about the two presidential candidates by the end of July. If the program discussed here can be properly executed it may be of help in getting them to make up their minds *the right way.*"

Beyond the Rowe/Clifford strategy document, the Truman campaign planners started with several assumptions. The press would be hostile. Truman expected fully 90 percent of the media to oppose him "as most were owned, operated, or subsidized by the same private interests that always benefited from Republican economic policies." Businessmen and corporation executives, especially utility moguls, would help the Republicans through advertising attacks on New Deal and Fair Deal programs. Truman's poor standing in public opinion polls was directly attributable to the drumfire of adverse press comment (or so the President felt, anyway); they did not represent farmers and workers. Overcoming the "false propaganda" would require taking the Democratic program directly to the voters.

One professional politician who sensed the impact of Truman's man-to-man rapport was Gael Sullivan, a young Chicago liberal working as staff director of the Democratic National Committee. In mid-1947 he advised the White House how to "capitalize fully on the President's impact on the people."

> Sometime before the National Convention in 1948 the President should show himself to the nation via the back platform of a cross-country train.
>
> The easy manner of speaking when speaking informally has been lost in translation to the people via radio and speaking tours.
>
> The entire approach to the President's speeches should be changed. It would be well to gain more natural delivery, even if some rhetorical effects are lost.

The White House began casting around for an excuse for the President to make a "nonpolitical" cross-country tour. With the Democrats flat broke, the trip would have to be made at public expense, hence the White House needed some nonpartisan draping. By happenstance, Dr. Robert Gordon Sproul, president of the University of California in Berkeley, wanted a commencement speaker, and when he called the White House to inquire whether Truman was interested, the President literally jumped at the offer. So on June 3 an eighteen-car train, the *Presidential Special,* rolled out of Washington's Union Station in one of the more thinly disguised political trips of the century. The only bow in the direction of propriety was the absence of J. Howard McGrath, the national chairman. But the itinerary took Truman through eighteen strategic states, during which he made major speeches in Chicago, Omaha, Seattle, Berkeley, and Los Angeles. Politicians bounded aboard at every stop to meet the President and to ride along for part of the route, with Truman quipping to the crowd, tongue in cheek, about the "nonpartisan, bipartisan trip we are making" and then proceeding to ask, for example, that Frank Lausche, standing alongside him, be reelected Ohio governor. At most stops Truman joked he was on his way "fur to get me a degree," whereupon columnist Thomas Stokes wrote a theme song for the trip, to the tune of "Oh, Susanna!":

They can't prove nothing. They ain't got a thing on me,
I'm going down to Berkeley, fur to get me a degree.

Truman talked tough, both at the Republican-controlled Eightieth Congress and at stay-at-home Democrats who cost the party the 1946 election. Speaking to a convention of the Communication Workers of America in Seattle, Truman said he shared unionists' dislike for the Taft–Hartley Act, but he wouldn't take blame for it. "You know the reason for that is in November 1946, just one-third of the population voted. The people were not interested in what might happen to them. . . . We have the law now, and I am the President and I have to enforce it. Your only remedy is November 1948, and if you continue that law in effect, that is your fault and not mine, because I don't want it." At Grand Coulee Dam he told a vast crowd that he favored reclamation and public power projects for the Pacific Northwest but he wasn't getting any help from Congress.

That is partly your fault. In the election of 1946 you believed all the lies that were published about your president and two-thirds of you didn't even go out and vote. Look what the other third gave you. You deserved it. If you let that sort of situation continue— you have a chance to remedy it this fall—I won't have any sympathy with you. You will get what you deserve.

All along the route Truman lashed at congressional inaction on housing and rent controls, its refusal to raise the minimum wage, its agricultural policies, its restrictive immigration legislation. Station-by-station he lambasted the 80th Congress as the "worst" in history:

Tacoma: "Congress is interested in the welfare of the better classes, and passed a rich man's tax bill."
Olympia: "If you want to continue the policies of the 80th Congress, it'll be your funeral. . . . The Republican Congress believes in the theory of Daniel Webster that the West is no good and there is no use spending money on it."
Albuquerque: "The issue in this country is between special privilege and the people."
East St. Louis: "I think they are hunting for a boom and bust."
Butte, Montana: Referring to Senator Robert A. Taft, "I guess he'd let you starve. I'm not that kind."

The trip had its rough moments as Truman's inexperienced entourage learned the tricks of cross-country campaigning. In Omaha, poor advance work brought only 1,000 persons into the cavernous Ak-Sar-Ben Auditorium, and press photographs showed Truman staring at row upon row of empty seats. In dedicating an airport at Carey, Idaho, the patriotic decorations misled the President, and he spoke of the "brave boy who died fighting for his country." There was an awkward silence, and a tearful woman standing near the President interrupted: the dedicatee was her sixteen-year-old daughter. Embarrassed, Truman said he was "more honored to dedicate the airport to the young woman who bravely gave her life to her country." The mother tugged his arm again. "No, no, our Wilma was killed right here," in the crash of her sweetheart's private plane while joyriding. All Truman could do was apologize to the shaken parents. During the off-the-cuff speech in Eugene, he said of Stalin, in a remark the Republicans were to hurl back at him for months, "I like old Joe. He's a decent fellow, but he's a prisoner of the Politburo."

But these incidents didn't diminish Truman's zest for political combat. He told his audiences he was on the road to "dispel the lies and misinformation" the press was spreading about him. "I am coming out here so you can look at me and hear what I have to say and then make up your mind as to whether you should believe some of the things that have been said about your President." The crowds were large (50,000 in Berkeley; in Los Angeles a million saw him between the railroad station and the Ambassador Hotel, where he spoke) and responsive, shouting "Pour it on!" when he talked rough about Congress. In Spokane, cub reporter Rhea Felknor of the Spokane *Spokesman Review* was in the midst of an impromptu trainside interview with Truman when Democratic Senator Warren Magnuson passed the President a copy of the paper. Truman skimmed it as Felknor asked, "How does it feel to invade a Republican stronghold?" Felknor wrote Truman's reaction:

> Raising his head to glare down on the lone newspaperman, he asked, "Do you work for this paper, young man?" The President's voice became raspy for virtually the only time during his appearance here as he declared:
>
> "The Chicago *Tribune* and this paper are the worst in the United States. You've got just what you ought to have. You've got the worst Congress in the United States you've ever had. And the papers, this paper, are responsible for it."

Senator Robert Taft derided Truman for "blackguarding the Congress at every whistle stop in the country." Whereupon the Democratic National Committee polled mayors and chambers of commerce in thirty-five cities visited by Truman and asked for comment on Taft's statement. Some of the replies:

> *Eugene, Oregon:* "Must have wrong city. As the lumber capital of the world . . . our whistles never stop blowing."
> *Laramie, Wyoming:* "Characteristically, Senator Taft is confused, this time on whistles."

Pocatello, Idaho: "If Senator Taft referred to Pocatello as 'whistle stop' it is apparent that he has not visited progressing Pocatello since time of his father's 1908 campaign. . . ."

Berkeley, California: ". . . [H]ard to think of our city as a whistle stop unless the whistle be one of admiration which our soldier boys give to a girl of breathtaking beauty!"

Most newspapers treated Truman's trip as a crass vaudeville performance that demeaned his office. Even friendly editorialists chided him. The Washington *Post* said, "It would not be surprising if Democratic chieftains were beginning to echo that apt Goldwynism, 'He should have stood in bed!' " The Washington *Star* said, "The President in this critical hour is making a spectacle of himself on a political junket that would reflect discreditably on a ward heeler." But journalists who listened closely divined exactly what Truman was doing. "The New Deal—its preservation, perpetuation, and completion is what Harry S. Truman is pinning his hopes on," Barnet Nover wrote in the Denver *Post*. "He has begun to make an impression." The crowd response convinced the White House political strategy board that Truman could sell himself—if only he could get through to the voters.

23

The GOP: Dewey, Again

T
HE ROWE STRATEGY predicted flatly that Thomas E.
Dewey would be the Republican nominee, a prognosis seemingly sound at the time, but one that became exceedingly shaky during
preconvention maneuvering. Titular leader of his party by virtue of his
losing the 1944 race with Roosevelt, Dewey was the country's best-known
Republican. And even the defeat was no disgrace: reluctant to make a
suicidal race against a popular wartime commander, he did his duty to
the GOP, campaigned hard and well, and held the plurality to a surprising 3,600,000 votes, smallest in FDR's four campaigns. Dewey
rebounded to win reelection as New York governor in 1946 by almost
700,000 votes, largest in the state's history. Moreover, Dewey enjoyed
a superb public image. New Yorkers first knew him as the racket-busting
young district attorney who put corrupt Tammany chieftains in jail and
broke the infamous "Murder, Inc." ring. Dewey made a premature run
for the GOP nomination in 1940 but was crushed beneath the Wendell
Willkie bandwagon. Lowering his sights to a more realistic level, he won
the governorship in 1942 and ran a clean, efficient administration
slightly to the left of traditional Republicanism. He pushed through
New York's first law barring racial and religious discrimination in employment, and he managed to cut both business and personal taxes and
still end the way years with a $623 million reserve in the state treasury.
Energetic and young (Dewey was forty-six in 1948), he seemed just the
man to appeal to progressive urban voters who traditionally favored the
Democrats. Yet his conservative credentials were good enough to pass
inspection by all but the most neanderthal of Republicans.

And yet, Dewey had a major handicap—his personality. In the oft-
quoted words of the wife of Kenneth Simpson, GOP leader in New York
County, "You have to know Dewey really well to dislike him." "A blunt
fact about Mr. Dewey should be faced," wrote John Gunther. "It is that

many people do not like him. He is, unfortunately, one of the least seductive personalities in public life." Priggish, self-important, brusque, smarter than most people and unwilling to conceal it, Dewey acted as if holding high public office was a personal divinity-granted right. Dewey's world seemed divided into two parts: the press, servants, and the "lesser public"; and people who could help him politically. Politicians endured his haughtiness of necessity; after all, the man won elections, and a party exists for that purpose. But the stories circulated, and many of them got into print. One midnight Dewey and Republican leaders of the legislature sat before a blazing wood fire in the governor's mansion. A burning log rolled out onto the stone hearth, and one of the men instinctively reached for a poker. Dewey halted him with a silent motion, and pressed a buzzer. He resumed the conversation. The servant finally came, brushing sleep from his eyes, and restored the fallen log to the fire. As one of the legislators remarked later, "A thoughtful man would have handled the situation in a few seconds without getting some poor servant up from bed. Dewey just didn't think that way." Then there was the lady reporter from a Republican paper who received an ungallant brush-off from Dewey on Election Night 1944. The lady had traveled on the campaign train with Mr. and Mrs. Dewey and was on a first-name basis with them. She happened to get into an elevator at the Roosevelt Hotel with the Deweys and nodded and spoke. Mrs. Dewey said, "Good evening." Dewey looked above the door of the elevator and said chillingly, "We don't want to see any newspaper people." The morning after his nomination in 1944 Dewey was having breakfast in a Chicago hotel with Governor John Bricker of Ohio, who was to be his vice-presidential running mate, and movie and still cameramen tried to get pictures of the conference. "Shake hands with Governor Bricker, will you please?" a cameraman asked. "One does not," Dewey replied, with a certain reproof in his voice, "shake hands across a breakfast table."

Again, there was the 1946 campaign trip in upstate New York when a Republican state committeeman entered Dewey's private rail car to ask what he thought about having a certain man introduce him at a dinner that night. Dewey pondered a moment and then summoned an adviser, who told him, No, the man had friends who would be damaging to Dewey's name. "That's what I thought," Dewey said. Turning to the committeeman, he said, "He's out." "I didn't suggest him," the official explained. "Actually, your New York office asked me to ask—" Dewey interrupted, his voice a discernible pitch higher, and much colder. "I said he's out. We needn't discuss it further." He got up and took the adviser to the end of the car. In the words of a New York political journalist familiar with the incident, "The Republican fellow was terribly hurt. Tom Dewey may not have known he had hurt the man's feelings. If he did know, I'm not sure he would have cared much."

Warren Moscow, a political writer for the *New York Times* who knew Dewey well, said of him, "Mr. Dewey is a strange character—or perhaps I might say, he's a strange *lack* of character." According to Moscow, soon after Dewey became governor he received a report about an outbreak of amoebic dysentery at a state mental hospital. One patient had already died. A legislative leader asked Dewey privately what he intended to do. Dewey replied, "Oh, we'll let it slide a bit, let it coast for a little while, and then we'll make a bigger splurge when we clean it up." Seven deaths later Dewey acted, depicting the hospital situation as "typical of twenty years of dry rot and incompetence" of preceding Democratic administrations. "In my opinion," Moscow said, "it boils down to seven people dying so that Mr. Dewey could get his name in bigger headlines."

In a glowing campaign biography, author Rupert Hughes related that when Dewey proposed to his wife, Frances Eileen Hutt, a musical-comedy star, his letter was so clogged with legal phrases that it annoyed her. Dewey indignantly denied the story. He told Hughes, "We lived in the same town for four years before we got married, and as a matter of fact most of that time was spent in waiting until my income was sufficient to warrant matrimony."

One acutely sensitive subject for Dewey was his height. Although at five feet eight inches he was about average for the American male, the impression of shortness perhaps came from the fact that his head was somewhat large for his body, or that unadmiring photographers deliberately shot him from unflattering angles (*Life* once noted in a facetious caption that Dewey was sitting on two telephone books because he wasn't tall enough for his desk chair). Alice Roosevelt Longworth called him "the little man on the wedding cake," and Harold Ickes wrote in 1944 that "Dewey has thrown his diaper into the ring." Finally, the Dewey staff circulated a fact sheet trying to put down the unkind remarks about his youth and height: he was three inches taller than Joe Stalin, and only three-quarters of an inch shorter than Harry Truman; that Alexander the Great was governor of Macedonia at nineteen, and that Napoleon at thirty-five was master of all of Europe.

But one had to watch Tom Dewey closely—or very critically—before the personality flaws were obvious. As governor of the largest state, wealth and powerful people were at his command. Regardless of his coolness, wrote the critical Marquis Childs, on the radio and before mass audiences "he is a worthy rival of President Roosevelt. His voice is strong and true. Here, of course, his training as a singer in breathing and timing stands him in good stead."

Dewey's initial strategy was to await, rather than pursue, the Republican nomination, the same course he had followed in 1944 when he won without opposition. And indeed the field appeared clear for him in 1948. The Rowe campaign memorandum, for instance, wrote off Senator

Robert A. Taft as hopeless because his policies had alienated so many large voter blocs. If a Dewey-Taft deadlock did develop, Rowe saw as fall-back candidates Eisenhower, Senator Arthur Vandenberg of Michigan, or Governor Earl Warren of California. Eisenhower, of course, was saying emphatically he did not intend to run. Vandenberg's public image was that of Midwestern fuddy-duddy. Warren was a virtual unknown.

Completely overlooked—by every other professional politician in the country, in addition to Rowe—was another youthful figure of Republican politics, Harold Stassen: elected governor of Minnesota at age thirty-one; a wartime naval officer; a delegate to the founding conference of the United Nations, by appointment of President Roosevelt. Now forty-one, the hulking, moon-faced Stassen, who exuded a Midwestern warmth comparable to Eisenhower's, held no public office, which meant he had to campaign hard, and early, just to keep his name before the voters. Stassen formally declared his candidacy in December 1946 and during the next eighteen months traveled in forty states and made more than 250 speeches to any audience he could find, from garden clubs to college commencements. Stassen lived off his lecture fees (from $500 to $1,000) and spread a message of liberal Republicanism—confidence in the free enterprise system and international peace through the United Nations; social programs far to the left of anything ever contemplated by Taft; a mixture of toughness and conciliation toward the Soviets. The experts laughed at Stassen. *Time,* which thought him important enough (or curious enough) to warrant a cover story in August 1947, told a current quip:

Q. What politician believes Harold Stassen will be nominated?

A. Harold Stassen.

Stassen ignored the gibes, and he gradually built a campaign organization, run from the tenth floor of the Pillsbury Building in Minneapolis by a husky, handsome forty-year-old St. Paul lawyer named Warren Burger. Volunteers mailed 300,000 letters a day asking support.

Dewey, conversely, conducted a noncampaign, declining to spell out any specific programs and shunting off most press questions about politics. During a western trip in mid-1947 his sole political activity was off-the-record meetings with party leaders. His very announcement was indirect, via press secretary James Hagerty in January 1948: "I am informed that a group of Governor Dewey's friends in Oregon has entered his name in the preferential primary in that state." Hagerty said Dewey would not actively seek the nomination because of the press of legislative business but "if nominated he would accept." At a news conference a few days later Dewey said he would discuss issues at times and places of his own choosing. Asked about his attitude on the influence of military men in government, he replied, "The list of questions on things like that could last from here to San Francisco and back. You will have to take my views as I give them in my speeches—and elsewhere." How about Taft's record as Senate majority leader? "There are 435 congressmen and 95 other senators. It would take a long time to answer that question." So evasive was Dewey, Edward Folliard of the Washington *Post* reported, that foes called him "the Mr. Hush of Politics."

The first direct confrontation came in Wisconsin, an important primary because the state has blocs of both farm and industrial votes, and is large enough to provide an accurate gauge of a candidate's drawing power. The 1948 primary drew additional interest because of the belated entry of General Douglas MacArthur, then commanding occupation forces in Japan—an inscrutable war hero whose views on domestic issues were even less known than those of Eisenhower, but who enjoyed the loud backing of the Chicago *Tribune* and the Hearst newspapers, both influential in Wisconsin. The Hearst papers called for MacArthur's candidacy in a three-column front-page editorial calling him "The Man of the Hour." Republican right-wingers poked at the reclusive general for weeks, attempting to recruit him to halt the detested Dewey. They finally succeeded in mid-March, four weeks before the primary, when MacArthur elaborately announced his availability: "In this hour of momentous importance . . . I can say, and with due humility, that I would be recreant to all my concepts of good citizenship were I to shirk . . . accepting any public duty to which I might be called by the American people."

Once in the race, MacArthur could not run. As an active army officer, he was barred from campaigning, and indeed, he issued no further statements, relying instead upon the *Tribune* and the Milwaukee *Journal,* the Hearst outlet, to publicize him. Supporters managed somehow to present him as a "favorite son," by virtue of the fact that he briefly attended a high school in Milwaukee, and received his West Point appointment from the state. But just what MacArthur would do as President no one deigned to suggest (after all, the general hadn't even set foot in the United States since 1937). Nor was there any evidence of a grass-roots swell of support. A Chicago ex-GI started a "Veterans Against MacArthur" club which spread rapidly to a dozen cities; "Give him a medal, but not the White House," veterans chanted at a Boston protest rally. All MacArthur could do was sit in Tokyo and read cables. Army censors kept critical comments out of the Japanese press (there was no mention, for instance, of the opposing veterans; official scissors also snipped out such items as "the thinness of MacArthur's hair is hidden by careful combing").

Stassen, meanwhile, whirled around Wisconsin in a Greyhound bus, speaking from sunup to midnight at mass meetings, at factory gates, at any crossroads where people gathered. The GOP state organization supported him, and freshman Senator Joseph R. McCarthy headed his slate of delegates. The aloof Dewey responded to Stassen's frenzied campaigning by visiting Wisconsin for two brief days. Most observers gave the nod to MacArthur, the *New York Times,* for instance, predicting the week before the election he would win at least fourteen of twenty-seven delegates.

The experts were wrong. Stassen got nineteen delegates, MacArthur eight, Dewey none. The New York governor's noncampaign was suddenly in deep trouble (MacArthur's died outright). As the New York *Herald Tribune* editorialized, Stassen was "no longer a dark horse. All at once Mr. Stassen has emerged from the fringe of interesting possibility. From now on he is in the first division of contenders for the Republican presidential nomination." Naturally concerned, Dewey moved into Nebraska, the next primary state, in dead earnest, this time facing Taft as well as Stassen. Dewey campaigned three days, Taft, four; Stassen, in Nebraska frequently for two years, came in for the final days. Once again, a Stassen upset: more than 43 percent of a record vote, with Dewey second and Taft a weak third. Next, Ohio, and Stassen's first stumble. Flouting the unwritten political rule that an outsider shouldn't go into a "favorite son" state (for practical reasons, as well as courtesy), Stassen challenged Taft for twenty-three of fifty-three delegates. He won only nine, and his steamroller lost much momentum.

For Dewey, Oregon would be decisive; for he would have to balance the losses in Wisconsin and Nebraska and to prove he was attractive to voters outside New York. Stassen opened an early lead in the polls, then the Dewey money-blitz began: a barrage of billboards, newspaper ads, and radio spots that cost an estimated quarter of a million dollars, an astronomical sum by 1948 standards. Sensing the nomination slipping from him, Dewey imitated Stassen's bus-stop campaigning with a vigorous effort that covered 2,000 miles in three weeks; often he worked sixteen hours a day. At inestimable cost to his dignity, he even performed some of the foolish rituals demanded of a candidate. He posed in a ten-gallon hat and in an Indian headdress worn by Queen Marie of Rumania when she visited Oregon in the 1920's. He let his party be "ambushed" by a mob of "cavemen"—clad in tattered furs and carrying clubs—participating in a local pageant.

The pivotal event, however, was a Dewey-Stassen radio debate broadcast live from Portland to some 900 stations around the country, the first ever in a presidential campaign. The ground rules, subject of intense negotiation, restricted the audience to newsmen, and provided each man with an opening presentation of twenty minutes, and then eight and a half minutes of rebuttal. The subject: whether the Communist Party should be outlawed, a subject of intense national interest because of the Mundt-Nixon Bill then before the House of Representatives. Stassen took the affirmative, Dewey the negative, and the former prosecutor chewed the former governor into forensic pieces. Stassen argued the Mundt-Nixon Bill would curb the party; Dewey retorted (by quoting the bill's legislative history) that the real purpose was to illegalize subversive acts, and through registration requirements force the party into the open. "This outlawing idea is not new," Dewey said. "It is as old as government. For thousands of years despots have shot, imprisoned, and exiled their people and their governments have always fallen into the dust." He argued for "keeping the Communist Party everlastingly out in the open so we can defeat it and all it stands for."* Stassen replied weakly that Dewey was "soft on communism," a statement so preposterous that newsmen in the studio stifled guffaws. Dewey walked away the clear victor, both in the debate and in the primary. He won 53 percent of the votes, and all twelve delegates. Harold Stassen's eighteen-month pursuit of the presidency was in grave trouble.

But what did America really know of Dewey as he stood on the brink of the Republican nomination? Very little, other than that he blamed Harry Truman for the nation's problems; just what Dewey would do differently he did not confide to the nation during his preconvention campaign. Alistair Cooke of the Manchester *Guardian* listened to Dewey closely and was not impressed: "He has gone after the presidency with the humorless calculation of a certified public accountant in pursuit of the Holy Grail. . . . He has a trick of hasty recovery, which makes many people feel that he is guided by no convictions but first wets his finger to the wind and then sticks his policies together, piece by fashionable piece."

At the convention, which opened in Philadelphia on June 21, the Dewey opposition was so fractionated it could not gather around a single candidate. Dewey came to town with 300 to 350 "sure votes" of the 548 needed, with many others secretly tucked away. Only Stassen, Taft, Warren, and Vandenberg survived as "serious candidates," and the latter said he would not campaign; if the Republicans wanted to nominate him, they knew his hotel room number. The facade of a contested convention lasted several days, with the lively combine of intrigue, frivolity, and bunkum that marks the American political process. Stassen supporters passed out 1,200 pounds of Swiss cheese supplied by friends in Wisconsin; a voluptuous blonde in nautical garb mock-rowed a boat across the lobby of the Bellevue-Stratford Hotel under a sign,

> Man the Oars and Ride the Crest
> Harold Stassen—He's the Best!

The Taft people paraded Little Eva, a baby elephant four feet tall, and even persuaded the august senator to shake its trunk at a press conference.

---

* Dewey turned out to be wrong. When the registration requirement became law in 1950 in the McCarran Act, the party went underground.

What solemnity existed stemmed from the universal conviction that the keynote speaker, Governor Dwight H. Green of Illinois, was indulging in more than traditional hyperbole when he declared, "We are here to nominate the thirty-fourth President of the United States." Former Representative Clare Boothe Luce called Truman "a gone goose." H. L. Mencken, with his usual disrespect for politicians and their craft, wrote, "The most earnest clapper-clawing, save at the end, followed the honorable gentleman's solemn promise that the new Republican president will clean out all the dubious characters who now hog at the public trough, feasting upon the taxpayers' vitals and disgracing the human race. . . . Most of the delegates and alternates have been pining and panting for office for fifteen long years and their pulses race every time they hear that succor is at hand."

The Dewey forces, meanwhile, noisily tossed big chips of delegates onto the table, and pursued fence straddlers with promises of federal judgeships and other patronage, and even cash (in the instance of a black delegate from Mississippi). Dewey began revealing his hidden delegate strength early, so as to build an unstoppable momentum. On Monday Senator Edward Martin of Pennsylvania, a favorite son, withdrew and gave Dewey thirty-five to fifty votes. On Wednesday New Jersey, Missouri, Massachusetts, and Indiana followed, and Dewey surged to the brink of the nomination. The opposition met, wrangled, and refused to join behind one man. On Thursday the first ballot gave Dewey 434 votes, Taft 224, Stassen 157, Vandenberg 62, Warren 59; favorite sons and fringers had the rest. An hour later the second ballot gave Dewey 515, Taft 274, Stassen 149, with minor candidates bringing up the rear. The total left Dewey 33 votes short of a majority. The anti-Dewey forces forced an overnight recess. Taft and Stassen talked; Stassen refused to withdraw until after the third ballot; Taft sat down and wrote a concession statement. When the convention reconvened on Friday Governor Bricker of Ohio read a message releasing Taft's delegates to Dewey, "a great Republican [who] . . . will be a great Republican President."

Facing the convention that evening, Dewey gave an address that foreshadowed the oratorical style he was to follow in the fall: rotund profundities which no one would question (nor, most likely, ever think about saying); no mention whatsoever of Democrats or Truman; no outline of the programs he would pursue if elected. Dewey's main theme was unity. "The unity we seek is more than material. It is more than a matter of things and measures. It is most of all spiritual. Our problem is not outside ourselves. Our problem is within ourselves. . . . Spiritually, we have yet to find the means to put together the world's broken pieces, to bind up its wounds, to make a good society. . . ." And so it went on, in the vein of a man who had won the presidency, not simply the nomination. Later that night Dewey completed the ticket by picking

Governor Warren as his running mate.* The Republicans were ready for November.

---

* In doing so, Dewey completed perhaps the crassest political double-cross of the decade. Several days earlier the Dewey brain trust (minus the Governor) had talked with Representative Charles Halleck, heading the Indiana delegation, sorely needed for continued momentum. J. Russel Sprague, the New York national committeeman, was blunt. "Charlie, do you believe that if we promise something we can deliver?" Yes, said Halleck. "Well," said Sprague, "you look to us like *the* vice-presidential nominee." All the Deweyites asked was that he deliver the Indiana delegation. Halleck did. Then Dewey said flatly, "Halleck won't do." Halleck heard the decision with bitter disbelief. "I can work for you and talk for you, but I can't run with you," he exclaimed to Dewey, who sat impassively. Later Leonard Hall, another New York politician, said to Dewey, "I don't know how I can face Charlie Halleck again." "Oh," Dewey replied, "I don't see that you did anything."

24

HST: The
Unwanted Man

FOR TRUMAN, nomination required hurdling a convention-
eve attempt to revive the Ike candidacy, under auspices of a
weird mélange of Dixiecrats, disillusioned New Dealers, and big city
bosses, united only by the common belief that disastrous defeat awaited
the President should he run again. Over the July 4 weekend James
Roosevelt, chairman of the California delegation, and eighteen prominent party leaders sent telegrams to each of the 1,592 convention delegates inviting them to caucus in Philadelphia on July 10, two days
before the formal opening, to select "the ablest and strongest man
available," that is, General Eisenhower. The signers included Mayor
Hubert Humphrey of Minneapolis; Chester Bowles, the former OPA
chief; city bosses Jacob Arvey of Chicago and Mayor William O'Dwyer
of New York; and a squad of southern governors: Ben Laney of Arkansas, Beauford Jester of Texas, William J. Tuck of Virginia, and J. Strom
Thurmond of South Carolina. Mayor Frank Hague of Jersey City announced he was ready to deliver New Jersey's thirty-six votes; the *New
York Times,* in a survey of southern states, found more than 200 votes
awaiting the general; strong Ike sentiment existed in California, Illinois,
New York, and elsewhere. The *Times'* James Hagerty concluded that
Truman "is facing a hard and possibly losing fight for the nomination."

Once again, however, Eisenhower raised a restraining hand: "I will
not, at this time, identify myself with any political party, and could not
accept nomination for any public office or participate in any partisan political contest." Supporters parsed the statement, declared they detected
signs of equivocation when comparing it with earlier disclaimers, and
pressed onward. Americans for Democratic Action members ringed
Eisenhower's home on the Columbia University campus with signs,
"Ike, You're A-1 with Us, Be 1-A in the Draft," and "Ike, You Favor

the Draft, We Favor It for You." John Bailey, the Democratic leader in Connecticut (and later Democratic national chairman in the Kennedy–Johnson years), noted Eisenhower didn't go so far as to say he would not serve if elected: nominate the general without his consent and run a campaign without his participation, Bailey suggested; Ike would never refuse the presidency under those terms. Senator Claude Pepper of Florida would convert the Democratic Party into a "national movement" and run Ike as a nonpartisan candidate. But such was not to be. On July 9 Eisenhower sent another telegram, this one even more emphatic, and intended to close off any semantic loopholes: "No matter under what terms, conditions or premises a proposal might be couched, I would refuse to accept the nomination." (One person who didn't heed the statement was an ex-GI named Marty Snyder, who identified himself as Ike's old mess sergeant. Snyder sat hopefully in a bright red jeep outside the Bellevue-Stratford all week, tormenting delegates with loud-speaker appeals for the general.)

The Truman foes still would not desist. Leon Henderson, national chairman of ADA, tried to swing the Ike support to Supreme Court Justice William O. Douglas,* who refused. "I never was a-runnin', I ain't a-runnin' now, and I ain't goin' tuh," Douglas said from his Pacific Northwest retreat. Senator Pepper announced he was running—and admitted he had only six and a half votes, from his native Florida. Even ADA was ready to call off the rebellion at this point. "We have already had two dark horses shot from under us," said Henderson. "Why the hell should we get up and ride on a red roan?"

The Democrats finally convened on July 12 in an atmosphere of political and physical misery. The City of Philadelphia had spent $250,000 refurbishing Convention Hall for the two conventions, none of which went for air-conditioning; the temperature at the speaker's rostrum opening day was ninety-three degrees. Describing Senator Alben Barkley, the keynote speaker, one journalist wrote, "Perspiration ran down his nose and dripped from his chin, and his elegant Palm Beach suit looked more and more like a wet towel." The hotel and street bunting, put up for the Republicans, was left in place for an intervening convention of Elks; faded and stained, it flapped listlessly. The Democrats put a huge papier-mâché donkey on the marquee of the Bellevue-

---

* After the Ike and Douglas booms collapsed, Truman tried to placate the liberals by offering Douglas the vice-presidency. He did so reluctantly. During convention week Truman wrote of Douglas: "He belongs to that crowd of Tommy Corcoran, Harold Ickes, Claude Pepper crackpots whose word is worth less than Jimmy Roosevelt's. I hope he has a more honorable political outlook. No professional liberal is intellectually honest. That's a real indictment—but true as the Ten Commandments." After Douglas refused the vice-presidential nomination, Truman was "inclined to give some credence to Tommy Corcoran's crack to Burt Wheeler [former Democratic senator from Wyoming] that Douglas had said he could 'not be a No. 2 man to a No. 2 man.' "

Stratford, a toothy Missouri mule with ears that waved back and forth, fire in his nostrils (provided by electric-light bulbs), and periodic puffs of smoke. Fittingly, even the donkey had trouble. In the careful words of the Washington *Post,* "The smoke that he now belches out of his nostrils in angry bursts was at first mistakenly inclined to emerge from the other end of the animal. Sweating mechanics got this repaired in a hurry." In midweek a thunderstorm shorted out the donkey altogether, leaving him standing stiff and still. The party's troubles were visible— and audible—at every hand. Wallace supporters circled the hotels in a truck carrying a merry-go-round on which Democratic donkeys and Republican elephants spun under a sign reading, "The Same Old Merry-Go-Round." A pennant on top said, "Wall Street." The girl with the microphone repeated again and again: Wallace's third-party convention would open in Philadelphia on July 23. Convention Hall, in turn, was ringed by black activists protesting segregation in the armed forces.

The abortive Ike boom, symptomatic as it was of the glum autumn facing the Democrats and of the inevitability of Truman's nomination, cut the spirit from the convention. "There is no enthusiasm, no jubilation, no confidence," wrote John C. O'Brian of the Philadelphia *Inquirer;* "rather, a 'what else can we do?' air of resignation." The Associated Press told of the Democrats who phoned room service for bourbon and scotch, only to find supplies exhausted. "Well," one of them said, "send up a bottle of embalming fluid. If we're going to hold a wake, we might as well do it right." "What is so strange about it all is that the heirs of Jefferson and Jackson . . . seem to have given up the fight even before it has started—and this in a year of roaring prosperity," marveled Edward Folliard of the Washington *Post.* "It is not merely defeatism; it is a creepy, funereal mood that baffles all who are veterans at these conclaves. Perhaps it should be called the 'cry-baby convention.'" Even Senator Alben Barkley's keynote address lacked the usual claim of victory: "We shall not follow the example so egotistically set by our opponents from this rostrum three short weeks ago, by announcing the result of the contest four months in advance." Raymond P. Brandt of the St. Louis *Post-Dispatch* thought it significant that corporate lobbyists stayed away (apart from those pushing an end to federal control of tidelands oil). During the GOP convention "the hotel lobbies and conference rooms were infested with the representatives of the oil, steel, real estate, railroad, and public utility groups that wanted to be in with the Republican crowd they thought would take over Washington in January."

Conservative and liberal columnists alike urged Truman to step aside even as the convention opened. The New York *Herald Tribune*'s Walter Lippmann, in a series of columns, berated Truman for even running. "The weakness of Truman is that he tends to repel Democrats, driving some to Wallace, some to the Republicans, some to stay at home, and that he does not attract the independents," he wrote. Lippmann felt that "stubborn pride" alone caused him to demand the nomination from an unwilling party; he suggested that the Democrats accept the fact they were going to lose, and nominate a congressional leader such as Barkley, who would be the party's voice until 1952. "This nomination would be a frank and honest acceptance of the realities of the political situation—that the Democrats are not out to win the presidency but to survive as the national party of opposition, to be critical, vigilant, but good-humored about the return of the Republicans and the rise of Dewey." Harold Ickes, vitriolic from the left, wrote, "Dictators have forced themselves upon reluctant peoples in other countries, but the U.S. has been free of any attempt similar to that being made by the little Caesar in the White House. He does not ask the Democratic leadership whether they want him; he orders them to accept him. . . . The political pygmies who surround the President and who could all be blown out by one sure breath, such as candles on a birthday cake, do their obeisances before an abridged version of a President who is too vain for his own good." Ickes repeated an earlier challenge that Truman conduct a secret poll of the Democratic National Committee, congressmen, and state governors on whether they wanted him, and abide by the results.

Truman, of course, intended to do no such thing. With the convention under his control, he sat in Washington and awaited his nomination, his only worries the platform and the selection of a running mate.

The platform plank on civil rights proved the major problem. Since his civil rights message in February Truman had resisted intense Dixiecrat pressures to backtrack, even when his inner circle warned that the South was sure to bolt if denied a face-saving sop. Publicly, Truman held fast. Privately, however, his lieutenants directing the convention made several conciliatory moves toward the South. First, the Truman-controlled credentials committee voted to seat the Mississippi delegation even though it was pledged to walk out if a strong civil rights plank was adopted. Barkley, presiding, refused liberal demands for a roll-call vote when the issue reached the floor, cut off the microphones, and announced Mississippi seated by voice vote. Next, the platform committee approved a civil rights plank (written in the White House) that repeated the generalities of the 1944 platform, rather than calling for passage of the legislative package Truman had sent Congress in February. The key sentences "committed" the party to continue "its efforts" that racial and religious minorities have the right to live, work, and vote, and the "full and equal protection of the law, on a basis of equality with all citizens *as guaranteed by the Constitution.*" Without naming any specific items, it called on Congress "to exert its full authority *to the limits of its constitutional powers* to assure and protect these rights."

The emphasized sections caused the trouble, for they are the sort of legal ambiguities long utilized by southern legislators; by Dixie interpretation, states' rights overrode federal authority in such fields as voting and education. Americans for Democratic Action, meanwhile, worked for more emphatic language, its plank calling on Congress to "support our President" in working for equal rights to vote, to work, to security, and to service in the armed forces.

The moderate plank prevailed in committee, so ADA mobilized a floor fight under Minneapolis Mayor Humphrey, who was running for the Senate against incumbent Joseph Ball, and Andrew J. Biemiller, former Socialist congressman from Wisconsin. Truman loyalists warned off the thirty-seven-year-old Humphrey, saying that fighting the President on the sensitive issue could permanently blight his standing in the party. Senator Scott Lucas of Illinois angrily called Humphrey a "pip-squeak." Many of his close friends echoed the advice that Humphrey should not take issue with Truman. Orville Freeman, one of his state's delegates,* argued with him until five o'clock on the morning of the vote. Freeman quoted him as saying, finally, "If there is one thing I believe in in this crazy business, it's civil rights. Regardless of what happens, we're going to do it. Now get the hell out of here and let me write a speech and get some sleep."

Humphrey came to Convention Hall expecting to lose, but as he sat on the platform, awaiting his turn to speak, Ed Flynn, the taciturn Democratic boss of the Bronx, beckoned him over. Flynn read Humphrey's minority report and told him, "Young man, that's just what this party needs." He sent runners to the floor for three other big-city bosses: Jacob Arvey of Chicago, David Lawrence of Pennsylvania, and Frank Hague of New Jersey, all of whom said they would support "the kids."

Nervous and perspiring, but his confidence buoyed by the last-minute support of the party's heavy guns, Humphrey spoke for less than ten minutes, yet he electrified the convention as no Democrat had done since William Jennings Bryan's famed "Cross of Gold" speech in 1896. Radio made him a national figure overnight, a rising saint of American liberals. Humphrey expressed "respect and admiration" for Southerners who disagreed with him on civil rights. Then Humphrey got tough. Speaking through bursts of applause, he built to a climax:

> There are those who say to you—we are rushing this issue of civil rights. I say we are a hundred and seventy-two years late.
> There are those who say—this issue of civil rights is an infringement on states' rights.

* In 1976 Biemiller is the AFL-CIO's chief lobbyist in Washington; Freeman, later governor of Minnesota, served the Kennedy and Johnson administrations as secretary of agriculture.

The time has arrived for the Democratic Party to get out of the shadow of states' rights and walk forthrightly into the bright sunshine of human rights.

Rebutting, Southerners urged adoption of the moderate plank to "preserve party unity." They were, in turn, conciliatory and belligerent, with Alabama and Mississippi making plain their intention to bolt if the liberal version passed. As Dixie amendments were voted down, one by one, Alabama chairman Handy Ellis demanded recognition so he could announce his delegation was walking out. Speaker Sam Rayburn, presiding, looked right at Ellis and ignored his shouts. Then the floor microphones went dead. Furious, Ellis turned to fellow delegate Eugene (Bull) Connor, the Birmingham public safety director.

"Raise some hell, Bull," he said.

Connor did. Sweaty, in shirt sleeves with buttons undone, his necktie off, Connor grabbed the Alabama placard, hopped on the seat of his chair, wigwagged furiously, and bellowed time and again, "Mr. Chairman! Mr. Chairman! Mr. Chairman!" The proceedings droned on, Rayburn looked the other way, and Connor got even madder, "hollering like the devil's own loudspeaker," in the words of Baltimore *Sun* reporter Lee McCardell. Connor, yelling all the while, was fumbling with the dead microphone when Rayburn announced the liberal plank had passed, 651½ to 582½.* "Damn thing won't work—they cut it off!— Mr. Chairman!" Connor yelled. Rayburn banged the gavel and announced adjournment. "Bull looked like he was about to bust," McCardell wrote. "His eyes popped out. The mighty vocal cords swelled up, blue and scarlet, in his open shirt collar. 'Well, I be damned,' he bellowed in the greatest blast yet, and disappeared under a mob of converging newsreel and camera men."

That evening, Alabama finally got a live microphone, and Chairman Ellis calmly announced the delegates had been selected on a pledge not to enact a civil rights plank, and not to nominate Truman. They were pledged to walk out, they held no malice for fellow Democrats, but they were leaving. Dins of boos and cheers echoed in the hall as Rayburn futilely banged for order, and most of the Alabama and Mississippi delegates trooped out in noisy procession. At that moment the Dixiecrat revolt was formal.

---

* The opposing votes came from an odd mixture of Southerners and Truman loyalists (Truman's Missouri, national chairman McGrath's Rhode Island, Barkley's Kentucky, and Sam Rayburn's Texas). Truman, in his memoirs, played loose with the truth, taking credit for the plank he actually opposed. Referring to the legislative proposals in his February civil rights message he wrote, "I incorporated these recommendations into the 1948 platform of the Democratic Party. . . . I was perfectly willing to risk defeat in 1948 by sticking to the civil rights plank in my platform." In fact, the combination of liberals and big-city bosses forced Truman to accept the Humphrey–Biemiller plank.

A Dixie rearguard remained to offer token opposition to Truman's nomination, but he won on the first ballot, with 947½ votes to 263 for Senator Richard Russell of Georgia. Next the delegates formalized Truman's choice of Senator Barkley for vice-president. Not until nearly two o'clock in the morning did the balloting end. But Truman brought the wilted convention back to life with a roar when he declaimed, in high, strident tones, "Senator Barkley and I will win this election and make the Republicans like it—don't you forget it. We will do that because they are wrong and we are right." Ad-libbing in short, punchy sentences, Truman flailed the Republicans as the party of "special privilege" and scorned its record in the Congress. Then Truman threw out a surprise challenge. On July 26 he intended to call Congress back in special session. "Now, my friends, if there is any reality behind that Republican platform, we ought to get some action from a short session of the Eightieth Congress. They can do this job in fifteen days, if they want to do it. They will still have time to go out and run for office."

Truman's fighting speech enabled the Democrats to end on a high note. "For that night, at least," Helen Fuller wrote in the *New Republic,* "Harry Truman was a real leader."

In the bright light of morning, however, the old problems remained all too visible. Railroad heir Cornelius Vanderbilt, serving as assistant secretary of the air force, had been expected to become campaign treasurer, and write a check for whatever deficit remained. He refused, and so did two other name moneymen. Not until late July did Washington lawyer Louis Johnson agree to take the post. "The Democratic donkey was still on its feet when it moved out of Philadelphia this week," W. H. Lawrence wrote in the *New York Times.* "However, all the medicaments in Doctor Truman's bag seemed likely only to alleviate, not cure, the basic organic ills afflicting the beast. Political buzzards were circling in the sky, waiting for the animal to drop by the roadside." John O'Donnell of the New York *Daily News* felt the Democrats "managed to make more people mad" than at any convention since 1860, when slavery splintered the party into factions supporting three separate presidential candidates. Only a handful of political journalists were not prepared to bury Truman, notably the astute Frank R. Kent of the Baltimore *Sun,* who found it "worth repeating that one of the most potent influences in American politics is sympathy. Certainly there is a disposition among the voters . . . to feel for the 'underdog'—provided he is a decent sort of underdog making as good a fight as he can without squeaks or squawls." Kent concluded:

The spectacle of a battered little man with his back to the wall, scorning the idea of surrender, refusing to let adversity overwhelm him, fighting with everything there is in him, is a moving one.

Perhaps it will not be moving enough to transform defeat into victory. But it is not one whose appeal should be lightly dismissed.

The immediate postconvention script went as anticipated. Angry Dixiecrats gathered in Birmingham for a loosely run convention which offered "credentials" to anyone interested in the southern cause; many "delegates" were curious college students and tourists. Prominent Southerners such as Senator Harry Byrd of Virginia, Governor Herman Talmadge of Georgia, and boss Ed Crump of Tennessee stayed away. The keynoter, former Governor Frank M. Dixon of Alabama, cursed Truman's civil rights program as a plot "to reduce us to the status of a mongrel, inferior race, mixed in blood, our Anglo-Saxon heritage a mockery." The Dixiecrats waved Confederate flags and chanted support of Governor Thurmond for President and Governor Fielding Wright of Mississippi for vice-president. The platform called for "the segregation of the races and the racial integrity of each race."

The Dixiecrats' racism, their failure to entice southern titans such as Byrd out of the Democratic Party, their embracing of super bigot Gerald L. K. Smith (who said in a convention speech that "there are not enough troops in the army to force the southern people to admit the Negroes into our theaters, our swimming pools, and homes") caused most editorialists to sniff disdainfully and look away. H. L. Mencken, no admirer of the South ("a sewer of imbecility . . . [that] has supported every major aberration, whether political or social, that has afflicted the country . . ."), cautioned that the Dixiecrats deserved more sober attention; that they represented a serious, and rational, regional movement. The more intelligent Southerners, Mencken wrote, "are painfully aware of what went on in the Seventies, and they are naturally fearful of a repetition, with Northerner jobholders, most of them dishonest and nearly all of them jackasses, substituted for the carpetbaggers of the first canto. They believe that they have some civil rights, too. . . . I must confess that I sympathize with them, despite my life-long devotion to exposing their deficiencies."

"Gideon's Army"—that is, the Wallace people—occupied Convention Hall a few days after the Democrats left Philadelphia, with Communist-liners swiftly taking control of the new Progressive Party. The platform committee, steered by Lee Pressman (who was fired as general counsel of the CIO for leftism, and who was to admit later he had been a Communist), repudiated the Marshall Plan in language closely tracking that passed by the Communist Party at its convention earlier in the summer. Representative Vito Marcantonio of Harlem ran the rules committee and wrote the keynote speech, delivered by Charles Howard, a Des Moines attorney who had been suspended by his bar association for misuse of funds. Wallace, who spent much of his time meditating in his hotel room, professed not to see any evidence of Communists at the convention. "I would say that the Communists are the closest things to the early Christian martyrs," he said at a press conference. "But I can truthfully say that the Communists have not come to me, as such. I saw one hurriedly in a railroad station not long ago. I don't recall his name. I told him I believed in progressive capitalism. That stopped him and I haven't heard from the Communists since." Other Progressive planks were in the tradition of American radicalism—nationalization of monopolistic industries, a $1 per hour minimum wage, strong civil rights and liberties laws, regional development authorities modeled after TVA, and enlarged social security programs.

Unfortunately, Wallace spent much of convention week—and the following months as well—bogged down in questions as to whether he had the intellectual stability demanded of a President. The questions harked back to an early episode in Wallace's New Deal days. While secretary of agriculture, Wallace had developed an interest in a Russian mystic named Nicholas Konstantinovich Roerich, guru of a religious sect devoted to theosophy: a charlatan to serious theologians, though venerated by such devout followers as the composer Igor Stravinsky. In 1934 Wallace hired Roerich as a government consultant and sent him on a mission to Outer Mongolia, supposedly to search for a strain of drought-resistant grass (although some of Wallace's colleagues, years later, were to intimate that Roerich's true mission was to look for evidence signaling an imminent second coming of Christ). Wallace and Roerich eventually fell out, and Wallace dismissed him from the government job.

These events transpired without public notice. Then, during the 1940 campaign, when Wallace was running for vice-president, Republican politicians turned up a sheaf of letters that Wallace supposedly wrote to Roerich. Stated charitably, the letters sounded downright peculiar. Chockful of mystical mumbo-jumbo, they addressed Roerich as "Dear Guru," and contained mysterious code references to prominent persons. President Roosevelt was "The Flaming One"; Winston Churchill, "The Roaring Lion"; Cordell Hull, "The Sour One." There was an account of how the writer cured himself of headaches at formal Senate dinners by passing a Tibetan amulet over his forehead, and a long discourse on the mystic potency of certain symbols, including the Christian cross, the Mongolian lama's reliquary, and the Indian medicine man's charms. A typical sentence read:

I have been thinking of you holding the casket—the sacred, most precious casket. And I have thought of the new country going forth, to meet the seven stars under the sign of the three stars. And I have thought of the admonition, "Await the stones."

Aware that the letters could destroy Wallace politically if authenticated, wary Republicans gave them to handwriting experts for study. Several said Wallace wrote them; others declared them to be forgeries. When a journalist intermediary bearded Wallace with the documents he laughed and denied authorship. After much agonizing the Republicans decided not to risk using them. The national chairman, Joe Martin, said privately that to do so would be "mud slinging." The Republicans' hesitancy also reflected doubts as to the authorship of the letters; if Wallace could indeed prove them to be forgeries, the episode could backfire on the GOP. The 1940 campaign passed without publication of the letters.

In 1948, however, the letters came to columnist Westbrook Pegler, who happily put them into print with the question as to whether Wallace still regarded Roerich "as a god or supernatural master of mankind as many of your associates in the cult did." Pegler quoted hundreds of words from the letters, and explicitly accepted them as authentic. But he wrote without the benefit of comment from Wallace, so the columnist sought to raise his questions directly at Wallace's first press conference in Philadelphia. Wallace flushed and his voice tightened at the sight of Pegler. "I do not answer questions put to me by Westbrook Pegler," he said. Whereupon Martin Hayden of the Detroit *News* asked the same question: Did Wallace write the letters? "I don't answer questions put to me by a stooge of Westbrook Pegler, either," Wallace replied. H. L. Mencken arose and asked, "Mr. Wallace, do you consider me a stooge of Westbrook Pegler?" Wallace didn't. Mencken continued: "Then I should like to hear, did you or did you not write the Guru letters?" Wallace would not answer. Other reporters persisted, with Wallace shouting back that he would answer in his own way and his own time. "Why not answer now?" asked Mencken. "We are all here." "Stooges of the world, unite!" a reporter yelled. Eventually the reporters got up and left, leaving Wallace alone with writers for Communist publications.

Thus was the Wallace campaign sidetracked onto the twin rails of communism and personal idiosyncrasy, to the dismay of uncountable thousands of Americans who wanted a true alternative to Truman. Even Wallace's press critics did not deny the sincerity of the young people who rode buses to Philadelphia, ate from brown paper bags and at Automats, and lived in tents in Fairmount Park and cheap hotel rooms, all to follow a man who spoke of lofty ideals. James Rowe, in his strategy memorandum for President Truman, acknowledged Wallace's appeal "particularly . . .[to] the young voters who are attracted by the idealism that he—and he alone—is talking and who regard war as the one evil greater than any other." Dramatic gimmicks helped Wallace. Though the preliminaries of Wallace rallies were conventional politics, when the time came for his appearance the houselights dimmed and the music became low and solemn, emphasizing a suspense-building roll of drums. A single spotlight would seek out the door, and there would be Wallace, suddenly aglow. "The spotlight ceremony of lighting the path of the savior as when he treads his way among the multitude," in the words of Gardner Jackson. As he strode down the aisle the drums came to a frenzied crescendo. Jack Redding, publicist for the Democratic National Committee, compared these theatrics with Nazi rallies for Hitler; and he encouraged newsmen to write about "phony and un-American showmanship." But the people present seemed moved.

All in all, however, the press dismissed the Progressive Party convention as curiosa, a political freak show bringing together "poets, female chiropractors, a gentleman who sought the abolition of interest on mortgages, an artist of renown who wanted art socialized, Negro Elks, members of Greek letter fraternities." The writer, of course, was H. L. Mencken, covering the last political convention of his newspaper career,* happily witnessing nightly confirmation of his dictum that politics is a carnival of buncombe, and that conventions are "political, homilectical, and patrio-inspirational orgies . . . as fascinating as a revival or a hanging." Mencken did not desire to entrust the republic to Gideon's Army:

> *On Wallace* he wrote: "If . . . he suddenly sprouts wings and begins flapping about the hall, no one will be surprised."
> *On running mate Glen Taylor:* "Soak a radio clown for ten days and ten nights in the rectified juices of all the cow-state Messiahs ever heard of, and you will have him to the life."
> *On the convention itself:* "The percentage of downright half-wits has been definitely lower than in, say, the Democratic convention of 1924."

The Progressives did not find Mencken amusing, and the Maryland delegation offered a resolution condemning his acid reporting. Nothing came of it. Nor, for that matter, did anything come of the Wallace candidacy.

---

* In April Mencken, then sixty-seven, said he intended to cover the conventions. "I'm an old reporter and I can't stand by. I'll probably end up coming home on a shutter. Oh, well, it's a heroic death." Three months after the Progressives' convention he suffered a stroke and could not write, read, or speak until his death in 1956.

25

The Loneliest Campaign

NOTHING CAME OF THE special session of Congress either. The Republicans recognized the Truman move as a political mousetrap, denounced it with suitably harsh oratory ("the last hysterical gasp of an expiring administration," said Senator Vandenberg), and ignored Truman's program. The only legislation passed during the truncated two-week session was a $65-million loan for construction of the United Nations headquarters building and two minor bills on powers of the Federal Reserve Bank. A few days after the session ended Truman picked up a reporter's phraseology and agreed it had been a "do-nothing" Congress. Harry Truman was ready for the fall.

"It looks like another four years of slavery," Harry Truman wrote his sister on September 2, when everyone in the country was predicting his defeat. "I'd be much better off personally if we lose the election but I fear the country would go to hell and I have to try to prevent that." For Truman, "trying" meant a campaign modeled on his western trip of the spring—to get on a special train, stop it wherever people would gather to listen, stage formal rallies in larger cities, and aim at groups with the votes to keep him in office: big-city blacks and union members, farmers, Southerners so ingrained with the Democratic tradition that they would not vote Dixiecrat, and progressive-minded Westerners.

Harry Truman worked. Six times during the next two months his special train rolled out of Washington's Union Station—sixteen cars plus the *Ferdinand Magellan,* a lavish armored suite the railroads had given to President Roosevelt—a combined traveling White House, political headquarters, and press room, with sleeping accommodations of varied comfort for the President, his wife and daughter Margaret, twenty-odd staff members, and three to four dozen reporters. Truman worked. He spent all or part of forty-four days* away from Washington

* Truman is overly modest in his memoirs, claiming only thirty-five days. But his "one-day" Labor Day trip to Michigan and north Ohio began late Sunday afternoon and did not end until he returned to Washington around dawn on Tuesday.

roaming America like a frenzied Flying Dutchman. Often he made his first rear-platform talk before six o'clock in the morning. Even after night rallies the train would stop at a smaller town down the line, and he would come out (frequently in a bathrobe) and talk to people waiting in the darkness. On one day alone he gave sixteen speeches. By Truman's computation he traveled 31,700 miles—all by rail, a statistic that evokes empathic fatigue in anyone ever exposed to American trains—and made 356 speeches, averaging ten per full working day. The Labor Day swing. A long trip to the West Coast and back between September 17 and October 2, through eighteen states. A fast four days in Delaware, Pennsylvania, New Jersey, and New York. To the Midwest again on October 9–16, to capitalize on rising farmer rage. A one-day dart to Pittsburgh and its heavy labor vote on October 23, a big-city tour (Chicago, Cleveland, Boston, New York, and St. Louis) that began October 24 and continued to Election Eve.

The morning Truman left on his long western trip Senator Barkley, his running mate, came down to wish the President well. "Go out there and mow 'em down," Barkley said.

"I'll mow 'em down, Alben," Truman replied, "and I'll give 'em hell."

Reporters heard the exchange and used it in their stories, and by the time Truman reached the West Coast people in the crowds were shouting, "Give 'em hell, Harry."

Truman smiled, and Truman obliged. Truman ran against business as hard as he did against the Republicans—"Wall Street reactionaries," "gluttons of privilege," "the economic tapeworm of big business." Truman constantly denounced his adversaries in the Eightieth Congress. In Fresno, California, he told an audience that "you have got a terrible congressman here in this district. . . . He is one of the worst obstructionists in the Congress. He has done everything he possibly could to cut the throats of the farmer and the laboring man. If you send him back, that will be your fault if you get your throats cut." Speaking to a vast throng at the National Plowing Contest, in Dexter, an Iowa hamlet forty miles from Des Moines, he charged that "this Republican Congress has already stuck a pitchfork in the farmer's back." He called the Republicans "tools of the most reactionary elements," silent and cunning men "who would skim the cream from our natural resources to satisfy their own greed . . . who would tear our country apart . . . bloodsuckers with offices in Wall Street, princes of privilege, plunderers."

Schematically, the whistle-stop* appearances followed a set pattern. Truman said a few kind words about the local candidate for Congress or the Senate, and worked in a reference to the town or the state, and

* After ridiculing Taft for using the term, the Democrats adopted it as their very own.

made some nice remarks about the Democratic Party. Then he would kick around the Republicans, telling how messed up the country was before 1933, how the New Deal made Americans prosperous again, and how the "do-nothing" Congress and the Republican/big business alliance were trying to undo Democratic accomplishments. Then Truman would call "Mrs. Truman" out to say hello to the crowd and smile, and then "my daughter Margaret" (or "Miss Margaret," before southern crowds). Truman often ended on a surprisingly personal note. In Provo, Utah, for instance, he called on the crowd to exercise "that God-given right . . . to go to the polls on the second of November and cast your ballot for the Democratic ticket—and then I can stay in the White House another four years." In Ogden, Utah, he asked the voters' help to "keep me from suffering from a housing shortage on January 20, 1949."

Most of the platform speeches were extemporaneous, Truman using only notes jotted on cards to insure that he didn't mix up local references (no one wanted a repeat of the Idaho airport embarrassment of the spring) and to remind himself of issues he wanted to stress. John E. Barriere, a young staff member of the Democratic National Committee, put together a background book containing a one-page memorandum on each town Truman was to visit, his basic source being Works Progress Administration guidebooks from the District of Columbia public library. Truman scanned the book each evening for tidbits to drop into his speeches. For the more formal folks, recalls Truman speech writer James L. Sundquist,* "we wrote in what was called jocularly 'Missouri English,' designed to incorporate his extemporaneous style into the manuscripts. What that meant really was short sentences and short words where we didn't have to have big ones. His secretary, Rose Conway, devised a way of typing these so that they almost read themselves. Her trick was to put the natural pauses always at the ends of lines, so Mr. Truman could read one line to the end, pause, then read the next line to the end and then pause, and so on. The pauses came out naturally."

Sundquist once was writing frantically on the train when he sensed someone standing behind him. He turned. It was the President. "He smiled at me benignly and said, 'Don't get up, I just wondered what stuff you're planning to put in the President's mouth tomorrow.' I assumed he wanted to know and started out to tell him, but he shushed me and said, 'That's all right, young man, I'm sure that what you're coming up with is going to be a lot better than anything I could suggest.' And he strode jauntily away." Another Truman writer, Charles S. Murphy, felt that Truman's best speeches were the ones delivered off-the-cuff, although the President always insisted on having an outline before him as a reminder, or as a fallback in case he "just decided to read." Several

* A Brookings Institution fellow in the 1970's.

times, according to Murphy, transcriptions of the impromptu speeches were adapted for use as future texts, "a sort of in-voice editing process by the President."

In faded transcript form, Truman's speeches are choppy, sometimes disjointed, even corny. He rambled. He often sounded like a garrulous old uncle telling what he had done on his travels. He could be so effusively praiseful of wherever he happened to be ("the great state of Iowa" or "the great city of Chicago") that only the most dedicated booster could take him seriously. Yet it worked. In blunt, sassy, Anglo-Saxon speech Truman told the American people what he thought they should hear, and apparently they agreed with him. They heard, for instance, from the rear of his train beginning at five minutes before midnight on September 6, the last speech of his Labor Day trip. Truman had already given five set speeches that day, and waved and paraded in the presence of upward of half a million people. No "give 'em hell" speech can be called archetypical, but the Toledo oration, delivered the very first day of Truman's formal campaign, is a classic of the genre:

It is a very great pleasure to me to have the opportunity to stop here in Toledo tonight. I didn't expect to see that half the population of northwest Ohio would be here. It looks as if it is. In every city I have been to in Michigan today, I thought I would see half the population of the State of Michigan, yet it never stopped growing in population all day long. I don't know what these people will say about the crowds. You know, when I made the trip across the country, on an inspection tour to see how things were going—a nonpolitical trip, if you remember—one of these great magazines took a picture of a soldier facing a vacant lot and said that was the kind of reception I got. There never was a crowd much less than this at any place where I stopped.

I think people want to see what the President of the United States looks like, and I think they are vitally interested in finding out what the President of the United States stands for.

You see, it is most difficult to get the facts and the truth to the public under present conditions, and I am not saying that in a critical manner at all. I am merely telling you what are facts.

Now, before this campaign is over, I expect to visit every whistle stop in the United States. You remember, on that western trip, I went to Omaha, Cheyenne, Wyoming, various towns in Idaho, Butte, Montana, and Spokane, Seattle, San Francisco, and Los Angeles, and Albuquerque, New Mexico, and stopped in Columbus, Ohio, too on the way back. And the senior senator from Ohio said I was stopping at every whistle stop.

Well, Toledo is right in that same class. If all the rest of these cities are whistle stops, so is Toledo. And I don't think we class Toledo as a whistle stop, what I know about it.

In fact, I wonder just how the Toledo ball team stands? [Laughter] You see, Kansas City is a suburb of my home town at home, and Kansas City is in that same American Association, too.

I have appeared before six Labor Day audiences in Michigan today, and I am glad to finish up today in this great State of Ohio. This may be the end of Labor Day, but I am just beginning the most important labor of my life. I am going to make the most important campaign that this country has witnessed since the Lincoln-Douglas debates. I intend to cover the length and breadth of this land, and take to the American people a message of the utmost significance. I am going to tell you the facts.

The message concerns November second. The question before you people is whether you want to go forward with the Democratic Party, or whether you want to go back to the past, go back to the horse-and-buggy days of the Republican Party.

I stopped in Pontiac today, and you know Pontiac—a city where they used to make buggies and wagons. They have been making automobiles up there for about forty years. And I asked them if they wanted to make that sort of a change, if they would like to go back to making buggies and wagons in an automobile and airplane age. They didn't want to do that.

These are not just words. Let me give you two vital illustrations of what I mean.

Most of you people are working people, just as I have been all my life. I have had to work for everything I ever received. I never went into a political campaign in my life that I didn't have a fight to obtain what I thought was real and for the benefit of the people.

I have only been defeated once and that was for township committeeman in Washington Township in Missouri, back in 1912.

It does you a lot of good, sometimes, to understand just exactly what defeat means. In 1940 I had the bitterest campaign for reelection to the United States Senate that I think any man had in the history of this country. I had every newspaper in the state against me, the governor of the state and his organization was against me, and at eleven o'clock that night, all the radio broadcasters and the papers said that I was defeated by eleven thousand votes. I went to bed, got up next morning and found out I had been nominated, which was equivalent to election by more than eight thousand votes. I know just exactly what it feels like to be defeated for major office.

I don't want to have that experience this time. I would like to go to bed elected on November second.

The Republican Eightieth Congress has struck you people deadly blows in each of the major fields. You are interested in security, good wages, and in the prices you are paying to support your family.

The Taft–Hartley Act was passed by the Republican Congress for the sole purpose of making it harder for organized labor to bargain for better wages and better living conditions. It was done with that express purpose in view. I vetoed that bill, and I set out in that veto just exactly what I thought the final result would be. And labor is just now beginning to feel the effects of that Taft–Hartley law.

Big business was getting worried about the strength of the organization of the people who work with their hands. The Republican Congress, that Eightieth "do-nothing" Republican Congress, joined with big business at the top to weaken organized labor.

What is more, it is just the opening gun in the Republican plan to go back to the days when big business held the upper hand and forced the working man to take only what they wanted to give him. I can remember that day very well—remember the Colorado Fuel and Iron strike, the Homestead strike, and a lot of other things. I was a little bit of a boy when the Pullman strike took place. These were historical events, and some of these people would like to turn the clock back just that far.

And if you people on November second do not exercise your God-given duty to go to the polls and vote, if you do not get yourselves on the books where registration is required, and you get what you got in 1946 by staying at home, you will deserve everything you get; and I won't be a bit sorry, for I will be at home enjoying myself.

I think you will find that the vast majority of labor is going to vote for me. Labor knows which side its bread is buttered on. Labor knows what is best for the country. And the best thing for the country is to go forward with the Democratic administration, and not go backward into the past with a lot of backward-looking Republicans who want to get control of this country for their own selfish interests.

Look at the tax bill they passed—the rich man's tax bill, the tax bill that helped the rich and hurt the poor.

Then what did they do about prices? You know, my sympathies are all with the mothers and wives of this country who have to buy books for the children, clothes at outrageous prices. I don't see how they do it. I just wonder how they do it. But they do manage it, some way.

I tried to get that Eightieth Republican "do-nothing" Congress to give you some help on that, and I couldn't get it done. In fact, they went to Philadelphia, after they had adjourned, after I had sent them message after message on what I thought would be the best thing for the welfare of the country. They went to Philadelphia and passed a platform in which they said they wanted to do all the things that I had been asking them to do for a year and a half!

I never was as exasperated in my life as when I read that cynical platform. I called them back into session, and they didn't do one single thing.

You know what they said? They said that platform was made to run on, and if they took any action on it at all, they would take it in 1949, after they had elected a Republican President.

Now, do you believe that? Do you believe that?

You know very well that they will do just exactly what they did with the Eightieth "do-nothing" Congress. They will turn the clock off a few hours further back than it is now.

Remember, then, November second is the day. I want to say to you that if everybody who is entitled to cast his ballot on that day casts it, I will be entirely satisfied with the result, for I can assure you that we will have a Congress that will work in the interests of the people, and I will still be in the White House.

But wasn't Harry Truman wasting his time? On September 9, a week before his long western trip, pollster Elmo Roper wrote that "Thomas E. Dewey is almost as good as elected" and that the chance of an upset could be largely disregarded. Roper continued, "That being so, I can think of nothing duller or more intellectually barren than acting like a sports announcer who feels he must pretend he is witnessing a neck-and-neck race that will end up in a photo finish or a dramatic upset for the favorite—and then finally have to announce that the horse which was eight lengths ahead at the turns is still eight lengths ahead." Roper gave Dewey 44.2 percent, Truman 31.4 percent, Wallace 3.6 percent, Thurmond 4.4 percent. Roper intended to continue polling but "to stop reporting . . . [results] unless something really interesting happens. My silence on this point can be construed as an indication that Mr. Dewey is still so clearly ahead that we might just as well get ready to listen to his inaugural. . . ."

Fletcher Knebel spent much of the campaign on the Truman train as a reporter for the Cowles newspapers. As was true with most reporters, he accepted the polls about Dewey's "insurmountable lead" as gospel, a feeling reflected in his daily stories. Yet there were times when Knebel wondered whether he should stop listening to politicians and public opinion experts and trust his reportorial instincts.

"Early on in the campaign we visited this plowing contest in Iowa, a hell of a big mob of people spread out as far as you could see in a hot, indescribably dusty field. The reporters stuck fairly close to the campaign train, for Truman didn't speak from a text, and we wanted to be sure to get what he said. One man who did go out into the crowd was a Scripps-Howard reporter and he came back shaking his head. These were Midwestern farm people, the bankers and grain dealers as well as the farmers, and you weren't supposed to find more than one Democrat every hundred miles or so. But the Scripps-Howard man talked to a hundred people, and he found a solid majority behind Truman. We decided it was a statistical fluke, that he had wandered into a chance gathering of Democrats, and we laughed; I don't think he even wrote the story himself.

"Later on, the Truman train stopped at dawn one morning in a pretty little hamlet in the mountains of Kentucky or Tennessee, I forget which. The early morning haze was still hanging over the hills, and the sun wasn't up. But gathered around the railroad tracks, as far as you could see in any direction, was this incredible crowd of people—men holding kids up on their shoulders so they could see, little boys climbing trees and roofs, old grandpappies and men in overalls. Of course, we experts in the press car talked about the crowd, and we finally decided it didn't mean a damned thing. 'Anybody will come out to see a man who is President of the United States, just to say they've seen one in the flesh. But that doesn't mean they'd vote for Harry Truman.' He was going to lose. We believed it, because we wrote it every day."

So, too, did Tom Dewey, who didn't even begin campaigning until September 19, only six weeks before Election Day, and who behaved more as an incumbent than a challenger for a party that had been out of office for sixteen years. In 1944 Dewey had run as a prosecutor and he had failed. This time he shelved his combative instincts and ran as a statesman, calling for national unity, never mentioning Truman, and avoiding issues that could cause trouble in his own party. The polls and the Wallace/Dixiecrat defections gave Dewey an ample supply of confidence, one most visible among the political mechanics on his campaign train. As key strategist Elliott Bell was to recall later, "Dewey was in and the thing to do was not stir up too much controversy and run the risk of losing votes." The plan was to ignore Truman's attacks: answering him would only direct more attention to him and conceivably create underdog sympathy for him. By remaining silent on specific issues, Dewey would not alarm independent voters into thinking he would reverse some of the enormously popular reforms of the New Deal.

As did Truman, Dewey traveled by train, but the differences were profound. For one thing, he made only about half as many rear-platform appearances, fifty to Truman's 140 on their first transcontinental trips. Dewey started his campaign day in gentlemanly leisure at 10 A.M.; Truman was up and speaking at the crack of dawn. Not even a crowd could arouse Dewey from his slumbers ahead of time. When the Dewey campaign trail rolled into Terre Haute, Indiana, at 7 A.M., a crowd was on hand in the expectation he would appear and say a few words, as Truman had done earlier. Many of the farmers had driven for miles to see Dewey. When word was passed he would not come out, they pelted his car with tomatoes and cabbage heads. Dewey tended to be forced and awkward when speaking from the rear of a train. Although he was a superb public speaker on formal occasions, a master of pace and modulation, in the impromptu talks he seemed determined to say as little as possible, and even that in high-sounding platitudes festooned with clichés. Dewey promised miracles but no specific reforms or plans. For instance, he told one audience that "national income is now at such high levels that we can build up our military strength, reduce our debt, and still see to it that taxes are less of a burden on our people and less of a throttle to their enterprise." But Dewey did not confide any mathematical formulae revealing how this was to be accomplished.

After ten days of campaigning, Dewey's use of banalities was so profuse that the Democratic National Committee generously undertook the expense of distributing a collection of them to the nation's political reporters. A sampling:

> "Our streams abound with fish."
> "The miners in our country are vital to our welfare."
> "Everybody that rides in a car or bus uses gasoline and oil."
> "You and I have a great responsibility to our children and towards generations to come."
> "We are troubled by high prices and we must end the maladjustments which caused them."
> "We need more homes for our people."
> "I firmly believe that depressions need not be inevitable."
> "The Communists have a long range scheme."
> "You know that your future is still ahead of you."
> "Ours is a magnificent land. Every part of it."

In a single "major" speech to a New York audience in October, Dewey put together a string of sentences with the ring of a commencement address, or a careful sermon to an ecumenical congregation.

> "Nature has a wonderful way of keeping her house in order. Her forces interplay and depend upon each other."
> "Obviously we cannot turn [our ranges] back to the buffalo and the antelope."

"Through all history water has meant life or death in the lives of nations. . . . The garden of Eden is believed to have flourished where the entire Babylonian civilization once thrived."

"Peace is a blessing that we all share."

"America will stand before the world as one country and one people believing deeply in the cause of peace."

Near the end of the speech Dewey reached a climax of sorts with these sentences: "By a simple rediscovery of our devotion to human rights and the protection of others from the abuse of those rights, we can draw a line through every conflict and draw it straight and true. It can be drawn so that both civil liberty and social responsibility complement and fortify each other. . . . The highest purpose to which we could dedicate ourselves is to rediscover the everlasting variety among us."

Columnist Frank Kingdon of the New York *Post* called such utterances "Dr. Dewey's soothing syrup . . . just too, too sweet." Edward Folliard of the Washington *Post* said that Dewey's "talks at the whistle stops are amazingly alike; so much so that the reporters hardly ever bother to make notes on them." In comparison, they kept pencils poised when Truman spoke, for he was almost sure to say something nastily new about the Eightieth Congress or make a sarcastic reference to "Dewey's lullaby talk about mother and home." Dewey's campaign people admitted the platform talks were dull but did not think it made any difference: people did not come to a rail yard to hear a candidate, but to see him. The only "joke" Dewey told—and he used it repeatedly, from coast to coast—went this way:

"Your welcome here [wherever he happened to be] is as cordial as the one I got up in Salem, Oregon. As I came down the steps of the state capitol, an elderly gentleman elbowed his way through the crowd, stuck out his hand and said, 'Hello, Dewey, I'm glad to see you. I've been waiting to vote for Dewey for President ever since you licked them Spaniards in Manila Bay.' "

Only once did Dewey show any emotion in public, and that moment was remembered. On October 12 he had just begun to speak from the rear platform in a small Illinois town, when the train suddenly moved backward into the crowd a few feet. No one was injured, and most persons took the mishap good-naturedly. But Dewey's temper flared. "That's the first lunatic I've had for an engineer," he said. "He probably ought to be shot at sunrise but I guess we can let him off because no one was hurt." The Democrats, of course, promptly capitalized upon the incident, Truman saying with a dead pan that "I was highly pleased when I found out . . . that the train crew on this train are all Democrats. . . . We have had wonderful train crews all around the country and they've been just as kind to us as they could possibly be." In a radio broadcast a few days later (financed by a union) Truman said, "We have been hearing about engineers again recently from the Republican candidate. He objects to having engineers back up. He doesn't mention, however, that under the 'Great Engineer' [a popular nickname of former President Herbert Hoover] we backed up into the worse depression in our history."

Dewey yawned and stayed on the high road, so sure of victory that his staff was uncertain whether he should "waste" the last week of the campaign with another trip. "Their real concern was over what Harry Truman might do between now and January to upset the country, particularly in its foreign relations," pontificated *Time*. "The responsibilities of power already weighed on them so heavily that a newsman inquired blandly, 'How long is Dewey going to tolerate Truman's interference in the government?' " Dewey campaigned "with an air of duty." In background sessions with newsmen he began giving sketches of people he would appoint to the cabinet. *Time* worried about Truman strategist Clark Clifford. "It was hard to understand how handsome Mr. Clifford could look so happy and knowing in view of the political debacle" facing Truman. To Truman's attacks, Dewey would say only he was "campaigning against Joe Stalin, not Harry S. Truman."

The Moss department store chain in California ran a "panty poll," Time *reported, grasping for omens as the campaign peaked. Pairs embroidered "Dewey-Warren" outsold "Truman-Barkley" eight-to-five.*

The fringe campaigns, meanwhile, spluttered along ineffectively, of interest mainly as curiosities certain to siphon Democratic votes from Truman. Truman kept out of the South altogether and made no attempts, overt or otherwise, to win segregationist support. In fact, he did just the opposite. Advance men invited blacks to a Truman rally at the Dallas baseball park, the first integrated political rally ever held there. When reporters traveling with Truman didn't mention the fact in their stories, the Truman staff quietly advised them of the historic first.

Candidates Thurmond and Wright whooped around the South, denouncing Truman as a "carpetbagger" and worse, but adding nothing of substance to the denunciations of the spring. More ominously for Truman, electors and officials in several states moved to sabotage his chances of receiving Democratic votes even if they were cast for him. All the "Democratic" electors in Alabama, Mississippi, and South Carolina announced in October they would not vote for Truman, regardless of how the state balloting went; so did four of eight electors in Florida, and three of ten in Tennessee. In Louisiana, the Democratic State Committee briefly succeeded in substituting the names of Thurmond-Wright on the ballot for Truman-Barkley; Governor Earl Long eventually called the legislature into special session to reverse the decision. The Republicans mischievously cheered on the Dixiecrats when possible. In Indiana, for instance, Republican State Chairman Clark Springer admitted (when caught) that petitions used by the Dixiecrats to get on the Indiana ballot were prepared in a GOP office.

In his campaign Thurmond pridefully pointed to his relatively progressive record on race relations as governor of South Carolina, and tried to keep racism out of his campaign. He even objected to the term "Dixiecrat,"* saying his crusade was national, not regional, and intended to protect "all Americans" from the intrusion of "Washington bureaucratic rule." The Truman civil rights program, he argued, would set precedents having nothing to do with race. The anti-poll tax provision would invade the rights of states to elect their own officials. The antilynching provision would usurp the police powers of states ("Would you want an antigangster law in New York? Didn't you resent prohibition laws?"). The Fair Employment Practices Commission would empower an "army of federal police . . . to spy into the affairs of each business enterprise, to control the hiring and firing of employees." Thurmond did advocate continued segregation as the natural choice of most Americans: "otherwise there would be no Harlem in New York City, no Chinatown in San Francisco, no South Side in Chicago." To demonstrate that states' rights was not a southern issue alone, Thurmond got on the ballot in North Dakota.

But political realities doomed the Thurmond-Wright ticket. The leading hotheads of the spring—Governors Laney of Arkansas, Jester of Texas, Cherry of North Carolina, and Millard Caldwell of Florida— came back to the Democratic Party. Only a handful of low-rung congressmen spoke for the Dixiecrats even in the four states (Alabama, Mississippi, South Carolina, and Louisiana) of hard-core support. The only name politicians working actively for Thurmond were Ed Crump of Memphis and former governors Albert B. (Happy) Chandler of Kentucky and Dan Moody of Texas. Most Democratic senators and congressmen, although certain of reelection themselves regardless of what happened to Truman, feared loss of seniority if they bolted the party. And soberer heads noted that the Republican platform went even further on civil rights than had Truman, and that Dewey had established a strong FEPC in New York.

Most southern newspapers denounced the Dixiecrat venture as futile. Douglas Southall Freeman, the noted southern historian, disassociated the Confederacy from the Dixiecrats. Writing in the Richmond *News Leader,* Virginia's most influential newspaper, he said, "When those

---

* No creation of the rebels. Bill Weisner, a telegraph editor for the Charlotte *News,* coined the word when he could not make the formal "States Rights Democrats" fit into a headline.

enemies of the Truman regime unfurled the Confederate flag and held up an engraving of General Lee as if it had been an ikon, they went too far. General Lee was not in Birmingham in spirit. He had no part before or after the War of 1861–65 in sowing the seeds of hate between races and sections." The Birmingham *Age-Herald* thought the Dixiecrat movement "a wild dream." The Raleigh *News Observer* considered the Dixiecrats and the Wallaceites equally daft: "Dixie and the Internationale make strange music when played together." And other Southerners felt the cause was being used as a stalking horse by interests with no legitimate concern for their states. The Anniston (Alabama) *Star* felt the states' rights doctrine was sound when first proposed but "in later days it became the refuge of predatory interests. It might be said . . . that a states' righter today is a pleader for a special interest who craves the power that is being exercised by a progressive opponent." The St. Louis *Post-Dispatch,* agreeing, said control of tidelands oil, not civil rights, was bringing conservative money to the Dixicrats. "The Texas oil men want the Democrats defeated because they think—in fact, they have been promised—that the Republicans will turn this up-to-thirty-billion-dollar plum over to them for the picking," the *Post-Dispatch* said. "As far as the oil men are concerned, there is something to be said in their defense. All they are out for is a killing." Thurmond steadfastly denied any alliance with the oil men and noted the Dixiecrat platform was silent on the tidelands. But by late autumn it was obvious the Dixiecrats were dead except in the four states where citizens were not able to vote for Truman even if they wished to do so.

So, too, was Henry Wallace, who suddenly found himself running without the labor and liberal support crucial to his campaign. Crowds melted. In the winter Wallace had drawn 8,000 supporters to a rally in Milwaukee; when he returned as a candidate, only 2,000 turned out. Wallace sensed his popular support was slipping away, but he acted as if he was accomplishing a "mission of conscience." As the New York *Post* observed, "His demeanor is exuberant. He speaks of Mr. Truman's impending defeat in joyous tones, as if convinced the political punishment neatly fits the crime." In Wilkes-Barre, Pennsylvania, Wallace gloated of Truman, "He is going to take the worst licking any Democrat has ever taken."

The detractors, however, could not fault Wallace's physical and political courage. In September he embarked upon a trip to the South intended to challenge racist mores: he would insist upon holding unsegregated meetings, and he would challenge Jim Crow in his own roost. Bull Connor of Birmingham warned, "I ain't going to allow darkies and white people to segregate together," and the Jackson *Daily News* declared, "To say that he would be as welcome as a common prostitute at a family reunion or a skunk under the church at prayer meeting night is putting it too mildly." Oddly, however, Wallace had minute pockets of support scattered throughout the South—labor organizers in the textile mills who had received no support from the moss-bound AFL; the few civil rights activists; blacks who risked their lives to participate in the political process; students whose social consciences had been stirred by wartime experiences.

In the latter category was Paul Moorhead,* a young navy veteran doing graduate work at the University of North Carolina in Chapel Hill. Two events stirred Moorhead from his apolitical conservatism: hearing an officer being called to task for criticizing President Roosevelt ("I was brought up on the idea that you could say anything you damn well pleased!") and Truman's "holding many navy people on active duty in late 1945 and early 1946 to break a strike by the National Maritime Union." Moorhead began reading In Fact, *Gilbert Seldes' muckraking journal, and he was pleased when Henry Wallace opposed U.S. aid to Greece and Turkey—"a rather rotten deal, an attempt to shore up British imperialism." Moorhead was in a minority. "I'm afraid the more typical reaction was that of my roommate at Southwestern University [in Memphis, Tennessee, where Moorhead had done his undergraduate work]. He said, 'Did you see what that son of a bitch did to Truman?'*

"When I arrived at Chapel Hill, Wallace had spoken there the day before, and there was general support for him against the Cold War. So some of us started a Wallace for President Club. The nucleus was persons active in the Southern Conference on Human Welfare, which had fought racism in the South for years. We ran the gamut from Trotskyites to Social Democrats and pacifists to people fighting universal military training. I was impressed because this was the first campus experience I had where you dealt with issues, rather than the esoteric campus crap. A mixed bag: Junius Scales, chairman of the Communist Party in North Carolina, was a member.

"When the Wallace campaign got underway we worked to get him on the ballot. The Democratic organization used all the tricks in the book. For instance, although the constitution said petition signers had to be of 'voting age,' the attorney general ruled they must have voted in the last election, and be registered. When blacks and low-income whites came in to register, the local registrars would say, 'We're closed for lunch.' Or they'd tell them, 'If you sign the Wallace petition, you must withdraw your Democratic registration'—which wasn't true. In canvassing we'd start in the black areas and work out, because we were likely to be run out by the police; you wanted to get the sure ones first. People would slam doors in your face. One man said, 'I'm going to get my gun.' A black shook his head and refused to sign. Later, when I had crossed the

* Now a professor at the University of Pennsylvania in Philadelphia.

street, he looked out at me and beckoned me over, and left the door open. I went on in and he gave me a registration list: he was the handkerchief head Democratic chairman, but he wanted to make it easier for us, because we could only take signatures from registered voters. We managed to get the 20,000 signatures.

"In the summer Wallace announced a trip through the South to speak on racism. His objective was to hold integrated luncheons and social events all through the South. This made my hair stand on end—I thought he was out of his mind.

"Wallace's plan for Carolina was to have an evening speech in Durham, then to spend the next day in a motorcade clear down the state, hitting Chapel Hill, Hillsboro, Winston-Salem, Greensboro, Charlotte, and Asheville. I thought his body would be flown north from Charlotte.

"The harassment started the first day, in Durham. The Progressive Party had rented a hall for the speech. A few hours before he arrived, they returned our check and said we could not use it because of the integrated dinner. After some negotiations, we got a federal national guard armory. My roommate, Mike Pochna, was sent to put up a sign on the first hall telling people where to go. Up went the sign, and the police arrested him for defacing public property, and down went the sign.

"I went to the armory around six o'clock, two hours early, to see how things were going. What a mob! Many Duke University students had come over to jeer at Wallace, and there were fifty or sixty people you'd have to call goons—rough rednecks with some professionally printed signs: 'Wall-ass,' 'Nigger-lover,' 'Communist,' that sort of stuff. They were marching four abreast along the sidewalk outside the armory.

"We immediately organized an 'anti-goon goon squad' to protect Mr. Wallace. My assignment was to sit on the front of the stage and take a chair and knock the hell out of anybody who tried to rush Wallace. It was wild: the parking lot was filled with government vehicles, and the national guardsmen had rifles. I asked an officer what he would do in case of trouble. 'Our orders are to protect government property,' he said, staring straight ahead. That's all I could get out of him.

"As it got close to eight o'clock the goons took over the front door. Here would come the local blacks, dressed in their Sunday clothes, walking the gauntlet, looking neither to the left nor the right, with people yelling at them and spitting at them.

"I was standing there with the goons, when a naïve kid from our group ran out and said, 'Come on, you and I are supposed to get a cab and go after Mr. Wallace.' I wanted to go through the pavement. As he started away the goons followed, yelling and cursing. I followed. If he was going to be killed, I'd be with him.

"Six of them jumped us, swinging and kicking. One drew a knife and caught my friend around the midriff and pulled it across his stomach.

The police, who were standing about thirty feet away watching, decided then to do something. They pulled off the goon and told him to get the hell out of there, and they arrested my friend. I ran away, back into the armory. (The friend wasn't hurt badly; he was released the next day.)

"We finally managed to get a black cab driver who sped over to the place where Wallace was staying, and we slipped him in through a rear door. As he began to speak the goons rushed the front door. Our people held the doors, the goons battered at them. At one point the goons broke through, and you could see this mass of heads and placards and flying fists. A national guardsman held his rifle sidewise and put it against the whole crowd and shoved everyone back out the door.

"Wallace's speech, actually, wasn't that rousing or inflammatory. He talked about the Cold War and racism and the things that, say, Mc-Govern talked about in 1972—the need for peace and justice. We got him out of the armory without any further incident.

"The next day, when we started the motorcade, the atmosphere was quite different. The press made a lot of outcry about the treatment of Wallace—after all, he had been a vice-president of the United States—and the police were out in force to escort us.

"There were still some rough times. At Winston-Salem, the main event was a fried chicken picnic in a park, two to three acres cordoned off by a hundred or more policemen. Someone from the Progressive Party had to identify you before you could pass in. The blacks and the others sat on the grass with Wallace and ate fried chicken—a nervous way to have a picnic.

"At the other places Wallace would go to the courthouse and speak, usually to a mostly black audience. Our anti-goon goon squad would mix with the crowd and watch for guns and knives. The worst thing that happened to Wallace was being hit with eggs but he just laughed about it.

"At Charlotte the shocking thing was that the crowd was middle-class business people—all full of hate—who lined the downtown streets to curse Wallace. All of it was racial. You were a Communist for proposing that 'the niggers eat with us,' and everyone knew that all Communists were spies for Russia.

"Our psychology for getting out of town after a rally was a lot like what happens when two dogs square away for a fight: if a dog breaks off, he must walk away with confidence, as if he is in control, otherwise he'll be jumped. So we would get into the cars simultaneously so that no one would be left behind and be picked off. One time a white business-man came running up to the car shouting and waving as we drove away and reached in, as if he was grabbing for Wallace. I rolled up the window and caught his hand. We were picking up speed, I had to roll the window down again, in a hurry, or we would have dragged him out

of town. He put a note in another car: 'I just want to shake your hand. I think Wallace is great.' But, you never knew.

"By Asheville, Aubrey Williams, Jr., and I were in charge of the sound truck. We had to go in first, like the first wave on the beach in an invasion. There'd be hostile crowds yelling and spitting as we drove through the small towns. I told Aubrey, 'Let's pretend we're with the sound company, not Wallace.' For self-protection we took off the Wallace buttons when we'd go into a town.

"Our squad had barely returned to Chapel Hill when the Wallace people recalled us for duty; to fly to Atlanta and meet Wallace, and accompany him for another week. They asked if we were married, and we said no. The implication was that then it would be OK if we were killed.

"By this time the various towns were practically running a contest to make sure Wallace wouldn't be killed within their boundaries. It was damned uncomfortable. Our protectors were state troopers wearing Dixiecrat buttons who couldn't care less about our survival.

"The cross-South caravan had twenty or so cars. Pete Seeger was with us, and some of the songs had an extra meaning: 'We'll all understand better bye and bye,' and 'So long, it's been good to know ya.' The idea was to have a rally, then an integrated function, a luncheon or a dinner, and then to get out alive.

"In Birmingham, Bull Connor, the police chief, had police everywhere with sirens wailing. He must have brought Wallace through town at ninety miles an hour, to a rally held on the outskirts. So technically Birmingham was pure: the 'nigger-rally' wasn't held within its limits.

"In Little Rock, Harry Ashmore, the editor, agreed to interview Wallace on the radio. Now I grew up in Little Rock, knew the town, so I knew where to go. We raced across town, sirens and red lights, and the caravan parked on the side of the street across from the station. The idea was to get him out of the car and into the building as rapidly as possible. So everyone jumped out of the car—Wallace in the middle—and ran into the first door they saw, which happened to be a bank. Here you are—a dozen or so excited men bursting into the lobby, followed closely by a mob of police—the bank guard staring, the tellers falling out of their cages with fright. I said, 'No, no, it's across the street.' 'Oh,' they said, and we turned and ran out the door to the right building.

"In Memphis, after the speech, we left in the police chief's limousine—Wallace in the back, our anti-goon goon squad on jump seats—and right away the car stuck in a muddy place. Twenty to thirty young men were running alongside the car, banging on it and yelling. When it stopped they began rocking it from side to side and pulling at the door. A city detective in the car pulled his gun and said, 'I hope that SOB does open the door, I'll kill him.' I was glad when the wheels finally caught

and we drove away. Later that night a reporter asked Wallace this profound question: How many eggs had hit him during the tour? Wallace looked at him and said, 'Do you want me to break it down by leghorns and pullets?'

"In Knoxville, the Ku Klux Klan announced a rally the night Wallace was to speak at a black church. We didn't know what they had in mind. By this time we had switched to a chartered bus. The driver, a white Southerner, didn't care much for us. We came over a hill and saw thousands of people, many of them with torches, spread out as far as you could see. My heart stopped. These couldn't be supporters; Wallace didn't have that many friends in the whole damned world. It had to be a lynch mob. Sweat actually jumped out on the driver's face, for he knew he was going to be hanged, too.

"But it turned out to be all blacks. The community had blocked off its neighborhood and dared any whites to come in and interrupt Wallace. Not even the police were around. It was a triumphant finish—the church overflowing, and people outside on the lawn listening.

"I didn't digest any food for six days of the trip. I spent the entire time with a lump in my stomach. That is the reason I couldn't go when the civil rights movement started again in the fifties. I took my risk earlier—someone else could do it, not me. I was with a bunch of Yankees who didn't know the South. I hated to be with them, because they scared me. They'd go into a restaurant and talk loudly about how rotten the South was—you don't get converts that way.

"Did Wallace really expect to win? He wasn't that naïve. He mainly ran meetings like a preacher espousing the Christian ethic, saying 'you don't treat people that way.' It was a message, not a campaign. But the 'campaign' was a vehicle that enabled him to call a spade a spade. I was very disappointed that he only got around a million votes. We had expected three or four million. Giving Harry Truman a black eye was the main political goal. The cleverness of the cold warriors was to put the Communist label on anyone who disagreed with them. In a way Wallace played into their hands. He would not repudiate Communist support; he felt he could use them for short-term advantage without getting into bed with them. Many of us saw no reason to worry about 'Communist' support—after all, we were outnumbered, and we were working for achievable ends in such areas as racism. That we lost the election wasn't all that important. We did teach the Democratic Party that the left couldn't be taken for granted."

Despite its surface appearance of an in-progress disaster, the Truman campaign was buoyed by two circumstances either overlooked or discounted by the press and the professional politicians: farm discontent and feverish labor activity on behalf of the President. James Rowe's strategy memo a year earlier had called both blocs vital to Truman's chances, and said they could be won, if prosperity did not keep them from voting.

The farm situation was so grotesquely complex—the inevitable nature of agricultural economic questions—as to be beyond the comprehension of most city dwellers, if not the farmers themselves. In simplified fashion, the problem developed as follows. Under the price support system begun in the New Deal, the government guaranteed farmers a certain "support price" for such basic crops as wheat and corn. If the market price proved higher, the farmer sold his produce through commercial channels without government involvement. But if prices dipped below the support level, he could obtain a loan based upon the guaranteed level, and pledge his crops as collateral. If the market recovered, he sold the crop and repaid the loan; otherwise, he simply forfeited the collateral and kept the money. To be eligible for the loan, however, the farmer had to store his crop in a facility approved by the government—either a commercial bin or one operated by the Commodity Credit Corporation. And here arose the problem. At the end of the war CCC began liquidating its storage space, dropping from 292 million bushels capacity to less than 50 million. When CCC's charter came up for renewal in the middle of 1948, the economy-minded House Banking and Currency Committee, noting that CCC was selling, not buying, space, prohibited it from acquiring any new storage bins. When the bill reached the floor, two farm-state Republicans objected briefly about the provision but it passed; not a Democratic voice was heard in opposition. Nor did any of the major farm organizations say anything.

Then came the deluge. The 1948 corn crop of 3,681,000,000 bushels was the largest in history, 55 percent above 1947. The wheat crop was the second largest in history. The bumper crops quickly filled all available commercial facilities; when the farmers turned to CCC, the traditional overflow storage, no space was available. Concurrently, prices plunged. Corn went from $2.46 a bushel in January to $1.78 in mid-September; wheat, from $2.81 to $1.97. Hence farmers faced the paradox of financial disaster during a bonanza year. And, incredibly, as tempers rose in the farm belt, the Republicans, through Harold Stassen, attacked the Truman Administration for shoring *up* farm prices through big grain purchases for export. "I believe that it was a deliberate step to stop the downward trend of food prices that followed the report of large crops," Stassen said. He said food prices would have dropped within a few months had not the Administration made the purchases.

The Stassen statement conceivably pleased a handful of housewives—assuming any had the acumen to link up the farm support program with supermarket prices—but it was a disaster in the farm states. Democrats distributed texts of the speech by the scores of thousands, and Truman came down hard on the issue in an Iowa speech:

When the Republicans rewrote the charter of the Commodity Credit Corporation this year, there were certain lobbyists in Washington representing the speculative grain trade. These big-business lobbyists and speculators persuaded the Congress not to provide storage bins for the farmer: . . .

They don't want the farmer to be prosperous. . . . What they have taken away from you thus far will only be an appetizer for the economic tapeworm of big business.

Republican spokesmen are not complaining that my Administration is trying to keep food prices up. They have given themselves away. They are ready to let the bottom drop out of farm prices.

The support price has nothing to do with the price the common man is paying for his bread. When wheat prices went up the price of bread went up steadily, from ten cents to fourteen cents. Now wheat prices have fallen a dollar a bushel but the price of bread has not come down. There you have the policy of reactionary big business. Pay as little as you can to the farmer and charge the consumer all he can bear.

Grain prices continued to drop as the weeks passed, and Truman blamed the Republicans in speech after speech. "Farmers all over the country are being forced to drop their grain as distress grain or let it rot on the ground because the CCC no longer has the power to provide emergency storage space for a bumper crop," he said. "While you sat here on a powder keg waiting for prices to blow up they lit the fuse." Dewey strategists tried to warn their candidate of the volatility of the issue. The evidence suggests he did not listen. Not until three weeks before election did the Dewey command create a farm division; it accomplished nothing. A "Dewey-Warren Farm Committee" was treated to a breakfast with Dewey, but he asked no questions. Dewey brushed aside entreaties that he make a strong statement, and as late as October 25 Tom O'Neill of the Baltimore *Sun* reported only that a "trace of concern" existed on the campaign train that the farm issue could help Truman.

Similarly, Dewey did not bestir himself for labor votes (indeed, his "labor committee" was headed by Barak Mattingly, a utilities and corporate lawyer from St. Louis). Dewey's "shot at sunrise" crack about the railroad engineer was evidence to many people that he had little regard for human beings—and especially laboring people; Dewey indeed had the imperiousness of a man born to command. Besides the erratic John L. Lewis of the mine workers, the only major union leader to back Dewey was Alvanley Johnston of the Brotherhood of Locomotive Engineers, whose 80,000 members were one-third the number of *active* campaign workers fielded by the CIO's Political Action Committee (PAC).

Labor's main contribution to Truman was manpower. The PAC,

under director Jack Kroll, concentrated first on voter registration, then on getting unionists and friends to the polls. PAC used as an incentive Taft–Hartley and other Republican congressional actions. The PAC hired fleets of cars to carry people to Truman's whistle stops, and it helped produce crowds for his rallies. Techniques varied. In Cleveland, whose Indians were in a hot chase for the American League pennant, the unions had the baseball announcers urge "Go out and register" in their between-innings chatter. In one Ohio town construction unions would not let a man work until he produced a voter registration card. PAC literature (an estimated 10 million pieces) depicted Truman dressed informally, with his homey smile, and Dewey in a tuxedo, looking rather stern.

For the American Federation of Labor, 1948 marked its first formal entry into a presidential election. The AFL long had followed founder Samuel Gompers' dictum, "Reward our friends and punish our enemies" —but not very energetically. The AFL periodically created a "non-partisan campaign committee" to work for Democratic presidential candidates, but its executive council never endorsed even such a labor friend as Franklin D. Roosevelt. The rival CIO, meanwhile, became so active beginning with the 1944 campaign that it acted as a de facto labor wing of the Democratic Party (so much so that when Truman was suggested as a running mate, Roosevelt replied, "Clear it with Sidney," meaning Sidney Hillman, the PAC chairman).

The Democratic debacle in the 1946 congressional elections, and labor's subsequent failure to find enough votes to sustain Truman's veto of the Taft–Hartley Act, brought the AFL into national politics with a roar. The AFL was scared. George Meany, the federation's number-two man, as secretary-treasurer, recalled meeting a Wall Street executive in a bar one evening after a speech. "My name must have rung a bell somewhere. He said, 'Oh, you are the labor guy.' 'Yes, that's me.' He said, 'Well, come the first of the year you fellows will be put in your place. There is going to be a very simple rule. The people that put the money into business in this country are going to make the rules.' " Under prodding from Meany, the AFL executive council created Labor's League for Political Education (LLPE), with a permanent staff and authority to raise money from affiliated unions. Joseph Keenan, a veteran of Chicago politics, signed on as director, and cajoled and goaded the big national unions to free manpower and money for Truman. In its literature and speeches LLPE stressed the Republican labor record. As did the PAC, the LLPE asked each AFL member to contribute a dollar for politics. Republicans raised a public alarm about a "$7 million labor boss slush fund," but in actuality LLPE got only a fraction of that amount: $360,000 from its 7,000,000 AFL members. PAC spent $513,000 nationally, its local affiliates another $500,000. Although the AFL executive council followed tradition and did not endorse Truman outright (its decision *not* to do so remained unpublicized, at Meany's suggestion), LLPE integrated itself into the Truman campaign, Keenan riding along on the train for many days, helping with labor crowds at the whistle stops.

Peculiarly, despite its feverish activity labor received little press attention during the campaign. There were several reasons. Labor did not wish to tie itself directly to a candidate it feared might lose; consequently, it did no flamboyant public campaigning for Truman, instead concentrating on the dull but essential work of voter registration and the like. Labor wanted to avoid becoming an oratorical whipping boy, as it had been in the 1944 campaign when Republicans used the "Clear it with Sidney" quotation to charge that labor "owned" the Democratic Party. So both PAC and LLPE let local organizations do the grass-roots work with as little visible national coordination as possible. Regardless of whether Truman won or lost, labor wanted a friendlier Congress, so much of the activity was for House and Senate candidates—work certain to stir votes for the head of the ticket as well. In many large cities where local Democratic bosses were cool to Truman, labor in effect created its own precinct organizations. The manpower involved was staggering: PAC alone claimed to have had a quarter of a million block workers active on Election Day.

Joseph Keenan began to realize by mid-October that the election would be closer than the "experts" predicted. "When the President went to Pittsburgh the crowds were so incredible that I just knew he was going to win. You don't get that sort of turnout, even in a Democratic city for a Democratic President, unless the tides are running very strongly." So, too, did the PAC's Jack Kroll, who made public predictions that Truman would win.

Few other persons in America would agree. The polls showed Dewey holding his strong lead. The Democrats showed signs of desperation. Truman, in a speech at Fresno, California, pointedly noted that he had volunteered for the army at age thirty-three and served overseas in combat. In doing so, he implicitly invited attention to the fact that Dewey spent the war years in Albany, while 16,000,000 other Americans served their country, and that he campaigned for the presidency in 1944 at the vigorous age of forty-two. Democratic National Chairman Howard McGrath added his bit of innuendo with a bland statement that Truman hated war because he had fought in a war. At a press conference, Mrs. India Edwards, head of the women's division of the Democratic National Committee, said with transparent relish that Truman had ordered the Democrats not to discuss Dewey's lack of military service or his draft status during the war. Why? "Innate decency," Mrs. Edwards said. "He didn't want to bring that up." Once raised, of course, the issue was discussed. Former Congressman Hamilton Fish, a Republican who disliked Dewey, called him a "chocolate soldier," and added, "Mr. Dewey did not serve. Alibis and excuses are of no avail now." The Republicans worried about whether organized veterans would make Dewey's lack of service an issue, and at one point prepared an elaborate chart showing that because of various changes in the selective service laws, Dewey at no time was subject to the draft. No outcry arose, and the chart was never released. The issue faded.

Dewey, in turn, passed up a chance to make a frontal attack on Truman for a serious foreign policy blunder in early October. Talks in Paris between the western powers and the Soviets over the Berlin blockade had broken down. A low-level staff adviser suggested that Truman break the impasse by sending Chief Justice Fred Vinson to Moscow to talk with Stalin. Truman liked the idea. He queried Secretary of State George C. Marshall in Paris, who objected. Truman decided to go ahead anyway, and asked the radio networks for time to make the announcement. Unwilling to give the President half an hour of free air time during a campaign without advance guarantees the talk would be nonpolitical, the networks forced the White House to reveal the subject in confidence. Before Truman went on the air, however, Marshall and the French and British objected that the Vinson mission would undercut the existing Allied policy toward Russia. Marshall pointedly reminded Truman the United States had agreed to hold no bilateral talks with the Russians until they lifted the blockade. Truman canceled the mission. Several days later news of the plan leaked out, and critics such as the New York Times and the Washington Post accused Truman of political grandstanding. The abortive affair seemed a case study of poor foreign policy planning, of disunity within the Administration, and of Truman's willingness to exploit foreign policy for political purposes.

Dewey, however, chose to remain on the high road of platitudes. In a public statement in which he appeared to lay claim to being spokesman for the entire nation, he said "the people of America" supported the work of the Paris delegation and that the "American people are in fact united in their foreign policy." In an off-the-record chat with reporters, however, Dewey sounded much different—so much so, in fact, that veteran correspondent Edwin A. Lahey of the Chicago Daily News called the event the moment "when God got off Dewey": "He deplored the visit, he said the Soviet Politburo was almost evenly divided, and that a shift of one or two votes could plunge the world into war. And he said, 'If Harry Truman would just keep his hands off things for another few weeks! Particularly if he will keep his hands off foreign policy, about which he knows considerably less than nothing!'

"Jesus, my eyes began to pop out. I was looking at Eddie [Folliard] of the [Washington] Post, who'd come up that same afternoon with me, and we couldn't believe our ears. Here was this man saying that the

President of the United States should keep his hands off foreign policy until this bum was elected, the world would be safe. "That's the night the angels switched. Somebody in heaven said, 'We gotta flatten this bum.' And that's what happened."

The fact of divine intervention, if indeed it existed, was not apparent to Lahey or other journalists at the time. During the last week of the campaign, *Newsweek* polled fifty top political writers; all gave victory to Dewey, with an average of 366 electoral votes, a flat hundred more than he needed. The *New York Times* predicted 345. *Life* captioned a full-page photograph of Dewey, "The next President travels by ferryboat over the broad waters of San Francisco Bay." Drew Pearson's column the day before the voting said a Truman victory was "impossible"; the day after the election his column began, "I surveyed the closely knit group around Tom Dewey who will take over the White House eighty-six days from now." The Alsop brothers, in a column published the same day, said, "The first postelection question is how the government can get through the next ten weeks." The insider pieces were seemingly endless. "Government will remain big, active, and expensive under President Thomas E. Dewey," the *Wall Street Journal* told its readers. *Changing Times,* published by the Kiplinger organization, proclaimed on its cover "What Dewey Will Do," and gave a full issue of predictions. "You've got to live with him for four years, possibly eight. He will influence your life, your thinking, your work, your business." A note on the last page suggested the special issue "will have historical value in the future. Perhaps you should put a copy away for your children or grandchildren."

The polls saw no chance of a Truman victory. The last published findings of the major organizations were as follows:

	Dewey	Truman	Wallace	Thurmond	Undecided and other
Roper	52.2	37.1	3.2	1.7	5.8
Gallup	49.5	44.5	4	2	—
Crossley	49.9	44.8	3.3	1.6	.4

But the size and enthusiasm of the Truman crowds nagged many persons, even among Dewey strategists: 50,000 in Dayton; 60,000 in Akron, many of whom stood two hours to await the train; 55,000 in Duluth, half the population of the town along a two-mile route; 15,000 in the auditorium at St. Paul, and another 6,000 outside; 200,000 in Miami. Dewey attracted 1,500 to the rail yards in Hammond, Indiana, Truman 20,000. In Chicago, Democratic chieftain Jacob Arvey turned out a crowd of half a million persons to line a motorcade route from the Blackstone Hotel to Chicago Stadium, where Truman spoke to 23,000 people. Six Medal of Honor winners rode in the parade, and one reporter noted "the route was lined by more policemen than Chicagoans could ever remember seeing at one time." Events started with a $50,000 fireworks display, then a twelve-foot heart was rolled onto the platform. Out hopped Lois Nettleton, Miss Chicago of 1948, who handed a flower to the laughing Truman as he began speaking.

Editorially, the vast majority of the nation's press supported Dewey— 65 percent of the dailies, with 78 percent of the circulation. Only 15 percent supported Truman; the rest were neutral. The *New York Times* and the Cleveland *Plain-Dealer,* which had opposed Dewey in 1944, now moved behind him. The St. Louis *Post-Dispatch,* in Truman's home state, said he did not have the "stature, the vision, the social and eco-nomic grasp, the sense of history required to lead the nation in a time of crisis." The Oregon *Journal* said that Truman, "in descending to his Missouri training in campaign vilification, has lost leadership of the nation." The Chicago *Tribune,* although it thought Dewey suspiciously liberal, decided he was the "least worst" of the candidates.

Working newsmen, conversely, worried about the sort of President Dewey would make. The cold efficiency of his staff, the lack of any human depth in Dewey, his ego and his unwillingness to discuss the issues raised by Truman, an overall shallowness of character and mind—should this man become President? Edwin Lahey, who traveled extensively with Dewey, said, "He made me vomit. I mean, he made me physically ill." Lahey's dislike for Dewey built during the campaign and peaked during a climactic rally at the old Madison Square Garden be-tween 49th and 50th Streets, the night before the election. "Suffering physically" from watching Dewey ("this little bug-eyed candidate with the ruby-red lips"), he wrote his story and left before the rally ended. As he walked away from the Garden toward Seventh Avenue, loud-speakers carried Dewey's voice to crowds outside. "I walked into the little chapel of St. Malachy's Church on Forty-ninth Street, just to make a visit to see if I could collect my senses. And I'll be goddamned, you know, he seemed to follow me down like a snake. I could hear the rally as I knelt before the Blessed Virgin's altar. Here some clown from Hollywood was making jokes about Truman, and I began to get real desperate. I left the chapel and walked upstairs, pretty close to panic by now. I had this sense of something following me . . . like being fol-lowed by an assassin you can't escape.

"As I stood on the curb wondering where the hell to turn, just like a man in a television panic show, there was a broad came by. She was dragging a guy with her. The guy didn't want to go to the meeting, but she was pulling him down toward the Garden, and as she passed me she said, 'Come on, kid, this is history.'

"It broke the spell, and I went over to the Roosevelt Hotel and went to bed."

The veteran political writer Thomas F. Reynolds, with Dewey in the final campaign days, was amazed at the candidate's arrogance, his refusal to make whistle-stop talks when his train passed through Ohio and Indiana, even though crowds could be easily assembled. "When Dewey's organization calculates an area is in the bag* it wastes neither action nor words. . . . After many years of campaigning this correspondent has never seen quite the counterpart of the spirit in the Dewey camp. In 1940, when fighting Wendell Willkie, Roosevelt was worried and alert. In 1944 . . . Roosevelt was outwardly confident, but inwardly a little doubtful and very tired." The only "competition" recognized on the Dewey train was the staff pool on the electoral vote.

Neale Roach, a veteran staff member of the Democratic National Committee,† managed the 1948 convention, and then went on to New York to run the national finance headquarters in the Biltmore Hotel. The New York newspapers wrote knowingly all fall about Truman's imminent defeat—information that did not jibe with reports Roach heard from people in the field, especially when the Truman crowds swelled to epic size late in the campaign.

"I had a nice deal in the Biltmore bar. Each evening, right before five o'clock, I'd find a comfortable stool and wait for the rush of tired executives who were hot for Dewey. Invariably the talk would get around to politics. I was the only one in the damned place who had anything nice to say about Truman. These executives were Dewey people, to a man, and they knew he was going to win because they read it in the New York Herald Tribune.

"I'd bait them a little bit, say how I thought Truman was a good man—that would turn up their tempers—and that he should win. 'Back your mouth with your money,' they'd say. I'd hem and haw and they'd get more eager. 'OK,' I'd say, 'I'll take your damned money.'

"We got the Biltmore manager to hold the money. In a couple of weeks I put down $4,000—money I didn't have—that Truman would win. I believed it."

* Dewey was to lose Ohio—and its 25 electoral votes—by a margin of 7,107 votes.
† In the 1970's a Washington lobbyist for the American Trucking Association.

26

A National Crow Feast

O N N O V E M B E R 2, Harry Truman voted in Independence, lunched with friends at a country club, then slipped away to a resort hotel at Excelsior Springs for a Turkish bath and relaxation. About 4:30 in the afternoon, hours before the polls closed, Herbert Brownell, Dewey's campaign manager, confidently announced that the record vote meant that Dewey had been overwhelmingly elected.

Truman had a light snack and went to bed in the early evening.

Dewey dined with family and friends in a New York hotel and began scratching out early vote totals on a pad. Downstairs, an early and confident crowd gathered, and the Dewey staff mimeographed hundreds of copies of the victory statement. It stressed national unity. Six secret service agents arrived to protect the new President.

The radio networks had hoped to announce the Dewey victory by 9 P.M., prime time in the East. They decided they had best wait. Truman was winning not only in the South (except the four Dixiecrat states) but was making a strong run in the Republican Midwest.

At 9:30 P.M. Herbert Brownell claimed 295 electoral votes, enough for victory. People began to filter into the Democratic headquarters in the Biltmore. People began to act a bit edgy in the Republican headquarters in the Roosevelt. Radio commentators could not find any Dewey officials to interview.

At 11 P.M. Truman led in Illinois and in the farm states of Iowa and Wisconsin. Although Truman carried New York City by half a million votes, Henry Wallace siphoned away enough support to threaten to throw the state to the Republicans. Brownell said a "pattern indicative of Republican victory is developing."

At midnight, Missouri time, Harry Truman rolled over and turned on the radio. Commentator H. V. Kaltenborn reported he was leading by 1,200,000 votes, but that he could not win: rural votes would turn the tide. Truman grunted and went back to sleep. In New York an elevator operator at the Roosevelt Hotel, the Dewey headquarters, cynically told a reporter, "The cops are spreading nets outside of the windows of the upper floors."

At 1:30 A.M. New York definitely went to Dewey, and Herbert Brownell said Dewey "will be the next President of the United States." In Independence, crowds gathered outside the Truman home, and Margaret went out in her best black dress and ballet slippers to fend off the reporters. "Daddy isn't here," she said.

At 4 A.M. James Rowley, head of Truman's secret service detail, could not stand any more suspense. He shook Truman awake and turned on the radio. H. V. Kaltenborn, in his excited Germanic tones, said Truman now led by 2,000,000 votes, but could not win because the "rural vote" would soon be coming in. Truman knew otherwise. He dressed and returned to his Kansas City headquarters. Among the many calls he took in the predawn hours was one from George E. Allen, a member of his poker crowd. "I want to be the first fellow that says that I didn't think you had a chance," Allen told the President. Truman laughed. Dewey, meanwhile, had gone to bed.

At 10:30 A.M. Dewey arose to find he had lost Ohio, Illinois, and California—and with them, the election. He talked with Brownell and other aides for perhaps half an hour; what disappointments he expressed, if any, are lost to history. At 11:14 A.M. Dewey sent the telegram: "My heartiest congratulations to you on your election. . . ." A couple of hours later, at a brief meeting with the press, Dewey displayed no outward signs of chagrin at having lost a "can't-lose" election. "I am as much surprised as you are," he told the reporters. "I have read your stories. We were all wrong together." Herbert Brownell could not be found for comment.

Truman had won twenty-eight states with 304 electoral votes,* Dewey sixteen states with 189 votes, Thurmond his four Dixiecrat states with 39 votes. In the popular vote Truman polled 24,179,345 to Dewey's 21,991,291, a plurality of 2,188,054. Wallace received a mere 1,157,326 votes, Thurmond, 1,176,126. But these were enough to deny Truman a majority: he got 49.6 percent of the popular vote to Dewey's 45.1 percent. Paradoxes abounded. Truman lost four of the largest industrial states (New York, Pennsylvania, New Jersey, and Michigan) that had been central to Roosevelt's victories. Yet he won three Midwestern states (Iowa, Ohio, and Wisconsin), dominated by farm votes, that Dewey had won in 1944. Truman's winning combination tracked closely the pattern James Rowe laid down in his 1947 memorandum: every state in the West except Oregon; seven of the eleven southern states, the border states of West Virginia, Missouri, Kentucky and Oklahoma, and five Midwestern states. In the Northeast, he won only Massachusetts and Rhode Island. Wallace votes cost him Michigan and Maryland in addition to New York.

* Later reduced to 303 when a Tennessee elector voted for Thurmond.

To Dewey, defeat was especially galling because a selective shift of fewer than 30,000 votes in three states would have given him victory in the electoral college, Truman's wide popular majority notwithstanding. Truman carried Ohio by 7,107 votes, California by 17,865, Illinois by 33,612. Had these states shifted to Dewey—which would have been accomplished had he received only one vote more than half his losing margin—he would have won by 267 electoral votes to 225 for Truman. A switch of even two of the states would have denied Truman the 266 electoral votes needed for victory and thrown the election into the House of Representatives. But such did not happen: Harry Truman had won what Joseph and Stewart Alsop called "the loneliest campaign," and he was ready to savor victory.

In the early afternoon Dewey and family and friends went to Grand Central Station to board a train for Albany. He smiled, gamely and politely, for the photographers. No, he did not intend to seek the presidency again. Would he wave for the photographers? No, he preferred not to do so.

On the train back to Washington a few days later Truman wandered into the press car and sneaked up behind the Associated Press correspondent, Tony Vaccaro, an old friend, brushed off his hat, and with a laugh shoved his face down, almost into the typewriter keys. As one witness wrote, "Before Mr. Vaccaro resorted to expletives he recognized the Chief Executive." Truman laughed along with everyone else and hoisted himself onto a table and sat there with legs dangling for almost half an hour, tickled over the victory, teasing the "prophets of the press."

For the Republicans, the sting of defeat was mitigated by the knowledge that probably 95 percent of the people in the country had guessed wrong. Recriminations were few, and mostly confined to intrafamilial griping by the Republicans. Hugh Scott, the figurehead Republican national chairman,* snapped as he watched the returns, "It's a good thing. Those mastodons won't listen to me. They had to learn their lesson. Now, maybe, they'll go out and [back] some social legislation." But the rest of the country laughed at—and with—itself. When Truman returned to Washington he found the streets crammed with 750,000 persons, including government workers and schoolchildren dismissed for the day. His motorcade passed the Washington *Post* building, festooned with a sign:

---

* By Scott's own account, Dewey pushed him for the chairmanship "with a commendatory reference to [my] sea duty as a source of good future publicity. I would be the only war veteran on the national committee. In 1948, the vote of recently returned war veterans was important." Scott was told bluntly that he would do nothing more than appease party factions: *"You* keep the party happy. Brownell runs the campaign." Scott accepted. In four months he attended one strategy meeting.

MR. PRESIDENT, WE ARE READY TO EAT CROW
WHENEVER YOU ARE READY TO SERVE IT

Truman laughed and waved at *Post* employees in the windows.

In fact, almost everyone was laughing. Tallulah Bankhead sent Truman a telegram: "The people have put you in your place." A bookstore in Mayfield, Kentucky, offered framed pictures of Truman: "Were $1.98. Now $10." In suburban New York, the Nassau County Federation of Republican Women canceled a talk on "Our New Republican President" and substituted "It Pays to Be Ignorant." In Louisville, William F. Hollinger, a GOP precinct chairman, paid off a bet by jumping into the Ohio River holding a picture of Dewey. Comedians had a field day with the public-opinion polls. "This year the polls went to the dogs, rather than the other way around," said Fred Allen. "Truman is the first President to lose in a Gallup and win in a walk," said another. The Chicago *Daily News* told of the woman bus passenger who put down her newspaper, turned to a friend, and said, "Now I don't know whether to believe even the Kinsey Report."*

Harry Truman's many shortcomings as a President notwithstanding, the 1948 election must rank as the most significant of modern American political history. His victory meant the majority of the voting public accepted the social reforms of the New Deal as institutionalized national standards. It ended, for all practical purposes, the South's death grip on the moral throat of the Democratic Party. It demonstrated that a Democratic candidate could fashion a winning majority from components other than the traditional city/labor/black/South coalition. It forced the Republican Party away from blind conservatism and toward the mainstream of American politics; not until 1964 did the conservatives gain enough force within the party to nominate their own candidate. And, perhaps most important, Truman's victory was one of *issues* over *power*. Truman beat more than Thomas E. Dewey. He beat the established centers of American power—industries and banks, the rich and the professional, the press and the academic elites. Harry Truman indeed was democracy personified.

* John Fenton of the Gallup organization said later the chief error was that most of the polls stopped interviewing too early. Gallup, for instance, finished its last survey on October 15, eighteen days before the election. Thus "the survey did not catch the last-minute trend to the Democrats among such groups as Midwestern farmers, disillusioned Wallace supporters, and wavering voters who made up their mind after hearing one of Truman's 'give 'em hell' speeches in the closing days. . . ." A post-election analysis showed that at least 4.5 million Truman voters—almost one of five of his total vote—was based on decisions made *after* the middle of October, Fenton said. The polls' fallibility is further illustrated by results of separate surveys in the spring of 1948. In March, Gallup interviewers asked, "Do you think that prices will be higher, lower, or about the same in the coming months?" The results: higher, 14 percent; lower, 39 percent; the same, 36 percent. The next month Roper asked the same question (substituting "prices of things you buy"). His results, published in *Fortune:* higher, 54 percent; lower, 9 percent; the same, 22 percent.

America paid a price. Other Presidents had used the majesty of their office for political benefit; Truman did so on a scale unsurpassed in history, with the American taxpayer financing his whistle-stop tour in an election year—a precedent followed, to one extent or another, by every succeeding President. Truman's harsh campaign oratory, necessary though it may have been for victory, brought the specter of class warfare to America. Truman's senseless scheme to send Chief Justice Vinson to Moscow revealed a willingness to manipulate foreign policy for selfish political gains; subsequent history is littered with similarly suspicious international episodes on election eve, ranging from the Gulf of Tonkin incident in 1964 that cast President Johnson as a man who would take a restrained approach to the Vietnam War, to the premature "peace is at hand" declaration of Henry Kissinger in 1972, when the nation cried out for an end to America's Indochinese venture. And Truman's campaign oratory, exciting though it was, did grave damage to the truth.

Nonetheless, Truman's victory served as an affirmation of public satisfaction with the status quo. Despite the tribulations and irritations of the postwar period, the meat shortages and the strikes, the foreign unrest and the fears of domestic subversion, a majority of the American people said, via their ballots, that what they enjoyed in 1948 was close enough to being the best years of their lives, so why change?

As it turned out, Truman's election in his own right brought only fleeting respite from the wide public belief that he was a narrow politician, unsuited temperamentally or intellectually to be President. Truman's stubborn loyalty to his friends, even when they were wrong, added to his problems; indeed the President at times seemed to take perverse delight in aggravating situations with cocky statements when the very wisdom of the ages cried out for silence or discretion. Typical was an episode in early 1950 when General Harry Vaughan, the White House military aide, accepted a medal from the Argentine dictator Juan Peron, despite a constitutional ban on officers receiving decorations from a foreign government.* Drew Pearson, the columnist, criticized Vaughan, and many newspapers joined in. A few nights later, at a military dinner honoring Vaughan, Truman said Pearson's attacks were aimed at him as President. "If any SOB thinks he can get me to discharge any of my staff or cabinet by some smart-aleck statement over the air, he has got another think coming," Truman declared. The comment, of course, fanned a triviality into a noisy cause célèbre, with Truman roundly condemned for "unpresidential language."

---

* A State Department protocol officer told Vaughan to take the medal lest the Argentines be offended. The same medal had gone earlier to Generals Eisenhower and Bradley and Admiral Chester Nimitz, among others, without incident.

Vaughan caused Truman more serious problems because of his involvement with people caught up in what came to be known as the "five-percenter" scandals. A clique of influence peddlers—politicians, former government officials, outright con men—claimed contacts who could speed contracts and other favors from the government, in return for five percent of the money involved. Long a Washington landmark, the fixer seemed especially prevalent in the postwar years. And one of the most prominent, a former army quartermaster colonel named James V. Hunt, boasted close friendship with Vaughan. According to Senate testimony in 1949–50, Hunt enjoyed access to Vaughan's office and often telephoned him for a social chat while awed clients listened. Vaughan made phone calls and wrote letters for Hunt, he graced cocktail and dinner parties for Hunt's clients, he even took Hunt into his poker club. When reporters asked Vaughan about these favors, he shot back, "What the hell business is it of yours?" and asked a photographer, "How would you like a punch in the nose?" He warned the reporters against writing unfriendly stories. "After all," he said, "I am the President's military aide. You guys will want favors at the White House some day."

Embarrassing disclosures tumbled out of the Senate for months. Albert Joseph Gross, a minor-league industrialist from Wisconsin and a Hunt client, admitted sending deep freezes to such Truman intimates (and officeholders) as Vaughan, John Snyder, Matthew Connelly, and James K. Vardaman, as well as the White House staff dining room. John Maragon, a onetime Kansas City shoeshine boy and an "expediter" in wartime Washington, used Vaughan's White House stationery to help along a perfume importation business, among other ventures. Builder William Helis persuaded Vaughan to intervene to have the government release to him $150,000 worth of lumber for a race track, at a time when Administration policy was to put all materials possible into home construction. But nothing seemed to shake Vaughan. In Senate testimony in September 1949 he denied doing any favors for Hunt, Maragon, or anyone else; he said Truman knew nothing of letters he wrote for them; he called the deep freezes and other gifts "an expression of friendship and nothing more." The committee could not prove otherwise, and Vaughan stayed on Truman's staff until the day the President left office. When the *Saturday Evening Post* called him a crook, he sued, and he collected $10,000.*

---

* The five-percenter and deep freeze scandals proved but the tip of an iceberg of corruption that crashed down on the Truman Administration in 1951–52, years beyond our purview. The Reconstruction Finance Corporation, a Depression-era agency created to provide loans to ailing but sound businesses, was one focus. Congressional testimony showed that William M. Boyle, Jr., the Democratic national chairman, and Donald Dawson, Truman's assistant for patronage, leaned on RFC to insure that Democratic contributors received loans. Truman stood behind both men, although he did have Boyle resign once the storm blew over. Corruption permeated the tax service. During and immediately after the Truman Adminis-

Harry Vaughan won in court—but Harry Truman lost in public respect. What especially galled the President was that the chief inquisitors in this instance were Democratic senators and congressmen. For months during the 1948 campaign the President had stormed that "special interests" tried to destroy his Administration. Now the attackers were of his own party, and the President withdrew into a bristly, defensive shell. Truman could—would—see no wrong in his underlings, even when sworn testimony revealed breaches of official propriety not seen in Washington since the Teapot Dome scandals. In less than two years the luster of the 1948 election victory had vanished, and Truman had so fallen in public esteem that Republican congressional candidates could campaign against him in the fall of 1950 (as did Dwight D. Eisenhower two years later) on grounds of "corruption."

Yet aside from providing a noisy sideshow for the press and that percentage of the public that worried about honesty in government, did the deep freezes and the five-percenters make any discernible impact upon the American psyche? As the best years neared the end of the decade, the mass public seemingly had its eyes fixed on material comfort. Happiness cannot be measured by statistics alone, but fruits of the postwar era were suddenly available for the picking. Some raw data suggests the economic situation of Americans in 1950 as compared with 1945. In July 1945 the average weekly salary for a worker in manufacturing was $45.42; for nonmanufacturing, $47.47, ranging from $59.64 in the auto industry to $24.40 for retail trade workers. In midsummer 1950 the manufacturing wage was $60.32, up almost $15; for nonmanufacturing, $65.41, up almost $18. Auto workers earned $75.74 weekly; retail clerks, $42.17. Overall, wages and salaries had increased about 23 percent.

Employment was at an all-time high, 61,400,000; the unemployment rate was 5.2 percent. Retail prices increased 49.6 percent; the cost-of-living index 36.2 percent. After-tax corporate profits increased 104.6 percent—more than four times as much as wages and salaries. The average single-family house cost $7,950 in 1950, exclusive of land costs. An electric washing machine sold for $168; six twelve-ounce bottles of Pepsi-Cola for twenty-five cents (nineteen cents on weekend specials). A hamburger cost a dime; gasoline eighteen or twenty cents a gallon; bread seventeen cents for a pound-and-a-half loaf; a bottle of beer twenty or twenty-five cents; five pounds of sugar, forty-nine cents; a best-selling novel such as *Prince of Foxes,* by Samuel Shellabarger, $3; a one-year subscription to *Life,* $5.50; a carton of cigarettes, $1.79; a Dr.

---

tration, 177 revenue officers were fired for misconduct; more than a dozen officials involved in tax matters went to jail, including T. Lamar Caudle, the assistant attorney general in charge of the Justice Department's tax division, and Matthew Connelly, Truman's appointments secretary.

West toothbrush, fifty cents; a Van Heusen dress shirt, $2.95 to $4.50; a package of Ex-Lax, ten cents. Between 1945 and 1950 Americans bought 5,500,000 passenger cars; 5,076,800 houses; 20,207,000 refrigerators; 17,549,000 vacuum cleaners; 5,451,000 electric ranges. During the five years, American technology gave the world the long-playing phonograph record (33⅓ revolutions per minute, to replace the 78); the automatic transmission for the automobile;* the electric clothes drier; the garbage disposal unit for the kitchen sink; the hula hoop; the bazooka.

Yet history must be known for its spiritual progeny as well as by its physical relics. And what did Americans carry out of the best years?

---

* Or the first workable one, at any rate—the hydraulic torque converter. Earlier versions were so expensive and unreliable they never got into wide use.

Epilogue:
How We Ended

T HERE NEVER WAS a country more fabulous than America," the British historian Robert Payne wrote after an extensive visit in 1948–49. "She bestrides the world like a Colossus: no other power at any time in the world's history has possessed so varied or so great an influence on other nations. . . . [I]t is already an axiom that the decisions of the American government affect the lives and the livelihood of the remotest people. Half the wealth of the world, more than half the productivity, nearly two-thirds of the world's machines are concentrated in American hands; the rest of the world lies in the shadow of American industry, and with each day the shadow looms larger, more portentous, more dangerous. . . ."

In the Prologue I wrote that the title *The Best Years* posed an implicit question that I would attempt to answer in due course, that is, was the period 1945–50 indeed "the best years" of the American experience? America did achieve a material well-being unsurpassed in the prior history of mankind. The postwar economic boom acted as a sort of booster rocket for the industrialization that started after the Civil War. Mass production techniques, economic planning at the national level, a new appreciation for research and applied science—America came out of the decade with the mechanical capability for comfort and prosperity.

During countless interviews in the last three years I asked person after person whether those years were in fact "the best years" for them personally, in terms of general satisfaction with life. The responses fell into a pattern: a review of "what I was doing then"—in college after the military, starting a business, establishing a home and family; an attempt to remember "what was happening"—the landmark events tended to be Truman beating Dewey, the end of rationing, the first postwar automobile, such trivia as the 1946 World Series between the St. Louis

Cardinals and the St. Louis Browns, and movie actresses; then a quantum jump to foreign affairs—The Bomb, trouble with the Russians, the Marshall Plan, the Berlin blockade. And almost invariably the interviewees came around to the same answer, couched in roughly the following language:

> Yes, they *were* good years, because I was putting my life together, and making enough money to get by on, and we weren't fighting a war. I didn't have all the things I wanted; those came later, in the fifties and the sixties, but the postwar period was the necessary preparation.
>
> The HUAC investigations disturbed me, for I thought many people were mistreated. But like a lot of people, I was scared of the Communists, and I was happy that someone was trying to get spies out of government. Besides, nobody I knew personally got into trouble with HUAC.
>
> I would have preferred that we not go back into the war business, but someone had to take on the job of stopping the Russians, and we were the only country around. It didn't make me especially happy, but it didn't worry me an awful lot either.

Yet the best years left memories elsewhere that were not nearly so pleasant. Thus the shabby maliciousness of the inquisitors who drove such men as the falsely-maligned Laurence Duggan to ruin or death, their unfeeling violation of the standards by which decent people live, stand as a tombstone for the decade—a more meaningful one, in the perspective of history, than the gadgetry of Detroit and Mr. Levitt's houses. A silent majority of Americans tolerated an ideological pogrom whose perpetrators followed highly subjective standards when selecting victims; indeed, people who should have known better cheered them on. In April 1950 Senator Joseph McCarthy, just beginning his rise to national fame, drew sustained applause when he said in a speech that General George C. Marshall, the wartime commander of all the U.S. military, was "pathetic and completely unfitted" to be secretary of state, and that his appointment "was a crime." McCarthy's audience was the American Society of Newspaper Editors. What followed thereafter, essentially, is that for a full decade, that of the 1950's, America went into a holding period—intellectually, morally, politically. Perhaps the pause was inevitable, even necessary; the nation was weary from depression, war, and reconversion, and the Eisenhower years proved singularly undemanding. The result, regardless, was a generation content to put its trust in government and in authority, to avoid deviant political ideas, to enjoy material comfort without undue worry about the invisible intrinsic costs. America misplaced, somewhere and somehow, the driving moral force it had carried out of the world war. American foreign policy, in a

lineal extension of the Truman Doctrine, relied upon massive retaliation, not the United Nations. There were times, during the 1950's, when
the entire nation seemed to be saying, "Leave me alone."

The psychic dangers of living with the nagging daily terror of atomic
warfare, as Americans did from 1945 on, even before the Soviets acquired the bomb, are subtle, but nonetheless real. "What do you want to
be when you grow up?" a magazine reporter asked an eight-year-old boy
in 1946 when doing an article on atomic bombs. "Alive," the lad responded. The commentator Raymond Swing feared that the very existence of atomic weaponry would drug America into fatal lethargy. "We
are like a man lost in a blizzard who is combating the numbness of his
limbs and the furtive thoughts that tell him he might as well succumb
and stop striving to keep going," he wrote in 1948. Norman Cousins, in
a widely discussed *Saturday Review* editorial in August 1945, went so
far as to argue, "man is obsolete." Prime Minister Clement Attlee,
speaking to Commons on November 22, 1945, said, "I think it is well
that we should make up our minds that if the world is again involved in
a war on a scale comparable with that from which we have just emerged,
every weapon will be used. We may confidently expect full-scale atomic
warfare which will result in the destruction of great cities, in the death of
millions, and the setting back of civilization to an unimaginable extent."
Yet the Truman Administration decided, and the mass public agreed,
that the atomic secret would be a tool of power politics, not international cooperation.

So, too, the fate of world government. The idealistic young veteran
Cord Meyer, Jr., wrote in 1947, "The institution that is ultimately responsible for two world wars within a generation and the growing
danger of a third is the sovereign nation-state. . . . Either some measure of world government will be achieved by voluntary consent or our
particular civilization will be destroyed."* Raymond Swing felt that at
the time of the San Francisco conference for formation of the United
Nations, "More people, I think, were ready . . . for a world federation
than our politicians have any idea of. They had been drilled in the logic
that there must be a law above nations, if an end is to be put to the
anarchy of war." And these persons, opined Swing, were "not so small a
minority as the so-called 'practical' folks thought." Yet Senator Tom C.
Connally of Texas, ranking Democrat on the Senate Foreign Relations
Committee, bellowed during debate over the UN that he was not going
to run after "some butterfly" of world government. ("That remark suggests that the mind that made it might be functioning inside a cocoon,"

---

* In the early 1950's the disillusioned Meyer tried a new route. He joined the
Central Intelligence Agency and worked in covert posts until his assignment as
London station chief in 1973. One of his responsibilities was funneling agency
money to student and other groups through cover foundations.

someone commented afterward.) Connally continued, "There are some 300,000,000 persons in India, 400,000,000 in China, and 175,000,000 in Russia, who would outnumber us in any world government. I don't want a world government, ever."

In postwar America, the Tom Connallys prevailed, not the Cord Meyers. The Truman Administration went along with formation of the United Nations, soon grew disillusioned with its practical capabilities, and in 1947 struck out on its own as world policeman, in the decision to support the Greek and Turkish governments against communism. The justification for the Truman Doctrine was that weak but legitimate governments were threatened by external forces. If this in fact was true (and in the instance of Greece, the Truman Doctrine relied upon a reed-weak case), the UN clearly had jurisdiction. But after 1947 only the hopelessly naïve took the UN seriously.

That America's foreign policy came to be built around the Truman Doctrine, rather than the United Nations, was possible* because American leaders in and out of government "bombarded the American people with a 'hate the enemy' campaign rarely seen in our history; never, certainly, in peacetime," in the words of a contemporary congressional committee. A panel headed by Representative Forrest A. Harness concluded a long study of government "information activities" in 1947: "Government propaganda distorts facts with such authority that the person becomes prejudiced or biased in the direction which the government propagandists wish to lead national thinking." (Lest the Harness conclusions be dismissed as vapory illusions of the left, one might listen to another authority, General Douglas MacArthur, addressing the same subject a decade later: "Our government has kept us in a perpetual state of fear—kept us in a continuous stampede of patriotic fervor—with the cry of a grave national emergency. . . . Yet, in retrospect, these disasters seem never to have happened, seem never to have been quite real.") The elite community of American policy makers "fell in love with its Cold War plan," in the opinion of James P. Warburg, a conservative analyst of foreign affairs, and sold it to the public.

The Cold War, by its very nature, inescapably became a protracted conflict without visible battlefields or discernible results, one in which the individual citizen felt he played no direct part—and with which,

---

* I use the words "was possible" rather than "was caused" because of an antipathy to revisionist historians who insist Truman provoked the Cold War against a blameless Soviet Union because of an imperialistic itch for wealth and warfare. My own conclusion is that Truman's foreign policy errors are attributable to a crippling combination of conservatism of thought and impetuousness of action. Nothing in Truman's character suggests he was a tool of the "corporate interests and monopolists" who would benefit from a warfare state; indeed, these interests worked feverishly to throw him out of office in 1948. The Truman Doctrine happened to be the panacea the nation's supposedly wisest men of the era were peddling. The President trusted them, and accepted it.

consequently, he soon became bored. Thus succumbed the national unity that marked the collective adventure of the Second World War. Another phenomenon—this one detected by the public opinion polls and professional sociologists—was the demise of the devil-may-care attitudes found in homecoming veterans in 1945–46. Disgusted with the ultimate regimentation of the military, a majority of the veterans had declared they intended to work for no one but themselves; they wanted their own farms, their own insurance agencies, their own shops. But as the decade ended the same veterans thought differently. The social scientist Harvey Olsen, after a study of 8,900 veterans, reported, "Many of these men came out of the service with a 'ho-ho' attitude towards life; they learned they could be the sole proprietors of their fortunes. They were not as bound by pre-war dogmas as their fathers; they opted for their own lives." Unfortunately, reported Olsen, most of the vets quickly reverted to pre-war thinking, settling into the "familiar old patterns rather than seeking out what they really wanted." But he found that "the ones who are the happiest, the most-balanced, in the long run, are those who obeyed their instincts and made new lives, even at the cost of passing psychic discomfort." *Fortune,* in a survey of graduating college seniors in June 1949, found similar confusion. The 1949 graduating class found the class "has turned its back on what its elders automatically assume is . . . one of the most cherished prerogatives of youth. Forty-nine is taking no chances." Only 2 percent of the graduates planned businesses for themselves. "The men of Forty-nine everywhere seem haunted by the fear of a recession. . . . 'I know AT&T might not be very exciting,' explains one senior, 'but there'll always be an AT&T.'" The graduates seemed little concerned with making vast amounts of money. "Forty-niners simply will not talk of the future in terms of the dollar. In terms of the Good Life, however, they are most articulate." The Good Life meant marriage, three children, a comfortable home, "a little knockabout for the wife," a summer cottage, an annual income of $10,000 a year (the median family income in 1950 was $6,405 for white families; $3,449 for blacks). The blandness of the graduates worried *Fortune:* Would they "furnish any quota of free-swinging s.o.b.'s we seem to need for leavening the economy? The answers will be a long time in coming."

I didn't read the Fortune *article until a near quarter-century later, but had it come to my attention in the summer of 1950, I would have laughed out loud. Security indeed! My immediate concern that summer, as I neared my last years in high school, was to "get out of Marshall," to insure that I did not spend the rest of my life as a checker and stock clerk in the Childs' Piggly Wiggly grocery on U.S. 80 four blocks north of the courthouse square, my after-school-and-summers job for five* *years. What inequities of capitalism convert an apolitical teen-ager into a muckraking journalist? Piggly Wiggly did its full share. During summers the "normal" work day was eleven hours, except on Monday, when the warehouse supply truck arrived at 6:30 P.M., our ostensible quitting time, and we spent two to three hours unloading cases of canned goods and stacking 60-pound bags of sugar to a height outstretched-arms distance above my head; and on Wednesday, Double S&H Green Stamp Day, when we stayed open until nine o'clock; and on Saturday, another late-closing day. Piggly Wiggly lacked air-conditioning, and on hot July afternoons, when the temperature inside the store crept to 100°, 115°, even 118°, canned goods turned warm to the touch, and we invented errands to the produce storage vault to find fleeting moments of refrigerated relief. (I envied my classmate, Billy Don Moyers,* who toiled for the seemingly cooler A&P, two blocks distant; the A&P kids, although they worked as hard and as long as we did, nonetheless seemed to look a bit fresher when we passed on the street.) For these labors, a minimum of 70 hours weekly, Piggly Wiggly paid me $35, and the manager, Mr. J. B. Cannon, a raucous bantam of a man with five children, a worn-out Plymouth, and a tired back, suggested I'd be wasting my time going to the University of Texas. "You're not going to amount to nothing, trying to keep up with those rich kids down in Austin. Stay with Piggly Wiggly, and I'll see that they make you assistant produce manager over at Henderson. You might even have your own store some day." Cannon made this offer one night about eleven o'clock as we worked on an inventory. I declined.*

Not too many routes led away from Marshall—and Piggly Wiggly— and some of them, in fact, appeared to be even deeper traps than a grocery checkout stand. A brief courtship of the daughter of a wealthy soft-drink bottler—a lady of high Episcopalian character whom my friends called "the Dr. Pepper heiress"—taught me that the hardest way to go about making money was to marry it. My mother at one time talked glowingly of career opportunities at the phone company and Sears, Roebuck. "They never lay off anybody, and they have good retirement plans," she reasoned. The bitterest realization was that although I had the physique of Marty "Slats" Marion, the shortstop for the St. Louis Cardinals, I did not share his fielding skills, and thus would be of no use to the world of professional baseball.

Logistical obstacles aside, the America that lay ahead of me in 1950 was not especially threatening. The Second World War by now was so remote, in memory if not in time, that people simply did not talk about it anymore. In Marshall everyone seemed to have a job, and a semblance of an automobile; even after savings for college, my Piggly

* Later an aide to President Johnson and a television journalist, among other things.

Wiggly earnings produced enough surplus to finance a 1939 Ford and to give me more "walking-around money"—for movie dates, hot dogs, and an occasional bootlegged six-pack of beer—than most other kids in town had. I knew that once I finished the University of Texas, I would become a newspaper reporter, hopefully even a statehouse correspondent for the Dallas News. The possibility of being drafted wasn't all that ominous, for despite the periodic Russian scares, we in East Texas decided early on that a nation of semibarbaric Asians would never start a war with the mighty United States, regardless of how badly Truman and Acheson bungled our foreign policy.

As if by paradox, what had happened, essentially, was that America appeared ready to give me the best years of my life.

Harry Truman shared my confidence. In a "nonpolitical" whistle-stop tour of western states in the spring of 1950, preparing for the congressional elections, he happily told his audiences, "The world is more settled now than in 1946." Perhaps it was. Western Europe had apparently stabilized, with the Communists losing pivotal elections in Italy and France. The Communists had prevailed in China, to be sure, an inevitability the Administration had expected since 1946. The blockade of Berlin had been broken by the air lift. Truman's foreign policy advisers puffed with pride over the good job they were doing. "The Cold War is a good war," declared Paul Hoffman, head of the Economic Cooperation Administration, the Marshall Plan agency. Hoffman expanded:

> It is the only war in history where the question of destruction doesn't enter into it at all. Everything we are doing is building up. We have rebuilt Europe, not destroyed it. . . . If the Marshall Plan had not been in effect you could have had at least part of Western Europe under the domination of the Kremlin and we would have spent much more for increased defense than we have spent for the Marshall Plan. Now, if we can carry on a smart, resourceful cold war, the kind of war free people can carry on, Russia will be contained.

But worries nagged Washington nonetheless. In late April Dean Acheson, the secretary of state, confided to a Republican senator that he feared trouble in South Korea, Berlin, and Burma. The likely trigger spot, Acheson said, was Berlin, where the Communists were expected to try to march half a million youth organization members into the western sector to oust the Allies. The United States, France, and Britain were ready to resist with force if necessary, Acheson said. Francis Matthews, secretary of the navy, warned, "There is nothing in the current international picture to justify the assumption that we shall not again be called upon to defend ourselves." General Omar Bradley, chairman of the Joint Chiefs of Staff, felt that "even if events are not worse, the accumulation of them makes the situation worse."

The first week of May the military staged a training exercise at Fort Bragg, North Carolina, that pointed up the depleted status of U.S. strategic might. The exercise was built around some 32,000 ground soldiers from the 82d and 11th Airborne Divisions, both at reduced strength, and a regimental combat team from the 3d Infantry Division—"just about all the Sunday punch the United States can mobilize in the first critical hours after a Cold War opening shot," in the words of one observer. The Carolina exercise assembled virtually all the troop carrier and cargo planes that would be available should the United States come under attack; getting the men and planes into place took four months. Military strength elsewhere included two half-sized Marine divisions; the 2d Army, so widely deployed at domestic posts as to be "wholly unready"; four occupation divisions in Germany and Japan; and twenty-seven National Guard divisions, a year from combat readiness. In 1950 the United States was spending $12.5 million for guided missiles for the army, and $34.1 million for peanut price supports.

But why should America worry? Truman's strategy of containment was working, for the media said so. In its cover story for May 29, 1950, *Time* told the American public even more supportive news:

> The United States now has a new frontier and a new ally in the Cold War. The place is Indo-China, a Southeast Asian jungle, mountain and delta land that includes the Republic of Viet Nam and the smaller neighboring kingdoms of Laos and Cambodia, all parts of the French Union.*

A week later *Time* expressed optimism about events in yet another part of Asia:

> Six months ago South Korea, bedeviled by guerrilla raids, galloping inflation and the daily threat of invasion from the North, looked like a candidate for the same mortuary as Nationalist China. Now the Republic of Korea looks more like a country on its way to healthy survival. . . . It has trained and equipped a first-rate ground army. . . . [U.S.] advisers have tried to give the Koreans Yankee self-sufficiency as well as Yankee organization and equipment.
>
> The policy has paid off. . . . Most observers now rate the 100,000-man South Korean army as the best of its size in Asia. Its fast-moving columns have mopped up all but a few of the Commu-

* In actuality, *Time* was saying that the French told the United States they could not hold off insurgents without help, so the Truman Administration agreed to underwrite the war there.

nist guerrilla bands . . . and no one believes that the Russian-trained North Korean army could pull off a quick, successful invasion of the south without heavy reinforcements.

On Sunday morning, June 25, 1950, Mrs. Ida Hamme wept as she stood before her Sunday school class at the First Methodist Church in Weslaco, Texas. A gentle woman in her thirties, with two young sons, Mrs. Hamme talked about the strange war that had begun during the night in a far-away place called Korea. She asked her class, all preteen children, to pray that peace would be swiftly restored.

Mrs. Hamme's grief so disturbed two of the children, Jody Corns and Anne Caskey, both twelve, that when class ended they went home instead of to church services. They found Maurine Corns, ten, and Kindred Caskey, eight, and walked the seven blocks to the Corns home. They spread the Sunday newspapers on the living-room floor and read the war news, and tried to understand what was happening and why.

"Our main question," Jody Corns remembered a quarter of a century later, "was whether our daddies would have to go back to war."

The best years were over.

Sources and
Acknowledgments

SEVERAL YEARS AGO, while researching a biography of George Meany, the labor leader, I constantly found myself having trouble keeping my mind on the business at hand: Meany's career in the immediate postwar period. I would turn the microfilm to an account of an American Federation of Labor convention, or one of John L. Lewis' periodic onslaughts against public tranquility, only to find my eyes flitting to adjacent columns, and stories about the Kaiser-Frazer automobile, or a polio epidemic, or efforts of rainmakers to break a horrendous drought in the Midwest. Some of the headlines stirred faint memories; others could have come from a planet other than the one on which I spent my boyhood. Someday, I said to myself, I'd like to go back and learn what I missed as a child.

One advantage of being a professional writer is that you can satisfy your curiosity and earn a living simultaneously. With *Meany* finished, I mentioned my fascination with the forties to Mike Bessie, then the president of Atheneum. We were having a prelunch drink at the Federal City Club in Washington, and Bessie fell silent and swirled the ice around in his glass. Then he said, "Quite a few of us were coming back to new lives in 1945 and 1946, not knowing what to expect, or what to make of ourselves." Another pause. "In fact, those years still confuse me. Let's do a book."

The Best Years, more than three years later, is the result, and the preceding pages are an amalgam of what I read, what I was told, what I remember, and what I think. At the outset I made a single rule: to the extent possible, I intended to avoid applying hindsight wisdom to the postwar years. My aim was to recreate the ambience of the five years as they *were,* rather than what they should or might have been. I didn't always succeed, for I find it difficult to maintain personal detachment when writing about outrageous situations (see, for instance, the sections on HUAC and the concluding pages of the account of the 1948 election).

The literature of the Truman years is voluminous, and growing, and I made liberal use of it. Some printed sources of continuing value included *The Crucial Decade* by Eric F. Goldman (Vintage edition, 1960); *The Great Leap* by John Brooks (Harper Colophon Books edition, 1966); *Inside U.S.A.* by John Gunther (Harper and Brothers, 1947); *The Crucial Years 1940–1945* by William Kenny (MacFadden Books edition, 1962); *The American People in the Twentieth Century* by Oscar Handlin (Beacon Press edition, 1963); and *Actions and Passions* by Max Lerner (Kennikat Press, 1969). Truman's two-volume presidential memoir—*Year of Decisions* and *Years of Trial and Hope,* both published by Doubleday—is lifeless and suffers sorely from a lack of candor; nonetheless it does give a view of the Truman Administration as seen by President Truman. (References to these works in the notes are as *Memoirs I* and *Memoirs II.*) Much more useful are *Harry S. Truman* by Margaret Truman (William Morrow and Company, 1973); *The Truman Presidency* by Cabell Phillips (Macmillan, 1966); *Beyond the New Deal: Harry S. Truman and American Liberalism,* by Alonzo L. Hamby (Columbia University Press, 1973); *Man of Independence,* Jonathan Daniels (Lippincott, 1950); *Harry Truman and the Crisis Presidency* by Bert Cochran (Funk and Wagnalls, 1973); *Plain Speaking* by Merle Miller (Berkley-Putnam, 1974); and *Report on America* by Robert Payne (John Day Company, 1949). One book of which I made use in virtually every chapter is *In Your Opinion* by John Fenton (Little, Brown and Company, 1969). Fenton, managing editor of the Gallup Poll, synthesized various survey findings into a narrative that gives a vivid picture of what Americans thought during the postwar years, and beyond; the Gallup surveys I have quoted, for the most part, come from his book.

For purposes of conciseness, I have tried to hold chapter notes to a minimum. If a source is obvious in the text, or derived from contemporary press coverage or standard reference works, I do not repeat it. Economic and other statistics are from the annual *Statistical Abstract of the United States.* With one exception (that of William Nation in Chapter 6) the first-person narrations in each chapter are from personal interviews; in two instances, persons asked that their names not be used because of the personal nature of what they said.

Among persons who helped with this book, in professional and personal capacities, are Dr. R. W. Coakley, Moreau D. Chambers, Detmar Finke, and Charles B. MacDonald, of the United States Army Center of Military History; Dr. Jonathan Grossman, historian of the Department of Labor; Philip Lauderquist, Marlene White, Elizabeth Costin, Dennis Bilger and Erwin J. Mueller, of the Harry S. Truman Memorial Library,

Independence, Missouri; June Willenz, national executive director, and Linda Goldberg, of the American Veterans Committee; Mrs. Claire R. Tedesco, chief librarian, and Alfred Sieminski, of the Veterans Administration library; Jerome Finster and James Paulauskas, of the National Archives; Mrs. Jeanne Fox, Mrs. Claire B. Waters, Mrs. Dianna Goldstein, and Mrs. Nancy Owens, of the Westover branch of the Arlington County Public Library; Hiram O. Lucy of the Department of the Army; George and Phylllis Belk, David Linton, Dick and Peggy Mullan, Paul and Betty Moorhead, Richardson Dilworth, Bob and Nancy Salgado, Michael Pakenham, B. A. Bergman, William B. Collins, Bill D. Moyers, June and Paul Heise, Mike and Ann Reynolds, Les and Roxanne Cramer, Brad and Kathy Dismukes, John Sullivan, John and Leah Shick, Betsy and Oliver Hailey, Gael M. Sullivan, Davida Maron, James Chatfield, formerly of the American Bar Association, Fred Trimble, Judith and Peter Espenschied, fellow bibliophiles, Carey McWilliams, Norman and Susan Gall, Alvin and Phyllis Richman, and especially my good Swedish diplomatic friends, Lars Georgsson and Lars Lonnbach, who arranged an interview with Prime Minister Olof Palme. Carol Brandt was most gracious in obtaining some good West Coast interviews. Carl Younger, of Brandt & Brandt, devoted much energy to obtaining permission for use of copyrighted musical material. Mrs. Inez Hughes, who was a demanding (and understanding) editor as my high school English teacher, helped chase down some obscure facts about Marshall in her present capacity as head of the Harrison County Historical Society. And, for the eighth book, I owe a special obligation to Jody Goulden.

I am also indebted to Mike Bessie, who got the idea going; Charles P. Corn, editor and friend; Irene King, who did her usual good job of typing; Mary Jane Alexander, for deft copy editing; and Carl D. Brandt, who kept me on the ridgeline and leveled out some pretty rugged descents. And I also owe an unpayable obligation to the scores of persons who tolerated my questions about the forties the past three years, and especially to those who gave me monologues that are in the preceding pages.

Prologue

The story of the origin of *The Best Years of Our Lives* comes from an interview with Harold Russell and an RKO General Pictures advertisement published in various periodicals in conjunction with the film's release in the autumn of 1946 (for instance, *Time*, October 28, 1946).

4 "The war left 14,648 soldiers." Veterans Administration annual report, June 30, 1947.

7 "Americans read the Sunday supplement features." A good discussion of the technological miracles promised Americans in the postwar period, and what they actually received in the years immediately after peace, is in "What Happened to the Dream World?" *Fortune*, July 1947.

7 "American industry built 297,000 planes." Final report of the Office of War Mobilization and Reconversion, June 30, 1947.

8 "Shortage of shipyard workers." *Time*, July 23, 1945; also the Los Angeles *Times*, July 14 and 17, 1945.

Chapter One

The most valuable single document for tracing the planning and execution of demobilization was *History of Personnel Demobilization in the United States Army* by John C. Sparrow (Department of the Army publication 20–210, July 1952); Sparrow's study contains a useful compendium of press, public and political comment on demobilization problems. Other government documents that proved helpful were *The American Soldier: Combat and Its Aftermath*, Volume II, by Samuel A. Stouffer *et al.*, based upon data collected by the Research Branch, Information and Education Division, War Department, during the Second World War (Princeton University Press, 1949); *Demobilizing the Ground Army*, by William G. Weaver, and *Redeployment Training*, by Major Bell I. Wiley, both in a special studies series, Historical Section, Army Ground Forces, 1948; *Résumé of Army Roll-Up Following World War Two* by Robert Coakley, Ernest F. Fisher, Karl E. Cocke and Daniel P. Griffin, published by the Office of the Chief of Military History in October 1968; "Demobilization and Transportation of Military Personnel," hearings, Senate Committee on Naval Affairs, November 13–15, 1945; "Demobilization of the Army," hearings, House Military Affairs Committee, January 1946; "Surplus Property Abroad," hearings, special Senate subcommittee to investigate the national defense program, January 1945; and annual reports of the Veterans Administration from 1943 to 1950. A useful academic study is *Preparing for Ulysses: Politics and Veterans During World War Two* by David R. B. Ross (Columbia University Press, 1969). Marshall's role is told in *George C. Marshall, Organizer of Victory, 1943–45*, by Forrest C. Pogue (Viking, 1973).

19 "No people in history." Truman, *Memoirs I*.

23 "The flow of discharges." "Demobilization and Transportation of Military Personnel," hearings, Senate Committee on Naval Affairs, November 13–15, 1945. Descriptions of homecoming scenes on the docks are from *Time* and *Newsweek*, various issues, June–August 1945.

24 "One person repelled." *Daily Worker*, January 10, 1946.

25 "For men in the Pacific." "Demobilization and Transportation of Military Personnel," *op. cit.*

26 "A Pullman Company advertisement." *Time*, July 23, 1945.

35 "General Marshall recalled the tribulations." Marshall speech to National Preparedness Orientation Conference, Washington, November 30, 1950.

Chapter Two

Of the many books published after 1945 about the "veteran problem," I found two to be the most useful: *Out of Uniform* by Benjamin C. Bowker (W. W. Norton Company, 1946); and *The American Veteran Back Home* by Robert J. Havighurst, John W. Baughman, Walter H. Eaton, and Ernest W. Burgess (Longmans, Green, 1951). The Bowker book especially contains a plethora of contemporary comment on the homecoming veteran. For the general ambience of the period vis-à-vis the veteran, I recommend *That Winter* by Merle Miller (William Sloane Associates, 1948). Almost every issue of the *American Legion Magazine* during 1945–50 contained information of value, and especially: "Elmira and the Ex-GI" by J. C. Furnas (February 1945); "So You Want to Be a Civilian" by Harold L. Elfenbein (June 1945); "Memorials That Live" by Louis Bromfield (May 1945); "Can You Deal with the Veterans Administration?" by T. W. Brickett (November 1948); "I'm a Veteran, Judge" by Roberta Rose (March 1946); and "How GI Employment Laws Work" by Jack Sher (August 1948). *Sex Problems of the Returned Veteran* by Howard Kitching, M.D. (Emerson Books, 1946), and *Shipmate*, alumni publication of the United States Naval Academy, Annapolis, were also helpful.

37 "The Boston *Post* found a psychologist." Boston *Post*, February 25, 1945.
38 "A Bill Mauldin cartoon." Bill Mauldin, *Back Home*, William Sloane Associates, 1947.
38 "AP would refrain." *Bulletin* of the California Department of Veteran Affairs, April 1947.
39 "A slim, pocket-sized booklet." Described in *Newsweek*, July 9, 1945.
39 "Gather close, our returning warriors." Philadelphia *Inquirer*, September 3, 1945.
41 "Hurried, lonely people." *Newsweek*, July 2, September 13, and October 7, 1945.
46 "A War Department survey." Stouffer, *The American Soldier*.
46 "Whether the war changed 'your own life.'" *Opinion News*, February 18, 1947.

Chapter Three

Two persons who were especially helpful in interviews, beyond credit given in the text, were Harry W. Colmery, of Topeka, Kansas, an attorney and a past national commander of the American Legion who did much of the legal draftsmanship of the GI Bill, and Charles G. Bolte, the first chairman of the American Veterans Committee. Although in his eighties Colmery granted me a "dinner" interview that lasted until four o'clock the next morning; he also supplied a 23-page memorandum about the origins of the GI Bill. Bolte's book, *The New Veteran* (Reynal & Hitchcock, 1945), is a moving exposition on the origins and philosophy of the AVC. The Hearst papers' role in passage of the GI Bill, and the political infighting, are detailed in a series of articles, "I Saw the GI Bill Written," by David

Camelon in *The American Legion Magazine* (September, October and November 1949).

Two extraordinarily critical—and readable—studies of the American Legion are in *The Inside Story of the Legion,* by Justin Gray (Boni and Gaer, 1948); and *Back Home* by Bill Mauldin.

52   "There aren't going to be any apple sellers." Washington *Post,* April 22, 1944.

52   "Why not give veterans' preferences." *Ibid.,* July 11, 1944.

52   "Marked tendency toward longevity." Gray, *The Inside Story of the Legion.*

57   "The bill's formal title." Chester Bowles, *Promises to Keep,* Harper & Row, 1971.

59   "Despite its defects." A good summary of benefits paid under the GI Bill is a fact sheet, "Thirty Years of Service to Those Who Served," Veterans Administration information service, June 1974.

Chapter Four

School & Society, a magazine for educational administrators, was invaluable for insight into how colleges planned for the postwar years, and especially "The Place of the College in Educating the Veteran for Civilian Life" by Paul Klapper (March 24, 1945); "Education and the Older Veteran" by Henry G. Kobs (February 23, 1946); "To What Extent Will Colleges Adjust to the Needs of Veterans?" by Loren S. Hadley (February 23, 1946); "They Know What They Want" by Nicholas M. McKnight (December 21, 1946); "The College Versus the Veteran" by Frederic W. Ness (December 21, 1946); "A New Angle in Higher Education" by Doris P. Merrill (February 1, 1947); and "The Veteran Flunks the Professor: A GI Indictment of Our Institutions of Higher Learning" by S. N. Vinocour (April 7, 1947). A good sociological study of the veteran in college is *Adjustment to College: A Study of 10,000 Veterans and Non-veteran Students in Sixteen American Colleges* by Norman Frederiksen and W. B. Schrader (Education Testing Service, 1951).

67   "In a study of postwar vets." Fredericksen and Schrader, *Adjustment to College.*

68   "Memorandum from Morningside." Servicemen's responses to the Columbia questionnaires are quoted in McKnight, "They Know What They Want."

78   "The veterans lobby put forth a bill." "Increasing Subsistence Allowances for Education," hearings, House Committee on Veterans Affairs, February 1947.

80   "One must speculate at the magnitude." "Let's Give the Veterans an Education," by Bayard Quincy Morgan, *The Pacific Spectator,* Winter 1948.

Chapter Five

The Truman Administration's reconversion policy was detailed in a study, "From War to Peace: A Challenge," issued by the Office of War Mobilization and Reconversion in August 1945. The report was written by Robert R. Nathan, OWMR deputy director. Nathan, now a consulting economist in Washington, provided further background in an interview, as did Leon H. Keyserling, vice-chairman of the Council of Economic Advisers during the Truman years. The course of Truman's economic policies can be traced in semiannual reports of the Council of Economic Advisers beginning in January 1947; the first five of these reports, crucial to our period, are compiled in a book, *The Economic Reports of the President* (Harcourt, Brace and Company, 1949). At the Truman library, I found valuable information in files of the Office of Price Administration, White House correspondence files (the latter, with communiqués from both citizens and officials, give vivid insight into the turbulent daily workings of the controls program), and in oral history interviews with three Truman-era economic officials: Roger W. Jones, of the Bureau of the Budget; William K. Divers, chairman of the Federal Home Loan Bank Board; and Dr. Walter S. Salant, staff economist for the Council of Economic Advisers. Other useful books on the CEA are *Economics in the Public Service* by Edwin G. Nourse (Harcourt, Brace and Company, 1953); *Economic Advice and Presidential Leadership* by Edward S. Flash, Jr. (Columbia University Press, 1965); and *The Postwar American Economy* by Alvin H. Hansen (W. W. Norton and Company, 1964). Background on the controls program was derived from *Promises to Keep,* by Chester Bowles (Harper & Row, 1971). *Fortune*'s continuing economic surveys were of immense value.

94 "Bowles feared a repetition." Bowles radio broadcast, August 15, 1945.
95 "Single most important collection of American fascists." *Time,* May 6, 1946.
96 "Touring the Midwest for the *New York Times.*" The *New York Times,* June 29, 1946.
99 "Snyder lacked an overall picture." William V. Shannon and Robert S. Allen, *The Truman Merry-Go-Round,* Vanguard, 1950.
101 "Danger ahead, Americans." Washington Post, October 26, 1945.
102 "The idea of government by press." Marquis Childs, the Washington *Post,* November 25, 1945.
103 "Passage put Truman in a dilemma." Cabell Philips, *The Truman Presidency,* Macmillan, 1966.
104 "It is with the greatest of pleasure." *Time,* July 15, 1946.
105 "OPA ticked off." OPA report to Truman, July 10, 1946.
106 "For established packers." The butcher vignettes are from *Time* and *Newsweek,* various issues, August–November 1946; the Cooney letter was to Matt Connelly of the White House staff, June 18, 1946.
"On the last business day." Washington *Post,* November 26, 1946.

Chapter Six

The general background for labor unrest during the 1940's draws heavily upon my *Meany* (Atheneum, 1972) which in turn was based upon research in files of the American Federation of Labor and interviews with a host of persons active in the labor movement at the time. Labor histories of value included *Labor in America* by Foster Rhea Dulles (Thomas Y. Crowell, 1955); *A History of American Labor* by Joseph G. Rayback (The Macmillan Company, 1964); and *The AFL from the Death of Gompers to the Merger* by Philip Taft (Harper and Brothers, 1959). For an understanding of the complexities of John L. Lewis, I am indebted to *John L. Lewis: An Authorized Biography* by Saul Alinsky (Vintage Books edition, 1970). Other sources include *Reuther* by Frank Cormier and William J. Eaton (Prentice-Hall, 1970); *Ford: An Unconventional Biography of the Men and Their Times*, by Booton Herndon (Weybright & Talley, 1969); and *Labor Baron* by James Wechsler (William Morrow Company, 1944). Labor reportage in *The Nation* was consistently incisive, especially that by Helen Fuller and Tris Coffin. Files of the United States Employment Service in the National Archives were also helpful.

111   "One executive told *PM*." *PM*, January 15, 1946.
111   "*Time* had continuing sport." *Time*'s treatment of Petrillo is typified by its story of April 22, 1946.
112   "A typical Petrillo maneuver." The Chicago *Tribune*, December 26, 1945.
112   "Is Anybody Interested." New York *Daily News*, November 2, 1945.
113   "One problem is that we got used." New York *Sun*, November 4, 1945.
113   "People are somewhat befuddled." Quoted in *Harry S. Truman* by Margaret Truman, William Morrow and Company, 1973.
114   "At one point William H. Davis." The story of Davis' firing was told by Walter Salant in his oral history interview, Truman library.
116   "If such a principle were sound." Henry Hazlitt in the *New York Times*, December 24, 1945.
117   "Obviously those who control." Riesel in the New York *Post*, January 23, 1946.
118   The Nation profile is based upon *Fortune*, August 1946.
120   "Organized labor has taken his measure." Louis Stark in the *New York Times*, September 9, 1945.
125   "Truman had come to detest Lewis." Margaret Truman, *Harry S. Truman.*
125   "Truman moved out of the picture entirely." Truman's strategy for dealing with Lewis was detailed by Edward T. Folliard in the Washington *Post*, December 11, 1946, in an article that obviously benefited from White House help.
125   "The instructions were to fight." Margaret Truman, *Harry S. Truman.*
127   "Well, John L. Lewis had to fold up." *Ibid.*
127   "While the strife in big industrial centers." Material on southern labor unrest and changing black attitudes is from the United States Employment Service's press clipping service and periodic reports from USES field offices in the south.

Chapter Seven

Statistics on postwar housing are from *A History of the Veterans Emergency Housing Program,* Office of the Housing Expediter, 1948. General background on trends in the building industry—policies and building techniques—came from *The American Builder* and *Architectural Forum. The Crack in the Picture Window* by John Keats (Houghton Mifflin Company, 1957) is a savage attack on tract developers, and they deserve every word of it. White House correspondence files in the Truman library contain thousands of angry citizen letters about the housing shortage. The profile of William Levitt was based on articles in *The American Builder* (December 1946), and *Time* (December 23, 1946, January 31, 1949, and April 17, 1950). Good overviews of postwar housing are in *Fortune,* "The Housing Mess" (January 1947), and "Rents and the Real Estate Lobby" (September 1947).

133 "Walter B. Mansfield, a marine captain." The Hartford *Courant,* November 30, 1945. Other perceptive housing shortage stories are in the Buffalo *Courier-Express,* December 3, 1945; and *Veteran View,* publication of the California Department of Veterans Affairs, January 1947.
134 "Contractor Clarke Daniel duplicated." Washington *Star,* December 2, 1945.
136 "The Legion's first worry." "Should Veterans Come First in Housing?" by Clarence Woodbury, the *American Legion Magazine,* January 1948.
141 "The psychic toll and social cost." The Winslow study is quoted in Keats, *Crack in the Picture Window.*

Chapter Eight

Quotations from specific programs are from the radio script collection, Library of Congress, and *The Serials* by Raymond William Steadman (University of Oklahoma Press, 1971). The latter was most useful for background on the soap opera industry. A good general history of broadcasting is *The Golden Web: A History of Broadcasting in the United States,* Volume II, 1933–53, by Erik Barnouw (Oxford University Press, 1968). A lighter look is *Tune In Tomorrow* by Mary Jane Higby (Cowles, 1968). Also most helpful were *The Great Audience* by Gilbert Seldes (Viking, 1950); and *Radio's Second Chance* by Charles A. Siepmann (Little, Brown, 1946).

148 "Christopher Morley complained." Both the Morley and John Mason Brown quotes are from essays in *Information Please Almanac,* 1947.
149 "The soap operas stood as an industry." *Time,* February 25, 1946.
149 "The brain trust of the soaps." Derived from Steadman, *The Serials.*
153 "I am reminded of an old." "The Revolt Against Radio," *Fortune,* March 1947.
155 "My sister married." *Time,* March 11, 1946.
157 "That's a joke, son." John Gunther, *Inside U.S.A.,* Harper and Brothers, 1947.

158   "As the radio critic John Crosby." Quoted in *Information Please Almanac*, 1946.
161   "Federal courts struck down the ban." RCA *v.* Whitman *et al.*, 114 Fed. 2d 86.
161   "American radio is the product." Quoted in Siepmann, *Radio's Second Chance.*
166   "At its best, radio offered." Ruark quoted in *Fortune*, March 1947.
167   "What have you gentlemen done." Chicago *Tribune*, October 28, 1946.

Chapter Nine

The Barnouw and Seldes books cited in the Chapter 8 notes were also useful for their commentary on the development of television, as was *David Sarnoff, a Biography*, by Eugene Lyons (Harper and Row, 1966).

170   "Soon after television came to Manhattan." *Time*, May 24, 1948.
171   "This damned Ferris wheel." Interview with Earl Muntz, June 25, 1973.
174   "Mimeographed warning to speakers." New York *Herald Tribune*, July 13, 1948.
174   "Democrats brought along Hal King." Washington *Star*, July 11, 1948.
176   "When these two stand up and slug it out." *Time*, April 19, 1948.
177   "Cone blamed these early crudities." Fairfax Cone, *With All Its Faults*, Little, Brown, 1970.

Chapter Ten

The discussion of book censorship draws on *Sex, Pornography, and Justice* by Albert Gerber (Lyle Stuart, Inc., 1966). Background on Albert Kinsey and his sex research are in *Dr. Kinsey and the Institute for Sex Research* by Wardell B. Pomeroy (Signet edition, 1972). Three contemporary books of commentary are *American Sexual Behavior and the Kinsey Report* by Morris L. Ernst and David Loth (Bantam Books, 1948); *An Analysis of the Kinsey Reports* edited by Donald Porter Geddes (Mentor, 1954); and *About the Kinsey Report* edited by Donald Porter Geddes and Enid Curie (Signet, 1948). Quotes from the male report are from the Saunders edition, 1948.

181   "It was hard to get other things." Edward Scherman, interview, Columbia Oral History Project.
182   "The first distinctive shift." Dorothy Canfield Fisher, interview, Columbia Oral History Project.
183   "I may as well confess." Norman Mailer, *Advertisements for Myself*, Putnam, 1959.
184   Quotes from *The Naked and the Dead* are from the Rinehart edition, 1948.
185   "Disillusion with a vengeance." *Information Please Almanac*, 1949.

186 "Notable for its gusto." *Dictionary of American Biography*, Harper and Row, 1974.
187 Quotes from *Memoirs of Hecate County* are from the Signet edition, 1961 (marked "Not For Sale in New York State").
194 "Actualities of sexual behavior." *American Journal of Psychiatry*, June 1948.
195 "Because of the socio-economic standards." Quoted in Geddes, *An Analysis of the Kinsey Reports*.

Chapter Eleven

Guidance on the movie industry in the postwar years came in interviews with King Vidor, Adela Rogers St. John, H. M. Swanson and Robert Thom. Among books that were useful were *The Western from Silents to the Seventies* by George N. Fenin and William K. Everson (Grossman, 1973); *Motion Pictures: The Development of an Art from Silent Films to the Age of Television* by A. R. Fulton (University of Oklahoma Press, 1960); *Hollywood in the Forties* by Charles Higham and Joel Greenburg (Paperback Library, 1970); *Shooting Star: A Biography of John Wayne* by Maurice Zolotow (Simon & Schuster, 1974); *See No Evil* by Jack Vizzard (Simon & Schuster, 1970); *Saturday Afternoon at the Bijou* by David Zinman (Arlington House, 1973); and *The Great Audience* by Gilbert Seldes (Viking, 1950).

197 "During the filming." John Keats, *Howard Hughes*, Random House, 1966.
201 "Also known as Rita Hayworth." Winston Sargeant, "The Cult of the Love Goddess in America," *Life*, November 10, 1947.
204 "The movies had degenerated." Shell Finger-tip Tours, Southern California tourism collection, Los Angeles public library.

Chapter Twelve

In addition to the general studies of the Truman era, books useful in this chapter (and succeeding ones) included *The Price of Vision: The Diary of Henry A. Wallace, 1942–46* by John Morton Blum (Houghton Mifflin, 1973); *The Journals of David A. Lilienthal: Volume Two, the Atomic Energy Years, 1946–50* (Harper and Row, 1964); *The Truman Era* by I. F. Stone (Vintage, 1972); *An Uncommon Man: Henry A. Wallace and Sixty Million Jobs* by Frank Kingdon (Longmans, Green, 1945); and *Henry Wallace: The Man and the Myth* by Dwight Macdonald (Vanguard, 1948).

212 "Now I wish you were at the helm." The Humphrey and Eleanor Roosevelt letters are quoted in *Beyond the New Deal: Harry S. Truman and American Liberalism* by Alonzo L. Hamby, Columbia University Press, 1973.
213 "For that matter, however." The Clifford quotations are in Lilienthal, *Journals*.
213 "I don't know how." Jonathan Daniels, *Man of Independence*, Lippincott, 1950.
213 "At the working level." Allen and Shannon, *Truman Merry-Go-Round*.

214   "A visit to official Washington." Willard Shelton in the Chicago *Sun-Times,* November 28, 1945.

215   "Power behind that drone." Victor Riesel in the Philadelphia *Inquirer,* December 4, 1945.

215   "Fewer than a hundred letters." *Time,* January 14, 1946.

215   "American myth and legend." Lippmann, in the New York *Herald Tribune,* January 14, 1946.

215   "The Tragedy of Truman." New York *Journal-American,* December 17, 1945.

217   "Ickes signed on." New York *Post,* August 1, 1948.

218   "Prepare meals out of soybeans." Louis Bean interviews, Columbia Oral History Project and Truman library; Bean also gave me an appraisal of Wallace in an interview.

218   "To believe that he talked for God." Quoted in Hamby, *Beyond the New Deal.*

218   "I have faith that divine providence." "Iowa Cycle," by Charles M. Wilson, *The Commonweal,* November 10, 1933.

219   "From Truman's vantage point." Margaret Truman, *Harry S. Truman.*

222   "Wallace's troubles escalated." A good summary of press and public reaction to the Wallace episode is an Associated Press story that appeared in many papers on September 17, 1946 (see, for instance, the St. Louis *Post-Dispatch*).

223   "As fundamentally sound intellectually." Quoted in Margaret Truman, *Harry S. Truman.*

Chapter Thirteen

For daily coverage of the 1946 campaign I made extensive use of the voluminous newspaper clipping file the Democratic National Committee deposited in the Truman library. The DNC files also contain texts of major statements made by both parties during the campaign.

226   "Look into the matter." Marquis Childs in the Washington *Post,* December 2, 1946.

228   "Threw out the military pictures." *Nixon,* Earl Mazo and Stephen Hess, Harper and Row, 1968. Quotes from the 1946 Nixon campaign are in *The Facts About Nixon,* William Costello, Viking, 1960.

229   "Joe McCarthy was a tail-gunner." The description of the 1946 McCarthy campaign is from *When Even Angels Wept,* Lately Thomas, William Morrow and Company, 1973.

230   "Truman was dubious." Margaret Truman, *Harry S. Truman.*

230   "HAD ENOUGH?" Boston *Globe,* September 9, 1946.

232   "Although this suggestion exploded." Fulbright's plan to put a Republican in the presidency is in *Fulbright: The Dissenter,* Haynes Johnson and Bernard W. Gwertzman, Doubleday, 1966.

Chapter Fourteen

Background on Robert A. Taft, and a Republican-oriented interpretation of the Eightieth Congress, are in *Mr. Republican: A Biography of Robert A. Taft,* by

James T. Patterson (Houghton Mifflin, 1972). Profiles of the leading congressional Republicans are in "Background on GOP Contenders," *Fortune,* April 1947.

236 "Wherry once got into a loud." Allen and Shannon, *Truman Merry-Go-Round.*
237 "One man calling the signals." *Time,* January 20, 1947.
237 "When provoked Taft's temper." *Sketches from Life,* Dean Acheson, Popular Library edition, 1962.
237 "Senator is talking tommyrot." *The Eisenhower Years,* Richard Rovere, Farrar, Straus and Cudahy, 1956.
238 The Lahey quotes from interview, Columbia Oral History Project.
239 "In terms of concrete legislation." Goulden, *Meany.*
240 "Pursuit of corruption." Keats, *Howard Hughes.*
243 "Only one scalp of passing importance." *Time,* December 1, 1947, and March 22, 1948.

Chapter Fifteen

General background of foreign policy developments, in this and other chapters, came from the series, *The United States in World Affairs,* published annually by Harper and Row under sponsorship of the Council on Foreign Relations. Other volumes of help included *Memoirs 1925–50* by George F. Kennan (Little Brown, 1967); *Present at the Creation* by Dean Acheson (W. W. Norton, 1969); *The United States in the World Arena* by Walt W. Rostow (Harper and Row, 1960); *The Great Globe Itself* by William C. Bullitt (Scribner's, 1946); *Meeting at Potsdam* by Charles L. Mee, Jr. (M. Evans and Company, 1975); *Speaking Frankly* by James Byrnes (Harper and Brothers, 1947); *The Tragedy of American Diplomacy* by William Appleman Williams (Delta Books edition, 1971); *From Yalta to Vietnam* by David Horowitz (Penguin Books, 1965); *Blockade: Berlin and the Cold War* by Eric Morris (Stein and Day, 1973); and *The Cold War as History* by Louis Halle (Harper and Row, 1967).

249 "According to a systematic study." "Public Opinion and Foreign Affairs," Alvin Richman, in *Communication in International Politics,* University of Illinois Press, 1972. I am grateful to Dr. Richman also for permitting me to read his doctoral dissertation from the University of Pennsylvania, "The Changing American Image of the Soviet Union," 1968, and other papers derived from his on-going studies.
250 "Two major battles three months apart." The *New York Times,* June 22 and September 12, 1942.
251 "It is true that American thought." Winston Churchill, *Triumph and Tragedy,* Houghton Mifflin, 1953.
252 "While the staff officers were disappointed." The *New York Times,* May 2, 1945.
252 "Barbarian invasion of Europe." Harry S. Truman, *Memoirs I.*
253 "Could go to hell." Quoted in Margaret Truman, *Harry S. Truman.*
254 "Funny to watch him." Harry S. Truman, *Memoirs I.*
255 "During an interlude at Potsdam." Margaret Truman, *Harry S. Truman.*
256 "Declaration of World War Three." Walter Millis, editor, *The Forrestal Diaries,* Viking, 1951.
257 "Dozens of war-weary little people." The Fischer quotes are from his *Why They Behave Like Russians,* Harper and Row, 1947.
257 "Stalin sent him a private note." Denver *Post,* February 9, 1948.
259 "Disillusioned fellow traveler." *Time,* July 7, 1947.

Chapter Sixteen

United States nuclear policy is detailed in *The Scorpion and the Tarantula* by Joseph I. Lieberman (Houghton Mifflin, 1970); *The New Force* by Ralph Lapp (Harper and Brothers, 1953); *Brighter Than a Thousand Suns* by Robert Jungk (Harcourt, Brace and Company, 1958); "The Baruch Plan: U.S. Diplomacy Enters the Nuclear Age" (Library of Congress study for the House Committee on Foreign Affairs, August 1972); and *Fortune*, January 1949. Candid discussions of the Greek and Turkish aid programs are in "Legislative Origins of the Truman Doctrine," hearings, Senate Foreign Relations Committee, March and April 1947, published January 12, 1973, as part of a historical series on Truman-era foreign policy decisions. *The Bulletin of the Atomic Scientists* was a useful, if consistently unobjective, source.

265 "Half the delivered papers." Quoted in Jungk, *Brighter Than a Thousand Suns.*
267 "First forgery by air power." *The Nation*, October 5, 1946.
272 "In another vein." Walter Lippmann columns in the New York *Herald Tribune*, May 1947.
273 "Domestic considerations as well." *Report on America*, Robert Payne, John Day Company, 1949.
275 "The persuasion carried Vandenberg." Gunther, *Inside U.S.A.*
275 "It is time to rally." *Time*, December 8, 1947.
275 "On the Democratic left." *I Vote My Conscience*, Vito Marcantonio, The Vito Marcantonio Memorial, 1956.
276 "I believe that the American people." Barbara Ward in the *New York Times Magazine*, January 11, 1948.

Chapter Seventeen

The *Amerasia* case is detailed in "The *Amerasia* Papers: A Clue to the Catastrophe of China," a two-volume report by the Internal Security Subcommittee of the Senate Judiciary Committee, January 26, 1970. The 1,819-page report contains a lengthy essay by Dr. Anthony Kubek on the origins of the case, as well as the texts of government documents seized from the *Amerasia* offices. Further background on *Amerasia*, the Institute of Pacific Relations, and their principals, are in "Institute of Pacific Relations," hearings, Internal Security Subcommittee, July and August 1951. A good critical history of the China Lobby is *The China Lobby in American Politics* by Ross Y. Koen (Harper and Row, 1974).* *While You Slept* by John T. Flynn (Devin-Adair Company, 1951) is the sort of thing Koen complained about. An exhaustive study of the Gouzenko case, with supporting documents, is in "The Report of the Royal Commission," June 27, 1946, a Canadian government publication.

* Harper and Row's 1974 edition contains a note by editor Richard C. Kagan: "Ross Y. Koen's book was first printed in 1960, but its distribution was enjoined owing to pressures from the China lobby; over 4,000 copies were destroyed by the publisher; less than 800 circulated. Many of these were stolen from libraries by right-wing groups. . . . Others were placed under lock and key in rare book rooms in university libraries throughout the country."

282 "Such was not to be the case." Joseph W. Esherick, ed., *Last Chance in China: The World War Two Dispatches of John Stewart Service*, Ran-

dom House, 1974.

284 "Luce was particularly obstinate." Luce's troubles with White, or vice versa, are told in *Luce and His Empire*, W. A. Swanberg, Scribner's, 1972.

285 "Emerging mouthpiece for the China Lobby." See, for instance, *China Monthly*, July and August 1945 issues.

Chapter Eighteen

When beginning this chapter I spent a solid week at the Library of Congress, reading printed hearing reports of the House Un-American Activities Committee, a summer pastime I do not recommend. For less masochistic historians, two books contain lengthy (if somewhat selective) excerpts that give the flavor of HUAC's activities: *Thirty Years of Treason*, selected and edited by Eric Bentley (Viking, 1971); and *The Committee* by Walter Goodman (Farrar, Straus and Giroux, 1968). An invaluable book for the Hollywood hearings is *Report on Blacklisting: Volume I, Movies* by John Cogley (The Fund for the Republic, Inc., 1956). I am indebted to Cogley for background not only on the HUAC hearings, but also for the history of Hollywood unionism. A good study of the Truman Administration's loyalty review program is in *The Loyalty of Free Men* by Alan Barth (Pocket Books edition, 1952); files of the loyalty review boards remain closed to researchers. On successive days in June 1973 I benefited from interviews with Adela Rogers St. John, who as a writer for the Hearst newspapers tried to stir up trouble for the Hollywood Ten, and with Robert Kenny, who as an attorney tried to keep them out of jail. Both were hospitable as well as helpful. *The Golden Web* by Erik Barnouw (Oxford University Press, 1968) was informative about radio blacklisting. Also helpful were two books by Louis Budenz, *This Is My Story* (McGraw-Hill, 1947); and *Men Without Faces* (Harper and Brothers, 1950); and *The Communist Party Versus the CIO* by Max Kampelman (Praeger, 1957).

304 Agee on "Mission to Moscow." *The Nation*, May 22, 1943.

304 "Had failed to establish." *Time*, November 10, 1947.

304 "None of the 159 films." "Communism and the Movies: A Study of Film Content," Dorothy B. Jones, printed as an appendix to the Cogley report.

Jones was chief of the film reviewing and analysis section of the Office of War Information during the Second World War.

306 "Sometime after his joust." Interview with Alger Hiss, May 28, 1975.

307 "Corporations ignored the consulting firms." *The Judges and the Judged*, Merle Miller, Doubleday, 1952.

307 "When a known pro-Soviet apologist." James F. O'Neil, "How You Can Fight Communism," *American Legion Magazine*, August 1948.

308 "Internal passport system in Chile." William LaVarre, "You Have to Be Yourself in Chile," *American Legion Magazine*, July 1949.

314 "No citizen is entitled." The *New York Times*, April 12, 1948.

Chapter Nineteen

The factual outline of the Bentley case and her HUAC dealings relies heavily upon *The FBI Nobody Knows* by Fred J. Cook (Macmillan, 1964), plus contemporary coverage by the New York *World-Telegram*, which was enthusiastic about her cause. The Bentley and Goodman books cited above were also useful.

315 "Soviet recruiters readily." Background on the Coplon trial is from *Time*, May 9 and June 27, 1949.
318 "Was urging me in the Dewey campaign." The *New York Times*, February 8, 1955.
318 "The closest relationship exists." Quoted in Cook, *The FBI Nobody Knows*.

Chapter Twenty

As of this writing Alger Hiss is on the verge of receiving access to some 53,000 pages of FBI documents relating to his investigation and trial. He is adamant that they will exonerate him, and so argues, convincingly, to many persons who listen to him. He might be right. Yet the ultimate truth of the Hiss case—if any can ever be found—is beyond the purview of *The Best Years*. My account is intended to present the case as it appeared to the public at the time. Two basic sources are books by the protagonists: *Witness* by Whittaker Chambers (Random House, 1952); and *In the Court of Public Opinion* by Hiss (Knopf, 1957). Unfortunately for Hiss, Chambers was much the better writer, and he made a good case for himself. Among contemporary journalistic accounts, the best is *A Generation on Trial* by Alistair Cooke (Knopf, 1950). Cooke, a Britisher, accepted the jury verdict, but was disturbed by its implications, and refused to "join the cheering squad of one side or the other." Ralph de Toledano and Victor Lasky had no such qualms. Their *Seeds of Treason* (Funk and Wagnall, 1950) is an unabashed huzzah for Chambers and the FBI. Fred Cook's FBI study, cited above, was also helpful. The Hiss chapter in *Six Crises* by Richard M. Nixon (Doubleday, 1962) has been partially disavowed by the former President, although it does purport to give insight into Nixon's thinking as the case progressed. In addition to an interview with Hiss I also benefited, to a minor extent, from an afternoon with a former HUAC staff member who was involved in the investigation, but who desired to speak from anonymity.

324 "I remember Alger Hiss." Murray Kempton quoted in Miller, *Plain Speaking*.
331 "*Time* Magazine shared his discomfort." Swanberg, *Luce and His Empire*.
334 "I am going to believe in Alger Hiss." Eleanor Roosevelt, quoted in Hamby, *Beyond the New Deal*.
335 "Journalist James Reston visited." The *New York Times*, June 9, 1949.
339 "Many prominent liberals." Derived from Hamby, *Beyond the New Deal*.

Chapter Twenty-one

A fruitful source of this chapter, and the five that follow, was the files of the Democratic National Committee at the Truman library—internal party papers, newspaper clippings, and texts of major documents. *Out of the Jaws of Victory* by Jules Abels (Henry Holt and Company, 1959), although suffering from a lack of insider-information, is a good daily chronology of the election, and offers an analysis of the vote. *Inside the Democratic Party* by Jack Redding (Bobbs-Merrill,

1958) is rich with campaign anecdotes. Much of the background on Henry Wallace is drawn from Dwight Macdonald's critical profile cited earlier. Eisenhower's off-again, on-again attitude toward politics is revealed in his *Mandate for Change* (Doubleday, 1961).

347 "I have a hunch." Wallace's statements during his foreign trip are from *Newsweek*, April 28, 1947, and the *New York Times*, April 12 and 21, 1947.
351 "The man won because." Interview, Louis Bean, April 24, 1975.
353 "Negro men literally saw the world." George W. Crockett in the Michigan *Chronicle*, December 22, 1945.
355 "My very stomach turned over." Quoted in Margaret Truman, *Harry S. Truman*.
359 "Professional academicians also looked askance." *School and Society*, October 1947. Eisenhower's response is in *Time*, October 27, 1947.
361 "Samuel Rosenman, who continued." Oral history interview, the Truman library.

Chapter Twenty-two

I am grateful to Stephen J. Springarn, who worked on the Truman staff in the White House, for alerting me to the authorship of the 1948 campaign-strategy memorandum. Both the Rowe and Clifford versions are in the Truman library. Clark Clifford was helpful in an informal interview.

Chapter Twenty-three

Background on Dewey's personality is from an interview with Warren Moscow, Columbia Oral History Project; "The Dewey Personality" by Marquis Childs (*Liberty*, October 7, 1944); and "Barefoot Boy with Screws On" by Hard S. Corners (a pseudonym), (New York *Star*, October 17, 1948).

Chapter Twenty-four

382 "He belongs to that crowd of Tommy Corcoran." Quoted in Margaret Truman, *Harry S. Truman*.
385 "The moderate plank prevailed in committee." Humphrey's civil rights battle is described in *Almost to the Presidency*, Albert Eisele, Piper Publishing Company, 1972.
389 "Unfortunately Wallace spent much of convention week." A good account of the "guru letters" controversy is in *Fair Enough: The Life of Westbrook Pegler*, Finis Farr, Arlington House, 1975.

Chapter Twenty-five

392 "Another four years of slavery." Quoted in Margaret Truman, *Harry S. Truman.*

393 "Give 'em hell, Harry." Edward T. Folliard in the Washington *Post,* April 28, 1975.

394 "Another Truman writer." Experiences of the Truman speechwriters are told in oral history interviews with Charles S. Murphy, John E Barriere, and James L. Sundquist, Truman library.

398 "Wasting his time." The Roper Poll, with its forget-Truman quotes, is in the New York *Herald Tribune,* September 9, 1948.

403 "Republican Chairman Clark Sprnger." Louisville *Courier-Journal,* September 9, 1948.

414 "God got off Dewey." The Lahey quotes here and elsewhere in the section are from his interview, Columbia Oral History Project.

Chapter Twenty-six

419 "I want to be the first to tell you." George E. Allen interview, oral history project, Truman library.

420 "The loneliest campaign." Joseph and Stewart Alsop in the Washington *Post,* July 7, 1948.

420 "The sting of defeat." Hugh Scott, *Come to the Party,* Prentice-Hall, 1968.

422 "As it turned out." A good discussion of Truman's postelection troubles in his official family is in *The Truman Scandals,* Jules Abels, Regnery, 1955.

Epilogue

426 "There never was a country." Robert Payne, *Report on America,* John Day Company, 1949.

428 "The psychic dangers." Quoted in Jungk, *Brighter Than a Thousand Suns.*

428 "We are like a man lost." Raymond Swing, *In the Name of Sanity,* Harper and Brothers, 1946.

428 "The fate of world government." Cord Meyer, Jr., *Peace or Anarchy?,* Little Brown, 1947.

428 "Functioning inside a cocoon." Quoted in Swing, *In the Name of Sanity.*

430 "Many of these men came out." Dr. Harvey Olsen, "After the Decision," *Future Musings Bulletin,* November 19, 1955.

Index